SAMU   Mary,
Devo   d talker
as a c   where
he beg   poems,
and J   y and
togetl   nded
in An   oems
were   'The
Eolia   in the same year,
althou   age was an unhappy one. He first met Dorothy and
William Wordsworth in 1797 and a close association developed between
them. Coleridge wrote his famous 'Kubla Khan' in the same year, followed
in 1798 by 'Frost at Midnight'. In 1799 he and Wordsworth published the
Lyrical Ballads, which marked a conscious break with eighteenth-century
tradition and included one of Coleridge's greatest poems, *The Rime of
the Ancient Mariner*. During a visit to the Wordsworths in 1799 he met
Sara Hutchinson, who became his lifelong love and the subject of his
Asra poems. In the following year Coleridge and his family settled at
Greta Hall, Keswick, where he wrote the second part of *Christabel*, begun
in 1798, and also became addicted to opium. In 1804 he separated from
his wife and spent the following years in the Mediterranean or London,
returning in 1808 to live with the Wordsworths in Grasmere. In 1809 he
established *The Friend*, a political, literary and philosophical weekly
journal, which he published regularly over the next year. After a disagree-
ment with Wordsworth in 1810 Coleridge left the Lake District for ever,
centring his life thereafter in London, where he gave his *Shakespeare
Lectures*. He presented his literary and philosophical theories in the
two-volume *Biographia Literaria*, published in 1817, and collected his
poems in *Sibylline Leaves*. In an attempt to control his opium addiction
he entered the household and care of Dr James Gillman at Highgate in
1816. Here he was to remain for the last eighteen years of his life, writing

a number of late confessional poems and prose works, including *Aids to Reflection*, published in 1825. Coleridge died in 1834 having overseen a final edition of his *Poetical Works*.

Poet, philosopher and critic, Coleridge stands as one of the seminal figures of his time. William Hazlitt wrote: 'His thoughts did not seem to come with labour and effort; but as if borne on the gusts of genius, and as if the wings of his imagination lifted him from off his feet', and Wordsworth called him 'the only wonderful man I ever knew'.

WILLIAM KEACH was born in Robstown, south Texas. He was educated in the local schools, then studied at the universities of Texas (Austin), Oxford and Yale. From 1970 until 1985 he taught in the English Department at Rutgers University, and since 1986 he has been Professor of English at Brown University in Providence, Rhode Island. He has published books and articles on Renaissance and Romantic literature and culture and he is currently writing a book about language and politics in the English Romantic period.

SAMUEL TAYLOR COLERIDGE

The Complete Poems

Edited by WILLIAM KEACH

PENGUIN BOOKS

rk 10014, USA
Penguin Books Australia Ltd, 250 Camberwell Road, Camberwell, Victoria 3124, Australia
Penguin Books Canada Ltd, 10 Alcorn Avenue, Toronto, Ontario, Canada M4V 3B2
Penguin Books India (P) Ltd, 11 Community Centre, Panchsheel Park, New Delhi – 110 017, India
Penguin Books (NZ) Ltd, Cnr Rosedale and Airborne Roads, Albany, Auckland, New Zealand
Penguin Books (South Africa) (Pty) Ltd, 24 Sturdee Avenue, Rosebank 2196, South Africa

Penguin Books Ltd, Registered Offices: 80 Strand, London WC2R 0RL, England

www.penguin.com

This edition first published 1997
Reprinted 2004
12

The moral right of the editor has been asserted

Set in 9.25/10.5 pt PostScript Monotype Ehrhardt
Typeset by Rowland Phototypesetting Ltd, Bury St Edmunds, Suffolk
Printed in England by Clays Ltd, St Ives plc

CONTENTS

INTRODUCTION

At first glance it might appear to be easier to produce a complete and textually accurate edition of the poems of Coleridge than of the other canonically dominant Romantic poets. He issued three editions of his *Poetical Works* near the end of his life – in 1828, in 1829, and (with the help of his nephew and son-in-law, Henry Nelson Coleridge) in 1834, the year of his death. Between 1834 and 1880 seven editions containing previously unpublished poems appeared, the most important of which were edited by H. N. Coleridge, by Coleridge's daughter Sara, and then by his youngest son Derwent – all of whom had intimate knowledge of Coleridge's attitudes towards his verse and distinctive access to his manuscripts. James Dykes Campbell in 1893 and Ernest Hartley Coleridge (the poet's grandson) in 1912 published annotated scholarly editions of the poems and plays that represent, according to the Modern Language Association's *English Romantic Poets: A Review of Research and Criticism* (1985), 'specimens of the best of late nineteenth-century editorial practice'. An unusually full and authoritative basis for a good modern edition had been established by the beginning of the twentieth century.

But several complications arising from Coleridge's characteristic habits as a writer of verse stand between the basis laid by these earlier editions and the kinds of editions we need today. Coleridge's notebooks and letters are full of verse unpublished by him and by his subsequent editors. Much of this verse is fragmentary; much of it is translated or adapted from other writers. But it constitutes, in any case, writing that many readers of Coleridge's poetry want to have ready access to. Furthermore, early in his career Coleridge published a number of poems in magazines and newspapers that he never included in collected editions. The fact that Coleridge never collected these poems is important. In some instances their textual status is ineluctably suspect because no manuscript version is known to exist and because they were never published under Coleridge's direct editorial supervision. These circumstances do not of course mean that poems of this kind should be excluded from editions that aim to meet reasonable standards of completeness.

But the most important and interesting complication that an edition of the poems has to contend with is Coleridge's relentless revising. Sometimes he wrote several different versions of what he and we want to think of as the same poem; sometimes he rewrote passages or added

new passages for subsequent published versions, or included such passages
in letters or notebooks; sometimes he revised or added passages in his
own or someone else's copy of his poems. This aspect of Coleridge's
poetic practice is the major concern of Jack Stillinger's recent *Coleridge
and Textual Instability* (1994). Concentrating exclusively on 'the facts and
issues raised by the existence of a great many different versions' of
Coleridge's seven most widely read poems ('The Rime of the Ancient
Mariner', 'Kubla Khan', 'Christabel', 'The Eolian Harp', 'This Lime-
Tree Bower my Prison', 'Frost at Midnight' and 'Dejection: An Ode'),
Stillinger argues that Coleridge 'produced a new definitive version, the
"final" text that he intended to stand at the moment, every time he
revised a text'. 'We have more versions of Coleridge's poems than we
have for the works of most other major writers', Stillinger contends; the
instability of Coleridge's texts is not primarily 'a function of missing
materials' but 'of a surplus of materials'.

Stillinger emphasizes the limitations of editions that privilege either
the latest or the earliest versions of poems, and his analysis, in addition
to containing a wealth of information and insight regarding the seven
major poems he discusses in detail, suggests more generally the critical
importance of taking Coleridge's multiple revisions into account. But any
editor, even an editor who aspires to produce a complete edition with
variant readings, will in the end have to present reading texts based on
principles that privilege one version over others. This edition, in keeping
with the Penguin English Poets series as a whole, privileges the latest
text published in Coleridge's lifetime, or the latest manuscript version
known to exist in cases of poems that Coleridge never published at all.
The notes contain full, though not exhaustive, information about variants
from earlier printed and manuscript versions. (I have, for example,
included variants of punctuation only when they might be thought to
have an important bearing on the meaning of a line or passage.) Readers are
encouraged to follow Stillinger's lead and explore the rich consequences of
Coleridge's revisions. In four especially significant instances ('Monody
on the Death of Chatterton', 'The Eolian Harp', 'The Rime of the Ancient
Mariner' and 'Dejection: An Ode') the latest printed version is preceded
by the most important earlier version.

The *Poetic Works* of 1834 provides the copy text for all the poems that
Coleridge included in that edition. There has been some controversy on
this point: for his edition of 1893 Campbell followed the text of the 1829
edition, claiming that because of Coleridge's illness during the last year
of his life this was the last edition 'upon which he was able to bestow
personal care and attention'. But there is substantial evidence to indicate
that though he was ill and strongly dependent on the help of his nephew,
Coleridge (as Stillinger puts it) 'had a hand in revisions up to the very

end', and that E. H. Coleridge was right to follow the 1834 edition in his Oxford University Press edition of 1912.

I have here followed as closely as possible the 1834 edition, including what Stillinger calls its 'distinctive accidentals' (far fewer initial capitals in nouns than in earlier collections, for example), and I have modified the punctuation and spelling only in cases where not to do so would prove confusing to a reader today. Since Coleridge's spelling hovers characteristically between older and more modern practice, obsolete and in some instances eccentric spellings have not been modernized except in cases where Coleridge's actual spelling might have impeded comprehension. Where ampersands appear in poems as they were originally printed in Coleridge's lifetime, they have been expanded to 'and'; ampersands have been retained, however, when they appear in poems left in manuscript at the time of his death.

For poems not included in the 1834 edition the latest text published in Coleridge's lifetime has been followed, or, in the case of unpublished poems, the most authoritative versions of manuscripts printed in recent standard editions of Coleridge's writing. Titles assigned to poems in later editions (after 1834) and having no clear basis in a manuscript source are given in square brackets. The style of titles from the early editions is reflected here by the use of different type-size and -style and capitalization patterns to distinguish main titles from subtitles and subsidiary title prose. I have usually retained Coleridge's double punctuation at the ends of clauses (,– or :–), because I believe he meant something rhetorically in using such punctuation and because it is rarely confusing. The closest thing we have to a set of Coleridgean principles on punctuation is an informal unpublished essay, dated 1809 by Kathleen Coburn in her edition of the *Notebooks*, now in the Victoria College Library at the University of Toronto (see Appendix 2). While I have consulted some Coleridge manuscript material directly, I have not been able to edit every unpublished poem anew and have relied heavily on Earl Leslie Grigg's edition of the *Collected Letters* and on Kathleen Coburn's edition of the *Notebooks*.

This edition includes all the poems known to have been published by Coleridge, with the exception of some of the epigrams, translations and adaptations that he himself never collected. It also includes a substantial selection of verse that remained in manuscript at the time of his death. I worked on this edition from the outset knowing that J. C. C. Mays would soon publish what will become the most complete and authoritative edition of the poems and plays in the Bollingen–Princeton *Collected Coleridge*. This edition was published in 2002 and contains among other things, a great deal of previously unpublished verse, as well as previously unknown or lost versions of published poems. Readers will obviously want to consult Mays's edition for such new material, as well as for the wealth of new textual information it offers. I should also mention here my indebtedness to John Beer's revised and expanded Everyman edition of the *Poems*. Since Beer was able to consult Mays's dates of composition for Coleridge's poems, the chronological ordering in the revised Everyman edition is particularly valuable.

Organizing an edition according to chronological order of composition will produce anomalies and uncertainties, especially with a poet such as Coleridge who kept revising his poems over a long period of time. 'The Eolian Harp', to cite one obvious instance, appears here among the poems of 1795 (it was first published in the *Poems* of 1796), even though it assumed its final form only when Coleridge revised it for *Sibylline Leaves* of 1817. One advantage of this procedure for the present edition is that it coincides with the view that Coleridge himself expressed in discussing the last edition of his poems with his nephew: 'After all you can say, I still think the chronological order the best for arranging a poet's works. All your divisions are in particular instances inadequate, and they destroy the interest which arises from watching the progress, maturity, and even the decay of genius' (*Table Talk*, 1 January 1834).

ACKNOWLEDGEMENTS

Like anyone working on Coleridge and his poetry, I am particularly indebted to the editors of the *Collected Coleridge* and to Kathleen Coburn for her edition of the *Notebooks*. Kelvin Everest and Jack Stillinger offered very helpful general advice on undertaking this edition, as well as more specific assistance at various stages of the work. James C. McKusick brought to my attention Coleridge's previously uncollected verse translation of 'The Song of Deborah', which I am pleased to include in this volume. For different kinds of help I wish to thank Anthony Arnove, Megan Behrent, Julia Deisler, Paul Magnuson, Lance Newman, Eric Ruder, Henry Spiller, Jeanne Spiller and Annie Zirin. Sheila Emerson's abiding interest and support were, and are, surpassingly important. From the beginning Christopher Ricks, the General Editor of this series, gave me his attentive encouragement; near the end, he gave the typescript a generously careful reading. Antony Wood and Annamaria Formichella provided excellent editorial assistance in the final stages of preparing the text for publication.

For permission to publish copyright material, I am grateful to Oxford University Press for quotations from E. H. Coleridge's edition of *Coleridge: Poetical Works* (1912) and from Earl Leslie Griggs's edition of the *Collected Letters of Samuel Taylor Coleridge* (1956–71); to Princeton University Press for material from the *Collected Coleridge* and from Coburn's edition of the *Notebooks*; and to Edinburgh University Press for Anthea Morrison's English translation of Coleridge's prize-winning Greek ode on the slave trade.

TABLE OF DATES

1795 *January* Lives in Bristol with George Burnett.
February Begins political lectures eventually published as *Conciones ad Populum. Or Addresses to the People*.
August Meets William Wordsworth.
August–September Quarrels with Southey; Pantisocracy scheme falls through.
4 October Marries Sara Fricker.
December Publishes 'An Answer to "A Letter to Edward Long Fox"' and 'Plot discovered'; plans a periodical to be called *The Watchman*.

1796 *9 January–13 February* Tour through Midlands to sell subscriptions to *The Watchman*; meets Erasmus Darwin, the painter Joseph Wright of Derby.
1 March–13 May *The Watchman* published in ten numbers.
March Takes laudanum for two weeks to relieve a painful eye infection.
16 April *Poems on Various Subjects* published.
19 September Birth of first son, David Hartley. Reconciliation with Southey.
December Moves to Nether Stowey, Somerset, near Thomas Poole.
31 December 'Ode on the Departing Year' published in the *Cambridge Intelligencer*.

1797 *March* William Wordsworth visits STC at Stowey; the two have developed a close friendship.
June Visits William and Dorothy Wordsworth at Racedown, Dorset.
July The Wordsworths settle at Alfoxden House, near Stowey.
16 October Completes the drama *Osorio*, publishes a second edition of *Poems, to which Are Now Added, Poems by Charles Lamb and Charles Lloyd*.
November Agrees to contribute regularly to the *Morning Post*, and publishes verse there including 'The Visions of the Maid of Orleans'.
13–16 November STC and William Wordsworth take an extended walk to Lynton, plan and begin composition of the 'Ancient Mariner'; these discussions form the germ of *Lyrical Ballads*.

1798 *January* Delivers Unitarian sermons at Shrewsbury, where he first meets William Hazlitt; accepts £150 annuity from the Wedgwood family.
March Completes 'Ancient Mariner', decides to go to Germany with the Wordsworths.

14 May Second son, Berkeley, is born.

18 September Lyrical Ballads is published, anonymously; STC and the Wordsworths sail to Hamburg on 19 September.

1799   *April* At the University of Göttingen; homesickness leads to extended bouts of drinking and opium-taking. Receives news that his infant son Berkeley has died.

29 July Returns to England and Stowey.

September–October Walking tour in Devon with Southey; meets Humphry Davy in Bristol.

26 October Meets Sara Hutchinson.

October–November First walking tour of the Lake District with Wordsworth.

10 November Receives offer from his friend Daniel Stuart, editor of the *Morning Post*, to work for the paper in London on full salary; arrives in London on 27 November, resumes friendship with Charles Lamb (an old school-friend from Christ's Hospital), becomes friends with William Godwin.

1800   *January–April* Works as a reporter and leader-writer for the *Morning Post*; translates Schiller's play *Wallenstein* (1797–9).

March STC's wife Sara leaves London; STC lives at Pentonville with Lamb; offered a proprietary share in the *Morning Post* but declines.

April Visits the Wordsworths at Grasmere.

May–June Visit to Stowey and Bristol.

24 July Moves with his family to Greta Hall, Keswick.

14 September Third son, Derwent, is born.

September–October Oversees printing of the second edition of *Lyrical Ballads*.

1801   *January* Second edition of *Lyrical Ballads* published; extended illness.

21 January Returns to London, where he lives and works during most of this year.

July–August In Lake District; affection for Sara Hutchinson deepens.

1802   *January* After Christmas visit to Stowey, returns to London with Poole, under the care of Stuart.

March–November Returns to Lake District; severe tension between STC and his wife.

4 April Writes 'A Letter to—[Sara Hutchinson]', which is published in the *Morning Post* on 4 October as 'Dejection: an Ode'.

Late November Returns to London for three days, then takes a

trip through South Wales with Tom and Sally Wedgwood.
23 December First daughter, Sara, is born.

1803 *June* A third edition of *Poems* is published. Visited at Greta Hall by Sir George and Lady Beaumont, Samuel Rogers, and William Hazlitt.
15–29 August Goes on a Scottish tour with William and Dorothy Wordsworth.
September–October First indication in notebooks of a plan 'to write my metaphysical works, as *my Life*'.

1804 Health further deteriorates.
April Sails to Malta, where (from July) he serves as under-secretary to Alexander Hall, British High Commissioner.
August–November Goes to Sicily, where he stays with G. F. Leckie and makes two ascents of Mount Etna.

1805 *January* Appointed Acting Public Secretary in Malta.
September–December In Sicily again; visits Naples in December.

1806 *January* Visits Rome, where he meets Wilhelm von Humboldt, Ludwig Tieck, Friedrich Schlegel; later visits Florence, Pisa.
23 June Sails from Livorno for England, where he arrives on 17 August.
Late October Returns to Lake District, where he determines to separate from his wife; becomes disillusioned with and alienated from William Wordsworth and Sara Hutchinson.

1807 *Late January* At Coleorton, hears Wordsworth read *The Prelude*, writes 'Lines to William Wordsworth'.
June Visits his family at Stowey.
August Meets Thomas De Quincey.
Autumn Returns to London.

1808 *January–June* Lives in rooms above *The Courier* office in the Strand (*The Courier* had been bought by Daniel Stuart in 1799). Lectures at Royal Institution on 'Poetry and Principles of Taste'; frequently ill.
Late summer Returns to the Lake District.
November Publishes first prospectus for *The Friend*, a weekly periodical.

1809 Publishes *The Friend*.

1810 *15 March* Last number of *The Friend* is published.
October Goes to London intending to live with Basil Montagu, whose remarks about Wordsworth's concern over this arrangement

precipitate a serious estrangement between STC and Wordsworth. Lives instead with the family of John Morgan, a Unitarian and wealthy wine-shipper originally from Bristol; begins a long friendship with Henry Crabb Robinson.

1811   Continues to write for *The Courier*.
November Begins lectures on Shakespeare and Milton to the London Philosophical Society at Scot's Corporation Hall.

1812   *February–March* Last journey to the Lake District.
May–August Lectures on drama in Willis's Rooms, London. In May his quarrel with Wordsworth is ameliorated through Lamb and Crabb Robinson.
November Lectures on Shakespeare begin at Surrey Institution; half of the Wedgwood annuity is withdrawn. With Southey, publishes *Omniana*, a collection of miscellaneous prose and verse. Goes to Bristol to lecture; serious depression and illness.

1813   *23 January* Drama *Remorse*, a revision of the earlier *Osorio*, opens at Drury Lane.
October–November Lectures on Shakespeare and on education in Bristol.
December Serious illness.

1814   *April* Lectures in Bristol on Milton, Cervantes, and on Napoleon, and the French Revolution; under medical care for opium addiction and suicidal depression.
1 August *Remorse* performed in Bristol.
August–September Essays 'On the Principles of Genial Criticism' published in *Felix Farley's Bristol Journal*. Moves with the Morgans to Calne, Wiltshire.

1815   *Spring* Living at Calne, STC plans to collect his poems with a new 'preface'.
July–September 'Preface' to poems develops into 'an Autobiographia literaria, or Sketches of my literary Life & opinions, as far as Poetry and *poetical* Criticism is concerned'.
19 September Sends MS of *Biographia Literaria* to printer.
October Printing of *BL* begins, to be published together with *Sibylline Leaves* (1817).

1816   *February* Receives financial help from the Literary Fund and from Byron.
March Returns to London, ill.
April–May Owing to technical problems *BL* and *1817* are to be issued separately.

15 April Accepted as a patient and lodger by Dr and Mrs James Gillman, Highgate.

May–June Christabel volume is published.

July Further problems develop with the publishing of *BL*.

December Publishes *Statesman's Manual; or The Bible the Best Guide to Political Skill and Foresight*, sharply criticized by Hazlitt in the *Examiner* and the *Edinburgh Review*.

1817 *January–June* Gale and Fenner, the new publishers of *BL*, ask STC for additional material for volume 2.

Summer Meets and becomes close friends with J. H. Green, young admirer.

July BL and *1817* are finally published.

November Drama *Zapolya* is published; visited by Ludwig Tieck in Highgate.

1818 *January* 'Treatise on Method' appears in the *Encyclopedia Metropolitana*.

April Writes pamphlets supporting the bill against exploitation of child labour.

November Three-volume edition of *The Friend* is published.

December Lectures alternately on the history of philosophy and on literature (until March 1819).

1819 *March* Rest Fenner, one of the publishers of *BL*, goes bankrupt, leaving STC with a serious loss.

11 April Meets Keats.

14 April Hartley Coleridge elected Fellow of Oriel College, Oxford.

1820 *March* Again plans to write a *magnum opus*.

May Hartley Coleridge's Oriel fellowship is not renewed.

October Derwent Coleridge enters St John's College, Cambridge.

1821 *July* Visits his brother, the Rev. George Coleridge.

Autumn Refuses an invitation to lecture in Dublin.

1822 *Spring* Begins receiving visitors in Highgate and holding a 'Thursday-evening class' on philosophy.

November STC's wife and daughter visit him in Highgate.

Late December Nephew H. N. Coleridge begins recording STC's *Table Talk*; Derwent Coleridge leaves Cambridge suddenly.

1823 *December* The Gillmans move to 3 The Grove, Highgate, adding a new attic study for STC.

1824   *March* Elected Fellow of the Royal Society of Literature with an annuity of £100.
June Visited by Thomas Carlyle and Dante Gabriel Rossetti in Highgate. Derwent Coleridge returns to Cambridge and receives his BA.

1825   *May* Publishes *Aids to Reflection*.
18 May Delivers the Royal Society of Literature lecture 'On the *Prometheus* of Aeschylus'.

1827   *May* Becomes seriously ill; visit from his old friend Thomas Poole. Derwent Coleridge marries Mary Pridham. Sir George Beaumont dies, leaving STC's wife £100.

1828   *22 April* STC receives a visit from James Fenimore Cooper.
21 June–7 August Rhine tour with William Wordsworth and his daughter Dora.
June–July Publishes *Poetical Works* in three volumes.

1829   *May* Publishes a second edition of *Poetical Works*.
Poetical Works of Coleridge, Shelley, and Keats issued by Galignani in Paris.
3 September Daughter Sara marries her cousin, H. N. Coleridge.
December On the Constitution of Church and State published.

1830   *June* Sara and H. N. Coleridge settle near STC in Hampstead.
July Makes his will.

1831   Last meetings between STC and Wordsworth.

1832   Receives a legacy of £300 from Adam Steinmetz.

1833   Hartley Coleridge publishes *Poems*, dedicated to STC.
24 May–9 June Visits Cambridge for a meeting of the British Association.
5 August Receives a visit from Ralph Waldo Emerson in Highgate.

1834   *March–July* Works on a third edition of the *Poetical Works* with the assistance of H. N. Coleridge.
25 July Dies in Highgate.

FURTHER READING

Collected Works and Prose

The standard version of STC's works, still in progress, is the *Collected Works*, general editor Kathleen Coburn, published for the Bollingen Foundation by Princeton University Press from 1969. Bollingen and Princeton are also the publishers of the *Notebooks*, edited by Coburn (four double volumes, text and notes, have so far been published), and of the recently published *Poetical Works*, edited by J. C. C. Mays (Part I, *Poems*, Reading Text; Part II, *Poems*, Variorum; Part III, *Plays*, edited with Joyce Crick, 2002). For prose works not yet available in this series, the seven-volume *Complete Works* edited by W. G. T. Shedd, 1853 (reprinted 1871, 1875, 1884) may be consulted. Useful collections of STC's prose include *Biographia Literaria*, edited by John Shawcross, Oxford University Press, 1907 (the second volume includes some of STC's essays on aesthetic theory); *Coleridge's Shakespearean Criticism*, edited by T. M. Raysor, 1930, revised edition, London, Everyman's Library, 1960; *Coleridge's Miscellaneous Criticism*, edited by Raysor, Cambridge, MA, Harvard University Press, 1936; and *Inquiring Spirit: A New Presentation of Coleridge from his Published and Unpublished Prose Writings*, edited by Kathleen Coburn, London, Routledge & Kegan Paul, 1951, revised edition, University of Toronto Press, 1979. The standard edition of STC's letters is the *Collected Letters*, edited by Earl Leslie Griggs, six volumes, Oxford University Press, 1956–71.

Editions of the Poems

Editions of STC's poems published in his lifetime and later in the nineteenth century are listed at the beginning of the Notes. The three most important subsequent editions prior to Mays's edition of the *Poetical Works* are *The Poetical Works of Samuel Taylor Coleridge*, edited by James Dykes Campbell, London, Macmillan, 1893; *The Complete Poetical Works of Samuel Taylor Coleridge*, edited by Ernest Hartley Coleridge, two volumes, Oxford University Press, 1912; and the Everyman Library edition of the *Poems*, edited by John Beer, London, 1963; revised edition 1993. The best selected editions are *Selected Poetry and Prose*, edited by Elisabeth Schneider, New York, Holt, Rinehart & Winston, 1951, reprinted 1971; *Coleridge's Verse: A Selection*, edited by William Empson and David Pirie, London, Faber, 1972; and the Oxford Authors *Samuel Taylor Coleridge*, edited by H. J. Jackson, Oxford University Press, 1985. Very much worth consulting are the freshly edited texts of STC's seven most widely read poems in Jack Stillinger's *Coleridge and Textual Instability*, Oxford University Press, 1994.

Biographies

Campbell's biographical introduction to the *Poetical Works* (1893) is still an important account; it was published separately in 1894 as *Coleridge: A Narrative of the Events of His Life*. Walter Jackson Bate's *Coleridge*, Toronto, Macmillan, 1968, is the best modern critical biography. Of particular interest among the many more specialized biographical studies are Richard Holmes's *Coleridge: Early Visions*, New York, Viking Penguin, 1989, and Nicholas Roe's *Wordsworth and Coleridge: The Radical Years*, Oxford, Clarendon Press, 1988. See also *Coleridge the Talker*, edited by Richard W. Armour and Raymond F. Howes, 1940; revised edition, New York and London, Johnson Reprint, 1969.

Criticism

This is a selective list of twentieth-century critical books. Essays of particular critical or scholarly pertinence are mentioned in the Notes. For Coleridge's contemporary and nineteenth-century reputation, see *Coleridge: The Critical Heritage*, edited by J. R. de J. Jackson, London, Routledge & Kegan Paul, 1970, reprinted 1991. The most useful bibliographies of Coleridge criticism and scholarship are those in volume 3 of the *New Cambridge Bibliography of English Literature* (covers work published before 1967), David Erdman's bibliography *The Romantic Movement* published as an annual supplement to *English Language Notes* until 1980 and then as a separate volume by Garland Publishing, New York, and the section on Coleridge in *The English Romantic Poets: A Review of Research and Criticism*, edited by Frank Jordan, New York, Modern Language Association of America, 1985. John Beer's brief discussion of 'Coleridge and His Critics' in the Everyman edition of the *Poems*, pp. 497–513 offers a helpful guide to some of the important nineteenth-century criticism.

J. A. Appleyard, *Coleridge's Philosophy of Literature: The Development of a Concept of Poetry 1791–1819*, Cambridge, MA, Harvard University Press, 1965

Rosemary Ashton, *The Life of Samuel Taylor Coleridge*, Oxford, Blackwell, 1996

Owen Barfield, *What Coleridge Thought*, 2nd edition, London, Oxford University Press, 1965

J. Robert Barth, *Coleridge and Christian Doctrine*, Cambridge, MA, Harvard University Press, 1969

John Beer, *Coleridge's Poetic Intelligence*, London, Macmillan, 1977

Alan Bewell, *Romanticism and Colonial Disease*, Baltimore, The Johns Hopkins University Press, 2000

Julie Carlson, *In the Theatre of Romanticism: Coleridge, Nationalism, Women*, Cambridge, Cambridge University Press, 1994

Jerome Christensen, *Coleridge's Blessed Machine of Language*, Ithaca, Cornell University Press, 1981

Timothy Corrigan, *Coleridge, Language, and Criticism*, Athens, University of Georgia Press, 1982

Susan Eilenberg, *Strange Powers of Speech: Wordsworth, Coleridge, and Literary Possession* (New York, Oxford University Press, 1992)

Kelvin Everest, *Coleridge's Secret Ministry*, Sussex, Harvester Press; New York, Barnes & Noble, 1979

Richard Harter Fogle, *The Idea of Coleridge's Criticism*, Berkeley and Los Angeles, University of California Press, 1962

Jennifer Ford, *Coleridge on Dreaming: Dreams and the Medical Imagination*. Cambridge, Cambridge University Press, 1997

Norman Fruman, *Coleridge the Damaged Archangel*, New York, George Braziller, 1971

A. C. Goodson, *Verbal Imagination: Coleridge and the Language of Modern Criticism*, New York, Oxford University Press, 1988

Paul Hamilton, *Coleridge's Poetics*, Stanford, Stanford University Press, 1983

John A. Hodgson, *Coleridge, Shelley, and Transcendental Inquiry*, Lincoln and London, University of Nebraska Press, 1989

Humphry House, *Coleridge*, London, Rupert Hart-Davis, 1953

Edward Kessler, *Coleridge's Metaphors of Being*, Princeton, Princeton University Press, 1979

Nigel Leask, *The Politics of Imagination in Coleridge's Thought*, London, Macmillan, 1988

T. H. Levere, *Poetry Realized in Nature: Samuel Taylor Coleridge and Early Nineteenth-Century Science*, Cambridge University Press, 1981

Laurence S. Lockridge, *Coleridge the Moralist*, Ithaca, Cornell University Press, 1977

J. L. Lowes, *The Road to Xanadu: A Study in the Ways of the Imagination*, London, Constable, 1927

Thomas McFarland, *Coleridge and the Pantheist Tradition*, Oxford, Clarendon Press, 1969

James C. McKusick, *Coleridge's Philosophy of Language*, New Haven, Yale University Press, 1986

Emerson R. Marks, *Coleridge on the Language of Verse*, Princeton, Princeton University Press, 1981

Raimonda Modiano, *Coleridge and the Concept of Nature*, Tallahassee, Florida State University Press, 1985

Lucy Newlyn, *Coleridge, Wordsworth and the Language of Allusion*, Oxford, Clarendon Press, 1986

Reeve Parker, *Coleridge's Meditative Art*, Ithaca, Cornell University Press, 1975

Stephen Prickett, *Coleridge and Wordsworth: The Poetry of Growth*, Cambridge University Press, 1977

Arden Reed, *Romantic Weather: The Climates of Coleridge and Baudelaire*, Hanover and London, University Press of New England, 1983

I. A. Richards, *Coleridge on Imagination*, London, Routledge & Kegan Paul, 1934

Elisabeth Schneider, *Coleridge, Opium and 'Kubla Khan'*, Chicago, University of Chicago Press, 1953

M. F. Schultz, *The Poetic Voice of Coleridge*, Detroit, Wayne State University Press, 1963

Marshall Suther, *Visions of Xanadu*, New York and London, Columbia University Press, 1965

Jeanie Watson, *Risking Enchantment: Coleridge's Symbolic World of Faery*, Lincoln and London, University of Nebraska Press, 1990

Carl Woodring, *Politics in the Poetry of Coleridge*, Madison, University of Wisconsin Press, 1961

Ian Wylie, *Young Coleridge and the Philosophers of Nature*, Oxford, Clarendon Press, 1989

Geoffrey Yarlott, *Coleridge and the Abyssinian Maid*, London, Methuen, 1967

THE POEMS

Easter Holidays

I

Hail! festal Easter, that dost bring
Approach of sweetly smiling spring,
  When Nature's clad in green:
When feather'd songsters through the grove
With beasts confess the power of love,
  And brighten all the scene.

II

Now Youths the breaking stages load,
That swiftly rattling o'er the road
  To Greenwich haste away;
While some with sounding oars divide
Of smoothly flowing Thames the tide:
  All sing the festive lay.

III

With mirthful dance they beat the ground,
Their shouts of joy the hills resound
  And catch the jocund noise:
Without a tear, without a sigh,
Their moments all in transport fly
  Till evening ends their joys.

IV

But little think their joyous hearts
Of dire Misfortune's varied smarts,
  Which youthful years conceal;
Thoughtless of bitter smiling woe,
Which all mankind are born to know,
  And they themselves must feel.

V

Yet he, who wisdom's paths shall keep,
And virtue firm, that scorns to weep
  At ills in fortune's power;
Through this life's variegated scene,
In raging storms – or calms serene,
  Shall cheerful spend the hour.

VI
While steady virtue guides his mind,
Heav'n born content he still shall find,
    That never sheds a tear:
Without respect to any tide,
His hours away in bliss shall glide,
    Like Easter all the year.

Dura navis

To tempt the dangerous deep, too venturous youth,
Why does thy breast with fondest wishes glow?
No tender parent there thy cares shall sooth,
No much-lov'd Friend shall share thy every woe.
Why does thy mind with hopes delusive burn?
Vain are thy Schemes by heated Fancy plann'd:
Thy promis'd joy thou'lt see to Sorrow turn
Exil'd from Bliss, and from thy native land.

Hast thou foreseen the Storm's impending rage,
When to the Clouds the Waves ambitious rise,
And seem with Heaven a doubtful war to wage,
Whilst total darkness overspreads the skies;
Save when the lightnings darting wingèd Fate
Quick bursting from the pitchy clouds between
In forkèd Terror, and destructive state
Shall show with double gloom the horrid scene?

Shalt thou be at this hour from danger free?
Perhaps with fearful force some falling Wave
Shall wash thee in the wild tempestuous Sea,
And in some monster's belly fix thy grave;
Or (woful hap!) against some wave-worn rock
Which long a Terror to each Bark had stood
Shall dash thy mangled limbs with furious shock
And stain its craggy sides with human blood.

Yet not the Tempest, or the Whirlwind's roar
Equal the horrors of a Naval Fight,
When thundering Cannons spread a sea of Gore
And varied deaths now fire and now affright:

The impatient shout, that longs for closer war,
Reaches from either side the distant shores;
Whilst frighten'd at His streams ensanguin'd far
Loud on his troubled bed huge Ocean roars.

What dreadful scenes appear before my eyes!
Ah! see how each with frequent slaughter red,
Regardless of his dying fellows' cries
O'er their fresh wounds with impious order tread!
From the dread place does soft Compassion fly!
The Furies fell each alter'd breast command;
Whilst Vengeance drunk with human blood stands by
And smiling fires each heart and arms each hand.

Should'st thou escape the fury of that day
A fate more cruel still, unhappy, view.
Opposing winds may stop thy luckless way,
And spread fell famine through the suffering crew,
Canst thou endure th' extreme of raging Thirst
Which soon may scorch thy throat, ah! thoughtless Youth?
Or ravening hunger canst thou bear which erst
On its own flesh hath fix'd the deadly tooth?

Dubious and fluttering 'twixt hope and fear
With trembling hands the lot I see thee draw,
Which shall, or sentence thee a victim drear,
To that gaunt Plague which savage knows no law:
Or, deep thy dagger in the friendly heart,
Whilst each strong passion agitates thy breast,
Though oft with Horror back I see thee start,
Lo! Hunger *drives* thee to th' inhuman feast.

These are the ills, that may the course attend –
Then with the joys of home contented rest –
Here, meek-eyed Peace with humble Plenty lend
Their aid united still, to make thee blest.
To ease each pain, and to increase each joy –
Here mutual Love shall fix thy tender wife,
Whose offspring shall thy youthful care employ
And gild with brightest rays the evening of thy Life.

Nil pejus est caelibe vita

I

What pleasures shall he ever find?
What joys shall ever glad his heart?
Or who shall heal his wounded mind,
If tortur'd by Misfortune's smart?
Who Hymeneal bliss will never prove,
That more than friendship, friendship mix'd with love.

II

Then without child or tender wife,
To drive away each care, each sigh,
Lonely he treads the paths of life
A stranger to Affection's tie:
And when from Death he meets his final doom
No mourning wife with tears of love shall wet his tomb.

III

Tho' Fortune, Riches, Honours, Pow'r,
Had giv'n with every other toy,
Those gilded trifles of the hour,
Those painted nothings sure to cloy:
He dies forgot, his name no son shall bear
To show the man so blest once breath'd the vital air.

Sonnet
TO THE AUTUMNAL MOON

Mild Splendour of the various-vested Night!
Mother of wildly-working visions! hail!
I watch thy gliding, while with watery light
Thy weak eye glimmers through a fleecy veil;
And when thou lovest thy pale orb to shroud
Behind the gathered blackness lost on high;
And when thou dartest from the wind-rent cloud
Thy placid lightning o'er the awakened sky.

Ah such is Hope! as changeful and as fair!
10   Now dimly peering on the wistful sight;
Now hid behind the dragon-winged Despair:
But soon emerging in her radiant might
She o'er the sorrow-clouded breast of Care
Sails, like a meteor kindling in its flight.

Julia

Medio de fonte leporum
Surgit amari aliquid.

Julia was blest with beauty, wit, and grace:
Small poets lov'd to sing her blooming face.
Before her altars, lo! a numerous train
Preferr'd their vows; yet all preferr'd in vain,
Till charming Florio, born to conquer, came
And touch'd the fair one with an equal flame.
The flame she felt, and ill could she conceal
What every look and action would reveal.
With boldness then, which seldom fails to move,
10   He pleads the cause of Marriage and of Love:
The course of Hymeneal joys he rounds,
The fair one's eyes danc'd pleasure at the sounds.
Nought now remain'd but 'Noes' – how little meant!
And the sweet coyness that endears consent.
The youth upon his knees enraptur'd fell:
The strange misfortune, oh! what words can tell?
Tell! ye neglected sylphs! who lap-dogs guard,
Why snatch'd ye not away your precious ward?
Why suffer'd ye the lover's weight to fall
20   On the ill-fated neck of much-lov'd Ball?
The favourite on his mistress casts his eyes,
Gives a short melancholy howl, and – dies.
Sacred his ashes lie, and long his rest!
Anger and grief divide poor Julia's breast.
Her eyes she fixt on guilty Florio first:
On him the storm of angry grief must burst.

That storm he fled: he wooes a kinder fair,
Whose fond affections no dear puppies share.
'Twere vain to tell, how Julia pin'd away:
30   Unhappy Fair! that in one luckless day –
From future Almanacks the day be crost! –
At once her Lover and her Lap-dog lost.

Quae nocent docent

O! mihi praeteritos referat si Jupiter annos!

Oh! might my ill-passed hours return again!
No more, as then, should Sloth around me throw
    Her soul-enslaving, leaden chain!
No more the precious time would I employ
In giddy revels, or in thoughtless joy,
A present joy producing future woe.

But o'er the midnight Lamp I'd love to pore,
I'd seek with care fair Learning's depths to sound,
    And gather scientific Lore:
10   Or to mature the embryo thoughts inclin'd,
That half-conceiv'd lay struggling in my mind,
The cloisters' solitary gloom I'd round.

'Tis vain to wish, for Time has ta'en his flight –
For follies past be ceas'd the fruitless tears:
    Let follies past to future care incite.
Averse maturer judgements to obey
Youth owns, with pleasure owns, the Passions' sway,
But sage Experience only comes with years.

The Nose

Ye souls unus'd to lofty verse,
    Who sweep the earth with lowly wing,
Like sand before the blast disperse –
    A Nose! a mighty Nose I sing!

As erst Prometheus stole from heaven the fire
   To animate the wonder of his hand;
Thus with unhallow'd hands, O muse, aspire,
   And from my subject snatch a burning brand!
So like the Nose I sing – my verse shall glow –
Like Phlegethon my verse in waves of fire shall flow!

   Light of this once all darksome spot
     Where now their glad course mortals run,
   First-born of Sirius begot
     Upon the focus of the sun –
I'll call thee ——! for such thy earthly name –
   What name so high, but what too low must be?
Comets, when most they drink the solar flame
   Are but faint types and images of thee!
Burn madly Fire! o'er earth in ravage run,
Then blush for shame more red by fiercer —— outdone!

   I saw when from the turtle feast
     The thick dark smoke in volumes rose!
   I saw the darkness of the mist
     Encircle thee, O Nose!
Shorn of thy rays thou shott'st a fearful gleam
   (The turtle quiver'd with prophetic fright)
Gloomy and sullen thro' the night of steam:–
   So Satan's Nose when Dunstan urg'd to flight,
Glowing from gripe of red hot pincers dread
Athwart the smokes of Hell disastrous twilight shed!

   The furies to madness my brain devote –
     In robes of ice my body wrap!
   On billowy flames of fire I float,
     Hear ye my entrails how they snap?
Some power unseen forbids my lungs to breathe!
   What fire–clad meteors round me whizzing fly!
I vitrify thy torrid zone beneath,
   Proboscis fierce! I am calcin'd! I die!
Thus, like great Pliny, in Vesuvius' fire,
I perish in the blaze while I the blaze admire.

Life

As late I journied o'er the extensive plain
    Where native Otter sports his scanty stream,
Musing in torpid woe a sister's pain,
    The glorious prospect woke me from the dream.

At every step it widen'd to my sight,
    Wood, Meadow, verdant Hill, and dreary Steep,
Following in quick succession of delight,
    Till all – at once – did my eye ravish'd sweep!

May this (I cried) my course through Life portray!
New scenes of wisdom may each step display,
    And knowledge open as my days advance!
Till what time Death shall pour the undarken'd ray,
    My eye shall dart thro' infinite expanse,
And thought suspended lie in rapture's blissful
        Trance.

To the Muse

Tho' no bold flights to thee belong;
And tho' thy lays with conscious fear,
Shrink from Judgment's eye severe,
Yet much I thank thee, Spirit of my song!
For, lovely Muse! thy sweet employ
Exalts my soul, refines my breast,
Gives each pure pleasure keener zest,
And softens sorrow into pensive Joy.
From thee I learn'd the wish to bless,
From thee to commune with my heart;
From thee, dear Muse! the gayer part,
To laugh with Pity at the crowds that press
Where Fashion flaunts her robes by Folly spun,
Whose hues gay-varying wanton in the sun.

Destruction of the Bastile

I

Heard'st thou yon universal cry,
    And dost thou linger still on Gallia's shore?
Go, Tyranny! beneath some barbarous sky
    Thy terrors lost, and ruin'd power deplore!
        What tho' through many a groaning age
        Was felt thy keen suspicious rage,
        Yet Freedom rous'd by fierce Disdain
        Has wildly broke thy triple chain,
And like the storm which earth's deep entrails hide,
At length has burst its way and spread the ruins wide.

*   *   *

IV

In sighs their sickly breath was spent; each gleam
    Of Hope had cease'd the long long day to cheer;
Or if delusive, in some flitting dream,
    It gave them to their friends and children dear –
        Awak'd by lordly Insult's sound
        To all the doubled horrors round,
        Oft shrunk they from Oppression's band
        While anguish rais'd the desperate hand
For silent death; or lost the mind's control,
Thro' every burning vein would tides of Frenzy roll.

V

But cease, ye pitying bosoms, cease to bleed!
    Such scenes no more demand the tear humane;
I see, I see! glad Liberty succeed
    With every patriot virtue in her train!
        And mark yon peasant's raptured eyes;
        Secure he views his harvests rise;
        No fetter vile the mind shall know,
        And Eloquence shall fearless glow.
Yes! Liberty the soul of Life shall reign,
Shall throb in every pulse, shall flow thro' every vein!

VI
Shall France alone a Despot spurn?
   Shall she alone, O Freedom, boast thy care?
Lo, round thy standard Belgia's heroes burn,
   Tho' Power's blood-stain'd streamers fire the air,
      And wider yet thy influence spread,
      Nor e'er recline thy weary head,
     Till every land from pole to pole
     Shall boast one independent soul!
And still, as erst, let favour'd Britain be
40 First ever of the first and freest of the free!

Anthem
FOR THE CHILDREN OF CHRIST'S HOSPITAL

   Seraphs! around th' Eternal's seat who throng
      With tuneful ecstacies of praise:
   O! teach our feeble tongues like yours the song
      Of fervent gratitude to raise –
   Like you, inspir'd with holy flame
   To dwell on that Almighty name
Who bade the child of woe no longer sigh,
And Joy in tears o'erspread the Widow's eye.

   Th' all-gracious Parent hears the wretch's prayer;
10   The meek tear strongly pleads on high;
   Wan Resignation struggling with despair
     The Lord beholds with pitying eye;
   Sees cheerless want unpitied pine,
   Disease on earth its head recline,
And bids compassion seek the realms of woe
To heal the wounded, and to raise the low.

   She comes! she comes! the meek-eyed power I see
      With liberal hand that loves to bless;
   The clouds of sorrow at her presence flee;
20   Rejoice! rejoice! ye children of distress!
   The beams that play around her head
   Thro' want's dark vale their radiance spread:
The young uncultur'd mind imbibes the ray,
And vice reluctant quits th' expected prey.

Cease, thou lorn mother! cease thy wailings drear;
    Ye babes! the unconscious sob forego;
Or let full gratitude now prompt the tear
    Which erst did sorrow force to flow.
    Unkindly cold and tempest shrill
30   In life's morn oft the traveller chill,
But soon his path the sun of Love shall warm;
And each glad scene look brighter for the storm!

Progress of Vice

Deep in the gulph of Vice and Woe
Leaps man at once with headlong throw?
Him inborn Truth and Virtue guide,
    Whose guards are shame and conscious pride;
In some gay hour Vice steals into the breast;
Perchance she wears some softer Virtue's vest.
By unperceiv'd degrees she tempts to stray,
Till far from Virtue's path she leads the feet away.

Then swift the soul to disenthrall
10   Will Memory the past recall,
    And fear before the Victim's eyes
    Bid future ills and dangers rise.
But hark! the voice, the lyre, their charms combine –
Gay sparkles in the cup the generous wine;
Th' inebriate dance the fair frail nymph inspires,
And Virtue vanquish'd – scorn'd – with hasty flight retires.

But soon to tempt the pleasures cease;
Yet shame forbids return to peace,
And stern necessity will force
20   Still to urge on the desperate course.
The drear black paths of Vice the wretch must try,
Where Conscience flashes horror on each eye,
Where Hate – where Murder scowl – where starts Affright!
Ah! close the scene – ah! close – for dreadful is the sight.

Monody on the Death of Chatterton
[FIRST VERSION]

Cold penury repress'd his noble rage,
And froze the genial current of his soul.

    Now prompts the Muse poetic lays,
      And high my bosom beats with love of Praise!
    But, Chatterton! methinks I hear thy name,
For cold my Fancy grows, and dead each Hope of Fame.

    When Want and cold Neglect had chill'd thy soul,
Athirst for Death I see thee drench the bowl!
      Thy corpse of many a livid hue
      On the bare ground I view,
    Whilst various passions all my mind engage;
10   Now is my breast distended with a sigh,
        And now a flash of Rage
Darts through the tear, that glistens in my eye.

    Is this the land of liberal Hearts!
    Is this the land, where Genius ne'er in vain
    Pour'd forth her soul-enchanting strain?
    Ah me! yet Butler 'gainst the bigot foe
      Well-skill'd to aim keen Humour's dart,
      Yet Butler felt Want's poignant sting;
      And Otway, Master of the Tragic art,
20   Whom Pity's self had taught to sing,
      Sank beneath a load of Woe;
    This ever can the generous Briton hear,
And starts not in his eye th' indignant Tear?

    Elate of Heart and confident of Fame,
From vales where Avon sports, the Minstrel came,
      Gay as the Poet hastes along
      He meditates the future song,
How Ælla battled with his country's foes,
      And whilst Fancy in the air
30   Paints him many a vision fair
His eyes dance rapture and his bosom glows.

With generous joy he views th' ideal gold:
  He listens to many a Widow's prayers,
    And many an Orphan's thanks he hears;
      He soothes to peace the care-worn breast,
      He bids the Debtor's eyes know rest,
      And Liberty and Bliss behold:
And now he punishes the heart of steel,
And her own iron rod he makes Oppression feel.

40   Fated to heave sad Disappointment's sigh,
To feel the Hope now rais'd, and now deprest,
To feel the burnings of an injur'd breast,
  From all thy Fate's deep sorrow keen
  In vain, O Youth, I turn th' affrighted eye;
  For powerful Fancy evernigh
The hateful picture forces on my sight.
  There, Death of every dear delight,
  Frowns Poverty of Giant mien!
In vain I seek the charms of youthful grace,
50 Thy sunken eye, thy haggard cheeks it shows,
The quick emotions struggling in the Face
  Faint index of thy mental Throes,
When each strong Passion spurn'd controll,
And not a Friend was nigh to calm thy stormy soul.

Such was the sad and gloomy hour
When anguish'd Care of sullen brow
Prepared the Poison's death-cold power.
Already to thy lips was rais'd the bowl,
When filial Pity stood thee by,
60 Thy fixèd eyes she bade thee roll
On scenes that well might melt thy soul –
Thy native cot she held to view,
Thy native cot, where Peace ere long
Had listen'd to thy evening song;
Thy sister's shrieks she bade thee hear,
And mark thy mother's thrilling tear,
She made thee feel her deep-drawn sigh,
And all her silent agony of Woe.

And from *thy* Fate shall such distress ensue?
70 Ah! dash the poison'd chalice from thy hand!
And thou had'st dash'd it at her soft command;
But that Despair and Indignation rose,
And told again the story of thy Woes,
Told the keen insult of th' unfeeling Heart,
The dread dependence on the low-born mind,
Told every Woe, for which thy breast might smart,
Neglect and grinning scorn and Want combin'd –
      Recoiling back, thou sent'st the friend of Pain
To roll a tide of Death thro' every freezing vein.

80   O Spirit blest!
      Whether th' eternal Throne around,
      Amidst the blaze of Cherubim,
      Thou pourest forth the grateful hymn,
      Or, soaring through the blest Domain,
      Enraptur'st Angels with thy strain, –
      Grant me, like thee, the lyre to sound,
      Like thee, with fire divine to glow –
      But ah! when rage the Waves of Woe,
      Grant me with firmer breast t'oppose their hate,
90   And soar beyond the storms with upright eye elate!

Monody on the Death of Chatterton
[SECOND VERSION]

O what a wonder seems the fear of death,
Seeing how gladly we all sink to sleep,
Babes, Children, Youths, and Men,
Night following night for threescore years and ten!
But doubly strange, where life is but a breath
To sigh and pant with, up Want's rugged steep.

Away, Grim Phantom! Scorpion King, away!
Reserve thy terrors and thy stings display
For coward Wealth and Guilt in robes of State!
10 Lo! by the grave I stand of one, for whom
A prodigal Nature and a niggard Doom

(That all bestowing, this withholding all)
Made each chance knell from distant spire or dome
Sound like a seeking Mother's anxious call,
Return, poor Child! Home, weary Truant, home!

Thee, Chatterton! these unblest stones protect
From want, and the bleak freezings of neglect.
Too long before the vexing Storm-blast driven
Here hast thou found repose! beneath this sod!
Thou! O vain word! thou dwell'st not with the clod!
Amid the shining Host of the Forgiven
Thou at the throne of Mercy and thy God
The triumph of redeeming Love dost hymn
(Believe it, O my Soul!) to harps of Seraphim.

Yet oft, perforce ('tis suffering Nature's call),
I weep, that heaven-born Genius so should fall;
And oft, in Fancy's saddest hour, my soul
Averted shudders at the poisoned bowl.
Now groans my sickening heart, as still I view
        Thy corse of livid hue;
Now indignation checks the feeble sigh,
Or flashes through the tear that glistens in mine eye!

Is this the land of song-ennobled line?
Is this the land, where Genius ne'er in vain
        Poured forth his lofty strain?
Ah me! yet Spenser, gentlest bard divine,
Beneath chill Disappointment's shade,
His weary limbs in lonely anguish laid;
        And o'er her darling dead
        Pity hopeless hung her head,
While 'mid the pelting of that merciless storm',
Sunk to the cold earth Otway's famished form!

Sublime of thought, and confident of fame,
From vales where Avon winds the Minstrel came.
        Light-hearted youth! aye, as he hastes along,
            He meditates the future song,

20

30

40

How dauntless Ælla fray'd the Dacyan foe;
  And while the numbers flowing strong
    In eddies whirl, in surges throng,
50   Exulting in the spirit's genial throe
In tides of power his life-blood seems to flow.

And now his cheeks with deeper ardours flame,
His eyes have glorious meanings, that declare
More than the light of outward day shines there,
A holier triumph and a sterner aim!
Wings grow within him; and he soars above
Or Bard's or Minstrel's lay of war or love.
Friends to the friendless, to the Sufferer health,
He hears the widow's prayer, the good man's praise;
60   To scenes of bliss transmutes his fancied wealth,
And young and old shall now see happy days.
On many a waste he bids trim Gardens rise,
Gives the blue sky to many a prisoner's eyes;
And now in wrath he grasps the patriot steel,
And her own iron rod he makes Oppression feel.

Sweet Flower of Hope! free Nature's genial child!
That didst so fair disclose thy early bloom,
Filling the wide air with a rich perfume!
For thee in vain all heavenly aspects smil'd;
70   From the hard world brief respite they could win –
The frost nipp'd sharp without, the canker prey'd within!
Ah! where are fled the charms of vernal Grace,
And Joy's wild gleams that lighten'd o'er thy face?
Youth of tumultuous soul, and haggard eye!
Thy wasted form, thy hurried steps I view,
On thy wan forehead starts the lethal dew,
And oh! the anguish of that shuddering sigh!

    Such were the struggles of the gloomy hour,
      When Care, of withered brow,
80   Prepared the poison's death-cold power:
    Already to thy lips was raised the bowl,
      When near thee stood Affection meek
      (Her bosom bare, and wildly pale her cheek)
    Thy sullen gaze she bade thee roll
    On scenes that well might melt thy soul;
Thy native cot she flashed upon thy view,

Thy native cot, where still, at close of day,
Peace smiling sate, and listened to thy lay;
Thy Sister's shrieks she bade thee hear,
And mark thy mother's thrilling tear;
        See, see her breast's convulsive throe,
        Her silent agony of woe!
Ah, dash the poisoned chalice from thy hand!

And thou hadst dashed it, at her soft command,
But that Despair and Indignation rose,
And told again the story of thy woes;
Told the keen insult of the unfeeling heart;
The dread dependence on the low-born mind;
Told every pang, with which thy soul must smart,
Neglect, and grinning Scorn, and Want combined!
Recoiling quick, thou badst the friend of pain
Roll the black tide of Death through every freezing vein!

                O Spirit blest!
Whether the Eternal's throne around,
Amidst the blaze of Seraphim,
Thou pourest forth the grateful hymn;
Or soaring thro' the blest domain
Enrapturest Angels with thy strain –
Grant me, like thee, the lyre to sound,
Like thee with fire divine to glow;
But ah! when rage the waves of woe,
Grant me with firmer breast to meet their hate,
And soar beyond the storm with upright eye elate!

Ye woods! that wave o'er Avon's rocky steep,
To Fancy's ear sweet is your murmuring deep!
For here she loves the cypress wreath to weave
Watching, with wistful eye, the saddening tints of eve.
Here, far from men, amid this pathless grove,
In solemn thought the Minstrel wont to rove,
Like star-beam on the slow sequestered tide
Long-glittering, through the high tree branching wide.

And here, in Inspiration's eager hour,
When most the big soul feels the mastering power,
        These wilds, these caverns roaming o'er,
        Round which the screaming sea-gulls soar,

With wild unequal steps he passed along,
Oft pouring on the winds a broken song:
Anon, upon some rough rock's fearful brow
Would pause abrupt – and gaze upon the waves below.

130   Poor Chatterton! he sorrows for thy fate
Who would have praised and loved thee, ere too late.
Poor Chatterton! farewell! of darkest hues
This chaplet cast I on thy unshaped tomb;
But dare no longer on the sad theme muse,
Lest kindred woes persuade a kindred doom:
For oh! big gall-drops, shook from Folly's wing,
Have blackened the fair promise of my spring;
And the stern Fate transpierced with viewless dart
The last pale Hope that shivered at my heart!

140   Hence, gloomy thoughts! no more my soul shall dwell
On joys that were! No more endure to weigh
The shame and anguish of the evil day.
Wisely forgetful! O'er the ocean swell
Sublime of Hope I seek the cottaged dell
Where Virtue calm with careless step may stray;
And, dancing to the moon-light roundelay,
The wizard passions weave a holy spell!

O Chatterton! that thou wert yet alive!
Sure thou would'st spread the canvass to the gale,
150   And love with us the tinkling team to drive
O'er peaceful Freedom's undivided dale;
And we, at sober eve, would round thee throng,
Would hang, enraptured, on thy stately song,
And greet with smiles the young-eyed Poesy
All deftly masked, as hoar Antiquity.
Alas, vain Phantasies! the fleeting brood
Of Woe self-solaced in her dreamy mood!
Yet will I love to follow the sweet dream,
Where Susquehana pours his untamed stream;
160   And on some hill, whose forest-frowning side
Waves o'er the murmurs of his calmer tide,
Will raise a solemn Cenotaph to thee,
Sweet Harper of time-shrouded Minstrelsy!
And there, soothed sadly by the dirgeful wind,
Muse on the sore ills I had left behind.

An Invocation

Sweet Muse! companion of my every hour!
Voice of my Joy! Sure soother of the sigh!
Now plume thy pinions, now exert each power,
And fly to him who owns the candid eye.

And if a smile of Praise thy labour hail
(Well shall thy labours then my mind employ)
Fly fleetly back, sweet Muse! and with the tale
O'erspread my Features with a flush of Joy!

Anna and Harland

Within these wilds was Anna wont to rove
   While Harland told his love in many a sigh,
   But stern on Harland roll'd her brother's eye,
They fought, they fell – her brother and her love!

To Death's dark house did grief-worn Anna haste,
   Yet here her pensive ghost delights to stay;
   Oft pouring on the winds the broken lay –
And hark, I hear her – 'twas the passing blast.

I love to sit upon her tomb's dark grass,
   Then Memory backward rolls Time's shadowy tide;
   The tales of other days before me glide:
With eager thought I seize them as they pass;
For fair, tho' faint, the forms of Memory gleam,
Like Heaven's bright beauteous bow reflected in the stream.

To the Evening Star

O meek attendant of Sol's setting blaze,
   I hail, sweet star, thy chaste effulgent glow;
On thee full oft with fixèd eye I gaze
   Till I, methinks, all spirit seem to grow.

O first and fairest of the starry choir,
   O loveliest 'mid the daughters of the night,
Must not the maid I love like thee inspire
   Pure joy and *calm* Delight?

   Must she not be, as is thy placid sphere,
10   Serenely brilliant? Whilst to gaze a while
Be all my wish 'mid Fancy's high career
   E'en till she quit this scene of earthly toil;
Then Hope perchance might fondly sigh to join
Her spirit in thy kindred orb, O Star benign!

Pain

Once could the Morn's first beams, the healthful breeze,
All nature charm, and gay was every hour –
But ah! not Music's self, nor fragrant bower
Can glad the trembling sense of wan disease.
Now that the frequent pangs my frame assail,
Now that my sleepless eyes are sunk and dim,
And seas of pain seem waving through each limb –
Ah what can all Life's gilded scenes avail?
I view the crowd, whom youth and health inspire,
10 Hear the loud laugh, and catch the sportive lay,
Then sigh and think – I too could laugh and play
And gaily sport it on the Muse's lyre,
Ere Tyrant Pain had chas'd away delight,
Ere the wild pulse throbb'd anguish thro' the night!

On a Lady Weeping

Lovely gems of radiance meek
Trembling down my Laura's cheek,
As the streamlets silent glide
Thro' the Mead's enamell'd pride,
Pledges sweet of pious woe,
Tears which Friendship taught to flow,
Sparkling in yon humid light
Love embathes his pinions bright:

There amid the glitt'ring shower
10   Smiling sits th' insidious Power;
As some wingèd Warbler oft
When Spring-clouds shed their treasures soft
Joyous tricks his plumes anew,
And flutters in the fost'ring dew.

Monody on a Tea-Kettle

O muse who sangest late another's pain,
To griefs domestic turn thy coal-black steed!
With slowest steps thy funeral steed must go,
Nodding his head in all the pomp of woe:
Wide scatter round each dark and deadly weed,
And let the melancholy dirge complain,
(While Bats shall shriek and Dogs shall howling run)
The tea-kettle is spoilt and Coleridge is undone!

Your cheerful songs, ye unseen crickets cease!
10   Let songs of grief your alter'd minds engage!
For he who sang responsive to your lay,
What time the joyous bubbles 'gan to play,
The sooty swain has felt the fire's fierce rage –
Yes he is gone, and all my woes increase;
I heard the Water issuing from the Wound –
No more the Tea shall pour its flagrant steams around!

O Goddess best beloved, delightful Tea!
With thee compar'd what yields the madd'ning vine?
Sweet power! who know'st to spread the calm delight,
20   And the pure joy prolong to midmost night!
Ah! must I all thy varied sweets resign?
Enfolded close in grief thy form I see
No more wilt thou extend thy willing arms,
Receive the fervent Jove and yield him all thy charms!

How sink the mighty low by Fate opprest!
Perhaps O Kettle! thou by scornful toe
Rude urg'd t' ignoble place with plaintive din,
May'st rust obscure midst heaps of vulgar tin –
As if no joy had ever seiz'd my breast

30   When from thy spout the streams did arching fly –
        As if infus'd thou ne'er hadst known t' inspire
        All the warm raptures of poetic fire!

        But hark! or do I fancy the glad voice –
        'What tho' the swain did wondrous charms disclose –
        (Not such did Memnon's sister sable drest)
        Take these bright arms with royal face imprest.
        A better Kettle shall thy soul rejoice,
        And with Oblivion's wings o'erspread thy woes!'
        Thus Fairy Hope can soothe distress and toil;
40   On empty Trivets she bids fancied Kettles boil!

Genevieve

Maid of my Love, sweet Genevieve!
In Beauty's light you glide along:
Your eye is like the star of eve,
And sweet your Voice, as Seraph's song.
Yet not your heavenly Beauty gives
This heart with passion soft to glow:
Within your soul a Voice there lives!
It bids you hear the tale of Woe.
When sinking low the Sufferer wan
10   Beholds no hand outstretcht to save,
Fair, as the bosom of the Swan
That rises graceful o'er the wave,
I've seen your breast with pity heave,
And therefore love I you, sweet Genevieve!

On Receiving an Account
THAT HIS ONLY SISTER'S DEATH WAS INEVITABLE

The tear which mourn'd a brother's fate scarce dry –
Pain after pain, and woe succeeding woe –
Is my heart destin'd for another blow?
O my sweet sister! and must thou too die?

Ah! how has Disappointment pour'd the tear
O'er infant Hope destroy'd by early frost!
How are ye gone, whom most my soul held dear!
Scarce had I lov'd you, ere I mourn'd you lost;
Say, is this hollow eye, this heartless pain,
Fated to rove thro' Life's wide cheerless plain –
Nor father, brother, sister meets its ken –
My woes, my joys unshar'd! Ah! long ere then
On me thy icy dart, stern Death, be prov'd –
Better to die, than live and not be lov'd!

On Seeing a Youth
AFFECTIONATELY WELCOMED BY A SISTER

I too a sister had! too cruel Death!
How sad remembrance bids my bosom heave!
Tranquil her soul, as sleeping Infant's breath;
Meek were her manners as a vernal Eve.
Knowledge, that frequent lifts the bloated mind,
Gave her the treasure of a lowly breast,
And Wit, to venom'd Malice oft assign'd,
Dwelt in her bosom in a Turtle's nest.
Cease, busy Memory! cease to urge the dart;
Nor on my soul her love to me impress!
For oh I mourn in anguish – and my heart
Feels the keen pang, th' unutterable distress.
Yet wherefore grieve I that her sorrows cease,
For Life was misery, and the Grave is Peace!

A Mathematical Problem

If Pegasus will let thee only ride him,
Spurning my clumsy efforts to o'erstride him,
Some fresh expedient the Muse will try,
And walk on stilts, although she cannot fly.

Dear Brother,
I have often been surprised that Mathematics, the quintessence of
Truth, should have found admirers so few and so languid. Frequent

consideration and minute scrutiny have at length unravelled the case; viz. that though Reason is feasted, Imagination is starved; whilst Reason is luxuriating in its proper Paradise, Imagination is wearily travelling on a dreary desert. To assist Reason by the stimulus of Imagination is the design of the following production. In the execution of it much may be objectionable. The verse (particularly in the introduction of the ode) may be accused of unwarrantable liberties, but they are liberties equally homogeneal with the exactness of Mathematical disquisition, and the boldness of Pindaric daring. I have three strong champions to defend me against the attacks of Criticism; the Novelty, the Difficulty, and the Utility of the work. I may justly plume myself, that I first have drawn the nymph Mathesis from the visionary caves of abstracted Idea, and caused her to unite with Harmony. The first-born of this Union I now present to you; with interested motives indeed – as I expect to receive in return the more valuable offspring of your Muse.

March 31, 1791.   Thine ever,
To the Rev. G. C.   S. T. C.

This is now – this was erst,
Proposition the first – and Problem the first.

I
   On a given finite line
Which must no way incline;
      To describe an equi –
      – lateral Tri –
      – A, N, G, E, L, E.
         Now let A. B.
      Be the given line
Which must no way incline;
      The great Mathematician
10   Makes this Requisition,
         That we describe an Equi –
         – lateral Tri –
         – angle on it;
Aid us Reason – aid us Wit!

II

From the centre A. at the distance A. B.
Describe the circle B. C. D.
At the distance B. A. from B. the centre
The round A. C. E. to describe boldly venture.
(Third postulate see.)
And from the point C.
In which the circles make a pother
Cutting and slashing one another,
Bid the straight lines a journeying go.
C. A. C. B. those lines will show
To the points, which by A. B. are reckon'd,
And postulate the second
For Authority ye know.
A. B. C.
Triumphant shall be
An Equilateral Triangle,
Not Peter Pindar carp, nor Zoilus can wrangle.

III

Because the point A. is the centre
Of the circle B. C. D.
And because the point B. is the centre
Of the circular A. C. E.
A. C. to A. B. and B. C. to B. A.
Harmoniously equal for ever must stay;
Then C. A. and B. C.
Both extend the kind hand
To the basis A. B,
Unambitiously join'd in Equality's Band.
But to the same powers, when two powers are equal,
My mind forebodes the sequel;
My mind does some celestial impulse teach,
And equalizes each to each.
Thus C. A. with B. C. strikes the same sure alliance,
That C. A. and B. C. had with A. B. before;
And in mutual affiance
None attempting to soar

50   Above another,
          The unanimous three
        C. A. and B. C. and A. B.
     All are equal, each to his brother,
        Preserving the balance of power so true:
     Ah! the like would the proud Autocratix do!
     At taxes impending not Britain would tremble,
     Nor Prussia struggle her fear to dissemble;
        Nor the Mah'met-sprung wight
          The great Mussulman
60   Would stain his Divan
     With Urine the soft-flowing daughter of Fright.

IV

But rein your stallion in, too daring Nine!
     Should Empires bloat the scientific line?
Or with dishevell'd hair all madly do ye run
     For transport that your task is done?
     For done it is – the cause is tried!
     And Proposition, gentle maid,
Who soothly ask'd stern Demonstration's aid,
        Has prov'd her right, and A. B. C.
70   Of Angles three
          Is shown to be of equal side;
And now our weary steed to rest in fine,
'Tis raised upon A. B. the straight, the given line.

Honour

O, Curas hominum! O, quantum est in rebus inane!

The fervid Sun had more than halv'd the day,
When gloomy on his couch Philedon lay;
His feeble frame consumptive as his purse,
His aching head did wine and women curse;
His fortune ruinèd and his wealth decay'd,
Clamorous his Duns, his gaming debts unpaid,
The youth indignant seiz'd his tailor's bill,
And on its back thus wrote with moral quill:
'Various as colours in the rainbow shown,
10   Or similar in emptiness alone,

How false, how vain are Man's pursuits below!
Wealth, Honour, Pleasure – what can ye bestow?
Yet see, how high and low, and young and old
Pursue the all delusive power of Gold.
Fond man! should all Peru thy empire own,
For thee tho' all Golconda's jewels shone,
What greater bliss could all this wealth supply?
What, but to eat and drink and sleep and die?
Go, tempt the stormy sea, the burning soil –
20 Go, waste the night in thought, the day in toil,
Dark frowns the rock, and fierce the tempests rave –
Thy ingots go the unconscious deep to pave!
Or thunder at thy door the midnight train,
Or death shall knock that never knocks in vain.
Next Honour's sons come bustling on amain;
I laugh with pity at the idle train.
Infirm of soul! who think'st to lift thy name
Upon the waxen wings of human fame –
Who for a sound, articulated breath –
30 Gazest undaunted in the face of death!
What art thou but a Meteor's glaring light –
Blazing a moment and then sunk in night?
Caprice which rais'd thee high shall hurl thee low,
Or envy blast the laurels on thy brow.
To such poor joys could ancient Honour lead
When empty fame was toiling Merit's mead;
To Modern Honour other lays belong;
Profuse of joy and Lord of right and wrong,
Honour can game, drink, riot in the stew,
40 Cut a friend's throat – what cannot Honour do?
Ah me – the storm within can Honour still
For Julio's death, whom Honour made me kill?
Or will this lordly Honour tell the way
To pay those debts, which Honour makes me pay?
Or if with pistol and terrific threats
I make some traveller pay on Honour's debts,
A med'cine for this wound can Honour give?
Ah, no! my Honour dies to make my Honour live.
But see! young Pleasure and her train advance,
50 And joy and laughter wake the inebriate dance;
Around my neck she throws her fair white arms,
I meet her loves, and madden at her charms.

For the gay grape can joys celestial move,
And what so sweet below as Woman's love?
With such high transport every moment flies,
I curse experience, that he makes me wise;
For at his frown the dear deliriums flew,
And the chang'd scene now wears a gloomy hue.
A hideous hag th' Enchantress Pleasure seems,
60   And all her joys appear but feverous dreams.
The vain Resolve still broken and still made,
Disease and loathing and remorse invade;
The charm is vanish'd and the bubble's broke –
A slave to pleasure is a slave to smoke!'
Such lays repentant did the Muse supply;
When as the Sun was hastening down the sky,
In glittering state twice fifty guineas come –
His Mother's plate antique had rais'd the sum.
Forth leap'd Philedon of new life possest:
70   'Twas Brookes's all till two – 'twas Hackett's all the rest!

On Imitation

All are not born to soar – and ah! how few
In tracks where Wisdom leads their paths pursue!
Contagious when to wit or wealth allied,
Folly and Vice diffuse their venom wide.
5   On Folly every fool his talent tries;
It asks some toil to imitate the wise;
Tho' few like Fox can speak – like Pitt can think –
Yet all like Fox can game – like Pitt can drink.

Inside the Coach

'Tis hard on Bagshot Heath to try
Unclos'd to keep the weary eye;
But ah! Oblivion's nod to get
In rattling coach is harder yet.
Slumbrous God of half shut eye!
Who lov'st with Limbs supine to lie;

Soother sweet of toil and care
Listen, listen to my prayer;
And to thy votary dispense
Thy soporific influence!
What tho' around thy drowsy head
The seven-fold cap of night be spread,
Yet lift that drowsy head awhile
And yawn propitiously a smile;
In drizzly rains poppean dews
O'er the tir'd inmates of the Coach diffuse;
And when thou'st charm'd our eyes to rest
Pillowing the chin upon the breast,
Bid many a dream from thy dominions
Wave its various-painted pinions,
Till ere the splendid visions close
We snore quartettes in ecstacy of nose.
While thus we urge our airy course,
Oh may no jolt's electric force
Our fancies from their steeds unhorse,
And call us from thy fairy reign
To dreary Bagshot Heath again!

Devonshire Roads

The indignant Bard compos'd this furious ode,
As tired he dragg'd his way thro' Plimtree road!
        Crusted with filth and stuck in mire
        Dull sounds the Bard's bemudded lyre;
        Nathless Revenge and Ire the Poet goad
        To pour his imprecations on the road.
    Curst road! whose execrable way
    Was darkly shadow'd out in Milton's lay,
    When the sad fiends thro' Hell's sulphureous roads
    Took the first survey of their new abodes;
    Or when the fall'n Archangel fierce
    Dar'd through the realms of Night to pierce,
    What time the Blood Hound lur'd by Human scent
Thro' all Confusion's quagmires floundering went.

Nor cheering pipe, nor Bird's shrill note
Around thy dreary paths shall float;
Their boding songs shall scritch owls pour
To fright the guilty shepherds sore,
Led by the wandering fires astray
20   Thro' the dank horrors of thy way!
While they their mud-lost sandals hunt
May all the curses, which they grunt
In raging moan like goaded hog,
Alight upon thee, damnèd Bog!

Music

Hence, soul-dissolving Harmony
    That lead'st th' oblivious soul astray –
Though thou sphere descended be –
    Hence away!
Thou mightier Goddess, thou demand'st my lay,
    Born when earth was seiz'd with cholic;
Or as more sapient sages say,
    What time the Legion diabolic
        Compelled their beings to enshrine
10   In bodies vile of herded swine,
        Precipitate adown the steep
        With hideous rout were plunging in the deep,
And hog and devil mingling grunt and yell
    Seiz'd on the ear with horrible obtrusion;
Then if aright old legendaries tell,
    Wert thou begot by Discord on Confusion!

What tho' no name's sonorous power
Was given thee at thy natal hour –
Yet oft I feel thy sacred might,
20 While concords wing their distant flight.
    Such power inspires thy holy son
        Sable clerk of Tiverton.
And oft where Otter sports his stream,
I hear thy banded offspring scream.
Thou Goddess! thou inspir'st each throat;
'Tis thou who pour'st the scritch owl note!
Transported hear'st thy children all

Scrape and blow and squeak and squall,
And while old Otter's steeple rings,
30   Clappest hoarse thy raven wings!

Absence
A FAREWELL ODE ON QUITTING SCHOOL FOR JESUS COLLEGE, CAMBRIDGE

Where graced with many a classic spoil
Cam rolls his reverend stream along,
I haste to urge the learned toil
That sternly chides my love-lorn song:
Ah me! too mindful of the days
Illumed by Passion's orient rays,
When peace, and Cheerfulness, and Health
Enriched me with the best of wealth.

Ah fair Delights! that o'er my soul
10   On Memory's wing, like shadows fly!
Ah Flowers! which Joy from Eden stole
While Innocence stood smiling by!
But cease, fond Heart! this bootless moan:
Those Hours on rapid Pinions flown
Shall yet return, by Absence crowned,
And scatter livelier roses round.

The Sun who ne'er remits his fires
On heedless eyes may pour the day:
The Moon, that oft from Heaven retires,
20   Endears her renovated ray.
What though she leave the sky unblest
To mourn awhile in murky vest?
When she relumes her lovely Light,
We bless the Wanderer of the Night.

Sonnet on the Same

Farewell parental scenes! a sad farewell!
To you my grateful heart still fondly clings,
Tho' fluttering round on Fancy's burnish'd wings
Her tales of future Joy Hope loves to tell.
Adieu, adieu! ye much lov'd cloisters pale!
Ah! would those happy days return again,
When 'neath your arches, free from every stain,
I heard of guilt and wonder'd at the tale!
Dear haunts! where oft my simple lays I sang,
Listening meanwhile the echoings of my feet,
Lingering I quit you, with as great a pang,
As when erewhile, my weeping childhood, torn
By early sorrow from my native seat,
Mingled its tears with hers – my widow'd Parent lorn.

Happiness

On wide or narrow scale shall Man
Most happily describe life's plan?
Say, shall he bloom and wither there,
Where first his infant buds appear;
Or upwards dart with soaring force,
And tempt some more ambitious course?
   Obedient now to Hope's command,
I bid each humble wish expand,
And fair and bright Life's prospects seem,
While Hope displays her cheering beam,
And Fancy's vivid colourings stream,
While Emulation stands me nigh
The Goddess of the eager eye.
   With foot advanc'd and anxious heart
Now for the fancied goal I start –
Ah! why will Reason intervene
Me and my promised joys between!
She stops my course, she chains my speed,
While thus her forceful words proceed.
   'Ah! listen, youth, ere yet too late,
What evils on thy course may wait!

To bow the head, to bend the knee,
A minion of Servility,
At low Pride's frequent frowns to sigh,
And watch the glance in Folly's eye;
To toil intense, yet toil in vain,
And feel with what a hollow pain
Pale Disappointment hangs her head
O'er darling Expectation dead!
30   'The scene is changed and Fortune's gale
Shall belly out each prosperous sail.
Yet sudden wealth full well I know
Did never Happiness bestow.
That wealth to which we were not born
Dooms us to sorrow or to scorn.
Behold yon flock which long had trod
O'er the short grass of Devon's sod,
To Lincoln's rank rich meads transferr'd,
And in their fate thy own be fear'd;
40   Through every limb contagions fly,
Deform'd and chok'd they burst and die.
      'When Luxury opens wide her arms,
And smiling wooes thee to those charms,
Whose fascination thousands own,
Shall thy brows wear the stoic frown?
And when her goblet she extends
Which madd'ning myriads press around,
What power divine thy soul befriends
That thou shouldst dash it to the ground?
50   No, thou shalt drink, and thou shalt know
Her transient bliss, her lasting woe,
Her maniac joys, that know no measure,
And riot rude and painted pleasure;
Till (sad reverse!) the Enchantress vile
To frowns converts her magic smile;
Her train impatient to destroy,
Observe her frown with gloomy joy;
On thee with harpy fangs they seize
The hideous offspring of Disease,
60   Swoll'n Dropsy ignorant of Rest,
And Fever garb'd in scarlet vest,
Consumption driving the quick hearse,
And Gout that howls the frequent curse,

With Apoplex of heavy head
That surely aims his dart of lead.
　'But say Life's joys unmix'd were given
To thee some favourite of Heaven:
Within, without, tho' all were health –
Yet what e'en thus are Fame, Power, Wealth,
70　But sounds that variously express,
What's thine already – Happiness!
'Tis thine the converse deep to hold
With all the famous sons of old;
And thine the happy waking dream
While Hope pursues some favourite theme,
As oft when Night o'er Heaven is spread,
Round this maternal seat you tread,
Where far from splendour, far from riot,
In silence wrapt sleeps careless quiet.
80　'Tis thine with fancy oft to talk,
And thine the peaceful evening walk;
And what to thee the sweetest are –
The setting sun, the evening star –
The tints, which live along the sky,
And Moon that meets thy raptur'd eye,
Where oft the tear shall grateful start,
Dear silent pleasures of the Heart!
Ah! Being blest, for Heaven shall lend
To share thy simple joys a friend!
90　Ah! doubly blest, if Love supply
His influence to complete thy joy,
If chance some lovely maid thou find
To read thy visage in thy mind.
　'One blessing more demands thy care –
Once more to Heaven address the prayer:
For humble independence pray
The guardian genius of thy way;
Whom (sages say) in days of yore
Meek competence to wisdom bore,
100　So shall thy little vessel glide
With a fair breeze adown the tide,
And Hope, if e'er thou 'ginst to sorrow,
Remind thee of some fair to-morrow,
Till death shall close thy tranquil eye
While Faith proclaims "thou shalt not die!" '

A Wish Written in Jesus Wood, Feb. 10th, 1792

Lo! thro' the dusky silence of the groves,
Thro' vales irriguous, and thro' green retreats,
With languid murmur creeps the placid stream,
          And works its secret way!

Awhile meand'ring round its native fields
It rolls the playful wave, and winds its flight:
Then downward flowing with awaken'd speed
          Embosoms in the Deep!

Thus thro' its silent tenor may my Life
10 Smooth its meek stream, by sordid Wealth unclogg'd,
Alike unconscious of forensic storms,
          And Glory's blood-stain'd palm!

And when dark Age shall close Life's little day,
Satiate of sport, and weary of its toils,
E'en thus may slumbrous Death my decent limbs
          Compose with icy hand!

An Ode in the Manner of Anacreon

As late in wreaths gay flowers I bound,
Beneath some roses LOVE I found,
And by his little frolic pinion
As quick as thought I seiz'd the minion,
Then in my Cup the prisoner threw,
And drank him in its sparkling dew:
And sure I feel my angry Guest
Flutt'ring his Wings within my breast!

To Disappointment

Hence! thou fiend of gloomy sway,
   That lov'st on withering blast to ride
   O'er fond Illusion's air-built pride,
Sullen Spirit! Hence! Away!

Where Avarice lurks in sordid cell,
   Or mad Ambition builds the dream,
   Or Pleasure plots th' unholy scheme,
There with Guilt and Folly dwell!

But oh! when Hope on Wisdom's wing
10   Prophetic whispers pure delight,
   Be distant far thy cank'rous blight,
Daemon of envenom'd sting!

Then haste thee, Nymph of balmy gales!
   Thy poet's prayer, sweet May! attend!
   Oh! place my Parent and my Friend
'Mid her lovely native vales.

Peace, that lists the woodlark's strains,
   Health, that breathes divinest treasures,
   Laughing Hours, and social Pleasures,
20 Wait my friend in Cambria's plains.

Affection there with mingled ray
   Shall pour at once the raptures high
   Of Filial and Maternal Joy –
Haste thee then, Delightful May!

And oh! may Spring's fair flowrets fade,
   May Summer cease her limbs to lave
   In cooling stream, may Autumn grave
Yellow o'er the corn-cloath'd glade,

Ere from sweet retirement torn
30   She seek again the crowded mart!
   Nor thou, my selfish selfish heart,
Dare her slow return to mourn!

A Fragment Found in a Lecture-Room

Where deep in mud Cam rolls his slumbrous stream,
And Bog and Desolution reign supreme,
Where all Boe[o]tia clouds the misty brain,
The Owl Mathesis pipes her loathsome strain.
Far far aloof the frighted Muses fly,
Indignant Genius scowls and passes by:
The frolic Pleasures start amid their dance,
And Wit congealed stands fix'd in Wintry trance.
But to the sounds with duteous haste repair
10   Cold Industry, and wary-footed Care,
And Dullness, dosing on a couch of Lead,
Pleas'd with the song uplifts her heavy head,
The sympathetic numbers lists awhile,
Then yawns propitiously a frosty smile . . .

                              Cetera desunt.

Ode

Ye Gales, that of the Lark's repose
The impatient Silence break,
To yon poor Pilgrim's wearying Woes
Your gentle Comfort speak!
He heard the midnight whirlwind die,
He saw the sun-awaken'd Sky
Resume its slowly-purpling Blue:
And ah! he sigh'd – that I might find
The cloudless Azure of the Mind
10   And Fortune's brightning Hue!

Where'er in waving Foliage hid
The Bird's gay Charm ascends,
Or by the fretful current chid
Some giant Rock impends –
There let the lonely Cares respire
As small airs thrill the mourning Lyre

And teach the Soul her native Calm;
While Passion with a languid Eye
Hangs o'er the fall of Harmony
20   And drinks the sacred Balm.

Slow as the fragrant whisper creeps
    Along the lilied Vale,
The alter'd Eye of Conquest weeps,
    And ruthless War grows pale
Relenting that his Heart forsook
Soft Concord of auspicious Look,
And Love, and social Poverty;
The Family of tender Fears,
The Sigh, that saddens and endears,
30   And Cares, that sweeten Joy.

Then cease, thy frantic Tumults cease,
Ambition, Sire of War!
Nor o'er the mangled Corse of Peace
Urge on thy scythèd Car.
And oh! that Reason's voice might swell
With whisper'd Airs and holy Spell
    To rouse thy gentler Sense,
As bending o'er the chilly bloom
The Morning wakes its soft Perfume
40   With breezy Influence.

A Lover's Complaint to his Mistress

The dubious light sad glimmers o'er the sky:
'Tis Silence all. By lonely anguish torn
With wandering feet to gloomy groves I fly,
And wakeful Love still tracks my course forlorn.

Ah! will you, cruel Julia! will you go?
And trust you to the Ocean's dark dismay?
Shall the wide wat'ry world between us flow?
And Winds unpitying snatch my Hopes away?

Thus could you sport with my too easy heart?
Yet tremble, lest not unavenged I grieve!
The Winds may learn your own delusive art,
And faithless Ocean smile – but to deceive.

With Fielding's Amelia

Virtues and Woes alike too great for man
  In the soft tale oft claim the useless sigh;
For vain the attempt to realize the plan,
  On folly's wings must imitation fly.
With other aim has Fielding here display'd
  Each social duty and each social care;
With just yet vivid colouring portray'd
  What every wife should be, what many are.
And sure the Parent of a race so sweet
With double pleasure on the page shall dwell,
Each scene with sympathizing breast shall meet,
While Reason still with smiles delights to tell
Maternal hope, that her lov'd Progeny
In all but Sorrows shall Amelias be!

Written After a Walk Before Supper

Tho' much averse, dear Jack, to flicker,
To find a likeness for friend V—ker,
I've made thro' Earth, and Air, and Sea,
A Voyage of Discovery!
And let me add (to ward off strife)
For V—ker and for V—ker's Wife –
SHE large and round beyond belief,
A superfluity of Beef!
Her mind and body of a piece,
And both composed of kitchen-grease.
In short, Dame Truth might safely dub her
Vulgarity enshrin'd in blubber!

He, meagre Bit of Littleness,
All snuff, and musk, and politesse;
So thin, that strip him of his clothing,
He'd totter on the edge of NOTHING!
In case of foe, he well might hide
Snug in the collops of her side.

Ah then, what simile will suit?
20   Spindle-leg in great jack-boot?
Pismire crawling in a rut?
Or a spigot in a butt?
Thus I humm'd and ha'd awhile,
When Madam Memory with a smile
Thus twitch'd my ear – 'Why sure, I ween,
In London streets thou oft hast seen
The very image of this Pair:
A little Ape with huge She-Bear
Link'd by hapless chain together:
30   An unlick'd mass the one – the other
An antic small with nimble crupper —'
But stop, my Muse! for here comes Supper.

Imitated from Ossian

The stream with languid murmur creeps,
    In Lumin's flowery vale:
Beneath the dew the Lily weeps
    Slow-waving to the gale.

'Cease, restless gale!' it seems to say,
    'Nor wake me with thy sighing!
The honours of my vernal day
    On rapid wing are flying.

Tomorrow shall the Traveller come
10   Who late beheld me blooming:
His searching eye shall vainly roam
    The dreary vale of Lumin.'

With eager gaze and wetted cheek
　　My wonted haunts along,
Thus, faithful Maiden! thou shalt seek
　　The Youth of simplest song.

But I along the breeze shall roll
　　The voice of feeble power;
And dwell, the Moon-beam of thy soul,
20　　In Slumber's nightly hour.

The Complaint of Ninathòma, from the Same

How long will ye round me be swelling,
　　O ye blue-tumbling waves of the sea?
Not always in caves was my dwelling,
　　Nor beneath the cold blast of the tree.
Through the high-sounding halls of Cathlòma
　　In the steps of my beauty I strayed;
The warriors beheld Ninathòma,
　　And they blessed the white-bosomed Maid!

A Ghost! by my cavern it darted!
10　　In moon-beams the Spirit was drest –
For lovely appear the departed
　　When they visit the dreams of my rest!
But disturbed by the tempest's commotion
　　Fleet the shadowy forms of delight –
Ah cease, thou shrill blast of the Ocean!
　　To howl through my cavern by night.

The Rose

As late each flower that sweetest blows
I plucked, the Garden's pride!
Within the petals of a Rose
A sleeping Love I spied.

Around his brows a beamy wreath
Of many a lucent hue;
All purple glowed his cheek, beneath,
Inebriate with dew.

I softly seized the unguarded Power,
Nor scared his balmy rest:
And placed him, caged within the flower,
On spotless Sara's breast.

But when unweeting of the guile
Awoke the prisoner sweet,
He struggled to escape awhile
And stamped his faery feet.

Ah! soon the soul-entrancing sight
Subdued the impatient boy!
He gazed! he thrilled with deep delight!
Then clapped his wings for joy.

'And O!' he cried – 'of magic kind
What charms this Throne endear!
Some other Love let Venus find –
I'll fix my empire here.'

Kisses

Cupid, if storying Legends tell aright,
Once fram'd a rich Elixir of Delight.
A Chalice o'er love-kindled flames he fix'd,
And in it Nectar and Ambrosia mix'd:
With these the magic dews which Evening brings,
Brush'd from the Idalian star by faery wings:
Each tender pledge of sacred Faith he join'd,
Each gentler Pleasure of th' unspotted mind –
Day-dreams, whose tints with sportive brightness glow,
And Hope, the blameless parasite of Woe.
The eyeless Chemist heard the process rise,
The steamy Chalice bubbled up in sighs;
Sweet sounds transpired, as when the enamour'd Dove
Pours the soft murmuring of responsive Love.

The finish'd work might Envy vainly blame,
And 'Kisses' was the precious Compound's name.
With half the God his Cyprian Mother blest,
And breath'd on Sara's lovelier lips the rest.

Sonnet

Thou gentle Look, that didst my soul beguile,
Why hast thou left me? Still in some fond dream
Revisit my sad heart, auspicious Smile!
As falls on closing flowers the lunar beam:
What time, in sickly mood, at parting day
I lay me down and think of happier years;
Of Joys, that glimmered in Hope's twilight ray,
Then left me darkling in a vale of tears.
O pleasant days of hope – for ever gone! –
Could I recall you! – But that thought is vain.
Availeth not Persuasion's sweetest tone
To lure the fleet-winged Travellers back again:
Yet fair, though faint, their images shall gleam
Like the bright Rainbow on a willowy stream.

Sonnet to the River Otter

Dear native brook! wild streamlet of the West!
    How many various-fated years have past,
    What happy and what mournful hours, since last
I skimmed the smooth thin stone along thy breast,
Numbering its light leaps! yet so deep imprest
Sink the sweet scenes of childhood, that mine eyes
    I never shut amid the sunny ray,
But straight with all their tints thy waters rise,
    Thy crossing plank, thy marge with willows grey,
And bedded sand that, veined with various dyes,
Gleamed through thy bright transparence! On my way,
    Visions of childhood! oft have ye beguiled
Lone manhood's cares, yet waking fondest sighs:
    Ah! that once more I were a careless child!

Lines on an Autumnal Evening

O thou wild Fancy, check thy wing! No more
Those thin white flakes, those purple clouds explore!
Nor there with happy spirits speed thy flight
Bathed in rich amber-glowing floods of light;
Nor in yon gleam, where slow descends the day,
With western peasants hail the morning ray!
Ah! rather bid the perished pleasures move,
A shadowy train, across the soul of Love!
O'er Disappointment's wintry desert fling
Each flower that wreathed the dewy locks of Spring,
When blushing, like a bride, from Hope's trim bower
She leapt, awakened by the pattering shower.
Now sheds the sinking Sun a deeper gleam,
Aid, lovely Sorceress! aid thy Poet's dream!
With faery wand O bid the Maid arise,
Chaste Joyance dancing in her bright-blue eyes;
As erst when from the Muses' calm abode
I came, with Learning's meed not unbestowed;
When as she twined a laurel round my brow,
And met my kiss, and half returned my vow,
O'er all my frame shot rapid my thrilled heart,
And every nerve confessed the electric dart.

O dear Deceit! I see the Maiden rise,
Chaste Joyance dancing in her bright-blue eyes!
When first the lark high soaring swells his throat,
Mocks the tired eye, and scatters the loud note,
I trace her footsteps on the accustomed lawn,
I mark her glancing mid the gleam of dawn.
When the bent flower beneath the night dew weeps
And on the lake the silver lustre sleeps,
Amid the paly radiance soft and sad,
She meets my lonely path in moon-beams clad.
With her along the streamlet's brink I rove;
With her I list the warblings of the grove;
And seems in each low wind her voice to float,
Lone whispering Pity in each soothing note!

Spirits of Love! ye heard her name! Obey
The powerful spell, and to my haunt repair.
Whether on clustering pinions ye are there,
Where rich snows blossom on the Myrtle trees,
Or with fond languishment around my fair
Sigh in the loose luxuriance of her hair;
O heed the spell, and hither wing your way,
Like far-off music, voyaging the breeze!
Spirits! to you the infant Maid was given
Formed by the wonderous Alchemy of Heaven!
No fairer Maid does Love's wide empire know,
No fairer Maid e'er heaved the bosom's snow.
A thousand Loves around her forehead fly;
A thousand Loves sit melting in her eye;
Love lights her smile – in Joy's red nectar dips
His myrtle flower, and plants it on her lips.
She speaks! and hark that passion-warbled song –
Still, Fancy! still that voice, those notes prolong.
As sweet as when that voice with rapturous falls
Shall wake the softened echoes of Heaven's Halls!

O (have I sighed) were mine the wizard's rod,
Or mine the power of Proteus, changeful God!
A flower-entangled Arbour I would seem
To shield my Love from Noontide's sultry beam:
Or bloom a Myrtle, from whose odorous boughs
My Love might weave gay garlands for her brows.
When Twilight stole across the fading vale,
To fan my Love I'd be the Evening Gale;
Mourn in the soft folds of her swelling vest,
And flutter my faint pinions on her breast!
On Seraph wing I'd float a Dream by night,
To soothe my Love with shadows of delight –
Or soar aloft to be the Spangled Skies,
And gaze upon her with a thousand eyes!

As when the savage, who his drowsy frame
Had basked beneath the Sun's unclouded flame,
Awakes amid the troubles of the air,
The skiey deluge, and white lightning's glare –

Aghast he scours before the tempest's sweep,
And sad recalls the sunny hour of sleep:
So tossed by storms along Life's wildering way,
Mine eye reverted views that cloudless day,
When by my native brook I wont to rove,
80   While Hope with kisses nursed the Infant Love.

Dear native brook! like Peace, so placidly
Smoothing through fertile fields thy current meek!
Dear native brook! where first young Poesy
Stared wildly-eager in her noontide dream!
Where blameless pleasures dimple Quiet's cheek,
As water-lilies ripple thy slow stream!
Dear native haunts! where Virtue still is gay,
Where Friendship's fix'd star sheds a mellowed ray,
Where Love a crown of thornless Roses wears,
90   Where softened Sorrow smiles within her tears;
And Memory, with a Vestal's chaste employ,
Unceasing feeds the lambent flame of joy!
No more your sky-larks melting from the sight
Shall thrill the attunèd heart-string with delight –
No more shall deck your pensive Pleasures sweet
With wreaths of sober hue my evening seat.
Yet dear to Fancy's eye your varied scene
Of wood, hill, dale, and sparkling brook between!
Yet sweet to Fancy's ear the warbled song,
100   That soars on Morning's wing your vales among.

Scenes of my Hope! the aching eye ye leave
Like yon bright hues that paint the clouds of eve!
Tearful and saddening with the saddened blaze
Mine eye the gleam pursues with wistful gaze:
Sees shades on shades with deeper tint impend,
Till chill and damp the moonless night descend.

To Fortune
ON BUYING A TICKET IN THE IRISH LOTTERY

*Composed during a walk to and from the Queen's Head, Gray's Inn
Lane, Holborn, and Hornsby's and Co., Cornhill.*

Promptress of unnumber'd sighs,
O snatch that circling bandage from thine eyes!
O look, and smile! No common prayer
Solicits, Fortune! thy propitious care!
For, not a silken son of dress
I clink the gilded chains of *politesse*,
Nor ask thy boon what time I scheme
Unholy Pleasure's frail and feverish dream;
Nor yet my view life's *dazzle* blinds –
Pomp! – Grandeur! Power! – I give you to the winds!
Let the little bosom cold
Melt only at the sunbeam ray of gold –
My pale cheeks glow – the big drops start –
The rebel *Feeling* riots at my heart!
And if in lonely durance pent,
Thy poor mite mourn a brief imprisonment –
That mite at Sorrow's faintest sound
Leaps from its scrip with an elastic bound!
But oh! if ever song thine ear
Might soothe, O haste with fost'ring hand to rear
One Flower of Hope! At Love's behest,
Trembling, I plac'd it in my secret breast:
And thrice I've view'd the vernal gleam,
Since oft mine eye, with Joy's electric beam,
Illum'd it – and its sadder hue
Oft moisten'd with the Tear's ambrosial dew!
Poor wither'd floweret! on its head
Has dark Despair his sickly mildew shed!
But thou, O Fortune! canst relume
Its deaden'd tints – and thou with hardier bloom
May'st haply tinge its beauties pale,
And yield the unsunn'd stranger to the western gale!

Perspiration: A Travelling Eclogue

The Dust flies smothering, as on clatt'ring Wheels
Loath'd Aristocracy careers along.
The distant Track quick vibrates to the Eye,
And white and dazzling undulates with heat.
Where scorching to th' unwary Traveller's touch
The stone-fence flings its narrow Slip of Shade,
Or where the worn sides of the chalky Road
Yield their scant excavations (sultry Grots!),
Emblem of languid Patience, we behold
10   The fleecy Files faint-ruminating lie.

Lines

WRITTEN AT THE KING'S ARMS, ROSS, FORMERLY THE
HOUSE OF THE 'MAN OF ROSS'

Richer than Miser o'er his countless hoards,
Nobler than Kings, or king-polluted Lords,
Here dwelt the Man of Ross! O Traveller, hear!
Departed Merit claims a reverent tear.
Friend to the friendless, to the sick man health,
With generous joy he viewed his modest wealth;
He heard the widow's heaven-breathed prayer of praise,
He marked the sheltered orphan's tearful gaze,
Or where the sorrow-shrivelled captive lay,
10   Pour'd the bright blaze of Freedom's noon-tide ray.
Beneath this roof if thy cheered moments pass,
Fill to the good man's name one grateful glass:
To higher zest shall Memory wake thy soul,
And Virtue mingle in the ennobled bowl.
But if, like me, through life's distressful scene
Lonely and sad thy pilgrimage hath been;
And if thy breast with heart-sick anguish fraught,
Thou journeyest onward tempest-tossed in thought;
Here cheat thy cares! in generous visions melt,
20   And dream of Goodness, thou hast never felt!

Imitated from the Welsh

If, while my passion I impart,
    You deem my words untrue,
O place your hand upon my heart –
    Feel how it throbs for you!

Ah no! reject the thoughtless claim
    In pity to your Lover!
That thrilling touch would aid the flame,
    It wishes to discover.

Lines
TO A BEAUTIFUL SPRING IN A VILLAGE

Once more, sweet Stream! with slow foot wandering near,
I bless thy milky waters cold and clear.
Escaped the flashing of the noontide hours,
With one fresh garland of Pierian flowers
(Ere from thy zephyr-haunted brink I turn)
My languid hand shall wreath thy mossy urn.
For not through pathless grove with murmur rude
Thou soothest the sad wood-nymph, Solitude;
Nor thine unseen in cavern depths to well,
10   The hermit-fountain of some dripping cell!
Pride of the Vale! thy useful streams supply
The scattered cots and peaceful hamlet nigh.
The elfin tribe around thy friendly banks
With infant uproar and soul-soothing pranks,
Released from school, their little hearts at rest,
Launch paper navies on thy waveless breast.
The rustic here at eve with pensive look
Whistling lorn ditties leans upon his crook,
Or starting pauses with hope-mingled dread
20   To list the much-loved maid's accustomed tread:
She, vainly mindful of her dame's command,
Loiters, the long-filled pitcher in her hand.

Unboastful Stream! thy fount with pebbled falls
The faded form of past delight recalls,
What time the morning sun of Hope arose,
And all was joy; save when another's woes
A transient gloom upon my soul imprest,
Like passing clouds impictured on thy breast.
Life's current then ran sparkling to the noon,
30   Or silvery stole beneath the pensive Moon:
Ah! now it works rude brakes and thorns among,
Or o'er the rough rock bursts and foams along!

Imitations Ad Lyram
(CASIMIR, BOOK II, ODE 3)

The solemn-breathing air is ended –
    Cease, O Lyre! thy kindred lay!
From the poplar-branch suspended
    Glitter to the eye of Day!

On thy wires hov'ring, dying,
    Softly sighs the summer wind:
I will slumber, careless lying,
    By yon waterfall reclin'd.

In the forest hollow-roaring
10   Hark! I hear a deep'ning sound –
Clouds rise thick with heavy low'ring!
    See! th' horizon blackens round!

Parent of the soothing measure,
    Let me seize thy wetted string!
Swiftly flies the flatterer, Pleasure,
    Headlong, ever on the wing.

The Sigh

When Youth his faery reign began
Ere sorrow had proclaimed me man;
While Peace the present hour beguiled,
And all the lovely Prospect smiled;
Then Mary! 'mid my lightsome glee
I heav'd the painless Sigh for thee.

And when, along the waves of woe,
My harassed Heart was doomed to know
The frantic burst of Outrage keen,
And the slow Pang that gnaws unseen;
Then shipwrecked on Life's stormy sea
I heaved an anguished Sigh for thee!

But soon Reflection's power imprest
A stiller sadness on my breast;
And sickly hope with waning eye
Was well content to droop and die:
I yielded to the stern decree,
Yet heaved a languid Sigh for thee!

And though in distant climes to roam,
A wanderer from my native home,
I fain would soothe the sense of Care,
And lull to sleep the Joys that were,
Thy Image may not banished be –
Still, Mary! still I sigh for thee.

The Kiss

One kiss, dear maid! I said and sighed –
Your scorn the little boon denied.
Ah why refuse the blameless bliss?
Can danger lurk within a kiss?

Yon viewless Wanderer of the vale,
The Spirit of the Western Gale,
At Morning's break, at Evening's close
Inhales the sweetness of the Rose,
And hovers o'er the uninjured Bloom
10 Sighing back the soft perfume.
Vigour to the Zephyr's wing
Her nectar-breathing Kisses fling;
And He the glitter of the Dew
Scatters on the Rose's hue.
Bashful lo! she bends her head,
And darts a blush of deeper Red!

Too well those lovely lips disclose
The triumphs of the opening Rose;
O fair! O graceful! bid them prove
20 As passive to the breath of Love.
In tender accents, faint and low,
Well-pleased I hear the whispered 'No!'
The whispered 'No' – how little meant!
Sweet Falsehood that endears Consent!
For on those lovely lips the while
Dawns the soft relenting smile,
And tempts with feigned dissuasion coy
The gentle violence of Joy.

To a Young Lady,
WITH A POEM ON THE FRENCH REVOLUTION

Much on my early youth I love to dwell,
Ere yet I bade that friendly dome farewell,
Where first, beneath the echoing cloisters pale
I heard of guilt and wondered at the tale!
Yet though the hours flew by on careless wing,
Full heavily of Sorrow would I sing.
Aye as the star of evening flung its beam
In broken radiance on the wavy stream,
My soul amid the pensive twilight gloom
10 Mourned with the breeze, O Lee Boo! o'er thy tomb.

Where'er I wandered, Pity still was near,
Breathed from the heart and glistened in the tear:
No knell that tolled, but filled my anxious eye,
And suffering Nature wept that one should die!

Thus to sad sympathies I soothed my breast,
Calm, as the rainbow in the weeping West:
When slumbering Freedom roused by high Disdain
With giant fury burst her triple chain!
Fierce on her front the blasting Dog-star glowed;
20   Her banners, like a midnight meteor, flowed;
Amid the yelling of the storm-rent skies
She came, and scattered battles from her eyes!
Then Exultation waked the patriot fire
And swept with wild hand the Tyrtæan lyre:
Red from the Tyrant's wound I shook the lance,
And strode in joy the reeking plains of France!

Fallen is the oppressor, friendless, ghastly, low,
And my heart aches, though Mercy struck the blow.
With wearied thought once more I seek the shade,
30   Where peaceful Virtue weaves the myrtle braid.
And O! if Eyes whose holy glances roll,
Swift messengers, and eloquent of soul;
If Smiles more winning, and a gentler Mien
Than the love-wildered Maniac's brain hath seen
Shaping celestial forms in vacant air,
If these demand the impassion'd Poet's care –
If Mirth and softened Sense and Wit refined,
The blameless features of a lovely mind;
Then haply shall my trembling hand assign
40   No fading wreath to Beauty's saintly shrine.
Nor, Sara! thou these early flowers refuse –
Ne'er lurked the snake beneath their simple hues;
No purple bloom the Child of Nature brings
From Flattery's night-shade: as he feels he sings.

Translation

OF WRANGHAM'S 'HENDECASYLLABI AD BRUNTONAM
E GRANTA EXITURAM'

Maid of unboastful charms! whom white-robed Truth
Right onward guiding through the maze of youth,
Forbade the Circe Praise to witch thy soul,
And dash'd to earth th' intoxicating bowl:
Thee meek-eyed Pity, eloquently fair,
Clasp'd to her bosom with a mother's care;
And, as she lov'd thy kindred form to trace,
The slow smile wander'd o'er her pallid face.

For never yet did mortal voice impart
10   Tones more congenial to the sadden'd heart:
Whether, to rouse the sympathetic glow,
Thou pourest lone Monimia's tale of woe;
Or haply clothest with funereal vest
The bridal loves that wept in Juliet's breast.
O'er our chill limbs the thrilling Terrors creep,
Th' entranced Passions their still vigil keep;
While the deep sighs, responsive to the song,
Sound through the silence of the trembling throng.

But purer raptures lighten'd from thy face,
20   And spread o'er all thy form an holier grace,
When from the daughter's breasts the father drew
The life he gave, and mix'd the big tear's dew.
Nor was it thine th' heroic strain to roll
With mimic feelings foreign from the soul:
Bright in thy parent's eye we mark'd the tear;
Methought he said, 'Thou art no Actress here!
A semblance of thyself the *Grecian* dame,
And Brunton and Euphrasia still the same!'

O soon to seek the city's busier scene,
30   Pause thee awhile, thou chaste-eyed maid serene,
Till Granta's sons from all her sacred bowers
With grateful hand shall weave Pierian flowers
To twine a fragrant chaplet round thy brow,
Enchanting ministress of virtuous woe!

To Miss Brunton
WITH THE PRECEDING TRANSLATION

That darling of the Tragic Muse,
  When Wrangham sung her praise,
Thalia lost her rosy hues,
  And sicken'd at her lays:

But transient was th' unwonted sigh;
  For soon the Goddess spied
A sister-form of mirthful eye,
  And danc'd for joy and cried:

'Meek Pity's sweetest child, proud dame,
  The fates have given to you!
Still bid your Poet boast her name;
  I have *my* Brunton too.'

10

Epitaph on an Infant

Ere Sin could blight or Sorrow fade,
  Death came with friendly care;
The opening bud to Heaven conveyed,
  And bade it blossom there.

[Pantisocracy]

    No more my Visionary Soul shall dwell
On Joys that were! No more endure to weigh
The Shame and Anguish of the evil Day,
Wisely forgetful! O'er the Ocean swell
Sublime of Hope I seek the cottag'd Dell,
Where Virtue calm with careless step may stray,
And dancing to the moonlight Roundelay
The Wizard Passions weave an holy Spell.

Eyes that have ach'd with Sorrow! ye shall weep
10   Tears of doubt-mingled Joy, like theirs who start
From Precipices of distemper'd Sleep,
On which the fierce-eyed Fiends their Revels keep,
And see the rising Sun, and feel it dart
New Rays of Pleasance trembling to the Heart.

On the Prospect of Establishing a Pantisocracy in America

Whilst pale Anxiety, corrosive Care,
The tear of Woe, the gloom of sad Despair,
   And deepen'd Anguish generous bosoms rend –
Whilst patriot souls their country's fate lament;
Whilst mad with rage demoniac, foul intent,
   Embattled legions Despots vainly send
To arrest the immortal mind's expanding ray
   Of everlasting Truth – I other climes
Where dawns, with hope serene, a brighter day
10   Than e'er saw Albion in her happiest times,
With mental eye exulting now explore,
   And soon with kindred minds shall haste to enjoy
(Free from the ills which here our peace destroy)
Content and Bliss on Transatlantic shore.

Elegy,
IMITATED FROM ONE OF AKENSIDE'S BLANK-VERSE
INSCRIPTIONS

Near the lone pile with ivy overspread,
   Fast by the rivulet's sleep-persuading sound,
Where 'sleeps the moonlight' on yon verdant bed –
   O humbly press that consecrated ground!

For there does Edmund rest, the learnèd swain!
   And there his spirit most delights to rove:
Young Edmund! famed for each harmonious strain,
   And the sore wounds of ill-requited love.

Like some tall tree that spreads its branches wide,
10   And loads the west-wind with its soft perfume,
His manhood blossomed: till the faithless pride
      Of fair Matilda sank him to the tomb.

But soon did righteous Heaven her guilt pursue!
      Where'er with wildered step she wandered pale,
Still Edmund's image rose to blast her view,
      Still Edmund's voice accused her in each gale.

With keen regret, and conscious guilt's alarms,
      Amid the pomp of affluence she pined;
Nor all that lured her faith from Edmund's arms
20   Could lull the wakeful horror of her mind.

Go, Traveller! tell the tale with sorrow fraught:
      Some tearful maid perchance, or blooming youth,
May hold it in remembrance; and be taught
      That riches cannot pay for Love or Truth.

The Faded Flower

Ungrateful he, who pluck'd thee from thy stalk,
Poor faded flow'ret! on his careless way;
Inhal'd awhile thy odours on his walk,
Then onward pass'd and left thee to decay.
Ah! melancholy emblem! had I seen
Thy modest beauties dew'd with Evening's gem,
I had not rudely cropp'd thy parent stem,
But left thee, blushing, 'mid the enliven'd green.
And now I bent me o'er thy wither'd bloom,
10   And drop the tear – as Fancy, at my side,
Deep-sighing, points the fair frail Abra's tomb –
'Like thine, sad Flower, was that poor wanderer's pride!
Oh! lost to Love and Truth, whose selfish joy
Tasted her vernal sweets, but tasted to destroy!'

Sonnet

Pale Roamer through the night! thou poor Forlorn!
Remorse that man on his death-bed possess,
Who in the credulous hour of tenderness
Betrayed, then cast thee forth to want and scorn!
The world is pitiless: the chaste one's pride
Mimic of Virtue scowls on thy distress:
Thy Loves and they, that envied thee, deride:
And Vice alone will shelter wretchedness!
O! I could weep to think, that there should be
10   Cold-bosomed lewd ones, who endure to place
Foul offerings on the shrine of misery,
And force from famine the caress of Love;
May He shed healing on the sore disgrace,
He, the great Comforter that rules above!

Domestic Peace

Tell me, on what holy ground
May Domestic Peace be found –
Halcyon Daughter of the skies!
Far on fearful wings she flies,
From the pomp of sceptered State,
From the Rebel's noisy hate;
In a cottaged vale She dwells
Listening to the Sabbath bells!
Still around her steps are seen
10   Spotless Honour's meeker mien,
Love, the sire of pleasing fears,
Sorrow smiling through her tears,
And conscious of the past employ
Memory, bosom-spring of joy.

Sonnet

Thou bleedest, my poor Heart! and thy distress
Reasoning I ponder with a scornful smile,
And probe thy sore wound sternly, though the while
Swoln be mine eye and dim with heaviness.
Why didst thou listen to Hope's whisper bland?
Or, listening, why forget the healing tale,
When Jealousy with feverous fancies pale
Jarred thy fine fibres with a maniac's hand?
Faint was that Hope, and rayless! – Yet 'twas fair,
10   And soothed with many a dream the hour of rest:
Thou shouldst have loved it most, when most opprest,
And nursed it with an agony of care,
Even as a Mother her sweet infant heir
That wan and sickly droops upon her breast!

Sonnet
TO THE AUTHOR OF THE 'ROBBERS'

Schiller! that hour I would have wished to die,
If through the shuddering midnight I had sent
From the dark dungeon of the tower time-rent
That fearful voice, a famished Father's cry –
Lest in some after moment aught more mean
Might stamp me mortal! A triumphant shout
Black Horror screamed, and all her goblin rout
Diminished shrunk from the more withering scene!
Ah! Bard tremendous in sublimity!
10   Could I behold thee in thy loftier mood
Wandering at eve with finely frenzied eye
Beneath some vast old tempest-swinging wood!
Awhile with mute awe gazing I would brood:
Then weep aloud in a wild ecstasy!

Melancholy
A FRAGMENT

Stretch'd on a mouldered Abbey's broadest wall,
　　Where ruining ivies propped the ruins steep –
Her folded arms wrapping her tattered pall,
　　Had melancholy mus'd herself to sleep.
　　　The fern was press'd beneath her hair,
　　　The dark green adder's tongue was there;
And still as passed the flagging sea-gale weak,
The long lank leaf bowed fluttering o'er her cheek.

That pallid cheek was flushed: her eager look
10　　Beamed eloquent in slumber! Inly wrought,
　　　Imperfect sounds her moving lips forsook,
　　And her bent forehead worked with troubled thought.
　　　Strange was the dream –

Songs of the Pixies

The Pixies, in the superstition of Devonshire, are a race of beings invisibly small, and harmless or friendly to man. At a small distance from a village in that county, half way up a wood-covered hill, is an excavation called the Pixies' Parlour. The roots of old trees form its ceiling; and on its sides are innumerable cyphers, among which the author discovered his own and those of his brothers, cut by the hand of their childhood. At the foot of the hill flows the river Otter.

To this place the Author, during the Summer months of the year 1793, conducted a party of young ladies; one of whom, of stature elegantly small, and of complexion colourless yet clear, was proclaimed the Faery Queen. On which occasion the following Irregular Ode was written.

I

　　Whom the untaught Shepherds call
　　　Pixies in their madrigal,
　　Fancy's children, here we dwell:
　　　Welcome, Ladies! to our cell.

Here the wren of softest note
　　Builds its nest and warbles well;
Here the blackbird strains his throat;
　　Welcome, Ladies! to our cell.

II

When fades the moon to shadowy-pale,
And scuds the cloud before the gale,
Ere the Morn, all gem-bedight,
Hath streak'd the East with rosy light,
We sip the furze-flower's fragrant dews
Clad in robes of rainbow hues:
Or sport amid the shooting gleams
To the tune of distant-tinkling teams,
While lusty Labour scouting sorrow
Bids the Dame a glad good-morrow,
Who jogs the accustomed road along,
And paces cheery to her cheering song.

III

　　But not our filmy pinion
We scorch amid the blaze of day,
When Noontide's fiery-tressed minion
　　　Flashes the fervid ray.
　　Aye from the sultry heat
　　We to the cave retreat
O'ercanopied by huge roots intertwined
With wildest texture, blackened o'er with age:
Round them their mantle green the ivies bind,
　　Beneath whose foliage pale
　　Fanned by the unfrequent gale
We shield us from the Tyrant's mid-day rage.

IV

Thither, while the murmuring throng
Of wild-bees hum their drowsy song,
By Indolence and Fancy brought,
A youthful Bard, 'unknown to Fame',
Wooes the Queen of Solemn Thought,

And heaves the gentle misery of a sigh
    Gazing with tearful eye,
40   As round our sandy grot appear
    Many a rudely sculptured name
      To pensive Memory dear!
Weaving gay dreams of sunny-tinctured hue
    We glance before his view:
O'er his hush'd soul our soothing witcheries shed
And twine the future garland round his head.

V

    When Evening's dusky car
    Crowned with her dewy star
Steals o'er the fading sky in shadowy flight;
50   On leaves of aspen trees
    We tremble to the breeze
Veiled from the grosser ken of mortal sight.
    Or, haply, at the visionary hour,
Along our wildly-bowered sequestered walk,
We listen to the enamoured rustic's talk;
Heave with the heavings of the maiden's breast,
Where young-eyed Loves have hid their turtle nest;
    Or guide of soul-subduing power
The glance, that from the half-confessing eye
60 Darts the fond question or the soft reply.

VI

    Or through the mystic ringlets of the vale
    We flash our faery feet in gamesome prank;
    Or, silent-sandal'd, pay our defter court,
    Circling the Spirit of the Western Gale,
    Where wearied with his flower-caressing sport,
    Supine he slumbers on a violet bank;
Then with quaint music hymn the parting gleam
By lonely Otter's sleep-persuading stream;
Or where his wave with loud unquiet song
70 Dashed o'er the rocky channel froths along;
Or where, his silver waters smoothed to rest,
The tall tree's shadow sleeps upon his breast.

VII

        Hence thou lingerer, Light!
        Eve saddens into Night.
Mother of wildly-working dreams! we view
    The sombre hours, that round thee stand
    With down-cast eyes (a duteous band!)
Their dark robes dripping with the heavy dew.
      Sorceress of the ebon throne!
80   Thy power the Pixies own,
        When round thy raven brow
        Heaven's lucent roses glow,
  And clouds in watery colours drest
Float in light drapery o'er thy sable vest:
What time the pale moon sheds a softer day
Mellowing the woods beneath its pensive beam:
For mid the quivering light 'tis ours to play,
Aye dancing to the cadence of the stream.

VIII

        Welcome, Ladies! to the cell
90   Where the blameless Pixies dwell:
But thou, sweet Nymph! proclaimed our Faery Queen,
      With what obeisance meet
      Thy presence shall we greet?
For lo! attendant on thy steps are seen
      Graceful Ease in artless stole,
      And white-robed Purity of soul,
        With Honour's softer mien;
  Mirth of the loosely-flowing hair,
And meek-eyed Pity eloquently fair,
100   Whose tearful cheeks are lovely to the view,
        As snow-drop wet with dew.

IX

Unboastful Maid! though now the Lily pale
   Transparent grace thy beauties meek;
Yet ere again along the impurpling vale,
The purpling vale and elfin-haunted grove,
Young Zephyr his fresh flowers profusely throws,
   We'll tinge with livelier hues thy cheek;
And, haply, from the nectar-breathing Rose
        Extract a Blush for Love!

To a Young Ass,
ITS MOTHER BEING TETHERED NEAR IT

Poor little Foal of an oppressèd Race!
I love the languid Patience of thy face:
And oft with gentle hand I give thee bread,
And clap thy ragged Coat, and pat thy head.
But what thy dullèd Spirits hath dismayed,
That never thou dost sport along the glade?
And (most unlike the nature of things young)
That earthward still thy moveless head is hung?
Do thy prophetic Fears anticipate,
Meek Child of Misery! thy future fate?
The starving meal, and all the thousand aches
'Which patient Merit of the Unworthy takes?'
Or is thy sad heart thrilled with filial pain
To see thy wretched Mother's shortened Chain?
And truly, very piteous is her Lot –
Chained to a Log within a narrow spot,
Where the close-eaten Grass is scarcely seen,
While sweet around her waves the tempting Green!
Poor Ass! thy master should have learnt to show
Pity – best taught by fellowship of Woe!
For much I fear me that He lives like thee,
Half famished in a land of Luxury!
How askingly its footsteps hither bend;
It seems to say, 'And have I then one Friend?'
Innocent Foal! thou poor despised Forlorn!
I hail thee Brother – spite of the fool's scorn!
And fain would take thee with me, in the Dell
Of Peace and mild Equality to dwell,
Where Toil shall call the charmer Health his bride,
And Laughter tickle Plenty's ribless side!
How thou wouldst toss thy heels in gamesome play,
And frisk about, as lamb or kitten gay!
Yea! and more musically sweet to me
Thy dissonant harsh bray of joy would be,
Than warbled melodies that soothe to rest
The aching of pale Fashion's vacant breast!

Lines on a Friend
WHO DIED OF A FRENZY FEVER INDUCED BY CALUMNIOUS REPORTS

Edmund! thy grave with aching eye I scan,
And inly groan for Heaven's poor outcast – Man!
'Tis tempest all or gloom: in early youth
If gifted with the Ithuriel lance of Truth
We force to start amid her feigned caress
Vice, siren-hag! in native ugliness;
A Brother's fate will haply rouse the tear,
And on we go in heaviness and fear!
But if our fond hearts call to Pleasure's bower
10   Some pigmy Folly in a careless hour,
The faithless guest shall stamp the enchanted ground,
And mingled forms of Misery rise around:
Heart-fretting Fear, with pallid look aghast,
That courts the future woe to hide the past;
Remorse, the poisoned arrow in his side,
And loud lewd Mirth, to Anguish close allied:
Till Frenzy, fierce-eyed child of moping pain,
Darts her hot lightning-flash athwart the brain.
Rest, injur'd shade! Shall Slander squatting near
20   Spit her cold venom in a dead Man's ear?
'Twas thine to feel the sympathetic glow
In Merit's joy, and Poverty's meek woe;
Thine all, that cheer the moment as it flies,
The zoneless Cares, and smiling Courtesies.
Nursed in thy heart the firmer Virtues grew,
And in thy heart they withered! Such chill dew
Wan Indolence on each young blossom shed;
And Vanity her filmy net-work spread,
With eye that rolled around in asking gaze,
30   And tongue that trafficked in the trade of praise.
Thy follies such! the hard world marked them well!
Were they more wise, the proud who never fell?
Rest, injured shade! the poor man's grateful prayer
On heaven-ward wing thy wounded soul shall bear.
As oft at twilight gloom thy grave I pass,
And sit me down upon its recent grass,
With introverted eye I contemplate
Similitude of soul, perhaps of – fate;

To me hath Heaven with bounteous hand assigned
40   Energic Reason and a shaping mind,
The daring ken of Truth, the Patriot's part,
And Pity's sigh, that breathes the gentle heart.
Sloth-jaundiced all! and from my graspless hand
Drop Friendship's precious pearls, like hour-glass sand.
I weep, yet stoop not! the faint anguish flows,
A dreamy pang in Morning's feverous doze.

Is this piled earth our Being's passless mound?
Tell me, cold grave! is death with poppies crowned?
Tired Sentinel! mid fitful starts I nod,
50   And fain would sleep, though pillowed on a clod!

To a Friend
TOGETHER WITH AN UNFINISHED POEM

Thus far my scanty brain hath built the rhyme
Elaborate and swelling: yet the heart
Not owns it. From thy spirit-breathing powers
I ask not now, my friend! the aiding verse,
Tedious to thee, and from thy anxious thought
Of dissonant mood. In fancy (well I know)
From business wandering far and local cares,
Thou creepest round a dear-lov'd Sister's bed
With noiseless step, and watchest the faint look,
10   Soothing each pang with fond solicitude,
And tenderest tones medicinal of love.
I too a Sister *had*, an only Sister –
She lov'd me dearly, and I doted on her!
To her I pour'd forth all my puny sorrows
(As a sick Patient in a Nurse's arms)
And of the heart those hidden maladies
That e'en from Friendship's eye will shrink asham'd.
O! I have wak'd at midnight, and have wept,
Because she was not! – Cheerily, dear Charles!
20   Thou thy best friend shalt cherish many a year:
Such warm presages feel I of high Hope.
For not uninterested the dear Maid
I've view'd – her soul affectionate yet wise,
Her polish'd wit as mild as lambent glories

That play around a sainted infant's head.
He knows (the Spirit that in secret sees,
Of whose omniscient and all-spreading Love
Aught to *implore* were impotence of mind)
That my mute thoughts are sad before his throne,
30   Prepar'd, when he his healing ray vouchsafes,
Thanksgiving to pour forth with lifted heart,
And praise Him Gracious with a Brother's Joy!

SONNETS ON EMINENT CHARACTERS

1. To the Honourable Mr Erskine

When British Freedom for a happier land
Spread her broad wings, that fluttered with affright,
Erskine! thy voice she heard, and paused her flight
Sublime of hope! For dreadless thou didst stand
(Thy censer glowing with the hallowed flame)
A hireless Priest before the insulted shrine,
And at her altar pour the stream divine
Of unmatched eloquence. Therefore thy name
Her sons shall venerate, and cheer thy breast
10   With blessings heaven-ward breathed. And when the doom
Of Nature bids thee die, beyond the tomb
Thy light shall shine: as sunk beneath the West
Though the great Summer Sun eludes our gaze,
Still burns wide Heaven with his distended blaze.

2. Burke

As late I lay in slumber's shadowy vale,
With wetted cheek and in a mourner's guise,
I saw the sainted form of Freedom rise:
She spake! not sadder moans the autumnal gale –

'Great Son of Genius! sweet to me thy name,
Ere in an evil hour with altered voice
Thou bad'st Oppression's hireling crew rejoice
Blasting with wizard spell my laurelled fame.
Yet never, Burke! thou drank'st Corruption's bowl!
Thee stormy Pity and the cherished lure
Of Pomp, and proud Precipitance of soul
Wildered with meteor fires. Ah Spirit pure!
That error's mist had left thy purgèd eye:
So might I clasp thee with a Mother's joy!'

10

3. Priestley

Though roused by that dark Vizir Riot rude
Have driven our Priestley o'er the ocean swell;
Though Superstition and her wolfish brood
Bay his mild radiance, impotent and fell;
Calm in his halls of brightness he shall dwell!
For lo! Religion at his strong behest
Starts with mild anger from the Papal spell,
And flings to earth her tinsel-glittering vest,
Her mitred state and cumbrous pomp unholy;
And Justice wakes to bid the Oppressor wail
Insulting aye the wrongs of patient Folly:
And from her dark retreat by Wisdom won
Meek Nature slowly lifts her matron veil
To smile with fondness on her gazing son!

10

4. La Fayette

As when far off the warbled strains are heard
That soar on Morning's wing the vales among,
Within his cage the imprisoned matin bird
Swells the full chorus with a generous song:
He bathes no pinion in the dewy light,
No Father's joy, no Lover's bliss he shares,
Yet still the rising radiance cheers his sight;
His fellows' freedom soothes the captive's cares!

Thou, Fayette! who didst wake with startling voice
10   Life's better sun from that long wintry night,
Thus in thy Country's triumphs shalt rejoice,
And mock with raptures high the dungeon's might:
For lo! the morning struggles into day,
And Slavery's spectres shriek and vanish from the ray!

5. Koskiusko

O what a loud and fearful shriek was there,
As though a thousand souls one death-groan poured!
Ah me! they saw beneath a hireling's sword
Their Koskiusko fall! Through the swart air
(As pauses the tired Cossac's barbarous yell
Of triumph) on the chill and midnight gale
Rises with frantic burst or sadder swell
The dirge of murdered Hope! while Freedom pale
Bends in such anguish o'er her destined bier,
10   As if from eldest time some Spirit meek
Had gathered in a mystic urn each tear
That ever on a Patriot's furrowed cheek
Fit channel found, and she had drained the bowl
In the mere wilfulness, and sick despair of soul!

6. Pitt

Not always should the Tear's ambrosial dew
    Roll its soft anguish down thy furrow'd cheek!
    Not always heaven-breath'd tones of Suppliance meek
Beseem thee, Mercy! Yon dark Scowler view,
Who with proud words of dear-lov'd Freedom came –
    More blasting than the mildew from the South!
    And kiss'd his country with Iscariot mouth
(Ah! foul apostate from his Father's fame!)
Then fix'd her on the Cross of deep distress,
10   And at safe distance marks the thirsty Lance

Pierce her big side! But O! if some strange trance
The eye-lids of thy stern-brow'd Sister press,
   Seize, Mercy! thou more terrible the brand,
   And hurl her thunderbolts with fiercer hand!

7. To the Rev. W. L. Bowles

[FIRST VERSION]

My heart has thank'd thee, BOWLES! for those soft strains,
   That, on the still air floating, tremblingly
   Wak'd in me Fancy, Love, and Sympathy!
For hence, not callous to a Brother's pains

Thro' Youth's gay prime and thornless paths I went;
   And, when the *darker* day of life began,
   And I did roam, a thought-bewilder'd man
Thy kindred Lays an healing solace lent,

Each lonely pang with dreamy joys combin'd,
10   And stole from vain REGRET her scorpion stings;
   While shadowy PLEASURE, with mysterious wings,
Brooded the wavy and tumultuous mind,

Like that great Spirit, who with plastic sweep
Mov'd on the darkness of the formless Deep!

[REVISED VERSION]

My heart has thanked thee, Bowles! for those soft strains
Whose sadness soothes me, like the murmuring
Of wild-bees in the sunny showers of spring!
For hence not callous to the mourner's pains
Through Youth's gay prime and thornless paths I went:
And when the mightier throes of mind began,
And drove me forth, a thought-bewildered man,
Their mild and manliest melancholy lent
A mingled charm, such as the pang consigned
10 To slumber, though the big tear it renewed;
Bidding a strange mysterious Pleasure brood

Over the wavy and tumultuous mind,
As the great Spirit erst with plastic sweep
Moved on the darkness of the unformed deep.

8. Mrs Siddons

As when a child on some long Winter's night
    Affrighted clinging to its Grandam's knees
    With eager wond'ring and perturb'd delight
Listens strange tales of fearful dark decrees

Mutter'd to wretch by necromantic spell;
    Or of those hags, who at the witching time
    Of murky Midnight ride the air sublime,
And mingle foul embrace with fiends of Hell:

Cold Horror drinks its blood! Anon the tear
10   More gentle starts, to hear the Beldame tell
    Of pretty Babes, that lov'd each other dear,
Murder'd by cruel Uncle's mandate fell:

Even such the shiv'ring joys thy tones impart,
Even so thou, SIDDONS! meltest my sad heart!

9. To William Godwin
AUTHOR OF 'POLITICAL JUSTICE'

O form'd t' illume a sunless world forlorn,
    As o'er the chill and dusky brow of Night,
    In Finland's wintry skies the Mimic Morn
Electric pours a stream of rosy light,

Pleas'd I have mark'd OPPRESSION, terror-pale,
    Since, thro' the windings of her dark machine,
    Thy steady eye has shot its glances keen –
And bade th' All-lovely 'scenes at distance hail'.

Nor will I not thy holy guidance bless,
10   And hymn thee, GODWIN! with an ardent lay;
    For that thy voice, in Passion's stormy day,
When wild I roam'd the bleak Heath of Distress,

Bade the bright form of Justice meet my way –
And told me that her name was HAPPINESS.

10. *To Robert Southey*

OF BALLIOL COLLEGE, OXFORD, AUTHOR OF THE
'RETROSPECT', AND OTHER POEMS

SOUTHEY! thy melodies steal o'er mine ear
    Like far-off joyance, or the murmuring
    Of wild bees in the sunny showers of Spring –
Sounds of such mingled import as may cheer

The lonely breast, yet rouse a mindful tear:
    Wak'd by the Song doth Hope-born FANCY fling
    Rich showers of dewy fragrance from her wing,
Till sickly PASSION's drooping Myrtles sear

Blossom anew! But O! more thrill'd, I prize
10   Thy sadder strains, that bid in MEMORY's Dream
The faded forms of past Delight arise;
    Then soft, on Love's pale cheek, the tearful gleam

    Of Pleasure smiles – as faint yet beauteous lies
    The imag'd Rainbow on a willowy stream.

11. *To Richard Brinsley Sheridan, Esq.*

It was some Spirit, Sheridan! that breathed
O'er thy young mind such wildly various power!
My soul hath marked thee in her shaping hour,
Thy temples with Hymettian flow'rets wreathed:

And sweet thy voice, as when o'er Laura's bier
Sad music trembled through Vauclusa's glade;
Sweet, as at dawn the love-lorn Serenade
That wafts soft dreams to Slumber's listening ear.
Now patriot rage and indignation high
Swell the full tones! And now thine eye-beams dance
Meanings of Scorn and Wit's quaint revelry!
Writhes inly from the bosom-probing glance
The Apostate by the brainless rout adored,
As erst that elder Fiend beneath great Michael's sword.

12. To Lord Stanhope
ON READING HIS LATE PROTEST IN THE HOUSE OF LORDS

STANHOPE! I hail, with ardent Hymn, thy name!
    Thou shalt be bless'd and lov'd, when in the dust
    Thy corse shall moulder – Patriot pure and just!
And o'er thy tomb the grateful hand of FAME

Shall grave: – 'Here sleeps the Friend of Humankind!'
    For thou, untainted by CORRUPTION's bowl,
    Or foul AMBITION, with undaunted soul
Hast spoke the language of a Free-born mind

Pleading the cause of Nature! Still pursue
Thy path of Honour! – To thy Country true,

Still watch th' expiring flame of Liberty!
    O Patriot! still pursue thy virtuous way,
    As holds his course the splendid Orb of Day,
Or thro' the stormy or the tranquil sky!

ONE OF THE PEOPLE

To Earl Stanhope

Not, STANHOPE! with the Patriot's doubtful name
  I mock thy worth – Friend of the Human Race!
  Since scorning Faction's low and partial aim
Aloof thou wendest in thy stately pace,

Thyself redeeming from that leprous stain,
  Nobility: and aye unterrify'd
  Pourest thine Abdiel warnings on the train
That sit complotting with rebellious pride

'Gainst *her* who from the Almighty's bosom leapt
10   With whirlwind arm, fierce Minister of Love!
  Wherefore, ere Virtue o'er thy tomb hath wept,
Angels shall lead thee to the Throne above:

And thou from forth its clouds shalt hear the voice,
Champion of Freedom and her God! rejoice!

Lines

TO A FRIEND IN ANSWER TO A MELANCHOLY LETTER

Away, those cloudy looks, that labouring sigh,
The peevish offspring of a sickly hour!
Nor meanly thus complain of Fortune's power,
When the blind gamester throws a luckless die.

Yon setting sun flashes a mournful gleam
Behind those broken clouds, his stormy train:
To-morrow shall the many-coloured main
In brightness roll beneath his orient beam!

Wild, as the autumnal gust, the hand of Time
10 Flies o'er his mystic lyre: in shadowy dance
The alternate groups of Joy and Grief advance
Responsive to his varying strains sublime!

Bears on its wing each hour a load of Fate;
The swain, who, lulled by Seine's mild murmurs, led
His weary oxen to their nightly shed,
To-day may rule a tempest-troubled State.

Nor shall not Fortune with a vengeful smile
Survey the sanguinary despot's might,
And haply hurl the pageant from his height
20   Unwept to wander in some savage isle.

There shiv'ring sad beneath the tempest's frown
Round his tired limbs to wrap the purple vest;
And mixed with nails and beads, an equal jest!
Barter for food the jewels of his crown.

To an Infant

Ah! cease thy tears and sobs, my little Life!
I did but snatch away the unclasped knife:
Some safer toy will soon arrest thine eye,
And to quick laughter change this peevish cry!
Poor stumbler on the rocky coast of woe,
Tutored by pain each source of pain to know!
Alike the foodful fruit and scorching fire
Awake thy eager grasp and young desire;
Alike the Good, the Ill offend thy sight,
10   And rouse the stormy sense of shrill affright!
Untaught, yet wise! mid all thy brief alarms
Thou closely clingest to thy Mother's arms,
Nestling thy little face in that fond breast
Whose anxious heavings lull thee to thy rest!
Man's breathing Miniature! thou mak'st me sigh –
A Babe art thou – and such a Thing am I!
To anger rapid and as soon appeased,
For trifles mourning and by trifles pleased,
Break Friendship's mirror with a tetchy blow,
20   Yet snatch what coals of fire on Pleasure's altar glow!

O thou that rearest with celestial aim
The future Seraph in my mortal frame,
Thrice holy Faith! whatever thorns I meet
As on I totter with unpractised feet,
Still let me stretch my arms and cling to thee,
Meek nurse of souls through their long infancy!

To the Rev. W. J. Hort
WHILE TEACHING A YOUNG LADY SOME SONG-TUNES
ON HIS FLUTE

I

Hush! ye clamorous Cares! be mute!
    Again, dear Harmonist! again
Thro' the hollow of thy flute
    Breathe that passion-warbled strain:
Till MEMORY each form shall bring
    The loveliest of her shadowy throng;
And HOPE, that soars on sky-lark wing,
    Carol wild her gladdest song!

II

O skill'd with magic spell to roll
The thrilling tones, that concentrate the soul!
Breathe thro' thy flute those tender notes again,
While near thee sits the chaste-eyed Maiden mild;
And bid her raise the Poet's kindred strain
In soft impassion'd voice, correctly wild.

III

In Freedom's UNDIVIDED dell,
Where *Toil* and *Health* with mellow'd *Love* shall dwell,
    Far from folly, far from men,
    In the rude romantic glen,
    Up the cliff, and thro' the glade,
Wand'ring with the dear-lov'd maid,
    I shall listen to the lay,
    And ponder on thee far away!

Still, as she bids those thrilling notes aspire
('Making my fond attunèd heart her lyre'),
Thy honour'd form, my Friend! shall reappear,
And I will thank thee with a raptur'd tear.

Sonnet

Sweet Mercy! how my very heart has bled
To see thee, poor Old Man! and thy grey hairs
Hoar with the snowy blast: while no one cares
To clothe thy shrivelled limbs and palsied head.
My Father! throw away this tattered vest
That mocks thy shivering! take my garment – use
A young man's arm! I'll melt these frozen dews
That hang from thy white beard and numb thy breast.
My Sara too shall tend thee, like a Child:
10 And thou shalt talk, in our fire-side's recess,
Of purple pride, that scowls on wretchedness.
He did not so, the Galilean mild,
Who met the Lazars turned from rich men's doors,
And called them Friends, and healed their noisome sores!

To the Nightingale

Sister of love-lorn Poets, Philomel!
How many Bards in city garret pent,
While at their window they with downward eye
Mark the faint lamp-beam on the kennell'd mud,
And listen to the drowsy cry of Watchmen
(Those hoarse unfeather'd Nightingales of Time!),
How many wretched Bards address *thy* name,
And hers, the full-orb'd Queen that shines above.
But I *do* hear thee, and the high bough mark,
10 Within whose mild moon-mellow'd foliage hid
Thou warblest sad thy pity-pleading strains.
O! I have listen'd, till my working soul,

Waked by those strains to thousand phantasies,
Absorb'd hath ceas'd to listen! Therefore oft,
I hymn thy name: and with a proud delight
Oft will I tell thee, Minstrel of the Moon!
'Most musical, most melancholy' Bird!
That all thy soft diversities of tone,
Tho' sweeter far than the delicious airs
20   That vibrate from a white-arm'd Lady's harp,
What time the languishment of lonely love
Melts in her eye, and heaves her breast of snow,
Are not so sweet as is the voice of her,
My Sara – best beloved of human kind!
When breathing the pure soul of tenderness,
She thrills me with the Husband's promis'd name!

Lines

COMPOSED WHILE CLIMBING THE LEFT ASCENT OF
BROCKLEY COOMB, SOMERSETSHIRE, MAY, 1795

With many a pause and oft reverted eye
I climb the Coomb's ascent: sweet songsters near
Warble in shade their wild-wood melody:
Far off the unvarying Cuckoo soothes my ear.
Up scour the startling stragglers of the Flock
That on green plots o'er precipices browse:
From the deep fissures of the naked rock
The Yew tree bursts! Beneath its dark green boughs
(Mid which the May-thorn blends its blossoms white)
10   Where broad smooth stones jut out in mossy seats,
I rest: – and now have gained the topmost site.
Ah! what a luxury of landscape meets
My gaze! Proud towers, and cots more dear to me,
Elm-shadow'd fields, and prospect-bounding sea!
Deep sighs my lonely heart: I drop the tear:
Enchanting spot! O were my Sara here!

Lines
IN THE MANNER OF SPENSER

O Peace, that on a lilied bank dost love
To rest thine head beneath an olive tree,
I would, that from the pinions of thy dove
One quill withouten pain yplucked might be!
For O! I wish my Sara's frowns to flee,
And fain to her some soothing song would write,
Lest she resent my rude discourtesy,
Who vowed to meet her ere the morning light,
But broke my plighted word – ah! false and recreant wight!

10 Last night as I my weary head did pillow
With thoughts of my dissevered Fair engrost,
Chill Fancy drooped wreathing herself with willow,
As though my breast entombed a pining ghost.
'From some blest couch, young Rapture's bridal boast,
Rejected Slumber! hither wing thy way;
But leave me with the matin hour, at most!
As night-closed floweret to the orient ray,
My sad heart will expand, when I the Maid survey.'

But Love, who heard the silence of my thought,
20 Contrived a too successful wile, I ween:
And whispered to himself, with malice fraught –
'Too long our Slave the Damsel's smiles hath seen:
To-morrow shall he ken her altered mien!'
He spake, and ambushed lay, till on my bed
The morning shot her dewy glances keen,
When as I 'gan to lift my drowsy head –
'Now, Bard! I'll work thee woe!' the laughing Elfin said.

Sleep, softly-breathing God! his downy wing
Was fluttering now, as quickly to depart;
30 When twanged an arrow from Love's mystic string,
With pathless wound it pierced him to the heart.
Was there some magic in the Elfin's dart?
Or did he strike my couch with wizard lance?
For straight so fair a Form did upwards start
(No fairer decked the bowers of old Romance)
That Sleep enamoured grew, nor moved from his sweet trance!

My Sara came, with gentlest look divine;
Bright shone her eye, yet tender was its beam:
I felt the pressure of her lip to mine!
40   Whispering we went, and Love was all our theme –
Love pure and spotless, as at first, I deem,
He sprang from Heaven! Such joys with Sleep did bide,
That I the living image of my dream
Fondly forgot. Too late I woke, and sigh'd –
'O! how shall I behold my Love at even-tide!'

To the Author of Poems
PUBLISHED ANONYMOUSLY AT BRISTOL IN
SEPTEMBER 1795

Unboastful Bard! whose verse concise yet clear
Tunes to smooth melody unconquer'd sense,
May your fame fadeless live, as 'never-sere'
The Ivy wreathes yon Oak, whose broad defence
Embowers me from Noon's sultry influence!
For, like that nameless Rivulet stealing by,
Your modest verse to musing Quiet dear
Is rich with tints heaven-borrow'd: the charm'd eye
Shall gaze undazzled there, and love the soften'd sky.

10   Circling the base of the Poetic mount
A stream there is, which rolls in lazy flow
Its coal-black waters from Oblivion's fount:
The vapour-poison'd Birds, that fly too low,
Fall with dead swoop, and to the bottom go.
Escaped that heavy stream on pinion fleet
Beneath the Mountain's lofty-frowning brow,
Ere aught of perilous ascent you meet,
A mead of mildest charm delays th' unlabouring feet.

Not there the cloud-climb'd rock, sublime and vast,
20   That like some giant king, o'er-glooms the hill;
Nor there the Pine-grove to the midnight blast
Makes solemn music! But th' unceasing rill

To the soft Wren or Lark's descending trill
Murmurs sweet undersong 'mid jasmin bowers.
In this same pleasant meadow, at your will
I ween, you wander'd – there collecting flowers
Of sober tint, and herbs of med'cinable powers!

There for the monarch-murder'd Soldier's tomb
You Wove th' unfinish'd wreath of saddest hues;
30   And to that holier chaplet added bloom
Besprinkling it with Jordan's cleansing dews.
But lo your Henderson awakes the Muse –
His Spirit beckon'd from the mountain's height!
You left the plain and soar'd mid richer views!
So Nature mourn'd when sunk the First Day's light,
With stars, unseen before, spangling her robe of night!

Still soar, my Friend, those richer views among,
Strong, rapid, fervent, flashing Fancy's beam!
Virtue and Truth shall love your gentler song;
40   But Poesy demands th' impassion'd theme:
Waked by Heaven's silent dews at Eve's mild gleam
What balmy sweets Pomona breathes around!
But if the vext air rush a stormy stream
Or Autumn's shrill gust moan in plaintive sound,
With fruits and flowers she loads the tempest-honour'd ground.

The Production of a Young Lady
ADDRESSED TO THE AUTHOR OF THE POEMS ALLUDED TO
IN THE PRECEDING EPISTLE

*She had lost her Silver Thimble, and her complaint being
accidentally overheard by him, her Friend, he immediately sent her
four others to take her choice of.*

As oft mine eye with careless glance
Has gallop'd thro' some old romance,
Of speaking Birds and Steeds with wings,
Giants and Dwarfs, and Fiends and Kings;
Beyond the rest with more attentive care
I've lov'd to read of elfin-favour'd Fair –

How if she long'd for aught beneath the sky
And suffer'd to escape one votive sigh,
Wafted along on viewless pinions aery
10   It laid itself obsequious at her Feet:
Such things, I thought, one might not hope to meet
Save in the dear delicious land of Faery!
But now (by proof I know it well)
There's still some peril in free wishing –
Politeness is a licenc'd *spell*,
And *you*, dear Sir! the Arch-magician.

You much perplex'd me by the various set:
They were indeed an elegant quartette!
My mind went to and fro, and waver'd long;
20   At length I've chosen (Samuel thinks me wrong)
That, around whose azure rim
Silver figures seem to swim,
Like fleece-white clouds, that on the skiey Blue,
Wak'd by no breeze, the self-same shapes retain;
Or ocean Nymphs with limbs of snowy hue
Slow-floating o'er the calm cerulean plain.

Just such a one, *mon cher ami*,
(The finger shield of industry)
Th' inventive Gods, I deem, to Pallas gave
30   What time the vain Arachne, madly brave,
Challeng'd the blue-eyed Virgin of the sky
A duel in embroider'd work to try.
And hence the thimbled Finger of grave Pallas
To th' erring Needle's point was more than callous.
But ah the poor Arachne! She unarm'd
Blundering thro' hasty eagerness, alarm'd
With all a *Rival's* hopes, a *Mortal's* fears,
Still miss'd the stitch, and stain'd the web with tears.
Unnumber'd punctures small yet sore
40   Full fretfully the maiden bore,
Till she her lily finger found
Crimson'd with many a tiny wound;
And to her eyes, suffus'd with wat'ry woe,
Her flower-embroider'd web danc'd dim, I wist,
Like blossom'd shrubs in a quick-moving mist:
Till vanquish'd the despairing Maid sunk low.

O Bard! whom sure no common Muse inspires,
I heard your Verse that glows with vestal fires!
And I from unwatch'd needle's erring point
50   Had surely suffer'd on each finger-joint
Those wounds, which erst did poor Arachne meet;
While he, the much-lov'd Object of my Choice
(My bosom thrilling with enthusiast heat),
Pour'd on mine ear with deep impressive voice,
How the great Prophet of the Desert stood
And preach'd of Penitence by Jordan's Flood;
On WAR; or else the legendary lays
In simplest measures hymn'd to ALLA's praise;
Or what the Bard from his heart's inmost stores
60   O'er his *Friend's* grave in loftier numbers pours:
Yes, Bard polite! you but obey'd the laws
Of Justice, when the thimble you had sent;
What wounds your thought-bewildering Muse might cause
'Tis well, your finger-shielding gifts prevent.

SARA

Effusion XXXV
COMPOSED AUGUST 20TH, 1795, AT CLEVEDON,
SOMERSETSHIRE

My pensive SARA! thy soft cheek reclin'd
Thus on mine arm, most soothing sweet it is
To sit beside our cot, our cot o'er grown
With white-flower'd Jasmin, and the broad-leav'd Myrtle,
(Meet emblems they of Innocence and Love!)
And watch the clouds, that late were rich with light,
Slow-sad'ning round, and mark the star of eve
Serenely brilliant (such should Wisdom be)
Shine opposite! How exquisite the scents
10   Snatch'd from yon bean-field! and the world *so* hush'd!
The stilly murmur of the distant Sea
Tells us of Silence. And that simplest Lute
Plac'd length-ways in the clasping casement, hark!
How by the desultory breeze caress'd,
Like some coy Maid half-yielding to her Lover,
It pours such sweet upbraidings, as must needs
Tempt to repeat the wrong! And now its strings

Boldlier swept, the long sequacious notes
Over delicious surges sink and rise,
20   Such a soft floating witchery of sound
As twilight Elfins make, when they at eve
Voyage on gentle gales from Faery Land,
Where *Melodies* round honey-dropping flowers
Footless and wild, like birds of Paradise,
Nor pause nor perch, hov'ring on untam'd wing.

And thus, my Love! as on the midway slope
Of yonder hill I stretch my limbs at noon
Whilst thro' my half-clos'd eyelids I behold
The sunbeams dance, like diamonds, on the main,
30   And tranquil muse upon tranquillity;
Full many a thought uncall'd and undetain'd,
And many idle flitting phantasies,
Traverse my indolent and passive brain
As wild and various, as the random gales
That swell or flutter on this subject Lute!
And what if all of animated nature
Be but organic Harps diversly fram'd,
That tremble into thought, as o'er them sweeps,
Plastic and vast, one intellectual Breeze,
40   At once the Soul of each, and God of all?
But thy more serious eye a mild reproof
Darts, O beloved Woman! nor such thoughts
Dim and unhallow'd dost thou not reject,
And biddest me walk humbly with my God.

Meek Daughter in the Family of Christ,
Well hast thou said and holily disprais'd
These shapings of the unregenerate mind,
Bubbles that glitter as they rise and break
On vain Philosophy's aye-babbling spring.
50   For never guiltless may I speak of Him,
Th' INCOMPREHENSIBLE! save when with awe
I praise him, and with Faith that inly *feels*;
Who with his saving mercies healed me,
A sinful and most miserable man
Wilder'd and dark, and gave me to possess
PEACE, and this COT, and THEE, heart-honour'd Maid!

The Eolian Harp
COMPOSED AT CLEVEDON, SOMERSETSHIRE

My pensive Sara! thy soft cheek reclined
Thus on mine arm, most soothing sweet it is
To sit beside our cot, our cot o'ergrown
With white-flowered jasmin, and the broad-leaved myrtle,
(Meet emblems they of Innocence and Love!)
And watch the clouds, that late were rich with light,
Slow saddening round, and mark the star of eve
Serenely brilliant (such should wisdom be)
Shine opposite! How exquisite the scents
Snatched from yon bean-field! and the world so hushed!
The stilly murmur of the distant sea
Tells us of silence.

        And that simplest lute,
Placed length-ways in the clasping casement, hark!
How by the desultory breeze caressed,
Like some coy maid half yielding to her lover,
It pours such sweet upbraiding, as must needs
Tempt to repeat the wrong! And now, its strings
Boldlier swept, the long sequacious notes
Over delicious surges sink and rise,
Such a soft floating witchery of sound
As twilight Elfins make, when they at eve
Voyage on gentle gales from Fairy-Land,
Where Melodies round honey-dropping flowers,
Footless and wild, like birds of Paradise,
Nor pause, nor perch, hovering on untamed wing!
O the one life within us and abroad,
Which meets all motion and becomes its soul,
A light in sound, a sound-like power in light
Rhythm in all thought, and joyance every where –
Methinks, it should have been impossible
Not to love all things in a world so filled;
Where the breeze warbles, and the mute still air
Is Music slumbering on her instrument.

And thus, my love! as on the midway slope
Of yonder hill I stretch my limbs at noon,
Whilst through my half-closed eye-lids I behold
The sunbeams dance, like diamonds, on the main,
And tranquil muse upon tranquillity;
Full many a thought uncalled and undetained,
And many idle flitting phantasies,
Traverse my indolent and passive brain,
As wild and various as the random gales
That swell and flutter on this subject lute!

And what if all of animated nature
Be but organic harps diversely framed,
That tremble into thought, as o'er them sweeps
Plastic and vast, one intellectual breeze,
At once the Soul of each, and God of All?

But thy more serious eye a mild reproof
Darts, O beloved woman! nor such thoughts
Dim and unhallowed dost thou not reject,
And biddest me walk humbly with my God.
Meek daughter in the family of Christ!
Well hast thou said and holily dispraised
These shapings of the unregenerate mind;
Bubbles that glitter as they rise and break
On vain Philosophy's aye-babbling spring.
For never guiltless may I speak of him,
The Incomprehensible! save when with awe
I praise him, and with Faith that inly feels;
Who with his saving mercies healed me,
A sinful and most miserable man,
Wildered and dark, and gave me to possess
Peace, and this cot, and thee, heart-honoured Maid!

Lines

WRITTEN AT SHURTON BARS, NEAR BRIDGEWATER,
SEPTEMBER, 1795, IN ANSWER TO A LETTER FROM BRISTOL

Good verse most good, and bad verse then seems better
Received from absent friend by way of Letter.
For what so sweet can laboured lays impart
As one rude rhyme warm from a friendly heart?
                                                    ANON.

Nor travels my meandering eye
The starry wilderness on high;
    Nor now with curious sight
I mark the glow-worm, as I pass,
Move with 'green radiance' through the grass,
    An emerald of light.

O ever present to my view!
My wafted spirit is with you,
    And soothes your boding fears:
I see you all oppressed with gloom
Sit lonely in that cheerless room –
    Ah me! You are in tears!

Beloved Woman! did you fly
Chilled Friendship's dark disliking eye,
    Or Mirth's untimely din?
With cruel weight these trifles press
A temper sore with tenderness,
    When aches the Void within.

But why with sable wand unblest
Should Fancy rouse within my breast
    Dim-visaged shapes of Dread?
Untenanting its beauteous clay
My Sara's soul has winged its way,
    And hovers round my head!

I felt it prompt the tender dream,
When slowly sank the day's last gleam;
    You roused each gentler sense,
As sighing o'er the blossom's bloom
Meek Evening wakes its soft perfume
30   With viewless influence.

And hark, my Love! The sea-breeze moans
Through yon reft house! O'er rolling stones
    In bold ambitious sweep,
The onward-surging tides supply
The silence of the cloudless sky
    With mimic thunders deep.

Dark reddening from the channelled Isle
(Where stands one solitary pile
    Unslated by the blast)
40 The watchfire, like a sullen star
Twinkles to many a dozing tar
    Rude cradled on the mast.

Even there – beneath that light-house tower –
In the tumultuous evil hour
    Ere Peace with Sara came,
Time was, I should have thought it sweet
To count the echoings of my feet,
    And watch the storm-vexed flame.

And there in black soul-jaundiced fit
50 A sad gloom-pampered Man to sit,
    And listen to the roar:
When mountain surges bellowing deep
With an uncouth monster leap
    Plunged foaming on the shore.

Then by the lightning's blaze to mark
Some toiling tempest-shattered bark;
    Her vain distress-guns hear;
And when a second sheet of light
Flashed o'er the blackness of the night –
60   To see no vessel there!

But Fancy now more gaily sings;
Or if awhile she droop her wings,
   As sky-larks 'mid the corn,
On summer fields she grounds her breast:
The oblivious poppy o'er her nest
   Nods, till returning morn.

O mark those smiling tears, that swell
The opened rose! From heaven they fell,
   And with the sun-beam blend.
70 Blest visitations from above,
Such are the tender woes of Love
   Fostering the heart they bend!

When stormy Midnight howling round
Beats on our roof with clattering sound,
   To me your arms you'll stretch:
Great God! you'll say – To us so kind,
O shelter from this loud bleak wind
   The houseless, friendless wretch!

The tears that tremble down your cheek,
80 Shall bathe my kisses chaste and meek
   In Pity's dew divine;
And from your heart the sighs that steal
Shall make your rising bosom feel
   The answering swell of mine!

How oft, my Love! with shapings sweet
I paint the moment, we shall meet!
   With eager speed I dart –
I seize you in the vacant air,
And fancy, with a husband's care
90 I press you to my heart!

'Tis said, in Summer's evening hour
Flashes the golden-coloured flower
   A fair electric flame:
And so shall flash my love-charged eye
When all the heart's big ecstasy
   Shoots rapid through the frame!

Reflections
ON HAVING LEFT A PLACE OF RETIREMENT

Sermoni propriora.
                          HOR.

Low was our pretty Cot: our tallest rose
Peeped at the chamber-window. We could hear
At silent noon, and eve, and early morn,
The sea's faint murmur. In the open air
Our myrtles blossomed; and across the porch
Thick jasmins twined: the little landscape round
Was green and woody, and refreshed the eye.
It was a spot which you might aptly call
The Valley of Seclusion! Once I saw
10   (Hallowing his Sabbath-day by quietness)
A wealthy son of commerce saunter by,
Bristowa's citizen: methought, it calmed
His thirst of idle gold, and made him muse
With wiser feelings: for he paused, and looked
With a pleased sadness, and gazed all around,
Then eyed our Cottage, and gazed round again,
And sighed, and said, it was a Blessed Place.
And we were blessed. Oft with patient ear
Long-listening to the viewless sky-lark's note
20   (Viewless, or haply for a moment seen
Gleaming on sunny wings) in whispered tones
I've said to my beloved, 'Such, sweet girl!
The inobtrusive song of happiness,
Unearthly minstrelsy! then only heard
When the soul seeks to hear; when all is hushed,
And the heart listens!'

                          But the time, when first
From that low dell, steep up the stony mount
I climbed with perilous toil and reached the top,
Oh! what a goodly scene! Here the bleak mount,
30   The bare bleak mountain speckled thin with sheep;
Gray clouds, that shadowing spot the sunny fields;
And river, now with bushy rocks o'erbrowed,
Now winding bright and full, with naked banks;
And seats, and lawns, the Abbey and the wood,

And cots, and hamlets, and faint city-spire;
The Channel there, the Islands and white sails,
Dim coasts, and cloud-like hills, and shoreless Ocean –
It seemed like Omnipresence! God, methought,
Had built him there a temple: the whole World
40 Seemed imaged in its vast circumference,
No wish profaned my overwhelmèd heart.
Blest hour! It was a luxury, – to be!

   Ah! quiet dell! dear Cot, and mount sublime!
I was constrained to quit you. Was it right,
While my unnumbered brethren toiled and bled,
That I should dream away the entrusted hours
On rose-leaf beds, pampering the coward heart
With feelings all too delicate for use?
Sweet is the tear that from some Howard's eye
50 Drops on the cheek of one he lifts from earth:
And he that works me good with unmoved face,
Does it but half: he chills me while he aids,
My benefactor, not my brother man!
Yet even this, this cold beneficence
Praise, praise it, O my Soul! oft as thou scann'st
The sluggard Pity's vision-weaving tribe!
Who sigh for wretchedness, yet shun the wretched,
Nursing in some delicious solitude
Their slothful loves and dainty sympathies!
60 I therefore go, and join head, heart, and hand,
Active and firm, to fight the bloodless fight
Of science, freedom, and the truth in Christ.

   Yet oft when after honourable toil
Rests the tired mind, and waking loves to dream,
My spirit shall revisit thee, dear Cot!
Thy jasmin and thy window-peeping rose,
And myrtles fearless of the mild sea-air.
And I shall sigh fond wishes – sweet abode!
Ah! – had none greater! And that all had such!
70 It might be so – but the time is not yet.
Speed it, O Father! Let thy kingdom come!

On Donne's Poetry

With Donne, whose muse on dromedary trots,
Wreathe iron pokers into true-love knots;
Rhyme's sturdy Cripple, Wit's Maze and Clue,
Thought's Forge and Furnace, Mangle-press and Screw.

The Hour When We Shall Meet Again

Composed during Illness, and in Absence.

Dim Hour! that sleep'st on pillowing clouds afar,
O rise and yoke the Turtles to thy car!
Bend o'er the traces, blame each lingering Dove,
And give me to the bosom of my Love!
My gentle Love, caressing and carest,
With heaving heart shall cradle me to rest!
Shed the warm tear-drop from her smiling eyes,
Lull with fond woe, and medicine me with sighs!
While finely-flushing float her kisses meek,
Like melted rubies, o'er my pallid cheek.
Chill'd by the night, the drooping Rose of May
Mourns the long absence of the lovely Day;
Young Day returning at her promis'd hour
Weeps o'er the sorrows of her favourite Flower;
Weeps the soft dew, the balmy gale she sighs,
And darts a trembling lustre from her eyes.
New life and joy th' expanding flow'ret feels:
His pitying Mistress mourns, and mourning heals!

The Destiny of Nations
A VISION

Auspicious Reverence! Hush all meaner song,
Ere we the deep preluding strain have poured
To the Great Father, only Rightful King,
Eternal Father! King Omnipotent!
To the Will Absolute, the One, the Good!
The I AM, the Word, the Life, the Living God!

Such symphony requires best instrument.
Seize, then, my soul! from Freedom's trophied dome
The harp which hangeth high between the shields
Of Brutus and Leonidas! With that
Strong music, that soliciting spell, force back
Man's free and stirring spirit that lies entranced.

For what is freedom, but the unfettered use
Of all the powers which God for use had given?
But chiefly this, him first, him last to view
Through meaner powers and secondary things
Effulgent, as through clouds that veil his blaze.
For all that meets the bodily sense I deem
Symbolical, one mighty alphabet
For infant minds; and we in this low world
Placed with our backs to bright reality,
That we may learn with young unwounded ken
The substance from its shadow. Infinite Love,
Whose latence is the plenitude of all,
Thou with retracted beams, and self-eclipse
Veiling, revealest thine eternal Sun.

But some there are who deem themselves most free
When they within this gross and visible sphere
Chain down the wingèd thought, scoffing ascent,
Proud in their meanness: and themselves they cheat
With noisy emptiness of learned phrase,
Their subtle fluids, impacts, essences,
Self-working tools, uncaused effects, and all
Those blind omniscients, those almighty slaves,
Untenanting creation of its God.

But properties are God: the naked mass
(If mass there be, fantastic guess or ghost)
Acts only by its inactivity.
Here we pause humbly. Others boldlier think
40   That as one body seems the aggregate
Of atoms numberless, each organized;
So by a strange and dim similitude
Infinite myriads of self-conscious minds
Are one all-conscious Spirit, which informs
With absolute ubiquity of thought
(His one eternal self-affirming act!)
All his involved Monads, that yet seem
With various province and apt agency
Each to pursue its own self-centring end.
50   Some nurse the infant diamond in the mine;
Some roll the genial juices through the oak;
Some drive the mutinous clouds to clash in air,
And rushing on the storm with whirlwind speed,
Yoke the red lightnings to their volleying car.
Thus these pursue their never-varying course,
No eddy in their stream. Others, more wild,
With complex interests weaving human fates,
Duteous or proud, alike obedient all,
Evolve the process of eternal good.

60   And what if some rebellious o'er dark realms
Arrogate power? yet these train up to God,
And on the rude eye, unconfirmed for day,
Flash meteor-lights better than total gloom.
As ere from Lieule-Oaive's vapoury head
The Laplander beholds the far-off sun
Dart his slant beam on unobeying snows,
While yet the stern and solitary night
Brooks no alternate sway, the Boreal Morn
With mimic lustre substitutes its gleam,
70   Guiding his course or by Niemi lake
Or Balda Zhiok, or the mossy stone
Of Solfar-kapper, while the snowy blast
Drifts arrowy by, or eddies round his sledge,
Making the poor babe at its mother's back
Scream in its scanty cradle: he the while
Wins gentle solace as with upward eye
He marks the streamy banners of the North,

Thinking himself those happy spirits shall join
Who there in floating robes of rosy light
80   Dance sportively. For Fancy is the power
That first unsensualizes the dark mind,
Giving it new delights; and bids it swell
With wild activity; and peopling air,
By obscure fears of beings invisible,
Emancipates it from the grosser thrall
Of the present impulse, teaching self-control,
Till Superstition with unconscious hand
Seat Reason on her throne. Wherefore not vain,
Nor yet without permitted power impressed,
90   I deem those legends terrible, with which
The polar ancient thrills his uncouth throng:
Whether of pitying Spirits that make their moan
O'er slaughtered infants, or that giant bird
Vuokho, of whose rushing wings the noise
Is tempest, when the unutterable shape
Speeds from the mother of Death, and utters once
That shriek, which never murderer heard, and lived.

Or if the Greenland Wizard in strange trance
Pierces the untravelled realms of Ocean's bed
100   Over the abysm, even to that uttermost cave
By mis-shaped prodigies beleaguered, such
As earth ne'er bred, nor air, nor the upper sea:
Where dwells the Fury Form, whose unheard name
With eager eye, pale cheek, suspended breath,
And lips half-opening with the dread of sound,
Unsleeping Silence guards, worn out with fear
Lest haply 'scaping on some treacherous blast
The fateful word let slip the elements
And frenzy Nature. Yet the wizard her,
110   Armed with Torngarsuck's power, the Spirit of Good,
Forces to unchain the foodful progeny
Of the Ocean stream; – thence thro' the realm of Souls,
Where live the Innocent, as far from cares
As from the storms and overwhelming waves
That tumble on the surface of the Deep,
Returns with far-heard pant, hotly pursued
By the fierce Warders of the Sea, once more,
Ere by the frost foreclosed, to repossess
His fleshly mansion, that had staid the while

120   In the dark tent within a cow'ring group
      Untenanted. – Wild phantasies! yet wise,
      On the victorious goodness of high God
      Teaching reliance, and medicinal hope,
      Till from Bethabra northward, heavenly Truth
      With gradual steps, winning her difficult way,
      Transfer their rude Faith perfected and pure.

      If there be beings of higher class than Man,
      I deem no nobler province they possess,
      Than by disposal of apt circumstance
130   To rear up kingdoms: and the deeds they prompt,
      Distinguishing from mortal agency,
      They choose their human ministers from such states
      As still the Epic song half fears to name,
      Repelled from all the minstrelsies that strike
      The palace-roof and soothe the monarch's pride.

      And such, perhaps, the Spirit, who (if words
      Witnessed by answering deeds may claim our faith)
      Held commune with that warrior-maid of France
      Who scourged the Invader. From her infant days,
140   With Wisdom, mother of retired thoughts,
      Her soul had dwelt; and she was quick to mark
      The good and evil thing, in human lore
      Undisciplined. For lowly was her birth,
      And Heaven had doomed her early years to toil
      That pure from tyranny's least deed, herself
      Unfeared by fellow-natures, she might wait
      On the poor labouring man with kindly looks,
      And minister refreshment to the tired
      Way-wanderer, when along the rough hewn bench
150   The sweltry man had stretched him, and aloft
      Vacantly watched the rudely pictured board
      Which on the mulberry-bough with welcome creak
      Swung to the pleasant breeze. Here, too, the Maid
      Learnt more than schools could teach: Man's shifting mind,
      His vices and his sorrows! And full oft
      At tales of cruel wrong and strange distress
      Had wept and shivered. To the tottering eld
      Still as a daughter would she run: she placed

His cold limbs at the sunny door, and loved
160   To hear him story, in his garrulous sort,
Of his eventful years, all come and gone.

So twenty seasons passed. The Virgin's form,
Active and tall, nor sloth nor luxury
Had shrunk or paled. Her front sublime and broad,
Her flexile eye-brows wildly haired and low,
And her full eye, now bright, now unillumed,
Spake more than Woman's thought; and all her face
Was moulded to such features as declared
That pity there had oft and strongly worked,
170   And sometimes indignation. Bold her mien,
And like a haughty huntress of the woods
She moved: yet sure she was a gentle maid!
And in each motion her most innocent soul
Beamed forth so brightly, that who saw would say
Guilt was a thing impossible in her!
Nor idly would have said – for she had lived
In this bad World, as in a place of tombs,
And touched not the pollutions of the dead.

'Twas the cold season when the rustic's eye
180   From the drear desolate whiteness of his fields
Rolls for relief to watch the skiey tints
And clouds slow varying their huge imagery;
When now, as she was wont, the healthful Maid
Had left her pallet ere one beam of day
Slanted the fog-smoke. She went forth alone
Urged by the indwelling angel-guide, that oft,
With dim inexplicable sympathies
Disquieting the heart, shapes out Man's course
To the predoomed adventure. Now the ascent
190   She climbs of that steep upland, on whose top
The Pilgrim-man, who long since eve had watched
The alien shine of unconcerning stars,
Shouts to himself, there first the Abbey-lights
Seen in Neufchatel's vale; now slopes adown
The winding sheep-track vale-ward: when, behold
In the first entrance of the level road
An unattended team! The foremost horse

Lay with stretched limbs; the others, yet alive
But stiff and cold, stood motionless, their manes
200   Hoar with the frozen night dews. Dismally
The dark-red dawn now glimmered; but its gleams
Disclosed no face of man. The maiden paused,
Then hailed who might be near. No voice replied.
From the thwart wain at length there reached her ear
A sound so feeble that it almost seemed
Distant: and feebly, with slow effort pushed,
A miserable man crept forth: his limbs
The silent frost had eat, scathing like fire.
Faint on the shafts he rested. She, mean time,
210   Saw crowded close beneath the coverture
A mother and her children – lifeless all,
Yet lovely! not a lineament was marred –
Death had put on so slumber-like a form!
It was a piteous sight; and one, a babe,
The crisp milk frozen on its innocent lips,
Lay on the woman's arm, its little hand
Stretched on her bosom.

                              Mutely questioning,
The Maid gazed wildly at the living wretch.
He, his head feebly turning, on the group
220   Looked with a vacant stare, and his eye spoke
The drowsy calm that steals on worn-out anguish.
She shuddered; but, each vainer pang subdued,
Quick disentangling from the foremost horse
The rustic bands, with difficulty and toil
The stiff cramped team forced homeward. There arrived,
Anxiously tends him she with healing herbs,
And weeps and prays – but the numb power of Death
Spreads o'er his limbs; and ere the noontide hour,
The hovering spirits of his wife and babes
230   Hail him immortal! Yet amid his pangs,
With interruptions long from ghastly throes,
His voice had faltered out this simple tale.

    The village, where he dwelt a husbandman,
By sudden inroad had been seized and fired
Late on the yester-evening. With his wife
And little ones he hurried his escape.
They saw the neighbouring hamlets flame, they heard

Uproar and shrieks! and terror-struck drove on
Through unfrequented roads, a weary way!
240 But saw nor house nor cottage. All had quenched
Their evening hearth-fire: for the alarm had spread.
The air clipped keen, the night was fanged with frost,
And they provisionless! The weeping wife
Ill hushed her children's moans; and still they moaned,
Till fright and cold and hunger drank their life.
They closed their eyes in sleep, nor knew 'twas death.
He only, lashing his o'er-wearied team,
Gained a sad respite, till beside the base
Of the high hill his foremost horse dropped dead.
250 Then hopeless, strengthless, sick for lack of food,
He crept beneath the coverture, entranced,
Till wakened by the maiden. – Such his tale.

Ah! suffering to the height of what was suffered,
Stung with too keen a sympathy, the Maid
Brooded with moving lips, mute, startful, dark!
And now her flushed tumultuous features shot
Such strange vivacity, as fires the eye
Of misery fancy-crazed! and now once more
Naked, and void, and fixed, and all within
260 The unquiet silence of confusèd thought
And shapeless feelings. For a mighty hand
Was strong upon her, till, in the heat of soul
To the high hill-top tracing back her steps,
Aside the beacon, up whose smouldered stones
The tender ivy-trails crept thinly, there,
Unconscious of the driving element,
Yea, swallowed up in the ominous dream, she sate
Ghastly as broad-eyed Slumber! a dim anguish
Breathed from her look! and still with pant and sob,
270 Inly she toil'd to flee, and still subdued,
Felt an inevitable Presence near.

Thus as she toiled in troublous ecstasy,
A horror of great darkness wrapt her round,
And a voice uttered forth unearthly tones,
Calming her soul, – 'O Thou of the Most High
Chosen, whom all the perfected in Heaven
Behold expectant –'

[The following fragments were intended to form part of the poem when finished.]

'Maid beloved of Heaven!
(To her the tutelary Power exclaimed)
280   Of Chaos the adventurous progeny
Thou seest; foul missionaries of foul sire,
Fierce to regain the losses of that hour
When Love rose glittering, and his gorgeous wings
Over the abyss fluttered with such glad noise,
As what time after long and pestful calms,
With slimy shapes and miscreated life
Poisoning the vast Pacific, the fresh breeze
Wakens the merchant-sail uprising. Night
A heavy unimaginable moan
290   Sent forth, when she the Protoplast beheld
Stand beauteous on confusion's charmèd wave.
Moaning she fled, and entered the Profound
That leads with downward windings to the cave
Of darkness palpable, desert of Death
Sunk deep beneath Gehenna's massy roots.
There many a dateless age the beldam lurked
And trembled; till engendered by fierce Hate,
Fierce Hate and gloomy Hope, a Dream arose,
Shaped like a black cloud marked with streaks of fire.
300   It roused the Hell-Hag: she the dew damp wiped
From off her brow, and through the uncouth maze
Retraced her steps; but ere she reached the mouth
Of that drear labyrinth, shuddering she paused,
Nor dared re-enter the diminished Gulf.
As through the dark vaults of some mouldered tower
(Which, fearful to approach, the evening hind
Circles at distance in his homeward way)
The winds breathe hollow, deemed the plaining groan
Of prisoned spirits; with such fearful voice
310   Night murmured, and the sound thro' Chaos went.
Leaped at her call her hideous-fronted brood!
A dark behest they heard, and rushed on earth;
Since that sad hour, in camps and courts adored,
Rebels from God, and tyrants o'er Mankind!'

                  From his obscure haunt
Shrieked Fear, of Cruelty the ghastly dam,
Feverous yet freezing, eager-paced yet slow,
As she that creeps from forth her swampy reeds,
Ague, the biform hag! when early Spring
320 Beams on the marsh-bred vapours.

          —————

        'Even so (the exulting Maiden said)
The sainted heralds of good tidings fell,
And thus they witnessed God! But now the clouds
Treading, and storms beneath their feet, they soar
Higher, and higher soar, and soaring sing
Loud songs of triumph! O ye spirits of God,
Hover around my mortal agonies!'
She spake, and instantly faint melody
Melts on her ear, soothing and sad, and slow,
330 Such measures, as at calmest midnight heard
By aged hermit in his holy dream,
Foretell and solace death; and now they rise
Louder, as when with harp amd mingled voice
The white-robed multitude of slaughtered saints
At Heaven's wide-opened portals gratulant
Receive some martyr'd patriot. The harmony
Entranced the Maid, till each suspended sense
Brief slumber seized, and confused ecstasy.

      At length awakening slow, she gazed around:
340 And through a mist, the relique of that trance
Still thinning as she gazed, an Isle appeared,
Its high, o'er-hanging, white, broad-breasted cliffs,
Glassed on the subject ocean. A vast plain
Stretched opposite, where ever and anon
The plough-man following sad his meagre team
Turned up fresh sculls unstartled, and the bones
Of fierce hate-breathing combatants, who there
All mingled lay beneath the common earth,
Death's gloomy reconcilement! O'er the fields
350 Stept a fair Form, repairing all she might,
Her temples olive-wreathed; and where she trod,
Fresh flowerets rose, and many a foodful herb.

But wan her cheek, her footsteps insecure,
And anxious pleasure beamed in her faint eye,
As she had newly left a couch of pain,
Pale convalescent! (Yet some time to rule
With power exclusive o'er the willing world,
That blest prophetic mandate then fulfilled –
Peace be on Earth!) A happy while, but brief,
360   She seemed to wander with assiduous feet,
And healed the recent harm of chill and blight,
And nursed each plant that fair and virtuous grew.

But soon a deep precursive sound moaned hollow:
Black rose the clouds, and now (as in a dream)
Their reddening shapes, transformed to warrior-hosts,
Coursed o'er the sky, and battled in mid-air.
Nor did not the large blood-drops fall from heaven
Portentous! while aloft were seen to float,
Like hideous features looming on the mist,
370   Wan stains of ominous light! Resigned, yet sad,
The fair Form bowed her olive-crownèd brow,
Then o'er the plain with oft reverted eye
Fled till a place of tombs she reached, and there
Within a ruined sepulchre obscure
Found hiding-place.

                    The delegated Maid
Gazed through her tears, then in sad tones exclaimed –
'Thou mild-eyed Form! wherefore, ah! wherefore fled?
The power of Justice like a name all light,
Shone from thy brow; but all they, who unblamed
380   Dwelt in thy dwellings, call thee Happiness.
Ah! why, uninjured and unprofited,
Should multitudes against their brethren rush?
Why sow they guilt, still reaping misery?
Lenient of care, thy songs, O Peace! are sweet,
As after showers the perfumed gale of eve,
That flings the cool drops on a feverous cheek;
And gay thy grassy altar piled with fruits.
But boasts the shrine of demon War one charm,
Save that with many an orgie strange and foul,
390   Dancing around with interwoven arms,
The maniac Suicide and giant Murder
Exult in their fierce union! I am sad,

And know not why the simple peasants crowd
Beneath the Chieftains' standard!' Thus the Maid.

   To her the tutelary Spirit said:
'When luxury and lust's exhausted stores
No more can rouse the appetites of kings;
When the low flattery of their reptile lords
Falls flat and heavy on the accustomed ear;
400   When eunuchs sing, and fools buffoonery make,
And dancers writhe their harlot-limbs in vain;
Then War and all its dread vicissitudes
Pleasingly agitate their stagnant hearts;
Its hopes, its fears, its victories, its defeats,
Insipid royalty's keen condiment!
Therefore uninjured and unprofited,
(Victims at once and executioners)
The congregated husbandmen lay waste
The vineyard and the harvest. As along
410   The Bothnic coast, or southward of the Line,
Though hushed the winds and cloudless the high noon,
Yet if Leviathan, weary of ease,
In sports unwieldy toss his island-bulk,
Ocean behind him billows, and before
A storm of waves breaks foamy on the strand.
And hence, for times and seasons bloody and dark,
Short Peace shall skin the wounds of causeless War,
And War, his strained sinews knit anew,
Still violate the unfinished works of Peace.
420   But yonder look! for more demands thy view!'
He said: and straightway from the opposite Isle
A vapour sailed, as when a cloud, exhaled
From Egypt's fields that steam hot pestilence,
Travels the sky for many a trackless league,
Till o'er some death-doomed land, distant in vain,
It broods incumbent. Forthwith from the plain,
Facing the Isle, a brighter cloud arose,
And steered its course which way the vapour went.

   The Maiden paused, musing what this might mean.
430   But long time passed not, ere that brighter cloud
Returned more bright; along the plain it swept;

And soon from forth its bursting sides emerged
A dazzling form, broad-bosomed, bold of eye,
And wild her hair, save where with laurels bound.
Not more majestic stood the healing God,
When from his bow the arrow sped that slew
Huge Python. Shriek'd Ambition's giant throng,
And with them hissed the locust-fiends that crawled
And glittered in Corruption's slimy track.
440   Great was their wrath, for short they knew their reign;
And such commotion made they, and uproar,
As when the mad tornado bellows through
The guilty islands of the western main,
What time departing from their native shores,
Eboe, or Koromantyn's plain of palms,
The infurate spirits of the murdered make
Fierce merriment, and vengeance ask of Heaven.
Warmed with new influence, the unwholesome plain
Sent up its foulest fogs to meet the morn:
450   The Sun that rose on Freedom, rose in blood!

   'Maiden beloved, and Delegate of Heaven!
(To her the tutelary Spirit said)
Soon shall the morning struggle into day,
The stormy morning into cloudless noon.
Much hast thou seen, nor all canst understand –
But this be thy best omen – Save thy Country!'
Thus saying, from the answering Maid he passed,
And with him disappeared the heavenly Vision.

   'Glory to Thee, Father of Earth and Heaven!
460   All conscious presence of the Universe!
Nature's vast ever-acting energy!
In will, in deed, impulse of All to All!
Whether thy Love with unrefracted ray
Beam on the Prophet's purgèd eye, or if
Diseasing realms the enthusiast, wild of thought,
Scatter new frenzies on the infected throng,
Thou both inspiring and predooming both,
Fit instruments and best, of perfect end:
Glory to Thee, Father of Earth and Heaven!'

———

470   And first a landscape rose
More wild and waste and desolate than where
The white bear, drifting on a field of ice,
Howls to her sundered cubs with piteous rage
And savage agony.

Religious Musings
A DESULTORY POEM, WRITTEN ON THE CHRISTMAS EVE OF 1794

This is the time, when most divine to hear,
The voice of adoration rouses me,
As with a Cherub's trump: and high upborne,
Yea, mingling with the choir, I seem to view
The vision of the heavenly multitude,
Who hymned the song of peace o'er Bethlehem's fields!
Yet thou more bright than all the angel blaze,
That harbingered thy birth, Thou, Man of Woes!
Despised Galilean! For the great
Invisible (by symbols only seen)
With a peculiar and surpassing light
Shines from the visage of the oppressed good man,
When heedless of himself the scourged Saint
Mourns for the oppressor. Fair the vernal mead,
Fair the high grove, the sea, the sun, the stars;
True impress each of their creating Sire!
Yet nor high grove, nor many-coloured mead,
Nor the green Ocean with his thousand isles,
Nor the starred azure, nor the sovran sun,
E'er with such majesty of portraiture
Imaged the supreme beauty uncreate,
As thou, meek Saviour! at the fearful hour
When thy insulted anguish winged the prayer
Harped by Archangels, when they sing of mercy!
Which when the Almighty heard from forth his throne
Diviner light filled Heaven with ecstasy!
Heaven's hymnings paused: and Hell her yawning mouth
Closed a brief moment.

10

20

                                Lovely was the death
       Of Him whose life was Love! Holy with power
30   He on the thought-benighted Sceptic beamed
       Manifest Godhead, melting into day
       What floating mists of dark idolatry
       Broke and misshaped the omnipresent Sire:
       And first by Fear uncharmed the drowsèd Soul.
       Till of its nobler nature it 'gan feel
       Dim recollections; and thence soared to Hope,
       Strong to believe whate'er of mystic good
       The Eternal dooms for his immortal sons.
       From Hope and firmer Faith to perfect Love
40   Attracted and absorbed: and centred there
       God only to behold, and know, and feel,
       Till by exclusive consciousness of God
       All self-annihilated it shall make
       God its identity: God all in all!
       We and our Father one!

                                And best are they,
       Who in this fleshly World, the elect of Heaven,
       Their strong eye darting through the deeds of men,
       Adore with steadfast unpresuming gaze
       Him Nature's essence, mind, and energy!
50   And gazing, trembling, patiently ascend
       Treading beneath their feet all visible things
       As steps, that upward to their Father's throne
       Lead gradual – else nor glorified nor loved.
       They nor contempt embosom nor revenge:
       For they dare know of what may seem deform
       The Supreme Fair sole operant: in whose sight
       All things are pure, his strong controlling Love
       Alike from all educing perfect good.
       Their's too celestial courage, inly armed –
60   Dwarfing Earth's giant brood, what time they muse
       On their great Father, great beyond compare!
       And marching onwards view high o'er their heads
       His waving banners of Omnipotence.

         Who the Creator love, created might
       Dread not: within their tents no terrors walk.
       For they are holy things before the Lord
       Aye unprofaned, though Earth should league with Hell;

God's altar grasping with an eager hand
Fear, the wild-visaged, pale, eye-starting wretch,
70   Sure-refuged hears his hot pursuing fiends
Yell at vain distance. Soon refreshed from Heaven
He calms the throb and tempest of his heart.
His countenance settles; a soft solemn bliss
Swims in his eye – his swimming eye upraised:
And Faith's whole armour glitters on his limbs!
And thus transfigured with a dreadless awe,
A solemn hush of soul, meek he beholds
All things of terrible seeming: yea, unmoved
Views e'en the immitigable ministers
80   That shower down vengeance on these latter days.
For kindling with intenser Deity
From the celestial Mercy-seat they come,
And at the renovating wells of Love
Have filled their vials with salutary wrath,
To sickly Nature more medicinal
Than what soft balm the weeping good man pours
Into the lone despoiled traveller's wounds!

Thus from the Elect, regenerate through faith,
Pass the dark Passions and what thirsty Cares
90   Drink up the Spirit, and the dim regards
Self-centre. Lo they vanish! or acquire
New names, new features – by supernal grace
Enrobed with Light, and naturalized in Heaven.
As when a shepherd on a vernal morn
Through some thick fog creeps timorous with slow foot,
Darkling he fixes on the immediate road
His downward eye: all else of fairest kind
Hid or deformed. But lo! the bursting Sun!
Touched by the enchantment of that sudden beam
100   Straight the black vapour melteth, and in globes
Of dewy glitter gems each plant and tree;
On every leaf, on every blade it hangs!
Dance glad the new-born intermingling rays,
And wide around the landscape streams with glory!

There is one Mind, one omnipresent Mind,
Omnific. His most holy name is Love.
Truth of subliming import! with the which
Who feeds and saturates his constant soul,

He from his small particular orbit flies
110   With blest outstarting! From Himself he flies,
Stands in the sun, and with no partial gaze
Views all creation; and he loves it all,
And blesses it, and calls it very good!
This is indeed to dwell with the most High!
Cherubs and rapture-trembling Seraphim
Can press no nearer to the Almighty's Throne.
But that we roam unconscious, or with hearts
Unfeeling of our universal Sire,
And that in his vast family no Cain
120   Injures uninjured (in her best-aimed blow
Victorious murder a blind suicide)
Haply for this some younger Angel now
Looks down on human nature: and, behold!
A sea of blood bestrewed with wrecks, where mad
Embattling interests on each other rush
With unhelmed rage!

           'Tis the sublime of man,
Our noontide majesty, to know ourselves
Parts and proportions of one wondrous whole!
This fraternizes man, this constitutes
130   Our charities and bearings. But 'tis God
Diffused through all, that doth make all one whole;
This the worst superstition, him except
Aught to desire, Supreme Reality!
The plenitude and permanence of bliss!
O Fiends of Superstition! not that oft
The erring priest hath stained with brother's blood
Your grisly idols, not for this may wrath
Thunder against you from the Holy One!
But o'er some plain that steameth to the sun,
140   Peopled with death; or where more hideous Trade
Loud-laughing packs his bales of human anguish;
I will raise up a mourning, O ye Fiends!
And curse your spells, that film the eye of Faith,
Hiding the present God; whose presence lost,
The moral world's cohesion, we become
An anarchy of Spirits! Toy-bewitched,
Made blind by lusts, disherited of soul,
No common centre Man, no common sire

Knoweth! A sordid solitary thing,
150   Mid countless brethren with a lonely heart
Through courts and cities the smooth savage roams
Feeling himself, his own low self the whole;
When he by sacred sympathy might make
The whole one self! self, that no alien knows!
Self, far diffused as Fancy's wing can travel!
Self, spreading still! Oblivious of its own,
Yet all of all possessing! This is Faith!
This the Messiah's destined victory!

But first offences needs must come! Even now
160   (Black Hell laughs horrible – to hear the scoff!)
Thee to defend, meek Galilean! Thee
And thy mild laws of Love unutterable,
Mistrust and enmity have burst the bands
Of social peace; and listening treachery lurks
With pious fraud to snare a brother's life;
And childless widows o'er the groaning land
Wail numberless; and orphans weep for bread!
Thee to defend, dear Saviour of mankind!
Thee, Lamb of God! Thee, blameless Prince of peace!
170   From all sides rush the thirsty brood of War –
Austria, and that foul Woman of the North,
The lustful murderess of her wedded lord!
And he, connatural mind! whom (in their songs
So bards of elder time had haply feigned)
Some Fury fondled in her hate to man,
Bidding her serpent hair in mazy surge
Lick his young face, and at his mouth imbreathe
Horrible sympathy! And leagued with these
Each petty German princeling, nursed in gore!
180   Soul-hardened barterers of human blood!
Death's prime slave-merchants! Scorpion-whips of Fate!
Nor least in savagery of holy zeal,
Apt for the yoke, the race degenerate,
Whom Britain erst had blushed to call her sons!
Thee to defend the Moloch priest prefers
The prayer of hate, and bellows to the herd
That Deity, accomplice Deity
In the fierce jealousy of wakened wrath,
Will go forth with our armies and our fleets

190   To scatter the red ruin on their foes!
O blasphemy! to mingle fiendish deeds
With blessedness!

                Lord of unsleeping Love,
From everlasting Thou! We shall not die.
These, even these, in mercy didst thou form,
Teachers of Good through Evil, by brief wrong
Making Truth lovely, and her future might
Magnetic o'er the fixed untrembling heart.

    In the primeval age a dateless while
The vacant Shepherd wandered with his flock,
200   Pitching his tent where'er the green grass waved.
But soon Imagination conjured up
A host of new desires: with busy aim,
Each for himself, Earth's eager children toiled.
So Property began, twy-streaming fount,
Whence Vice and Virtue flow, honey and gall.
Hence the soft couch, and many-coloured robe,
The timbrel, and arch'd dome and costly feast,
With all the inventive arts, that nursed the soul
To forms of beauty, and by sensual wants
210   Unsensualized the mind, which in the means
Learnt to forget the grossness of the end,
Best pleasured with its own activity.
And hence Disease that withers manhood's arm,
The daggered Envy, spirit-quenching Want,
Warriors, and Lords, and Priests – all the sore ills
That vex and desolate our mortal life.
Wide-wasting ills! yet each the immediate source
Of mightier good. Their keen necessities
To ceaseless action goading human thought
220   Have made Earth's reasoning animal her Lord;
And the pale-featured Sage's trembling hand
Strong as a host of armèd Deities,
Such as the blind Ionian fabled erst.

    From avarice thus, from luxury and war
Sprang heavenly science; and from science freedom.
O'er wakened realms Philosophers and Bards
Spread in concentric circles: they whose souls,
Conscious of their high dignities from God,

Brook not wealth's rivalry! and they who long
230 Enamoured with the charms of order hate
The unseemly disproportion: and whoe'er
Turn with mild sorrow from the victor's car
And the low puppetry of thrones, to muse
On that blest triumph, when the patriot Sage
Called the red lightnings from the o'er-rushing cloud
And dashed the beauteous terrors on the earth
Smiling majestic. Such a phalanx ne'er
Measured firm paces to the calming sound
Of Spartan flute! These on the fated day,
240 When, stung to rage by pity, eloquent men
Have roused with pealing voice the unnumbered tribes
That toil and groan and bleed, hungry and blind –
These hushed awhile with patient eye serene
Shall watch the mad careering of the storm;
Then o'er the wild and wavy chaos rush
And tame the outrageous mass, with plastic might
Moulding confusion to such perfect forms,
As erst were wont – bright visions of the day! –
To float before them, when, the summer noon,
250 Beneath some arch'd romantic rock reclined
They felt the sea breeze lift their youthful locks;
Or in the month of blossoms, at mild eve,
Wandering with desultory feet inhaled
The wafted perfumes, and the flocks and woods
And many-tinted streams and setting sun
With all his gorgeous company of clouds
Ecstatic gazed! then homeward as they strayed
Cast the sad eye to earth, and inly mused
Why there was misery in a world so fair.

260   Ah! far removed from all that glads the sense,
From all that softens or ennobles Man,
The wretched Many! Bent beneath their loads
They gape at pageant Power, nor recognise
Their cots' transmuted plunder! From the tree
Of Knowledge, ere the vernal sap had risen
Rudely disbranchèd! Blest Society!
Fitliest depictured by some sun-scorched waste,
Where oft majestic through the tainted noon
The Simoom sails, before whose purple pomp
270 Who falls not prostrate dies! And where by night,

Fast by each precious fountain on green herbs
The lion couches; or hyæna dips
Deep in the lucid stream his bloody jaws;
Or serpent plants his vast moon-glittering bulk,
Caught in whose monstrous twine Behemoth yells,
His bones loud-crashing!
                           O ye numberless,
Whom foul oppression's ruffian gluttony
Drives from life's plenteous feast! O thou poor wretch
Who nursed in darkness and made wild by want,
280   Roamest for prey, yea thy unnatural hand
Dost lift to deeds of blood! O pale-eyed form,
The victim of seduction, doomed to know
Polluted nights and days of blasphemy;
Who in loathed orgies with lewd wassailers
Must gaily laugh, while thy remembered home
Gnaws like a viper at thy secret heart!
O aged women! ye who weekly catch
The morsel tossed by law-forced charity,
And die so slowly, that none call it murder!
290   O loathly suppliants! ye, that unreceived
Totter heart-broken from the closing gates
Of the full Lazar-house: or, gazing, stand
Sick with despair! O ye to glory's field
Forced or ensnared, who, as ye gasp in death,
Bleed with new wounds beneath the vulture's beak!
O thou poor widow, who in dreams dost view
Thy husband's mangled corse, and from short doze
Start'st with a shriek; or in thy half-thatched cot
Waked by the wintry night-storm, wet and cold
300   Cow'rst o'er thy screaming baby! Rest awhile
Children of wretchedness! More groans must rise,
More blood must stream, or ere your wrongs be full.
Yet is the day of retribution nigh:
The Lamb of God hath opened the fifth seal:
And upward rush on swiftest wing of fire
The innumerable multitude of Wrongs
By man on man inflicted! Rest awhile,
Children of wretchedness! The hour is nigh;
And lo! the great, the rich, the mighty Men,
310   The Kings and the chief Captains of the World,
With all that fixed on high like stars of Heaven
Shot baleful influence, shall be cast to earth,

Vile and down-trodden, as the untimely fruit
Shook from the fig-tree by a sudden storm.
Even now the storm begins: each gentle name,
Faith and meek Piety, with fearful joy
Tremble far-off – for lo! the giant Frenzy
Uprooting empires with his whirlwind arm
Mocketh high Heaven; burst hideous from the cell
320   Where the old Hag, unconquerable, huge,
Creation's eyeless drudge, black ruin, sits
Nursing the impatient earthquake.
                     O return!
Pure Faith! meek Piety! The abhorred Form
Whose scarlet robe was stiff with earthly pomp,
Who drank iniquity in cups of gold,
Whose names were many and all blasphemous,
Hath met the horrible judgment! Whence that cry?
The mighty army of foul Spirits shrieked
Disherited of earth! For she hath fallen
330   On whose black front was written Mystery;
She that reeled heavily, whose wine was blood;
She that worked whoredom with the Demon Power,
And from the dark embrace all evil things
Brought forth and nurtured: mitred atheism!
And patient Folly who on bended knee
Gives back the steel that stabbed him; and pale Fear
Haunted by ghastlier shapings than surround
Moon-blasted Madness when he yells at midnight!
Return pure Faith! return meek Piety!
340   The kingdoms of the world are yours: each heart
Self-governed, the vast family of Love
Raised from the common earth by common toil
Enjoy the equal produce. Such delights
As float to earth, permitted visitants!
When in some hour of solemn jubilee
The massy gates of Paradise are thrown
Wide open, and forth come in fragments wild
Sweet echoes of unearthly melodies,
And odours snatched from beds of amaranth,
350   And they, that from the crystal river of life
Spring up on freshened wing, ambrosial gales!
The favoured good man in his lonely walk
Perceives them, and his silent spirit drinks
Strange bliss which he shall recognise in heaven.

And such delights, such strange beatitudes
Seize on my young anticipating heart
When that blest future rushes on my view!
For in his own and in his Father's might
The Saviour comes! While as the Thousand Years
360   Lead up their mystic dance, the Desert shouts!
Old Ocean claps his hands! The mighty Dead
Rise to new life, whoe'er from earliest time
With conscious zeal had urged Love's wondrous plan,
Coadjutors of God. To Milton's trump
The high groves of the renovated Earth
Unbosom their glad echoes: inly hushed,
Adoring Newton his serener eye
Raises to heaven: and he of mortal kind
Wisest, he first who marked the ideal tribes
370   Up the fine fibres through the sentient brain.
Lo! Priestley there, patriot, and saint, and sage,
Him, full of years, from his loved native land
Statesmen blood-stained and priests idolatrous
By dark lies maddening the blind multitude
Drove with vain hate. Calm, pitying he retired,
And mused expectant on these promised years.

O Years! the blest pre-eminence of Saints!
Ye sweep athwart my gaze, so heavenly bright,
The wings that veil the adoring Seraphs' eyes,
380   What time they bend before the Jasper Throne
Reflect no lovelier hues! Yet ye depart,
And all beyond is darkness! Heights most strange,
Whence Fancy falls, fluttering her idle wing.
For who of woman born may paint the hour,
When seized in his mid course, the Sun shall wane
Making noon ghastly! Who of woman born
May image in the workings of his thought,
How the black-visaged, red-eyed Fiend outstretched
Beneath the unsteady feet of Nature groans,
390   In feverous slumbers – destined then to wake,
When fiery whirlwinds thunder his dread name
And Angels shout, Destruction! How his arm
The last great Spirit lifting high in air
Shall swear by Him, the ever-living One,
Time is no more!

Believe thou, O my soul,
Life is a vision shadowy of Truth;
And vice, and anguish, and the wormy grave,
Shapes of a dream! The veiling clouds retire,
And lo! the Throne of the redeeming God
400 Forth flashing unimaginable day
Wraps in one blaze earth, heaven, and deepest hell.

Contemplant Spirits! ye that hover o'er
With untired gaze the immeasurable fount
Ebullient with creative Deity!
And ye of plastic power, that interfused
Roll through the grosser and material mass
In organizing surge! Holies of God!
(And what if Monads of the infinite mind)
I haply journeying my immortal course
410 Shall sometime join your mystic choir. Till then
I discipline my young and novice thought
In ministeries of heart-stirring song,
And aye on Meditation's heaven-ward wing
Soaring aloft I breathe the empyreal air
Of Love, omnific, omnipresent Love,
Whose day-spring rises glorious in my soul
As the great Sun, when he his influence
Sheds on the frost-bound waters – The glad stream
Flows to the ray and warbles as it flows.

From an Unpublished Poem

The early Year's fast-flying Vapours stray
In shadowing Trains across the orb of Day:
And we, poor Insects of a few short Hours,
    Deem it a world of Gloom.
Were it not better hope a nobler doom,
Proud to believe that with more active powers
On rapid many-coloured Wing
We thro' one bright perpetual Spring
Shall hover round the Fruits and Flowers
10 Screen'd by those Clouds and cherish'd by those Showers!

On Observing a Blossom on the First of February, 1796

Sweet Flower! that peeping from thy russet stem
Unfoldest timidly, (for in strange sort
This dark, frieze-coated, hoarse, teeth-chattering Month
Hath borrowed Zephyr's voice, and gazed upon thee
With blue voluptuous eye) alas, poor Flower!
These are but flatteries of the faithless year.
Perchance, escaped its unknown polar cave,
E'en now the keen North-East is on its way.
Flower that must perish! shall I liken thee
10   To some sweet girl of too too rapid growth
Nipped by consumption mid untimely charms?
Or to Bristowa's bard, the wondrous boy!
An amaranth, which Earth scarce seemed to own,
Till disappointment came, and pelting wrong
Beat it to Earth? or with indignant grief
Shall I compare thee to poor Poland's hope,
Bright flower of Hope killed in the opening bud?
Farewell, sweet blossom! better fate be thine
And mock my boding! Dim similitudes
20   Weaving in moral strains, I've stolen one hour
From anxious self, Life's cruel task-master!
And the warm wooings of this sunny day
Tremble along my frame, and harmonize
The attempered organ, that even saddest thoughts
Mix with some sweet sensations, like harsh tunes
Played deftly on a soft-toned instrument.

Verses

ADDRESSED TO J. HORNE TOOKE AND THE COMPANY
WHO MET ON JUNE 28TH, 1796, TO CELEBRATE HIS POLL
AT THE WESTMINSTER ELECTION

Britons! when last ye met, with distant streak
So faintly promis'd the pale Dawn to break;
So dim it stain'd the precincts of the Sky
E'en *Expectation* gaz'd with doubtful Eye.

But now such fair Varieties of Light
O'ertake the heavy-sailing Clouds of Night;
Th' Horizon kindles with so rich a red,
That, tho' the *Sun still hides* his glorious head,
Th' impatient Matin-bird *assur'd of Day*
Leaves his low nest to meet its earliest ray;
Loud the sweet song of Gratulation sings,
And high in air claps his rejoicing wings!
Patriot and Sage! whose breeze-like Spirit first
The lazy mists of Pedantry dispers'd
(Mists in which Superstition's *pigmy* band
Seem'd Giant Forms, the Genii of the Land!),
Thy struggles soon shall wak'ning Britain bless,
And Truth and Freedom hail thy wish'd success.
Yes, *Tooke!* tho' foul Corruption's wolfish throng
Outmalice Calumny's imposthum'd Tongue,
Thy Country's noblest and *determin'd* Choice,
Soon shalt thou thrill the Senate with thy voice;
With gradual Dawn bid Error's phantoms flit,
Or wither with the lightning flash of Wit;
Or with sublimer mien and tones more deep,
Charm sworded Justice from mysterious Sleep,
'By violated Freedom's loud Lament,
Her Lamps extinguish'd and her Temple rent;
By the forc'd tears her captive Martyrs shed;
By each pale Orphan's feeble cry for bread;
By ravag'd Belgium's corse-impeded Flood,
And Vendée steaming still with brothers' blood!'
And if amid the strong impassion'd Tale
Thy Tongue should falter and thy Lips turn pale;
If transient Darkness film thy aweful Eye,
And thy tir'd Bosom struggle with a sigh:
Science and Freedom shall demand to hear
Who practis'd on a Life so doubly dear;
Infus'd the unwholesome anguish drop by drop,
Pois'ning the sacred stream they could not stop!
Shall bid thee with recover'd strength relate
How dark and deadly is a Coward's Hate:
What seeds of Death by wan Confinement sown,
When prison-echoes mock'd Disease's groan!
Shall bid th' indignant Father flash dismay,
And drag the unnatural Villain into Day

Line numbers in left margin: 10, 20, 30, 40

Who to the sports of his flesh'd Ruffians left
Two lovely Mourners of their Sire bereft!
'Twas wrong, like this, which Rome's *first Consul* bore –
50   So by th' insulted Female's name *he* swore
Ruin (and rais'd her reeking dagger high)
Not to the *Tyrants* but the *Tyranny*!

On a Late Connubial Rupture in High Life

I sigh, fair injur'd Stranger! for thy fate –
But what shall Signs avail thee? Thy poor Heart
Mid all the pomp and circumstance of State
Shivers in nakedness! Unbidden start

Sad Recollections of Hope's garish dream
That shap'd a seraph form, and nam'd it Love –
Its hues gay-varying, as the Orient Beam
Varies the neck of Cytherea's Dove.

To one soft accent of domestic Joy,
10   Poor are the Shouts that shake the high-arch'd Dome:
The Plaudits that thy *public* path annoy,
Alas! they tell thee – Thou'rt a Wretch *at home*!

Then o! retire and weep! Their very Woes
Solace the guiltless. Drop the pearly Flood
On thy sweet Infant, as the full-blown Rose
Surcharg'd with dew bends o'er its neighb'ring BUD!

And ah! that Truth some holy spell could lend
To lure thy Wanderer from the syren's power:
Then bid your Souls inseparably blend,
20   Like two bright Dew-drops bosom'd in a flower!

Sonnet

WRITTEN ON RECEIVING LETTERS INFORMING ME OF
THE BIRTH OF A SON, I BEING AT BIRMINGHAM

When they did greet me Father, sudden Awe
Weigh'd down my spirit! I retir'd and knelt
Seeking the throne of grace, but inly felt
No heavenly visitation upwards draw
My feeble mind, nor cheering ray impart.
Ah me! before the eternal Sire I brought
Th' unquiet Silence of confusèd Thought
And shapeless feelings: my o'erwhelmèd Heart
Trembled: and vacant tears stream'd down my face.
And now once more, O Lord! to thee I bend,
Lover of Souls! and groan for future grace,
That, ere my Babe youth's perilous maze have trod,
Thy overshadowing Spirit may descend
And he be born again, a child of God!

Sonnet

COMPOSED ON A JOURNEY HOMEWARD; THE AUTHOR
HAVING RECEIVED INTELLIGENCE OF THE BIRTH OF A
SON, SEPT. 20TH, 1796

Oft o'er my brain does that strange fancy roll
   Which makes the present (while the flash doth last)
   Seem a mere semblance of some unknown past,
Mixed with such feelings, as perplex the soul
Self-questioned in her sleep; and some have said
   We lived, ere yet this robe of flesh we wore.
   O my sweet baby! when I reach my door,
If heavy looks should tell me thou art dead
(As sometimes, through excess of hope, I fear),
I think that I should struggle to believe
   Thou wert a spirit, to this nether sphere
Sentenced for some more venial crime to grieve;
Did'st scream, then spring to meet Heaven's quick reprieve,
   While we wept idly o'er thy little bier!

Sonnet

TO A FRIEND WHO ASKED, HOW I FELT WHEN THE NURSE
FIRST PRESENTED MY INFANT TO ME

Charles! my slow heart was only sad, when first
   I scanned that face of feeble infancy:
For dimly on my thoughtful spirit burst
   All I had been, and all my child might be!
But when I saw it on its mother's arm,
   And hanging at her bosom (she the while
   Bent o'er its features with a tearful smile)
Then I was thrilled and melted, and most warm
Impressed a father's kiss: and all beguiled
   Of dark remembrance and presageful fear,
   I seemed to see an angel-form appear –
'Twas even thine, beloved woman mild!
   So for the mother's sake the child was dear,
And dearer was the mother for the child.

Sonnet

[TO CHARLES LLOYD]

The piteous sobs that choke the Virgin's breath
   For him, the fair betrothèd Youth, who lies
   Cold in the narrow dwelling, or the cries
With which a Mother wails her darling's death,
These from our nature's common impulse spring,
   Unblam'd, unprais'd; but o'er the pilèd earth
   Which hides the sheeted corse of grey-hair'd Worth,
If droops the soaring Youth with slacken'd wing;
If he recall in saddest minstrelsy
   Each tenderness bestow'd, each truth imprest,
Such grief is Reason, Virtue, Piety!
And from the Almighty Father shall descend
   Comforts on his late evening, whose young breast
Mourns with no transient love the Agèd Friend.

To a Young Friend
ON HIS PROPOSING TO DOMESTICATE WITH THE AUTHOR.
COMPOSED IN 1796

A mount, not wearisome and bare and steep,
　　But a green mountain variously up-piled,
Where o'er the jutting rocks soft mosses creep,
Or coloured lichens with slow oosing weep;
　　Where cypress and the darker yew start wild;
And 'mid the summer torrent's gentle dash
Dance brightened the red clusters of the ash;
　　Beneath whose boughs, by those still sounds beguiled,
Calm Pensiveness might muse herself to sleep;
10　　Till haply startled by some fleecy dam,
That rustling on the bushy cliff above,
With melancholy bleat of anxious love,
　　Made meek enquiry for her wandering lamb:
　　Such a green mountain 'twere most sweet to climb,
E'en while the bosom ached with loneliness –
How more than sweet, if some dear friend should bless
　　The adventurous toil, and up the path sublime
Now lead, now follow: the glad landscape round,
Wide and more wide, increasing without bound!

20　　O then 'twere loveliest sympathy, to mark
The berries of the half-uprooted ash
Dripping and bright; and list the torrent's dash, –
　　Beneath the cypress, or the yew more dark,
Seated at ease, on some smooth mossy rock;
In social silence now, and now to unlock
The treasured heart; arm linked in friendly arm,
Save if the one, his muse's witching charm
Muttering brow-bent, at unwatched distance lag;
　　Till high o'er head his beckoning friend appears,
30　And from the forehead of the topmost crag
　　Shouts eagerly: for haply there uprears
That shadowing pine its old romantic limbs,
　　Which latest shall detain the enamoured sight
Seen from below, when eve the valley dims,
　　Tinged yellow with the rich departing light;

And haply, basoned in some unsunned cleft,
A beauteous spring, the rock's collected tears,
Sleeps sheltered there, scarce wrinkled by the gale!
    Together thus, the world's vain turmoil left,
40   Stretched on the crag, and shadowed by the pine,
      And bending o'er the clear delicious fount,
Ah! dearest youth! it were a lot divine
To cheat our noons in moralizing mood,
While west-winds fanned our temples toil-bedewed:
    Then downwards slope, oft pausing, from the mount,
To some lone mansion, in some woody dale,
Where smiling with blue eye, domestic bliss
Gives this the husband's, that the brother's kiss!

    Thus rudely versed in allegoric lore,
50   The Hill of Knowledge I essayed to trace;
That verdurous hill with many a resting-place,
And many a stream, whose warbling waters pour
    To glad and fertilize the subject plains;
That hill with secret springs, and nooks untrod,
And many a fancy-blest and holy sod
    Where Inspiration, his diviner strains
Low murmuring, lay; and starting from the rocks
Stiff evergreens, whose spreading foliage mocks
Want's barren soil, and the bleak frosts of age,
60   And bigotry's mad fire-invoking rage!
O meek retiring spirit! we will climb,
Cheering and cheered, this lovely hill sublime;
    And from the stirring world up-lifted high
(Whose noises, faintly wafted on the wind,
To quiet musings shall attune the mind,
    And oft the melancholy theme supply)
    There, while the prospect through the gazing eye
Pours all its healthful greenness on the soul,
We'll smile at wealth, and learn to smile at fame,
70   Our hopes, our knowledge, and our joys the same,
    As neighbouring fountains image each the whole:
Then when the mind hath drunk its fill of truth
    We'll discipline the heart to pure delight,
Rekindling sober joy's domestic flame.
They whom I love shall love thee, honoured youth!
    Now may Heaven realize this vision bright!

Addressed to a Young Man of Fortune
WHO ABANDONED HIMSELF TO AN INDOLENT AND
CAUSELESS MELANCHOLY

Hence that fantastic wantonness of woe,
    O Youth to partial Fortune vainly dear!
To plundered want's half-sheltered hovel go,
    Go, and some hunger-bitten infant hear
    Moan haply in a dying mother's ear:
Or when the cold and dismal fog-damps brood
O'er the rank church-yard with sear elm-leaves strewed,
Pace round some widow's grave, whose dearer part
    Was slaughtered, where o'er his uncoffined limbs
10 The flocking flesh-birds screamed! Then, while thy heart
    Groans, and thine eye a fiercer sorrow dims,
Know (and the truth shall kindle thy young mind)
What nature makes thee mourn, she bids thee heal!
    O abject! if, to sickly dreams resigned,
All effortless thou leave life's common-weal
    A prey to tyrants, murderers of mankind.

To a Friend
WHO HAD DECLARED HIS INTENTION OF WRITING NO
MORE POETRY

Dear Charles! whilst yet thou wert a babe, I ween
That Genius plunged thee in that wizard fount
Hight Castalie: and (sureties of thy faith)
That Pity and Simplicity stood by,
And promised for thee, that thou shouldst renounce
The world's low cares and lying vanities,
Steadfast and rooted in the heavenly Muse,
And washed and sanctified to Poesy.
Yes – thou wert plunged, but with forgetful hand
10 Held, as by Thetis erst her warrior son:
And with those recreant unbaptizèd heels
Thou'rt flying from thy bounden minist'ries –
So sore it seems and burthensome a task
To weave unwithering flowers! But take thou heed:
For thou art vulnerable, wild-eyed boy,

And I have arrows mystically dipt,
Such as may stop thy speed. Is thy Burns dead?
And shall he die unwept, and sink to earth
'Without the meed of one melodious tear?'
20 Thy Burns, and Nature's own belovèd bard,
Who to the 'Illustrious of his native Land
So properly did look for patronage.'
Ghost of Mæcenas! hide thy blushing face!
They snatched him from the sickle and the plough –
To gauge ale-firkins.
                    Oh! for shame return!
On a bleak rock, midway the Aonian mount,
There stands a lone and melancholy tree,
Whose agèd branches to the midnight blast
Make solemn music: pluck its darkest bough,
30 Ere yet the unwholesome night-dew be exhaled,
And weeping wreath it round thy Poet's tomb.
Then in the outskirts, where pollutions grow,
Pick the rank henbane and the dusky flowers
Of night-shade, or its red and tempting fruit,
These with stopped nostril and glove-guarded hand
Knit in nice intertexture, so to twine
The illustrious brow of Scotch Nobility.

Ode to the Departing Year

'Ιού, ιού, ὦ ὦ κακά.
'Υπ' αὖ μὲ δεινὸς ὀρθομαντείας πόνος
Στροβεῖ, ταράσσων φροιμίοις ἐφημίοις.

          *   *   *

Τὸ μέλλον ἥξει. Καὶ σύ μ' ἐν τάχει παρὼν
Ἄγαν γ' ἀληθόμαντιν οἰκτείρας ἐρεῖς.

                         ÆSCHYL. *Agam. 1225*

ARGUMENT

The Ode commences with an address to the Divine Providence, that
regulates into one vast harmony all the events of time, however calamitous
some of them may appear to mortals. The second Strophe calls on men to
suspend their private joys and sorrows, and devote them for a while to the
cause of human nature in general. The first Epode speaks of the Empress

of Russia, who died of an apoplexy on the 17th of November, 1796; having just concluded a subsidiary treaty with the Kings combined against France. The first and second Antistrophe describe the Image of the Departing Year, &c. as in a vision. The second Epode prophesies, in anguish of spirit, the downfall of this country.

I

Spirit who sweepest the wild harp of Time!
 It is most hard, with an untroubled ear
 Thy dark inwoven harmonies to hear!
Yet, mine eye fixed on Heaven's unchanging clime,
Long had I listened, free from mortal fear,
 With inward stillness, and a bowèd mind;
 When lo! its folds far waving on the wind,
I saw the train of the departing Year!
 Starting from my silent sadness
10 Then with no unholy madness
Ere yet the entered cloud foreclosed my sight,
I raised the impetuous song, and solemnized his flight.

II

 Hither, from the recent tomb,
 From the prison's direr gloom,
 From distemper's midnight anguish!
And thence, where poverty doth waste and languish!
 Or where, his two bright torches blending,
  Love illumines manhood's maze;
 Or where o'er cradled infants bending
20 Hope has fixed her wishful gaze;
  Hither, in perplexèd dance,
Ye Woes! ye young-eyed Joys! advance!
By Time's wild harp, and by the hand
 Whose indefatigable sweep
 Raises its fateful strings from sleep,
I bid you haste, a mixed tumultuous band!
 From every private bower,
  And each domestic hearth,
 Haste for one solemn hour;
30 And with a loud and yet a louder voice,
O'er Nature struggling in portentous birth,
  Weep and rejoice!
Still echoes the dread name that o'er the earth

Let slip the storm, and woke the brood of Hell:
    And now advance in saintly jubilee
Justice and Truth! They too have heard thy spell,
    They too obey thy name, divinest Liberty!

III

I marked Ambition in his war-array!
        I heard the mailèd Monarch's troublous cry –
40 'Ah! wherefore does the Northern Conqueress stay!
Groans not her chariot on its onward way?'
            Fly, mailèd Monarch, fly!
            Stunned by Death's twice mortal mace,
            No more on murder's lurid face
The insatiate hag shall gloat with drunken eye!
        Manes of the unnumbered slain!
        Ye that gasped on Warsaw's plain!
    Ye that erst at Ismail's tower,
When human ruin choked the streams,
50   Fell in conquest's glutted hour,
Mid women's shrieks and infants' screams!
        Spirits of the uncoffined slain,
            Sudden blasts of triumph swelling,
        Oft, at night, in misty train,
            Rush around her narrow dwelling!
        The exterminating fiend is fled –
            (Foul her life, and dark her doom)
        Mighty armies of the dead
            Dance, like death-fires, round her tomb!
60   Then with prophetic song relate,
    Each some tyrant-murderer's fate!

IV

Departing Year! 'twas on no earthly shore
    My soul beheld thy vision! Where alone,
    Voiceless and stern, before the cloudy throne,
Aye Memory sits: thy robe inscribed with gore,
With many an unimaginable groan
    Thou storied'st thy sad hours! Silence ensued,
    Deep silence o'er the ethereal multitude,
Whose locks with wreaths, whose wreaths with glories shone.

70   Then, his eye wild ardours glancing,
        From the choirèd gods advancing,
The Spirit of the Earth made reverence meet,
And stood up, beautiful, before the cloudy seat.

    V
        Throughout the blissful throng,
        Hushed were harp and song:
Till wheeling round the throne the Lampads seven,
        (The mystic Words of Heaven)
        Permissive signal make:
The fervent Spirit bowed, then spread his wings and spake!
80   'Thou in stormy blackness throning
        Love and uncreated Light,
    By the Earth's unsolaced groaning,
        Seize thy terrors, Arm of might!
    By peace with proffered insult scared,
            Masked hate and envying scorn!
            By years of havoc yet unborn!
And hunger's bosom to the frost-winds bared!
        But chief by Afric's wrongs,
            Strange, horrible, and foul!
90   By what deep guilt belongs
    To the deaf Synod, "full of gifts and lies!"
By wealth's insensate laugh! by torture's howl!
                Avenger, rise!
    For ever shall the thankless Island scowl,
    Her quiver full, and with unbroken bow?
Speak! from thy storm-black Heaven O speak aloud!
            And on the darkling foe
Open thine eye of fire from some uncertain cloud!
    O dart the flash! O rise and deal the blow!
100 The Past to thee, to thee the Future cries!
        Hark! how wide Nature joins her groans below!
        Rise, God of Nature! rise.'

    VI
        The voice had ceased, the vision fled;
        Yet still I gasped and reeled with dread.
        And ever, when the dream of night
        Renews the phantom to my sight,

Cold sweat-drops gather on my limbs;
 My ears throb hot; my eye-balls start;
My brain with horrid tumult swims;
110 Wild is the tempest of my heart;
 And my thick and struggling breath
 Imitates the toil of death!
No stranger agony confounds
 The soldier on the war-field spread,
When all foredone with toil and wounds,
 Death-like he dozes among heaps of dead!
(The strife is o'er, the day-light fled,
 And the night-wind clamours hoarse!
See! the starting wretch's head
120 Lies pillowed on a brother's corse!)

VII

Not yet enslaved, not wholly vile,
O Albion! O my mother Isle!
Thy valleys, fair as Eden's bowers,
Glitter green with sunny showers;
Thy grassy uplands' gentle swells,
 Echo to the bleat of flocks;
(Those grassy hills, those glittering dells
 Proudly ramparted with rocks)
And Ocean mid his uproar wild
130 Speaks safety to his island-child,
  Hence for many a fearless age
  Has social Quiet loved thy shore;
 Nor ever proud invader's rage
Or sacked thy towers, or stained thy fields with gore.

VIII

Abandoned of Heaven! mad avarice thy guide,
At cowardly distance, yet kindling with pride –
Mid thy herds and thy corn-fields secure thou hast stood,
And joined the wild yelling of famine and blood!
The nations curse thee! They with eager wondering
140 Shall hear Destruction, like a vulture, scream!
 Strange-eyed Destruction! who with many a dream
Of central fires through nether seas upthundering

Soothes her fierce solitude; yet as she lies
By livid fount, or red volcanic stream,
    If ever to her lidless dragon-eyes,
    O Albion! thy predestined ruins rise,
The fiend-hag on her perilous couch doth leap,
Muttering distempered triumph in her charmèd sleep.

IX

Away, my soul, away!
150   In vain, in vain the birds of warning sing –
And hark! I hear the famished brood of prey
Flap their lank pennons on the groaning wind!
                    Away, my soul, away!
    I unpartaking of the evil thing,
        With daily prayer and daily toil
        Soliciting for food my scanty soil,
        Have wailed my country with a loud Lament.
Now I recentre my immortal mind
        In the deep sabbath of meek self-content;
160   Cleansed from the vaporous passions that bedim
God's Image, sister of the Seraphim.

The Raven

A CHRISTMAS TALE, TOLD BY A SCHOOL-BOY TO
HIS LITTLE BROTHERS AND SISTERS

Underneath an old oak tree
There was of swine a huge company,
That grunted as they crunched the mast:
For that was ripe, and fell full fast.
Then they trotted away, for the wind grew high:
One acorn they left, and no more might you spy.
Next came a Raven, that liked not such folly:
He belonged, they did say, to the witch Melancholy!
Blacker was he than blackest jet,
10   Flew low in the rain, and his feathers not wet.

He picked up the acorn and buried it straight
By the side of a river both deep and great.
> Where then did the Raven go?
> He went high and low,
Over hill, over dale, did the black Raven go.
> Many Autumns, many Springs
> Travelled he with wandering wings:
> Many Summers, many Winters –
> I can't tell half his adventures.

20   At length he came back, and with him a She,
And the acorn was grown to a tall oak tree.
They built them a nest in the topmost bough,
And young ones they had, and were happy enow.
But soon came a woodman in leathern guise,
His brow, like a pent-house, hung over his eyes.
He'd an axe in his hand, not a word he spoke,
But with many a hem! and a sturdy stroke,
At length he brought down the poor Raven's own oak.
His young ones were killed; for they could not depart,
30   And their mother did die of a broken heart.
The boughs from the trunk the woodman did sever;
And they floated it down on the course of the river.
They sawed it in planks, and its bark they did strip,
And with this tree and others they made a good ship.
The ship, it was launched; but in sight of the land
Such a storm there did rise as no ship could withstand.
It bulged on a rock, and the waves rushed in fast:
Round and round flew the Raven, and cawed to the blast.
He heard the last shriek of the perishing souls –
40   See! See! o'er the topmast and mad water rolls!
> Right glad was the Raven, and off he went fleet,
And Death riding home on a cloud he did meet,
And he thank'd him again and again for this treat:
> They had taken his all, and Revenge it was sweet!

To an Unfortunate Woman at the Theatre

Maiden, that with sullen brow
   Sitt'st behind those virgins gay,
Like a scorched and mildewed bough,
   Leafless 'mid the blooms of May!

Him who lured thee and forsook,
   Oft I watched with angry gaze,
Fearful saw his pleading look,
   Anxious heard his fervid phrase.

Soft the glances of the youth,
   Soft his speech, and soft his sigh;
But no sound like simple truth,
   But no true love in his eye.

Loathing thy polluted lot,
   Hie thee, Maiden, hie thee hence!
Seek thy weeping Mother's cot,
   With a wiser innocence.

Thou hast known deceit and folly,
   Thou hast felt that vice is woe:
With a musing melancholy
   Inly armed, go, Maiden! go.

Mother sage of self-dominion,
   Firm thy steps, O Melancholy!
The strongest plume in wisdom's pinion
   Is the memory of past folly.

Mute the sky-lark and forlorn,
   While she moults the firstling plumes,
That had skimmed the tender corn,
   Or the beanfield's odorous blooms.

Soon with renovated wing
   Shall she dare a loftier flight,
Upward to the day-star spring,
   And embathe in heavenly light.

To an Unfortunate Woman,
WHOM THE AUTHOR HAD KNOWN IN THE DAYS OF HER
INNOCENCE

Myrtle-leaf that, ill besped,
　Pinest in the gladsome ray,
Soiled beneath the common tread,
　Far from thy protecting spray!

When the partridge o'er the sheaf
　Whirred along the yellow vale,
Sad I saw thee, heedless leaf!
　Love the dalliance of the gale.

Lightly didst thou, foolish thing!
　　Heave and flutter to his sighs,
While the flatterer, on his wing,
　Wooed and whispered thee to rise.

Gaily from thy mother-stalk
　Wert thou danced and wafted high –
Soon on this unsheltered walk
　Flung to fade, to rot and die.

10

To the Rev. George Coleridge
OF OTTERY ST MARY, DEVON. WITH SOME POEMS

Notus in fratres animi paterni.
　　　　HOR. *Carm. lib. 1. 2.*

A blessèd lot hath he, who having passed
His youth and early manhood in the stir
And turmoil of the world, retreats at length,
With cares that move, not agitate the heart,
To the same dwelling where his father dwelt;
And haply views his tottering little ones
Embrace those agèd knees and climb that lap,
On which first kneeling his own infancy
Lisped its brief prayer. Such, O my earliest Friend!
Thy lot, and such thy brothers too enjoy.

10

At distance did ye climb life's upland road,
Yet cheered and cheering: now fraternal love
Hath drawn you to one centre. Be your days
Holy, and blest and blessing may ye live!

To me the Eternal Wisdom hath dispensed
A different fortune and more different mind –
Me from the spot where first I sprang to light
Too soon transplanted, ere my soul had fixed
Its first domestic loves; and hence through life
20   Chasing chance-started friendships. A brief while
Some have preserved me from life's pelting ills;
But, like a tree with leaves of feeble stem,
If the clouds lasted, and a sudden breeze
Ruffled the boughs, they on my head at once
Dropped the collected shower; and some most false,
False and fair foliaged as the Manchineel,
Have tempted me to slumber in their shade
E'en mid the storm; then breathing subtlest damps,
Mixed their own venom with the rain from Heaven,
30   That I woke poisoned! But, all praise to Him
Who gives us all things, more have yielded me
Permanent shelter; and beside one friend,
Beneath the impervious covert of one oak,
I've raised a lowly shed, and know the names
Of husband and of father; not unhearing
Of that divine and nightly-whispering voice,
Which from my childhood to maturer years
Spake to me of predestinated wreaths,
Bright with no fading colours!

                           Yet at times
40   My soul is sad, that I have roamed through life
Still most a stranger, most with naked heart
At mine own home and birth-place: chiefly then,
When I remember thee, my earliest friend!
Thee, who didst watch my boyhood and my youth;
Didst trace my wanderings with a father's eye;
And boding evil yet still hoping good,
Rebuked each fault, and over all my woes
Sorrowed in silence! He who counts along
The beatings of the solitary heart,
50   That being knows, how I have loved thee ever,

Loved as a brother, as a son revered thee!
Oh! 'tis to me an ever new delight,
To talk of thee and thine: or when the blast
Of the shrill winter, rattling our rude sash,
Endears the cleanly hearth and social bowl;
Or when as now, on some delicious eve,
We in our sweet sequestered orchard-plot
Sit on the tree crooked earth-ward; whose old boughs,
That hang above us in an arborous roof,
60   Stirred by the faint gale of departing May,
Send their loose blossoms slanting o'er our heads!

    Nor dost not thou sometimes recall those hours,
When with the joy of hope thou gav'st thine ear
To my wild firstling-lays. Since then my song
Hath sounded deeper notes, such as beseem
Or that sad wisdom folly leaves behind,
Or such as, tuned to these tumultuous times,
Cope with the tempest's swell!

                              These various strains,
Which I have framed in many a various mood,
70   Accept, my brother! and (for some perchance
Will strike discordant on thy milder mind)
If aught of error or intemperate truth
Should meet thine ear, think thou that riper age
Will calm it down, and let thy love forgive it!

On the Christening of a Friend's Child

This day among the faithful plac'd
    And fed with fontal manna;
O with maternal title grac'd
    Dear Anna's dearest Anna!

While others wish thee wise and fair,
    A maid of spotless fame,
I'll breathe this more compendious prayer –
    May'st thou deserve thy name!

Thy mother's name, a potent spell,
That bids the Virtues hie
From mystic grove and living cell
Confest to Fancy's eye;

Meek QUIETNESS without offence;
CONTENT in homespun kirtle;
TRUE LOVE; and True Love's Innocence,
White Blossom of the Myrtle!

Associates of thy name, sweet Child!
These Virtues may'st thou win;
With face as eloquently mild
To say, they lodge within.

So, when her tale of days all flown,
Thy Mother shall be miss'd here;
When Heaven at length shall claim its own,
And Angels snatch their Sister;

Some hoary-headed Friend, perchance,
May gaze with stifled breath;
And oft, in momentary trance,
Forget the waste of death.

Ev'n thus a lovely rose I view'd
In summer-swelling Pride;
Nor mark'd the bud, that green and rude
Peep'd at the Rose's side.

It chanc'd, I pass'd again that way
In Autumn's latest hour,
And wond'ring saw the self-same spray
Rich with the self-same flower –

Ah fond deceit! the rude green Bud
Alike in shape, place, name,
Had bloom'd, where bloom'd its parent stud,
Another and the same!

Inscription by the Rev. W. L. Bowles
IN NETHER STOWEY CHURCH

TRANSLATION
Depart in joy from this world's noise and strife
To the deep quiet of celestial life!
Depart! – Affection's self reproves the tear
Which falls, O honour'd Parent! on thy bier; –
Yet Nature will be heard, the heart will swell,
And the voice tremble with a last Farewell!

This Lime-Tree Bower My Prison

In the June of 1797, some long-expected Friends paid a visit to the author's cottage; and on the morning of their arrival, he met with an accident, which disabled him from walking during the whole time of their stay. One evening, when they had left him for a few hours, he composed the following lines in the garden-bower.

Well, they are gone, and here must I remain,
This lime-tree bower my prison! I have lost
Beauties and feelings, such as would have been
Most sweet to my remembrance even when age
Had dimmed mine eyes to blindness! They, meanwhile,
Friends, whom I never more may meet again,
On springy heath, along the hill-top edge,
Wander in gladness, and wind down, perchance,
To that still roaring dell, of which I told;
10 The roaring dell, o'erwooded, narrow, deep,
And only speckled by the mid-day sun;
Where its slim trunk the ash from rock to rock
Flings arching like a bridge; – that branchless ash,
Unsunned and damp, whose few poor yellow leaves
Ne'er tremble in the gale, yet tremble still,
Fanned by the water-fall! and there my friends
Behold the dark green file of long lank weeds,
That all at once (a most fantastic sight!)
Still nod and drip beneath the dripping edge
20 Of the blue clay-stone.

                          Now, my friends emerge
Beneath the wide wide Heaven – and view again
The many-steepled tract magnificent
Of hilly fields and meadows, and the sea,
With some fair bark, perhaps, whose sails light up
The slip of smooth clear blue betwixt two Isles
Of purple shadow! Yes! they wander on
In gladness all; but thou, methinks, most glad,
My gentle-hearted Charles! for thou hast pined
And hungered after Nature, many a year,
30 In the great City pent, winning thy way
With sad yet patient soul, through evil and pain
And strange calamity! Ah! slowly sink
Behind the western ridge, thou glorious sun!
Shine in the slant beams of the sinking orb,
Ye purple heath-flowers! richlier burn, ye clouds!
Live in the yellow light, ye distant groves!
And kindle, thou blue ocean! So my Friend
Struck with deep joy may stand, as I have stood,
Silent with swimming sense; yea, gazing round
40 On the wide landscape, gaze till all doth seem
Less gross than bodily; and of such hues
As veil the Almighty Spirit, when yet he makes
Spirits perceive his presence.

                          A delight
Comes sudden on my heart, and I am glad
As I myself were there! Nor in this bower,
This little lime-tree bower, have I not marked
Much that has soothed me. Pale beneath the blaze
Hung the transparent foliage; and I watched
Some broad and sunny leaf, and loved to see
50 The shadow of the leaf and stem above
Dappling its sunshine! And that walnut-tree
Was richly tinged, and a deep radiance lay
Full on the ancient ivy which usurps
Those fronting elms, and now, with blackest mass
Makes their dark branches gleam a lighter hue
Through the late twilight: and though now the bat
Wheels silent by, and not a swallow twitters,
Yet still the solitary humble bee
Sings in the bean-flower! Henceforth I shall know
60 That Nature ne'er deserts the wise and pure;

No plot so narrow, be but Nature there,
No waste so vacant, but may well employ
Each faculty of sense, and keep the heart
Awake to Love and Beauty! and sometimes
'Tis well to be bereft of promised good,
That we may lift the Soul, and contemplate
With lively joy the joys we cannot share.
My gentle-hearted Charles! when the last rook
Beat its straight path along the dusky air
70   Homewards, I blest it! deeming, its black wing
(Now a dim speck, now vanishing in light)
Had crossed the mighty orb's dilated glory,
While thou stood'st gazing; or when all was still,
Flew creeking o'er thy head, and had a charm
For thee, my gentle-hearted Charles, to whom
No sound is dissonant which tells of Life.

The Foster-Mother's Tale
A DRAMATIC FRAGMENT

FOSTER-MOTHER
I never saw the man whom you describe.

MARIA
'Tis strange, he spake of you familiarly,
As mine and Albert's common Foster-Mother.

FOSTER-MOTHER
Now blessings on the man, whoe'er he be,
That joined your names with mine! O my sweet lady!
As often as I think of those dear times,
When you two little ones would stand at eve
On each side of my chair, and make me learn
All you had learnt in the day, and how to talk
10   In gentle phrase, then bid me sing to you –
'Tis more like heaven to come than what has been.

MARIA

O my dear Mother! this strange man has left me
Troubled with wilder fancies, than the Moon
Breeds in the love-sick maid who gazes at it,
Till lost in inward vision, with wet eye
She gazes idly – But that entrance, Mother!

FOSTER-MOTHER

Can no one hear? It is a perilous tale!

MARIA

No one.

FOSTER-MOTHER

My husband's father told it me,
Poor old Leoni: Angels, rest his soul!
20   He was a woodman, and could fell, and saw,
With lusty arm. You know that huge round beam
Which props the hanging-wall of the old chapel?
Beneath that tree, while yet it was a tree,
He found a baby, wrapt in mosses lined
With thistle-beards, and such small locks of wool
As hang on brambles. Well, he brought him home,
And reared him at the then Lord Valez' cost;
And so the babe grew up a pretty boy –
A pretty boy, but most unteachable –
30   And never learnt a prayer nor told a bead;
But knew the names of birds, and mocked their notes,
And whistled, as he were a bird himself!
And all the autumn 'twas his only play
To gather seeds of wild-flowers, and to plant them
With earth and water on the stumps of trees.
A Friar, who oft cull'd simples in the wood,
A grey-haired man – he loved this little boy:
The boy loved him – and, when the Friar taught him,
He soon could write with the pen; and from that time
40   Lived chiefly at the Convent or the Castle.
So he became a very learnèd youth.
But oh! poor wretch! he read, and read, and read,
Till his brain turned – and ere his twentieth year,
He had unlawful thoughts of many things:

And though he prayed, he never loved to pray
With holy men, or in a holy place;
But yet his speech, it was so soft and sweet,
The late Lord Valez ne'er was wearied with him:
And once, as by the north side of the chapel
50   They stood together, chained in deep discourse,
The earth heaved under them with such a groan,
That the wall tottered, and had well nigh fallen
Right on their heads. My Lord was sorely frightened;
A fever seized him, and he made confession
Of all the heretical and lawless talk
Which brought this judgment. So the youth was seized
And cast into that hole. My husband's father
Sobbed like a child – it almost broke his heart;
And once, as he was working in the cellar,
60   He hear'd a voice distinctly; 'twas the youth's,
Who sung a doleful song about green fields,
How sweet it were on lake or wild savannah
To hunt for food, and be a naked man,
And wander up and down at liberty.
He always doted on the youth, and now
His love grew desperate; and defying death,
He made that cunning entrance I described;
And the young man escaped.

MARIA

                              'Tis a sweet tale:
Such as would lull a listening child to sleep,
70   His rosy face besoiled with unwiped tears.
And what became of him?

FOSTER-MOTHER

                              He went on ship-board,
With those bold voyagers who made discovery
Of golden lands. Leoni's youngest brother
Went likewise; and when he returned to Spain,
He told Leoni, that the poor mad youth,
Soon after they arrived in that new world,
In spite of his dissuasion, seized a boat,
And, all alone, set sail by silent moonlight
Up a great river, great as any sea,
80   And ne'er was heard of more; but 'tis supposed,
He lived and died among the savage men.

The Dungeon

And this place our forefathers made for man!
This is the process of our love and wisdom,
To each poor brother who offends against us –
Most innocent, perhaps – and what if guilty?
Is this the only cure? Merciful God?
Each pore and natural outlet shrivell'd up
By ignorance and parching poverty,
His energies roll back upon his heart,
And stagnate and corrupt; till changed to poison,
They break out on him, like a loathsome plague-spot;
Then we call in our pamper'd mountebanks –
And this is their best cure! uncomforted
And friendless solitude, groaning and tears,
And savage faces, at the clanking hour,
Seen through the steams and vapour of his dungeon,
By the lamp's dismal twilight! So he lies
Circled with evil, till his very soul
Unmoulds its essence, hopelessly deformed
By sights of ever more deformity!

With other ministrations thou, O nature!
Healest thy wandering and distempered child:
Thou pourest on him thy soft influences,
Thy sunny hues, fair forms, and breathing sweets,
Thy melodies of woods, and winds, and waters,
Till he relent, and can no more endure
To be a jarring and a dissonant thing,
Amid this general dance and minstrelsy;
But, bursting into tears, wins back his way,
His angry spirit healed and harmonized
By the benignant touch of love and beauty.

SONNETS ATTEMPTED IN THE MANNER OF CONTEMPORARY WRITERS

Sonnet I

Pensive at eve, on the *hard* world I mused,
And *my poor* heart was sad; so at the MOON
I gazed, and sighed, and sighed; for ah how soon
Eve saddens into night! mine eyes perused
With tearful vacancy the *dampy* grass
That wept and glitter'd in the *paly* ray:
And I *did pause me*, on my lonely way
And *mused me*, on the *wretched ones* that pass
O'er the bleak heath of sorrow. But alas!
10   Most of *myself* I thought! when it befel,
That the *soothe* spirit of the *breezy* wood
Breath'd in mine ear: 'All this is very well,
But much of ONE thing, is for NO thing good.'
Oh *my poor heart's* INEXPLICABLE SWELL!

Sonnet II

Oh I do love thee, meek SIMPLICITY!
For of thy lays the lulling simpleness
Goes to my heart, and soothes each small distress,
Distress tho' small, yet haply great to me.
'Tis true on Lady Fortune's gentlest pad
I amble on; and yet I know not why
So sad I am! but should a friend and I
Frown, pout and part, then I am *very* sad.
And then with sonnets and with sympathy
10   My dreamy bosom's mystic woes I pall;
Now of my false friend plaining plaintively,
Now raving at mankind in general;
But whether sad or fierce, 'tis simple all,
All very simple, meek SIMPLICITY!

Sonnet III

And this reft house is that, the which he built,
Lamented Jack! and here his malt he pil'd,
Cautious in vain! these rats, that squeak so wild,
Squeak not unconscious of their father's guilt.
Did he not see her gleaming thro' the glade!
Belike 'twas she, the maiden all forlorn,
What tho' she milk no cow with crumpled horn,
Yet, *aye* she haunts the dale where *erst* she stray'd:
And *aye*, beside her stalks her amorous knight!
Still on his thighs their wonted brogues are worn,
And thro' those brogues, still tatter'd and betorn,
His hindward charms gleam an unearthly white.
Ah! thus thro' broken clouds at night's high Noon
Peeps in fair fragments forth the full-orb'd harvest-moon!

*   *   *

Parliamentary Oscillators

Almost awake? Why, what is this, and whence,
    O ye right loyal men, all undefilèd?
Sure, 'tis not possible that Common Sense,
    Has hitch'd her pullies to each heavy eye-lid?

Yet wherefore else that start, which discomposes
    The drowsy waters lingering in your eye?
    And are you *really* able to descry
That precipice three yards beyond your noses?

Yet flatter you I cannot, that your wit
    Is much improved by this long loyal dosing;
And I admire, no more than Mr PITT,
    Your jumps and starts of patriotic prosing –

Now cluttering to the Treasury Cluck, like chicken,
    Now with small beaks the ravenous *Bill* opposing;
With serpent-tongue now stinging, and now licking,
    Now semi-sibilant, now smoothly glozing –

Now having faith implicit that he can't err,
  Hoping his hopes, alarm'd with his alarms;
And now believing him a sly inchanter,
20   Yet still afraid to break his brittle charms,

Lest some mad Devil suddenly unhamp'ring,
  Slap-dash! the imp should fly off with the steeple,
On revolutionary broom-stick scampering. –
  O ye soft-headed and soft-hearted people,

If you can stay so long from slumber free,
  My muse shall make an effort to salute 'e:
For lo! a very dainty simile
  Flash'd sudden through my brain, and 'twill just suit 'e!

You know that water-fowl that cries, Quack! quack!?
30   Full often have I seen a waggish crew
Fasten the Bird of Wisdom on its back,
  The ivy-haunting bird, that cries, Tu-whoo!

Both plunged together in the deep mill-stream,
  (Mill-stream, or farm-yard pond, or mountain-lake)
Shrill, as a *Church and Constitution* scream,
  TU-WHOO! quoth BROAD-FACE, and down dives the Drake!

The green-neck'd Drake once more pops up to view,
  Stares round, cries Quack! and makes an angry pother;
Then shriller screams the bird with eye-lids blue,
40   The broad-faced bird! and deeper dives the other.
Ye *quacking* Statesmen! 'tis even so with you –
  One peasecod is not liker to another.

Even so on Loyalty's Decoy-pond, each
  Pops up his head, as fir'd with British blood,
Hears once again the Ministerial screech,
  And once more seeks the bottom's blackest mud!

The Rime of the Ancyent Marinere (1798)
IN SEVEN PARTS

ARGUMENT

How a Ship having passed the Line was driven by Storms to the cold
Country towards the South Pole; and how from thence she made her
course to the tropical Latitude of the Great Pacific Ocean; and of the
strange things that befell; and in what manner the Ancyent Marinere came
back to his own Country.

I

It is an ancyent Marinere,
   And he stoppeth one of three:
'By thy long grey beard and thy glittering eye
   Now wherefore stoppest me?

The Bridegroom's doors are open'd wide
   And I am next of kin;
The Guests are met, the Feast is set, –
   May'st hear the merry din.'

But still he holds the wedding-guest –
10   There was a Ship, quoth he –
'Nay, if thou'st got a laughsome tale,
   Marinere! come with me.'

He holds him with his skinny hand,
   Quoth he, there was a Ship –
'Now get thee hence, thou grey-beard Loon!
   Or my Staff shall make thee skip.'

He holds him with his glittering eye –
   The wedding-guest stood still
And listens like a three year's child;
20   The Marinere hath his will.

The wedding-guest sate on a stone,
   He cannot chuse but hear:
And thus spake on that ancyent man,
   The bright-eyed Marinere.

The Ship was cheer'd, the Harbour clear'd –
  Merrily did we drop
Below the Kirk, below the Hill,
  Below the Light-house top.

30
The Sun came up upon the left,
  Out of the Sea came he:
And he shone bright, and on the right
  Went down into the Sea.

Higher and higher every day,
  Till over the mast at noon –
The wedding-guest here beat his breast,
  For he heard the loud bassoon.

The Bride hath pac'd into the Hall,
  Red as a rose is she;
Nodding their heads before her goes
40
  The merry Minstralsy.

The wedding-guest he beat his breast,
  Yet he cannot chuse but hear:
And thus spake on that ancyent Man,
  The bright-eyed Marinere.

Listen, Stranger! Storm and Wind,
  A Wind and Tempest strong!
For days and weeks it play'd us freaks –
  Like Chaff we drove along.

Listen, Stranger! Mist and Snow,
50
  And it grew wond'rous cauld:
And Ice mast-high came floating by
  As green as Emerauld.

And thro' the drifts the snowy clifts
  Did send a dismal sheen;
Ne shapes of men ne beasts we ken –
  The Ice was all between.

The Ice was here, the Ice was there,
   The Ice was all around:
It crack'd and growl'd, and roar'd and howl'd –
60   Like noises of a swound.

At length did cross an Albatross,
   Thorough the Fog it came;
And an it were a Christian Soul,
   We hail'd it in God's name.

The Marineres gave it biscuit-worms,
   And round and round it flew:
The Ice did split with a Thunder-fit;
   The Helmsman steer'd us thro'.

And a good south wind sprung up behind,
70   The Albatross did follow;
And every day for food or play
   Came to the Marinere's hollo!

In mist or cloud on mast or shroud
   It perch'd for vespers nine,
Whiles all the night thro' fog smoke-white
   Glimmer'd the white moon-shine.

'God save thee, ancyent Marinere!
   From the fiends that plague thee thus –
Why look'st thou so?' – with my cross bow
80   I shot the Albatross.

II

The Sun came up upon the right,
   Out of the Sea came he;
And broad as a weft upon the left
   Went down into the Sea.

And the good south wind still blew behind,
   But no sweet Bird did follow
Ne any day for food or play
   Came to the Marinere's hollo!

And I had done an hellish thing
90   And it would work 'em woe;
For all averr'd, I had kill'd the Bird
    That made the Breeze to blow.

Ne dim ne red, like God's own head,
    The glorious Sun uprist:
Then all averr'd, I had kill'd the Bird
    That brought the fog and mist.
'Twas right, said they, such birds to slay
    That bring the fog and mist.

The breezes blew, the white foam flew,
100   The furrow follow'd free:
We were the first that ever burst
    Into that silent Sea.

Down dropt the breeze, the Sails dropt down,
    'Twas sad as sad could be
And we did speak only to break
    The silence of the Sea.

All in a hot and copper sky
    The bloody sun at noon,
Right up above the mast did stand,
110   No bigger than the moon.

Day after day, day after day,
    We stuck, ne breath ne motion,
As idle as a painted Ship
    Upon a painted Ocean.

Water, water, every where
    And all the boards did shrink;
Water, water every where,
    Ne any drop to drink.

The very deeps did rot: O Christ!
120   That ever this should be!
Yea, slimly things did crawl with legs
    Upon the slimy Sea.

About, about, in reel and rout
   The Death-fires danc'd at night;
The water, like a witch's oils,
   Burnt green and blue and white.

And some in dreams assurèd were
   Of the Spirit that plagued us so:
Nine fathom deep he had follow'd us
130   From the Land of Mist and Snow.

And every tongue thro' utter drouth
   Was wither'd at the root;
We could not speak no more than if
   We had been choked with soot.

Ah wel-a-day! what evil looks
   Had I from old and young;
Instead of the Cross the Albatross
   About my neck was hung.

III

I saw a something in the Sky
140   No bigger than my fist;
At first it seem'd a little speck
   And then it seem'd a mist:
It mov'd and mov'd, and took at last
   A certain shape, I wist.

A speck, a mist, a shape, I wist!
   And still it ner'd and ner'd;
And, an it dodg'd a water-sprite,
   It plung'd and tack'd and veer'd.

With throat unslack'd, with black lips bak'd
150   Ne could we laugh, ne wail:
Then while thro' drouth all dumb they stood
I bit my arm and suck'd the blood
   And cry'd, A sail! a sail!

With throat unslack'd, with black lips bak'd
   Agape they hear'd me call:
Gramercy! they for joy did grin
And all at once their breath drew in
   As they were drinking all.

She doth not tack from side to side –
160   Hither to work us weal
Withouten wind, withouten tide
   She steddies with upright keel.

The western wave was all a flame,
   The day was well nigh done!
Almost upon the western wave
   Rested the broad bright Sun;
When that strange shape drove suddenly
   Betwixt us and the Sun.

And strait the Sun was fleck'd with bars
170   (Heaven's mother send us grace)
As if thro' a dungeon grate he peer'd
   With broad and burning face.

Alas! (thought I, and my heart beat loud)
   How fast she neres and neres!
Are those *her* Sails that glance in the Sun
   Like restless gossameres?

Are those *her* naked ribs, which fleck'd
   The sun that did behind them peer?
And are those two all, all the crew,
180   That woman and her fleshless Pheere?

His bones were black with many a crack,
   All black and bare, I ween;
Jet-black and bare, save where with rust
Of mouldy damps and charnel crust
   They're patch'd with purple and green.

Her lips are red, *her* looks are free,
 Her locks are yellow as gold:
Her skin is as white as leprosy,
And she is far liker Death than he;
190 Her flesh makes the still air cold.

The naked Hulk alongside came
 And the Twain were playing dice;
'The Game is done! I've won, I've won!'
 Quoth she, and whistled thrice.

A gust of wind sterte up behind
 And whistled thro' his bones;
Thro' the holes of his eyes and the hole of his mouth
 Half-whistles and half-groans.

With never a whisper in the Sea
200 Oft darts the Spectre-ship;
While clombe above the Eastern bar
The hornèd Moon, with one bright Star
 Almost atween the tips.

One after one by the hornèd Moon
 (Listen, O Stranger! to me)
Each turn'd his face with a ghastly pang
 And curs'd me with his ee.

Four times fifty living men,
 With never a sigh or groan.
210 With heavy thump, a lifeless lump
 They dropp'd down one by one.

Their souls did from their bodies fly, –
 They fled to bliss or woe;
And every soul it pass'd me by,
 Like the whiz of my Cross-bow.

IV

'I fear thee, ancyent Marinere!
 I fear thy skinny hand;
And thou art long and lank and brown
 As is the ribb'd Sea-sand.

220   I fear thee and thy glittering eye
      And thy skinny hand so brown – '
  Fear not, fear not, thou wedding-guest!
      This body dropt not down.

  Alone, alone, all all alone
      Alone on the wide wide Sea;
  And Christ would take no pity on
      My soul in agony.

  The many men so beautiful,
      And they all dead die lie!
230   And a million million slimy things
      Liv'd on – and so did I.

  I look'd upon the rotting Sea,
      And drew my eyes away;
  I look'd upon the eldritch deck,
      And there the dead men lay.

  I look'd to Heaven, and try'd to pray;
      But or ever a prayer had gusht,
  A wicked whisper came and made
      My heart as dry as dust.

240   I clos'd my lids and kept them close,
      Till the balls like pulses beat;
  For the sky and the sea, and the sea and the sky
  Lay like a load on my weary eye,
      And the dead were at my feet.

  The cold sweat melted from their limbs,
      Ne rot, ne reek did they;
  The look with which they look'd on me,
      Had never pass'd away.

  An orphan's curse would drag to Hell
250   A spirit from on high:
  But O! more horrible than that
      Is the curse in a dead man's eye!
  Seven days, seven nights I saw that curse,
      And yet I could not die.

The moving Moon went up the sky
   And no where did abide:
Softly she was going up
   And a star or two beside –

Her beams bemock'd the sultry main
260   Like morning frosts yspread;
But where the ship's huge shadow lay,
The charmèd water burnt alway
   A still and awful red.

Beyond the shadow of the ship
   I watch'd the water-snakes:
They mov'd in tracks of shining white;
And when they rear'd, the elfish light
   Fell off in hoary flakes.

Within the shadow of the ship
270   I watch'd their rich attire:
Blue, glossy green, and velvet black
They coil'd and swam; and every track
   Was a flash of golden fire.

O happy living things! no tongue
   Their beauty might declare:
A spring of love gusht from my heart,
   And I bless'd them unaware!
Sure my kind saint took pity on me,
   And I bless'd them unaware.

280   The self-same moment I could pray;
   And from my neck so free
The Albatross fell off, and sank
   Like lead into the sea.

V

O sleep, it is a gentle thing
   Belov'd from pole to pole!
To Mary-queen the praise be yeven
She sent the gentle sleep from heaven
   That slid into my soul.

The silly buckets on the deck
    That had so long remain'd,
290 I dreamt that they were fill'd with dew
    And when I awoke it rain'd.

My lips were wet, my throat was cold,
    My garments all were dank;
Sure I had drunken in my dreams
    And still my body drank.

I mov'd and could not feel my limbs,
    I was so light, almost
I thought that I had died in sleep,
300   And was a blessed Ghost.

The roaring wind! it roar'd far off,
    It did not come anear;
But with its sound it shook the sails
    That were so thin and sere.

The upper air bursts into life,
    And a hundred fire-flags sheen
To and fro they are hurried about;
And to and fro, and in and out
    The stars dance on between.

310 The coming wind doth roar more loud;
    The sails do sigh, like sedge:
The rain pours down from one black cloud
    And the Moon is at its edge.

Hark! hark! the thick black cloud is cleft,
    And the Moon is at its side:
Like waters shot from some high crag,
The lightning falls with never a jag
    A river steep and wide.

The strong wind reach'd the ship: it roar'd
320   And dropp'd down, like a stone!
Beneath the lightning and the moon
    The dead men gave a groan.

They groan'd, they stirr'd, they all uprose,
  Ne spake, ne mov'd their eyes:
It had been strange, even in a dream
  To have seen those dead men rise.

The helmsman steerd, the ship mov'd on;
  Yet never a breeze up-blew;
The Marineres all 'gan work the ropes,
330 Where they were wont to do:
They rais'd their limbs like lifeless tools –
  We were a ghastly crew.

The body of my brother's son
  Stood by me knee to knee:
The body and I pull'd at one rope,
  But he said nought to me –
And I quak'd to think of my own voice
  How frightful it would be!

The day-light dawn'd – they dropp'd their arms,
340 And cluster'd round the mast:
Sweet sounds rose slowly thro' their mouths
  And from their bodies pass'd.

Around, around, flew each sweet sound,
  Then darted to the sun:
Slowly the sounds came back again
  Now mix'd, now one by one.

Sometimes a dropping from the sky
  I heard the Lavrock sing;
Sometimes all little birds that are
350 How they seem'd to fill the sea and air
  With their sweet jargoning.

And now 'twas like all instruments,
  Now like a lonely flute;
And now it is an angel's song
  That makes the heavens be mute.

It ceas'd: yet still the sails made on
  A pleasant noise till noon,
A noise like of a hidden brook
  In the leafy month of June,
360 That to the sleeping woods all night
  Singeth a quiet tune.

Listen, O listen, thou Wedding-guest!
  'Marinere! thou hast thy will:
For that, which comes out of thine eye, doth make
  My body and soul to be still.'

Never sadder tale was told
  To a man of woman born:
Sadder and wiser thou wedding-guest!
  Thou'lt rise to-morrow morn.

370 Never sadder tale was heard
  By a man of woman born:
The Marineres all return'd to work
  As silent as beforne.

The Marineres all 'gan pull the ropes,
  But look at me they n'old:
Thought I, I am as thin as air –
  They cannot me behold.

Till noon we silently sail'd on
  Yet never a breeze did breathe:
380 Slowly and smoothly went the ship
  Mov'd onward from beneath.

Under the keel nine fathom deep
  From the land of mist and snow
The spirit slid: and it was He
  That made the Ship to go.
The sails at noon left off their tune
  And the Ship stood still also.

The sun right up above the mast
  Had fix'd her to the ocean:
390 But in a minute she 'gan stir
  With a short uneasy motion –
Backwards and forwards half her length
  With a short uneasy motion.

Then, like a pawing horse let go,
  She made a sudden bound:
It flung the blood into my head,
  And I fell into a swound.

How long in that same fit I lay,
  I have not to declare;
400 But ere my living life return'd,
I heard and in my soul discern'd
  Two voices in the air,

'Is it he?' quoth one, 'Is this the man?
  By him who died on cross,
With his cruel bow he lay'd full low
  The harmless Albatross.

'The spirit who 'bideth by himself
  In the land of mist and snow,
He lov'd the bird that lov'd the man
410   Who shot him with his bow.'

The other was a softer voice,
  As soft as honey-dew:
Quoth he the man hath penance done,
  And penance more will do.

VI

First voice
'But tell me, tell me! speak again,
  Thy soft response renewing –
What makes that ship drive on so fast?
  What is the Ocean doing?'

Second voice
'Still as a Slave before his Lord,
    The Ocean hath no blast:
420 His great bright eye most silently
    Up to the moon is cast –

'If he may know which way to go,
    For she guides him smooth or grim.
See, brother, see! how graciously
    She looketh down on him.'

First voice
'But why drives on that ship so fast
    Withouten wave or wind?'

Second voice
'The air is cut away before,
430   And closes from behind.

Fly, brother, fly! more high, more high,
    Or we shall be belated.
For slow and slow that ship will go,
    When the Marinere's trance is abated.'

I woke, and we were sailing on
    As in a gentle weather:
Twas night, calm night, the moon was high;
    The dead men stood together.

All stood together on the deck,
440   For a charnel-dungeon fitter:
All fix'd on me their stony eyes
    That in the moon did glitter.

The pang, the curse, with which they died,
    Had never pass'd away:
I could not draw my een from theirs
    Ne turn them up to pray.

And in its time the spell was snapt,
    And I could move my een:
I look'd far-forth, but little saw
450   Of what might else be seen.

Like one, that on a lonely road
    Doth walk in fear and dread,
And having once turn'd round, walks on
    And turns no more his head:
Because he knows, a frightful fiend
    Doth close behind him tread.

But soon there breath'd a wind on me,
    Ne sound ne motion made:
Its path was not upon the sea
460   In ripple or in shade.

It rais'd my hair, it fann'd my cheek,
    Like a meadow-gale of spring –
It mingled strangely with my fears,
    Yet it felt like a welcoming.

Swiftly, swiftly flew the ship,
    Yet she sail'd softly too:
Sweetly, sweetly blew the breeze –
    On me alone it blew.

O dream of joy! is this indeed
470   The light-house top I see?
Is this the Hill? Is this the Kirk?
    Is this mine own countrèe?

We drifted o'er the Harbour-bar,
    And I with sobs did pray –
'O let me be awake, my God!
    Or let me sleep alway!'

The harbour-bay was clear as glass,
    So smoothly it was strewn!
And on the bay the moonlight lay,
480   And the shadow of the moon.

The moonlight bay was white all o'er,
    Till rising from the same,
Full many shapes, that shadows were,
    Like as of torches came.

A little distance from the prow
   Those dark-red shadows were;
But soon I saw that my own flesh
   Was red as in a glare.

I turn'd my head in fear and dread,
490   And by the holy rood,
The bodies had advanc'd, and now
   Before the mast they stood.

They lifted up their stiff right arms,
   They held them strait and tight;
And each right-arm burnt like a torch,
   A torch that's borne upright.
Their stony eye-balls glitter'd on
   In the red and smoky light.

I pray'd and turn'd my head away
500   Forth looking as before.
There was no breeze upon the bay,
   No wave against the shore.

The rock shone bright, the kirk no less
   That stands above the rock:
The moonlight steep'd in silentness
   The steady weathercock.

And the bay was white with silent light,
   Till rising from the same
Full many shapes, that shadows were,
510   In crimson colours came.

A little distance from the prow
   Those crimson shadows were:
I turn'd my eyes upon the deck –
   O Christ! what saw I there?

Each corse lay flat, lifeless and flat;
   And by the Holy rood
A man all light, a seraph-man,
   On every corse there stood.

This seraph-band, each wav'd his hand:
    It was a heavenly sight:
They stood as signals to the land,
    Each one a lovely light:

This seraph-band, each wav'd his hand,
    No voice did they impart –
No voice; but O! the silence sank,
    Like music on my heart.

Eftsones I heard the dash of oars,
    I heard the pilot's cheer:
My head was turn'd perforce away
    And I saw a boat appear.

Then vanish'd all the lovely lights;
    The bodies rose anew:
With silent pace, each to his place,
    Came back the ghastly crew.
The wind, that shade nor motion made,
    On me alone it blew.

The pilot, and the pilot's boy
    I heard them coming fast:
Dear Lord in Heaven! it was a joy,
    The dead men could not blast.

I saw a third – I heard his voice:
    It is the Hermit good!
He singeth loud his godly hymns
    That he makes in the wood.
He'll shrieve my soul, he'll wash away
    The Albatross's blood.

VII

This Hermit good lives in that wood
    Which slopes down to the Sea.
How loudly his sweet voice he rears!
He loves to talk with Marineres
    That come from a far Contrèe.

He kneels at morn and noon and eve –
   He hath a cushion plump:
It is the moss, that wholly hides
   The rotted old Oak-stump.

The Skiff-boat ne'rd: I heard them talk,
   'Why, this is strange, I trow!
Where are those lights so many and fair
   That signal made but now?'

560   'Strange, by my faith!' the Hermit said –
   'And they answer'd not our cheer.
The planks look warp'd, and see those sails
   How thin they are and sere!
I never saw aught like to them
   Unless perchance it were

'The skeletons of leaves that lag
   My forest brook along:
When the Ivy-tod is heavy with snow,
And the Owlet whoops to the wolf below
570   That eats the she-wolf's young.'

'Dear Lord! it has a fiendish look –'
   (The Pilot made reply)
'I am a-fear'd.' – 'Push on, push on!'
   Said the Hermit cheerily.

The Boat came closer to the Ship,
   But I ne spake ne stirr'd!
The Boat came close beneath the Ship,
   And strait a sound was heard!

Under the water it rumbled on,
580   Still louder and more dread:
It reach'd the Ship, it split the bay;
   The Ship went down like lead.

Stunn'd by that loud and dreadful sound,
    Which sky and ocean smote:
Like one that hath been seven days drown'd
    My body lay afloat:
But, swift as dreams, myself I found
    Within the Pilot's boat.

Upon the whirl, where sank the Ship,
590   The boat spun round and round:
And all was still, save that the hill
    Was telling of the sound.

I mov'd my lips: the Pilot shriek'd
    And fell down in a fit.
The Holy Hermit rais'd his eyes
    And pray'd where he did sit.

I took the oars: the Pilot's boy,
    Who now doth crazy go,
Laugh'd loud and long, and all the while
600   His eyes went to and fro,
'Ha! ha!' quoth he – 'full plain I see,
    The devil knows how to row.'

And now all in mine own Countrèe
    I stood on the firm land!
The Hermit stepp'd forth from the boat,
    And scarcely he could stand.

'O shrieve me, shrieve me, holy Man!'
    The Hermit cross'd his brow –
'Say quick,' quoth he, 'I bid thee say
610   What manner man art thou?'

Forthwith this frame of mine was wrench'd
    With a woeful agony,
Which forc'd me to begin my tale
    And then it left me free.

Since then at an uncertain hour,
   Now oftimes and now fewer,
That anguish comes and makes me tell
   My ghastly aventure.

I pass, like night, from land to land;
620   I have strange power of speech;
The moment that his face I see
I know the man that must hear me;
   To him my tale I teach.

What loud uproar bursts from that door!
   The Wedding-guests are there;
But in the Garden-bower the Bride
   And Bride-maids singing are:
And hark the little Vesper-bell
   Which biddeth me to prayer.

630 O Wedding-guest! this soul hath been
   Alone on a wide wide sea:
So lonely 'twas, that God himself
   Scarce seemèd there to be.

O sweeter than the Marriage-feast,
   'Tis sweeter far to me
To walk together to the Kirk
   With a goodly company.

To walk together to the Kirk
   And all together pray,
640 While each to his great father bends,
Old men, and babes, and loving friends,
   And Youths, and Maidens gay.

Farewell, farewell! but this I tell
   To thee, thou wedding-guest!
He prayeth well who loveth well,
   Both man and bird and beast.

He prayeth best who loveth best,
   All things both great and small:
For the dear God, who loveth us,
650   He made and loveth all.

The Marinere, whose eye is bright,
 Whose beard with age is hoar,
Is gone; and now the wedding-guest
 Turn'd from the bridegroom's door.

He went, like one that hath been stunn'd
 And is of sense forlorn:
A sadder and a wiser man
 He rose the morrow morn.

The Rime of the Ancient Mariner (1834)
IN SEVEN PARTS

Facile credo, plures esse Naturas invisibiles quam visibiles in rerum univer-
sitate. Sed horum omnium familiam quis nobis enarrabit, et gradus et
cognationes et discrimina et singulorum munera? Quid agunt? quæ loca
habitant? Harum rerum notitiam semper ambivit ingenium humanum,
nunquam attigit. Juvat, interea, non diffiteor, quandoque in animo, tanquam
in tabulâ, majoris et melioris mundi imaginem contemplari: ne mens
assuefacta hodiernæ vitæ minutiis se contrahat nimis, et tota subsidat in
pusillas cogitationes. Sed veritati interea invigilandum est, modusque
servandus, ut certa ab incertis, diem a nocte, distinguamus.

T. BURNET, Archæol. Phil., p. 68

PART I

It is an ancient Mariner,
And he stoppeth one of three.
'By thy long grey beard and glittering eye,
Now wherefore stopp'st thou me?

An ancient Mariner meeteth three gallants bidden to a wedding-feast, and detaineth one.

'The Bridegroom's doors are opened wide,
And I am next of kin;
The guests are met, the feast is set:
May'st hear the merry din.'

 He holds him with his skinny hand,
10 'There was a ship,' quoth he.
'Hold off! unhand me, grey-beard loon!'
Eftsoons his hand dropt he.

He holds him with his glittering eye –
The Wedding-Guest stood still,
And listens like a three years' child:
The Mariner hath his will.

The wedding-guest is spell-bound by the eye of the old sea-faring man, and constrained to hear his tale.

The Wedding-Guest sat on a stone:
He cannot choose but hear;
And thus spake on that ancient man,
20   The bright-eyed Mariner.

The ship was cheered, the harbour cleared,
Merrily did we drop
Below the kirk, below the hill,
Below the light-house top.

The sun came up upon the left,
Out of the sea came he!
And he shone bright, and on the right
Went down into the sea.

The Mariner tells how the ship sailed southward with a good wind and fair weather, till it reached the line.

Higher and higher every day,
30   Till over the mast at noon –
The Wedding-Guest here beat his breast,
For he heard the loud bassoon.

The bride hath paced into the hall,
Red as a rose is she;
Nodding their heads before her goes
The merry minstrelsy.

The wedding-guest heareth the bridal music; but the Mariner continueth his tale.

The Wedding-Guest he beat his breast,
Yet he cannot choose but hear;
And thus spake on that ancient man,
40   The bright-eyed Mariner.

And now the storm-blast came, and he
Was tyrannous and strong:
He struck with his o'ertaking wings,
And chased us south along.

The ship drawn by a storm toward the south pole.

With sloping masts and dipping prow,
As who pursued with yell and blow
Still treads the shadow of his foe,
And forward bends his head,
The ship drove fast, loud roared the blast,
50   And southward aye we fled.

And now there came both mist and snow,
And it grew wondrous cold:
And ice, mast-high, came floating by,
As green as emerald.

And through the drifts the snowy clifts
Did send a dismal sheen:
Nor shapes of men nor beasts we ken –
The ice was all between.

The land of ice, and of fearful sounds where no living thing was to be seen.

The ice was here, the ice was there,
60   The ice was all around:
It cracked and growled, and roared and howled,
Like noises in a swound!

At length did cross an Albatross,
Thorough the fog it came;
As if it had been a Christian soul,
We hailed it in God's name.

Till a great sea-bird, called the Albatross, came through the snow-fog, and was received with great joy and hospitality.

It ate the food it ne'er had eat,
And round and round it flew.
The ice did split with a thunder-fit;
70   The helmsman steered us through!

And a good south wind sprung up behind;
The Albatross did follow,
And ever day, for food or play,
Came to the mariner's hollo!

And lo! the Albatross proveth a bird of good omen, and followeth the ship as it returned northward through fog and floating ice.

In mist or cloud, on mast or shroud,
It perched for vespers nine;
Whiles all the night, through fog-smoke white,
Glimmered the white moon-shine.

'God save thee, ancient Mariner!
From the fiends, that plague thee thus! –
Why look'st thou so?' – With my cross-bow
I shot the Albatross.

80

The ancient Mariner inhospitably killeth the pious bird of good omen.

PART II

The Sun now rose upon the right:
Out of the sea came he,
Still hid in mist, and on the left
Went down into the sea.

And the good south wind still blew behind,
But no sweet bird did follow,
Nor any day for food or play
Came to the mariners' hollo!

90

And I had done a hellish thing,
And it would work 'em woe:
For all averred, I had killed the bird
That made the breeze to blow.
Ah wretch! said they, the bird to slay,
That made the breeze to blow!

His ship-mates cry out against the ancient Mariner, for killing the bird of good luck.

Nor dim nor red, like God's own head,
The glorious Sun uprist:
Then all averred, I had killed the bird
That brought the fog and mist.
'Twas right, said they, such birds to slay,
That bring the fog and mist.

100

But when the fog cleared off, they justify the same, and thus make themselves accomplices in the crime.

The fair breeze blew, the white foam flew,
The furrow followed free;
We were the first that ever burst
Into that silent sea.

The fair breeze continues; the ship enters the Pacific Ocean, and sails northward, even till it reaches the Line.

Down dropt the breeze, the sails dropt down,
'Twas sad as sad could be;
And we did speak only to break
The silence of the sea!

110

The ship hath been suddenly becalmed.

All in a hot and copper sky,
The bloody Sun, at noon,
Right up above the mast did stand,
No bigger than the Moon.

Day after day, day after day,
We stuck, nor breath nor motion;
As idle as a painted ship
Upon a painted ocean.

Water, water, every where,
120　And all the boards did shrink;
Water, water, every where,
Nor any drop to drink.

And the Albatross
begins to be
avenged.

The very deep did rot: O Christ!
That ever this should be!
Yea, slimy things did crawl with legs
Upon the slimy sea.

About, about, in reel and rout
The death-fires danced at night;
The water, like a witch's oils,
130　Burnt green, and blue and white.

And some in dreams assurèd were
Of the spirit that plagued us so;
Nine fathom deep he had followed us
From the land of mist and snow.

A spirit had
followed them; one
of the invisible
inhabitants of this
planet, neither
departed souls nor
angels; concerning whom the learned Jew, Josephus, and the Platonic
Constantinopolitan, Michael Psellus, may be consulted. They are very numerous,
and there is no climate or element without one or more.

And every tongue, through utter drought,
Was withered at the root;
We could not speak, no more than if
We had been choked with soot.

Ah! well a-day! what evil looks
140　Had I from old and young!
Instead of the cross, the Albatross
About my neck was hung.

The ship-mates, in their sore distress, would fain throw the whole guilt on the ancient Mariner: in sign whereof they hang the dead sea-bird round his neck.

PART III

There passed a weary time. Each throat
Was parched, and glazed each eye.
A weary time! a weary time!
How glazed each weary eye,
When looking westward, I beheld
A something in the sky.

The ancient Mariner beholdeth a sign in the element afar off.

At first it seemed a little speck,
150　And then it seemed a mist;
It moved and moved, and took at last
A certain shape, I wist.

A speck, a mist, a shape, I wist!
And still it neared and neared:
As if it dodged a water-sprite,
It plunged and tacked and veered.

With throats unslaked, with black lips baked,
We could nor laugh nor wail;
Through utter drought all dumb we stood!
160　I bit my arm, I sucked the blood,
And cried, A sail! a sail!

At its nearer approach, it seemeth him to be a ship; and at a dear ransom he freeth his speech from the bonds of thirst.

With throats unslaked, with black lips baked,
Agape they heard me call:
Gramercy! they for joy did grin,
And all at once their breath drew in,
As they were drinking all.

A flash of joy;

See! see! (I cried) she tacks no more!
Hither to work us weal;
Without a breeze, without a tide,
170　She steadies with upright keel!

And horror follows. For can it be a ship that comes onward without wind or tide?

The western wave was all a-flame.
The day was well nigh done!
Almost upon the western wave
Rested the broad bright Sun;
When that strange shape drove suddenly
Betwixt us and the Sun.

And straight the Sun was flecked with bars,
(Heaven's Mother send us grace!)
As if through a dungeon-grate he peered
180   With broad and burning face.

> It seemeth him but the skeleton of a ship.

Alas! (thought I, and my heart beat loud)
How fast she nears and nears!
Are those her sails that glance in the Sun,
Like restless gossameres?

Are those her ribs through which the Sun
Did peer, as through a grate?
And is that Woman all her crew?
Is that a Death? and are there two?
Is Death that woman's mate?

> And its ribs are seen as bars on the face of the setting Sun. The spectre-woman and her death-mate, and no other on board the skeleton-ship.

190   Her lips were red, her looks were free,
Her locks were yellow as gold:
Her skin was as white as leprosy,
The Night-mare Life-in-Death was she,
Who thicks man's blood with cold.

> Like vessel, like crew!

The naked hulk alongside came,
And the twain were casting dice;
'The game is done! I've, I've won!'
Quoth she, and whistles thrice.

> Death and Life-in-death have diced for the ship's crew, and she (the latter) winneth the ancient Mariner.

The Sun's rim dips; the stars rush out:
200   At one stride comes the dark;
With far-heard whisper, o'er the sea,
Off shot the spectre-bark.

> No twilight within the courts of the Sun.

We listened and looked sideways up!
Fear at my heart, as at a cup,
My life-blood seemed to sip!
The stars were dim, and thick the night,
The steersman's face by his lamp gleamed white;
From the sails the dew did drip –
Till clomb above the eastern bar
210　The hornèd Moon, with one bright star
Within the nether tip.

At the rising of the Moon.

One after one, by the star-dogged Moon,
Too quick for groan or sigh,
Each turned his face with a ghastly pang,
And cursed me with his eye.

One after another,

Four times fifty living men,
(And I heard nor sigh nor groan)
With heavy thump, a lifeless lump,
They dropped down one by one.

His ship-mates drop down dead.

220　The souls did from their bodies fly, –
They fled to bliss or woe!
And every soul, it passed me by,
Like the whizz of my cross-bow!

But Life-in-Death begins her work on the ancient Mariner.

PART IV

'I fear thee, ancient Mariner!
I fear thy skinny hand!
And thou art long, and lank, and brown,
As is the ribbed sea-sand.

The wedding-guest feareth that a spirit is talking to him.

I fear thee and thy glittering eye,
And thy skinny hand, so brown.' –
230　Fear not, fear not, thou Wedding-Guest!
This body dropt not down.

But the ancient Mariner assureth him of his bodily life, and proceedeth to relate his horrible penance.

Alone, alone, all, all alone,
Alone on a wide wide sea!
And never a saint took pity on
My soul in agony.

The many men, so beautiful!
And they all dead did lie:
And a thousand thousand slimy things
Lived on; and so did I.

He despiseth the creatures of the calm.

240   I looked upon the rotting sea,
And drew my eyes away;
I looked upon the rotting deck,
And there the dead men lay.

And envieth that they should live, and so many lie dead.

I looked to heaven, and tried to pray;
But or ever a prayer had gusht,
A wicked whisper came, and made
My heart as dry as dust.

I closed my lids, and kept them close,
And the balls like pulses beat;
250   For the sky and the sea, and the sea and the sky
Lay like a load on my weary eye,
And the dead were at my feet.

The cold sweat melted from their limbs,
Nor rot nor reek did they:
The look with which they looked on me
Had never passed away.

But the curse liveth for him in the eye of the dead men.

An orphan's curse would drag to hell
A spirit from on high;
But oh! more horrible than that
260   Is the curse in a dead man's eye!
Seven days, seven nights, I saw that curse,
And yet I could not die.

The moving Moon went up the sky,
And no where did abide:
Softly she was going up,
And a star or two beside –

In his loneliness and fixedness he yearneth towards the journeying Moon, and the stars that still sojourn,

yet still move onward; and every where the blue sky belongs to them, and is their appointed rest, and their native country and their own natural homes, which they enter unannounced, as lords that are certainly expected and yet there is a silent joy at their arrival.

Her beams bemocked the sultry main,
Like April hoar-frost spread;
But where the ship's huge shadow lay,
270   The charmèd water burnt alway
A still and awful red.

Beyond the shadow of the ship,
I watched the water-snakes:
They moved in tracks of shining white,   By the light of the
And when they reared, the elfish light   Moon he beholdeth
Fell off in hoary flakes.   God's creatures of
                                            the great calm.

Within the shadow of the ship
I watched their rich attire:
Blue, glossy green, and velvet black,
280   They coiled and swam; and every track
Was a flash of golden fire.

O happy living things! no tongue   Their beauty and
Their beauty might declare: their happiness.
A spring of love gushed from my heart,
And I blessed them unaware: He blesseth them in
Sure my kind saint took pity on me,   his heart.
And I blessed them unaware.

The selfsame moment I could pray;   The spell begins to
And from my neck so free   break.
290   The Albatross fell off, and sank
Like lead into the sea.

PART V

Oh sleep! it is a gentle thing,
Beloved from pole to pole!
To Mary Queen the praise be given!
She sent the gentle sleep from Heaven,
That slid into my soul

The silly buckets on the deck,   By grace of the holy
That had so long remained,   Mother, the ancient
I dreamt that they were filled with dew;   Mariner is refreshed
                                            with rain.
300   And when I awoke, it rained.

My lips were wet, my throat was cold,
My garments all were dank;
Sure I had drunken in my dreams,
And still my body drank.

I moved, and could not feel my limbs:
I was so light – almost
I thought that I had died in sleep,
And was a blessed ghost.

And soon I heard a roaring wind:
310 It did not come anear;
But with its sound it shook the sails,
That were so thin and sere.

He heareth sounds and seeth strange sights and commotions in the sky and the element.

The upper air burst into life!
And a hundred fire-flags sheen,
To and fro they were hurried about!
And to and fro, and in and out,
The wan stars danced between.

And the coming wind did roar more loud,
And the sails did sigh like sedge;
320 And the rain poured down from one black cloud;
The Moon was at its edge.

The thick black cloud was cleft, and still
The Moon was at its side:
Like waters shot from some high crag,
The lightning fell with never a jag,
A river steep and wide.

The loud wind never reached the ship,
Yet now the ship moved on!
Beneath the lightning and the moon
330 The dead men gave a groan.

The bodies of the ship's crew are inspired, and the ship moves on;

They groaned, they stirred, they all uprose,
Nor spake, nor moved their eyes;
It had been strange, even in a dream,
To have seen those dead men rise.

The helmsman steered, the ship moved on;
Yet never a breeze up blew;
The mariners all 'gan work the ropes,
Where they were wont to do;
They raised their limbs like lifeless tools –
340   We were a ghastly crew.

The body of my brother's son
Stood by me, knee to knee:
The body and I pulled at one rope,
But he said nought to me.

'I fear thee, ancient Mariner!'
Be calm, thou Wedding-Guest!
'Twas not those souls that fled in pain,
Which to their corses came again,
But a troop of spirits blest:

350   For when it dawned – they dropped their
            arms,
And clustered round the mast;
Sweet sounds rose slowly through their mouths,
And from their bodies passed.

But not by the souls of the men, nor by demons of earth or middle air, but by a blessed troop of angelic spirits, sent down by the invocation of the guardian saint.

Around, around, flew each sweet sound,
Then darted to the Sun;
Slowly the sounds came back again,
Now mixed, now one by one.

Sometimes a-dropping from the sky
I heard the sky-lark sing;
360   Sometimes all little birds that are,
How they seemed to fill the sea and air
With their sweet jargoning!

And now 'twas like all instruments,
Now like a lonely flute;
And now it is an angel's song,
That makes the heavens be mute.

It ceased; yet still the sails made on
A pleasant noise till noon,
A noise like of a hidden brook
370   In the leafy month of June,
That to the sleeping woods all night
Singeth a quiet tune.

Till noon we quietly sailed on,
Yet never a breeze did breathe:
Slowly and smoothly went the ship,
Moved onward from beneath.

Under the keel nine fathom deep,
From the land of mist and snow,
The spirit slid: and it was he
380   That made the ship to go.
The sails at noon left off their tune,
And the ship stood still also.

The lonesome spirit from the south pole carries on the ship as far as the line, in obedience to the angelic troop, but still requireth vengeance.

The Sun, right up above the mast,
Had fixed her to the ocean:
But in a minute she 'gan stir,
With a short uneasy motion –
Backwards and forwards half her length
With a short uneasy motion.

Then like a pawing horse let go,
390   She made a sudden bound:
It flung the blood into my head,
And I fell down in a swound.

How long in that same fit I lay,
I have not to declare;
But ere my living life returned,
I heard, and in my soul discerned
Two voices in the air.

The Polar Spirit's fellow demons, the invisible inhabitants of the element, take part in his wrong; and two of them relate, one to the other, that penance long and heavy for the ancient Mariner hath been accorded to the Polar Spirit, who returneth southward.

'Is it he?' quoth one, 'Is this the man?
By him who died on cross,
With his cruel bow he laid full low
The harmless Albatross.

'The spirit who bideth by himself
In the land of mist and snow,
He loved the bird that loved the man
Who shot him with his bow.'

The other was a softer voice,
As soft as honey-dew:
Quoth he, 'The man hath penance done,
And penance more will do.'

PART VI

First voice
But tell me, tell me! speak again,
Thy soft response renewing –
What makes that ship drive on so fast?
What is the ocean doing?

Second voice
Still as a slave before his lord,
The ocean hath no blast;
His great bright eye most silently
Up to the Moon is cast –

If he may know which way to go;
For she guides him smooth or grim.
See, brother, see! how graciously
She looketh down on him.

First voice
But why drives on that ship so fast,
Without or wave or wind?

Second voice
The air is cut away before,
And closes from behind.

The Mariner hath been cast into a trance; for the angelic power causeth the vessel to drive northward faster than human life could endure.

Fly, brother, fly! more high, more high!
Or we shall be belated:
For slow and slow that ship will go,
When the Mariner's trance is abated.

430 I woke, and we were sailing on
As in a gentle weather:
'Twas night, calm night, the moon was high;
The dead men stood together.

All stood together on the deck,
For a charnel-dungeon fitter:
All fixed on me their stony eyes,
That in the Moon did glitter.

The pang, the curse, with which they died,
Had never passed away:
440 I could not draw my eyes from theirs,
Nor turn them up to pray.

And now this spell was snapt: once more
I viewed the ocean green,
And looked far forth, yet little saw
Of what had else been seen –

Like one, that on a lonesome road
Doth walk in fear and dread,
And having once turned round walks on,
And turns no more his head;
450 Because he knows, a frightful fiend
Doth close behind him tread.

But soon there breathed a wind on me,
Nor sound nor motion made:
Its path was not upon the sea,
In ripple or in shade.

It raised my hair, it fanned my cheek
Like a meadow-gale of spring –
It mingled strangely with my fears,
Yet it felt like a welcoming.

The supernatural
motion is retarded;
the Mariner awakes,
and his penance
begins anew.

The curse is finally
expiated.

460 Swiftly, swiftly flew the ship,
Yet she sailed softly too:
Sweetly, sweetly blew the breeze –
On me alone it blew.

Oh! dream of joy! is this indeed
The light-house top I see?
Is this the hill? is this the kirk?
Is this mine own countree?

And the ancient Mariner beholdeth his native country.

We drifted o'er the harbour-bar,
And I with sobs did pray –
470 O let me be awake, my God!
Or let me sleep alway.

The harbour-bay was clear as glass,
So smoothly it was strewn!
And on the bay the moonlight lay,
And the shadow of the moon.

The rock shone bright, the kirk no less,
That stands above the rock:
The moonlight steeped in silentness
The steady weathercock.

480 And the bay was white with silent light
Till rising from the same,
Full many shapes, that shadows were,
In crimson colours came.

The angelic spirits leave the dead bodies,

A little distance from the prow
Those crimson shadows were:
I turned my eyes upon the deck –
Oh, Christ! what saw I there!

And appear in their own forms of light.

Each corse lay flat, lifeless and flat,
And, by the holy rood!
490 A man all light, a seraph-man,
On every corse there stood.

This seraph-band, each waved his hand:
It was a heavenly sight!
They stood as signals to the land,
Each one a lovely light;

This seraph-band, each waved his hand,
No voice did they impart –
No voice; but oh! the silence sank
Like music on my heart.

500 But soon I heard the dash of oars,
I heard the Pilot's cheer;
My head was turned perforce away,
And I saw a boat appear.

The Pilot and the Pilot's boy,
I heard them coming fast:
Dear Lord in Heaven! it was a joy
The dead men could not blast.

I saw a third – I heard his voice:
It is the Hermit good!
510 He singeth loud his godly hymns
That he makes in the wood.
He'll shrieve my soul, he'll wash away
The Albatross's blood.

PART VII

This Hermit good lives in that wood   The Hermit of the
Which slopes down to the sea.   wood,
How loudly his sweet voice he rears!
He loves to talk with marineres
That come from a far countree.

He kneels at morn, and noon, and eve –
520 He hath a cushion plump:
It is the moss that wholly hides
The rotted old oak-stump.

The skiff-boat neared: I heard them talk,
'Why, this is strange, I trow!
Where are those lights so many and fair,
That signal made but now?'

'Strange, by my faith!' the Hermit said –   Approacheth the
'And they answered not our cheer!   ship with wonder.
The planks looked warped! and see those sails,
530   How thin they are and sere!
I never saw aught like to them,
Unless perchance it were

Brown skeletons of leaves that lag
My forest-brook along;
When the ivy-tod is heavy with snow,
And the owlet whoops to the wolf below,
That eats the she-wolf's young.'

'Dear Lord! it hath a fiendish look –
(The Pilot made reply)
540   I am a-feared' – 'Push on, push on!'
Said the Hermit cheerily.

The boat came closer to the ship,
But I nor spake nor stirred;
The boat came close beneath the ship,
And straight a sound was heard.

Under the water it rumbled on,   The ship suddenly
Still louder and more dread: sinketh.
It reached the ship, it split the bay;
The ship went down like lead.

550   Stunned by that loud and dreadful sound,   The ancient
Which sky and ocean smote,   Mariner is saved in
Like one that hath been seven days drowned   the Pilot's boat.
My body lay afloat;
But swift as dreams, myself I found
Within the Pilot's boat.

Upon the whirl, where sank the ship,
The boat spun round and round;
And all was still, save that the hill
Was telling of the sound.

560   I moved my lips – the Pilot shrieked
And fell down in a fit;
The holy Hermit raised his eyes,
And prayed where he did sit.

I took the oars: the Pilot's boy,
Who now doth crazy go,
Laughed loud and long, and all the while
His eyes went to and fro.
'Ha! ha!' quoth he, 'full plain I see,
The Devil knows how to row.'

570   And now, all in my own countree,
I stood on the firm land!
The Hermit stepped forth from the boat,
And scarcely he could stand.

'O shrieve me, shrieve me, holy man!'
The Hermit crossed his brow.
'Say quick,' quoth he, 'I bid thee say –
What manner of man art thou?'

The ancient Mariner earnestly entreateth the Hermit to shrieve him; and the penance of life falls on him.

Forthwith this frame of mine was wrenched
With a woful agony,
580   Which forced me to begin my tale;
And then it left me free.

Since then, at an uncertain hour,
That agony returns:
And till my ghastly tale is told,
This heart within me burns.

And ever and anon throughout his future life an agony constraineth him to travel from land to land.

I pass, like night, from land to land;
I have strange power of speech;
That moment that his face I see,
I know the man that must hear me:
590   To him my tale I teach.

What loud uproar bursts from that door!
The wedding-guests are there:
But in the garden-bower the bride
And bride-maids singing are:
And hark the little vesper bell,
Which biddeth me to prayer!

O Wedding-Guest! this soul hath been
Alone on a wide wide sea:
So lonely 'twas, that God himself
600   Scarce seemèd there to be.

O sweeter than the marriage-feast,
'Tis sweeter far to me,
To walk together to the kirk
With a goodly company! –

To walk together to the kirk,
And all together pray,
While each to his great Father bends,
Old men, and babes, and loving friends,
And youths and maidens gay!

610   Farewell, farewell! but this I tell
To thee, thou Wedding-Guest!
He prayeth well, who loveth well
Both man and bird and beast.

And to teach, by his own example, love and reverence to all things that God made and loveth.

He prayeth best, who loveth best
All things both great and small;
For the dear God who loveth us,
He made and loveth all.'

The Mariner, whose eye is bright,
Whose beard with age is hoar,
620   Is gone: and now the Wedding-Guest
Turned from the bridegroom's door.

He went like one that hath been stunned,
And is of sense forlorn:
A sadder and a wiser man,
He rose the morrow morn.

Christabel

PREFACE

The first part of the following poem was written in the year 1797, at Stowey, in the county of Somerset. The second part, after my return from Germany, in the year 1800, at Keswick, Cumberland. It is probable, that if the poem had been finished at either of the former periods, or if even the first and second part had been published in the year 1800, the impression of its originality would have been much greater than I dare at present expect. But for this, I have only my own indolence to blame. The dates are mentioned for the exclusive purpose of precluding charges of plagiarism or servile imitation from myself. For there is amongst us a set of critics, who seem to hold, that every possible thought and image is traditional; who have no notion that there are such things as fountains in the world, small as well as great; and who would therefore charitably derive every rill they behold flowing, from a perforation made in some other man's tank. I am confident, however, that as far as the present poem is concerned, the celebrated poets whose writings I might be suspected of having imitated, either in particular passages, or in the tone and the spirit of the whole, would be among the first to vindicate me from the charge, and who, on any striking coincidence, would permit me to address them in this doggerel version of two monkish Latin hexameters.

'Tis mine and it is likewise yours;
But an if this will not do;
Let it be mine, good friend! for I
Am the poorer of the two.

I have only to add, that the metre of the Christabel is not, properly speaking, irregular, though it may seem so from its being founded on a new principle: namely, that of counting in each line the accents, not the syllables. Though the latter may vary from seven to twelve, yet in each line the accents will be found to be only four. Nevertheless this occasional variation in number of syllables is not introduced wantonly, or for the mere ends of convenience, but in correspondence with some transition, in the nature of the imagery or passion.

PART I

'Tis the middle of night by the castle clock,
And the owls have awakened the crowing cock;
Tu – whit! – Tu – whoo!
And hark, again! the crowing cock,
How drowsily it crew.

Sir Leoline, the Baron rich,
Hath a toothless mastiff bitch;
From her kennel beneath the rock
She maketh answer to the clock,
10   Four for the quarters, and twelve for the hour;
Ever and aye, by shine and shower,
Sixteen short howls, not over loud;
Some say, she sees my lady's shroud.

Is the night chilly and dark?
The night is chilly, but not dark.
The thin gray cloud is spread on high,
It covers but not hides the sky.
The moon is behind, and at the full;
And yet she looks both small and dull.
20   The night is chill, the cloud is gray:
'Tis a month before the month of May,
And the Spring comes slowly up this way.

The lovely lady, Christabel,
Whom her father loves so well,
What makes her in the wood so late,
A furlong from the castle gate?
She had dreams all yesternight
Of her own betrothèd knight;
And she in the midnight wood will pray
30   For the weal of her lover that's far away.

She stole along, she nothing spoke,
The sighs she heaved were soft and low,
And naught was green upon the oak,
But moss and rarest misletoe:
She kneels beneath the huge oak tree,
And in silence prayeth she.

The lady sprang up suddenly,
The lovely lady, Christabel!
It moaned as near, as near can be,
But what it is, she cannot tell. –
On the other side it seems to be,
Of the huge, broad-breasted, old oak tree.

The night is chill; the forest bare;
Is it the wind that moaneth bleak?
There is not wind enough in the air
To move away the ringlet curl
From the lovely lady's cheek –
There is not wind enough to twirl
The one red leaf, the last of its clan,
That dances as often as dance it can,
Hanging so light, and hanging so high,
On the topmost twig that looks up at the sky.

Hush, beating heart of Christabel!
Jesu, Maria, shield her well!
She folded her arms beneath her cloak,
And stole to the other side of the oak.
        What sees she there?

There she sees a damsel bright,
Drest in a silken robe of white,
That shadowy in the moonlight shone:
The neck that made that white robe wan,
Her stately neck, and arms were bare;
Her blue-veined feet unsandal'd were,
And wildly glittered here and there
The gems entangled in her hair.
I guess, 'twas frightful there to see
A lady so richly clad as she –
Beautiful exceedingly!

Mary mother, save me now!
(Said Christabel) And who art thou?

The lady strange made answer meet,
And her voice was faint and sweet: –
'Have pity on my sore distress,
I scarce can speak for weariness:

Stretch forth thy hand, and have no fear!'
Said Christabel, 'How camest thou here?'
And the lady, whose voice was faint and sweet,
Did thus pursue her answer meet: –

'My sire is of a noble line,
80   And my name is Geraldine:
Five warriors seized me yestermorn,
Me, even me, a maid forlorn:
They choked my cries with force and fright,
And tied me on a palfrey white.
The palfrey was as fleet as wind,
And they rode furiously behind.
They spurred amain, their steeds were white:
And once we crossed the shade of night.
As sure as Heaven shall rescue me,
90   I have no thought what men they be;
Nor do I know how long it is
(For I have lain entranced I wis)
Since one, the tallest of the five,
Took me from the palfrey's back,
A weary woman, scarce alive.
Some muttered words his comrades spoke:
He placed me underneath this oak;
He swore they would return with haste;
Whither they went I cannot tell –
100   I thought I heard, some minutes past,
Sounds as of a castle bell.
Stretch forth thy hand' (thus ended she),
'And help a wretched maid to flee.'

Then Christabel stretched forth her hand
And comforted fair Geraldine:
'O well, bright dame! may you command
The service of Sir Leoline;
And gladly our stout chivalry
Will he send forth and friends withal
110   To guide and guard you safe and free
Home to your noble father's hall.'

She rose: and forth with steps they passed
That strove to be, and were not, fast.
Her gracious stars the lady blest,

And thus spake on sweet Christabel:
'All our household are at rest,
The hall as silent as the cell;
Sir Leoline is weak in health,
And may not well awakened be,
120   But we will move as if in stealth,
And I beseech your courtesy,
This night, to share your couch with me.'

They crossed the moat, and Christabel
Took the key that fitted well;
A little door she opened straight,
All in the middle of the gate;
The gate that was ironed within and without,
Where an army in battle array had marched out
The lady sank, belike through pain,
130   And Christabel with might and main
Lifted her up, a weary weight,
Over the threshold of the gate:
Then the lady rose again,
And moved, as she were not in pain.

So free from danger, free from fear,
They crossed the court: right glad they were.
And Christabel devoutly cried
To the Lady by her side;
'Praise we the Virgin all divine
140   Who hath rescued thee from thy distress!'
'Alas, alas!' said Geraldine,
'I cannot speak for weariness.'
So free from danger, free from fear,
They crossed the court: right glad they were.

Outside her kennel the mastiff old
Lay fast asleep, in moonshine cold.
The mastiff old did not awake,
Yet she an angry moan did make!
And what can ail the mastiff bitch?
150   Never till now she uttered yell
Beneath the eye of Christabel.
Perhaps it is the owlet's scritch:
For what can ail the mastiff bitch?

They passed the hall, that echoes still,
Pass as lightly as you will!
The brands were flat, the brands were dying,
Amid their own white ashes lying;
But when the lady passed, there came
A tongue of light, a fit of flame;
160 And Christabel saw the lady's eye,
And nothing else saw she thereby,
Save the boss of the shield of Sir Leoline tall,
Which hung in a murky old niche in the wall.
'O softly tread, said Christabel,
My father seldom sleepeth well.'

Sweet Christabel her feet doth bare,
And, jealous of the listening air,
They steal their way from stair to stair,
Now in glimmer, and now in gloom,
170 And now they pass the Baron's room,
As still as death with stifled breath!
And now have reached her chamber door;
And now doth Geraldine press down
The rushes of the chamber floor.

The moon shines dim in the open air,
And not a moonbeam enters here.
But they without its light can see
The chamber carved so curiously,
Carved with figures strange and sweet,
180 All made out of the carver's brain,
For a lady's chamber meet:
The lamp with twofold silver chain
Is fastened to an angel's feet.
The silver lamp burns dead and dim;
But Christabel the lamp will trim.
She trimmed the lamp, and made it bright,
And left it swinging to and fro,
While Geraldine, in wretched plight,
Sank down upon the floor below.

190 'O weary lady, Geraldine,
I pray you, drink this cordial wine!
It is a wine of virtuous powers;
My mother made it of wild flowers.'

'And will your mother pity me,
Who am a maiden most forlorn?'
Christabel answered – 'Woe is me!
She died the hour that I was born.
I have heard the grey-haired friar tell,
How on her death-bed she did say,
200 That she should hear the castle-bell
Strike twelve upon my wedding day.
O mother dear! that thou wert here!'
'I would,' said Geraldine, 'she were!'

But soon with altered voice, said she –
'Off, wandering mother! Peak and pine!
I have power to bid thee flee.'
Alas! what ails poor Geraldine?
Why stares she with unsettled eye?
Can she the bodiless dead espy?
210 And why with hollow voice cries she,
'Off, woman, off! this hour is mine –
Though thou her guardian spirit be,
Off, woman off! 'tis given to me.'

Then Christabel knelt by the lady's side,
And raised to heaven her eyes so blue –
'Alas!' said she, 'this ghastly ride –
Dear lady! it hath wildered you!'
The lady wiped her moist cold brow,
And faintly said, ' 'tis over now!'

220 Again the wild-flower wine she drank:
Her fair large eyes 'gan glitter bright,
And from the floor whereon she sank,
The lofty lady stood upright;
She was most beautiful to see,
Like a lady of a far countrèe.

And thus the lofty lady spake –
'All they, who live in the upper sky,
Do love you, holy Christabel!
And you love them, and for their sake

230 And for the good which me befell,
Even I in my degree will try,
Fair maiden, to requite you well.
But now unrobe yourself; for I
Must pray, ere yet in bed I lie.'

Quoth Christabel, 'so let it be!'
And as the lady bade, did she.
Her gentle limbs did she undress,
And lay down in her loveliness.

But through her brain of weal and woe
240 So many thoughts moved to and fro,
That vain it were her lids to close;
So half-way from the bed she rose,
And on her elbow did recline
To look at the lady Geraldine.

Beneath the lamp the lady bowed,
And slowly rolled her eyes around;
Then drawing in her breath aloud
Like one that shuddered, she unbound
The cincture from beneath her breast:
250 Her silken robe, and inner vest,
Dropt to her feet, and full in view,
Behold! her bosom and half her side –
A sight to dream of, not to tell!
O shield her! shield sweet Christabel!

Yet Geraldine nor speaks nor stirs;
Ah! what a stricken look was hers!
Deep from within she seems half-way
To lift some weight with sick assay,
And eyes the maid and seeks delay;
260 Then suddenly as one defied
Collects herself in scorn and pride,
And lay down by the maiden's side! –
And in her arms the maid she took,
          Ah well-a-day!
And with low voice and doleful look
These words did say:

'In the touch of this bosom there worketh a spell,
Which is lord of thy utterance, Christabel!
Thou knowest to-night, and wilt know to-morrow,
270   This mark of my shame, this seal of my sorrow;
    But vainly thou warrest,
      For this is alone in
    Thy power to declare,
      That in the dim forest
    Thou heard'st a low moaning,
And found'st a bright lady, surpassingly fair:
And didst bring her home with thee in love and in charity,
To shield her and shelter her from the damp air.'

THE CONCLUSION TO PART I

It was a lovely sight to see
280   The lady Christabel, when she
Was praying at the old oak tree.
    Amid the jagged shadows
    Of mossy leafless boughs,
    Kneeling in the moonlight,
    To make her gentle vows;
Her slender palms together prest,
Heaving sometimes on her breast;
Her face resigned to bliss or bale –
Her face, oh call it fair not pale,
290   And both blue eyes more bright than clear,
Each about to have a tear.

With open eyes (ah woe is me!)
Asleep, and dreaming fearfully,
Fearfully dreaming, yet I wis,
Dreaming that alone, which is –
O sorrow and shame! Can this be she,
The lady, who knelt at the old oak tree?
And lo! the worker of these harms,
That holds the maiden in her arms,
300   Seems to slumber still and mild,
As a mother with her child.

A star hath set, a star hath risen,
O Geraldine! since arms of thine
Have been the lovely lady's prison.
O Geraldine! one hour was thine –
Thou'st had thy will! By tairn and rill,
The night-birds all that hour were still.
But now they are jubilant anew,
From cliff and tower, tu – whoo! tu – whoo!
310   Tu – whoo! tu – whoo! from wood and fell!

And see! the lady Christabel
Gathers herself from out her trance;
Her limbs relax, her countenance
Grows sad and soft; the smooth thin lids
Close o'er her eyes; and tears she sheds –
Large tears that leave the lashes bright!
And oft the while she seems to smile
As infants at a sudden light!
Yea, she doth smile, and she doth weep,
320   Like a youthful hermitess,
Beauteous in a wilderness,
Who, praying always, prays in sleep.
And, if she move unquietly,
Perchance, 'tis but the blood so free,
Comes back and tingles in her feet.
No doubt, she hath a vision sweet.
What if her guardian spirit 'twere?
What if she knew her mother near?
But this she knows, in joys and woes,
330   That saints will aid if men will call:
For the blue sky bends over all!

PART II

'Each matin bell, the Baron saith,
Knells us back to a world of death.'
These words Sir Leoline first said,
When he rose and found his lady dead:
These words Sir Leoline will say,
Many a morn to his dying day!

And hence the custom and law began,
That still at dawn the sacristan,
340   Who duly pulls the heavy bell,
Five and forty beads must tell
Between each stroke – a warning knell,
Which not a soul can choose but hear
From Bratha Head to Wyndermere.

Saith Bracy the bard, 'So let it knell!
And let the drowsy sacristan
Still count as slowly as he can!
There is no lack of such, I ween,
As well fill up the space between.
350   In Langdale Pike and Witch's Lair,
And Dungeon-ghyll so foully rent,
With ropes of rock and bells of air
Three sinful sextons' ghosts are pent,
Who all give back, one after t'other,
The death-note to their living brother;
And oft too, by the knell offended,
Just as their one! two! three! is ended,
The devil mocks the doleful tale
With a merry peal from Borodale.'

360   The air is still! through mist and cloud
That merry peal comes ringing loud;
And Geraldine shakes off her dread,
And rises lightly from the bed;
Puts on her silken vestments white,
And tricks her hair in lovely plight,
And nothing doubting of her spell
Awakens the lady Christabel.
'Sleep you, sweet lady Christabel?
I trust that you have rested well.'

370   And Christabel awoke and spied
The same who lay down by her side –
O rather say, the same whom she
Raised up beneath the old oak tree!

Nay, fairer yet! and yet more fair!
For she belike hath drunken deep
Of all the blessedness of sleep!
And while she spake, her looks, her air
Such gentle thankfulness declare,
That (so it seemed) her girded vests
380 Grew tight beneath her heaving breasts.
'Sure I have sinned!' said Christabel,
'Now heaven be praised if all be well!'
And in low faltering tones, yet sweet,
Did she the lofty lady greet
With such perplexity of mind
As dreams too lively leave behind.

So quickly she rose, and quickly arrayed
Her maiden limbs, and having prayed
That He, who on the cross did groan,
390 Might wash away her sins unknown,
She forthwith led fair Geraldine
To meet her sire, Sir Leoline.

The lovely maid and the lady tall
Are pacing both into the hall,
And pacing on through page and groom,
Enter the Baron's presence room.

The Baron rose, and while he prest
His gentle daughter to his breast,
With cheerful wonder in his eyes
400 The lady Geraldine espies,
And gave such welcome to the same,
As might beseem so bright a dame!

But when he heard the lady's tale,
And when she told her father's name,
Why waxed Sir Leoline so pale,
Murmuring o'er the name again,
Lord Roland de Vaux of Tryermaine?

Alas! they had been friends in youth;
But whispering tongues can poison truth;
410 And constancy lives in realms above;
And life is thorny; and youth is vain;
And to be wroth with one we love,
Doth work like madness in the brain.
And thus it chanced, as I divine,
With Roland and Sir Leoline.
Each spake words of high disdain
And insult to his heart's best brother:
They parted – ne'er to meet again!
But never either found another
420 To free the hollow heart from paining –
They stood aloof, the scars remaining,
Like cliffs which had been rent asunder;
A dreary sea now flows between; –
But neither heat, nor frost, nor thunder,
Shall wholly do away, I ween,
The marks of that which once hath been.

Sir Leoline, a moment's space,
Stood gazing on the damsel's face:
And the youthful Lord of Tryermaine
430 Came back upon his heart again.

O then the Baron forgot his age,
His noble heart swelled high with rage;
He swore by the wounds in Jesu's side,
He would proclaim it far and wide
With trump and solemn heraldry,
That they who thus had wronged the dame,
Were base as spotted infamy!
'And if they dare deny the same,
My herald shall appoint a week,
440 And let the recreant traitors seek
My tourney court – that there and then
I may dislodge their reptile souls
From the bodies and forms of men!'
He spake: his eye in lightning rolls!
For the lady was ruthlessly seized; and he kenned
In the beautiful lady the child of his friend!

And now the tears were on his face,
And fondly in his arms he took
Fair Geraldine, who met the embrace,
450 Prolonging it with joyous look.
Which when she viewed, a vision fell
Upon the soul of Christabel,
The vision of fear, the touch and pain!
She shrunk and shuddered, and saw again –
(Ah, woe is me! Was it for thee,
Thou gentle maid! such sights to see?)
Again she saw that bosom old,
Again she felt that bosom cold,
And drew in her breath with a hissing sound:
460 Whereat the Knight turned wildly round,
And nothing saw, but his own sweet maid
With eyes upraised, as one that prayed.

The touch, the sight, had passed away,
And in its stead that vision blest,
Which comforted her after-rest,
While in the lady's arms she lay,
Had put a rapture in her breast,
And on her lips and o'er her eyes
Spread smiles like light!
                              With new surprise,
470 'What ails then my beloved child?'
The Baron said – His daughter mild
Made answer, 'All will yet be well!'
I ween, she had no power to tell
Aught else: so mighty was the spell.

Yet he, who saw this Geraldine,
Had deemed her sure a thing divine.
Such sorrow with such grace she blended,
As if she feared, she had offended
Sweet Christabel, that gentle maid!
480 And with such lowly tones she prayed,
She might be sent without delay
Home to her father's mansion.
                                        'Nay!
Nay, by my soul!' said Leoline.
'Ho! Bracy, the bard, the charge be thine!

Go thou, with music sweet and loud,
And take two steeds with trappings proud,
And take the youth whom thou lov'st best
To bear thy harp, and learn thy song,
And clothe you both in solemn vest,
490   And over the mountains haste along,
Lest wandering folk, that are abroad,
Detain you on the valley road.
And when he has crossed the Irthing flood,
My merry bard! he hastes, he hastes
Up Knorren Moor, through Halegarth Wood,
And reaches soon that castle good
Which stands and threatens Scotland's wastes.

'Bard Bracy! bard Bracy! your horses are fleet,
Ye must ride up the hall, your music so sweet,
500   More loud than your horses' echoing feet!
And loud and loud to Lord Roland call,
Thy daughter is safe in Langdale hall!
Thy beautiful daughter is safe and free –
Sir Leoline greets thee thus through me.
He bids thee come without delay
With all thy numerous array;
And take thy lovely daughter home:
And he will meet thee on the way
With all his numerous array
510   White with their panting palfreys' foam:
And by mine honour! I will say,
That I repent me of the day
When I spake words of fierce disdain
To Roland de Vaux of Tryermaine! –
– For since that evil hour hath flown,
Many a summer's sun hath shone;
Yet ne'er found I a friend again
Like Roland de Vaux of Tryermaine.'

The lady fell, and clasped his knees,
520   Her face upraised, her eyes o'erflowing;
And Bracy replied, with faltering voice,
His gracious hail on all bestowing! –
'Thy words, thou sire of Christabel,
Are sweeter than my harp can tell;

Yet might I gain a boon of thee,
This day my journey should not be,
So strange a dream hath come to me;
That I had vowed with music loud
To clear yon wood from thing unblest,
530   Warned by a vision in my rest!
For in my sleep I saw that dove,
That gentle bird, whom thou dost love,
And call'st by thy own daughter's name –
Sir Leoline! I saw the same
Fluttering, and uttering fearful moan,
Among the green herbs in the forest alone.
Which when I saw and when I heard,
I wonder'd what might ail the bird;
For nothing near it could I see,
540   Save the grass and green herbs underneath the old tree.

'And in my dream methought I went
To search out what might there be found;
And what the sweet bird's trouble meant,
That thus lay fluttering on the ground.
I went and peered, and could descry
No cause for her distressful cry;
But yet for her dear lady's sake
I stooped, methought, the dove to take,
When lo! I saw a bright green snake
550   Coiled around its wings and neck,
Green as the herbs on which it couched,
Close by the dove's its head it crouched;
And with the dove it heaves and stirs,
Swelling its neck as she swelled hers!
I woke; it was the midnight hour,
The clock was echoing in the tower;
But though my slumber was gone by,
This dream it would not pass away –
It seems to live upon my eye!
560   And thence I vowed this self-same day,
With music strong and saintly song
To wander through the forest bare,
Lest aught unholy loiter there.'

Thus Bracy said: the Baron, the while,
Half-listening heard him with a smile;

Then turned to Lady Geraldine,
His eyes made up of wonder and love;
And said in courtly accents fine,
'Sweet maid, Lord Roland's beauteous dove,
570   With arms more strong than harp or song,
Thy sire and I will crush the snake!'
He kissed her forehead as he spake,
And Geraldine, in maiden wise,
Casting down her large bright eyes,
With blushing cheek and courtesy fine
She turned her from Sir Leoline;
Softly gathering up her train,
That o'er her right arm fell again;
And folded her arms across her chest,
580   And couched her head upon her breast,
And looked askance at Christabel –
Jesu Maria, shield her well!

A snake's small eye blinks dull and shy,
And the lady's eyes they shrunk in her head,
Each shrunk up to a serpent's eye,
And with somewhat of malice, and more of dread,
At Christabel she looked askance! –
One moment – and the sight was fled!
But Christabel in dizzy trance
590   Stumbling on the unsteady ground
Shuddered aloud, with a hissing sound;
And Geraldine again turned round,
And like a thing, that sought relief,
Full of wonder and full of grief,
She rolled her large bright eyes divine
Wildly on Sir Leoline.

The maid, alas! her thoughts are gone,
She nothing sees – no sight but one!
The maid, devoid of guile and sin,
600   I know not how, in fearful wise
So deeply had she drunken in
That look, those shrunken serpent eyes,
That all her features were resigned
To this sole image in her mind;
And passively did imitate
That look of dull and treacherous hate!

And thus she stood, in dizzy trance,
Still picturing that look askance
With forced unconscious sympathy
610   Full before her father's view –
As far as such a look could be,
In eyes so innocent and blue!
And when the trance was o'er, the maid
Paused awhile, and inly prayed:
Then falling at the Baron's feet,
'By my mother's soul do I entreat
That thou this woman send away!'
She said: and more she could not say:
For what she knew she could not tell,
620   O'er-mastered by the mighty spell.

Why is thy cheek so wan and wild,
Sir Leoline? Thy only child
Lies at thy feet, thy joy, thy pride,
So fair, so innocent, so mild;
The same, for whom thy lady died!
O by the pangs of her dear mother
Think thou no evil of thy child!
For her, and thee, and for no other,
She prayed the moment ere she died:
630   Prayed that the babe for whom she died,
Might prove her dear lord's joy and pride!
      That prayer her deadly pangs beguiled,
              Sir Leoline!
      And wouldst thou wrong thy only child,
              Her child and thine?

Within the Baron's heart and brain
If thoughts, like these, had any share,
They only swelled his rage and pain,
And did but work confusion there.
640   His heart was cleft with pain and rage,
His cheeks they quivered, his eyes were wild,
Dishonoured thus in his old age;
Dishonoured by his only child,
And all his hospitality
To the wrong'd daughter of his friend

By more than woman's jealousy
Brought thus to a disgraceful end –
He rolled his eye with stern regard
Upon the gentle minstrel bard,
650   And said in tones abrupt, austere –
'Why, Bracy! dost thou loiter here?
I bade thee hence!' The bard obeyed;
And turning from his own sweet maid,
The aged knight, Sir Leoline,
Led forth the lady Geraldine!

THE CONCLUSION TO PART II

A little child, a limber elf,
Singing, dancing to itself,
A fairy thing with red round cheeks,
That always finds, and never seeeks,
660   Makes such a vision to the sight
As fills a father's eyes with light;
And pleasures flow in so thick and fast
Upon his heart, that he at last
Must needs express his love's excess
With words of unmeant bitterness.
Perhaps 'tis pretty to force together
Thoughts so all unlike each other;
To mutter and mock a broken charm,
To dally with wrong that does no harm.
670   Perhaps 'tis tender too and pretty
At each wild word to feel within
A sweet recoil of love and pity.
And what, if in a world of sin
(O sorrow and shame should this be true!)
Such giddiness of heart and brain
Comes seldom save from rage and pain,
So talks as it's most used to do.

Lines to W. L.
WHILE HE SANG A SONG TO PURCELL'S MUSIC

While my young cheek retains its healthful hues,
    And I have many friends who hold me dear;
      L———! methinks, I would not often hear
Such melodies as thine, lest I should lose
All memory of the wrongs and sore distress,
    For which my miserable brethren weep!
    But should uncomforted misfortunes steep
My daily bread in tears and bitterness;
And if at death's dread moment I should lie
      With no belovèd face at my bed-side,
To fix the last glance of my closing eye,
    Methinks, such strains, breathed by my angel-guide,
Would make me pass the cup of anguish by,
    Mix with the blest, nor know that I had died!

The Three Graves
A FRAGMENT OF A SEXTON'S TALE

[The Author has published the following humble fragment, encouraged by the decisive recommendation of more than one of our most celebrated living Poets. The language was intended to be dramatic; that is suited to the narrator; and the metre corresponds to the homeliness of the diction. It is therefore presented as the fragment, not of a Poem, but of a common Ballad-tale. Whether this is sufficient to justify the adoption of such a style, in any metrical composition not professedly ludicrous, the Author is himself in some doubt. At all events, it is not presented as poetry, and it is in no way connected with the Author's judgment concerning poetic diction. Its merits, if any, are exclusively psychological. The story which must be supposed to have been narrated in the first and second parts is as follows.

Edward, a young farmer, meets at the house of Ellen her bosom-friend Mary, and commences an acquaintance, which ends in a mutual attachment. With her consent, and by the advice of their common friend Ellen, he announces his hopes and intentions to Mary's mother, a widow-woman bordering on her fortieth year, and from constant health, the possession of a competent property, and from having had no other children but Mary and another daughter (the father died in their infancy), retaining for the greater part, her personal attractions and comeliness of appearance; but a woman of low education and violent temper. The answer which she at once returned to Edward's application was remarkable – 'Well, Edward! you are a handsome young fellow, and you shall have my daughter.' From this time all their wooing passed under the mother's eye; and, in fine, she became herself enamoured of her future son-in-law, and practised every art, both of endearment and of calumny, to transfer his affections from her daughter to herself. (The outlines of the Tale are positive facts, and of no very distant date, though the author has purposely altered the names and the scene of action, as well as invented the characters of the parties and the detail of the incidents.) Edward, however, though perplexed by her strange detractions from her daughter's good qualities, yet in the innocence of his own heart still mistaking her increasing fondness for motherly affection; she at length, overcome by her miserable passion, after much abuse of Mary's temper and moral tendencies, exclaimed with violent emotion – 'O Edward! indeed, indeed, she is not fit for you – she has not a heart to love you as you deserve. It is I that love you! Marry me, Edward! and I will this very day settle all my property on you.' The Lover's eyes were now opened; and thus taken by surprise, whether from the effect of the horror which he felt, acting as it were hysterically on his nervous system, or that at the first moment he lost the sense of guilt of the proposal in the feeling of its strangeness and absurdity, he flung her from him and burst into a fit of laughter. Irritated by this almost to frenzy, the woman fell on her knees, and in a loud voice that approached to a scream, she prayed for a curse both on him and on her own child. Mary happened to be in the room directly above them, heard Edward's laugh, and her mother's blasphemous prayer, and fainted away. He, hearing the fall, ran up stairs, and taking her in his arms, carried her off to Ellen's home; and after some fruitless attempts on her part toward a reconciliation with her mother, she was married to him. – And here the third part of the Tale begins.

I was not led to choose this story from any partiality to tragic, much less to monstrous events (though at the time that I composed the verses, somewhat more than twelve years ago, I was less averse to such subjects than at present), but from finding it in a striking proof of the possible effect on the imagination, from an Idea violently and suddenly impressed on it. I had been reading Bryan Edwards's account of the effect of the Oby witchcraft on the Negroes in the West Indies, and Hearne's deeply interesting anecdotes of similar workings on the imagination of the Copper Indians (those of my readers who have it in their power will be well repaid for the trouble of referring to those works for the passages alluded to) and I conceived the design of showing that instances of this kind are not peculiar to savage or barbarous tribes, and of illustrating the mode in which the mind is affected in these cases, and the progress and symptoms of the morbid action on the fancy from the beginning.

The Tale is supposed to be narrated by an old Sexton, in a country church-yard, to a traveller whose curiosity had been awakened by the appearance of three grves, close by each other, to two only of which there were gravestones. On the first of these was the name, and dates, as usual: on the second, no name, but only a date, and the words, 'The Mercy of God is infinite.']   1818

[PART III]

The grapes upon the Vicar's wall
    Were ripe as ripe could be;
And yellow leaves in sun and wind
    Were falling from the tree.

On the hedge-elms in the narrow lane
    Still swung the spikes of corn:
Dear Lord! it seems but yesterday –
    Young Edward's marriage-morn.

Up through that wood behind the church,
10   There leads from Edward's door
A mossy track, all over boughed,
    For half a mile or more.

And from their house-door by that track
    The bride and bridegroom went;
Sweet Mary, though she was not gay,
    Seemed cheerful and content.

But when they to the church-yard came,
    I've heard poor Mary say,
As soon as she stepped into the sun,
20   Her heart it died away.

And when the Vicar joined their hands,
    Her limbs did creep and freeze;
But when they prayed, she thought she saw
    Her mother on her knees.

And o'er the church-path they returned –
    I saw poor Mary's back,
Just as she stepped beneath the boughs
    Into the mossy track.

Her feet upon the mossy track
    The married maiden set:
That moment – I have heard her say –
    She wished she could forget.

The shade o'er-flushed her limbs with heat –
    Then came a chill like death:
And when the merry bells rang out,
    They seemed to stop her breath.

Beneath the foulest mother's curse
    No child could ever thrive:
A mother is a mother still,
    The holiest thing alive.

So five months passed: the mother still
    Would never heal the strife;
But Edward was a loving man,
    And Mary a fond wife.

'My sister may not visit us,
    My mother says her nay:
O Edward! you are all to me,
I wish for your sake I could be
    More lifesome and more gay.

'I'm dull and sad! indeed, indeed
    I know I have no reason!
Perhaps I am not well in health,
    And 'tis a gloomy season.'

'Twas a drizzly time – no ice, no snow!
    And on the few fine days
She stirred not out, lest she might meet
    Her mother in the ways.

But Ellen, spite of miry ways
  And weather dark and dreary,
60 Trudged every day to Edward's house,
  And made them all more cheery.

Oh! Ellen was a faithful friend,
  More dear than any sister!
As cheerful too as singing lark;
And she ne'er left them till 'twas dark,
  And then they always missed her.

And now Ash-Wednesday came – that day
  But few to church repair:
For on that day you know we read
70   The Commination prayer.

Our late old Vicar, a kind man,
  Once, Sir, he said to me,
He wished that service was clean out
  Of our good liturgy.

The mother walked into the church –
  To Ellen's seat she went:
Though Ellen always kept her church
  All church-days during Lent.

And gentle Ellen welcomed her
80   With courteous looks and mild:
Thought she 'what if her heart should melt,
  And all be reconciled!'

The day was scarcely like a day –
  The clouds were black outright:
And many a night, with half a moon,
  I've seen the church more light.

The wind was wild; against the glass
  The rain did beat and bicker;
The church-tower swinging over head,
90   You scarce could hear the Vicar!

And then and there the mother knelt,
 And audibly she cried –
'Oh! may a clinging curse consume
 This woman by my side!

O hear me, hear me, Lord in Heaven,
 Although you take my life –
O curse this woman, at whose house
 Young Edward woo'd his wife.

By night and day, in bed and bower,
100 O let her cursèd be!'
So having prayed, steady and slow,
 She rose up from her knee,
And left the church, nor e'er again
 The church-door entered she.

I saw poor Ellen kneeling still,
 So pale, I guessed not why:
When she stood up, there plainly was
 A trouble in her eye.

And when the prayers were done, we all
110 Came round and asked her why:
Giddy she seemed, and sure, there was
 A trouble in her eye.

But ere she from the church-door stepped
 She smiled and told us why:
'It was a wicked woman's curse,'
 Quoth she, 'and what care I?'

She smiled, and smiled, and passed it off
 Ere from the door she stept –
But all agree it would have been
120 Much better had she wept.

And if her heart was not at ease,
 This was her constant cry –
'It was a wicked woman's curse –
 God's good, and what care I?'

There was a hurry in her looks,
    Her struggles she redoubled:
'It was a wicked woman's curse
    And why should I be troubled?'

These tears will come – I dandled her
130   When 'twas the merest fairy –
Good creature! and she hid it all:
    She told it not to Mary.

But Mary heard the tale: her arms
    Round Ellen's neck she threw;
'O Ellen, Ellen, she cursed me,
    And now she hath cursed you!'

I saw young Edward by himself
    Stalk fast adown the lee,
He snatched a stick from every fence,
140   A twig from every tree.

He snapped them still with hand or knee,
    And then away they flew!
As if with his uneasy limbs
    He knew not what to do!

You see, good sir! that single hill?
    His farm lies underneath:
He heard it there, he heard it all,
    And only gnashed his teeth.

Now Ellen was a darling love
150   In all his joys and cares:
And Ellen's name and Mary's name
Fast-linked they both together came,
    Whene'er he said his prayers.

And in the moment of his prayers
    He loved them both alike:
Yea, both sweet names with one sweet joy
    Upon his heart did strike!

He reach'd his home, and by his looks
   They saw his inward strife:
160 And they clung round him with their arms,
   Both Ellen and his wife.

And Mary could not check her tears,
   So on his breast she bowed;
Then frenzy melted into grief,
   And Edward wept aloud.

Dear Ellen did not weep at all,
   But closelier did she cling,
And turned her face and looked as if
   She saw some frightful thing.

PART IV

170 To see a man tread over graves
   I hold it no good mark;
'Tis wicked in the sun and moon,
   And bad luck in the dark!

You see that grave? The Lord he gives,
   The Lord he takes away:
O Sir! the child of my old age
   Lies there as cold as clay.

Except that grave, you scarce see one
   That was not dug by me;
180 I'd rather dance upon 'em all
   Than tread upon these three!

'Ay, Sexton! 'tis a touching tale.'
   You, Sir! are but a lad;
This month I'm in my seventieth year,
   And still it makes me sad.

And Mary's sister told it me,
   For three good hours and more;
Though I had heard it, in the main,
   From Edward's self before.

190   Well! it passed off! the gentle Ellen
        Did well nigh dote on Mary;
     And she went oftener than before,
     And Mary loved her more and more:
        She managed all the dairy.

     To market she on market-days,
        To church on Sundays came;
     All seemed the same: all seemed so, Sir!
        But all was not the same!

     Had Ellen lost her mirth? Oh! no!
200   But she was seldom cheerful;
     And Edward looked as if he thought
        That Ellen's mirth was fearful.

     When by herself, she to herself
        Must sing some merry rhyme;
     She could not now be glad for hours,
        Yet silent all the time.

     And when she soothed her friend, through all
        Her soothing words 'twas plain
     She had a sore grief of her own,
210   A haunting in her brain.

     And oft she said, I'm not grown thin!
        And then her wrist she spanned;
     And once when Mary was down-cast,
        She took her by the hand,
     And gazed upon her, and at first
        She gently pressed her hand;

     Then harder, till her grasp at length
        Did gripe like a convulsion!
     Alas! said she, we ne'er can be
220   Made happy by compulsion!

     And once her both arms suddenly
        Round Mary's neck she flung,
     And her heart panted, and she felt
        The words upon her tongue.

She felt them coming, but no power
  Had she the words to smother;
And with a kind of shriek she cried,
  'Oh Christ! you're like your mother!'

So gentle Ellen now no more
  Could make this sad house cheery;
230 And Mary's melancholy ways
  Drove Edward wild and weary.

Lingering he raised his latch at eve,
  Though tired in heart and limb:
He loved no other place, and yet
  Home was no home to him.

One evening he took up a book,
  And nothing in it read;
Then flung it down, and groaning cried,
240 'Oh! Heaven! that I were dead.'

Mary looked up into his face,
  And nothing to him said;
She tried to smile, and on his arm
  Mournfully leaned her head.

And he burst into tears, and fell
  Upon his knees in prayer:
'Her heart is broke! O God! my grief,
  It is too great to bear!'

'Twas such a foggy time as makes
250 Old sextons, Sir! like me,
Rest on their spades to cough; the spring
  Was late uncommonly.

And then the hot days, all at once,
  They came, we knew not how:
You looked about for shade, when scarce
  A leaf was on a bough.

It happened then; 'twas in the bower
    A furlong up the wood
(Perhaps you know the place, and yet
260   I scarce know how you should):

No path leads thither, 'tis not nigh
    To any pasture-plot;
But clustered near the chattering brook,
    Lone hollies marked the spot.

Those hollies of themselves a shape
    As of an arbour took,
A close, round arbour; and it stands
    Not three strides from a brook.

Within this arbour, which was still
270   With scarlet berries hung,
Were these three friends, one Sunday morn
    Just as the first bell rung.

'Tis sweet to hear a brook, 'tis sweet
    To hear the Sabbath-bell,
'Tis sweet to hear them both at once,
    Deep in a woody dell.

His limbs along the moss, his head
    Upon a mossy heap,
With shut-up senses, Edward lay:
280   That brook e'en on a working day
    Might chatter one to sleep.

And he had passed a restless night,
    And was not well in health;
The women sat down by his side,
    And talked as 'twere by stealth.

'The sun peeps through the close thick leaves,
    See, dearest Ellen! see!
'Tis in the leaves, a little sun,
    No bigger than your ee;

290 'A tiny sun, and it has got
    A perfect glory too;
Ten thousand threads and hairs of light,
Make up a glory, gay and bright,
    Round that small orb, so blue.'

And then they argued of those rays,
    What colour they might be;
Says this, 'they're mostly green'; says that,
    'They're amber-like to me.'

So they sat chatting, while bad thoughts
300   Were troubling Edward's rest;
But soon they heard his hard quick pants,
    And the thumping in his breast.

'A mother too!' these self-same words
    Did Edward mutter plain;
His face was drawn back on itself,
    With horror and huge pain.

Both groaned at once, for both knew well
    What thoughts were in his mind;
When he waked up, and stared like one
310   That hath been just struck blind.

He sat upright; and ere the dream
    Had had time to depart,
'O God, forgive me! (he exclaimed)
    I have torn out her heart.'

Then Ellen shrieked, and forthwith burst
    Into ungentle laughter;
And Mary shivered, where she sat,
    And never she smiled after.

Carmen reliquum in futurum tempus relegatum. To-morrow! and
To-morrow! and To-morrow! –

The Wanderings of Cain
PREFATORY NOTE

A prose composition, one not in metre at least, seems prima facie to require explanation or apology. It was written in the year 1798, near Nether Stowey, in Somersetshire, at which place (sanctum et amabile nomen! rich by so many associations and recollections) the author had taken up his residence in order to enjoy the society and close neighbourhood of a dear and honoured friend, T. Poole, Esq. The work was to have been written in concert with another, whose name is too venerable within the precincts of genius to be unnecessarily brought into connection with such a trifle, and who was then residing at a small distance from Nether Stowey. The title and subject were suggested by myself, who likewise drew out the scheme and the contents for each of the three books or cantos, of which the work was to consist, and which, the reader is to be informed, was to have been finished in one night! My partner undertook the first canto: I the second: and which ever had done first, was to set about the third. Almost thirty years have passed by; yet at this moment I cannot without something more than a smile moot the question which of the two things was the more impracticable, for a mind so eminently original to compose another man's thoughts and fancies, or for a taste so austerely pure and simple to imitate the Death of Abel? Methinks I see his grand and noble countenance as at the moment when having despatched my own portion of the task at full finger-speed, I hastened to him with my manuscript – that look of humorous despondency fixed on his almost blank sheet of paper, and then its silent mock-piteous admission of failure struggling with the sense of the exceeding ridiculousness of the whole scheme – which broke up in a laugh: and the Ancient Mariner was written instead.

Years afterward, however, the draft of the plan and proposed incidents, and the portion executed, obtained favour in the eyes of more than one person, whose judgment on a poetic work could not but have weighed with me, even though no parental partiality had been thrown into the same scale, as a make-weight: and I determined on commencing anew, and composing the whole in stanzas, and made some progress in realizing this intention, when adverse gales drove my bark off the 'Fortunate Isles' of the Muses: and then other and more momentous interests prompted a different voyage, to firmer anchorage and a securer port. I have in vain tried to recover the lines from the palimpsest tablet of my memory: and I can only offer the introductory stanza, which had been committed to writing for the purpose of procuring a friend's judgment on the metre, as a specimen.

Encinctured with a twine of leaves,
That leafy twine his only dress!
A lovely Boy was plucking fruits,
By moonlight, in a wilderness.
The moon was bright, the air was free,
And fruits and flowers together grew
On many a shrub and many a tree:
And all put on a gentle hue,
Hanging in the shadowy air
Like a picture rich and rare.
It was a climate where, they say,
The night is more belov'd than day.
But who that beauteous Boy beguil'd,
That beauteous Boy to linger here?
Alone, by night, a little child,
In place so silent and so wild –
Has he no friend, no loving mother near?

CANTO II

'A little further, O my father, yet a little further, and we shall
come into the open moonlight.' Their road was through a forest
of fir-trees; at its entrance the trees stood at distances from each
other, and the path was broad, and the moonlight and the moonlight
shadows reposed upon it, and appeared quietly to inhabit that
solitude. But soon the path winded and became narrow; the sun
at high noon sometimes speckled, but never illumined it, and now
it was dark as a cavern.

'It is dark, O my father!' said Enos, 'but the path under our feet
10   is smooth and soft, and we shall soon come out into the open
moonlight.'

'Lead on, my child!' said Cain: 'guide me, little child!' And the
innocent little child clasped a finger of the hand which had mur-
dered the righteous Abel, and he guided his father. 'The fir branches
drip upon thee, my son.' 'Yea, pleasantly, father, for I ran fast and
eagerly to bring thee the pitcher and the cake, and my body is not
yet cool. How happy the squirrels are that feed on these fir-trees!
they leap from bough to bough, and the old squirrels play round
their young ones in the nest. I clomb a tree yesterday at noon, O
20   my father, that I might play with them, but they leaped away from
the branches, even to the slender twigs did they leap, and in a
moment I beheld them on another tree. Why, O my father, would
they not play with me? I would be good to them as thou art good

to me: and I groaned to them even as thou groanest when thou givest me to eat, and when thou coverest me at evening, and as often as I stand at thy knee and thine eyes look at me?' Then Cain stopped, and stifling his groans he sank to the earth, and the child Enos stood in the darkness beside him.

And Cain lifted up his voice and cried bitterly, and said, 'The Mighty One that persecuteth me is on this side and on that; he pursueth my soul like the wind, like the sand-blast he passeth through me; he is around me even as the air! O that I might be utterly no more! I desire to die – yea, the things that never had life, neither move they upon the earth – behold! they seem precious to mine eyes. O that a man might live without the breath of his nostrils. So I might abide in darkness, and blackness, and an empty space! Yea, I would lie down, I would not rise, neither would I stir my limbs till I became as the rock in the den of the lion, on which the young lion resteth his head whilst he sleepeth. For the torrent that roareth far off hath a voice: and the clouds in heaven look terribly on me; the Mighty One who is against me speaketh in the wind of the cedar grove; and in silence am I dried up.' Then Enos spake to his father, 'Arise, my father, arise, we are but a little way from the place where I found the cake and the pitcher.' And Cain said, 'How knowest thou?' and the child answered – 'Behold the bare rocks are a few of thy strides distant from the forest; and while even now thou wert lifting up thy voice, I heard the echo.' Then the child took hold of his father, as if he would raise him: and Cain being faint and feeble rose slowly on his knees and pressed himself against the trunk of a fir, and stood upright and followed the child.

The path was dark till within three strides length of its termination, when it turned suddenly; the thick black trees formed a low arch, and the moonlight appeared for a moment like a dazzling portal. Enos ran before and stood in the open air; and when Cain, his father, emerged from the darkness, the child was affrighted. For the mighty limbs of Cain were wasted as by fire; his hair was as the matted curls on the bison's forehead, and so glared his fierce and sullen eye beneath: and the black abundant locks on either side, a rank and tangled mass, were stained and scorched, as though the grasp of a burning iron hand had striven to rend them; and his countenance told in a strange and terrible language of agonies that had been, and were, and were still to continue to be.

The scene around was desolate; as far as the eye could reach it was desolate: the bare rocks faced each other, and left a long and wide interval of thin white sand. You might wander on and look

round and round, and peep into the crevices of the rocks and discover nothing that acknowledged the influence of the seasons. There was no spring, no summer, no autumn: and the winter's
70 snow, that would have been lovely, fell not on these hot rocks and scorching sands. Never morning lark had poised himself over this desert; but the huge serpent often hissed there beneath the talons of the vulture, and the vulture screamed, his wings imprisoned within the coils of the serpent. The pointed and shattered summits of the ridges of the rocks made a rude mimicry of human concerns, and seemed to prophesy mutely of things that then were not; steeples, and battlements, and ships with naked masts. As far from the wood as a boy might sling a pebble of the brook, there was one rock by itself at a small distance from the main ridge. It had been
80 precipitated there perhaps by the groan which the Earth uttered when our first father fell. Before you approached, it appeared to lie flat on the ground, but its base slanted from its point, and between its point and the sands a tall man might stand upright. It was here that Enos had found the pitcher and cake, and to this place he led his father. But ere they had reached the rock they beheld a human shape: his back was towards them, and they were advancing unperceived, when they heard him smite his breast and cry aloud, 'Woe is me! woe is me! I must never die again, and yet I am perishing with thirst and hunger.'
90 Pallid, as the reflection of the sheeted lightning on the heavy-sailing night-cloud, became the face of Cain; but the child Enos took hold of the shaggy skin, his father's robe, and raised his eyes to his father, and listening whispered, 'Ere yet I could speak, I am sure, O my father, that I heard that voice. Have not I often said that I remembered a sweet voice? O my father! this is it': and Cain trembled exceedingly. The voice was sweet indeed, but it was thin and querulous, like that of a feeble slave in misery, who despairs altogether, yet can not refrain himself from weeping and lamentation. And, behold! Enos glided forward, and creeping softly round
100 the base of the rock, stood before the stranger, and looked up into his face. And the Shape shrieked, and turned round, and Cain beheld him, that his limbs and his face were those of his brother Abel whom he had killed! And Cain stood like one who struggles in his sleep because of the exceeding terribleness of a dream.

Thus as he stood in silence and darkness of soul, the Shape fell at his feet, and embraced his knees, and cried out with a bitter outcry, 'Thou eldest born of Adam, whom Eve, my mother, brought forth, cease to torment me! I was feeding my flocks in green pastures by the side of quiet rivers, and thou killedst me; and now

110 I am in misery.' Then Cain closed his eyes, and hid them with his
hands; and again he opened his eyes, and looked around him, and
said to Enos, 'What beholdest thou? Didst thou hear a voice, my
son?' 'Yes, my father, I beheld a man in unclean garments, and he
uttered a sweet voice, full of lamentation.' Then Cain raised up
the Shape that was like Abel, and said: – 'The Creator of our
father, who had respect unto thee, and unto thy offering, wherefore
hath he forsaken thee?' Then the Shape shrieked a second time,
and rent his garment, and his naked skin was like the white sands
beneath their feet; and he shrieked yet a third time, and threw
120 himself on his face upon the sand that was black with the shadow
of the rock, and Cain and Enos sate beside him; the child by his
right hand, and Cain by his left. They were all three under the
rock, and within the shadow. The Shape that was like Abel raised
himself up, and spake to the child: 'I know where the cold waters
are, but I may not drink, wherefore didst thou then take away my
pitcher?' But Cain said, 'Didst thou not find favour in the sight
of the Lord thy God?' The Shape answered, 'The Lord is God of
the living only, the dead have another God.' Then the child Enos
lifted up his eyes and prayed; but Cain rejoiced secretly in his
130 heart. 'Wretched shall they be all the days of their mortal life,'
exclaimed the shape, 'who sacrifice worthy and acceptable sacrifices
to the God of the dead; but after death their toil ceaseth. Woe is
me, for I was well beloved by the God of the living, and cruel wert
thou, O my brother, who didst snatch me away from his power
and his dominion.' Having uttered these words, he rose suddenly,
and fled over the sands: and Cain said in his heart, 'The curse of
the Lord is on me; but who is the God of the dead? and he ran
after the Shape, and the Shape fled shrieking over the sands, and
the sands rose like white mists behind the steps of Cain, but the
140 feet of him that was like Abel disturbed not the sands. He greatly
outrun Cain, and turning short, he wheeled round, and came again
to the rock where they had been sitting, and where Enos still stood;
and the child caught hold of his garment as he passed by, and he
fell upon the ground. And Cain stopped, and beholding him not,
said, 'he has passed into the dark woods,' and he walked slowly
back to the rocks; and when he reached it the child told him that
he had caught hold of his garment as he passed by, and that the
man had fallen upon the ground: and Cain once more sate beside
him, and said, 'Abel, my brother, I would lament for thee, but that
150 the spirit within me is withered, and burnt up with extreme agony.
Now, I pray thee, by thy flocks, and by thy pastures, and by the
quiet rivers which thou lovedst, that thou tell me all that thou

knowest. Who is the God of the dead? where doth he make his
dwelling? what sacrifices are acceptable unto him? for I have offered,
but have not been received; I have prayed, and have not been
heard; and how can I be afflicted more than I already am?' The
Shape arose and answered, 'O that thou hadst had pity on me as
I will have pity on thee. Follow me, Son of Adam! and bring thy
child with thee!'

160   And they three passed over the white sands between the rocks,
silent as the shadows.

Fire, Famine, and Slaughter
A WAR ECLOGUE. WITH AN APOLOGETIC PREFACE

The Scene a desolated Tract in la Vendée. FAMINE *is discovered
lying on the ground; to her enter* FIRE *and* SLAUGHTER.

Fam. Sisters! sisters! who sent you here?
Slau. [*to Fire*]. I will whisper it in her ear.
Fire. No! no! no!
Spirits hear what spirits tell:
'Twill make a holiday in Hell.
        No! no! no!
Myself, I named him once below,
And all the souls, that damnèd be,
Leaped up at once in anarchy,
10   Clapped their hands and danced for glee.
They no longer heeded me;
But laughed to hear Hell's burning rafters
Unwillingly re-echo laughters!
        No! no! no!
Spirits hear what spirits tell:
'Twill make a holiday in Hel!
Fam. Whisper it, sister! so and so!
In a dark hint, soft and slow.
Slau. Letters four do form his name –
20   And who sent you?
    Both.   The same! the same!
Slau. He came by stealth, and unlocked my den,
And I have drunk the blood since then
Of thrice three hundred thousand men.
Both. Who bade you do it?

Slau.   The same! the same!
Letters four do form his name.
He let me loose, and cried Halloo!
To him alone the praise is due.
Fam. Thanks, sister, thanks! the men have bled,
Their wives and their children faint for bread.

30   I stood in a swampy field of battle;
With bones and skulls I made a rattle,
To frighten the wolf and carrion-crow.
And the homeless dog – but they would not go.
So off I flew: for how could I bear
To see them gorge their dainty fare?
I heard a groan and a peevish squall,
And through the chink of a cottage-wall –
Can you guess what I saw there?
Both. Whisper it, sister! in our ear.

40   *Fam.* A baby beat its dying mother:
I had starved the one and was starving the other!
Both. Who bade you do't?
Fam.   The same! the same!
Letters four do form his name.
He let me loose, and cried, Halloo!
To him alone the praise is due.
Fire. Sisters! I from Ireland came!
Hedge and corn-fields all on flame,
I triumphed o'er the setting sun!
And all the while the work was done,

50   On as I strode with my huge strides,
I flung back my head and I held my sides,
It was so rare a piece of fun
To see the sweltered cattle run
With uncouth gallop through the night,
Scared by the red and noisy light!
By the light of his own blazing cot
Was many a naked rebel shot:
The house-stream met the flame and hissed,
While crash! fell in the roof, I wist,

60   On some of those old bed-rid nurses,
That deal in discontent and curses.
Both. Who bade you do't?
Fire.   The same! the same!
Letters four do form his name.

He let me loose, and cried Halloo!
To him alone the praise is due.
All. He let us loose, and cried Halloo!
How shall we yield him honour due?
Fam. Wisdom comes with lack of food.
I'll gnaw, I'll gnaw the multitude,
70   Till the cup of rage o'erbrim:
They shall seize him and his brood –
Slau. They shall tear him limb from limb!
Fire. O thankless beldames and untrue!
And is this all that you can do
For him, who did so much for you?
Ninety months he, by my troth!
Hath richly catered for you both;
And in an hour would you repay
An eight years' work? – Away! away!
80   I alone am faithful! I
Cling to him everlastingly.

The Old Man of the Alps

Stranger! whose eyes a look of pity shew,
Say, will you listen to a tale of woe?
A tale in no unwonted horrors drest;
But sweet is pity to an agèd breast.
This voice did falter with old age before;
Sad recollections make it falter more.
Beside the torrent and beneath a wood,
High in these Alps my summer cottage stood;
One daughter still remain'd to cheer my way,
10   The evening-star of life's declining day:
Duly she hied to fill her milking-pail,
Ere shout of herdsmen rang from cliff or vale;
When she return'd, before the summer shiel,
On the fresh grass she spread the dairy meal;
Just as the snowy peaks began to lose
In glittering silver lights their rosy hues.
Singing in woods or bounding o'er the lawn,
No blither creature hail'd the early dawn;
And if I spoke of hearts by pain oppress'd,
20   When every friend is gone to them that rest;

Or of old men that leave, when they expire,
Daughters, that should have perish'd with their sire –
Leave them to toil all day through paths unknown,
And house at night behind some sheltering stone;
Impatient of the thought, with lively cheer
She broke half-closed the tasteless tale severe.
She play'd with fancies of a gayer hue,
Enamour'd of the scenes her *wishes* drew;
And oft she prattled with an eager tongue
Of promised joys that would not loiter long,
Till with her tearless eyes so bright and fair,
She seem'd to see them realis'd in air!
In fancy oft, within some sunny dell,
Where never wolf should howl or tempest yell,
She built a little home of joy and rest,
And fill'd it with the friends whom she lov'd best:
She named the inmates of her fancied cot,
And gave to each his own peculiar lot;
Which with our little herd abroad should roam,
And which should tend the dairy's toil at home.
And now the hour approach'd which should restore
Her lover from the wars, to part no more.
Her whole frame fluttered with uneasy joy;
I long'd myself to clasp the valiant boy;
And though I strove to calm *her* eager mood,
It was my own sole thought in solitude.
I told it to the Saints amid my hymns –
For O! you know not, on an old man's limbs
How thrillingly the pleasant sun-beams play,
That shine upon his daughter's wedding-day.
I hoped, that those fierce tempests, soon to rave
Unheard, unfelt, around *my* mountain grave,
Not undelightfully would break *her* rest,
While she lay pillow'd on her lover's breast;
Or join'd his pious prayer for pilgrims driven
Out to the mercy of the winds of heaven.
Yes! now the hour approach'd that should restore
Her lover from the wars to part no more.
Her thoughts were wild, her soul was in her eye,
She wept and laugh'd as if she knew not why;
And she had made a song about the wars,
And sang it to the sun and to the stars!

30

40

50

60

But while she look'd and listen'd, stood and ran,
And saw him plain in every distant man,
By treachery stabbed, on NANSY's murderous day,
A senseless corse th' expected husband lay.
A wounded man, who met us in the wood,
Heavily ask'd her where *my* cottage stood,
And told us all: she cast her eyes around
70 As if his words had been but empty sound.
Then look'd to Heav'n, like one that would deny
That such a thing *could be* beneath the sky.
Again he ask'd her if she knew my name,
And instantly an anguish wrench'd her frame,
And left her mind imperfect. No delight
Thenceforth she found in any cheerful sight,
Not ev'n in those time-haunted wells and groves,
Scenes of past joy, and birth-place of her loves.
        · If to her spirit any sound was dear,
80 'Twas the deep moan that spoke the tempest near;
Or sighs which chasms of icy vales outbreathe,
Sent from the dark, imprison'd floods beneath.
She wander'd up the crag and down the slope,
But not, as in her happy days of hope,
To seek the churning-plant of sovereign power,
That grew in clefts and bore a scarlet flower!
She roam'd, without a purpose, all alone,
Thro' high grey vales unknowing and unknown.

        Kind-hearted stranger! patiently you hear
90 A tedious tale: I thank you for that tear.
May never other tears o'ercloud your eye,
Than those which gentle Pity can supply!
Did you not mark a towering convent hang,
Where the huge rocks with sounds of torrents rang?
Ev'n yet, methinks, its spiry turrets swim
Amid yon purple gloom ascending dim!
For thither oft would my poor child repair,
To ease her soul by penitence and prayer.
I knew that peace at good men's prayers returns
100 Home to the contrite heart of him that mourns,
And check'd her not; and often there she found
A timely pallet when the evening frown'd.
And there I trusted that my child would light
On shelter and on food, one dreadful night,

When there was uproar in the element,
And she was absent. To my rest I went:
I thought her safe, yet often did I wake
And felt my very heart within me ache.
No daughter near me, at this very door,
110 Next morn I listen'd to the dying roar.
Above, below, the prowling vulture wail'd,
And down the cliffs the heavy vapour sail'd.
Up by the wide-spread waves in fury torn,
Homestalls and pines along the vale were borne.
The Dalesmen in thick crowds appear'd below
Clearing the road, o'erwhelm'd with hills of snow.
At times to the proud gust's ascending swell,
A pack of blood-hounds flung their doleful yell:
For after nights of storm, that dismal train
120 The pious convent sends, with hope humane,
To find some out-stretch'd man – perchance to save,
Or give, at least, that last good gift, a grave!
But now a gathering crowd did I survey,
That slowly up the pasture bent their way;
Nor could I doubt but that their care had found
Some pilgrim in th' unchannel'd torrent drown'd.
And down the lawn I hasten'd to implore
That they would bring the body to my door;
But soon exclaim'd a boy, who ran before,
130 'Thrown by the last night's waters from their bed,
Your daughter has been found, and she is dead!'

    The old man paused – May he who, sternly just,
Lays at his will his creatures in the dust;
Some ere the earliest buds of hope be blown,
And some, when every bloom of joy is flown;
May he the parent to his child restore
In that unchanging realm, where Love reigns evermore!

March 8th, 1798   NICIAS ERYTHRAEUS

The Apotheosis, or The Snow-Drop

I

FEAR no more, thou timid flower!
　Fear thou no more the Winter's might;
The whelming thaw; the ponderous shower;
　The silence of the freezing night!
Since LAURA murmur'd o'er thy leaves
　The potent sorceries of song,
To thee, meek flow'ret! gentler gales
　And cloudless skies belong.

II

On thee with feelings unreprov'd
10　Her eye with tearful meanings fraught,
She gaz'd till all the body mov'd
　Interpreting the spirit's thought:
Now trembled with thy trembling stem;
　And, while thou droopè'st o'er thy bed,
With imitative sympathy
　Inclin'd the drooping head.

III

She droop'd her head, she stretch'd her arm,
　She whisper'd low her witching rhymes;
FAME unrebellious heard the charm,
20　And bore thee to Pierian climes.
Fear thou no more the matin frost
　That sparkled on thy bed of snow:
For there, mid laurels ever green,
　Immortal thou shalt blow.

IV

Thy petals boast a white more soft –
　The spell hath so perfumed thee,
That careless LOVE shall deem thee oft
　A blossom from his myrtle-tree;
Then laughing at the fair deceit
30　Shall race with some Etesian wind
To seek the woven arboret,
　Where LAURA lies reclin'd!

V

For them, whom LOVE and FANCY grace,
    When human eyes are clos'd in sleep,
Them oft the spirits of the place
    Waft up that strange unpathway'd steep;
On whose vast summit, smooth and broad,
    His nest the phoenix bird conceals,
And where by cypresses o'erhung
40   A heavenly Lethe steals.

VI

A sea-like sound the branches breathe,
    Stirr'd by the breeze that loiters there;
And all, who stretch their limbs beneath,
    Forget the coil of mortal care.
Such mists along the margin rise,
    As heal the guests, who thither come;
And fit the soul to re-endure
    Its earthly martyrdom.

VII

That marge, how dear to moonlight elves!
50   *There* zephyr-trembling lilies blow,
And bend to kiss their softer selves
    That tremble in the stream below!
There, nightly borne, does LAURA lie –
    A magic slumber heaves her breast!
Her arm, white wanderer of the harp,
    Beneath her cheek is prest!

VIII

The harp, uphung by golden chains,
    Of that low wind which whispers round,
With coy reproachfulness complains
60   In snatches of reluctant sound!
The music hovers half-perceiv'd,
    And only moulds the slumberer's dreams;
Remember'd loves light up her cheek
    With youth's returning gleams.

IX

The LOVES trip round her all the night;
   And PITY hates the morning's birth,
That rudely warns the ling'ring SPRITE
   Whose plumes must waft her back to earth!
Meek PITY, that foreruns relief,
   Yet still assumes the hues of woe;
Pale promiser of rosy Spring,
   A SNOW-DROP mid the snow.

FRANCINI

Frost at Midnight

The frost performs its secret ministry,
Unhelped by any wind. The owlet's cry
Came loud – and hark, again! loud as before.
The inmates of my cottage, all at rest,
Have left me to that solitude, which suits
Abstruser musings: save that at my side
My cradled infant slumbers peacefully.
'Tis calm indeed! so calm, that it disturbs
And vexes meditation with its strange
And extreme silentness. Sea, hill, and wood,
This populous village! Sea, and hill, and wood,
With all the numberless goings on of life,
Inaudible as dreams! the thin blue flame
Lies on my low burnt fire, and quivers not;
Only that film, which fluttered on the grate,
Still flutters there, the sole unquiet thing.
Methinks, its motion in this hush of nature
Gives it dim sympathies with me who live,
Making it a companionable form,
Whose puny flaps and freaks the idling Spirit
By its own moods interprets, every where
Echo or mirror seeking of itself,
And makes a toy of Thought.

But O! how oft,
How oft, at school, with most believing mind,
Presageful, have I gazed upon the bars,
To watch that fluttering stranger! and as oft
With unclosed lids, already had I dreamt
Of my sweet birth-place, and the old church-tower,
Whose bells, the poor man's only music, rang
30   From morn to evening, all the hot Fair-day,
So sweetly, that they stirred and haunted me
With a wild pleasure, falling on mine ear
Most like articulate sounds of things to come!
So gazed I, till the soothing things I dreamt
Lulled me to sleep, and sleep prolonged my dreams!
And so I brooded all the following morn,
Awed by the stern preceptor's face, mine eye
Fixed with mock study on my swimming book:
Save if the door half opened, and I snatched
40   A hasty glance, and still my heart leaped up,
For still I hoped to see the stranger's face,
Townsman, or aunt, or sister more beloved,
My play-mate when we both were clothed alike!

Dear Babe, that sleepest cradled by my side,
Whose gentle breathings, heard in this deep calm,
Fill up the interspersèd vacancies
And momentary pauses of the thought!
My babe so beautiful! it thrills my heart
With tender gladness, thus to look at thee,
50   And think that thou shalt learn far other lore
And in far other scenes! For I was reared
In the great city, pent 'mid cloisters dim,
And saw nought lovely but the sky and stars.
But thou, my babe! shalt wander like a breeze
By lakes and sandy shores, beneath the crags
Of ancient mountain, and beneath the clouds,
Which image in their bulk both lakes and shores
And mountain crags: so shalt thou see and hear
The lovely shapes and sounds intelligible
60   Of that eternal language, which thy God
Utters, who from eternity doth teach
Himself in all, and all things in himself.
Great universal Teacher! he shall mould
Thy spirit, and by giving make it ask.

Therefore all seasons shall be sweet to thee,
Whether the summer clothe the general earth
With greenness, or the redbreast sit and sing
Betwixt the tufts of snow on the bare branch
Of mossy apple-tree, while the nigh thatch
70 Smokes in the sun-thaw; whether the eve-drops fall
Heard only in the trances of the blast,
Or if the secret ministry of frost
Shall hang them up in silent icicles,
Quietly shining to the quiet Moon.

France. An Ode

I

Ye Clouds! that far above me float and pause,
    Whose pathless march no mortal may control!
    Ye Ocean-Waves! that, wheresoe'er ye roll,
Yield homage only to eternal laws!
Ye Woods! that listen to the night-birds singing,
    Midway the smooth and perilous slope reclined,
Save when your own imperious branches swinging,
    Have made a solemn music of the wind!
Where, like a man beloved of God,
10 Through glooms, which never woodman trod,
        How oft, pursuing fancies holy,
My moonlight way o'er flowering weeds I wound,
    Inspired, beyond the guess of folly,
By each rude shape and wild unconquerable sound!
O ye loud Waves! and O ye Forests high!
    And O ye Clouds that far above me soared!
Thou rising Sun! thou blue rejoicing Sky!
    Yea, every thing that is and will be free!
    Bear witness for me, wheresoe'er ye be,
20   With what deep worship I have still adored
        The spirit of divinest Liberty.

II

When France in wrath her giant-limbs upreared,
    And with that oath, which smote air, earth and sea,
    Stamped her strong foot and said she would be free,
Bear witness for me, how I hoped and feared!

With what a joy my lofty gratulation
   Unawed I sang, amid a slavish band:
And when to whelm the disenchanted nation,
   Like fiends embattled by a wizard's wand,
30   The Monarchs marched in evil day,
      And Britain joined the dire array;
   Though dear her shores and circling ocean,
Though many friendships, many youthful loves
   Had swol'n the patriot emotion
And flung a magic light o'er her hills and groves;
Yet still my voice, unaltered, sang defeat
   To all that braved the tyrant-quelling lance,
And shame too long delayed and vain retreat!
For ne'er, O Liberty! with partial aim
40 I dimmed thy light or damped thy holy flame;
   But blessed the pæans of delivered France,
And hung my head and wept at Britain's name.

III

'And what,' I said, 'though Blasphemy's loud scream
   With that sweet music of deliverance strove!
   Though all the fierce and drunken passions wove
A dance more wild than e'er was maniac's dream!
   Ye storms, that round the dawning east assembled,
The Sun was rising, though ye hid his light!'
   And when, to sooth my soul, that hoped and trembled,
50 The dissonance ceased, and all seemed calm and bright;
   When France her front deep-scarr'd and gory
   Concealed with clustering wreaths of glory;
     When, insupportably advancing,
   Her arm made mockery of the warrior's ramp;
     While timid looks of fury glancing,
   Domestic treason, crushed beneath her fatal stamp,
Writhed like a wounded dragon in his gore;
   Then I reproached my fears that would not flee;
'And soon,' I said, 'shall Wisdom teach her lore
60 In the low huts of them that toil and groan!
And, conquering by her happiness alone,
   Shall France compel the nations to be free,
Till Love and Joy look round, and call the Earth their own.'

IV

Forgive me, Freedom! O forgive those dreams!
   I hear thy voice, I hear thy loud lament,
   From bleak Helvetia's icy cavern sent –
I hear thy groans upon her blood-stained streams!
   Heroes, that for your peaceful country perished,
And ye that, fleeing, spot your mountain-snows
70   With bleeding wounds; forgive me, that I cherished
One thought that ever blessed your cruel foes!
   To scatter rage, and traitorous guilt,
   Where Peace her jealous home had built;
     A patriot-race to disinherit
Of all that made their stormy wilds so dear;
     And with inexpiable spirit
To taint the bloodless freedom of the mountaineer –
O France, that mockest Heaven, adulterous, blind,
   And patriot only in pernicious toils,
80   Are these thy boasts, Champion of human kind?
   To mix with Kings in the low lust of sway,
   Yell in the hunt, and share the murderous prey;
To insult the shrine of Liberty with spoils
   From freemen torn; to tempt and to betray?

V

   The Sensual and the Dark rebel in vain,
Slaves by their own compulsion! In mad game
They burst their manacles and wear the name
   Of Freedom, graven on a heavier chain!
O Liberty! with profitless endeavour
90 Have I pursued thee, many a weary hour;
   But thou nor swell'st the victor's strain, nor ever
Didst breathe thy soul in forms of human power.
   Alike from all, howe'er they praise thee,
   (Nor prayer, nor boastful name delays thee)
     Alike from Priestcraft's harpy minions,
And factious Blasphemy's obscener slaves,
     Thou speedest on thy subtle pinions,
The guide of homeless winds, and playmate of the waves!
And there I felt thee! – on that sea-cliff's verge,
100 Whose pines, scarce travelled by the breeze above,
Had made one murmur with the distant surge!

Yes, while I stood and gazed, my temples bare,
And shot my being through earth, sea and air,
   Possessing all things with intensest love,
     O Liberty! my spirit felt thee there.

Lewti,
OR THE CIRCASSIAN LOVE-CHAUNT

At midnight by the stream I roved,
To forget the form I loved.
Image of Lewti! from my mind
Depart; for Lewti is not kind.

The Moon was high, the moonlight gleam
   And the shadow of a star
Heaved upon Tamaha's stream;
   But the rock shone brighter far,
The rock half sheltered from my view
By pendent boughs of tressy yew –
So shines my Lewti's forehead fair,
Gleaming through her sable hair.
Image of Lewti! from my mind
Depart; for Lewti is not kind.

I saw a cloud of palest hue,
   Onward to the moon it passed;
Still brighter and more bright it grew,
With floating colours not a few,
   Till it reached the moon at last:
Then the cloud was wholly bright,
With a rich and amber light!
And so with many a hope I seek,
   And with such joy I find my Lewti;
And even so my pale wan cheek
   Drinks in as deep a flush of beauty!
Nay, treacherous image! leave my mind,
If Lewti never will be kind.

The little cloud – it floats away,
   Away it goes; away so soon?
Alas! it has no power to stay:
Its hues are dim, its hues are grey –

Away it passes from the moon!
How mournfully it seems to fly,
  Ever fading more and more,
To joyless regions of the sky –
  And now 'tis whiter than before!
As white as my poor cheek will be,
  When, Lewti! on my couch I lie,
A dying man for love of thee.
Nay, treacherous image! leave my mind –
And yet, thou did'st not look unkind.

I saw a vapour in the sky,
  Thin, and white, and very high;
I ne'er beheld so thin a cloud:
  Perhaps the breezes that can fly
  Now below and now above,
Have snatched aloft the lawny shroud
  Of Lady fair – that died for love.
For maids, as well as youths, have perished
From fruitless love too fondly cherished.
Nay, treacherous image! leave my mind –
For Lewti never will be kind.

Hush! my heedless feet from under
  Slip the crumbling banks for ever:
Like echoes to a distant thunder,
  They plunge into the gentle river.
The river-swans have heard my tread,
And startle from their reedy bed.
O beauteous birds! methinks ye measure
  Your movements to some heavenly tune!
O beauteous birds! 'tis such a pleasure
  To see you move beneath the moon,
I would it were your true delight
To sleep by day and wake all night.
I know the place where Lewti lies,
When silent night has closed her eyes:
  It is a breezy jasmine-bower,
The nightingale sings o'er her head:
  Voice of the night! had I the power
That leafy labyrinth to thread,
And creep, like thee, with soundless tread,

I then might view her bosom white
Heaving lovely to my sight,
As these two swans together heave
On the gently swelling wave.

Oh! that she saw me in a dream,
    And dreamt that I had died for care;
All pale and wasted I would seem,
    Yet fair withal, as spirits are!
80 I'd die indeed, if I might see
Her bosom heave, and heave for me!
Soothe, gentle image! soothe my mind!
To-morrow Lewti may be kind.

1795

To a Young Lady
ON HER RECOVERY FROM A FEVER

Why need I say, Louisa dear!
How glad I am to see you here,
    A lovely convalescent;
Risen from the bed of pain and fear,
    And feverish heat incessant.

The sunny showers, the dappled sky
The little birds that warble high,
    Their vernal loves commencing,
Will better welcome you than I
10   With their sweet influencing.

Believe me, while in bed you lay,
Your danger taught us all to pray:
    You made us grow devouter!
Each eye looked up and seemed to say,
    How can we do without her?

Besides, what vexed us worse, we knew,
They have no need of such as you
    In the place where you were going:
This World has angels all too few,
20   And Heaven is overflowing!

Fears in Solitude
WRITTEN IN APRIL, 1798, DURING THE ALARM OF AN
INVASION

A green and silent spot, amid the hills,
A small and silent dell! O'er stiller place
No singing sky-lark ever poised himself.
The hills are heathy, save that swelling slope,
Which hath a gay and gorgeous covering on,
All golden with the never-bloomless furze,
Which now blooms most profusely: but the dell,
Bathed by the mist, is fresh and delicate
As vernal corn-field, or the unripe flax,
When, through its half-transparent stalks, at eve,
The level sunshine glimmers with green light.
Oh! 'tis a quiet spirit-healing nook!
Which all, methinks, would love; but chiefly he,
The humble man, who, in his youthful years,
Knew just so much of folly, as had made
His early manhood more securely wise!
Here he might lie on fern or withered heath,
While from the singing-lark (that sings unseen
The minstrelsy that solitude loves best),
And from the sun, and from the breezy air,
Sweet influences trembled o'er his frame;
And he, with many feelings, many thoughts,
Made up a meditative joy, and found
Religious meanings in the forms of nature!
And so, his senses gradually wrapt
In a half sleep, he dreams of better worlds,
And dreaming hears thee still, O singing-lark;
That singest like an angel in the clouds!

My God! it is a melancholy thing
For such a man, who would full fain preserve
His soul in calmness, yet perforce must feel
For all his human brethren – O my God!
It weighs upon the heart, that he must think
What uproar and what strife may now be stirring
This way or that way o'er these silent hills –
Invasion, and the thunder and the shout,
And all the crash of onset; fear and rage,

And undetermined conflict – even now,
Even now, perchance, and in his native isle:
40   Carnage and groans beneath this blessed sun!
We have offended, Oh! my countrymen!
We have offended very grievously,
And been most tyrannous. From east to west
A groan of accusation pierces Heaven!
The wretched plead against us; multitudes
Countless and vehement, the sons of God,
Our brethren! Like a cloud that travels on,
Steamed up from Cairo's swamps of pestilence,
Even so, my countrymen! have we gone forth
50   And borne to distant tribes slavery and pangs,
And, deadlier far, our vices, whose deep taint
With slow perdition murders the whole man,
His body and his soul! Meanwhile, at home,
All individual dignity and power
Engulfed in courts, committees, institutions,
Associations and societies,
A vain, speech-mouthing, speech-reporting guild,
One benefit-club for mutual flattery,
We have drunk up, demure as at a grace,
60   Pollutions from the brimming cup of wealth;
Contemptuous of all honourable rule,
Yet bartering freedom and the poor man's life
For gold, as at a market! The sweet words
Of Christian promise, words that even yet
Might stem destruction, were they wisely preached,
Are muttered o'er by men, whose tones proclaim
How flat and wearisome they feel their trade:
Rank scoffers some, but most too indolent
To deem them falsehoods or to know their truth.
70   Oh! blasphemous! the book of life is made
A superstitious instrument, on which
We gabble o'er the oaths we mean to break;
For all must swear – all and in every place,
College and wharf, council and justice-court;
All, all must swear, the briber and the bribed,
Merchant and lawyer, senator and priest,
The rich, the poor, the old man and the young;
All, all make up one scheme of perjury,
That faith doth reel; the very name of God
80   Sounds like a juggler's charm; and, bold with joy,

Forth from his dark and lonely hiding-place,
(Portentous sight!) the owlet Atheism,
Sailing on obscene wings athwart the noon,
Drops his blue-fringed lids, and holds them close,
And hooting at the glorious sun in Heaven,
Cries out, 'Where is it?'

                Thankless too for peace
(Peace long preserved by fleets and perilous seas),
Secure from actual warfare, we have loved
To swell the war-whoop, passionate for war!
90   Alas! for ages ignorant of all
Its ghastlier workings (famine or blue plague,
Battle, or siege, or flight through wintry-snows),
We, this whole people, have been clamorous
For war and bloodshed; animating sports,
The which we pay for as a thing to talk of,
Spectators and not combatants! No guess
Anticipative of a wrong unfelt,
No speculation on contingency,
However dim and vague, too vague and dim
100   To yield a justifying cause; and forth
(Stuffed out with big preamble, holy names,
And adjurations of the God in Heaven),
We send our mandates for the certain death
Of thousands and ten thousands! Boys and girls,
And women, that would groan to see a child
Pull off an insect's leg, all read of war,
The best amusement for our morning-meal!
The poor wretch, who has learnt his only prayers
From curses, who knows scarcely words enough
110   To ask a blessing from his Heavenly Father,
Becomes a fluent phraseman, absolute
And technical in victories and defeats,
And all our dainty terms for fratricide;
Terms which we trundle smoothly o'er our tongues
Like mere abstractions, empty sounds to which
We join no feeling and attach no form!
As if the soldier died without a wound;
As if the fibres of this godlike frame
Were gored without a pang; as if the wretch,
120   Who fell in battle, doing bloody deeds,
Passed off to Heaven, translated and not killed;

As though he had no wife to pine for him,
No God to judge him! Therefore, evil days
Are coming on us, O my countrymen!
And what if all-avenging Providence,
Strong and retributive, should make us know
The meaning of our words, force us to feel
The desolation and the agony
Of our fierce doings!

          Spare us yet awhile,
130 Father and God! O! spare us yet awhile!
Oh! let not English women drag their flight
Fainting beneath the burthen of their babes,
Of the sweet infants, that but yesterday
Laughed at the breast! Sons, brothers, husbands, all
Who ever gazed with fondness on the forms
Which grew up with you round the same fire-side,
And all who ever heard the sabbath-bells
Without the infidel's scorn, make yourselves pure!
Stand forth! be men! repel an impious foe,
140 Impious and false, a light yet cruel race,
Who laugh away all virtue, mingling mirth
With deeds of murder; and still promising
Freedom, themselves too sensual to be free,
Poison life's amities, and cheat the heart
Of faith and quiet hope, and all that soothes
And all that lifts the spirit! Stand we forth;
Render them back upon the insulted ocean,
And let them toss as idly on its waves
As the vile sea-weed, which some mountain-blast
150 Swept from our shores! And oh! may we return
Not with a drunken triumph, but with fear,
Repenting of the wrongs with which we stung
So fierce a foe to frenzy!

          I have told
O Britons! O my brethren! I have told
Most bitter truth, but without bitterness.
Nor deem my zeal or factious or mis-timed;
For never can true courage dwell with them,
Who, playing tricks with conscience, dare not look
At their own vices. We have been too long
160 Dupes of a deep delusion! Some, belike,

Groaning with restless enmity, expect
All change from change of constituted power;
As if a Government had been a robe,
On which our vice and wretchedness were tagged
Like fancy-points and fringes, with the robe
Pulled off at pleasure. Fondly these attach
A radical causation to a few
Poor drudges of chastising Providence,
Who borrow all their hues and qualities
170 From our own folly and rank wickedness,
Which gave them birth and nursed them. Others, meanwhile,
Dote with a mad idolatry; and all
Who will not fall before their images,
And yield them worship, they are enemies
Even of their country!

              Such have I been deemed –
But, O dear Britain! O my Mother Isle!
Needs must thou prove a name most dear and holy
To me, a son, a brother, and a friend,
A husband, and a father! who revere
180 All bonds of natural love, and find them all
Within the limits of thy rocky shores.
O native Britain! O my Mother Isle!
How shouldst thou prove aught else but dear and holy
To me, who from thy lakes and mountain-hills,
Thy clouds, thy quiet dales, thy rocks and seas,
Have drunk in all my intellectual life,
All sweet sensations, all ennobling thoughts,
All adoration of the God in nature,
All lovely and all honourable things,
190 Whatever makes this mortal spirit feel
The joy and greatness of its future being?
There lives nor form nor feeling in my soul
Unborrowed from my country. O divine
And beauteous island! thou hast been my sole
And most magnificant temple, in the which
I walk with awe, and sing my stately songs,
Loving the God that made me!

              May my fears,
My filial fears, be vain! and may the vaunts
And menace of the vengeful enemy

200   Pass like the gust, that roared and died away
       In the distant tree: which heard, and only heard
       In this low dell, bowed not the delicate grass.

       But now the gentle dew-fall sends abroad
       The fruit-like perfume of the golden furze:
       The light has left the summit of the hill,
       Though still a sunny gleam lies beautiful,
       Aslant the ivied beacon. Now farewell,
       Farewell, awhile, O soft and silent spot!
       On the green sheep-track, up the heathy hill,
210   Homeward I wind my way; and lo! recalled
       From bodings that have well nigh wearied me,
       I find myself upon the brow, and pause
       Startled! And after lonely sojourning
       In such a quiet and surrounded nook,
       This burst of prospect, here the shadowy main,
       Dim tinted, there the mighty majesty
       Of that huge amphitheatre of rich
       And elmy fields, seems like society –
       Conversing with the mind, and giving it
220   A livelier impulse and a dance of thought!
       And now, beloved Stowey! I behold
       Thy church-tower, and, methinks, the four huge elms
       Clustering, which mark the mansion of my friend;
       And close behind them, hidden from my view,
       Is my own lowly cottage, where my babe
       And my babe's mother dwell in peace! With light
       And quickened footsteps thitherward I tend,
       Remembering thee, O green and silent dell!
       And grateful, that by nature's quietness
230   And solitary musings, all my heart
       Is softened, and made worthy to indulge
       Love, and the thoughts that yearn for human kind.

The Nightingale
A CONVERSATION POEM. APRIL, 1798

No cloud, no relique of the sunken day
Distinguishes the West, no long thin slip
Of sullen light, no obscure trembling hues.

Come, we will rest on this old mossy bridge!
You see the glimmer of the stream beneath,
But hear no murmuring: it flows silently,
O'er its soft bed of verdure. All is still,
A balmy night! and though the stars be dim,
Yet let us think upon the vernal showers
That gladden the green earth, and we shall find
A pleasure in the dimness of the stars.
And hark! the Nightingale begins its song,
'Most musical, most melancholy' bird!
A melancholy bird! Oh! idle thought!
In nature there is nothing melancholy.
But some night-wandering man whose heart was pierced
With the remembrance of a grievous wrong,
Or slow distemper, or neglected love,
(And so, poor wretch! filled all things with himself,
And made all gentle sounds tell back the tale
Of his own sorrow) he, and such as he,
First named these notes a melancholy strain.
And many a poet echoes the conceit;
Poet who hath been building up the rhyme
When he had better far have stretched his limbs
Beside a brook in mossy forest-dell,
By sun or moon-light, to the influxes
Of shapes and sounds and shifting elements
Surrendering his whole spirit, of his song
And of his fame forgetful! so his fame
Should share in Nature's immortality,
A venerable thing! and so his song
Should make all Nature lovelier, and itself
Be loved like Nature! But 'twill not be so;
And youths and maidens most poetical,
Who lose the deepening twilights of the spring
In ball-rooms and hot theatres, they still
Full of meek sympathy must heave their sighs
O'er Philomela's pity-pleading strains.

My Friend, and thou, our Sister! we have learnt
A different lore: we may not thus profane
Nature's sweet voices, always full of love
And joyance! 'Tis the merry Nightingale
That crowds, and hurries, and precipitates
With fast thick warble his delicious notes,

As he were fearful that an April night
Would be too short for him to utter forth
His love-chant, and disburthen his full soul
Of all its music!

              And I know a grove
50 Of large extent, hard by a castle huge,
Which the great lord inhabits not; and so
This grove is wild with tangling underwood,
And the trim walks are broken up, and grass,
Thin grass and king-cups grow within the paths.
But never elsewhere in one place I knew
So many nightingales; and far and near,
In wood and thicket, over the wide grove,
They answer and provoke each other's song,
With skirmish and capricious passagings,
60 And murmurs musical and swift jug jug,
And one low piping sound more sweet than all –
Stirring the air with such a harmony,
That should you close your eyes, you might almost
Forget it was not day! On moon-lit bushes,
Whose dewy leaflets are but half disclosed,
You may perchance behold them on the twigs,
Their bright, bright eyes, their eyes both bright and full,
Glistening, while many a glow-worm in the shade
Lights up her love-torch.

              A most gentle Maid,
70 Who dwelleth in her hospitable home
Hard by the castle, and at latest eve
(Even like a Lady vowed and dedicate
To something more than Nature in the grove)
Glides through the pathways; she knows all their notes,
That gentle Maid! and oft a moment's space,
What time the moon was lost behind a cloud,
Hath heard a pause of silence; till the moon
Emerging, hath awakened earth and sky
With one sensation, and these wakeful birds
80 Have all burst forth in choral minstrelsy,
As if some sudden gale had swept at once
A hundred airy harps! And she hath watched
Many a nightingale perched giddily

On blossomy twig still swinging from the breeze,
And to that motion tune his wanton song
Like tipsy joy that reels with tossing head.

Farewell, O Warbler! till to-morrow eve,
And you, my friends! farewell, a short farewell!
We have been loitering long and pleasantly,
90   And now for our dear homes. – That strain again!
Full fain it would delay me! My dear babe,
Who, capable of no articulate sound,
Mars all things with his imitative lisp,
How he would place his hand beside his ear,
His little hand, the small forefinger up,
And bid us listen! And I deem it wise
To make him Nature's play-mate. He knows well
The evening-star; and once, when he awoke
In most distressful mood (some inward pain
100   Had made up that strange thing, an infant's dream –)
I hurried with him to our orchard-plot,
And he beheld the moon, and, hushed at once,
Suspends his sobs, and laughs most silently,
While his fair eyes, that swam with undropped tears,
Did glitter in the yellow moon-beam! Well! –
It is a father's tale: But if that Heaven
Should give me life, his childhood shall grow up
Familiar with these songs, that with the night
He may associate joy. – Once more, farewell,
110   Sweet Nightingale! Once more, my friends! farewell.

The Ballad of the Dark Ladie
A FRAGMENT

Beneath yon birch with silver bark,
And boughs so pendulous and fair,
The brook falls scatter'd down the rock:
        And all is mossy there!

And there upon the moss she sits,
The Dark Ladie in silent pain;
The heavy tear is in her eye,
        And drops and swells again.

Three times she sends her little page
10   Up the castled mountain's breast,
If he might find the Knight that wears
      The Griffin for his crest.

The sun was sloping down the sky,
And she had lingered there all day,
Counting moments, dreaming fears –
      O wherefore can he stay?

She hears a rustling o'er the brook,
She sees far off a swinging bough!
' 'Tis He! 'Tis my betrothèd Knight!
20   Lord Falkland, it is Thou!'

She springs, she clasps him round the neck,
She sobs a thousand hopes and fears,
Her kisses glowing on his cheeks
      She quenches with her tears.

* * *

'My friends with rude ungentle words
They scoff and bid me fly to thee!
O give me shelter in thy breast!
      O shield and shelter me!

'My Henry, I have given thee much,
30   I gave what I can ne'er recall,
I gave my heart, I gave my peace,
      O Heaven! I gave thee all.'

The Knight made answer to the Maid,
While to his heart he held her hand,
'Nine castles hath my noble sire,
      None statelier in the land.

'The fairest one shall be my love's,
The fairest castle of the nine!
Wait only till the stars peep out,
40   The fairest shall be thine:

'Wait only till the hand of eve
Hath wholly closed yon western bars,
And through the dark we two will steal
    Beneath the twinkling stars!' –

'The dark? the dark? No! not the dark?
The twinkling stars? How, Henry? How?
O God! 'twas in the eye of noon
    He pledged his sacred vow!

'And in the eye of noon, my love,
50   Shall lead me from my mother's door,
Sweet boys and girls all clothed in white
    Strewing flow'rs before:

'But first the nodding minstrels go
With music meet for lordly bow'rs,
The children next in snow-white vests,
    Strewing buds and flow'rs!

'And then my love and I shall pace,
My jet black hair in pearly braids,
Between our comely bachelors
60   And blushing bridal maids.'

      *   *   *

Kubla Khan: Or, A Vision in a Dream
A FRAGMENT

In the summer of the year 1797, the Author, then in ill health, had retired
to a lonely farm house between Porlock and Linton, on the Exmoor confines
of Somerset and Devonshire. In consequence of a slight indisposition, an
anodyne had been prescribed, from the effect of which he fell asleep in
his chair at the moment that he was reading the following sentence, or
words of the same substance, in 'Purchas's Pilgrimage:' 'Here the Khan
Kubla commanded a palace to be built, and a stately garden thereunto:
and thus ten miles of fertile ground were inclosed with a wall.' The Author
continued for about three hours in a profound sleep, at least of the external
senses, during which time he has the most vivid confidence, that he could
not have composed less than from two to three hundred lines; if that indeed

can be called composition in which all the images rose up before him as things, with a parallel production of the correspondent expressions, without any sensation or consciousness of effort. On awaking he appeared to himself to have a distinct recollection of the whole, and taking his pen, ink, and paper, instantly and eagerly wrote down the lines that are here preserved. At this moment he was unfortunately called out by a person on business from Porlock, and detained by him above an hour, and on his return to his room, found, to his no small surprise and mortification, that though he still retained some vague and dim recollection of the general purport of the vision, yet, with the exception of some eight or ten scattered lines and images, all the rest had passed away like the images on the surface of a stream into which a stone had been cast, but, alas! without the after restoration of the latter:

> Then all the charm
> Is broken – all that phantom-world so fair
> Vanishes, and a thousand circlets spread,
> And each mis-shape the other. Stay awhile,
> Poor youth! who scarcely dar'st lift up thine eyes –
> The stream will soon renew its smoothness, soon
> The visions will return! And lo! he stays,
> And soon the fragments dim of lovely forms
> Come trembling back, unite, and now once more
> The pool becomes a mirror.

Yet from the still surviving recollections in his mind, the Author has frequently purposed to finish for himself what had been originally, as it were, given to him. Αὔριον ἅδιον ἄσω: but the to-morrow is yet to come.

As a contrast to this vision, I have annexed a fragment of a very different character, describing with equal fidelity the dream of pain and disease.

– 1816

Kubla Khan

In Xanadu did Kubla Khan
A stately pleasure-dome decree:
Where Alph, the sacred river, ran
Through caverns measureless to man
    Down to a sunless sea.
So twice five miles of fertile ground
With walls and towers were girdled round:

And there were gardens bright with sinuous rills
Where blossomed many an incense-bearing tree;
10   And here were forests ancient as the hills,
Enfolding sunny spots of greenery.

But oh! that deep romantic chasm which slanted
Down the green hill athwart a cedarn cover!
A savage place! as holy and enchanted
As e'er beneath a waning moon was haunted
By woman wailing for her demon-lover!
And from this chasm, with ceaseless turmoil seething,
As if this earth in fast thick pants were breathing,
A mighty fountain momently was forced:
20   Amid whose swift half-intermitted burst
Huge fragments vaulted like rebounding hail,
Or chaffy grain beneath the thresher's flail:
And mid these dancing rocks at once and ever
It flung up momently the sacred river.
Five miles meandering with a mazy motion
Through wood and dale the sacred river ran,
Then reached the caverns measureless to man,
And sank in tumult to a lifeless ocean:
And 'mid this tumult Kubla heard from far
30   Ancestral voices prophesying war!

The shadow of the dome of pleasure
Floated midway on the waves;
Where was heard the mingled measure
From the fountain and the caves.
It was a miracle of rare device,
A sunny pleasure-dome with caves of ice!

A damsel with a dulcimer
In a vision once I saw:
It was an Abyssinian maid,
40   And on her dulcimer she played,
Singing of Mount Abora.
Could I revive within me
Her symphony and song,
To such a deep delight 'twould win me
That with music loud and long,
I would build that dome in air,
That sunny dome! those caves of ice!

And all who heard should see them there,
And all should cry, Beware! Beware!
His flashing eyes, his floating hair!
Weave a circle round him thrice,
And close your eyes with holy dread,
For he on honey-dew hath fed,
And drunk the milk of Paradise.

[Lines from a notebook – September 1798]

The silence of a City – How awful at midnight –
Mute as the battlements & crags & towers
That fancy makes in the clouds – yea as mute
As the moonlight that sleeps on the steady Vanes –
The cell of a departed Anchoret,
His skeleton & flitting ghost are there,
Sole tenants –
And all the City, silent as the moon
That steeps in quiet light the steady Vanes
Of her huge temples –

[Hexameters:] William, My Teacher, My Friend!

William, my teacher, my friend! dear William and dear
    Dorothea!
Smooth out the folds of my letter, and place it on desk or on
    table;
Place it on table or desk; and your right hands loosely
    half-closing,
Gently sustain them in air, and extending the digit didactic,
Rest it a moment on each of the forks of the five-forkèd left
    hand,
Twice on the breadth of the thumb, and once on the tip of each
    finger;
Read with a nod of the head in a humouring recitativo;
And, as I live, you will see my hexameters hopping before you.
This is a galloping measure; a hop, and a trot, and a gallop!

All my hexameters fly, like stags pursued by the stag-hounds,
Breathless and panting, and ready to drop, yet flying still
    onwards.

I would full fain pull in my hard-mouthed runaway hunter;
But our English Spondeans are clumsy yet impotent curb-reins;
And so to make him go slowly, no way have I left but to lame
    him.

William, my head and my heart! dear Poet that feelest and
    thinkest!
Dorothy, eager of soul, my most affectionate sister!
Many a mile, O! many a wearisome mile are ye distant,
Long, long, comfortless roads, with no one eye that doth know
    us.
O! it is all too far to send to you mockeries idle:
20   Yea, and I feel it not right! But O! my friends, my beloved!
Feverish and wakeful I lie, – I am weary of feeling and thinking.
Every thought is worn *down*, – I am weary, yet cannot be vacant.
Five long hours have I tossed, rheumatic heats, dry and flushing,
Gnawing behind in my head, and wandering and throbbing
    about me,
Busy and tiresome, my friends, as the beat of the boding
    night-spider.

[I forget the beginning of the line:]
                              . . . my eyes are a burthen,
Now unwillingly closed, now open and aching with darkness.
O! what a life is the eye! what a fine and inscrutable essence!
Him that is utterly blind, nor glimpses the fire that warns him;
30   Him that never beheld the swelling breast of his mother;
Him that ne'er smiled at the bosom as babe that smiles in its
    slumber;
Even to him it exists, it stirs and moves in its prison;
Lives with a separate life, and 'Is it the spirit?' he murmurs:
'Sure, it has thoughts of its own, and to see is only its language.'

[There was a great deal more, which I have forgotten, as I never
wrote it down. No doubt, much better might be written; but these
will still give you some idea of them. The last line which I wrote
I remember, and write it for the truth of the sentiment, scarcely
less true in company than in pain and solitude:]

William, my head and my heart! dear William and dear
    Dorothea!
You have all in each other; but I am lonely, and want you!

[Translation of a passage in Ottfried's metrical paraphrase of the Gospel]

She gave with joy her virgin breast;
She hid it not, she bared the breast,
Which suckled that divinest babe!
Blessed, blessed were the breasts
Which the Saviour infant kiss'd;
And blessed, blessed was the mother
Who wrapp'd his limbs in swaddling clothes,
Singing placed him on her lap,
Hung o'er him with her looks of love,
And soothed him with a lulling motion.
Blessed! for she shelter'd him
From the damp and chilling air;
Blessed, blessed! for she lay
With such a babe in one blest bed,
Close as babes and mothers lie!
Blessed, blessed evermore,
With her virgin lips she kiss'd,
With her arms, and to her breast
She embraced the babe divine,
Her babe divine the virgin mother!
There lives not on this ring of earth
A mortal, that can sing her praise.
Mighty mother, virgin pure,
In the darkness and the night
For us she *bore* the heavenly Lord!

[Fragmentary translation of the Song of Deborah]

The Song of Deborah, translated in the ‡ parallelisms of the Original /
(‡ that is, so that each Line or member of a sentence is counter-balanced
by the following, either by difference, or similitude, or by the repetition
of the same thought in different words or with a different Image).

Then sang Deborah,
And Barak, Abinoam's Son,
On that day sang they thus:

That the Leaders of Israel led on,
And the People willingly followed
    Praise ye the Lord!

————

I

Ye Monarchs, hear!
Give ear, ye Princes!
I sing to the Everlasting,
10   To the Everlasting will I play & sing praises,
    To the Lord God of Israel.

II

Lord God, Eternal!
When thou marchedst out from Seir,
When thou marchedst on thro' Edom,
    The Earth trembled,
    The Heavens dissolved,
    The Clouds poured,
Mountains melted away from the Lord,
Mount Sina from before the face of Jehovah,
20   The Lord God of Israel.

————

III

In the days of Samgar, the Son of Anath,
In the days of Jael lay waste the High roads,
The Travellers went not save by crooked by-ways
Suspended were the assemblies of Israel,
They ceased, till I arose, Deborah,
Till that I arise, a mother in Israel.

IV

To themselves they had chosen strange Gods;
And close to their gates came War.
Not a Shield was there seen, nor a Spear
30   Among the twice twenty Thousand of Israel.

————

V

My Heart, it swells high to the Rulers of Israel,
O ye, who offered yourselves freely among the People,
    Praise the Everlasting One.

Ye that ride on white asses,
Ye that sit on seats of costly Coverings, or embroidered Seats
Ye that walk on the High roads, frame a Song.

———————

VI

A Song for the Voice of the herdsmen, who beside thee draw wells
    Draw water for the Herds & Flocks!
For there will they sing the Deeds of Jehovah,
His deeds will the People of Israel praise.

40

Catullian Hendecasyllables

Hear, my beloved, an old Milesian story! –
High, and embosom'd in congregated laurels,
Glimmer'd a temple upon a breezy headland;
In the dim distance amid the skiey billows
Rose a fair island; the god of flocks had plac'd it.
From the far shores of the bleat-resounding island
Oft by the moonlight a little boat came floating,
Came to the sea-cave beneath the breezy headland,
Where amid myrtles a pathway stole in mazes
Up to the groves of the high embosom'd temple.
There in a thicket of dedicated roses,
Oft did a priestess, as lovely as a vision,
Pouring her soul to the son of Cytherea,
Pray him to hover around the slight canoe-boat,
And with invisible pilotage to guide it
Over the dusk wave, until the nightly sailor
Shivering with ecstasy sank upon her bosom.

10

The Homeric Hexameter Described and Exemplified

Strongly it bears us along in swelling and limitless billows,
Nothing before and nothing behind but the sky and the Ocean.

The Ovidian Elegiac Metre Described and Exemplified

In the hexameter rises the fountain's silvery column;
In the pentameter aye falling in melody back.

On a Cataract

FROM A CAVERN NEAR THE SUMMIT OF A
MOUNTAIN PRECIPICE

STROPHE
Unperishing youth!
Thou leapest from forth
The cell of thy hidden nativity;
Never mortal saw
The cradle of the strong one;
Never mortal heard
The gathering of his voices;
The deep-murmured charm of the son of the rock,
That is lisp'd evermore at his slumberless fountain.
10   There's a cloud at the portal, a spray-woven veil
At the shrine of his ceaseless renewing;
It embosoms the roses of dawn,
It entangles the shafts of the noon,
And into the bed of its stillness
The moonshine sinks down as in slumber,
That the son of the rock, that the nursling of heaven
May be born in a holy twilight!

ANTISTROPHE
The wild goat in awe
Looks up and beholds
20   Above thee the cliff inaccessible; –
Thou at once full-born
Madd'nest in thy joyance,
Whirlest, shatter'st, splitt'st,
Life invulnerable.

Tell's Birth-Place
IMITATED FROM STOLBERG

I

Mark this holy chapel well!
The birth-place, this, of William Tell.
Here, where stands God's altar dread,
Stood his parents' marriage-bed.

II

Here, first, an infant to her breast,
Him his loving mother prest;
And kissed the babe, and blessed the day,
And prayed as mothers use to pray.

III

'Vouchsafe him health, O God! and give
10   The child thy servant still to live!'
But God had destined to do more
Through him, than through an armèd power.

IV

God gave him reverence of laws,
Yet stirring blood in Freedom's cause –
A spirit to his rocks akin,
The eye of the hawk, and the fire therein!

V

To Nature and to Holy Writ
Alone did God the boy commit:
Where flashed and roared the torrent, oft
20   His soul found wings, and soared aloft!

VI

The straining oar and chamois chase
Had formed his limbs to strength and grace:
On wave and wind the boy would toss,
Was great, nor knew how great he was!

VII
He knew not that his chosen hand,
Made strong by God, his native land
Would rescue from the shameful yoke
Of Slavery – the which he broke!

The Visit of the Gods
IMITATED FROM SCHILLER

> Never, believe me,
>   Appear the Immortals,
>   Never alone:
> Scarce had I welcomed the sorrow-beguiler,
> Iacchus! but in came boy Cupid the smiler;
> Lo! Phœbus the glorious descends from his throne!
> They advance, they float in, the Olympians all!
>   With divinities fills my
>   Terrestrial hall!

10
>   How shall I yield you
>   Due entertainment,
>   Celestial quire?
> Me rather, bright guests! with your wings of upbuoyance
> Bear aloft to your homes, to your banquets of joyance,
> That the roofs of Olympus may echo my lyre!
> Hah! we mount! on their pinions they waft up my soul!
>   O give me the nectar!
>   O fill me the bowl!

>   Give him the nectar!
20
>   Pour out for the poet,
>   Hebe! pour free!
> Quicken his eyes with celestial dew,
> That Styx the detested no more he may view,
> And like one of us Gods may conceit him to be!
> Thanks, Hebe! I quaff it! Io Pæan, I cry!
>   The wine of the Immortals
>   Forbids me to die!

On an Infant
WHICH DIED BEFORE BAPTISM

'Be, rather than be called, a child of God,'
Death whispered! – with assenting nod,
Its head upon its mother's breast,
   The Baby bowed, without demur –
Of the kingdom of the Blest
   Possessor, not inheritor.

Something Childish, but Very Natural
WRITTEN IN GERMANY

If I had but two little wings,
   And were a little feathery bird,
     To you I'd fly, my dear!
But thoughts like these are idle things,
       And I stay here.

But in my sleep to you I fly:
   I'm always with you in my sleep!
     The world is all one's own.
But then one wakes, and where am I?
10   All, all alone.

Sleep stays not, though a monarch bids:
   So I love to wake ere break of day:
     For though my sleep be gone,
Yet while 'tis dark, one shuts one's lids,
       And still dreams on.

Home-Sick
WRITTEN IN GERMANY

'Tis sweet to him, who all the week
   Through city-crowds must push his way,
To stroll alone through fields and woods,
   And hallow thus the Sabbath-day.

And sweet it is, in summer bower,
    Sincere, affectionate and gay,
One's own dear children feasting round,
    To celebrate one's marriage-day.

But what is all, to his delight,
10   Who having long been doomed to roam,
Throws off the bundle from his back,
    Before the door of his own home?

Home-sickness is a wasting pang;
    This feel I hourly more and more:
There's healing only in thy wings,
    Thou Breeze that play'st on Albion's shore!

The Virgin's Cradle-Hymn
COPIED FROM A PRINT OF THE VIRGIN, IN A ROMAN CATHOLIC VILLAGE IN GERMANY

Dormi, Jesu! Mater ridet
Quæ tam dulcem somnum videt,
    Dormi, Jesu! blandule!
Si non dormis, Mater plorat,
Inter fila cantans orat,
    Blande, veni, somnule.

ENGLISH
Sleep, sweet babe! my cares beguiling:
Mother sits beside thee smiling;
    Sleep, my darling, tenderly!
If thou sleep not, mother mourneth,
Singing as her wheel she turneth:
    Come, soft slumber, balmily!

Lines

WRITTEN IN THE ALBUM AT ELBINGERODE,
IN THE HARTZ FOREST

I stood on Brocken's sovran height, and saw
Woods crowding upon woods, hills over hills,
A surging scene, and only limited
By the blue distance. Heavily my way
Downward I dragged through fir groves evermore,
Where bright green moss heaves in sepulchral forms
Speckled with sunshine; and, but seldom heard,
The sweet bird's song became a hollow sound;
And the breeze, murmuring indivisibly,
10   Preserved its solemn murmur most distinct
From many a note of many a waterfall,
And the brook's chatter; 'mid whose islet stones
The dingy kidling with its tinkling bell
Leaped frolicsome, or old romantic goat
Sat, his white beard slow waving. I moved on
In low and languid mood: for I had found
That outward forms, the loftiest, still receive
Their finer influence from the Life within; –
Fair cyphers else: fair, but of import vague
20   Or unconcerning, where the heart not finds
History or prophecy of friend, or child,
Or gentle maid, our first and early love,
Or father, or the venerable name
Of our adored country! O thou Queen,
Thou delegated Deity of Earth,
O dear, dear England! how my longing eye
Turned westward, shaping in the steady clouds
Thy sands and high white cliffs!

My native Land!
Filled with the thought of thee this heart was proud,
30   Yea, mine eye swam with tears: that all the view
From sovran Brocken, woods and woody hills,
Floated away, like a departing dream,
Feeble and dim! Stranger, these impulses
Blame thou not lightly; nor will I profane,
With hasty judgment or injurious doubt,
That man's sublimer spirit, who can feel

That God is everywhere! the God who framed
Mankind to be one mighty family,
Himself our Father, and the World our Home.

The British Stripling's War-Song
IMITATED FROM STOLBERG

Yes, noble old Warrior! this heart has beat high,
   Since you told of the deeds which our countrymen wrought;
O lend me the sabre that hung by thy thigh,
   And I too will fight as my forefathers fought.

Despise not my youth, for my spirit is steel'd,
   And I know there is strength in the grasp of my hand;
Yea, as firm as thyself would I march to the field,
   And as proudly would die for my dear native land.

In the sports of my childhood I mimick'd the fight,
10   The sound of a trumpet suspended my breath;
And my fancy still wander'd by day and by night,
   Amid battle and tumult, 'mid conquest and death.

My own shout of onset, when the Armies advance,
   How oft it awakes me from visions of glory;
When I meant to have leapt on the Hero of France,
   And have dash'd him to earth, pale and breathless and gory.

As late thro' the city with banners all streaming
   To the music of trumpets the Warriors flew by,
With helmet and scimitars naked and gleaming,
20   On their proud-trampling, thunder-hoof'd steeds did they fly;

I sped to yon heath that is lonely and bare,
   For each nerve was unquiet, each pulse in alarm;
And I hurl'd the mock-lance thro' the objectless air,
   And in open-eyed dream proved the strength of my arm.

Yes, noble old Warrior! this heart has beat high,
   Since you told of the deeds that our countrymen wrought;
O lend me the sabre that hung by thy thigh,
   And I too will fight as my forefathers fought!

Names

I asked my fair one happy day,
What I should call her in my lay;
   By what sweet name from Rome or Greece;
Lalage, Neæra, Chloris,
Sappho, Lesbia, or Doris,
   Arethusa or Lucrece.

'Ah!' replied my gentle fair,
'Beloved, what are names but air?
   Choose thou whatever suits the line;
Call me Sappho, call me Chloris,
Call me Lalage or Doris,
   Only, only call me Thine.'

The Devil's Thoughts

I

From his brimstone bed at break of day
   A walking the Devil is gone,
To visit his snug little farm the Earth,
   And see how his stock goes on.

II

Over the hill and over the dale,
   And he went over the plain.
And backward and forward he switched his long tail
   As a gentleman switches his cane.

III

And how then was the Devil drest?
Oh! he was in his Sunday's best:
His jacket was red and his breeches were blue,
And there was a hole where the tail came through.

IV

He saw a Lawyer killing a viper
   On a dung hill hard by his own stable;
And the Devil smiled, for it put him in mind
   Of Cain and his brother Abel.

V

He saw an Apothecary on a white horse
   Ride by on his vocations;
And the Devil thought of his old friend
20   Death in the Revelations.

VI

He saw a cottage with a double coach-house,
   A cottage of gentility;
And the Devil did grin, for his darling sin
   Is pride that apes humility.

VII

He peep'd into a rich bookseller's shop,
   Quoth he! 'We are both of one college!
For I sate myself, like a cormorant, once
   Hard by the tree of knowledge.'

VIII

Down the river did glide, with wind and with tide,
30   A pig with vast celerity;
And the Devil look'd wise as he saw how the while,
It cut its own throat. 'There!' quoth he with a smile,
   'Goes England's commercial prosperity.'

IX

As he went through Cold-Bath Fields he saw
   A solitary cell;
And the Devil was pleased, for it gave him a hint
   For improving his prisons in Hell.

X

He saw a Turnkey in a trice
   Unfetter a troublesome blade;
40   'Nimbly' quoth he, 'do the fingers move
   If a man be but used to his trade.'

XI

He saw the same Turnkey unfetter a man
    With but little expedition,
Which put him in mind of the long debate
    On the Slave-trade abolition.

XII

He saw an old acquaintance
    As he pass'd by a Methodist meeting; –
She holds a consecrated key,
    And the Devil nods her a greeting.

XIII

50   She turned up her nose, and said,
        'Avaunt! my name's Religion,'
    And she looked to Mr ———
        And leered like a love-sick pigeon.

XIV

He saw a certain minister
    (A minister to his mind)
Go up into a certain House,
    With a majority behind.

XV

The Devil quoted Genesis,
    Like a very learned clerk,
60   How 'Noah and his creeping things
        Went up into the Ark.'

XVI

He took from the poor,
    And he gave to the rich,
And he shook hands with a Scotchman,
    For he was not afraid of the —

                * * *

XVII

General ——————— burning face
    He saw with consternation,
And back to hell his way did he take,
For the Devil thought by a slight mistake
70   It was general conflagration.

Lines Composed in a Concert-Room

Nor cold, nor stern, my soul! yet I detest
   These scented rooms, where, to a gaudy throng,
Heaves the proud harlot her distended breast
   In intricacies of laborious song.

These feel not Music's genuine power, nor deign
   To melt at Nature's passion-warbled plaint;
But when the long-breathed singer's uptrilled strain
   Bursts in a squall – they gape for wonderment.

Hark! the deep buzz of vanity and hate!
   Scornful, yet envious, with self-torturing sneer
My lady eyes some maid of humbler state,
   While the pert captain, or the primmer priest,
   Prattles accordant scandal in her ear.

O give me, from this heartless scene released,
   To hear our old musician, blind and gray
(Whom stretching from my nurse's arms I kissed),
   His Scottish tunes and warlike marches play,
By moonshine, on the balmy summer-night,
   The while I dance amid the tedded hay
With merry maids, whose ringlets toss in light.

Or lies the purple evening on the bay
Of the calm glossy lake, O let me hide
   Unheard, unseen, behind the alder-trees,
For round their roots the fisher's boat is tied,
   On whose trim seat doth Edmund stretch at ease,
And while the lazy boat sways to and fro,
   Breathes in his flute sad airs, so wild and slow,
That his own cheek is wet with quiet tears.

But O, dear Anne! when midnight wind careers,
   And the gust pelting on the out-house shed
   Makes the cock shrilly on the rain storm crow,
   To hear thee sing some ballad full of woe,
Ballad of ship-wrecked sailor floating dead,
   Whom his own true-love buried in the sands!

Thee, gentle woman, for thy voice re-measures
Whatever tones and melancholy pleasures
   The things of Nature utter; birds or trees
Or moan of ocean-gale in weedy caves,
Or where the stiff grass mid the heath-plant waves,
40   Murmur and music thin of sudden breeze.

The Exchange

We pledged our hearts, my love and I, –
   I in my arms the maiden clasping;
I could not tell the reason why,
   But, oh! I trembled like an aspen.

Her father's love she bade me gain;
   I went, and shook like any reed!
I strove to act the man – in vain!
   We had exchanged our hearts indeed.

[Paraphrase of Psalm 46. Hexameters]

Gōd ĭs oŭr Strēngth ănd oŭr Rēfŭge: thērefŏre wĭll wĕ nŏt
   trēmblĕ,

Thō' thĕ Eārth bĕ rĕmōvĕd; ănd thō' thĕ pĕrpētŭăl Moūntains,
Sink in the Swell of the Ocean! God is our Strength & our
   Refuge.
There is a River, the Flowing whereof shall gladden the City,
Hallelujah! the City of God! Jehova shall help her.

Thē Īdōlătĕrs ragĕd, the Kingdoms were moving in fury –
But He utter'd his Voice: Earth melted away from beneath
   them.
Halleluja! th' Eternal is with us, Almighty Jehova!

Fearful the works of the Lord, yea, fearful his Desolations –
10 But *He* maketh the Battle to cease, he burneth the Spear & the
   Chariot.
Halleluja! th' Eternal is with us, the God of our Fathers!

Hymn to the Earth
HEXAMETERS

Earth! thou mother of numberless children, the nurse and the
    mother,
Hail! O Goddess, thrice hail! Blest be thou! and, blessing, I
    hymn thee!
Forth, ye sweet sounds! from my harp, and my voice shall float
    on your surges –
Soar thou aloft, O my soul! and bear up my song on thy pinions.

Travelling the vale with mine eyes – green meadows and lake
    with green island,
Dark in its basin of rock, and the bare stream flowing in
    brightness,
Thrilled with thy beauty and love in the wooded slope of the
    mountain,
Here, great mother, I lie, thy child, with his head on thy bosom!
Playful the spirits of noon, that rushing soft through thy tresses,
Green-haired goddess! refresh me; and hark! as they hurry or
    linger,
Fill the pause of my harp, or sustain it with musical murmurs.
Into my being thou murmurest joy, and tenderest sadness
Shedd'st thou, like dew, on my heart, till the joy and the
    heavenly sadness
Pour themselves forth from my heart in tears, and the hymn of
    thanksgiving.
Earth! thou mother of numberless children, the nurse and the
    mother,
Sister thou of the stars, and beloved by the sun the rejoicer!
Guardian and friend of the moon, O Earth, whom the comets
    forget not,
Yea, in the measureless distance wheel round and again they
    behold thee!
Fadeless and young (and what if the latest birth of creation?)
Bride and consort of Heaven, that looks down upon thee
    enamoured!
Say, mysterious Earth! O say, great mother and goddess,
Was it not well with thee then, when first thy lap was ungirdled,
Thy lap to the genial Heaven, the day that he wooed thee and
    won thee!

Fair was thy blush, the fairest and first of the blushes of
    morning!
Deep was the shudder, O Earth! the throe of thy self-retention:
Inly thou strovest to flee, and didst seek thyself at thy centre!
Mightier far was the joy of thy sudden resilience; and forthwith
Myriad myriads of lives teemed forth from the mighty
    embracement.
Thousand-fold tribes of dwellers, impelled by thousand-fold
    instincts,
30   Filled, as a dream, the wide waters; the rivers sang on their
    channels;
Laughed on their shores the hoarse seas; the yearning ocean
    swelled upward;
Young life lowed through the meadows, the woods, and the
    echoing mountains,
Wandered bleating in valleys, and warbled on blossoming
    branches.

Mahomet

Utter the song, O my soul! the flight and return of Mohammed,
Prophet and priest, who scatter'd abroad both evil and blessing,
Huge wasteful empires founded and hallow'd slow persecution,
Soul-withering, but crush'd the blasphemous rites of the Pagan
And idolatrous Christians. – For veiling the Gospel of Jesus,
They, the best corrupting, had made it worse than the vilest.
Wherefore Heaven decreed th' enthusiast warrior of Mecca,
Choosing good from iniquity rather than evil from goodness.
Loud the tumult in Mecca surrounding the fane of the idol; –
10   Naked and prostrate the priesthood were laid – the people with
    mad shouts
Thundering now, and now with saddest ululation
Flew, as over the channel of rock-stone the ruinous river
Shatters its waters abreast, and in mazy uproar bewilder'd,
Rushes dividuous all – all rushing impetuous onward.

Ode to Georgiana,

DUCHESS OF DEVONSHIRE, ON THE TWENTY-FOURTH
STANZA IN HER 'PASSAGE OVER MOUNT GOTHARD'

And hail the chapel! hail the platform wild
    There Tell directed the avenging dart,
With well strung arm, that first preserved his child,
    Then aimed the arrow at the tyrant's heart.

Splendour's fondly fostered child!
And did you hail the platform wild,
    Where once the Austrian fell
    Beneath the shaft of Tell!
O Lady, nursed in pomp and pleasure!
Whence learn'd you that heroic measure?

Light as a dream your days their circlets ran,
From all that teaches brotherhood to Man
Far, far removed! from want, from hope, from fear!
Enchanting music lulled your infant ear,
Obeisance, praises soothed your infant heart:
    Emblasonments and old ancestral crests,
With many a bright obtrusive form of art,
    Detained your eye from nature: stately vests,
That veiling strove to deck your charms divine,
Rich viands and the pleasurable wine,
Were yours unearned by toil; nor could you see
The unenjoying toiler's misery.
And yet, free Nature's uncorrupted child,
You hailed the chapel and the platform wild,
    Where once the Austrian fell
    Beneath the shaft of Tell!
O Lady, nursed in pomp and pleasure!
Whence learn'd you that heroic measure?

There crowd your finely-fibred frame,
    All living faculties of bliss;
And Genius to your cradle came,
His forehead wreathed with lambent flame,
    And bending low, with godlike kiss

30   Breath'd in a more celestial life;
But boasts not many a fair compeer,
    A heart as sensitive to joy and fear?
And some, perchance, might wage an equal strife,
Some few, to nobler being wrought,
Corrivals in the nobler gift of thought.
            Yet these delight to celebrate
            Laurelled war and plumy state;
            Or in verse and music dress
            Tales of rustic happiness –
40   Pernicious tales! insidious strains!
            That steel the rich man's breast,
            And mock the lot unblest,
        The sordid vices and the abject pains,
            Which evermore must be
        The doom of ignorance and penury!
But you, free Nature's uncorrupted child,
You hailed the chapel and the platform wild,
            Where once the Austrian fell
            Beneath the shaft of Tell!
50   O Lady, nursed in pomp and pleasure!
    Whence learn'd you that heroic measure?

You were a mother! That most holy name,
    Which Heaven and Nature bless,
    I may not vilely prostitute to those
        Whose infants owe them less
    Than the poor caterpillar owes
        Its gaudy parent fly.
You were a mother! at your bosom fed
    The babes that loved you. You, with laughing eye,
60   Each twilight-thought, each nascent feeling read,
    Which you yourself created. Oh! delight!
        A second time to be a mother,
            Without the mother's bitter groans:
        Another thought, and yet another,
            By touch, or taste, by looks or tones
        O'er the growing sense to roll,
        The mother of your infant's soul!
The Angel of the Earth, who, while he guides
    His chariot-planet round the goal of day,
70   All trembling gazes on the eye of God,
    A moment turned his awful face away;

And as he viewed you, from his aspect sweet
  New influences in your being rose,
Blest intuitions and communions fleet
    With living Nature, in her joys and woes!
      Thenceforth your soul rejoiced to see
      The shrine of social Liberty!
      O beautiful! O Nature's child!
      'Twas thence you hailed the platform wild,
80   Where once the Austrian fell
        Beneath the shaft of Tell!
      O Lady, nursed in pomp and pleasure!
      Thence learn'd you that heroic measure.

A Christmas Carol

I

    The shepherds went their hasty way,
      And found the lowly stable-shed
  Where the Virgin-Mother lay:
      And now they checked their eager tread,
For to the Babe, that at her bosom clung,
A mother's song the Virgin-Mother sung.

II

    They told her how a glorious light,
      Streaming from a heavenly throng,
  Around them shone, suspending night!
10   While sweeter than a mother's song,
Blest Angels heralded the Saviour's birth,
Glory to God on high! and Peace on Earth.

III

    She listened to the tale divine,
      And closer still the Babe she prest;
  And while she cried, 'the Babe is mine!'
      The milk rushed faster to her breast:
Joy rose within her, like a summer's morn;
Peace, Peace on Earth! the Prince of Peace is born.

IV

Thou Mother of the Prince of Peace,
20 Poor, simple, and of low estate!
That strife should vanish, battle cease,
  O why should this thy soul elate?
Sweet music's loudest note, the poet's story, –
Did'st thou ne'er love to hear of fame and glory?

V

And is not War a youthful king,
  A stately hero clad in mail?
Beneath his footsteps laurels spring;
  Him Earth's majestic monarchs hail
Their friend, their playmate! and his bold bright eye
30 Compels the maiden's love-confessing sigh.

VI

'Tell this in some more courtly scene,
  To maids and youths in robes of state!
I am a woman poor and mean,
  And therefore is my soul elate.
War is a ruffian, all with guilt defiled,
That from the aged father tears his child!

VII

'A murderous fiend, by fiends adored,
  He kills the sire and starves the son;
The husband kills, and from her board
40 Steals all his widow's toil had won;
Plunders God's world of beauty; rends away
All safety from the night, all comfort from the day.

VIII

'Then wisely is my soul elate,
  That strife should vanish, battle cease:
I'm poor and of a low estate,
  The Mother of the Prince of Peace.
Joy rises in me, like a summer's morn:
Peace, Peace on Earth! the Prince of Peace is born.'

On an Insignificant

No doleful faces here, no sighing –
Here rots a thing that *won* by dying:
'Tis Cypher lies beneath this crust –
Whom Death *created* into dust.

Job's Luck

Sly Beelzebub took all occasions
To try Job's constancy and patience;
He took his honours, took his health,
He took his children, took his wealth,
His camels, horses, asses, cows –
And the sly Devil did not take his spouse.

But Heaven that brings out good from evil,
And loves to disappoint the Devil,
Had predetermined to restore
10 Twofold all Job had before,
His children, camels, horses, cows –
Short-sighted Devil, not to take his spouse!

Love

All thoughts, all passions, all delights,
Whatever stirs this mortal frame,
All are but ministers of Love,
    And feed his sacred flame.

Oft in my waking dreams do I
Live o'er again that happy hour,
When midway on the mount I lay,
    Beside the ruined tower.

The moonshine, stealing o'er the scene
Had blended with the lights of eve;
And she was there, my hope, my joy,
 My own dear Genevieve!

She lean'd against the armèd man,
The statue of the armèd knight;
She stood and listened to my lay,
 Amid the lingering light.

Few sorrows hath she of her own,
My hope! my joy! my Genevieve!
She loves me best, whene'er I sing
 The songs that make her grieve.

I played a soft and doleful air,
I sang an old and moving story –
An old rude song, that suited well
 That ruin wild and hoary.

She listened with a flitting blush,
With downcast eyes and modest grace;
For well she knew, I could not choose
 But gaze upon her face.

I told her of the Knight that wore
Upon his shield a burning brand;
And that for ten long years he wooed
 The Lady of the Land.

I told her how he pined: and ah!
The deep, the low, the pleading tone
With which I sang another's love,
 Interpreted my own.

She listened with a flitting blush,
With downcast eyes, and modest grace;
And she forgave me, that I gazed
 Too fondly on her face!

But when I told the cruel scorn
That crazed that bold and lovely Knight,
And that he crossed the mountain-woods,
    Nor rested day nor night;

That sometimes from the savage den,
And sometimes from the darksome shade,
And sometimes starting up at once
    In green and sunny glade, –

There came and looked him in the face
50   An angel beautiful and bright;
And that he knew it was a Fiend,
    This miserable Knight!

And that unknowing what he did,
He leaped amid a murderous band,
And saved from outrage worse than death
    The Lady of the Land; –

And how she wept, and clasped his knees;
And how she tended him in vain –
And ever strove to expiate
60   The scorn that crazed his brain; –

And that she nursed him in a cave;
And how his madness went away,
When on the yellow forest-leaves
    A dying man he lay; –

His dying words – but when I reached
That tenderest strain of all the ditty,
My faltering voice and pausing harp
    Disturbed her soul with pity!

All impulses of soul and sense
70   Had thrilled my guileless Genevieve;
The music and the doleful tale,
    The rich and balmy eve;

And hopes, and fears that kindle hope,
An undistinguishable throng,
And gentle wishes long subdued,
    Subdued and cherished long!

She wept with pity and delight,
She blushed with love, and virgin shame;
And like the murmur of a dream,
80   I heard her breathe my name.

Her bosom heaved – she stepped aside,
As conscious of my look she stept –
Then suddenly, with timorous eye
    She fled to me and wept.

She half inclosed me with her arms,
She pressed me with a meek embrace;
And bending back her head, looked up,
    And gazed upon my face.

'Twas partly love, and partly fear,
90   And partly 'twas a bashful art,
That I might rather feel, than see,
    The swelling of her heart.

I calmed her fears, and she was calm,
And told her love with virgin pride;
And so I won my Genevieve,
    My bright and beauteous Bride.

The Madman and the Lethargist, an Example

Quoth Dick to me, as once at College
We argued on the use of Knowledge,
'In old king Olim's reign, I've read,
There lay two Patients in one bed.
The one in fat lethargic trance
Lay wan and motionless as lead:
The other, like the Folks in France,
Possess'd a different disposition –
In short, the plain truth to confess,

10   The man was madder than mad Bess.
But both diseases, none disputed,
Were unmedicinably rooted.
Yet so it chanc'd, by Heaven's Permission,
Each prov'd the other's true Physician.'

'Fighting with a ghastly stare
Troops of Despots in the air,
Obstreporously Jacobinical
The Madman froth'd & foam'd & roar'd:
The other, snoring octaves cynical,
20   Like good John Bull, in posture clinical
Seem'd living only when he snor'd.
The *Citizen*, enrag'd to see
This fat Insensibility,
Or tir'd with solitary Labour,
Determin'd to *convert* his Neighbour.
So up he sprung, & to 't he fell
Like Devil piping hot from hell;
With indefatigable Fist
Belab'ring the poor Lethargist,
30   Till his own Limbs were stiff & sore,
And Sweatdrops roll'd from every pore.
Yet still, with "flying fingers" fleet –
Duly accompanied by feet,
With some short Interludes of Biting
He executes the self-same Strain,
Till the Slumb'rer woke for pain
And half prepar'd himself for Fighting,
That moment, that his mad Colleague
Sunk down & slept thro' pure fatigue.
40   So both were cur'd: & this example,
Gives demonstration full & ample,
That Chance may bring a thing to bear
When Art sits down in flat Despair.'
'That's true enough, Dick!' – answer'd I –
'But as for th'example, 'tis a Lie!'

On a Volunteer Singer

Swans sing before they die: 'twere no bad thing,
Should certain persons die before they sing.

Talleyrand to Lord Grenville
A METRICAL EPISTLE

To the Editor of *The Morning Post*.

MR EDITOR, – An unmetrical letter from Talleyrand to Lord Grenville
has already appeared, and from an authority too high to be questioned:
otherwise I could adduce some arguments for the exclusive authenticity
of the following metrical epistle. The very epithet which the wise ancients
used, '*aurea carmina*,' might have been supposed likely to have determined
the choice of the French minister in favour of verse; and the rather when
we recollect that this phrase of '*golden verses*' is applied emphatically to
the works of that philosopher who imposed *silence* on all with whom he
had to deal. Besides is it not somewhat improbable that Talleyrand should
have preferred prose to rhyme, when the latter alone *has got the chink*? Is
it not likewise curious that in our official answer no notice whatever is
taken of the Chief Consul, Bonaparte, as if there had been no such person
existing; notwithstanding that his existence is pretty generally admitted,
nay that some have been so rash as to believe that he has created as great
a sensation in the world as Lord Grenville, or even the Duke of Portland?
But the Minister of Foreign Affairs, Talleyrand, *is* acknowledged, which, in
our opinion, could not have happened had he written only that insignificant
prose-letter, which seems to precede Bonaparte's, as in old romances a
dwarf always ran before to proclaim the advent or arrival of knight or
giant. That Talleyrand's character and practices more resemble those of
some *regular* Governments than Bonaparte's I admit; but this of itself does
not appear a satisfactory explanation. However, let the letter speak for
itself. The second line is supererogative in syllables, whether from the
oscitancy of the transcriber, or from the trepidation which might have
overpowered the modest Frenchman, on finding himself in the act of
writing to so *great* a man, I shall not dare to determine. A few Notes are
added by

Your servant,
GNOME

P.S. – As mottoes are now fashionable, especially if taken from out of the way books, you may prefix, if you please, the following lines from Sidonius Apollinaris:

'Saxa et robora, corneasque fibras
Mollit dulciloquâ canorus arte!'

TALLEYRAND, MINISTER OF FOREIGN AFFAIRS AT PARIS,
TO LORD GRENVILLE, SECRETARY OF STATE IN GREAT
BRITAIN FOR FOREIGN AFFAIRS, AUDITOR OF THE
EXCHEQUER, A LORD OF TRADE, AN ELDER BROTHER OF
TRINITY HOUSE, ETC.

My Lord! though your Lordship repel deviation
From forms long establish'd, yet with high consideration,
I plead for the honour to hope that no blame
Will attach, should this letter *begin* with my name.
I dar'd not presume on your Lordship to bounce,
But thought it more *exquisite* first to *announce*!

My Lord! I've the honour to be Talleyrand,
And the letter's from *me*! you'll not draw back your hand
Nor yet take it up by the rim in dismay,
As boys pick up ha'pence on April fool-day.
I'm no Jacobin foul, or red-hot Cordelier
That your Lordship's *un*gauntleted fingers need fear
An infection or burn! Believe me, 'tis true,
With a scorn like another I look down on the crew
That bawl and hold up to the mob's detestation
The most delicate wish for a *silent persuasion*.
A form long-establish'd these Terrorists call
Bribes, perjury, theft, and the devil and all!
And yet spite of all that the Moralist prates,
'Tis the keystone and cement of *civilized States*.
Those American *Reps*! And i' faith, they were serious!
It shock'd us at Paris, like something mysterious,
That men who've a Congress – But no more of 't! I'm proud
To have stood so distinct from the Jacobin crowd.

My Lord! though the vulgar in wonder be lost at
My transfigurations, and name me *Apostate*,
Such a meaningless nickname, which never incens'd me,
Cannot prejudice you or your Cousin against me:

I'm Ex-bishop. What then? Burke himself would agree
30   That I left not the Church – 'twas the Church that left me.
My titles prelatic I lov'd and retain'd,
As long as what *I* meant by Prelate remain'd:
And tho' Mitres no longer will *pass* in our mart,
I'm *episcopal* still to the core of my heart.
No time from my name this my motto shall sever:
'Twill be *Non sine pulvere palma* for ever!

Your goodness, my Lord, I conceive as excessive,
Or I dar'd not present you a scroll so digressive;
And in truth with my pen thro' and thro' I should strike it;
40   But I hear that your Lordship's own style is just like it.
Dear my Lord, we are right: for what charms can be shew'd
In a thing that goes straight like an old Roman road?
The tortoise crawls straight, the hare doubles about;
And the true line of beauty still winds in and out.
It argues, my Lord! of fine thoughts such a brood in us
To split and divide into heads multitudinous,
While charms that surprise (it can ne'er be denied us)
Sprout forth from each head, like the ears from King Midas.
Were a genius of rank, like a commonplace dunce,
50   Compell'd to drive on to the main point at once,
What a plentiful vintage of initiations
Would Noble Lords lose in your Lordship's orations.
My fancy transports me! As mute as a mouse,
And as fleet as a pigeon, I'm borne to the house
Where all those who *are* Lords, from father to son,
Discuss the affairs of all those who are none.
I behold you, my Lord! of your feelings quite full,
'Fore the woolsack arise, like a sack full of wool!
You rise on each Anti-Grenvillian Member,
60   Short, thick and blustrous, like a day in November!
Short in person, I mean: for the length of your speeches
Fame herself, that most famous reporter, ne'er reaches.
Lo! Patience beholds you contemn her brief reign,
And Time, that all-panting toil'd after in vain,
(Like the Beldam who raced for a smock with her grand-child)
Drops and cries: 'Were such lungs e'er assign'd to a man-child?'
Your strokes at her vitals pale Truth has confess'd,
And Zeal unresisted entempests your breast!
Though some noble Lords may be wishing to sup,
70   Your merit self-conscious, my Lord, *keeps you up*,

Unextinguish'd and swoln, as a balloon of paper
Keeps aloft by the smoke of its own farthing taper.
Ye SIXTEENS of Scotland, your snuffs ye must trim;
Your Geminies, fix'd stars of England! grow dim,
And but for *a form long-establish'd*, no doubt
Twinkling faster and faster, ye all would *go out*.

    Apropos, my dear Lord! a ridiculous blunder
Of some of our Journalists caused us some wonder:
It was said that in aspect malignant and sinister
80 In the Isle of Great Britain a great Foreign Minister
Turn'd as pale as a journeyman miller's frock coat is
On observing a star that appear'd in BOOTES!
When the whole truth was this (O those ignorant brutes!)
Your Lordship had made his appearance in boots.
You, my Lord, with your star, sat in boots, and the Spanish
Ambassador thereupon thought fit to vanish.

    But perhaps, dear my Lord, among other worse crimes,
The whole was no more than a lie of *The Times*.
It is monstrous, my Lord! in a civilis'd state
90 That such Newspaper rogues should have license to prate.
Indeed printing in general – but for the taxes,
Is in theory false and pernicious in praxis!
You and I, and your Cousin, and Abbé Sieyès,
And all the great Statesmen that live in these days,
Are agreed that no nation secure is from vi'lence
Unless all who must think are maintain'd all in silence.
This printing, my Lord – but 'tis useless to mention
What we both of us think – 'twas a cursèd invention,
And Germany might have been honestly prouder
100 Had she left it alone, and found out only powder.
My Lord! when I think of our labours and cares
Who rule the Department of foreign affairs,
And how with their libels these journalists bore us,
Though Rage I acknowledge than scorn less decorous;
Yet their presses and types I could shiver in splinters,
Those Printers' black Devils! those Devils of Printers!
In case of a peace – but perhaps it were better
To proceed to the absolute point of my letter:
For the deep wounds of France, Bonaparte, my master,
110 Has found out a new sort of *basilicon* plaister.

But your time, my dear Lord! is your nation's best treasure,
I've intruded already too long on your leisure;
If so, I entreat you with penitent sorrow
To pause, and resume the remainder to-morrow.

The Two Round Spaces on the Tomb-Stone

See the apology for the 'Fire, Famine, and Slaughter,' in first volume.
This is the first time the author ever published these lines. He would have
been glad, had they perished; but they have now been printed repeatedly
in magazines, and he is told that the verses will not perish. Here, therefore,
they are owned, with a hope that they will be taken – as assuredly as they
were composed – in mere sport.

The Devil believes that the Lord will come,
Stealing a march without beat of drum,
About the same time that he came last,
On an old Christmas-day in a snowy blast:
Till he bids the trump sound, neither body nor soul stirs,
For the dead men's heads have slipt under their bolsters.

Oh! ho! brother Bard, in our church-yard,
Both beds and bolsters are soft and green;
Save one alone, and that's of stone,
10   And under it lies a Counsellor keen.
'Twould be a square tomb, if it were not too long,
And 'tis fenced round with irons sharp, spearlike, and strong.

This fellow from Aberdeen hither did skip,
With a waxy face, and a blubber lip,
And a black tooth in front, to show in part
What was the colour of his whole heart.
          This Counsellor sweet,
          This Scotchman complete,
      (The Devil scotch him for a snake)
20   I trust he lies in his grave awake.

On the sixth of January,
  When all around is white with snow,
    As a Cheshire yeoman's dairy;
      Brother Bard, ho! ho!
      Believe it, or no,
On that stone tomb to you I'll show
Two round spaces void of snow.
I swear by our Knight, and his forefathers' souls,
That in size and shape they are just like the holes
30   In the house of privity
      Of that ancient family.
On those two places void of snow,
There have sate in the night for an hour or so,
Before sunrise, and after cock-crow,
He kicking his heels, she cursing her corns,
All to the tune of the wind in their horns,
      The Devil, and his Grannam,
      With a snow-blast to fan 'em;
Expecting and hoping the trumpet to blow,
40 For they are cock-sure of the fellow below.

The Mad Monk

I heard a voice from Etna's side,
  Where o'er a cavern's mouth
  That fronted to the south
A chesnut spread its umbrage wide:

A hermit or a monk the man might be;
  But him I could not see:
And thus the music flow'd along,
In melody most like to old Sicilian song:

'There was a time when earth, and sea, and skies,
10   The bright green vale, and forest's dark recess,
With all things, lay before mine eyes
  In steady loveliness:
But now I feel, on earth's uneasy scene,
  Such sorrows as will never cease; –
  I only ask for peace;
If I must live to know that such a time has been!'

A silence then ensued:
   Till from the cavern came
   A voice; – it was the same!
20 And thus, in mournful tone, its dreary plaint renew'd:

'Last night, as o'er the sloping turf I trod,
   The smooth green turf, to me a vision gave
Beneath mine eyes, the sod –
   The roof of Rosa's grave!

'My heart has need with dreams like these to strive,
   For, when I woke, beneath mine eyes I found
   The plot of mossy ground,
On which we oft have sat when Rosa was alive. –
Why must the rock, and margin of the flood,
30   Why must the hills so many flow'rets bear,
Whose colours to a *murder'd* maiden's blood,
   Such sad resemblance wear? –

'*I struck the wound*, – this hand of mine!
For Oh, thou maid divine,
   I lov'd to agony!
The youth whom thou call'd'st thine
   Did never love like me!

'Is it the stormy clouds above
   That flash'd so red a gleam?
40   On yonder downward trickling stream? –
'Tis not the blood of her I love. –
The sun torments me from his western bed,
   Oh, let him cease for ever to diffuse
   Those crimson spectre hues!
Oh, let me lie in peace, and be for ever dead!'

Here ceas'd the voice. In deep dismay,
Down thro' the forest I pursu'd my way.

A Stranger Minstrel
WRITTEN [TO MRS ROBINSON] A FEW WEEKS
BEFORE HER DEATH

As late on Skiddaw's mount I lay supine,
Midway th' ascent, in that repose divine
When the soul centred in the heart's recess
Hath quaff'd its fill of Nature's loveliness,
Yet still beside the fountain's marge will stay
   And fain would thirst again, again to quaff;
Then when the tear, slow travelling on its way,
   Fills up the wrinkles of a silent laugh –
In that sweet mood of sad and humorous thought
10 A form within me rose, within me wrought
With such strong magic, that I cried aloud,
'Thou ancient Skiddaw by thy helm of cloud,
And by thy many-colour'd chasms deep,
And by their shadows that for ever sleep,
By yon small flaky mists that love to creep
Along the edges of those spots of light,
Those sunny islands of thy smooth green height,
   And by yon shepherds with their sheep,
   And dogs and boys, a gladsome crowd,
20   That rush e'en now with clamour loud
   Sudden from forth thy topmost cloud,
   And by this laugh, and by this tear,
   I would, old Skiddaw, she were here!
   A lady of sweet song is she,
   Her soft blue eye was made for thee!
   O ancient Skiddaw, by this tear,
   I would, I would that she were here!'

Then ancient Skiddaw, stern and proud,
   In Sullen majesty replying,
30 Thus spake from out his helm of cloud
   (His voice was like an echo dying!): –
'She dwells belike in scenes more fair,
And scorns a mount so bleak and bare.'

I only sigh'd when this I heard;
Such mournful thoughts within me stirr'd
That all my heart was faint and weak,
    So sorely was I troubled!
No laughter wrinkled on my cheek,
    But O the tears were doubled!
40 But ancient Skiddaw green and high
Heard and understood my sigh;
And now, in tones less stern and rude,
As if he wish'd to end the feud,
Spake he, the proud response renewing
(His voice was like a monarch wooing): –
'Nay, but thou dost not know her might,
    The pinions of her soul how strong!
But many a stranger in my height
    Hath sung to me her magic song,
50   Sending forth his ecstasy
        In her divinest melody,
    And hence I know her soul is free,
    She is where'er she wills to be,
    Unfetter'd by mortality!
Now to the "haunted beach" can fly,
    Beside the threshold scourged with waves,
    Now where the maniac wildly raves,
"*Pale moon, thou spectre of the sky!*"
    No wind that hurries o'er my height
60 Can travel with so swift a flight.
        I too, methinks, might merit
        The presence of her spirit!
        To me too might belong
    The honour of her song and witching melody,
        Which most resembles me,
        Soft, various, and sublime,
        Exempt from wrongs of Time!'

Thus spake the mighty Mount, and I
Made answer, with a deep-drawn sigh: –
70 'Thou ancient Skiddaw, by this tear,
I would, I would that she were here!'

Inscription for a Seat by the Road Side Half-Way Up a Steep Hill Facing South

Thou who in youthful vigour rich, and light
With youthful thoughts dost need no rest! O thou,
To whom alike the valley and the hill
Present a path of ease! Should e'er thine eye
Glance on this sod, and this rude tablet, stop!
'Tis a rude spot, yet here, with thankful hearts,
The foot-worn soldier and his family
Have rested, wife and babe, and boy, perchance
Some eight years old or less, and scantly fed,
10 Garbed like his father, and already bound
To his poor father's trade. Or think of him
Who, laden with his implements of toil,
Returns at night to some far distant home,
And having plodded on through rain and mire
With limbs o'erlaboured, weak from feverish heat,
And chafed and fretted by December blasts,
Here pauses, thankful he hath reached so far,
And 'mid the sheltering warmth of these bleak trees
Finds restoration – or reflect on those
20 Who in the spring to meet the warmer sun
Crawl up this steep hill-side, that needlessly
Bends double their weak frames, already bowed
By age or malady, and when, at last,
They gain this wished-for turf, this seat of sods,
Repose – and, well-admonished, ponder here
On final rest. And if a serious thought
Should come uncalled – how soon *thy* motions high,
Thy balmy spirits and thy fervid blood
Must change to feeble, withered, cold and dry –
30 Cherish the wholesome sadness! And where'er
The tide of Life impel thee, O be prompt
To make thy present strength the staff of all,
Their staff and resting-place – so shalt thou give
To Youth the sweetest joy that Youth can know;
And for thy future self thou shalt provide
Through every change of various life, a seat,
Not built by hands, on which thy inner part,
Imperishable, many a grievous hour,

Or bleak or sultry may repose – yea, sleep
40 The sleep of Death, and dream of blissful worlds,
Then wake in Heaven, and find the dream all true.

Apologia Pro Vita Sua

The poet in his lone yet genial hour
Gives to his eyes a magnifying power:
Or rather he emancipates his eyes
From the black shapeless accidents of size –
In unctuous cones of kindling coal,
Or smoke upwreathing from the pipe's trim bole,
    His gifted ken can see
    Phantoms of sublimity.

The Night-Scene:
A DRAMATIC FRAGMENT

Sandoval. You loved the daughter of Don Manrique?
Earl Henry.   Loved?
Sandoval. Did you not say you wooed her?
Earl Henry.   Once I loved
Her whom I dared not woo!
Sandoval.   And wooed, perchance,
One whom you loved not!
Earl Henry.   Oh! I were most base,
Not loving Oropeza. True, I wooed her,
Hoping to heal a deeper wound; but she
Met my advances with impassioned pride,
That kindled love with love. And when her sire,
Who in his dream of hope already grasped
10 The golden circlet in his hand, rejected
My suit with insult, and in memory
Of ancient feuds poured curses on my head,
Her blessings overtook and baffled them!
But thou art stern, and with unkindly countenance
Art inly reasoning whilst thou listenest to me.
Sandoval. Anxiously, Henry! reasoning anxiously.
But Oropeza –

Earl Henry.
                    Blessings gather round her!
Within this wood there winds a secret passage,
Beneath the walls, which opens out at length
20   Into the gloomiest covert of the garden. –
The night ere my departure to the army,
She, nothing trembling, led me through that gloom,
And to that covert by a silent stream,
Which, with one star reflected near its marge,
Was the sole object visible around me.
No leaflet stirred; the air was almost sultry;
So deep, so dark, so close, the umbrage o'er us!
No leaflet stirred; – yet pleasure hung upon
The gloom and stillness of the balmy night-air.
30   A little further on an arbour stood,
Fragrant with flowering trees – I well remember
What an uncertain glimmer in the darkness
Their snow-white blossoms made – thither she led me,
To that sweet bower! Then Oropeza trembled –
I heard her heart beat – if 'twere not my own.
Sandoval. A rude and scaring note, my friend!
Earl Henry.   Oh! no!
I have small memory of aught but pleasure.
The inquietudes of fear, like lesser streams
Still flowing, still were lost in those of love:
40   So love grew mightier from the fear, and Nature,
Fleeing from pain, sheltered herself in joy.
The stars above our heads were dim and steady,
Like eyes suffused with rapture. – Life was in us:
We were all life, each atom of our frames
A living soul – I vowed to die for her:
With the faint voice of one who, having spoken,
Relapses into blessedness, I vowed it:
That solemn vow, a whisper scarcely heard,
A murmur breathed against a lady's ear.
50   Oh! there is joy above the name of pleasure,
Deep self-possession, an intense repose.
Sandoval [*with a sarcastic smile*]. No other than as eastern sages
          paint,
The God, who floats upon a lotos leaf,
Dreams for a thousand ages; then awaking,
Creates a world, and smiling at the bubble,
Relapses into bliss.

Earl Henry.   Ah! was that bliss
Feared as an alien, and too vast for man?
For suddenly, impatient of its silence,
Did Oropeza, starting, grasp my forehead.
60 I caught her arms; the veins were swelling on them.
Through the dark bower she sent a hollow voice; –
'Oh! what if all betray me? what if thou?'
I swore, and with an inward thought that seemed
The purpose and the substance of my being,
I swore to her, that were she red with guilt,
I would exchange my unblenched state with hers. –
Friend! by that winding passage, to that bower
I now will go – all objects there will teach me
Unwavering love, and singleness of heart.
70 Go, Sandoval! I am prepared to meet her –
Say nothing of me – I myself will seek her –
Nay, leave me, friend! I cannot bear the torment
And keen inquiry of that scanning eye. –

[*Earl Henry retires into the wood.*]

Sandoval [*alone*]. O Henry! always striv'st thou to be great
By thine own act – yet art thou never great
But by the inspiration of great passion.
The whirl-blast comes, the desert-sands rise up
And shape themselves: from earth to heaven they stand,
As though they were the pillars of a temple,
80 Built by Omnipotence in its own honour!
But the blast pauses, and their shaping spirit
Is fled: the mighty columns were but sand,
And lazy snakes trail o'er the level ruins!

On Revisiting the Sea-Shore
AFTER LONG ABSENCE, UNDER STRONG MEDICAL
RECOMMENDATION NOT TO BATHE

God be with thee, gladsome Ocean!
    How gladly greet I thee once more!
Ships and waves, and ceaseless motion,
    And men rejoicing on thy shore.

Dissuading spake the mild physician,
  'Those briny waves for thee are death!'
But my soul fulfilled her mission,
  And lo! I breathe untroubled breath!

Fashion's pining sons and daughters,
10   That seek the crowd they seem to fly,
Trembling they approach thy waters;
  And what cares Nature, if they die?

Me a thousand hopes and pleasures,
  A thousand recollections bland,
Thoughts sublime, and stately measures,
  Revisit on thy echoing strand:

Dreams (the soul herself forsaking),
  Tearful raptures, boyish mirth;
Silent adorations, making
20   A blessed shadow of this Earth!

O ye hopes, that stir within me,
  Health comes with you from above!
God is with me, God is in me!
  I cannot die, if Life be Love.

Inscription

FOR A FOUNTAIN ON A HEATH

This Sycamore, oft musical with bees, –
Such tents the Patriarchs loved! O long unharmed
May all its aged boughs o'er-canopy
The small round basin, which this jutting stone
Keeps pure from falling leaves! Long may the Spring,
Quietly as a sleeping infant's breath,
Send up cold waters to the traveller
With soft and even pulse! Nor ever cease
Yon tiny cone of sand its soundless dance,
10 Which at the bottom, like a Fairy's page,
As merry and no taller, dances still,

Nor wrinkles the smooth surface of the Fount.
Here twilight is and coolness: here is moss,
A soft seat, and a deep and ample shade.
Thou may'st toil far and find no second tree.
Drink, Pilgrim, here; Here rest! and if thy heart
Be innocent, here too shalt thou refresh
Thy Spirit, listening to some gentle sound,
Or passing gale or hum of murmuring bees!

Drinking versus Thinking
OR, A SONG AGAINST THE NEW PHILOSOPHY

My Merry men all, that drink with glee
This fanciful Philosophy,
    Pray tell me what good is it?
If *antient Nick* should come and take,
The same across the Stygian Lake,
    I guess we ne'er should miss it.

Away, each pale, self-brooding spark
That goes truth-hunting in the dark,
    Away from our carousing!
To Pallas we resign such fowls –
Grave birds of Wisdom! ye're but owls,
    And all your trade but *mousing*!

My merry men all, here's punch and wine,
And spicy bishop, drink divine!
    Let's live while we are able.
While Mirth and Sense sit, hand in glove,
This Don Philosophy we'll shove
    Dead drunk beneath the table!

An Ode to the Rain

Composed before day-light, on the morning appointed for the departure of a very worthy, but not very pleasant Visitor; whom it was feared the rain might detain.

I

I know it is dark; and though I have lain
Awake, as I guess, an hour or twain,
I have not once open'd the lids of my eyes,
But I lie in the dark, as a blind man lies.
O Rain! that I lie listening to,
    You're but a doleful sound at best:
I owe you little thanks, 'tis true,
    For breaking thus my needful rest!
Yet if, as soon as it is light,
O Rain! you will but take your flight,
I'll neither rail, nor malice keep,
Tho' sick and sore for want of sleep:
But only now, for this one day,
Do go, dear Rain! do go away!

II

O Rain! with your dull two-fold sound,
The clash hard by, and the murmur all round!
You know, if you know aught, that we,
Both night and day, but ill agree:
For days, and months, and almost years,
Have limp'd on thro' this vale of tears,
Since body of mine, and rainy weather,
Have liv'd on easy terms together.
Yet if, as soon as it is light,
O Rain! you will but take your flight,
Though you should come again to-morrow,
And bring with you both pain and sorrow;
Tho' stomach should sicken, and knees should swell –
I'll nothing speak of you but well.
But only now for this one day,
Do go, dear Rain! do go away!

III

Dear Rain! I ne'er refus'd to say
You're a good creature in your way.
Nay, I could write a book myself,
Would fit a parson's lower shelf,
Shewing, how very good you are –
What then? sometimes it must be fair!
And if sometimes, why not to day?
Do go, dear Rain! do go away!

IV

Dear Rain! if I've been cold and shy,
40   Take no offence! I'll tell you, why.
A dear old Friend e'en now is here,
And with him came my sister dear;
After long absence now first met,
Long months by pain and grief beset –
We three dear friends! in truth, we groan
Impatiently to be alone.
We three, you mark! and not one more!
The strong wish makes my spirit sore.
We have so much to talk about,
50   So many sad things to let out;
So many tears in our eye-corners,
Sitting like little Jacky Horners –
In short, as soon as it is day,
Do go, dear Rain! do go away.

V

And this I'll swear to you, dear Rain!
Whenever you shall come again,
Be you as dull as e'er you cou'd
(And by the bye 'tis understood,
You're not so pleasant, as you're good),
60   Yet, knowing well your worth and place,
I'll welcome you with cheerful face;
And though you stay'd a week or more,
Were ten times duller than before;
Yet with kind heart, and right good will,
I'll sit and listen to you still;

Nor should you go away, dear Rain!
Uninvited to remain.
But only now, for this one day,
Do go, dear Rain! do go away.

The Wills of the Wisp
A SAPPHIC

Vix ea nostra voco

Lunatic Witch-fires! Ghosts of Light and Motion!
Fearless I see you weave your wanton dances
Near me, far off me; you, that tempt the traveller
                        Onward and onward.

Wooing, retreating, till the swamp beneath him
Groans – and 'tis dark! – This woman's wile – I know it!
Learnt it from *thee*, from *thy* perfidious glances!
                        Black-ey'd Rebecca!

Ode to Tranquillity

Tranquillity! thou better name
Than all the family of Fame!
Thou ne'er wilt leave my riper age
To low intrigue, or factious rage;
For oh! dear child of thoughtful Truth,
To thee I gave my early youth,
And left the bark, and blest the steadfast shore,
Ere yet the tempest rose and scared me with its roar.

Who late and lingering seeks thy shrine,
On him but seldom, Power divine,
Thy spirit rests! Satiety
And Sloth, poor counterfeits of thee,
Mock the tired worldling. Idle hope
And dire remembrance interlope,
To vex the feverish slumbers of the mind:
The bubble floats before, the spectre stalks behind.

But me thy gentle hand will lead
At morning through the accustomed mead;
And in the sultry summer's heat
20   Will build me up a mossy seat;
And when the gust of Autumn crowds,
And breaks the busy moonlight clouds,
Thou best the thought canst raise, the heart attune,
Light as the busy clouds, calm as the gliding moon.

The feeling heart, the searching soul,
To thee I dedicate the whole!
And while within myself I trace
The greatness of some future race,
Aloof with hermit-eye I scan
30   The present works of present man –
A wild and dream-like trade of blood and guile,
Too foolish for a tear, too wicked for a smile!

A Letter to ——
April 4, 1802. – Sunday Evening

[*1834* lines]

Well! if the Bard was weatherwise, who made   1
The grand old Ballad of Sir Patrick Spence,   2
This Night, so tranquil now, will not go hence   3
Unrous'd by winds, that ply a busier trade   4
Than that, which moulds yon clouds in lazy flakes,   5
Or the dull sobbing Draft, that drones & rakes   6
Upon the Strings of this Eolian Lute,   7
    Which better far were mute.   8
For, lo! the New Moon, winter-bright!   9
10   And overspread with phantom Light,   10
(With swimming phantom Light o'erspread   11
But rimm'd & circled with a silver Thread)   12
I see the Old Moon in her Lap, foretelling   13
The coming-on of Rain & squally Blast –   14
O! Sara! that the Gust ev'n now were swelling,   15
And the slant Night-shower driving loud & fast!   16

¶

[*1834* lines]

A Grief without a pang, void, dark, & drear,	21
A stifling, drowsy, unimpassion'd Grief	22
That finds no natural Outlet, no Relief	23
In word, or sigh, or tear –	24

20

This, Sara! well thou know'st,
Is that sore Evil, which I dread the Most,
And oft'nest suffer! In this heartless Mood,   26
To other thoughts by yonder Throstle woo'd,
That pipes within the Larch-tree, not unseen,
(The Larch, which pushes out in tassels green
Its bundled Leafits) woo'd to mild Delights
By all the tender Sounds & gentle Sights
Of this sweet Primrose-month – & *vainly* woo'd

30 O dearest Sara! in this heartless Mood	25
All this long Eve, so balmy & serene,	27
Have I been gazing on the western Sky	28
And it's peculiar Tint of Yellow Green –	29
And still I gaze – & with how blank an eye!	30
And those thin Clouds above, in flakes & bars,	31
That give away their Motion to the Stars;	32
Those Stars, that glide behind them, or between,	33
Now sparkling, now bedimm'd, but always seen;	34
Yon crescent Moon, as fix'd as if it grew	35
40 In it's own cloudless, starless Lake of Blue –	36

A boat becalm'd! dear William's Sky Canoe!
– I see them all, so excellently fair!   37
  I see, not feel, how beautiful they are.   38

My genial Spirits fail –	39
And what can these avail	40
To lift the smoth'ring Weight from off my Breast?	41
It were a vain Endeavour,	42
Tho' I should gaze for ever	43
On that Green Light which lingers in the West!	44
50 I may not hope from outward Forms to win	45
The Passion & the Life whose Fountains are within!	46

These lifeless Shapes, around, below, Above,
  O what can they impart?
When even the gentle Thought, that thou, my Love!

Art gazing now, like me,
And see'st the Heaven, I see –
Sweet Thought it is – yet feebly stirs my Heart!

Feebly! O feebly! – Yet
(I well remember it)
60 In my first Dawn of Youth that Fancy stole
With many secret Yearnings on my Soul.
At eve, sky-gazing in 'ecstatic fit'
(Alas! for cloister'd in a city School
The Sky was all, I knew, of Beautiful)
At the barr'd window often did I sit,
And oft upon the leaded School-roof lay,
And to myself would say –
There does not live the Man so stripp'd of good affections
As not to love to see a Maiden's quiet Eyes
70 Uprais'd, and linking on sweet Dreams by dim Connections
To Moon, or Evening Star, or glorious western Skies –
While yet a Boy, this Thought would so pursue me
That often it became a kind of Vision to me!

Sweet Thought! and dear of old
To Hearts of finer Mould!
Ten thousand times by Friends & Lovers blest!
I spake with rash Despair,
And ere I was aware,
The Weight was somewhat lifted from my Breast!
80 O Sara! in the weather-fended Wood,
Thy lov'd haunt! where the Stock-doves coo at Noon,
I guess, that thou hast stood
And watch'd yon Crescent, & its ghost-like Moon.
And yet, far rather in my present Mood
I would, that thou'dst been sitting all this while
Upon the sod-built Seat of Camomile –
And tho' thy Robin may have ceas'd to sing,
Yet needs for *my* sake must thou love to hear
The Bee-hive murmuring near,
90 That ever-busy & most quiet Thing
Which I have heard at Midnight murmuring.

I feel my spirit moved –
And wheresoe'er thou be,
O Sister! O Beloved!

    Those dear mild Eyes, that see
    Even now the Heaven, *I* see –
There is a Prayer in them! It is for *me* –
And I, dear Sara – *I* am blessing *thee*!

It was as calm as this, that happy night
100 When Mary, thou, & I together were,
The low decaying Fire our only Light,
And listen'd to the Stillness of the Air!
O that affectionate & blameless Maid,
Dear Mary! on her Lap my head she lay'd –
    Her Hand was on my Brow,
    Even as my own is now;
And on my Cheek I felt thy eye-lash play.
Such Joy I had, that I may truly say,
My Spirit was awe-stricken with the Excess
110 And trance-like Depth of it's brief Happiness.

Ah fair Remembrances, that so revive
The Heart, & fill it with a living Power,
Where were they, Sara? – or did I not strive
To win them to me? – on the fretting Hour
Then when I wrote thee that complaining Scroll
Which even to bodily Sickness bruis'd thy Soul!
And yet thou blam'st thyself alone! And yet
    Forbidd'st me all Regret!

And must I not regret, that I distress'd
120 Thee, best belov'd! who lovest me the best?
My better mind had fled, I know not whither –
For O! was this an Absent Friend's Employ
To send from far both Pain & Sorrow thither
Where still his Blessings should have call'd down Joy!
I read thy guileless Letter o'er again –
I hear thee of thy blameless Self complain –
And only this I learn – & this, alas! I know –
That thou art weak & pale with Sickness, Grief, & Pain –
    And *I* – *I* made thee so!

130 O for my own sake I regret perforce
Whatever turns thee, Sara! from the course
Of calm Well-being & a Heart at rest!
When thou, & with thee those, whom thou lov'st best,

Shall dwell together in one happy Home,
One House, the dear *abiding* Home of All,
I too will crown me with a Coronal –
Nor shall this Heart in idle Wishes roam
    Morbidly soft!
No! let me trust, that I shall wear away
140 In no inglorious Toils the manly Day,
And only now & then, & not too oft,
Some dear & memorable Eve will bless
Dreaming of all your Loves & Quietness.

Be happy, & I need thee not in sight.
Peace in thy Heart, & Quiet in thy Dwelling,
Health in thy Limbs, & in thine Eyes the Light
Of Love, & Hope, & honorable Feeling –
Wharee'er I am, I shall be well content!
Not near thee, haply shall be more content!
150 To all things I prefer the Permanent.
And better seems it for a heart, like mine,
Always to *know*, than sometimes to behold,
    Their Happiness & thine –
For Change doth trouble me with pangs untold!
To see thee, hear thee, feel thee – then to part
    Oh! – it weighs down the Heart!
To *visit* those, I love, as I love thee,
Mary, & William, & dear Dorothy,
It is but a temptation to repine –
160 The transientness is Poison in the Wine,
Eats out the pith of Joy, makes all Joy hollow,
All Pleasure a dim Dream of Pain to follow!
My own peculiar Lot, my house-hold Life
It is, & will remain, Indifference or Strife –
While *ye* are *well* & *happy*, 'twould but wrong you
If I should fondly yearn to be among you –
Wherefore, O wherefore! should I wish to be
A wither'd branch upon a blossoming Tree?

But (let me say it! for I vainly strive
170 To beat away the Thought) but if thou pin'd,
Whate'er the Cause, in body or in mind,
I were the miserablest Man alive
To know it & be absent! Thy Delights

[*1834* lines]

Far off, or near, alike I may partake –
But O! to mourn for thee, & to forsake
All power, all hope of giving comfort to thee –
To know that thou art weak & worn with pain,
And not to hear thee, Sara! not to view thee
  Not sit beside thy Bed,
180 Not press thy aching Head,
  Not bring thee Health again –
  At least to hope, to try –
By this Voice, which thou lov'st, & by this earnest Eye –
Nay, wherefore did I let it haunt my Mind   94
  The dark distressful Dream!   95
I turn from it, & listen to the Wind   96
Which long has rav'd unnotic'd! What a Scream 97
Of agony by Torture lengthen'd out   98
That Lute sent forth! O thou wild Storm without! 99
190 Jagg'd Rock, or mountain Pond, or blasted Tree, 100
Or Pine-grove, whither Woodman never clomb, 101
Or lonely House, long held the Witches' Home, 102
Methinks were fitter Instruments for Thee, 103
Mad Lutanist! that in this month of Showers, 104
Of dark brown Gardens, & of peeping Flowers, 105
Mak'st Devil's Yule, with worse than wintry Song 106
The Blossoms, Buds, and timorous Leaves among! 107
Thou Actor, perfect in all tragic Sounds! 108
Thou mighty Poet, even to frenzy bold! 109
200 What tell'st thou now about?   110
'Tis of the Rushing of an Host in Rout – 111
And many Groans from men with smarting Wounds – 112
At once they groan with smart, and shudder with the Cold! 113
'Tis hush'd! there is a Trance of deepest Silence – 114
Again! but all that Sound, as of a rushing Crowd, 115
And Groans & tremulous Shudderings, all are over – 116
And it has other Sounds, and all less deep, less loud! 117
  A Tale of less Affright,   118
  And temper'd with Delight,   119
210 As William's Self had made the tender Lay – 120
  'Tis of a little Child   121
  Upon a heathy Wild,   122
Not far from home – but it has lost its way – 123
And now moans low in utter grief & fear – 124
And now screams loud, & hopes to make its Mother hear! 125

[*1834* lines]

'Tis Midnight! and small Thoughts have I of Sleep.   126

Full seldom may my Friend such Vigils keep –   127
O breathe She softly in her gentle Sleep!
Cover her, gentle Sleep! with wings of Healing –   128

220   And be this Tempest but a Mountain Birth!   129
May all the Stars hang bright above her Dwelling,   130
Silent, as tho' they watch'd the sleeping Earth!   131
Healthful & light, my Darling! may'st thou rise   132
    With clear & cheerful Eyes –   133
And of the same good Tidings to me send!
    For, oh! beloved Friend!
I am not the buoyant Thing, I was of yore –
When like an own Child, I to JOY belong'd;
For others mourning oft, myself oft sorely wrong'd,

230   Yet bearing all things then, as if I nothing bore!

    Yes, dearest Sara! yes!
There *was* a time when tho' my path was rough,   76
The Joy within me dallied with Distress;   77
And all Misfortunes were but as the Stuff   78
Whence Fancy made me Dreams of Happiness: 79
For Hope grew round me, like the climbing Vine,   80
And Leaves & Fruitage, not my own, seem'd mine!   81
But now Ill Tidings bow me down to earth –   82
Nor care I, that they rob me of my Mirth –   83
    But oh! each Visitation   84

240   Suspends what Nature gave me at my Birth,   85
    My shaping Spirit of Imagination!   86
I speak not now of those habitual Ills
That wear out Life, when two unequal Minds
Meet in one House, & two discordant Wills –
    This leaves me, where it finds,
Past cure, & past Complaint – a fate austere
Too fix'd & hopeless to partake of Fear!

But thou, dear Sara! (dear indeed thou art,
My Comforter! A Heart within my Heart!)

250   Thou, & the Few, we love, tho' few ye be,
Make up a world of Hopes & Fears for me.
And if Affliction, or distemp'ring Pain,
Or wayward Chance befall you, I complain

[*1834* lines]

Not that I mourn – O Friends, most dear! most true!
    Methinks to weep with you
Were better far than to rejoice alone –
But that my coarse domestic Life has known
No Habits of heart-nursing Sympathy,
No Griefs, but such as dull and deaden me,
No mutual mild Enjoyments of it's own,
No Hopes of it's own Vintage, None, O! none –
Whence when I mourn'd for you, my Heart might borrow
Fair forms & living Motions for it's Sorrow.
For not to think of what I needs must feel,   87
But to be still & patient all I can;   88
And haply by abstruse Research to steal   89
From my own Nature all the Natural Man –   90
This was my sole Resource, my wisest plan!   91
And that, which suits a part, infects the whole,   92
And now is almost grown the Temper of my Soul.   83

    My little Children are a Joy, a Love,
        A good Gift from above!
But what is Bliss, that still calls up a Woe,
        And makes it doubly keen
Compelling me to *feel*, as well as *know*,
What a most blessed Lot mine might have been
Those little Angel Children (woe is me!)
There have been hours, when feeling how they bind
And pluck out the wing-feathers of my Mind,
Turning my Error to Necessity,
I have half-wish'd, they never had been born!
That seldom! But sad Thoughts they always bring,
And like the Poet's Philomel, I sing
My Love-song, with my breast against a Thorn.

With no unthankful Spirit I confess,
This clinging Grief too, in it's turn, awakes
That Love, and Father's Joy; but O! it makes
The Love the greater, & the Joy far less.
These Mountains too, these Vales, these Woods, these Lakes,
Scenes full of Beauty & of Loftiness

Line numbers in left margin: 260, 270, 280, 290

[*1834* lines]

Where all my Life I fondly hop'd to live –
I were sunk low indeed, did they *no* solace give;
But oft I seem to feel, & evermore I fear,
They are not to me the Things, which once they were.

O Sara! we receive but what we give,   47
And in *our* Life alone does Nature live.   48
Our's is her Wedding Garment, our's her Shroud –   49
And would we aught behold of higher Worth   50
Than that inanimate cold World allow'd   51
To the poor loveless ever-anxious Crowd,   52
Ah! from the Soul itself must issue forth   53
A Light, a Glory, and a luminous Cloud   54
   Enveloping the Earth!   55
And from the Soul itself must there be se[nt]   56
A sweet & potent Voice, of it's own Bir[th,]   57
Of all sweet Sounds the Life & Element.   58
O pure of Heart! thou need'st not ask of me   59
What this strong music in the Soul may be,   60
   What, & wherein it doth exist,   61
This Light, this Glory, this fair luminous Mist,   62
This beautiful & beauty-making Power!   63
Joy, innocent Sara! Joy, that ne'er was given   64
Save to the Pure, & in their purest Hour,   65
Joy, Sara! is the Spirit & the Power,   67
That wedding Nature to us gives in Dower   68
   A new Earth & new Heaven   69
Undreamt of by the Sensual & the Proud!   70
Joy is that strong Voice, Joy that luminous Cloud –   71
   We, we ourselves rejoice!   72
And thence flows all that charms or ear or sight,   73
All melodies the Echoes of that Voice,   74
All Colours a Suffusion of that Light.   75

Sister & Friend of my devoutest Choice!
Thou being innocent & full of love,
And nested with the Darlings of thy Love,
And feeling in thy Soul, Heart, Lips, & Arms
Even what the conjugal & mother Dove
That borrows genial Warmth from those, she warms,
Feels in her thrill'd wings, blessedly outspread –
Thou free'd awhile from Cares & human Dread

300

310

320

330

[*1834* lines]

By the Immenseness of the Good & Fair
    Which thou see'st every where –
Thus, thus should'st thou rejoice!
To thee would all Things live from Pole to Pole,   135
Their Life the Eddying of thy living Soul.   136
O dear! O Innocent! O full of Love!   [137]
A very Friend! A Sister of my Choice –   138
O dear, as Light & Impulse from above,   [137]
Thus may'st thou ever, evermore rejoice!   139
                    S. T. C.

Dejection: An Ode

Late, late yestreen I saw the new Moon,
With the old Moon in her arms;
And I fear, I fear, my Master dear!
We shall have a deadly storm.

Ballad of Sir Patrick Spence

I

Well! If the Bard was weather-wise, who made
    The grand old ballad of Sir Patrick Spence,
  This night, so tranquil now, will not go hence
Unroused by winds, that ply a busier trade
Than those which mould yon cloud in lazy flakes,
Or the dull sobbing draft, that moans and rakes,
    Upon the strings of this Eolian lute,
    Which better far were mute.
  For lo! the New-moon winter-bright!
    And overspread with phantom light,
    (With swimming phantom light o'erspread
    But rimmed and circled by a silver thread)
I see the old Moon in her lap, foretelling
  The coming on of rain and squally blast.
And oh! that even now the gust were swelling,
  And the slant night-shower driving loud and fast!
Those sounds which oft have raised me, whilst they awed,
    And sent my soul abroad,
Might now perhaps their wonted impulse give,
Might startle this dull pain, and make it move and live!

II

A grief without a pang, void, dark, and drear,
　　A stifled, drowsy, unimpassioned grief,
　　Which finds no natural outlet, no relief,
　　　　In word, or sigh, or tear –
O Lady! in this wan and heartless mood,
To other thoughts by yonder throstle woo'd,
　　All this long eve, so balmy and serene,
Have I been gazing on the western sky,
　　And its peculiar tint of yellow green:
30　And still I gaze – and with how blank an eye!
And those thin clouds above, in flakes and bars,
That give away their motion to the stars;
Those stars, that glide behind them or between,
Now sparkling, now bedimmed, but always seen:
Yon crescent Moon as fixed as if it grew
In its own cloudless, starless lake of blue;
I see them all so excellently fair,
I see, not feel how beautiful they are!

III

　　　　My genial spirits fail;
40　　　And what can these avail
To lift the smothering weight from off my breast?
　　　　It were a vain endeavour,
　　　　Though I should gaze for ever
On that green light that lingers in the west:
I may not hope from outward forms to win
The passion and the life, whose fountains are within.

IV

O Lady! we receive but what we give,
And in our life alone does nature live:
Ours is her wedding-garment, ours her shroud!
50　　And would we aught behold, of higher worth,
Than that inanimate cold world allowed
To the poor loveless ever-anxious crowd,
　　Ah! from the soul itself must issue forth,
A light, a glory, a fair luminous cloud
　　　　Enveloping the Earth –
And from the soul itself must there be sent
　　A sweet and potent voice, of its own birth,
Of all sweet sounds the life and element!

V

O pure of heart! thou need'st not ask of me
60 What this strong music in the soul may be!
What, and wherein it doth exist,
This light, this glory, this fair luminous mist,
This beautiful and beauty-making power.
    Joy, virtuous Lady! Joy that ne'er was given,
Save to the pure, and in their purest hour,
Life, and Life's effluence, cloud at once and shower,
Joy, Lady! is the spirit and the power,
Which wedding Nature to us gives in dower,
    A new Earth and new Heaven,
70 Undreamt of by the sensual and the proud –
Joy is the sweet voice, Joy the luminous cloud –
        We in ourselves rejoice!
And thence flows all that charms or ear or sight,
    All melodies the echoes of that voice,
All colours a suffusion from that light.

VI

There was a time when, though my path was rough,
    This joy within me dallied with distress,
And all misfortunes were but as the stuff
    Whence Fancy made me dreams of happiness:
80 For hope grew round me, like the twining vine,
And fruits, and foliage, not my own, seemed mine.
But now afflictions bow me down to earth:
Nor care I that they rob me of my mirth,
        But oh! each visitation
Suspends what nature gave me at my birth,
    My shaping spirit of Imagination.
For not to think of what I needs must feel,
    But to be still and patient, all I can;
And haply by abstruse research to steal
90   From my own nature all the natural man –
    This was my sole resource, my only plan:
Till that which suits a part infects the whole,
And now is almost grown the habit of my soul.

VII

Hence, viper thoughts, that coil around my mind,
        Reality's dark dream!
I turn from you, and listen to the wind,

Which long has raved unnoticed. What a scream
Of agony by torture lengthened out
That lute sent forth! Thou wind, that ravest without,
100   Bare craig, or mountain-tairn, or blasted tree,
Or pine-grove whither woodman never clomb,
Or lonely house, long held the witches' home,
Methinks were fitter instruments for thee,
Mad Lutanist! who in this month of showers,
Of dark brown gardens, and of peeping flowers,
Mak'st Devils' yule, with worse than wintry song,
The blossoms, buds, and timorous leaves among.
Thou Actor, perfect in all tragic sounds!
Thou mighty Poet, e'en to frenzy bold!
110   What tell'st thou now about?
'Tis of the rushing of a host in rout,
With groans of trampled men, with smarting wounds –
At once they groan with pain, and shudder with the cold!
But hush! there is a pause of deepest silence!
And all that noise, as of a rushing crowd,
With groans, and tremulous shudderings – all is over –
It tells another tale, with sounds less deep and loud!
A tale of less affright,
And tempered with delight,
120   As Otway's self had framed the tender lay,
'Tis of a little child
Upon a lonesome wild,
Not far from home, but she hath lost her way:
And now moans low in bitter grief and fear,
And now screams loud, and hopes to make her mother hear.

VIII

'Tis midnight, but small thoughts have I of sleep:
Full seldom may my friend such vigils keep!
Visit her, gentle Sleep! with wings of healing,
And may this storm be but a mountain-birth,
130   May all the stars hang bright above her dwelling
Silent as though they watched the sleeping Earth!
With light heart may she rise,
Gay fancy, cheerful eyes,
Joy lift her spirit, joy attune her voice;
To her may all things live, from pole to pole,
Their life the eddying of her living soul!

O simple spirit, guided from above,
Dear Lady! friend devoutest of my choice,
Thus mayest thou ever, evermore rejoice.

[A Soliloquy of the full Moon, She being in a Mad Passion –]

Now as Heaven is my Lot, they're the Pests of the Nation!
Wherever they can come
With clankum and blankum
'Tis all Botheration, & Hell & Damnation,
With fun, jeering
Conjuring
Sky-staring,
Loungering,
And still to the tune of Transmogrification –
10   Those muttering
Spluttering
Ventriloquogusty
Poets
With no Hats
Or Hats that are rusty.
They're my Torment and Curse
And harass me worse
And bait me and bay me, far sorer I vow
Than the Screech of the Owl
20   Or the witch-wolf's long howl,
Or sheep-killing Butcher-dog's inward Bow wow
For me they all spite – an unfortunate Wight.
And the very first moment that I came to Light
A Rascal call'd Voss the more to his scandal,
Turn'd me into a sickle with never a handle.
A Night or two after a worse Rogue there came,
The head of the Gang, one Wordsworth by name –
'Ho! What's in the wind?' 'Tis the voice of a Wizzard!
I saw him look at me most terribly blue!
30   He was hunting for witch-rhymes from great A to Izzard,
And soon as he'd found them made no more ado
But chang'd me at once to a little Canoe.
From this strange Enchantment uncharm'd by degrees

I began to take courage & hop'd for some Ease,
When one Coleridge, a Raff of the self-same Banditti
Passed by – & intending no doubt to be witty,
Because I'd th' ill-fortune his taste to displease,
   He turn'd up his nose,
   And in pitiful Prose
40   Made me into the half of a small Cheshire Cheese.
Well, a night or two past – it was wind, rain & hail –
And I ventur'd abroad in a thick Cloak & veil –
But the very first Evening he saw me again
The last mentioned Ruffian popp'd out of his Den –
I was resting a moment on the bare edge of Naddle
I fancy the sight of me turn'd his Brains addle –
   For what was I now?
   A complete Barley-mow
And when I climb'd higher he made a long leg,
50   And chang'd me at once to an Ostrich's Egg –
But now Heaven be praised in contempt of the Loon,
I am I myself I, the jolly full Moon.
   Yet my heart is still fluttering –
   For I heard the Rogue muttering –
He was hulking and skulking at the skirt of a Wood
When lightly & brightly on tip-toe I stood
On the long level Line of a motionless Cloud
And ho! what a Skittle-ground! quoth he aloud
And wish'd from his heart nine-pins to see
60   In brightness & size just proportion'd to me.
So I fear'd from my soul,
That he'd make me a Bowl,
But in spite of his spite
This was more than his might
And still Heaven be prais'd! in contempt of the Loon
I am I myself I, the jolly full Moon.

Answer to a Child's Question

Do you ask what the birds say? The sparrow, the dove,
The linnet and thrush say, 'I love and I love!'
In the winter they're silent – the wind is so strong;
What it says, I don't know, but it sings a loud song.
But green leaves, and blossoms, and sunny warm weather,
And singing, and loving – all come back together.
But the lark is so brimful of gladness and love,
The green fields below him, the blue sky above,
That he sings, and he sings; and for ever sings he –
'I love my Love, and my Love loves me!'

A Day Dream

My eyes make pictures, when they are shut: –
I see a fountain, large and fair,
A willow and a ruinèd hut,
And thee, and me and Mary there.
O Mary! make thy gentle lap our pillow!
Bend o'er us, like a bower, my beautiful green willow!

A wild-rose roofs the ruined shed,
And that and summer well agree:
And lo! where Mary leans her head,
Two dear names carved upon the tree!
And Mary's tears, they are not tears of sorrow:
Our sister and our friend will both be here to-morrow.

'Twas day! But now few, large, and bright
The stars are round the crescent moon!
And now it is a dark warm night,
The balmiest of the month of June!
A glow-worm fallen, and on the marge remounting
Shines and its shadow shines, fit stars for our sweet fountain.

O ever – ever be thou blest!
20   For dearly, Asra, love I thee!
This brooding warmth across my breast,
      This depth of tranquil bliss – ah me!
Fount, tree and shed are gone, I know not whither,
But in one quiet room we three are still together.

The shadows dance upon the wall,
      By the still dancing fire-flames made;
And now they slumber, moveless all!
      And now they melt to one deep shade!
But not from me shall this mild darkness steal thee:
30   I dream thee with mine eyes, and at my heart I feel thee!

Thine eyelash on my cheek doth play –
      'Tis Mary's hand upon my brow!
But let me check this tender lay
      Which none may hear but she and thou!
Like the still hive at quiet midnight humming,
Murmur it to yourselves, ye two beloved women!

The Day-Dream
FROM AN EMIGRANT TO HIS ABSENT WIFE

If thou wert here, these tears were tears of light!
      But from as sweet a vision did I start
As ever made these eyes grow idly bright!
      And though I weep, yet still around my heart
A sweet and playful tenderness doth linger,
Touching my heart as with an infant's finger.

My mouth half open, like a witless man,
      I saw our couch, I saw our quiet room,
      Its shadows heaving by the fire-light gloom;
10   And o'er my lips a subtle feeling ran,
All o'er my lips a soft and breeze-like feeling –
I know not what – but had the same been stealing

Upon a sleeping mother's lips, I guess
    It would have made the loving mother dream
That she was softly bending down to kiss
    Her babe, that something more than babe did seem,
A floating presence of its darling father,
And yet its own dear baby self far rather!

Across my chest there lay a weight, so warm!
20   As if some bird had taken shelter there;
And lo! I seemed to see a woman's form –
    Thine, Sara, thine? O joy, if thine it were!
I gazed with stifled breath, and feared to stir it,
No deeper trance e'er wrapt a yearning spirit!

And now, when I seemed sure thy face to see,
    Thy own dear self in our own quiet home;
There came an elfish laugh, and wakened me:
    'Twas Frederic, who behind my chair had clomb,
And with his bright eyes at my face was peeping.
30   I blessed him, tried to laugh, and fell a-weeping!

To Asra

Are there two things, of all which men possess,
That are so like each other and so near,
As mutual Love seems like to Happiness?
Dear Asra, woman beyond utterance dear!
This Love which ever welling at my heart,
Now in its living fount doth heave and fall,
Now overflowing pours thro' every part
Of all my frame, and fills and changes all,
Like vernal waters springing up through snow,
10   This Love that seeming great beyond the power
Of growth, yet seemeth ever more to grow,
Could I transmute the whole to one rich Dower
Of Happy Life, and give it all to Thee,
Thy lot, methinks, were Heaven, thy age, Eternity!

The Happy Husband

Oft, oft methinks, the while with Thee
  I breathe, as from the heart, thy dear
  And dedicated name, I hear
A promise and a mystery,
  A pledge of more than passing life,
  Yea, in that very name of Wife!

A pulse of love, that ne'er can sleep!
  A feeling that upbraids the heart
  With happiness beyond desert,
10 That gladness half requests to weep!
  Nor bless I not the keener sense
  And unalarming turbulence

Of transient joys, that ask no sting
  From jealous fears, or coy denying;
  But born beneath Love's brooding wing,
And into tenderness soon dying,
  Wheel out their giddy moment, then
  Resign the soul to love again; –

A more precipitated vein
20   Of notes, that eddy in the flow
  Of smoothest song, they come, they go,
And leave their sweeter understrain
  Its own sweet self – a love of Thee
  That seems, yet cannot greater be!

A Thought Suggested by a View
OF SADDLEBACK IN CUMBERLAND

On stern Blencathra's perilous height
  The winds are tyrannous and strong;
And flashing forth unsteady light
From stern Blencathra's skiey height,
  As loud the torrents throng!

Beneath the moon, in gentle weather,
They bind the earth and sky together.
But oh! the sky and all its forms, how quiet!
The things that seek the earth, how full of noise and riot!

[Untitled]

Upon the mountain's Edge all lightly resting
There a brief while the Globe of splendour sits,
And seems a creature of this earth; but soon
   More changeful than the Moon
To Wane fantastic his great orb submits,
Or cone or mow of Fire, till sinking slowly
Even to a Star at length he lessens wholly.

Abrupt, as Spirits vanish, he is sunk
A soul-like breeze possesses all the wood;
10   The Boughs, the sprays have stood
As motionless, as stands the ancient Trunk,
But every leaf thro all the forest flutters,
And deep the Cavern of the Fountain mutters.

The Keepsake

The tedded hay, the first fruits of the soil,
The tedded hay and corn-sheaves in one field,
Show summer gone, ere come. The foxglove tall
Sheds its loose purple bells, or in the gust,
Or when it bends beneath the up-springing lark,
Or mountain-finch alighting. And the rose
(In vain the darling of successful love)
Stands, like some boasted beauty of past years,
The thorns remaining, and the flowers all gone.
10 Nor can I find, amid my lonely walk
By rivulet, or spring, or wet road-side,
That blue and bright-eyed floweret of the brook,
Hope's gentle gem, the sweet Forget-me-not!

So will not fade the flowers which Emmeline
With delicate fingers on the snow-white silk
Has worked (the flowers which most she knew I loved)
And, more beloved than they, her auburn hair.

    In the cool morning twilight, early waked
By her full bosom's joyous restlessness,
20   Softly she rose, and lightly stole along,
Down the slope coppice to the woodbine bower,
Whose rich flowers, swinging in the morning breeze,
Over their dim fast-moving shadows hung,
Making a quiet image of disquiet
In the smooth, scarcely moving river-pool.
There, in that bower where first she owned her love,
And let me kiss my own warm tear of joy
From off her glowing cheek, she sate and stretched
The silk upon the frame, and worked her name
30   Between the Moss-Rose and Forget-me-not –
Her own dear name, with her own auburn hair!
That forced to wander till sweet spring return,
I yet might ne'er forget her smile, her look,
Her voice (that even in her mirthful mood
Has made me wish to steal away and weep),
Nor yet the entrancement of that maiden kiss
With which she promised, that when spring returned,
She would resign one half of that dear name,
And own thenceforth no other name but mine!

The Picture,
OR THE LOVER'S RESOLUTION

Through weeds and thorns, and matted underwood
I force my way; now climb, and now descend
O'er rocks, or bare or mossy, with wild foot
Crushing the purple whorts; while oft unseen,
Hurrying along the drifted forest-leaves,
The scared snake rustles. Onward still I toil
I know not, ask not whither! A new joy,

Lovely as light, sudden as summer gust,
And gladsome as the first-born of the spring,
10   Beckons me on, or follows from behind,
Playmate, or guide! The master-passion quelled,
I feel that I am free. With dun-red bark
The fir-trees, and the unfrequent slender oak,
Forth from this tangle wild of bush and brake
Soar up, and form a melancholy vault
High o'er me, murmuring like a distant sea.

Here Wisdom might resort, and here Remorse;
Here too the love-lorn man, who, sick in soul,
And of this busy human heart aweary,
20   Worships the spirit of unconscious life
In tree or wild-flower. – Gentle lunatic!
If so he might not wholly cease to be,
He would far rather not be that, he is;
But would be something, that he knows not of,
In winds or waters, or among the rocks!

But hence, fond wretch! breathe not contagion here!
No myrtle-walks are these: these are no groves
Where Love dare loiter! If in sullen mood
He should stray hither, the low stumps shall gore
30   His dainty feet, the brier and the thorn
Make his plumes haggard. Like a wounded bird
Easily caught, ensnare him, O ye Nymphs,
Ye Oreads chaste, ye dusky Dryades!
And you, ye Earth-winds! you that make at morn
The dew-drops quiver on the spiders' webs!
You, O ye wingless Airs! that creep between
The rigid stems of heath and bitten furze,
Within whose scanty shade, at summer-noon,
The mother-sheep hath worn a hollow bed –
40   Ye, that now cool her fleece with dropless damp,
Now pant and murmur with her feeding lamb.
Chase, chase him, all ye Fays, and elfin Gnomes!
With prickles sharper than his darts bemock
His little Godship, making him perforce
Creep through a thorn-bush on yon hedgehog's back.

    This is my hour of triumph! I can now
With my own fancies play the merry fool,
And laugh away worse folly, being free.
Here will I seat myself, beside this old,
50   Hollow, and weedy oak, which ivy-twine
Clothes as with net-work: here will I couch my limbs,
Close by this river, in this silent shade,
As safe and sacred from the step of man
As an invisible world – unheard, unseen,
And listening only to the pebbly brook
That murmurs with a dead, yet tinkling sound;
Or to the bees, that in the neighbouring trunk
Make honey-hoards. The breeze, that visits me,
Was never Love's accomplice, never raised
60   The tendril ringlets from the maiden's brow,
And the blue, delicate veins above her cheek;
Ne'er played the wanton – never half disclosed
The maiden's snowy bosom, scattering thence
Eye-poisons for some love-distempered youth,
Who ne'er henceforth may see an aspen-grove
Shiver in sunshine, but his feeble heart
Shall flow away like a dissolving thing.

    Sweet breeze! thou only, if I guess aright,
Liftest the feathers of the robin's breast,
70   That swells its little breast, so full of song,
Singing above me, on the mountain-ash.
And thou too, desert stream! no pool of thine,
Though clear as lake in latest summer-eve,
Did e'er reflect the stately virgin's robe,
The face, the form divine, the downcast look
Contemplative! Behold! her open palm
Presses her cheek and brow! her elbow rests
On the bare branch of half-uprooted tree
That leans towards its mirror! Who erewhile
80   Had from her countenance turned, or looked by stealth
(For fear is true love's cruel nurse), he now
With steadfast gaze and unoffending eye,
Worships the watery idol, dreaming hopes
Delicious to the soul, but fleeting, vain,
E'en as that phantom-world on which he gazed,
But not unheeded gazed: for see, ah! see,
The sportive tyrant with her left hand plucks

The heads of tall flowers that behind her grow,
Lychnis, and willow-herb, and fox-glove bells:
90 And suddenly, as one that toys with time,
Scatters them on the pool! Then all the charm
Is broken – all that phantom-world so fair
Vanishes, and a thousand circlets spread,
And each mis-shape the other. Stay awhile,
Poor youth, who scarcely dar'st lift up thine eyes!
The stream will soon renew its smoothness, soon
The visions will return! And lo! he stays:
And soon the fragments dim of lovely forms
Come trembling back, unite, and now once more
100 The pool becomes a mirror; and behold
Each wild-flower on the marge inverted there,
And there the half-uprooted tree – but where,
O where the virgin's snowy arm, that leaned
On its bare branch? He turns, and she is gone!
Homeward she steals through many a woodland maze
Which he shall seek in vain. Ill-fated youth!
Go, day by day, and waste thy manly prime
In mad love-yearning by the vacant brook,
Till sickly thoughts bewitch thine eyes, and thou
110 Behold'st her shadow still abiding there,
The Naiad of the mirror!

                Not to thee,
O wild and desert stream! belongs this tale:
Gloomy and dark art thou – the crowded firs
Spire from thy shores, and stretch across thy bed,
Making thee doleful as a cavern-well:
Save when the shy king-fishers build their nest
On thy steep banks, no loves hast thou, wild stream!

    This be my chosen haunt – emancipate
From passion's dreams, a freeman, and alone,
120 I rise and trace its devious course. O lead,
Lead me to deeper shades and lonelier glooms.
Lo! stealing through the canopy of firs,
How fair the sunshine spots that mossy rock,
Isle of the river, whose disparted waves
Dart off asunder with an angry sound,
How soon to re-unite! And see! they meet,
Each in the other lost and found: and see

Placeless, as spirits, one soft water-sun
Throbbing within them, heart at once and eye!
130   With its soft neighbourhood of filmy clouds,
The stains and shadings of forgotten tears,
Dimness o'erswum with lustre! Such the hour
Of deep enjoyment, following love's brief feuds;
And hark, the noise of a near waterfall!
I pass forth into light – I find myself
Beneath a weeping birch (most beautiful
Of forest-trees, the lady of the woods)
Hard by the brink of a tall weedy rock
That overbrows the cataract. How bursts
140   The landscape on my sight! Two crescent hills
Fold in behind each other, and so make
A circular vale, and land-locked, as might seem,
With brook and bridge, and grey stone cottages,
Half hid by rocks and fruit-trees. At my feet,
The whortle-berries are bedewed with spray,
Dashed upwards by the furious waterfall.
How solemnly the pendent ivy-mass
Swings in its winnow; all the air is calm.
The smoke from cottage chimneys, tinged with light,
150   Rises in columns; from this house alone,
Close by the waterfall, the column slants,
And feels its ceaseless breeze. But what is this?
That cottage, with its slanting chimney-smoke,
And close beside its porch a sleeping child,
His dear head pillowed on a sleeping dog –
One arm between its fore legs, and the hand
Holds loosely its small handful of wild-flowers,
Unfilletted, and of unequal lengths.
A curious picture, with a master's haste
160   Sketched on a strip of pinky-silver skin,
Peeled from the birchen bark! Divinest maid!
Yon bark her canvass, and those purple berries
Her pencil! See, the juice is scarcely dried
On the fine skin! She has been newly here;
And lo! yon patch of heath has been her couch –
The pressure still remains! O blessed couch!
For this mayst thou flower early, and the sun,
Slanting at eve, rest bright, and linger long
Upon thy purple bells! O Isabel!
170   Daughter of genius! stateliest of our maids!

More beautiful than whom Alcæus wooed
The Lesbian woman of immortal song!
O child of genius! stately, beautiful,
And full of love to all, save only me,
And not ungentle e'en to me! My heart,
Why beats it thus? Through yonder coppice-wood
Needs must the pathway turn, that leads straightway
On to her father's house. She is alone!
The night draws on – such ways are hard to hit –
180   And fit it is I should restore this sketch,
Dropt unawares no doubt. Why should I yearn
To keep the relique? 'twill but idly feed
The passion that consumes me. Let me haste!
The picture in my hand which she has left;
She cannot blame me that I followed her:
And I may be her guide the long wood through.

Hymn
BEFORE SUN-RISE, IN THE VALE OF CHAMOUNI

Besides the Rivers, Arve and Arveiron, which have their sources in the
foot of Mont Blanc, five conspicuous torrents rush down its sides; and
within a few paces of the Glaciers, the Gentiana Major grows in immense
numbers with its 'flowers of loveliest blue'.

Hast thou a charm to stay the morning-star
In his steep course? So long he seems to pause
On thy bald awful head, O sovran Blanc!
The Arve and Arveiron at thy base
Rave ceaselessly; but thou, most awful Form!
Risest from forth thy silent sea of pines,
How silently! Around thee and above
Deep is the air and dark, substantial, black,
An ebon mass: methinks thou piercest it,
10   As with a wedge! But when I look again,
It is thine own calm home, thy crystal shrine,
Thy habitation from eternity!
O dread and silent Mount! I gazed upon thee,
Till thou, still present to the bodily sense,
Didst vanish from my thought: entranced in prayer
I worshipped the Invisible alone.

Yet, like some sweet beguiling melody,
So sweet, we know not we are listening to it,
Thou, the meanwhile, wast blending with my thought,
20 Yea, with my life and life's own secret joy:
Till the dilating Soul, enrapt, transfused,
Into the mighty vision passing – there
As in her natural form, swelled vast to Heaven!

Awake, my soul! not only passive praise
Thou owest! not alone these swelling tears,
Mute thanks and secret ecstasy! Awake,
Voice of sweet song! Awake, my Heart, awake!
Green vales and icy cliffs, all join my Hymn.

Thou first and chief, sole sovran of the Vale!
30 O struggling with the darkness all the night,
And visited all night by troops of stars,
Or when they climb the sky or when they sink:
Companion of the morning-star at dawn,
Thyself Earth's rosy star, and of the dawn
Co-herald: wake, O wake, and utter praise!
Who sank thy sunless pillars deep in Earth?
Who filled thy countenance with rosy light?
Who made thee parent of perpetual streams?

And you, ye five wild torrents fiercely glad!
40 Who called you forth from night and utter death,
From dark and icy caverns called you forth,
Down those precipitous, black, jagged Rocks,
For ever shattered and the same for ever?
Who gave you your invulnerable life,
Your strength, your speed, your fury, and your joy,
Unceasing thunder and eternal foam?
And who commanded (and the silence came),
Here let the billows stiffen, and have rest?

Ye ice-falls! ye that from the mountain's brow
50 Adown enormous ravines slope amain –
Torrents, methinks, that heard a mighty voice,
And stopped at once amid their maddest plunge!
Motionless torrents! silent cataracts!
Who made you glorious as the gates of Heaven
Beneath the keen full moon? Who bade the sun

Clothe you with rainbows? Who, with living flowers
Of loveliest blue, spread garlands at your feet? –
God! let the torrents, like a shout of nations,
Answer! and let the ice-plains echo, God!
60 God! sing ye meadow-streams with gladsome voice!
Ye pine-groves, with your soft and soul-like sounds!
And they too have a voice, yon piles of snow,
And in their perilous fall shall thunder, God!

Ye living flowers that skirt the eternal frost!
Ye wild goats sporting round the eagle's nest!
Ye eagles, play-mates of the mountain-storm!
Ye lightnings, the dread arrows of the clouds!
Ye signs and wonders of the element!
Utter forth God, and fill the hills with praise!

70 Thou too, hoar Mount! with thy sky-pointing peaks,
Oft from whose feet the avalanche, unheard,
Shoots downward, glittering through the pure serene
Into the depth of clouds, that veil thy breast –
Thou too again, stupendous Mountain! thou
That as I raise my head, awhile bowed low
In adoration, upward from thy base
Slow travelling with dim eyes suffused with tears,
Solemnly seemest, like a vapoury cloud,
To rise before me – Rise, O ever rise,
80 Rise like a cloud of incense, from the Earth!
Thou kingly Spirit throned among the hills,
Thou dread ambassador from Earth to Heaven,
Great hierarch! tell thou the silent sky,
And tell the stars, and tell yon rising sun,
Earth, with her thousand voices, praises God.

The Good, Great Man

'How seldom, friend! a good great man inherits
Honour or wealth with all his worth and pains!
It sounds like stories from the land of spirits
If any man obtain that which he merits
Or any merit that which he obtains.'

REPLY TO THE ABOVE

For shame, dear friend, renounce this canting strain!
What would'st thou have a good great man obtain?
Place? titles? salary? a gilded chain?
10   Or throne of corses which his sword had slain?
Greatness and goodness are not *means*, but *ends*!
Hath he not always treasures, always friends,
The good great man? *three* treasures, LOVE, and LIGHT,
    And CALM THOUGHTS, regular as infant's breath:
And three firm friends, more sure than day and night,
    HIMSELF, his MAKER, and the ANGEL DEATH!

The Knight's Tomb

Where is the grave of Sir Arthur O'Kellyn?
Where may the grave of that good man be? –
By the side of a spring, on the breast of Helvellyn,
Under the twigs of a young birch tree!
The oak that in summer was sweet to hear,
And rustled its leaves in the fall of the year,
And whistled and roared in the winter alone,
Is gone, – and the birch in its stead is grown. –
The Knight's bones are dust,
10   And his good sword rust; –
His soul is with the saints, I trust.

To Matilda Betham from a Stranger

Matilda! I have heard a sweet tune played
On a sweet instrument – thy Poesie –
Sent to my soul by Boughton's pleading voice,
Where friendship's zealous wish inspirited,
Deepened and filled the subtle tones of *taste*:
(So have I heard a Nightingale's fine notes
Blend with the murmur of a hidden stream!)
And now the fair, wild offspring of thy genius,
Those wanderers whom thy fancy had sent forth

10   To seek their fortune in this motley world,
Have found a little home within *my* heart,
And brought me, as the quit-rent of their lodging,
Rose-buds, and fruit-blossoms, and pretty weeds,
And timorous laurel leaflets half-disclosed,
Engarlanded with gadding woodbine tendrils!
A coronal, which, with undoubting hand,
I twine around the brows of patriot HOPE!

The Almighty, having first composed a Man,
Set him to music, framing Woman for him,
20   And fitted each to each, and made them one!
And 'tis my faith, that there's a natural bond
Between the female mind and measured sounds,
Nor do I know a sweeter Hope than this,
That this sweet Hope, by judgment unreproved,
That our own Britain, our dear mother Isle,
May boast one Maid, a poetess *indeed*,
Great as th' impassioned Lesbian, in sweet song,
And O! of holier mind, and happier fate.

Matilda! I dare twine *thy* vernal wreath
30   Around the brows of patriot Hope! But thou
Be wise! be bold! fulfil my auspices!
Tho' sweet thy measures, stern must be thy thought,
Patient thy study, watchful thy mild eye!
Poetic feelings, like the stretching boughs
Of mighty oaks, pay homage to the gales,
Toss in the strong winds, drive before the gust,
Themselves one giddy storm of fluttering leaves;
Yet, all the while self-limited, remain
Equally near the fixed and solid trunk
40   Of Truth and Nature in the howling storm,
As in the calm that stills the aspen grove.
Be bold, meek Woman! but be wisely bold!
Fly, ostrich-like, firm land beneath thy feet,
Yet hurried onward by thy wings of fancy
Swift as the whirlwind, singing in their quills.
Look round thee! look within thee! think and feel!
What nobler meed, Matilda! canst thou win,
Than tears of gladness in a BOUGHTON's eyes,
And exultation even in strangers' hearts?

Westphalian Song

The following is an almost literal translation of a very old and very favourite song among the Westphalian Boors. The turn at the end is the same with one of Mr Dibdin's excellent songs, and the air to which it is sung by the Boors is remarkably sweet and lively.

When thou to my true-love com'st
    Greet her from me kindly;
When she asks thee how I fare?
    Say, folks in Heaven fare finely.

When she asks, 'What! Is he sick?'
    Say, dead! – and when for sorrow
She begins to sob and cry,
    Say. I come to-morrow.

The Pains of Sleep

Ere on my bed my limbs I lay,
It hath not been my use to pray
With moving lips or bended knees;
But silently, by slow degrees,
My spirit I to Love compose,
In humble trust mine eye-lids close,
With reverential resignation,
No wish conceived, no thought exprest,
Only a sense of supplication;
10   A sense o'er all my soul imprest
That I am weak, yet not unblest,
Since in me, round me, every where
Eternal strength and wisdom are.

But yester-night I prayed aloud
In anguish and in agony,
Up-starting from the fiendish crowd
Of shapes and thoughts that tortured me:
A lurid light, a trampling throng,
Sense of intolerable wrong,
20   And whom I scorned, those only strong!

Thirst of revenge, the powerless will
Still baffled, and yet burning still!
Desire with loathing strangely mixed
On wild or hateful objects fixed.
Fantastic passions! maddening brawl!
And shame and terror over all!
Deeds to be hid which were not hid,
Which all confused I could not know,
Whether I suffered, or I did:
30   For all seemed guilt, remorse or woe,
My own or others still the same
Life-stifling fear, soul-stifling shame.

So two nights passed: the night's dismay
Saddened and stunned the coming day.
Sleep, the wide blessing, seemed to me
Distemper's worst calamity.
The third night, when my own loud scream
Had waked me from the fiendish dream,
O'ercome with sufferings strange and wild,
40   I wept as I had been a child;
And having thus by tears subdued
My anguish to a milder mood,
Such punishments, I said, were due
To natures deepliest stained with sin, –
For aye entempesting anew
The unfathomable hell within
The horror of their deeds to view,
To know and loathe, yet wish and do!
Such griefs with such men well agree,
50   But wherefore, wherefore fall on me?
To be beloved is all I need,
And whom I love, I love indeed.

[Lines from a notebook – September 1803]

Such love as mourning Husbands have.
To her whose spirit has been newly given/
To be his guardian Saint in Heaven/
Whose Beauty lieth in the Grave Unconquered/
as if the Soul could find no *purer* Tabernacle, nor place of Sojourn,

than the virgin Body it had before dwelt in, & wished to stay there
till the Resurrection – Far liker to a Flower now than when alive
– Cold to the Touch & blooming to the eye –

[Lines from a notebook – February–March 1804]

Sole Maid, associate sole, to me beyond
Compare, above all living Creatures Dear –

Thoughts which how found they harbour in thy Breast,
Sara, misthoughts of him to thee so dear.

I from the influence of thy Looks receive
Access in every Virtue, in thy sight
More wise, more watchful, stronger if need were
Of outward Strength/

[What is Life?]

Resembles life what once was deem'd of light,
Too ample in itself for human sight?
An absolute self – an element ungrounded –
All that we see, all colours of all shade
By encroach of darkness made? –
Is very life by consciousness unbounded?
And all the thoughts, pains, joys of mortal breath,
A war-embrace of wrestling life and death?

[Lines from a notebook – April 1805]

O th' oppressive, irksome weight
Felt in an uncertain State:
Comfort, peace, and rest adieu,
Should I prove at last untrue!

Self-confiding Wretch. I thought
I could love thee as I ought,
Win thee and deserve to feel
All the love, thou can'st reveal,
And still I chuse thee, follow still
10   Every notice [. . .]

[Lines from a notebook – May–June 1805]

O Beauty, in a beauteous Body dight!
Body! that veiling Brightness becom'st bright/
Fair Cloud which less we see, than by thee see the Light!

Phantom

All look and likeness caught from earth,
All accident of kin and birth,
Had pass'd away. There was no trace
Of aught on that illumined face,
Uprais'd beneath the rifted stone
But of one spirit all her own; –
She, she herself, and only she,
Shone thro' her body visibly.

[An Angel Visitant]

Within these circling Hollies Woodbine-clad –
Beneath this small blue Roof of vernal Sky
How warm, how still! tho' Tears should dim mine eye,
Yet will my Heart for days continue glad –
For here, my Love! thou art! and here am I!

Reason for Love's Blindness

I have heard of reasons manifold
   Why Love must needs be blind,
But this the best of all I hold –
   His eyes are in his mind.

What outward form and feature are
   He guesseth but in part;
But that within is good and fair
   He seeth with the heart.

[Untitled]

Friend, Lover, Husband, Sister, Brother!
Dear Names! close in upon each other!
Alas! poor Fancy's Bitter-sweet –
Our names, and *but* our names, can meet!

Constancy to an Ideal Object

Since all that beat about in Nature's range,
Or veer or vanish; why shouldst thou remain
The only constant in a world of change,
O yearning thought! that liv'st but in the brain?
Call to the hours, that in the distance play,
The faery people of the future day –
Fond thought! not one of all that shining swarm
Will breathe on thee with life-enkindling breath,
Till when, like strangers shelt'ring from a storm,
Hope and Despair meet in the porch of Death!
Yet still thou haunt'st me; and though well I see,
She is not thou, and only thou art she,
Still, still as though some dear embodied good,
Some living love before my eyes there stood

With answering look a ready ear to lend,
I mourn to thee and say – 'Ah! loveliest friend!
That this the meed of all my toils might be,
To have a home, an English home, and thee!'
Vain repetition! Home and Thou are one.
20 The peacefull'st cot, the moon shall shine upon,
Lulled by the thrush and wakened by the lark,
Without thee were but a becalmèd bark,
Whose helmsman on an ocean waste and wide
Sits mute and pale his mouldering helm beside.
And art thou nothing? Such thou art, as when
The woodman winding westward up the glen
At wintry dawn, where o'er the sheep-track's maze
The viewless snow-mist weaves a glist'ning haze,
Sees full before him, gliding without tread,
30 An image with a glory round its head;
The enamoured rustic worships its fair hues,
Nor knows he makes the shadow he pursues!

[Lines from a notebook – March 1806]

I know 'tis but a Dream, yet feel more anguish
Than if 'twere Truth. It has been often so,
Must I die under it? Is no one near?
Will no one hear these stifled groans, & wake me?

[Lines from a notebook – June 1806]

Come, come, thou bleak December Wind,
    And blow the dry Leaves from the Tree!
Flash, like a Love-thought, thro' me, Death
    And take a Life, that wearies me.

Farewell to Love

Farewell, sweet Love! yet blame you not my truth;
   More fondly ne'er did mother eye her child
Than I your form: *yours* were my hopes of youth,
   And as *you* shaped my thoughts I sighed or smiled.

While most were wooing wealth, or gaily swerving
   To pleasure's secret haunts, and some apart
Stood strong in pride, self-conscious of deserving,
   To you I gave my whole weak wishing heart.

And when I met the maid that realised
   Your fair creations, and had won her kindness,
Say, but for her if aught on earth I prized!
   Your dreams alone I dreamt, and caught your blindness.

O grief! – but farewell, Love! I will go play me
With thoughts that please me less, and less betray me.

Time, Real and Imaginary
AN ALLEGORY

On the wide level of a mountain's head,
(I knew not where, but 'twas some faery place)
Their pinions, ostrich-like, for sails outspread,
Two lovely children run an endless race,
     A sister and a brother!
     That far outstripp'd the other;
  Yet ever runs she with reverted face,
  And looks and listens for the boy behind:
     For he, alas! is blind!
O'er rough and smooth with even step he passed,
And knows not whether he be first or last.

[Lines from a notebook – 1806]

Bright clouds of reverence sufferably bright
That intercept the dazzle not the Light
That veil the finite form, the boundless power reveal
Itself an earthly sun, of pure intensest White . . .

[Lines from a notebook – October–November 1806]

His own fair countenance, his kingly forehead
His tender smiles, Love's day-dawn on his Lips
That put on such heavenly spiritual light
At the same moment in his steadfast eyes/
Were virtue's native crest, the innocent Soul's
Unconscious meek Self-heraldry – to man
Genial, and pleasant to his guardian angel –
He suffered, nor complain'd; tho' oft, with tears,
He mourn'd the oppression of his helpless Brethren, –
And sometimes with a deeper, holier grief
Mourn'd for the oppressor: but that in Sabbath Hours –
a solemn grief,
That like a Cloud at Sunset,
Was but the veil of inward meditation,
Pierc'd thro'
And saturate with the intellectual rays, it soften'd.

[Lines from a notebook – 1806]

Let Eagle bid the Tortoise sunward soar –
As vainly Strength speaks to a broken Mind.

[Lines from a notebook – November–December 1806]

As the shy Hind, the soft-eyed gentle Brute,
Now moves, now stops, approaching by degrees
At length emerges from the shelt'ring Trees,
Lur'd by her Hunter with the shepherd's Flute
Whose music travelling on the twilight Breeze,
    When all beside was mute,
She oft had heard unharm'd and ever loves to hear,
She, fearful Beast! but that no sound of Fear.

[Lines from a notebook – February 1807]

As some vast tropic Tree, itself a Wood,
That crests its Head with clouds, beneath the flood
Feeds its deep roots, and with the bulging flank
Of its wide Base controlls the fronting bank,
(By the slant current's pressure scoop'd away
The fronting Bank becomes a foam-piled Bay)
High in its Fork the uncouth Idol knits
His channel'd Brows: low murmurs stir by fits:
And dark below the horrid Faquir sits;
10 An Horror from its broad Head's branching Wreath
Broods o'er the rude Idolatry beneath. –

[Lines from a notebook – February 1807]

    And in Life's noisiest hour,
There whispers still the ceaseless Love of Thee,
The heart's *Self-solace*, and soliloquy.

    You mould my Hopes, you fashion me within;
      And to the leading Love-throb in the Heart
    Thro' all my being all my pulses beat.

You lie in all my many Thoughts, like Light
Like the fair Light of Dawn, or summer-Eve
On rippling Stream, or cloud-reflecting Lake.

And looking to the Heaven, that bends above you
How oft I bless the Lot, that made me love you.

[Lines from a manuscript – 1807–8]

The moon – how definite its orb!
Yet gaze again & with a steady gaze
'Tis there indeed – but where is it not –
It is suffused o'er all the sapphire Heaven,
Trees, herbage, snake-like Stream, unwrinkled Lake,
Whose very murmur does of it partake/
And low & close the broad smooth mountain
Is more a thing of Heaven than when
Distinct by one dim shade
10 yet undivided from the universal cloud
In which it towers, infinite in height/ –

[Lines from a notebook – July 1807]
INCLUDES LINES PREVIOUSLY PUBLISHED SEPARATELY AS
'COELI ENARRANT'

Life wakeful over all knew no gradation
That Bliss in its excess became a Dream;
For every sense, each thought, & each sensation
Lived in my eye, transfigured not supprest.
And Time drew out his subtle threads so quick,
And with such Spirit-speed & silentness,
That only in the web, of space like Time,
On the still spreading web I still diffused
Lay still commensurate –

10   For Memory & all undoubting Hope
      Sang the same note & in the selfsame Voice,
      with each sweet *now* of my Felicity,
      and blended momently,
      Like Milk that coming comes & in its easy stream
      Flows ever in, upon the mingling milk
      in the Babe's murmuring Mouth/
      or mirrors each reflecting each/ –

      What never is but only is to be
      This is not Life –
20   O Hopeless Hope, and Death's Hypocrisy!
      And with perpetual Promise, breaks its Promises. –

      The Stars that wont to start, as on a chase,
      And twinkling insult on Heaven's darkened Face,
      Like a conven'd Conspiracy of Spies
      Wink at each other with confiding eyes,
      Turn from the portent, all is blank on high,
      No constellations alphabet the Sky –
      The Heavens one large black Letter only shews,
      And as a Child beneath its master's Blows
30   Shrills out at once its Task and its Affright,
      The groaning world now learns to read aright,
      And with its Voice of Voices cries out, O!

[Lines from a notebook – January 1808]

The singing Kettle & the purring Cat,
The gentle Breathing of the cradled Babe,
The silence of the Mother's love-bright Eye,
And tender Smile answ'ring its smile of Sleep.

To William Wordsworth
COMPOSED ON THE NIGHT AFTER HIS RECITATION OF A
POEM ON THE GROWTH OF AN INDIVIDUAL MIND

Friend of the wise! and teacher of the good!
Into my heart have I received that lay
More than historic, that prophetic lay
Wherein (high theme by thee first sung aright)
Of the foundations and the building up
Of a Human Spirit thou hast dared to tell
What may be told, to the understanding mind
Revealable; and what within the mind
By vital breathings secret as the soul
Of vernal growth, oft quickens in the heart
Thoughts all too deep for words! –

                        Theme hard as high!
Of smiles spontaneous, and mysterious fears,
(The first-born they of Reason and twin-birth)
Of tides obedient to external force,
And currents self-determined, as might seem,
Or by some inner power; of moments awful,
Now in thy inner life, and now abroad,
When power streamed from thee, and thy soul received
The light reflected, as a light bestowed –
Of fancies fair, and milder hours of youth,
Hyblean murmurs of poetic thought
Industrious in its joy, in vales and glens
Native or outland, lakes and famous hills!
Or on the lonely high-road, when the stars
Were rising; or by secret mountain-streams,
The guides and the companions of thy way!

  Of more than Fancy, of the Social Sense
Distending wide, and man beloved as man,
Where France in all her towns lay vibrating
Like some becalmèd bark beneath the burst
Of Heaven's immediate thunder, when no cloud
Is visible, or shadow on the main.
For thou wert there, thine own brows garlanded,

10

20

30

Amid the tremor of a realm aglow,
Amid a mighty nation jubilant,
When from the general heart of human kind
Hope sprang forth like a full-born Deity!
—Of that dear Hope afflicted and struck down,
So summoned homeward, thenceforth calm and sure
40 From the dread watch-tower of man's absolute self,
With light unwaning on her eyes, to look
Far on – herself a glory to behold,
The Angel of the vision! Then (last strain)
Of Duty, chosen laws controlling choice,
Action and joy! – An Orphic song indeed,
A song divine of high and passionate thoughts
To their own music chanted!

O great Bard!
Ere yet that last strain dying awed the air,
With steadfast eye I viewed thee in the choir
50 Of ever-enduring men. The truly great
Have all one age, and from one visible space
Shed influence! They, both in power and act,
Are permanent, and Time is not with them,
Save as it worketh for them, they in it.
Nor less a sacred roll, than those of old,
And to be placed, as they, with gradual fame
Among the archives of mankind, thy work
Makes audible a linkèd lay of Truth,
Of Truth profound a sweet continuous lay,
60 Not learnt, but native, her own natural notes!
Ah! as I listened with a heart forlorn,
The pulses of my being beat anew:
And even as life returns upon the drowned,
Life's joy rekindling roused a throng of pains –
Keen pangs of Love, awakening as a babe
Turbulent, with an outcry in the heart;
And fears self-willed, that shunned the eye of hope;
And hope that scarce would know itself from fear;
Sense of past youth, and manhood come in vain,
70 And genius given, and knowledge won in vain;
And all which I had culled in wood-walks wild,
And all which patient toil had reared, and all,
Commune with thee had opened out – but flowers

Strewed on my corse, and borne upon my bier,
In the same coffin, for the self-same grave!

That way no more! and ill beseems it me,
Who came a welcomer in herald's guise,
Singing of glory, and futurity,
To wander back on such unhealthful road,
80   Plucking the poisons of self-harm! And ill
Such intertwine beseems triumphal wreaths
Strewed before thy advancing!

                  Nor do thou,
Sage Bard! impair the memory of that hour
Of thy communion with my nobler mind
By pity or grief, already felt too long!
Nor let my words import more blame than needs.
The tumult rose and ceased: for peace is nigh
Where wisdom's voice has found a listening heart.
Amid the howl of more than wintry storms,
90   The halcyon hears the voice of vernal hours
Already on the wing.

                  Eve following eve,
Dear tranquil time, when the sweet sense of Home
Is sweetest! moments for their own sake hailed
And more desired, more precious, for thy song,
In silence listening, like a devout child,
My soul lay passive, by thy various strain
Driven as in surges now beneath the stars,
With momentary stars of my own birth,
Fair constellated foam, still darting off
100 Into the darkness; now a tranquil sea,
Outspread and bright, yet swelling to the moon.

And when – O Friend! my comforter and guide!
Strong in thyself, and powerful to give strength! –
Thy long sustainèd Song finally closed,
And thy deep voice had ceased – yet thou thyself
Wert still before my eyes, and round us both
That happy vision of beloved faces –

Scarce conscious, and yet conscious of its close
I sate, my being blended in one thought
110 (Thought was it? or aspiration? or resolve?)
Absorbed, yet hanging still upon the sound –
And when I rose, I found myself in prayer.

Metrical Feet. Lesson for a Boy

Trōchĕe trīps frŏm lōng tŏ shōrt;
From long to long in solemn sort
Slōw Spōndēe stālks; strŏng fŏot! yet ill able
Ēvĕr tŏ cōme ŭp wĭth Dāctўl trĭsўllăblĕ.
Ĭāmbĭcs mārch frŏm shōrt tŏ lōng; –
Wĭth ă lēap ănd ă bōund thĕ swĭft Ănăpǽsts thrōng;
One syllable long, with one short at each side,
Ămphībrăchўs hāstes wĭth ă stātelў stride; –
Fīrst ănd lāst bēing lōng, mĭddlĕ shōrt, Ămphīmācer
10 Strīkes hĭs thūndērĭng hoofs līke ă prŏud hĭgh-brĕd Rācer.
If Derwent be innocent, steady, and wise,
And delight in the things of earth, water, and skies;
Tender warmth at his heart, with these metres to show it,
With sound sense in his brains, may make Derwent a poet, –
May crown him with fame, and must win him the love
Of his father on earth and his Father above.
My dear, dear child!
Could you stand upon Skiddaw, you would not from its whole
ridge
See a man who loves you as your fond S. T. COLERIDGE.

Recollections of Love

I
How warm this woodland wild Recess!
Love surely hath been breathing here;
And this sweet bed of heath, my dear!
Swells up, then sinks with faint caress,
As if to have you yet more near.

II

Eight springs have flown, since last I lay
  On sea ward Quantock's heathy hills,
  Where quiet sounds from hidden rills
Float here and there, like things astray,
10   And high o'er head the sky-lark shrills.

III

No voice as yet had made the air
  Be music with your name; yet why
  That asking look? that yearning sigh?
That sense of promise every where?
  Beloved! flew your spirit by?

IV

As when a mother doth explore
  The rose-mark on her long lost child,
  I met, I loved you, maiden mild!
As whom I long had loved before –
20   So deeply, had I been beguiled.

V

You stood before me like a thought,
  A dream remembered in a dream.
  But when those meek eyes first did seem
To tell me, Love within you wrought –
  O Greta, dear domestic stream!

VI

Has not, since then, Love's prompture deep,
  Has not Love's whisper evermore
  Been ceaseless, as thy gentle roar?
Sole voice, when other voices sleep,
30   Dear under-song in clamour's hour.

The Blossoming of the Solitary Date-Tree. A Lament

I seem to have an indistinct recollection of having read either in one of the ponderous tomes of George of Venice, or in some other compilation from the uninspired Hebrew writers, an apologue or Rabbinical tradition to the following purpose:

While our first parents stood before their offended Maker, and the last words of the sentence were yet sounding in Adam's ear, the guileful false serpent, a counterfeit and a usurper from the beginning, presumptuously took on himself the character of advocate or mediator, and pretending to intercede for Adam, exclaimed: 'Nay, Lord, in thy justice, not so! for the Man was the least in fault. Rather let the Woman return at once to the dust, and let Adam remain in this thy Paradise.' And the word of the Most High answered Satan: 'The tender mercies of the wicked are cruel. Treacherous Fiend! if with guilt like thine, it had been possible for thee to have the heart of a Man, and to feel the yearning of a human soul for its counterpart, the sentence, which thou now counsellest, should have been inflicted on thyself.'

The title of the following poem was suggested by a fact mentioned by Linnæus, of a date-tree in a nobleman's garden which year after year had put forth a full show of blossoms, but never produced fruit, till a branch from another date-tree had been conveyed from a distance of some hundred leagues. The first leaf of the MS. from which the poem has been transcribed, and which contained the two or three introductory stanzas, is wanting: and the author has in vain taxed his memory to repair the loss. But a rude draught of the poem contains the substance of the stanzas, and the reader is requested to receive it as the substitute. It is not impossible, that some congenial spirit, whose years do not exceed those of the author, at the time the poem was written, may find a pleasure in restoring the Lament to its original integrity by a reduction of the thoughts to the requisite metre.

I

Beneath the blaze of a tropical sun the mountain peaks are the thrones of frost, through the absence of objects to reflect the rays. 'What no one with us shares, seems scarce our own.' The presence of a one,

The best belov'd, who loveth me the best,

is for the heart, what the supporting air from within is for the hollow globe with its suspended car. Deprive it of this, and all without, that would have buoyed it aloft even to the seat of the gods, becomes a burthen and crushes it into flatness.

II

The finer sense for the beautiful and the lovely, and the fairer and lovelier the object presented to the sense, the more exquisite the individual's capacity of joy; and the more ample his means and opportunities of enjoyment, the more heavily will he feel the ache of solitariness, the more unsubstantial becomes the feast spread around him. What matters it, whether in fact the viands and the ministering graces are shadowy or real, to him who has not hand to grasp nor arms to embrace them?

III

Imagination; honourable aims;
Free commune with the choir that cannot die;
Science and song; delight in little things,
The buoyant child surviving in the man;
Fields, forests, ancient mountains, ocean, sky,
With all their voices – O dare I accuse
My earthly lot as guilty of my spleen,
Or call my destiny niggard! O no! no!
It is her largeness, and her overflow,
Which being incomplete, disquieteth me so!

IV

For never touch of gladness stirs my heart,
But tim'rously beginning to rejoice
Like a blind Arab, that from sleep doth start
In lonesome tent, I listen for thy voice.
Beloved! 'tis not thine; thou art not there!
Then melts the bubble into idle air,
And wishing without hope I restlessly despair.

V

The mother with anticipated glee
Smiles o'er the child, that, standing by her chair
And flatt'ning its round cheek upon her knee,
Looks up, and doth its rosy lips prepare
To mock the coming sounds. At that sweet sight
She hears her own voice with a new delight;
And if the babe perchance should lisp the notes aright,

VI

Then is she tenfold gladder than before!
But should disease or chance the darling take,
What then avail those songs, which sweet of yore
Were only sweet for their sweet echo's sake?
Dear maid! no prattler at a mother's knee
Was e'er so dearly prized as I prize thee:
Why was I made for Love and Love denied to me?

To Two Sisters
A WANDERER'S FAREWELL

To know, to esteem, to love, – and then to part –
Makes up life's tale to many a feeling heart;
Alas for some abiding-place of love,
O'er which my spirit, like the mother dove,
Might brood with warming wings!
                            O fair! O kind!
Sisters in blood, yet each with each intwined
More close by sisterhood of heart and mind!
Me disinherited in form and face
By nature, and mishap of outward grace;
Who, soul and body, through one guiltless fault
Waste daily with the poison of sad thought,
Me did you soothe, when solace hoped I none!
And as on unthaw'd ice the winter sun,
Though stern the frost, though brief the genial day,
You bless my heart with many a cheerful ray;
For gratitude suspends the heart's despair,
Reflecting bright though cold your image there.
Nay more! its music by some sweeter strain
Makes us live o'er our happiest hours again,
Hope re-appearing dim in memory's guise –
Even thus did you call up before mine eyes
Two dear, dear Sisters, prized all price above,
Sisters, like you, with more than sisters' love;
So like you *they*, and so in *you* were seen
Their relative statures, tempers, looks, and mien,
That oft, dear ladies! you have been to me
At once a vision and reality.
Sight seem'd a sort of memory, and amaze

Mingled a trouble with affection's gaze.
30   Oft to my eager soul I whisper blame,
A Stranger bid it feel the Stranger's shame –
My eager soul, impatient of the name,
No strangeness owns, no Stranger's form descries:
The chidden heart spreads trembling on the eyes.

First-seen I gazed, as I would look you thro'!
My best-beloved regain'd their youth in you, –
And still I ask, though now familiar grown,
Are you for *their* sakes dear, or for your own?
O doubly dear! may Quiet with you dwell!

40   In Grief I love you, yet I love you well!
Hope long is dead to me! an orphan's tear
Love wept despairing o'er his nurse's bier.
Yet she flutters o'er her grave's green slope:
For Love's despair is but the ghost of Hope!

Sweet Sisters! were you placed around one hearth
With those, your other selves in shape and worth,
Far rather would I sit in solitude,
Fond recollections all my fond heart's food,
And dream of *you*, sweet Sisters! (ah! not mine!)
50   And only *dream* of you (ah! dream and pine!)
Than boast the presence and partake the pride,
And shine in the eye, of all the world beside.

On Taking Leave of ——, *1817*

To know, to esteem, to love – and then to part,
Makes up life's tale to many a feeling heart!
O for some dear abiding-place of Love,
O'er which my spirit, like the mother dove,
Might brood with warming wings! – O fair as kind,
Were but one sisterhood with you combined
(Your very image they in shape and mind),
Far rather would I sit in solitude,
The forms of memory all my mental food,

10   And dream of you, sweet sisters (ah, not mine!)
And only dream of you (ah dream and pine!)
Than have the presence, and partake the pride,
And shine in the eye of all the world beside!

A Child's Evening Prayer

Ere on my bed my limbs I lay,
God grant me grace my prayers to say:
O God! preserve my mother dear
In strength and health for many a year;
And, O! preserve my father too,
And may I pay him reverence due;
And may I my best thoughts employ
To be my parents' hope and joy;
And, O! preserve my brothers both
10   From evil doings and from sloth,
And may we always love each other,
Our friends, our father, and our mother:
And still, O Lord, to me impart
An innocent and grateful heart,
That after my last sleep I may
Awake to thy eternal day!
                                        Amen.

Ad Vilmum Axiologum

This be the meed, that thy Song creates a thousandfold Echo!
Sweet as the warble of woods that awake at the gale of the
        Morning!
List! the Hearts of the Pure, like Caves in the ancient
        Mountains
Deep, deep *in* the Bosom, and *from* the Bosom resound it,
Each with a different Tone, complete or in musical fragments,
All have welcom'd thy Voice, and receive and retain and prolong
        it!

This is the word of the Lord! – it is spoken, and Beings Eternal
Live and are born, as an Infant – the Eternal begets the
    Immortal!
Love is the Spirit of Life, and Music the Life of the Spirit. –

Psyche

The butterfly the ancient Grecians made
The soul's fair emblem, and its only name –
But of the soul, escaped the slavish trade
Of mortal life! For in this earthly frame
Ours is the reptile's lot, much toil, much blame,
Manifold motions making little speed,
And to deform and kill the things, whereon we feed.

[Sonnet – translated from Marino]

Lady, to Death we're doom'd, our crime the same!
Thou, that in me thou kindledst such fierce Heat;
I, that my Heart did of a Sun so sweet
The Rays concentre to so hot a flame.
I, fascinated by an Adder's Eye,
Deaf as an Adder thou to all my Pain;
Thou obstinate in Scorn, in Passion I –
I lov'd too much, too much didst thou disdain.
Hear then our doom in Hell as just as stern,
Our sentence equal as our crimes conspire
Who living basked at Beauty's earthly Fire
In living flames eternal there must burn/ –
Hell for us both fit places too supplies –
In *my* Heart thou wilt burn, I roast before thine Eyes –

[Fragment: 'Two wedded Hearts']

[VERSION 1]

Two wedded Hearts, if e'er were such,
Imprison'd in adjoining cells
Across whose thin partition wall
The Builder left one narrow rent,
And there most content in discontent
A Joy with itself at strife,
Die into an intenser Life/

[VERSION 2]

The Builder left one narrow rent,
Two wedded Hearts, if e'er were such,
Contented most in discontent
There cling, and try in vain to touch!
O Joy with thy own Joy at Strife,
That yearning for the Realm above
Would'st die into intenser Life,
And union absolute of Love.

A Tombless Epitaph

'Tis true, Idoloclastes Satyrane!
(So call him, for so mingling blame with praise,
And smiles with anxious looks, his earliest friends,
Masking his birth-name, wont to character
His wild-wood fancy and impetuous zeal)
'Tis true that, passionate for ancient truths,
And honouring with religious love the great
Of elder times, he hated to excess,
With an unquiet and intolerant scorn,
The hollow puppets of a hollow age,
Ever idolatrous, and changing ever
Its worthless idols! learning, power, and time,
(Too much of all) thus wasting in vain war
Of fervid colloquy. Sickness, 'tis true,
Whole years of weary days, besieged him close,

Even to the gates and inlets of his life!
But it is true, no less, that strenuous, firm,
And with a natural gladness, he maintained
The citadel unconquered, and in joy
20 Was strong to follow the delightful Muse.
For not a hidden path, that to the shades
Of the beloved Parnassian forest leads,
Lurked undiscovered by him; not a rill
There issues from the fount of Hippocrene,
But he had traced it upward to its source,
Through open glade, dark glen, and secret dell,
Knew the gay wild flowers on its banks, and culled
Its med'cinable herbs. Yea, oft alone,
Piercing the long-neglected holy cave,
30 The haunt obscure of old Philosophy,
He bade with lifted torch its starry walls
Sparkle, as erst they sparkled to the flame
Of odorous lamps tended by Saint and Sage.
O framed for calmer times and nobler hearts!
O studious Poet, eloquent for truth!
Philosopher! contemning wealth and death,
Yet docile, childlike, full of Life and Love!
Here, rather than on monumental stone,
This record of thy worth thy Friend inscribes,
40 Thoughtful, with quiet tears upon his cheek.

On a Clock in a Market-Place

What now thou dost or art about to do
Will help to give thee peace or make thee rue,
When wav'ring o'er the dot this Hand shall tell
The Moment, that secures thee *Heaven* or *Hell*.

Separation

A sworded man whose trade is blood,
    In grief, in anger, and in fear,
Thro' jungle, swamp, and torrent flood,
    I seek the wealth you hold so dear!

The dazzling charm of outward form,
    The power of gold, the pride of birth,
Have taken Woman's heart by storm –
    Usurp'd the place of inward worth.

Is not true Love of higher price
10   Than outward Form, tho' fair to see,
Wealth's glittering fairy-dome of ice,
    Or echo of proud ancestry? –

O! Asra, Asra! couldst thou see
    Into the bottom of my heart,
There's such a mine of Love for thee,
    As almost might supply desert!

(This separation is, alas!
    Too great a punishment to bear;
O! take my life, or let me pass
20   That life, that happy life, with her!)

The perils, erst with steadfast eye
    Encounter'd, now I shrink to see –
Oh! I have heart enough to die –
    Not half enough to part from Thee!

The Visionary Hope

Sad lot, to have no hope! Though lowly kneeling
He fain would frame a prayer within his breast,
Would fain entreat for some sweet breath of healing,
That his sick body might have ease and rest;
He strove in vain! the dull sighs from his chest
Against his will the stifling load revealing,
Though Nature forced; though like some captive guest,
Some royal prisoner at his conqueror's feast,
An alien's restless mood but half concealing,
10 The sternness on his gentle brow confessed,
Sickness within and miserable feeling:
Though obscure pangs made curses of his dreams,
And dreaded sleep, each night repelled in vain,
Each night was scattered by its own loud screams:

Yet never could his heart command, though fain,
One deep full wish to be no more in pain.

That Hope, which was his inward bliss and boast
Which waned and died, yet ever near him stood,
Though changed in nature, wander where he would –
20   For Love's despair is but Hope's pining ghost!
For this one hope he makes his hourly moan,
He wishes and can wish for this alone!
Pierced, as with light from Heaven, before its gleams
(So the love-stricken visionary deems)
Disease would vanish, like a summer shower,
Whose dews fling sunshine from the noon-tide bower!
Or let it stay! yet this one Hope should give
Such strength that he would bless his pains and live.

[Lines from a notebook – March 1810]

When Hope but made Tranquillity be felt –
A Flight of Hopes for ever on the wing
But made Tranquillity a conscious Thing –
And wheeling round and round in sportive Coil,
Fann'd the calm Air upon the brow of Toil –

[Lines from a notebook – April–June 1810]

The body
    Eternal Shadow of the finite Soul/
    The Soul's self-symbol/its image of itself,
    Its own yet not itself –

[Lines from a notebook – May 1810]

                I have experienc'd
The worst, the World can wreak on me; the worst
That can make Life indifferent, yet disturb
With whisper'd Discontents the dying prayer.

I have beheld the whole of all, wherein
My Heart had any interest in this Life,
To be disrent and torn from off my Hopes
That nothing now is left. Why then live on?
That Hostage, which the world had in it's keeping
10   Given by me as a Pledge that I would live,
That Hope of Her, say rather, that pure Faith
In her fix'd Love, which held me to keep truce
With the Tyranny of Life – is gone ah whither?
What boots it to reply? – 'tis gone! and now
Well may I break this Pact, this League of Blood
That ties me to myself – and break I shall! –

Epitaph on an Infant

Its balmy lips the infant blest
Relaxing from its mother's breast,
How sweet it heaves the happy sigh
Of innocent satiety!

And such my infant's latest sigh!
O tell, rude stone! the passer by,
That here the pretty babe doth lie,
Death sang to sleep with Lullaby.

[Lines from a notebook – 1811]

As when the new or full moon urges
The high, long, large, unbreaking surges
Of the pacific Main.

[Fragment of an ode on Napoleon]

O'erhung with yew, midway the Muses mount
    From thy sweet murmurs far, O Hippocrene!
Turbid and black upboils an angry fount
    Tossing its shatter'd foam in vengeful spleen –

Phlegethon's rage Cocytus' wailings hoarse
Alternate now, now mixt, made known its headlong course:
   Thither with terror stricken and surprise,
(For sure such haunts were ne'er to Muse's choice)
   Euterpe led me. Mute with asking eyes
10 I stood expectant of her heavenly voice.
Her voice entranc'd my terror and made flow
In a rude understrain the maniac fount below.
'Whene'er (the Goddess said) abhorr'd of Jove
Usurping Power his hands in blood imbrues –'

[Lines inscribed on the fly-leaf of Benedetto Menzini's 'Poesie' (1782)]

I stand alone, nor tho' my Heart should break
Have I, to whom I may complain or speak.
Here I stand, a hopeless man and sad
Who hoped to have seen my Love, my Life.
And strange it were indeed, could I be glad
Remembring her, my Soul's betrothed Wife/
For in this World no creature, that has life,
Was e'er to me so gracious & so good/
Her Love was to my Heart, like the Heart-blood.

[Lines from a notebook – May–June 1811]

O mercy, O me miserable man!
Slowly my wisdom, & how slowly comes
My Virtue! and how rapidly pass off
My Joys, my Hopes, my Friendships, & my Love!

[Lines from a notebook – May–July 1811]

A low dead Thunder muttered thro' the Night,
As 'twere a Giant angry in his Sleep –
Nature! sweet Nurse! O take me in thy Lap –

And tell me of my Father yet unseen
Sweet Tales & True, that lull me into Sleep,
& leave me dreaming. –

[Lines from a notebook – May 1814?]

Seaward, white-gleaming thro' the busy Scud
With arching Wings the Sea-mew o'er my head
Posts on, as bent on speed; now passaging
Edges the stiffer Breeze, now yielding *drifts*,
Now floats upon the Air, and sends from far
A wildly-wailing Note.

[Lines from a notebook – 1815–16]

O! Superstition is the Giant Shadow
Which the Solicitude of weak Mortality
Its Back toward Religion's rising Sun,
Casts on the thin mist of the uncertain Future.

[Lines from a notebook – 1815–16]

Let klumps of Earth however glorified
Roll round & round & still renew their cycle/
Man rushes like a wingèd Cherub thro'
The infinite Space, and that which has been
Can therefore never be again –

On Donne's First Poem

Be proud, as Spaniards! and Leap for Pride, ye Fleas
Henceforth in Nature's *Minim* World Grandees,
In Phœbus' Archives registered are ye –
And this your Patent of Nobility.

No Skip-Jacks now, nor civiller Skip-Johns,
Dread Anthropophagi! Specks of living Bronze,
I hail you one & all, sans Pros or Cons,
Descendants from a noble Race of *Dons*.

What tho' that great ancestral Flea be gone
10   Immortal with immortalizing Donne –
His earthly Spots bleach'd off as Papists gloze,
In purgatory fire on Bardolph's Nose,
Or else starved out, his aery tread defied
By the dry Potticary's bladdery Hide,
Which cross'd unchang'd and still keeps in ghost-Light
Of lank Half-nothings his, the thinnest Sprite
The sole true *Something* this in Limbo Den
It frightens Ghosts as Ghosts here frighten men –
For skimming in the wake, it mock'd the care
20   Of the Old Boat-God for his Farthing Fare,
Tho' Irus' Ghost itself he neer frown'd blacker on,
The skin and skin-pent Druggist crost the Acheron,
Styx and with Puriphlegethon Cocytus:
The very names, methinks, might thither fright us –
Unchang'd it cross'd & shall, some fated Hour,
Be pulverized by Demogorgon's Power
And given as poison, to anni'late Souls –
Even now it shrinks them! they shrink in, as Moles
(Nature's mute Monks, live Mandrakes of the ground)
30   Creep back from Light, then listen for its Sound –
See but to dread, and dread they know not why
The natural Alien of their negative Eye.

Limbo

'Tis a strange place, this Limbo! – not a Place,
Yet name it so; – where Time and weary Space
Fettered from flight, with night-mare sense of fleeing,
Strive for their last crepuscular half-being; –
Lank Space, and scytheless Time with branny hands
Barren and soundless as the measuring sands,
Not mark'd by flit of Shades, – unmeaning they
As moonlight on the dial of the day!

But that is lovely – looks like human Time, –
10   An old man with a steady look sublime,
That stops his earthly task to watch the skies;
But he is blind – a statue hath such eyes;
Yet having moonward turn'd his face by chance,
Gazes the orb with moon-like countenance,
With scant white hairs, with foretop bald and high,
He gazes still, – his eyeless face all eye; –
As 'twere an organ full of silent sight,
His whole face seemeth to rejoice in light! –
Lip touching lip, all moveless, bust and limb –
20   He seems to gaze at that which seems to gaze on him!
     No such sweet sights doth Limbo den immure,
Wall'd round, and made a spirit-jail secure,
By the mere horror of blank Naught-at-all,
Whose circumambience doth these ghosts enthral.
A lurid thought is growthless, dull Privation,
Yet that is but a Purgatory curse;
Hell knows a fear far worse,
A fear – a future state; – 'tis positive Negation!

Moles

           They shrink in, as Moles
(Nature's mute monks, live mandrakes of the ground)
Creep back from Light – then listen for its sound; –
See but to dread, and dread they know not why –
The natural alien of their negative eye.

Ne plus ultra

           Sole Positive of Night!
           Antipathist of Light!
Fate's only essence! primal scorpion rod –
The one permitted opposite of God! –
Condensèd blackness and abysmal storm
           Compacted to one sceptre
           Arms the Grasp enorm –
           The Intercepter –

The Substance that still casts the shadow Death! –
10   The Dragon foul and fell –
          The unrevealable,
And hidden one, whose breath
Gives wind and fuel to the fires of Hell! –
      Ah! sole despair
      Of both th' eternities in Heaven!
Sole interdict of all-bedewing prayer,
      The all-compassionate!
      Save to the Lampads Seven
Reveal'd to none of all th' Angelic State,
20   Save to the Lampads Seven,
          That watch the throne of Heaven!

The Suicide's Argument

Ere the birth of my life, if I wished it or no,
No question was asked me – it could not be so!
If the life was the question, a thing sent to try,
And to live on be Yes; what can No be? to die.

NATURE'S ANSWER

Is't returned, as 'twas sent? Is't no worse for the wear?
Think first, what you are! Call to mind what you were!
I gave you innocence, I gave you hope,
Gave health, and genius, and an ample scope.
Return you me guilt, lethargy, despair?
10 Make out the invent'ry; inspect, compare!
Then die – if die you dare!

[An Invocation:
FROM 'REMORSE']

Hear, sweet Spirit, hear the spell,
Lest a blacker charm compel!
So shall the midnight breezes swell
With thy deep long-lingering knell.

And at evening evermore,
In a chapel on the shore,
Shall the chaunter, sad and saintly,
Yellow tapers burning faintly,
Doleful masses chaunt for thee,
10   Miserere Domine!

Hush! the cadence dies away
  On the quiet moonlight sea:
The boatmen rest their oars and say,
    Miserere Domine!

God's Omnipresence,
A HYMN

My Maker! of thy power the trace
In every creature's form and face
  The wond'ring soul surveys:
Thy wisdom, infinite above
Seraphic thought, a Father's love
  As infinite displays!

From all that meets or eye or ear,
There falls a genial holy fear
Which, like the heavy dew of morn,
10 Refreshes while it bows the heart forlorn!

Great God! thy works how wondrous fair!
Yet sinful man didst thou declare
  The whole Earth's voice and mind!
  If rootless thus, thus substanceless thy state,
Lord, ev'n as Thou all-present art,
O may we still with heedful heart
  Thy presence know and find!
Then, come what will, of weal or woe,
Joy's bosom-spring shall steady flow;
For though 'tis Heaven THYSELF to see,
20 Where but thy *Shadow* falls, Grief cannot be!

To a Lady.
WITH FALCONER'S 'SHIPWRECK'

Ah! not by Cam, or Isis, famous streams,
　　In archèd groves, the youthful poet's choice;
　　　Nor while half-listening, mid delicious dreams,
　　To harp and song from lady's hand and voice;

Nor yet while gazing in sublimer mood
　　On cliff, or cataract, in Alpine dell;
Nor in dim cave with bladdery sea-weed strewed,
　　Framing wild fancies to the ocean's swell;

Our sea-bard sang this song! which still he sings,
10　　And sings for thee, sweet friend! Hark, Pity, hark!
Now mounts, now totters on the tempest's wings,
　　Now groans, and shivers, the replunging bark!

'Cling to the shrouds!' In vain! The breakers roar –
　　Death shrieks! With two alone of all his clan
Forlorn the poet paced the Grecian shore,
　　No classic roamer, but a ship-wrecked man!

Say then, what muse inspired these genial strains,
　　And lit his spirit to so bright a flame?
The elevating thought of suffered pains,
20　　Which gentle hearts shall mourn; but chief, the name

Of gratitude! remembrances of friend,
　　Or absent or no more! shades of the Past,
Which Love makes substance! Hence to thee I send,
　　O dear as long as life and memory last!

I send with deep regards of heart and head,
　　Sweet maid, for friendship formed! this work to thee:
And thou, the while thou canst not choose but shed
　　A tear for Falconer, wilt remember me.

Human Life,

ON THE DENIAL OF IMMORTALITY

If dead, we cease to be; if total gloom
   Swallow up life's brief flash for aye, we fare
As summer-gusts, of sudden birth and doom,
   Whose sound and motion not alone declare,
But are their whole of being! If the breath
   Be life itself, and not its task and tent,
If even a soul like Milton's can know death;
   O Man! thou vessel purposeless, unmeant,
Yet drone-hive strange of phantom purposes!
10   Surplus of nature's dread activity,
Which, as she gazed on some nigh-finished vase,
Retreating slow, with meditative pause,
   She formed with restless hands unconsciously!
Blank accident! nothing's anomaly!
   If rootless thus, thus substanceless thy state,
Go, weigh thy dreams, and be thy hopes, thy fears,
The counter-weights! – Thy laughter and thy tears
   Mean but themselves, each fittest to create,
And to repay the other! Why rejoices
20   Thy heart with hollow joy for hollow good?
   Why cowl thy face beneath the mourner's hood,
Why waste thy sighs, and thy lamenting voices,
   Image of image, ghost of ghostly elf,
That such a thing as thou feel'st warm or cold?
Yet what and whence thy gain, if thou withhold
   These costless shadows of thy shadowy self?
Be sad! be glad! be neither! seek, or shun!
Thou hast no reason why! Thou canst have none;
Thy being's being is contradiction.

[Song

FROM 'ZAPOLYA']

A sunny shaft did I behold,
   From sky to earth it slanted:
And poised therein a bird so bold –
   Sweet bird, thou wert enchanted!

He sank, he rose, he twinkled, he trolled
    Within that shaft of sunny mist;
His eyes of fire, his beak of gold,
    All else of amethyst!

And thus he sang: 'Adieu! adieu!
Love's dreams prove seldom true.
The blossoms they make no delay:
The sparkling dew-drops will not stay.
    Sweet month of May,
      We must away;
        Far, far away!
          To-day! to-day!'

[Hunting Song
FROM 'ZAPOLYA']

Up, up! ye dames, and lasses gay!
To the meadows trip away.
'Tis you must tend the flocks this morn,
And scare the small birds from the corn.
    Not a soul at home may stay:
      For the shepherds must go
      With lance and bow
    To hunt the wolf in the woods to-day.

Leave the hearth and leave the house
To the cricket and the mouse:
Find grannam out a sunny seat,
With babe and lambkin at her feet.
    Not a soul at home may stay:
      For the shepherds must go
      With lance and bow
    To hunt the wolf in the woods to-day.

[Faith, Hope, and Charity
FROM THE ITALIAN OF GUARINI]

Faith

Let those whose low delights to Earth are given
    Chaunt forth their earthly Loves! but we
    Must make an holier minstrelsy,
And, heavenly-born, will sing the Things of Heaven.

Charity

But who for us the listening Heart shall gain?
    Inaudible as of the sphere
    Our music dies upon the ear,
Enchanted with the mortal Syren's strain.

Hope

Yet let our choral songs abound!
10   Th' inspiring Power, its living Source,
    May flow with them and give them force,
If, elsewhere all unheard, in Heaven they sound.

All

Aid thou our voice, Great Spirit! thou whose flame
    Kindled the Songster sweet of Israel,
    Who made so high to swell
Beyond a mortal strain thy glorious Name.

Charity and Faith

Though rapt to Heaven, our mission and our care
    Is still to sojourn on the Earth,
    To shape, to soothe, Man's second Birth,
20 And re-ascend to Heaven, Heaven's prodigal Heir!

Charity

What is Man's soul of Love deprived?

Hope, Faith

    It like a Harp untunèd is,
    That sounds, indeed, but sounds amiss.

Charity, Hope

From holy Love all good gifts are derived.

Faith
But 'tis time that every nation
Should hear how loftily we sing.

Faith. Hope. Charity
See, O World, see thy salvation!
Let the Heavens with praises ring.
Who would have a Throne above,
30   Let him hope, believe and love;
And whoso loves no earthly song,
But does for heavenly music long.
Faith, Hope, and Charity for him,
Shall sing like wingèd Cherubim.

Fancy in Nubibus
OR THE POET IN THE CLOUDS

O! it is pleasant, with a heart at ease,
   Just after sunset, or by moonlight skies,
To make the shifting clouds be what you please,
   Or let the easily persuaded eyes
Own each quaint likeness issuing from the mould
   Of a friend's fancy; or with head bent low
And cheek aslant see rivers flow of gold
   'Twixt crimson banks; and then, a traveller, go
From mount to mount through Cloudland, gorgeous land!
10   Or list'ning to the tide, with closèd sight,
Be that blind bard, who on the Chian strand
   By those deep sounds possessed with inward light,
Beheld the Iliad and the Odyssee
   Rise to the swelling of the voiceful sea.

Israel's Lament

A Hebrew Dirge, chaunted in the Great Synagogue, St James's Place,
Aldgate, on the day of the Funeral of Her Royal Highness the Princess
Charlotte. By Hyman Hurwitz, Master of the Hebrew Academy,
Highgate: with a Translation in English Verse, by S. T. Coleridge,
Esq., 1817.

Mourn, Israel! Sons of Israel, mourn!
   Give utt'rance to the inward throe!
As wails, of her first Love forlorn,
   The Virgin clad in robes of woe.

Mourn the young Mother, snatch'd away
   From Light and Life's ascending Sun!
Mourn for the Babe, Death's voiceless prey,
   Earn'd by long pangs and lost 'ere won.

Mourn the bright Rose, that bloom'd and went,
10   'Ere half disclos'd its vernal hue!
Mourn the green Bud, so rudely rent,
   It brake the stem on which it grew.

Mourn for the universal Woe
   With solemn dirge and falt'ring tongue:
For England's Lady is laid low,
   So dear, so lovely, and so young!

The Blossoms of her Tree of Life
   Shone with the dews of recent Bliss:
Transplanted in that deadly strife,
20   She plucks its fruits in Paradise.

Mourn for the widow'd Lord in chief,
   Who wails and will not solaced be!
Mourn for the childless Father's grief,
   The wedded Lover's Agony!

Mourn for the Prince, who rose at Morn
   To seek and bless the firstling Bud
Of his own Rose, and found the Thorn,
   Its point bedew'd with tears of blood.

O press again that murmuring string!
    Again bewail that princely Sire!
A destin'd Queen, a future King
    He mourns on one funereal pyre.

Mourn for Britannia's hopes decay'd,
    Her Daughters wail their dear Defence;
Their fair Example, prostrate lay'd,
    Chaste LOVE and fervid INNOCENCE.

While Grief in song shall seek repose,
    We will take up a Mourning yearly:
To wail the Blow that crush'd the Rose
    So dearly priz'd and lov'd so dearly.

Long as the Fount of Song o'erflows,
    Will I the yearly dirge renew:
Mourn for the firstling of the Rose,
    That snapt the stem on which it grew.

The proud shall pass, forgot; the chill,
    Damp, trickling Vault their only mourner!
Not so the regal Rose, that still
    Clung to the Breast which first had worn her!

———————

O Thou, who mark'st the Mourner's path,
    To sad Jeshurun's Sons attend!
Amid the Light'nings of thy Wrath
    The showers of Consolation send!

Jehovah frowns! the Islands bow!
    And Prince and People kiss the Rod! –
Their dread chastising Judge wert thou!
    Be thou their Comforter, O God!

A Character

A bird, who for his other sins
Had liv'd amongst the Jacobins;
Tho' like a kitten amid rats,
Or callow tit in nest of bats,
He much abhorr'd all democrats;
Yet nathless stood in ill report
Of wishing ill to Church and Court,
Tho' he'd nor claw, nor tooth, nor sting,
And learnt to pipe God save the King;
Tho' each day did new feathers bring,
All swore he had a leathern wing;
Nor polish'd wing, nor feather'd tail,
Nor down-clad thigh would aught avail;
And tho' – his tongue devoid of gall –
He civilly assur'd them all: –
'A bird am I of Phœbus' breed,
And on the sunflower cling and feed;
My name, good Sirs, is Thomas Tit!'
The bats would hail him brother cit,
Or, at the furthest, cousin-german.
At length the matter to determine,
He publicly denounced the vermin;
He spared the mouse, he prais'd the owl;
But bats were neither flesh nor fowl.
Blood-sucker, vampire, harpy, goul,
Came in full clatter from his throat,
Till his old nest-mates chang'd their note
To hireling, traitor, and turncoat, –
A base apostate who had sold
His very teeth and claws for gold; –
And then his feathers! – sharp the jest –
No doubt he feather'd well his nest!
'A Tit indeed! aye, tit for tat –
With place and title, brother Bat,
We soon shall see how well he'll play
Count Goldfinch, or Sir Joseph Jay!'
    Alas, poor Bird! and ill-bestarred –
Or rather let us say, poor Bard!

And henceforth quit the allegoric
40   With metaphor and simile,
For simple facts and style historic: –
Alas, poor Bard! no gold had he
Behind another's team he stept,
And plough'd and sow'd, while others reapt;
The work was his, but theirs the glory,
Sic vos non vobis, his whole story.
Besides, whate'er he wrote or said
Came from his heart as well as head;
And tho' he never left in lurch
50   His king, his country, or his church,
'Twas but to humour his own cynical
Contempt of doctrines Jacobinical;
To his own conscience only hearty,
'Twas but by chance he serv'd the party; –
The self-same things had said and writ,
Had Pitt been Fox, and Fox been Pitt;
Content his own applause to win
Would never dash thro' thick and thin,
And he can make, so say the wise,
60   No claim who makes no sacrifice; –
And bard still less: – what claim had he,
Who swore it vex'd his soul to see
So grand a cause, so proud a realm
With Goose and Goody at the helm;
Who long ago had fall'n asunder
But for their rivals baser blunder,
The coward whine and Frenchified
Slaver and slang of the other side? –
    Thus, his own whim his only bribe,
70   Our bard pursued his old A. B. C.
Contented if he could subscribe
In fullest sense his name Ἔστησε;
('Tis Punic Greek, for 'he hath stood!')
Whate'er the men, the cause was good;
And therefore with a right good will,
Poor fool, he fights their battles still.
Tush! squeak'd the Bats; – a mere bravado
To whitewash that base renegado;
'Tis plain unless you're blind or mad,
80   His conscience for the bays he barters; –

And true it is – as true as sad –
These circlets of green baize he had –
But then, alas! they were his garters!
   Ah, silly Bard, unfed, untended,
His lamp but glimmer'd in its socket;
He liv'd unhonour'd and unfriended
With scarce a penny in his pocket; –
Nay – tho' he hid it from the many –
With scarce a pocket for his penny!

Lines
TO A COMIC AUTHOR, ON AN ABUSIVE REVIEW

What though the chilly wide-mouth'd quacking chorus
From the rank swamps of murk Review-land croak:
So was it, neighbour, in the times before us,
When Momus, throwing on his Attic cloak,
Romped with the Graces; and each tickled Muse
(That Turk, Dan Phœbus, whom bards call divine,
Was married to – at least, he kept – all nine)
Fled, but still with reverted faces ran;
Yet, somewhat the broad freedoms to excuse,
They had allur'd the audacious Greek to use,
Swore they mistook him for their own good man.
This Momus – Aristophanes on earth
Men called him – maugre all his wit and worth
Was croaked and gabbled at. How, then, should you,
Or I, friend, hope to 'scape the skulking crew?
No! laugh, and say aloud, in tones of glee,
'I hate the quacking tribe, and they hate me!'

To Nature

It may indeed be phantasy, when I
   Essay to draw from all created things
   Deep, heartfelt, inward joy that closely clings;
And trace in leaves and flowers that round me lie

Lessons of love and earnest piety.
     So let it be; and if the wide world rings
     In mock of this belief, it brings
Nor fear, nor grief, nor vain perplexity.
So will I build my altar in the fields,
10   And the blue sky my fretted dome shall be,
And the sweet fragrance that the wild flower yields
     Shall be the incense I will yield to Thee,
Thee only God! and thou shalt not despise
Even me, the priest of this poor sacrifice.

The Tears of a Grateful People

A Hebrew Dirge and Hymn, chaunted in the Great Synagogue. St. James' pl. Aldgate, on the Day of the Funeral of King George III. of blessed memory. By Hyman Hurwitz of Highgate, Translated by a Friend.

DIRGE

Oppress'd, confused, with grief and pain,
     And inly shrinking from the blow,
In vain I seek the dirgeful strain,
     The wonted words refuse to flow.

A fear in every face I find,
     Each voice is that of one who grieves;
And all my Soul, to grief resigned,
     Reflects the sorrow it receives.

The Day-Star of our glory sets!
10   Our King has breathed his latest breath!
Each heart its wonted pulse forgets,
     As if it own'd the pow'r of death.

Our Crown, our heart's Desire is fled!
     Britannia's glory moults its wing!
Let us with ashes on our head,
     Raise up a mourning for our King.

Lo! of his beams the Day-Star shorn,
    Sad gleams the Moon through cloudy veil!
The Stars are dim! Our Nobles mourn;
20   The Matrons weep, their Children wail.

No age records a King so just,
    His virtues numerous as his days;
The Lord Jehovah was his trust,
    And truth with mercy ruled his ways.

His Love was bounded by no Clime;
    Each diverse Race, each distant Clan
He govern'd by this truth sublime,
    'God only knows the heart – not man.'

His word appall'd the sons of pride,
30   Iniquity far wing'd her way;
Deceit and fraud were scatter'd wide,
    And truth resum'd her sacred sway.

He sooth'd the wretched, and the prey
    From impious tyranny he tore;
He stay'd th' Usurper's iron sway,
    And bade the Spoiler waste no more.

Thou too, Jeshurun's Daughter! thou,
    Th' oppress'd of nations and the scorn!
Didst hail on his benignant brow
40   A safety dawning like the morn.

The scoff of each unfeeling mind,
    Thy doom was hard, and keen thy grief;
Beneath his throne, peace thou didst find,
    And blest the hand that gave relief.

E'en when a fatal cloud o'erspread
    The moonlight splendour of his sway,
Yet still the light remain'd, and shed
    Mild radiance on the traveller's way.

But he is gone – the Just! the Good!
50   Nor could a Nation's pray'r delay
The heavenly meed, that long had stood
      His portion in the realms of day.

Beyond the mighty Isle's extent
      The mightier Nation mourns her Chief:
Him Judah's Daughter shall lament,
      In tears of fervour, love and grief.

Britannia mourns in silent grief;
      Her heart a prey to inward woe.
In vain she strives to find relief,
60   Her pang so great, so great the blow.

Britannia! Sister! woe is me!
      Full fain would I console thy woe.
But, ah! how shall I comfort thee,
      Who need the balm I would bestow?

United then let us repair,
      As round our common Parent's grave;
And pouring out our heart in prayer,
      Our heav'nly Father's mercy crave.

Until Jehovah from his throne
70   Shall heed his suffering people's fears;
Shall turn to song the Mourner's groan,
      To smiles of joy the Nation's tears.

Praise to the Lord! Loud praises sing!
      And bless Jehovah's righteous hand!
Again he bids a George, our King,
      Dispense his blessings to the Land.

HYMN

O thron'd in Heav'n! Sole King of kings,
Jehovah! hear thy Children's prayers and sighs!
Thou Binder of the broken heart! with wings
80   Of healing on thy people rise!
        Thy mercies, Lord, are sweet;
        And Peace and Mercy meet,
        Before thy Judgment seat:
        Lord, hear us! we entreat!

When angry clouds thy throne surround,
E'en from the cloud thou bid'st thy mercy shine:
And ere thy righteous vengeance strikes the wound,
      Thy grace prepares the balm divine!
        Thy mercies, Lord, are sweet;
          etc.

90   The Parent tree thy hand did spare –
It fell not till the ripen'd fruit was won:
Beneath its shade the Scion flourish'd fair,
      And for the Sire thou gav'st the Son.
        etc.

This thy own Vine, which thou didst rear,
And train up for us from the royal root,
Protect, O Lord! and to the Nations near
      Long let it shelter yield, and fruit.
        etc.

Lord, comfort thou the royal line:
Let Peace and Joy watch round us hand and hand.
100 Our Nobles visit with thy grace divine,
      And banish sorrow from the land!
        Thy mercies, Lord, are sweet;
        And Peace and Mercy meet
        Before thy Judgment seat;
        Lord, hear us! we entreat!

First Advent of Love

O fair is Love's first hope to gentle mind!
As Eve's first star thro' fleecy cloudlet peeping;
And sweeter than the gentle south-west wind,
O'er willowy meads and shadow'd waters creeping,
And Ceres' golden fields; – the sultry hind
Meets it with brow uplift, and stays his reaping.

[Reason]

Whene'er the mist, that stands 'twixt God and thee
Defecates to a pure transparency,
That intercepts no light and adds no stain –
There Reason is, and then begins her reign!

But alas!
    – tu stesso ti fai grosso
  Col falso imaginar, sì che non vedi
  Ciò che vedresti, se l'avessi scosso.

DANTE, Paradiso, Canto I

[Lines from a notebook – 1822]

Where'er I find the Good, the True, the Fair,
I ask no names. God's Spirit dwelleth there!
The unconfounded, undivided Three.
Each for itself, and all in each, to see
In Man, and Nature is Philosophy.

From the German

Know'st thou the land where the pale citrons grow,
The golden fruits in darker foliage glow?
Soft blows the wind that breathes from that blue sky!
Still stands the myrtle and the laurel high!
Know'st thou it well that land, belovèd Friend?
Thither with thee, O, thither would I wend!

The Reproof and Reply

'Fie, Mr Coleridge! – and can this be you?
Break two commandments? and in church-time too!
Have you not heard, or have you heard in vain,
The birth and parentage-recording strain?
Confessions shrill, that out-shrill'd mack'rel drown –
Fresh from the drop, the youth not yet cut down.
Letter to sweet-heart – the last dying speech –
And didn't all this begin in Sabbath-breach?
You, that knew better! In broad open day.
Steal in, steal out, and steal our flowers away?
What could possess you? Ah! sweet youth, I fear
The chap with horns and tail was at your ear!'

Such sounds of late, accusing fancy brought
From fair ——— to the Poet's thought.
Now hear the meek Parnassian youth's reply: –
A bow, a pleading look, a downcast eye, –
And then:

          'Fair dame! a visionary wight,
Hard by your hill-side mansion sparkling white,
His thoughts all hovering round the Muses' home,
Long hath it been your poet's wont to roam,
And many a morn, on his becharmèd sense
So rich a stream of music issued thence
He deem'd himself, as it flowed warbling on,
Beside the vocal fount of Helicon!

But when, as if to settle the concern,
A nymph too he beheld, in many a turn,
Guiding the sweet rill from its fontal urn, –
Say, can you blame? – No! none that saw and heard
Could blame a bard, that he thus inly stirr'd;
30 A muse beholding in each fervent trait,
Took Mary ―――― for Polly Hymnia!
Or haply as there stood beside the maid
One loftier form in sable stole array'd,
If with regretful thought he hail'd in thee
―――――, his long-lost friend, Mol Pomene!
But most of you, soft warblings, I complain!
'Twas ye that from the bee-hive of my brain
Lured the wild fancies forth, a freakish rout,
And witch'd the air with dreams turn'd inside out.

40 'Thus all conspir'd – each power of eye and ear,
And this gay month, th' enchantress of the year,
To cheat poor me (no conjurer, God wot!)
And ――――'s self accomplice in the plot.
Can you then wonder if I went astray?
Not bards alone, nor lovers mad as they; –
All nature day-dreams in the month of May.
And if I pluck'd each flower that sweetest blows, –
Who walks in sleep, needs follow must his nose.
Thus, long accustom'd on the twy-fork'd hill,
50 To pluck both flower and floweret at my will;
The garden's maze, like No-man's-land, I tread,
Nor common law, nor statute in my head;
For my own proper smell, sight, fancy, feeling,
With autocratic hand at once repealing
Five Acts of Parliament 'gainst private stealing!
But yet from ―――― who despairs of grace?
There's no spring-gun or man-trap in that face!
Let Moses then look black, and Aaron blue,
That look as if they had little else to do:
60 For ――――speaks, "Poor youth! he's but a waif!
The spoons all right? the hen and chickens safe?
Well, well, he shall not forfeit our regards –
The Eighth Commandment was not made for Bards!" '

Youth and Age

Verse, a breeze mid blossoms straying,
Where Hope clung feeding, like a bee –
Both were mine! Life went a maying
    With Nature, Hope, and Poesy,
        When I was young!
When I was young? – Ah, woful when!
Ah! for the change 'twixt Now and Then!
This breathing house not built with hands,
This body that does me grievous wrong,
O'er aery cliffs and glittering sands,
How lightly then it flashed along: –
Like those trim skiffs, unknown of yore,
On winding lakes and rivers wide,
That ask no aid of sail or oar,
That fear no spite of wind or tide!
Nought cared this body for wind or weather
When Youth and I liv'd in't together.

Flowers are lovely; Love is flower-like;
Friendship is a sheltering tree;
O! the joys, that came down shower-like,
Of Friendship, Love, and Liberty,
        Ere I was old!
Ere I was old? Ah woful Ere,
Which tells me, Youth's no longer here!
O Youth! for years so many and sweet,
'Tis known, that Thou and I were one,
I'll think it but a fond conceit –
It cannot be, that Thou art gone!
Thy vesper-bell hath not yet toll'd: –
And thou wert aye a masker bold!
What strange disguise hast now put on,
To make believe, that Thou art gone?
I see these locks in silvery slips,
This drooping gait, this altered size:
But springtide blossoms on thy lips,
And tears take sunshine from thine eyes!
Life is but thought: so think I will
That Youth and I are house-mates still.

Dew-drops are the gems of morning,
40 But the tears of mournful eve!
Where no hope is, life's a warning
That only serves to make us grieve,
                          When we are old:
That only serves to make us grieve
With oft and tedious taking-leave,
Like some poor nigh-related guest,
That may not rudely be dismist.
Yet hath outstay'd his welcome while,
And tells the jest without the smile.

Desire

Where true Love burns Desire is Love's pure flame;
It is the reflex of our earthly frame,
That takes its meaning from the nobler part,
And but translates the language of the heart.

The Delinquent Travellers

Some are home-sick – some two or three,
Their third year on the Arctic Sea –
Brave Captain Lyon tells us so –
Spite of those charming Esquimaux.
But O, what scores are sick of Home,
Agog for Paris or for Rome!
Nay! tho' contented to abide,
You should prefer your own fireside;
Yet since grim War has ceas'd its madding,
10 And Peace has set John Bull agadding,
'Twould such a vulgar taste betray,
For very shame you must away!
'What? not yet seen the coast of France!
The folks will swear, for lack of bail,
You've spent your last five years in jail!'

Keep moving! Steam, or Gas, or Stage,
Hold, cabin, steerage, hencoop's cage –
Tour, Journey, Voyage, Lounge, Ride, Walk,
Skim, Sketch, Excursion, Travel-talk –
20   For move you must! 'Tis now the rage,
The law and fashion of the Age.
If you but perch, where Dover tallies,
So strangely with the coast of Calais,
With a good glass and knowing look,
You'll soon get matter for a book!
Or else, in Gas-car, take your chance
Like that adventurous king of France,
Who, once, with twenty thousand men
Went up – and then came down again;
30   At least, he moved if nothing more:
And if there's nought left to explore,
Yet while your well-greased wheels keep spinning,
The traveller's honoured name you're winning,
And, snug as Jonas in the Whale,
You may loll back and dream a tale.
Move, or be moved – there's no protection,
Our Mother Earth has ta'en the infection.
(That rogue Copernicus, 'tis said
First put the whirring in her head.)
40   A planet She, and can't endure
T"exist without her annual Tour:
The *name* were else a mere misnomer,
Since Planet is but Greek for *Roamer*.
The atmosphere, too, can do no less
Than ventilate her emptiness,
Bilks turn-pike gates, for no one cares,
And gives herself a thousand airs –
While streams and shopkeepers, we see,
Will have their run toward the sea –
50   And if, meantime, like old King Log,
Or ass with tether and a clog,
Must graze at home! to yawn and bray
'I guess we shall have rain to-day!'
Nor clog nor tether can be worse
Than the dead palsy of the purse.
Money, I've heard a wise man say,
Makes herself wings and flys away:

Ah! would She take it in her head
To make a pair for me instead!
At all events, the Fancy's free,
No traveller so bold as she.
From Fear and Poverty released
I'll saddle Pegasus, at least,
And when she's seated to her mind,
I within I can mount behind:
And since this outward I, you know,
Must stay because he cannot go,
My fellow-travellers shall be they
Who go because they cannot stay –
Rogues, rascals, sharpers, blanks and prizes,
Delinquents of all sorts and sizes,
Fraudulent bankrupts, Knights burglarious,
And demireps of means precarious –
All whom Law thwarted, Arms or Arts,
Compel to visit foreign parts,
All hail! No compliments, I pray,
I'll follow where you lead the way!
But ere we cross the main once more,
Methinks, along my native shore,
Dismounting from my steed I'll stray
Beneath the cliffs of Dumpton Bay,
Where, Ramsgate and Broadstairs between,
Rude caves and grated doors are seen:
And here I'll watch till break of day,
(For Fancy in her magic might
Can turn broad noon to starless night!)
When lo! methinks a sudden band
Of smock-clad smugglers round me stand.
Denials, oaths, in vain I try,
At once they gag me for a spy,
And stow me in the boat hard by.
Suppose us fairly now afloat,
Till Boulogne mouth receives our Boat.
But, bless us! what a numerous band
Of cockneys anglicise the strand!
Delinquent bankrupts, leg-bail'd debtors,
Some for the news, and some for letters –
With hungry look and tarnished dress,
French shrugs and British surliness.

100   Sick of the country for their sake
      Of them and France *French leave* I take –
      And lo! a transport comes in view
      I hear the merry motley crew,
      Well skill'd in pocket to make entry,
      Of Dieman's Land the elected Gentry,
      And founders of Australian Races. –
      The Rogues! I see it in their faces!
      Receive me, Lads! I'll go with you,
      Hunt the black swan and kangaroo,
110   And that New Holland we'll presume
      Old England with some elbow-room.
      Across the mountains we will roam,
      And each man make himself a home:
      Or, if old habits ne'er forsaking,
      Like clock-work of the Devil's making,
      Ourselves inveterate rogues should be,
      We'll have a virtuous progeny;
      And on the dunghill of our vices
      Raise human pine-apples and spices.
120   Of all the children of John Bull
      With empty heads and bellies full,
      Who ramble East, West, North and South,
      With leaky purse and open mouth,
      In search of varieties exotic
      The usefullest and most patriotic,
      And merriest, too, believe me, Sirs!
      Are your Delinquent Travellers!

Song, ex improviso
ON HEARING A SONG IN PRAISE OF A LADY'S BEAUTY

'Tis not the lily-brow I prize,
Nor roseate cheeks, nor sunny eyes,
    Enough of lilies and of roses!
A thousand-fold more dear to me
    The gentle look that Love discloses, –
The look that Love alone can see!

Work Without Hope
LINES COMPOSED 21ST FEBRUARY, 1827

All Nature seems at work. Slugs leave their lair –
The bees are stirring – birds are on the wing –
And Winter slumbering in the open air,
Wears on his smiling face a dream of Spring!
And I, the while, the sole unbusy thing,
Nor honey make, nor pair, nor build, nor sing.

Yet well I ken the banks where amaranths blow,
Have traced the fount whence streams of nectar flow.
Bloom, O ye amaranths! bloom for whom ye may,
10   For me ye bloom not! Glide, rich streams, away!
With lips unbrightened, wreathless brow, I stroll:
And would you learn the spells that drowse my soul?
Work without hope draws nectar in a sieve,
And hope without an object cannot live.

The Two Founts
STANZAS ADDRESSED TO A LADY ON HER RECOVERY
WITH UNBLEMISHED LOOKS, FROM A SEVERE ATTACK
OF PAIN

'Twas my last waking thought, how it could be,
That thou, sweet friend, such anguish shouldst endure;
When straight from Dreamland came a Dwarf, and he
Could tell the cause, forsooth, and knew the cure.

Methought he fronted me with peering look
Fix'd on my heart; and read aloud in game
The loves and griefs therein, as from a book;
And uttered praise like one who wished to blame.

In every heart (quoth he) since Adam's sin
10   Two Founts there are, of suffering and of cheer!
That to let forth, and this to keep within!
But she, whose aspect I find imaged here,

Of Pleasure only will to all dispense,
That Fount alone unlock, by no distress
Choked or turned inward, but still issue thence
Unconqueerd cheer, persistent loveliness.

As on the driving cloud the shiny bow,
That gracious thing made up of tears and light,
Mid the wild rack and rain that slants below
Stands smiling forth, unmoved and freshly bright; –

As though the spirits of all lovely flowers,
Inweaving each its wreath and dewy crown,
Or ere they sank to earth in vernal showers,
Had built a bridge to tempt the angels down.

Ev'n so, Eliza! on that face of thine,
On that benignant face, whose look alone
(The soul's translucence thro' her crystal shrine!)
Has power to soothe all anguish but thine own,

A beauty hovers still, and ne'er takes wing,
But with a silent charm compels the stern
And tort'ring Genius of the bitter spring,
To shrink aback, and cower upon his urn.

Who then needs wonder, if (no outlet found
In passion, spleen, or strife) the fount of pain
O'erflowing beats against its lovely mound,
And in wild flashes shoots from heart to brain?

Sleep, and the Dwarf with that unsteady gleam
On his raised lip, that aped a critic smile,
Had passed: yet I, my sad thoughts to beguile,
Lay weaving on the tissue of my dream;

Till audibly at length I cried, as though
Thou had'st indeed been present to my eyes,
O sweet, sweet sufferer; if the case be so,
I pray thee, be less good, less sweet, less wise!

In every look a barbèd arrow send,
On those soft lips let scorn and anger live!
Do any thing, rather than thus, sweet friend!
Hoard for thyself the pain, thou wilt not give!

The Pang More Sharp Than All
AN ALLEGORY

I

He too has flitted from his secret nest,
Hope's last and dearest Child without a name! –
Has flitted from me, like the warmthless flame,
That makes false promise of a place of rest
To the tir'd Pilgrim's still believing mind; –
Or like some Elfin Knight in kingly court,
Who having won all guerdons in his sport,
Glides out of view, and whither none can find!

II

Yes! He hath flitted from me – with what aim,
Or why, I know not! 'Twas a home of bliss,
And He was innocent, as the pretty shame
Of babe, that tempts and shuns the menaced kiss,
From its twy-cluster'd hiding place of snow!
Pure as the babe, I ween, and all aglow
As the dear hopes, that swell the mother's breast –
Her eyes down gazing o'er her claspèd charge; –
Yet gay as that twice happy father's kiss,
That well might glance aside, yet never miss,
Where the sweet mark emboss'd so sweet a targe –
Twice wretched he who hath been doubly blest!

III

Like a loose blossom on a gusty night
He flitted from me – and has left behind
(As if to them his faith he ne'er did plight)
Of either sex and answerable mind
Two playmates, twin-births of his foster-dame: –
The one a steady lad (Esteem he hight)
And Kindness is the gentler sister's name.
Dim likeness now, tho' fair she be and good,

Of that bright Boy who hath us all forsook; –
30   But in his full-eyed aspect when she stood,
And while her face reflected every look,
And in reflection kindled – she became
So like Him, that almost she seem'd the same!

IV

Ah! He is gone, and yet will not depart! –
Is with me still, yet I from Him exil'd!
For still there lives within my secret heart
The magic image of the magic Child,
Which there He made up-grow by his strong art,
As in that crystal orb – wise Merlin's feat, –
40   The wondrous 'World of Glass', wherein inisl'd
All long'd for things their beings did repeat; –
And there He left it, like a Sylph beguiled,
To live and yearn and languish incomplete!

V

Can wit of man a heavier grief reveal?
Can sharper pang from hate or scorn arise? –
Yes! one more sharp there is that deeper lies,
Which fond Esteem but mocks when he would heal.
Yet neither scorn nor hate did it devise,
But sad compassion and atoning zeal!
50   One pang more blighting-keen than hope betray'd!
And this it is my woful hap to feel,
When at her Brother's hest, the twin-born Maid
With face averted and unsteady eyes,
Her truant playmate's faded robe puts on;
And inly shrinking from her own disguise
Enacts the faery Boy that's lost and gone.
O worse than all! O pang all pangs above
Is Kindness counterfeiting absent Love!

Sancti Dominici Pallium
A DIALOGUE BETWEEN POET AND FRIEND

*Found written on the blank leaf at the beginning of Butler's
Book of the Church.*

Poet
I note the moods and feelings men betray,
And heed them more than aught they do or say;
The lingering ghosts of many a secret deed
Still-born or haply strangled in its birth;
These best reveal the smooth man's inward creed!
These mark the spot where lies the treasure Worth!

——made up of impudence and trick,
With cloven tongue prepared to hiss and lick,
Rome's brazen serpent – boldly dares discuss
10 The roasting of thy heart, O brave John Huss!
And with grim triumph and a truculent glee
Absolves anew the Pope-wrought perfidy,
That made an empire's plighted faith a lie,
And fix'd a broad stare on the Devil's eye –
(Pleas'd with the guilt, yet envy-stung at heart
To stand outmaster'd in his own black art!)
Yet——

Friend
          Enough of ——! we're agreed,
Who now defends would then have done the deed.
But who not feels persuasion's gentle sway,
20 Who but must meet the proffered hand half way
When courteous——

Poet (*aside*)
                              (Rome's smooth go-between!)

Friend
Laments the advice that soured a milky queen –
(For 'bloody' all enlighten'd men confess
An antiquated error of the press:)
Who rapt by zeal beyond her sex's bounds,
With actual cautery staunched the church's wounds!

And tho' he deems, that with too broad a blur
We damn the French and Irish massacre,
Yet blames them both – and thinks the Pope might err!
30   What think you now? Boots it with spear and shield
Against such gentle foes to take the field
Whose beck'ning hands the mild Caduceus wield?

Poet
What think I now? Ev'n what I thought before; –
What——boasts tho'——may deplore,
Still I repeat, words lead me not astray
When the shown feeling points a different way.
Smooth——can say grace at slander's feast,
And bless each haut-gout cook'd by monk or priest;
Leaves the full lie on——'s gong to swell,
40   Content with half-truths that do just as well;
But duly decks his mitred comrade's flanks,
And with him shares the Irish nation's thanks!

So much for you, my Friend! who own a Church,
And would not leave your mother in the lurch!
But when a Liberal asks me what I think –
Scar'd by the blood and soot of Cobbett's ink,
And Jeffrey's glairy phlegm and Connor's foam,
In search of some safe parable I roam –
An emblem sometimes may comprise a tome!

50   Disclaimant of his uncaught grandsire's mood,
I see a tiger lapping kitten's food:
And who shall blame him that he purrs applause,
When brother Brindle pleads the good old cause;
And frisks his pretty tail, and half unsheathes his claws!
Yet not the less, for modern lights unapt,
I trust the bolts and cross-bars of the laws
More than the Protestant milk all newly lapt,
Impearling a tame wild-cat's whisker'd jaws!

The Improvisatore
OR 'JOHN ANDERSON, MY JO, JOHN'

Scene – A spacious drawing-room, with music-room adjoining.

Katharine. What are the words?

Eliza. Ask our friend, the Improvisatore; here he comes. Kate has a favour to ask of you, Sir; it is that you will repeat the ballad that Mr —— sang so sweetly.

Friend. It is in Moore's Irish Melodies; but I do not recollect the words distinctly. The moral of them, however, I take to be this: –

> Love would remain the same if true,
> When we were neither young nor new;
> Yea, and in all within the will that came,
> By the same proofs would show itself the same.

Eliz. What are the lines you repeated from Beaumont and Fletcher, which my mother admired so much? It begins with something about two vines so close that their tendrils intermingle.

Fri. You mean Charles' speech to Angelina, in 'The Elder Brother.'

> We'll live together, like two neighbour vines,
> Circling our souls and loves in one another!
> We'll spring together, and we'll bear one fruit;
> One joy shall make us smile, and one grief mourn;
> One age go with us, and one hour of death
> Shall close our eyes, and one grave make us happy.

Kath. A precious boon, that would go far to reconcile one to old age – this love – if true! But is there any such true love?

Fri. I hope so.

Kath. But do you believe it?

Eliz. (*eagerly*). I am sure he does.

Fri. From a man turned of fifty, Katharine, I imagine, expects a less confident answer.

Kath. A more sincere one, perhaps.

Fri. Even though he should have obtained the nick-name of Improvisatore, by perpetrating charades and extempore verses at Christmas times?

Eliz. Nay, but be serious.

Fri. Serious! Doubtless. A grave personage of my years giving a love-lecture to two young ladies, cannot well be otherwise. The difficulty, I suspect, would be for them to remain so. It will be asked whether I am not the 'elderly gentleman' who sate 'despairing beside a clear stream', with a willow for his wig-block.

Eliz. Say another word, and we will call it downright affectation.

Kath. No! we will be affronted, drop a courtesy, and ask pardon for our presumption in expecting that Mr —— would waste his sense on two insignificant girls.

Fri. Well, well, I will be serious. Hem! Now then commences the discourse; Mr Moore's song being the text. Love, as distinguished from Friendship, on the one hand, and from the passion that too often usurps its name, on the other –

Lucius (*Eliza's brother, who had just joined the trio, in a whisper to the Friend*). But is not Love the union of both?

Fri. (*aside to Lucius*). He never loved who thinks so.

Eliz. Brother, we don't want you. There! Mrs H. cannot arrange the flower-vase without you. Thank you, Mrs Hartman.

Luc. I'll have my revenge! I know what I will say!

Eliz. Off! off! Now, dear sir, – Love, you were saying –

Fri. Hush! Preaching, you mean, Eliza.

Eliz. (*impatiently*). Pshaw!

Fri. Well then, I was saying that love, truly such, is itself not the most common thing in the world: and mutual love still less so. But that enduring personal attachment, so beautifully delineated by Erin's sweet melodist, and still more touchingly, perhaps, in the well-known ballad, 'John Anderson, my Jo, John', in addition to a depth and constancy of character of no every-day occurrence, supposes a peculiar sensibility and tenderness of nature; a constitutional communicativeness and utterancy of heart and soul; a delight in the detail of sympathy, in the outward and visible signs of the sacrament within – to count, as it were, the pulses of the life of love. But above all, it supposes a soul which, even in the pride and summer-tide of life – even in the lustihood of health and strength, had felt oftenest and prized highest that which age cannot take away, and which, in all our lovings, is *the* Love; –

Eliz. There is something here (*pointing to her heart*) that seems to understand you, but wants the word that would make it understand itself.

Kath. I, too, seem to feel what you mean. Interpret the feeling for us.

Fri. – I mean that willing sense of the unsufficingness of the self for itself, which predisposes a generous nature to see, in the total being of another, the supplement and completion of its own; – that quiet perpetual seeking which the presence of the beloved object modulates, not suspends, where the heart momently finds, and, finding, again seeks on; – lastly, when 'life's changeful orb has pass'd the full,' a confirmed faith in the nobleness of humanity, thus brought home and pressed, as it were, to the very bosom of hourly experience; it supposes, I say, a heartfelt reverence for worth, not the less deep because divested of its solemnity by habit, by familiarity, by mutual infirmities, and even by a feeling of modesty which will arise in delicate minds, when they are conscious of possessing the same or the correspondent excellence in their own characters. In short, there must be a mind, which, while it feels the beautiful and the excellent in the beloved as its own, and by right of love appropriates it, can call Goodness its playfellow; and dares make sport of time and infirmity, while, in the person of a thousand-foldly endeared partner, we feel for aged virtue the caressing fondness that belongs to the innocence of childhood, and repeat the same attentions and tender courtesies which had been dictated by the same affection to the same object when attired in feminine loveliness or in manly beauty.

Eliz. What a soothing – what an elevating thought!

Kath. If it be not only a mere fancy.

Fri. At all events, these qualities which I have enumerated, are rarely found united in a single individual. How much more rare must it be, that two such individuals should meet together in this wide world under circumstances that admit of their union as Husband and Wife. A person may be highly estimable on the whole, nay, amiable as neighbour, friend, housemate – in short, in all the concentric circles of attachment save only the last and inmost; and yet from how many causes be estranged from the highest perfection in this! Pride, coldness, or fastidiousness of nature, worldly cares, an anxious or ambitious disposition, a passion for display, a sullen temper, – one or the other – too often proves 'the dead fly in the compost of spices', and any one is enough to unfit it for the precious balm of unction. For some mighty good sort of people, too, there is not seldom a sort of solemn saturnine, or, if you will, ursine vanity, that keeps itself alive by sucking the paws of its own self-importance. And as this high sense, or rather sensation of their own value is, for the most part, grounded on negative qualities, so they have no better means of preserving the same but by negatives – that is, by not doing or saying any thing, that might be put down for fond, silly, or nonsensical; – or (to use their own phrase) by never forgetting themselves, which some of their acquaintance are uncharitable enough to think the most worthless object they could be employed in remembering.

Eliz. (*in answer to a whisper from Katharine*). To a hair! He must have sate for it himself. Save me from such folks! But they are out of the question.

Fri. True! but the same effect is produced in thousands by the too general insensibility to a very important truth; this, namely, that the misery of human life is made up of large massses, each separated from the other by certain intervals. One year, the death of a child; years after, a failure in trade; after another longer or shorter interval, a daughter may have married unhappily; – in all but the singularly unfortunate, the integral parts that compose the sum total of the unhappiness of a man's life, are easily counted, and distinctly remembered. The happiness of life, on the contrary, is made up of minute fractions – the little, soon-forgotten charities of a kiss, a smile, a kind look, a heartfelt compliment in the disguise of playful raillery, and the countless other infinitesimals of pleasurable thought and genial feeling.

Kath. Well, Sir; you have said quite enough to make me despair of finding a 'John Anderson, my Jo, John', with whom to totter down the hill of life.

Fri. Not so! Good men are not, I trust, so much scarcer than good women, but that what another would find in you, you may hope to find in another. But well, however, may that boon be rare, the possession of which would be more than an adequate reward for the rarest virtue.

Eliz. Surely, he, who has described it so well, must have possessed it?

Fri. If he were worthy to have possessed it, and had believingly anticipated and not found it, how bitter the disappointment! (Then, after a pause of a few minutes),

ANSWER, *ex improviso*

Yes, yes! that boon, life's richest treat,
He had, or fancied that he had;
Say, 'twas but in his own conceit –
   The fancy made him glad!
Crown of his cup, and garnish of his dish,
The boon, prefigured in his earliest wish,
The fair fulfilment of his poesy,
When his young heart first yearn'd for sympathy!

But e'en the meteor offspring of the brain
        Unnourished wane;
Faith asks her daily bread,

And Fancy must be fed.
Now so it chanced – from wet or dry,
It boots not how – I know not why –
She missed her wonted food; and quickly
Poor Fancy stagger'd and grew sickly.
Then came a restless state, 'twixt yea and nay,
His faith was fix'd, his heart all ebb and flow;
Or like a bark, in some half-shelter'd bay,
20   Above its anchor driving to and fro.

That boon, which but to have possest
In a belief, gave life a zest –
Uncertain both what it had been,
And if by error lost, or luck;
And what it was; – an evergreen
Which some insidious blight had struck,
Or annual flower, which, past its blow,
No vernal spell shall e'er revive;
Uncertain, and afraid to know,
30   Doubts toss'd him to and fro:
Hope keeping Love, Love Hope alive,
Like babes bewildered in the snow,
That cling and huddle from the cold
In hollow tree or ruin'd fold.

Those sparkling colours, once his boast
        Fading, one by one away,
Thin and hueless as a ghost,
        Poor Fancy on her sick bed lay;
Ill at distance, worse when near,
40   Telling her dreams to jealous Fear!
Where was it then, the sociable sprite
That crown'd the Poet's cup and deck'd his dish!
Poor shadow cast from an unsteady wish,
Itself a substance by no other right
But that it intercepted Reason's light;
It dimm'd his eye, it darken'd on his brow,
A peevish mood, a tedious time, I trow!
        Thank Heaven! 'tis not so now.

O bliss of blissful hours!
50   The boon of Heaven's decreeing,
While yet in Eden's bowers

Dwelt the first husband and his sinless mate!
The one sweet plant, which, piteous Heaven agreeing,
They bore with them thro' Eden's closing gate!
Of life's gay summer tide the sovran rose!
Late autumn's amaranth, that more fragrant blows
When passion's flowers all fall or fade;
If this were ever his, in outward being,
Or but his own true love's projected shade,
60   Now that at length by certain proof he knows,
That whether real or a magic show,
Whate'er it was, it is no longer so;
Though heart be lonesome, hope laid low,
Yet, Lady! deem him not unblest:
The certainty that struck hope dead,
Hath left contentment in her stead:
       And that is next to best!

Love's Burial-Place: A Madrigal

Lady. If Love be dead –
  Poet. And I aver it!
Lady. Tell me, Bard! where Love lies buried?
  Poet. Love lies buried where 'twas born:
Oh, gentle dame! think it no scorn
If, in my fancy, I presume
To call thy bosom poor Love's Tomb.
And on that tomb to read the line: –
'Here lies a Love that once seem'd mine
10   But caught a chill, as I divine,
And died at length of a Decline.'

Lines

SUGGESTED BY THE LAST WORDS OF BERENGARIUS. OB.
ANNO DOM. 1088

No more 'twixt conscience staggering and the Pope
Soon shall I now before my God appear,
By him to be acquitted, as I hope;
By him to be condemnèd, as I fear. –

REFLECTION ON THE ABOVE

Lynx amid moles! had I stood by thy bed,
Be of good cheer, meek soul! I would have said:
I see a hope spring from that humble fear.
All are not strong alike through storms to steer
Right onward. What? though dread of threaten'd death
10   And dungeon torture made thy hand and breath
Inconstant to the truth within thy heart?
That truth, from which, through fear, thou twice didst start,
Fear haply told thee, was a learned strife,
Or not so vital as to claim thy life:
And myriads had reached Heaven, who never knew
Where lay the difference 'twixt the false and true!

Ye, who secure 'mid trophies not your own,
Judge him who won them when he stood alone,
And proudly talk of recreant Berengare –
20   O first the age, and then the man compare!
That age how dark! congenial minds how rare!
No host of friends with kindred zeal did burn!
No throbbing hearts awaited his return!
Prostrate alike when prince and peasant fell,
He only disenchanted from the spell,
Like the weak worm that gems the starless night,
Moved in the scanty circlet of his light:
And was it strange if he withdrew the ray
That did but guide the night-birds to their prey?

30   The ascending day-star with a bolder eye
Hath lit each dew-drop on our trimmer lawn!
Yet not for this, if wise, shall we decry
The spots and struggles of the timid dawn;
Lest so we tempt th' approaching noon to scorn
The mists and painted vapours of our morn.

Epitaphium testamentarium

Τὸ τοῦ ῎ΕΣΤΗΣΕ τοῦ ἐπιθανοὺς Epitaphium testamentarium αὐτόγραφον.

Quae linquam, aut nihil, aut nihili, aut vix sunt mea. Sordes
Do Morti: reddo caetera, Christe! tibi.

Duty Surviving Self-Love
THE ONLY SURE FRIEND OF DECLINING LIFE.
A SOLILOQUY

Unchanged within to see all changed without
Is a blank lot and hard to bear, no doubt.
Yet why at others' wanings should'st thou fret?
Then only might'st thou feel a just regret,
Hadst thou withheld thy love or hid thy light
In selfish forethought of neglect and slight.
O wiselier then, from feeble yearnings freed,
While, and on whom, thou may'st – shine on! nor heed
Whether the object by reflected light
Return thy radiance or absorb it quite:
And though thou notest from thy safe recess
Old friends burn dim, like lamps in noisome air,
Love them for what they are; nor love them less,
Because to thee they are not what they were.

10

[Homeless]

'O! Christmas Day, Oh! happy day!
  A foretaste from above,
To him who hath a happy home
  And love returned from love!'

O! Christmas Day, O gloomy day,
  The barb in Memory's dart,
To him who walks alone through Life,
  The desolate in heart.

Ἔρως ἀεὶ λάληθρος ἑταῖρος

In many ways does the full heart reveal
The presence of the love it would conceal;
But in far more th' estrangèd heart lets know
The absence of the love, which yet it fain would shew.

Song

Tho' veiled in spires of myrtle wreath,
Love is a sword that cuts its sheath
And thro' the clefts, itself has made
We spy the flashes of the Blade!

But thro' the clefts, itself had made,
We likewise see Love's flashing blade
By rust consumed or snapt in twain:
And only Hilt and Stump remain.

Profuse Kindness

Νήπτιοι, οὐκ ἴσασιν ὅσῳ πλέον ἥμισυ παντός. – HESIOD.

What a spring-tide of Love to dear friends in a shoal!
Half of it to one were worth double the whole!

Written in an Album

PARRY seeks the polar ridge;
Rhymes seeks S. T. Coleridge,
Author of works, whereof – tho' not in Dutch –
The public little knows – the publisher too much.

To Mary Pridham

Dear tho' unseen! tho' I have left behind
Life's gayer views and all that stirs the mind,
Now I revive, Hope making a new start,
Since I have heard with most believing heart,
That all my glad eyes would grow bright to see,
My Derwent hath found realiz'd in thee,
The boon prefigur'd in his earliest wish
Crown of his cup and garnish of his dish!
The fair fulfilment of his poesy,
10   When his young heart first yearn'd for sympathy!
Dear tho' unseen! unseen, yet long portray'd!
A Father's blessing on thee, gentle Maid!

Verses Trivocular

Of one scrap of science I've evidence ocular.
A heart of one chamber they call unilocular,
And in a sharp frost, or when snow-flakes fall floccular,
Your wise man of old wrapp'd himself in a Roquelaure,
Which was called a Wrap-rascal when folks would be jocular.
And shell-fish, the small, Periwinkle and Cockle are,
So with them will I finish these verses trivocular.

Water Ballad
[FROM THE FRENCH]

'Come hither, gently rowing,
  Come, bear me quickly o'er
This stream so brightly flowing,
  To yonder woodland shore.
But vain were my endeavour
  To pay thee, courteous guide;
Row on, row on, for ever
  I'd have thee by my side.

'Good boatman, prithee haste thee,
   I seek my father-land.' –
'Say, when I there have placed thee,
   Dare I demand thy hand?' –
'A maiden's head can never
   So hard a point decide;
Row on, row on, for ever
   I'd have thee by my side.'

The happy bridal over
   The wanderer ceased to roam,
For, seated by her lover,
   The boat became her home.
And still they sang together
   As steering o'er the tide,
'Row on through wind and weather
   For ever by my side.'

Cologne

In Köhln, a town of monks and bones,
And pavements fang'd with murderous stones,
And rags, and hags, and hideous wenches;
I counted two and seventy stenches,
All well defined, and several stinks!
Ye Nymphs that reign o'er sewers and sinks,
The river Rhine, it is well known,
Doth wash your city of Cologne;
But tell me, Nymphs! what power divine
Shall henceforth wash the river Rhine?

On my Joyful Departure from the Same City

As I am rhymer,
And now at least a merry one,
    Mr Mum's Rudesheimer
    And the church of St. Geryon
    Are the two things alone
    That deserve to be known
In the body and soul-stinking town of Cologne.

[The Netherlands]

Water and windmills, greenness, Islets green; –
Willows whose Trunks beside the shadows stood
Of their own higher half, and willowy swamp: –
Farmhouses that at anchor seem'd – in the inland sky
The fog-transfixing Spires –
Water, wide water, greenness and green banks,
And water seen –

The Garden of Boccaccio

Of late, in one of those most weary hours,
When life seems emptied of all genial powers,
A dreary mood, which he who ne'er has known
May bless his happy lot, I sate alone;
And, from the numbing spell to win relief,
Call'd on the past for thought of glee or grief.
In vain! bereft alike of grief and glee,
I sate and cow'r'd o'er my own vacancy!
And as I watch'd the dull continuous ache,
10 Which, all else slumb'ring, seem'd alone to wake;
O Friend! long wont to notice yet conceal,
And soothe by silence what words cannot heal,
I but half saw that quiet hand of thine
Place on my desk this exquisite design,

Boccaccio's Garden and its faery,
The love, the joyaunce, and the gallantry!
An Idyll, with Boccaccio's spirit warm,
Framed in the silent poesy of form.

Like flocks adown a newly-bathèd steep
20 Emerging from a mist; or like a stream
Of music soft that not dispels the sleep,
But casts in happier moulds the slumberer's dream,
Gazed by an idle eye with silent might
The picture stole upon my inward sight.
A tremulous warmth crept gradual o'er my chest,
As though an infant's finger touch'd my breast.
And one by one (I know not whence) were brought
All spirits of power that most had stirr'd my thought
In selfless boyhood, on a new world tost
30 Of wonder, and in its own fancies lost;
Or charm'd my youth, that, kindled from above,
Loved ere it loved, and sought a form for love;
Or lent a lustre to the earnest scan
Of manhood, musing what and whence is man!
Wild strain of Scalds, that in the sea-worn caves
Rehearsed their war-spell to the winds and waves;
Or fateful hymn of those prophetic maids,
That call'd on Hertha in deep forest glades;
Or minstrel lay, that cheer'd the baron's feast;
40 Or rhyme of city pomp, of monk and priest,
Judge, mayor, and many a guild in long array,
To high-church pacing on the great saint's day.
And many a verse which to myself I sang,
That woke the tear yet stole away the pang,
Of hopes which in lamenting I renew'd.
And last, a matron now, of sober mien,
Yet radiant still and with no earthly sheen,
Whom as a faery child my childhood woo'd
Even in my dawn of thought – Philosophy;
50 Though then unconscious of herself, pardie,
She bore no other name than Poesy;
And, like a gift from heaven, in lifeful glee,
That had but newly left a mother's knee,
Prattled and play'd with bird and flower, and stone
As if with elfin playfellows well known,
And life reveal'd to innocence alone.

Thanks, gentle artist! now I can descry
Thy fair creation with a mastering eye,
And all awake! And now in fix'd gaze stand,
60   Now wander through the Eden of thy hand;
Praise the green arches, on the fountain clear
See fragment shadows of the crossing deer;
And with that serviceable nymph I stoop
The crystal from its restless pool to scoop.
I see no longer! I myself am there,
Sit on the ground-sward, and the banquet share.
'Tis I, that sweep that lute's love-echoing strings,
And gaze upon the maid who gazing sings:
Or pause and listen to the tinkling bells
70   From the high tower, and think that there she dwells.
With old Boccaccio's soul I stand possest,
And breathe an air like life, that swells my chest.

The brightness of the world, O thou once free,
And always fair, rare land of courtesy!
O Florence! with the Tuscan fields and hills,
And famous Arno, fed with all their rills;
Thou brightest star of star-bright Italy!
Rich, ornate, populous, all treasures thine,
The golden corn, the olive, and the vine.
80   Fair cities, gallant mansions, castles old
And forests, where beside his leafy hold
The sullen boar hath heard the distant horn,
And whets his tusks against the gnarlèd thorn;
Palladian palace with its storied halls;
Fountains, where Love lies listening to their falls;
Gardens, where flings the bridge its airy span,
And Nature makes her happy home with man;
Where many a gorgeous flower is duly fed
With its own rill, on its own spangled bed,
90   And wreathes the marble urn, or leans its head,
A mimic mourner, that with veil withdrawn
Weeps liquid gems, the presents of the dawn; –
Thine all delights, and every muse is thine;
And more than all, the embrace and intertwine
Of all with all in gay and twinkling dance!
Mid gods of Greece and warriors of romance,

See! Boccace sits, unfolding on his knees
The new-found roll of old Mæonides;
But from his mantle's fold, and near the heart,
100   Peers Ovid's holy book of Love's sweet smart!

   O all-enjoying and all-blending sage,
Long be it mine to con thy mazy page,
Where, half conceal'd, the eye of fancy views
Fauns, nymphs, and wingèd saints, all gracious to thy muse!

   Still in thy garden let me watch their pranks,
And see in Dian's vest between the ranks
Of the trim vines, some maid that half believes
The vestal fires, of which her lover grieves,
With that sly satyr peeping through the leaves!

Alice du Clos:
OR THE FORKED TONGUE. A BALLAD

One word with two meanings is the traitor's shield and shaft: and a slit
tongue be his blazon!

Caucasian proverb

'The Sun is not yet risen,
But the dawn lies red on the dew:
Lord Julian has stolen from the hunters away,
Is seeking, Lady, for you.
Put on your dress of green,
   Your buskins and your quiver;
Lord Julian is a hasty man,
   Long waiting brook'd he never.
I dare not doubt him, that he means
10   To wed you on a day,
Your lord and master for to be,
   And you his lady gay.
O Lady! throw your book aside!
   I would not that my Lord should chide.'

Thus spake Sir Hugh the vassal knight
   To Alice, child of old Du Clos,
As spotless fair, as airy light
   As that moon-shiny doe,
The gold star on its brow, her sire's ancestral crest!
20 For ere the lark had left his nest,
   She in the garden bower below
Sate loosely wrapt in maiden white,
Her face half drooping from the sight,
   A snow-drop on a tuft of snow!
O close your eyes, and strive to see
The studious maid, with book on knee, –
   Ah! earliest-open'd flower;
While yet with keen unblunted light
The morning star shone opposite
30   The lattice of her bower –
Alone of all the starry host,
   As if in prideful scorn
Of flight and fear he stay'd behind,
   To brave th' advancing morn.

O! Alice could read passing well,
   And she was conning then
Dan Ovid's mazy tale of loves,
   And gods, and beasts, and men.

The vassal's speech, his taunting vein,
40 It thrill'd like venom thro' her brain;
   Yet never from the book
She rais'd her head, nor did she deign
   The knight a single look.

'Off, traitor friend! how dar'st thou fix
   Thy wanton gaze on me?
And why, against my earnest suit,
   Does Julian send by thee?

'Go, tell thy Lord, that slow is sure:
   Fair speed his shafts to-day!
50 I follow here a stronger lure,
   And chase a gentler prey.'

She said: and with a baleful smile
 The vassal knight reel'd off –
Like a huge billow from a bark
 Toil'd in the deep sea-trough,
That shouldering sideways in mid plunge,
 Is travers'd by a flash.
And staggering onward, leaves the ear
 With dull and distant crash.

60 And Alice sate with troubled mien
A moment; for the scoff was keen,
 And thro' her veins did shiver!
Then rose and donn'd her dress of green,
 Her buskins and her quiver.

There stands the flow'ring may-thorn tree!
From thro' the veiling mist you see
 The black and shadowy stem; –
Smit by the sun the mist in glee
Dissolves to lightsome jewelry –
70 Each blossom hath its gem!

With tear-drop glittering to a smile,
The gay maid on the garden-stile
 Mimics the hunter's shout.
'Hip! Florian, hip! To horse, to horse!
 Go, bring the palfrey out.

'My Julian's out with all his clan,
 And, bonny boy, you wis,
Lord Julian is a hasty man,
 Who comes late, comes amiss.'

80 Now Florian was a stripling squire,
 A gallant boy of Spain,
That toss'd his head in joy and pride,
Behind his Lady fair to ride,
 But blush'd to hold her train.

The huntress is in her dress of green, –
And forth they go; she with her bow,
   Her buskins and her quiver! –
The squire – no younger e'er was seen –
With restless arm and laughing een,
90   He makes his javelin quiver.

And had not Ellen stay'd the race,
And stopp'd to see, a moment's space,
   The whole great globe of light
Give the last parting kiss-like touch
To the eastern ridge, it lack'd not much,
   They had o'erta'en the knight.

It chanced that up the covert lane,
   Where Julian waiting stood,
A neighbour knight prick'd on to join
100   The huntsmen in the wood.

And with him must Lord Julian go,
   Tho' with an anger'd mind:
Betroth'd not wedded to his bride,
In vain he sought, twixt shame and pride,
   Excuse to stay behind.

He bit his lip, he wrung his glove,
He look'd around, he look'd above,
   But pretext none could find or frame!
Alas! alas! and well-a-day!
110   It grives me sore to think, to say,
That names so seldom meet with Love,
   Yet Love wants courage without a name!

Straight from the forest's skirt the trees
   O'er-branching, made an aisle,
Where hermit old might pace and chaunt
   As in a minster's pile.

From underneath its leafy screen,
   And from the twilight shade,
You pass at once into a green,
120   A green and lightsome glade.

And there Lord Julian sate on steed;
   Behind him, in a round,
Stood knight and squire, and menial train;
Against the leash the greyhounds strain;
   The horses paw'd the ground.

When up the alley green, Sir Hugh
   Spurr'd in upon the sward,
And mute, without a word, did he
   Fall in behind his lord.

130   Lord Julian turn'd his steel half round. –
     'What! doth not Alice deign
To accept your loving convoy, knight?
Or doth she fear our woodland sleight,
   And joins us on the plain?'

With stifled tones the knight replied,
And look'd askance on either side, –
   'Nay, let the hunt proceed! –
The Lady's message that I bear,
I guess would scantly please your ear,
140   And less deserves your heed.

'You sent betimes. Not yet unbarr'd
   I found the middle door; –
Two stirrers only met my eyes,
   Fair Alice, and one more.

'I came unlook'd for: and, it seem'd,
   In an unwelcome hour;
And found the daughter of Du Clos
   Within the lattic'd bower.

'But hush! the rest may wait. If lost,
150   No great loss, I divine;
And idle words will better suit
   A fair maid's lips than mine.'

'God's wrath! speak out man,' Julian cried,
   O'ermaster'd by the sudden smart; –
And feigning wrath, sharp, blunt, and rude,
The knight his subtle shift pursued. –

'Scowl not at me; command my skill,
To lure your hawk back, if you will,
   But not a woman's heart.

160 ' "Go! (said she) tell him, – slow is sure;
   Fair speed his shafts to-day!
I follow here a stronger lure,
   And chase a gentler prey."

'The game, pardie, was full in sight,
That then did, if I saw aright,
   The fair dame's eye engage;
For turning, as I took my ways,
I saw them fix'd with steadfast gaze
   Full on her wanton page.'

170 The last word of the traitor knight
   It had but entered Julian's ear, –
From two o'erarching oaks between,
With glist'ning helm-like cap is seen,
   Borne on in giddy cheer,

A youth, that ill his steed can guide;
Yet with reverted face doth ride,
   As answering to a voice,
That seems at once to laugh and chide –
'Not mine, dear mistress,' still he cried,
180   ' 'Tis this mad filly's choice.'

With sudden bound, beyond the boy,
See! see! that face of hope and joy,
   That regal front! those cheeks aglow!
Thou needed'st but the crescent sheen,
A quiver'd Dian to have been,
   Thou lovely child of old Du Clos!

Dark as a dream Lord Julian stood,
Swift as a dream, from forth the wood,
   Sprang on the plighted Maid!
190 With fatal aim, and frantic force,
The shaft was hurl'd! – a lifeless corse,
Fair Alice from her vaulting horse,
   Lies bleeding on the glade.

Love, Hope, and Patience in Education

O'er wayward childhood would'st thou hold firm rule,
And sun thee in the light of happy faces;
Love, Hope, and Patience, these must be thy graces,
And in thine own heart let them first keep school.
For as old Atlas on his broad neck places
Heaven's starry globe, and there sustains it; – so
Do these upbear the little world below
Of Education, – Patience, Love, and Hope.
Methinks, I see them group'd in seemly show,
The straiten'd arms upraised, the palms aslope,
And robes that touching as adown they flow,
Distinctly blend, like snow emboss'd in snow.

O part them never! If Hope prostrate lie,
              Love too will sink and die.
But Love is subtle, and doth proof derive
From her own life that Hope is yet alive;
And bending o'er, with soul-transfusing eyes,
And the soft murmurs of the mother dove,
Woos back the fleeting spirit, and half supplies; –
Thus Love repays to Hope what Hope first gave to Love.

Yet haply there will come a weary day,
              When overtask'd at length
Both Love and Hope beneath the load give way.
Then with a statue's smile, a statue's strength,
Stands the mute sister, Patience, nothing loth,
And both supporting does the work of both.

[Lines
WRITTEN IN COMMONPLACE BOOK OF MISS BARBOUR,
DAUGHTER OF THE MINISTER OF THE USA TO ENGLAND*]*

Child of my muse! in Barbour's gentle hand
Go cross the main: thou seek'st no foreign land:
'Tis not the clod beneath our feet we name
Our country. Each heaven-sanctioned tie the same,
Laws, manners, language, faith, ancestral blood,

Domestic honour, awe of womanhood: –
With kindling pride thou wilt rejoice to see
Britain with elbow-room and doubly free!
Go seek thy countrymen! and if one scar
10   Still linger of that fratricidal war,
Look to the maid who brings thee from afar;
Be thou the olive-leaf and she the dove,
And say, I greet thee with a brother's love!

To Miss A. T.

Verse, pictures, music, thoughts both grave and gay,
Remembrances of dear-loved friends away,
On spotless page of virgin white displayed,
Such should thine Album be, for such art thou, sweet maid!

Love and Friendship Opposite

Her attachment may differ from yours in degree,
    Provided they are both of one kind;
But Friendship how tender so ever it be
    Gives no accord to Love, however refin'd.

Love, that meets not with Love, its true nature revealing,
    Grows asham'd of itself, and demurs:
If you cannot lift hers up to your state of feeling,
    You must lower down your state to hers.

Not at Home

That Jealousy may rule a mind
    Where Love could never be
I know; but ne'er expect to find
    Love without Jealousy.

She has a strange cast in her ee,
   A swart sour-visaged maid –
But yet Love's own twin-sister she
   His house-mate and his shade.

Ask for her and she'll be denied: –
10   What then? they only mean
Their mistress has lain down to sleep,
   And can't just then be seen.

W. H. Eheu!

Beneath this stone does William Hazlitt lie,
   Thankless of all that God or man could give.
He lived like one who never thought to die,
   He died like one who dared not hope to live.

Phantom or Fact?
A DIALOGUE IN VERSE

Author
A lovely form there sate beside my bed,
And such a feeding calm its presence shed,
A tender love so pure from earthly leaven
That I unnethe the fancy might control,
'Twas my own spirit newly come from heaven,
Wooing its gentle way into my soul!
But ah! the change – It had not stirr'd, and yet –
Alas! that change how fain would I forget!
That shrinking back, like one that had mistook!
10 That weary, wandering, disavowing look!
'Twas all another, feature, look, and frame,
And still, methought, I knew, it was the same!

Friend
This riddling tale, to what does it belong?
Is't history? vision? or an idle song?
Or rather say at once, within what space
Of time this wild disastrous change took place?

Author
Call it a moment's work (and such it seems)
This tale's a fragment from the life of dreams;
But say, that years matur'd the silent strife,
20   And 'tis a record from the dream of life.

Charity in Thought

To praise men as good, and to take them for such,
   Is a grace, which no soul can mete out to a tittle; –
Of which he who has not a little too much,
   Will by Charity's gage surely have much too little.

Humility the Mother of Charity

Frail creatures are we all! To be the best,
   Is but the fewest faults to have: –
Look thou then to thyself, and leave the rest
   To God, thy conscience, and the grave.

['Gently I took that which ungently came']

Beareth all things. – *1 Cor.* xiii, 7

Gently I took that which ungently came,
And without scorn forgave: – Do thou the same.
A wrong done to thee think a cat's eye spark
Thou wouldst not see, were not thine own heart dark.
Thine own keen sense of wrong that thirsts for sin,
Fear that – the spark self-kindled from within,
Which blown upon will blind thee with its glare,
Or smother'd stifle thee with noisome air.
Clap on the extinguisher, pull up the blinds,
10   And soon the ventilated spirit finds
Its natural daylight. If a foe have kenn'd,
Or worse than foe, an alienated friend,

A rib of dry rot in thy ship's stout side,
Think it God's message, and in humble pride
With heart of oak replace it; – thine the gains –
Give him the rotten timber for his pains!

Cholera Cured Before Hand

Or a premonition promulgated gratis for the use of the Useful Classes,
specially those resident in St Giles's, Saffron Hill, Bethnal Green, &c.;
and likewise, inasmuch as the good man is merciful even to the beasts, for
the benefit of the Bulls and Bears of the Stock Exchange.

Pains ventral, subventral,
In stomach or entrail,
Think no longer mere prefaces
For grins, groans, and wry faces;
But off to the doctor, fast as ye can crawl! –
Yet far better 'twoud be not to have them at all.

Now to 'scape inward aches,
Eat no plums nor plum-cakes;
Cry avaunt! new potatoe –
And don't drink, like old Cato.
Ah! Beware of Dispipsy,
And don't ye get tipsy!
For tho' gin and whiskey
May make you feel frisky,
They're but crimps to Dispipsy;
And nose to tail, with this gipsy
Comes, black as a porpus,
The diabolus ipse,
Call'd Cholery Morpus;
Who with horns, hoofs, and tail, croaks for carrion to feed him,
Tho' being a Devil, no one never has seed him!

Ah! then my dear honies,
There's no cure for you
For loves nor for monies: –
You'll find it too true.

Och! the hallabaloo!
Och! och! how you'll wail,
When the offal-fed vagrant
Shall turn you as blue
30   As the gas-light unfragrant,
That gushes in jets from beneath his own tail; –
'Till swift as the mail,
He at last brings the cramps on,
That will twist you like Samson.

So without further blethring,
Dear mudlarks! my brethren!
Of all scents and degrees,
(Yourselves and your shes)
Forswear all cabal, lads,
40   Wakes, unions, and rows,
Hot dreams, and cold salads
And don't pig in sties that would suffocate sows!
Quit Cobbett's, O'Connell's, and Beelzebub's banners,
And whitewash at once bowels, rooms, hands, and manners!

Love's Apparition and Evanishment
AN ALLEGORIC ROMANCE

Like a lone Arab, old and blind
Some caravan had left behind
Who sits beside a ruin'd well,
Where the shy sand-asps bask and swell;
And now he hangs his aged head aslant,
And listens for a human sound – in vain!
And now the aid, which Heaven alone can grant,
Upturns his eyeless face from Heaven to gain; –
Even thus, in vacant mood, one sultry hour,
10   Resting my eye upon a drooping plant,
With brow low bent, within my garden bower,
I sate upon the couch of camomile;
And – whether 'twas a transient sleep, perchance,
Flitted across the idle brain, the while
I watch'd the sickly calm with aimless scope,
In my own heart; or that, indeed a trance,
Turn'd my eye inward – thee, O genial Hope,

Love's elder sister! thee did I behold,
Drest as a bridesmaid, but all pale and cold,
20   With roseless cheek, all pale and cold and dim
    Lie lifeless at my feet!
And then came Love, a sylph in bridal trim,
    And stood beside my seat;
She bent, and kissed her sister's lips,
    As she was wont to do; –
Alas! 'twas but a chilling breath
Woke just enough of life in death
    To make Hope die anew.

To the Young Artist, Kayser of Kaserwerth

Kayser! to whom, as to a second self,
Nature, or Nature's next-of-kin, the Elf,
Hight Genius, hath dispens'd the happy skill
To cheer or soothe the parting friend's 'alas'!
Turning the blank scroll to a magic glass,
That makes the absent present at our will;
And to the shadowing of thy pencil gives
Such seeming substance, that it almost lives.

Well hast thou given the thoughtful Poet's face!
10 Yet hast thou on the tablet of his mind
A more delightful portrait left behind –
Ev'n thy own youthful beauty, and artless grace,
Thy natural gladness and eyes bright with glee!
      Kayser! farewell!
Be wise! be happy! and forget not me.

Know Thyself

– E cœlo descendit γνῶθι σεαυτόν. – JUVENAL

Γνῶθι σεαυτόν! – and is this the prime
And heaven-sprung adage of the olden time! –
Say, canst thou make thyself? – Learn first that trade; –
Haply thou mayst know what thyself had made.

What hast thou, Man, that thou dar'st call thine own? –
What is there in thee, Man, that can be known? –
Dark fluxion, all unfixable by thought,
A phantom dim of past and future wrought,
Vain sister of the worm, – life, death, soul, clod –
10   Ignore thyself, and strive to know thy God!

My Baptismal Birth-Day

God's child in Christ adopted, – Christ my all, –
What that earth boasts were not lost cheaply, rather
Than forfeit that blest name, by which I call
The Holy One, the Almighty God, my Father? –
Father! in Christ we live, and Christ in Thee –
Eternal Thou, and everlasting we.
The heir of heaven, henceforth I fear not death:
In Christ I live! in Christ I draw the breath
Of the true life! – Let then earth, sea, and sky
10   Make war against me! On my front I show
Their mighty master's seal. In vain they try
To end my life, that can but end its woe. –
Is that a death-bed where a Christian lies? –
Yes! but not his – 'tis Death itself there dies.

Epitaph

Stop, Christian Passer-by! – Stop, child of God,
And read with gentle breast. Beneath this sod
A poet lies, or that which once seem'd he. –
O, lift one thought in prayer for S. T. C.;
That he who many a year with toil of breath
Found death in life, may here find life in death!
Mercy for praise – to be forgiven for fame
He ask'd, and hoped, through Christ. Do thou the same!

9th November, 1833

APPENDICES

APPENDIX 1

On the Wretched Lot of the Slaves in the Isles of Western India

In the highest Assembly Jul. 3. 1792.

O Death, leaving the gates of darkness, come
hastening to a race yoked to misery; thou
wilt not be received with tearings of cheeks
or with lamentation, but, on the contrary,
with circles beating out the dance and with the
joy of songs: thou art Fearful indeed, but still thou
dwellest with Liberty, hateful Tyrant. Raised
10   on thy murky wings, through the rough swell of
the vast Ocean, let them fly to the dear
resorts of pleasure, and to their fatherland.
There, verily, beside the springs
beneath the citron groves, lovers tell to their
beloved what terrible things, being men,
they suffered from men. Alas! Islands
full of murderous excess, abounding in
evils ill to look upon, where Hunger is
20   sick, and a bloody blow roars,
woe for us; how often a mist has come over
the tearful eyes, and how often at the same time
the heart has groaned! For I grieve deeply
with the race of slaves suffering dire ills,
just as they groan with unspeakable grief,
so they circle round in eddies of loathsome
labours, children of Necessity.
30   Since burning Heat, and Plague, and insufferable
Weariness rage round them on loveless days, and
the relentless phantoms of baneful Memory.
Alas! the watchful Scourge drives them on
exhausted, before Dawn wakes the sun; and the
sweet-looking star of Day sets, but griefs
blossom for ever: for midnight terrors smite
the soul, breathing wrath; the eyes of the
40   wretched ones fall asleep, but Fear never sleeps.

And if they seek after any sweet delusion with the
shadows of hope that appear in dreams, as they
are roused they are promptly driven mad with
the torments of wanton violence.
O you who revel in the evils of Slavery, O you
who feed on the persecution of the wretched,
wanton children of Excess, snatching your
brother's blood, does not an inescapable Eye
50   behold? Does not Nemesis brandish fire-breathing
requital? Do you hear? Or do you not hear?
Because winds shake the earth from its foundations,
and the recesses of the earth moan, and the
depths bellow terribly, guaranteeing that those
below are angry with those who slay!
But what sweet-voiced echo, what throbbings
of the Dorian lyre, hovers towards me?
60   What soft voice lets fall a sweet whispering?
O! I see a Herald of Pity, his head shaded
with branches of olive! O! the golden joy of
thy words, Wilberforce, I hear! 'Holy spring
of Tears, now [there is] enough of thy drops:
smitten with the stranger-helping lightning
of Justice, the misery having been quelled
70   shall die. And the abominable thankless Favour of
Gold shall no longer fall upon African shores,
as the breath of Pestilence rides with
parching winds. Far from fatherland
and kinsfolk, old age shall not wrestle with
lawless labours, breathing out wild cries, ah! ah!
when life is setting.
No longer with prophetic fear shall the Mother
take her grimy babe to her breast: no; because
80   the Day of Slavery has already been stretched
too far. You who, Slaves of puffed-up Masters,
have never, wretches, seen a tear moisten pity's
cheek, [though] suffering things shattering to
hear, for you, your Children taste of [?] Justice,
gathering the roses of Tranquillity, and surely the holy
reverence for Liberty, mother of prizes.[']
90   Such [words] the breezes sent, more desirable
than the shouts of the multitudes round the
delayed chariot of Victory, on the day of
delightful Triumph. Hail, thou who guidest

well the rudder of Compassion! Love, setting
laughter within her tears, shall honour thee
with the wings of good deeds. And the Muse,
attendant of Virtue, shall love to remember
thee continuously; and with the blessings of
100   the sufferers thy name shall dart to heaven.

Translated from the Greek by
Anthea Morrison

APPENDIX 2

[Notebook draft of an essay on punctuation]

Punctuation. Four stops, two marks of movement, and a stroke, or expression of the indefinite or fragmentary –

Comma , Semicolon ; Colon : Period . Mark of Interrogation ? Note of Admiration ! Stroke – . It appears next to self-evident, that the first four or five characters can never be made to represent all the modes and subtle distinctions of connection, accumulation, disjunction, and completion of sense – it would be quite as absurd as to imagine that the ? and ! should designate all the moods of passion, that we convey by interrogation or wonder – as the simple question for information – the ironical – the impetuous – the ratiocinative &c – No! this must be left to the understanding of the Reader or Hearer. What then is their use? This will be more easily understood by supposing one person reading what a hundred or more are listening to. Their use is to enable the reader to regulate his *breath* foresightedly, & inclusively his Tones. This will become plain after <having> considered the use of each stop separately.

The comma is either [1.] simply addi<t>ive, and equivalent to the conjunction 'and'; or it is [2.] parenthetic, i.e. marks the insertion of a sentence, between a sentence uncompleted and its completion. [1] He, James, Harry, and I were going/= He *and* James and Harry and I – in such cases therefore I deem the comma before the and tautologic. 2. Parenthetic. He and I were going, *when* we met James, to visit Westminster Abbey.

The semicolon is accumulative, either when it is desired to draw more attention to each member of the cumulus: 'I would urge you to consider long and earnestly, the power of God; the omniscience & wisdom that direct his omnipotence; the ineffable Love, which makes the happiness of creatures a final cause of that self-sufficing Being, where knowledge & might are the efficient causes of all things; and above all, his long-suffering & tender Redemption, of sinful Creatures who by sin had forfeited all claims on his justice even for that only dire demand, which even an unfallen Angel could make on the justice of a Creator, viz. Annihilation!' – This sentence contains likewise the illustration of the second – namely, when the component parts of a cumulus contain more than a simple sentence, consequently, must have a comma, & therefore require something more than a comma in order to distinguish between the *parts* of the whole; and the parts of the part. – Here therefore in both cases the stop [semicolon] is used not to express a real logical difference of connection from the comma, for there is none; but to regulate the Breath, so as that the longer pause may mark the limbs of the Period, from the Joints of the Limbs. – This use of the Semicolon is far more common in the elder English Classics, from Elizabeth to William the 3rd than in modern writers – See Jeremy Taylor's Works. It was perhaps used in excess by them; but the disuse seems a worse evil – and I am glad to observe, in some of the best Articles of our Reviews, & in the later pamphlets of Sir J. Mackintosh, a moderated use of it in this form restored to our Language. Lord Bacon & Jer. Taylor are the two Authors, to be consulted – The second and more admitted use is to express exception or disjunction/and therefore commonly precedes *but*. To shew however that this primarily and essentially depends on the regulation of the Breath, and not on any logical symbolism, it is sufficient to consider, that when we except or disjoin the former sense as it exists in the foresight of the writer or speaker [it] is not compleat, & yet would for the moment appear complete to the Listener – the Speaker therefore naturally goes on more quickly to remove or prevent the misunderstanding, than when the sense is complete in itself; and only requires or permits a confirmation by the addition of the reason. Thence is it that the colon, <wch> precedes the causal connective, For, implies a larger pause than the ; [semicolon] – and thence too it would be pedantry to place the ; before a but, where the shortness & sense of the former sentence rendering its sense wholly incomplete, precludes all misunderstanding. Was it James? No! Not James, but Harry.

I have thus anticipated the use of the Colon – which is distinguished from the full stop by this, that tho' the sense is compleat, yet in that same moment of thought the speaker connects with it & during speaking it presses the grounds, cause, or reason or confirmation of it. Here I would use the Colon –. But when the sense is completed as far as it existed at that moment in the mind, and then the mind starting afresh either commences a new train or adds an argument, after a pause of Thought, then tho' the *For* or *But* should be [the] first word, I would use a full stop. – Instances from any good Writer –

In short, I look on the stops not as logical Symbols, but rather as dramatic *directions* representing the process of Thinking and Speaking conjointly – either therefore the regulation of the Breath simply, for in very long periods of exceedingly close reasoning this occurs; or as the movements in the Speaker's Thoughts make him regulate his Breath, pause longer or shorter, & prepare his voice before the pause for the pause – As for instance – 'No good man can contemplate the African Slave-Trade without horror, who has once read an account of the wars & atrocious kidnapping practised in the procuring of the Slaves, the horrors of the middle passage in the conveyance of them, or the outrage to our common nature in the too frequent and always possible final cruelty in employing & punishing them. Then, too, the fearful effect on the oppressors' own minds, the hardness, pride, proneness to frantic anger, sensuality, and the deadning of the moral sense – respecting the distinctions between Thing & Person will force the thoughts thro' a fresh Channel to the common Bay and Receptacle, in which the mind floats at anchor upon its accumulated Thoughts, deep & with a sure bottom of arguments & grounds, yet wavy with the pa[s]sions of honest Indignation.' Now here the later sense is equally the ground of the proposition with the former –; but the former might be, & is gracefully regarded as the whole, at the commencement in the Speaker's view. He pauses – then the activity of the mind, generating upon its generations, starts anew – & the pause is not, for which I am contending, at all *retrospective*, but always prospective – that is, the pause is not affected by what <actually> follows, but by what anterior to it was foreseen as following –

It is the first and simplest duty of a Writer, i.e. an artist in words, as a Statuary is in Marble, or a Painter in coloured Surfaces – to make the pauses, which the movements of his Thought require in order to be intelligible, consistent with an easy regulation of the Breath – not that the Stop depends on the Breath, but that it should prevent the Breath from making a stop from its own necessity. (Tho' in the modern French Writers and their English Imitators one might suppose the necessity of the Breath to be the sole principle of punctuation, & the powers of the Breath averaged from a nation of asthmatic patients.) – Supposing then therefore (& surely, it would be absurd to lay down rules for punctuating what ought not to have been written) I would say, that Punctuation expresses – say, rather – generally *hints* the sorts of pause which the Speaker makes, and the tones accompanying & leading to them from the Speaker's foresight of his own meaning. Punctuation therefore is always prospective: that is, it is not made according to the actual weight & difference or equality of the logical connections, but to the view which the Speaker is supposed to have at the moment, in which he speaks the particular sentence. Therefore I call them not symbols of Logic, but dramatic directions, enabling the reader more easily to place himself in the state of the writer or original Speaker.

NOTES

NOTES

The notes give the first publication of each poem, its subsequent publication during STC's lifetime and – when important – afterwards, and its main textual sources. They also indicate a poem's place in STC's life and development as a writer. Textual variants are given when they are of serious importance to the meaning and to a poem's genesis and existence in multiple versions. The notes attempt to identify echoes of and allusions to other poems and passages in STC's prose that enrich or enable our reading of a particular passage. In some instances critical positions and interpretive debates are noted.

ABBREVIATIONS

Editions of STC's poems

1796   *Poems on Various Subjects* (1796)

1797   *Poems, by S. T. Coleridge. Second Edition. To Which Are Now Added Poems by Charles Lamb and Charles Lloyd* (1797)

1798   *Fears in Solitude, Written in 1798, during the Alarm of an Invasion. To Which Are Added, France, An Ode; and Frost at Midnight* (1798)

LB   *Lyrical Ballads* (1798, 1800, 1802, 1805)

1803   *Poems* (1803)

1816   *Christabel; Kubla Khan, A Vision; The Pains of Sleep* (1816)

1817   *Sibylline Leaves: A Collection of Poems* (1817)

1828   *The Poetical Works of S. T. Coleridge*, 3 vols (1828)

1829   *The Poetical Works of S. T. Coleridge*, 3 vols (1829)

Galignani   *The Poetical Works of Coleridge, Shelley, and Keats*, published by A. and W. Galignani (Paris, 1829)

1834   *The Poetical Works of S. T. Coleridge*, 3 vols (1834)

LR   *Literary Remains* (1836)

1844   *The Poems of S. T. Coleridge*, edited by Mrs H. N. [Sara] Coleridge (1844)

1852   *The Poems of Samuel Taylor Coleridge*, edited by Derwent and Sara Coleridge (1852)

1877–80   *Poetical Works*, edited by Richard Herne Shepherd, 4 vols (1877–80)

1893   *The Poetical Works of Samuel Taylor Coleridge*, edited by James Dykes Campbell (1893)

1912   *The Complete Poetical Works of Samuel Taylor Coleridge*, edited by Ernest Hartley Coleridge, 2 vols (1912)

Asra Poems   *Coleridge, Sara Hutchinson, and the Asra Poems*, edited by George Whalley, Routledge & Kegan Paul (1955); contains 'Sara Hutchinson's Poets', a commonplace book mainly in the hand of Sara Hutchinson containing 11 poems by STC in his own hand

Inquiring Spirit   *Inquiring Spirit: A New Presentation of Coleridge from his Published and Unpublished Prose Writing*, edited by Kathleen Coburn, University of Toronto Press (revised edition 1979)

Everyman   *Poems*, edited by John Beer, Orion: Everyman's Library (revised edition 1993)

Stillinger   Jack Stillinger, *Coleridge and Textual Instability*, Oxford University Press (1994)

Volumes of STC early manuscripts frequently referred to

MS E   Notebook in STC's hand, inscribed 'S. Estlin – given to her by the Author – April 1795' (Bristol Reference Library)

MS O   Notebook in STC's hand, known as the 'Ottery Copybook'; probably written out by Coleridge for his family in 1792 or early 1793 (British Library)

MS O(c)   Transcript (mostly of MS O) known as the 'Green Ottery Copybook', possibly by John May; dated c. 1820 (Victoria College Library, Toronto)

Rugby MS   Composite volume in STC's hand, sent piecemeal to the publisher Joseph Cottle between August 1795 and early April 1796, including poems and preliminary matter for *1796* and *1797* (University of Texas, Austin)

Other editions and sources of STC's writing

BL   *Biographia Literaria*, edited by James Engell and W. Jackson Bate, 2 vols as no. 7 in *CC* (1983); 1 vol. paperback ed. with same pagination (1984)

CC   *The Collected Works of Samuel Taylor Coleridge* (*Collected Coleridge*), Princeton University Press for the Bollingen Foundation (1969–)

Index   *Index of English Literary Manuscripts*, vol. 4: 1800–1900, part I: *Arnold-Gissing*, compiled by Barbara Rosenbaum and Pamela White, London, Mansell (1982). References to entries in this volume are indicated by the abbreviation CoS followed by the entry number

L   *Collected Letters of Samuel Taylor Coleridge*, edited by Earl Leslie Griggs, Oxford University Press, 6 vols (1956–71)

N   *The Notebooks of Samuel Taylor Coleridge*, edited by Kathleen Coburn, Princeton University Press for the Bollingen Foundation, 4 vols to date (1957–)

Easter Holidays

First published in *1912*. Sent in a letter to Luke Coleridge dated 12 May 1787 (*L* 1: 3–4), from which the present text is taken. STC was fourteen and a student at Christ's Hospital in 1787.

7 *stages* stage-coaches.
17 *transport* 'transports' (*1912*).

Dura navis

First published in *1893*. There is a fair copy in the British Library with an annotation indicating that STC wrote this poem at the age of fifteen (see *Index* CoS 111), which would support the 1787 date of composition given in both *1893* and *1912*. STC's full annotations to this fair copy of 1823 are given below.

15 'This school exercise, written in the 15th year of my age, does not contain a line that any clever schoolboy might not have written, and like most school poetry is a *Putting of Thought into Verse*; for such Verses as *strivings* of mind and struggles after the Intense and Vivid are a fair Promise of better things' (STC's note, 1823).
32 'I well remember old Jemmy Bowyer [James Bowyer, Headmaster], the plagose Orbibus of Christ's Hospital, but an admirable educer no less than Educator of the Intellect, bade me leave out as many epithets as would turn the whole into eight-syllable lines, and then ask if the exercise would not be greatly improved. How often have I thought of the proposal since then, and how many thousand bloated and puffing lines have I read, that, by this process, would have tripped over the tongue excellently. Likewise I remember that he told me on the same occasion – "Coleridge! the connections of a Declamation are not the transitions of Poetry – bad, however, as they are, they are better than "Apostrophes" and "O thou's", for at the worst they are something like common sense. The others are the grimaces of Lunacy" ' (STC's note, 1823).

Nil pejus est caelibe vita

First published in *1893*, from the *Liber Aureus* or Christ's Hospital Book, into which Bowyer (see notes to 'Dura navis') required his students to transcribe their best exercises. Probably written in 1787; cf. 'Julia', 'Quae nocent docent', 'Progress of Vice' and 'Monody on the Death of Chatterton'. The title means 'nothing is worse than the celibate life'.

5 *Hymeneal* Hymen is the Greek and Roman god of marriage.

Sonnet to the Autumnal Moon

First published in *1796*, but excluded from *1797*, despite Charles Lamb's objections; included in *1803, 1828, 1829, 1834*. Marked 'aet. 16' by STC in an annotated copy of *1828*, so probably written in 1788. There is a later manuscript version entitled 'To the Moon in Autumn' and beginning 'Hail, softly-beaming Wand'rer of the Night!' on a leaf of the Christ's Hospital Book (dated c. 1794–6; see *Index* CoS 643). The rhyme scheme merges features of the Shakespearean and Petrarchan sonnet forms.

1 *various-vested* variously clothed, dressed.

Julia

First published in the Rev. William Trollope's *A History of the Royal Foundation Christ's Hospital* (1834). There is a fair copy in Bowyer's Christ's Hospital Book or *Liber Aureus*, where it is signed 'Sam. T. Coleridge, 1789'. The Latin epigraph means 'from the midst of the fountain of pleasures surges something bitter'.

1, 5 For *Julia* and *Florio*, see STC's note in *1796* to line 57 of 'Lines on an Autumnal Evening' (quoted below). *Julia* might also suggest the fictitious name of the beautiful young woman celebrated in Robert Herrick's poetry (Herrick, like STC, was from Devon).
11 *Hymeneal* See 'Nil pejus est caelibe vita' 5 (above).
17 *Tell! ye neglected sylphs!* From this line on, the poem is heavily indebted to Cantos 1 and 2 of Pope's *The Rape of the Lock* (Belinda's lapdog is called Shock).

Quae nocent docent

First published in *1893*; the present text is from *1912*. There is a fair copy in the Christ's Hospital Book, signed and dated 1789. The title means 'those [things] that harm instruct'; the epigraph is from Evander's speech in Virgil's *Aeneid*, VIII. 560: 'O if Jupiter would bring me back the years that are past!'

1 *ill-passed* 'ill-spent' (MS).
2 *Sloth* This early personification of Sloth importantly anticipates STC's later preoccupation with his own failures to sustain productive intensity; see especially 'The Eolian Harp' 34–41 and 'Dejection: An Ode', with its image of 'smothering weight' (41).
7 *midnight Lamp* Echoes Milton's 'Il Penseroso', as does *cloisters' solitary gloom* in line 12.

The Nose

First published in its entirety in *1834*; the third stanza appeared in the *Morning Post* for 2 January 1798 with the title 'To the Lord Mayor's Nose'. A version entitled 'A Rhapsody', different from the *1834* text in a few minor details, appears in MS O. In a transcription of lines 1–30 in MS O(c) the poem is marked 'aet. 17', suggesting that it was written in 1789. William Gill was Lord Mayor of London in 1788: in the MS version the blanks in lines 15 and 20 are spelled out 'Gill'.

10 *Phlegethon* in Greek and Roman mythology, the great river of fire in Hades.
13 *Sirius* the dog-star, principal star of the constellation Canis Major (Great Dog) and traditionally the brightest in the sky.
21 *turtle feast* a dinner featuring turtle soup; also called a 'turtle frolic' or simply a 'turtle' (OED).
28 *Satan's Nose ... Dunstan* Saint Dunstan (c. 924–88), English monk and eventually archbishop of Canterbury, became a royal counsellor to King Edred.

30 *disastrous twilight* Cf. *Paradise Lost* I. 597.

38 *Proboscis* nose, but normally applied to a long tubular nose used for feeding, such as the elephant's trunk; cf. *Paradise Lost* IV. 346.

calcin'd burned until reduced to powder or ashes.

39 *Pliny, in Vesuvius' fire* Pliny the Elder (c. AD 23–79), Roman naturalist, died of asphyxiation near Vesuvius where he had gone to investigate its eruption.

Life

First published in *1834*. The poem was included in a letter to George Coleridge of 22 June 1791, where it is entitled simply 'Sonnet' and dated 'Sept. 1789' (*L* 1: 14). There is a fair copy, headed 'Sonnet 2 Written September 1789', in MS O, and a later transcript not by STC in MS O(c) entitled 'Sonnet. Written just after the Author left the country in Sept: 1789 aetat. 15' (STC was in fact seventeen in September 1789 – the error appears elsewhere in MS O[c]).

2 *Otter* the River Otter, in Devonshire, near STC's birthplace, Ottery St Mary.

3 *sister's pain* See headnote below to 'On Receiving an Account that his Only Sister's Death Was Inevitable'.

6 *Wood, Meadow, verdant Hill* Cf. 'Frost at Midnight' 10, 11: 'Sea, hill, and wood . . .'

8 *my eye ravish'd sweep!* Both MSS read 'my ravish'd eye did sweep'.

12 *Till what time Death* A Miltonic locution meaning 'Until that time when Death'. Both in the letter to George Coleridge and in the later transcription this phrase reads 'Till, when death'.

To the Muse

First published in *1834*. There is a fair copy in MS O entitled 'Sonnet I. To my Muse'. The poem was probably written c. 1789.

2 *conscious* aware of what one is doing; cf. 'Anthem for the Children of Christ's Hospital' 26.

Destruction of the Bastile

First published in *1834*. There is a fair copy in MS O entitled 'An Ode on the destruction of the Bastile'. In this version stanza IV follows stanza I, as in the printed text, with part of the page torn away. In a later transcription not by STC, where asterisks appear in the printed text there is this note: 'Stanzas second and third are lost. We may gather from the context that they allude to the Bastille and its inhabitants' (MS O[c]). The Bastille fell on 14 July 1789, and most editors have assumed that the poem was written shortly after that date. This is, in any case, STC's earliest effort to articulate in verse his responses to the French Revolution.

2 *Gallia's* France's.

12 *long long* The fair copy has 'live-long', which seems more idiomatic.
33 *Belgia's heroes* early supporters of the French Revolution in Belgium.
39 *let favour'd Britain be* The storming of the Bastille and other early events of the French Revolution were at first welcomed in Britain, even by the Pitt government and other conservative forces which would soon turn violently against the Revolution.

Anthem for the Children of Christ's Hospital

First published in *1834*; probably written c. 1789. A fair copy in MS O, dated 1792-3, contains a heading indicating that 'This Anthem was written as if intended to have been sung by the Children of Christ's Hospital'.

23 *uncultur'd* uncultivated, unrefined.
26 *unconscious* here in the sense of 'unaware' or 'instinctive'.

Progress of Vice

First published in *1834*. There is a fair copy in the Christ's Hospital Book entitled 'Nemo repente turpissimus' ('no one so shameful may repent') and dated 1790, and another in MS O. There is also a later transcript not by STC in MS O(c).

6 *vest* vestment; costume.

Monody on the Death of Chatterton

The earliest version, first published in *1893*, was written c. 1790 and appears in the Christ's Hospital Book, in MS O, and in the Victoria College Library group of transcriptions. In 1794 a much revised version was published in an edition of Chatterton's *Poems*. The poem then appeared, with further additions and revisions, in *1796* and in all subsequent editions of the poems in STC's lifetime except *1817*. The second version presented here is from *1834*. Thomas Chatterton (1752-70), the remarkably precocious young Bristol poet whose proffered imitations of fifteenth-century writing were exposed as fabrications, poisoned himself at the age of seventeen; he was admired as a tragically misunderstood genius by many of STC's contemporaries. In Greek literature a *monody* was a lyric ode sung by a single voice; since the seventeenth century the term has referred to a poem in which the speaker laments someone's death (cf. the subtitle to Milton's *Lycidas*).

An Invocation

First published in *1893*, from a MS (at present unlocated) in STC's hand sent from Christ's Hospital to his brother George in 1790. The MS also included a copy of 'Monody on the Death of Chatterton' and 'Monody on a Tea-Kettle'.

4 *him who owns the candid eye* a fair, impartial, straightforward reader – or perhaps (taking 'candid' in an older sense still alive in the 1790s but now obsolete), a reader who is favourably disposed, kindly.

Anna and Harland

First published from MS in its present form in *1877–80*; included in *1893* and *1912*, where it is conjecturally dated 1790. Another version was published in the *Cambridge Intelligencer* for 25 October 1794 and is entitled 'Anna and Henry', but the sonnet was never included in any collection in STC's lifetime. The present text follows *1912*.

To the Evening Star

First published in *1877–80*, from MS O; conjecturally dated 1790 in *1893* and *1912*. The present text follows *1912*.

Pain

First published in *1834*; conjecturally dated 1790 in *1893* and *1912*. There is a fair copy in MS O entitled 'Pain: a Sonnet', and a later transcript in MS O(c) entitled 'Sonnet composed in sickness'. According to Dr Gillman STC recalled that, as a result of his having swum across the New River with his clothes on and let them dry on his body, 'full half his time from seventeen to eighteen [1789–90] was passed in the sick-ward of Christ's Hospital, afflicted with jaundice and rheumatic fever' (*The Life of Samuel Taylor Coleridge* [1838], p. 33). See headnote to 'Genevieve' below.

4 *glad* gladden, make happy.

On a Lady Weeping

First published in *1893*, from a transcript in MS O(c), with the subtitle 'Imitation from the Latin of Nicolaus Archius'. The present text follows *1912*, where the conjectured date of composition is 1790.

4 *the Mead's enamell'd pride* the meadow's brightly-coloured beauty; the conceit of the face as a beautiful meadow is common in Renaissance love poetry.
10 *th' insidious Power* 'Love' or Cupid, as in line 8. There is a play on 'sits' and 'insidious' (Latin *sedere*, 'to sit').
14 *fost'ring* nurturing, growth-inducing.

Monody on a Tea-Kettle

First published in *1834*, from a fair copy in MS O (the stanzaic division and lineation have been made consistent); written in 1790. Another version appears in the MS pages sent to STC's brother George along with 'Invocation' and

'Monody on the Death of Chatterton'. This version may have been meant as a parody of the poem about Chatterton: its title is 'Monody the Second, occasioned by a very recent Calamity'.

1 The opening line clearly refers to 'Monody on the Death of Chatterton'.
13 *The sooty swain* I.e. the kettle, here personified as if it were a dead poet (like Chatterton).
19 *who know'st to spread* Cf. Milton's *Lycidas* 10–11: 'he knew / Himself to sing, and build the lofty rhyme'.
35 *Memnon's sister sable drest* In Greek mythology, Memnon was king of the Ethiopians who fought on the Trojan side in the siege of Troy. He was killed by Achilles.

Genevieve

First published in the *Morning Chronicle* for 15 July 1793, where it is called 'Irregular Sonnet'; printed again in the *Cambridge Intelligencer* for 1 November 1794. It is included in *1796* with a note ('This little poem was written when the Author was a boy'), and in *1803*, *1828*, *1829* and *1834*. STC spent months in the sick ward of Christ's Hospital in 1789–90, and E. H. Coleridge accordingly dates the poem to this period. Campbell, however, says 'This seems to be the earliest composition of Coleridge which has been preserved. He has dated it as early as "aet. 14"' (*1893* 561; Campbell dates it 1786). This sonnet appears, with minor variants, in MS O, in MS E and in MS O(c). By tradition the title 'Genevieve', which first appeared in *1803*, has been thought to refer to the daughter of a Mrs Brewman, whom STC identifies in a letter of 18 December 1807 as 'a Nurse to one of the Wards in Christ's Hospital, at the time that I was an upper boy there' (*L* 3: 44).

On Receiving an Account that his Only Sister's Death Was Inevitable

First published in *1834*. There is a fair copy in MS O. Ann Coleridge (called Nancy by her family), STC's only sister and the daughter of his father's second marriage, died in March 1791 at the age of twenty-five. The opening line of the poem refers to the death of STC's brother, Luke Herman Coleridge, in 1790.

On Seeing a Youth Affectionately Welcomed by a Sister

First published in *1834*. Dated 1791 in *1912*; Campbell says it was 'probably written about 1792' but offers no evidence and groups the poem with the preceding one, for obvious reasons. In *1834* this poem is followed by lines 12–19 of 'To a Friend, Together with an Unfinished Poem' (see headnote to that poem below), which is printed as a separate poem under the title 'The Same'. The 'Friend' in that poem is Charles Lamb, the 'sister' Mary Lamb.

8 *Turtle's nest* the nest of a turtle-dove, a familiar figure of peace and love.

A Mathematical Problem

First published in *1834*, where the above title is given only in the table of contents. The poem is printed in *1834* as it appears in a letter to STC's brother George dated 31 March 1791 (*L* 1: 7–9); there is a transcript in MS O(c) headed 'Prospectus and Specimen of a translation of Euclid in a series of Pindaric Odes . . .'

5 *– A, N, G, E, L, E.* 'A EN GEE E EL E' (letter, where STC includes the following note on this misspelling for metrical purposes: 'Poetice for *Angle*'; *L* 1: 7).
21 *pother* disturbance, commotion, tumult; also specifically a verbal commotion or a mental perturbation.
31 *Peter Pindar* satirical poet whose actual name was John Wolcott (1738–1819); *Zoilus* was an ancient grammarian and critic of Homer, subsequently the type of the carping, envious critic.
48 *affiance* truth, faith, confidence; the text in the 1791 letter has 'alliance'.
55 *Autocratix* 'Th[e Empress of] the [Russians.]' (note to letter, where the word is 'Autocratorix'. The reference is to Catherine the Great, 1729–96).
58 *the Mah'met sprung wight* the man descended from the prophet Mohammed; an Islamic king or prince.
62 *Nine!* the nine muses.
68 *soothly* truthfully.
72 *in fine* in the end; at last.

Honour

First published in *1834*, where the title 'Honour' appears only in the table of contents. There is a fair copy in MS O headed 'O Curas hominum – O quantum est in rebus inane'; the original date of composition is probably 1791. In *1877–80* and *1893* the poem is entitled 'Philedon'.

6 *Duns* creditors demanding to be paid.
15 *should all Peru thy empire own* should all Peru acknowledge itself to be your empire.
16 *Golconda's jewels* Golconda was an ancient town in India, famous especially as a source of diamonds.
28 *waxen wings* like those of Icarus, which melted when he flew too near the sun.
36 *mead* reward.
39 *stew* brothel.
70 'Brookes's, a famous gaming-house in Fleet Street. Hackett's, a brothel under the Convent Garden Piazza' (STC's note in MS O).

On Imitation

First published in *1834*. In MS O lines 3–4 come at the end of the poem. In *1893* Campbell comments: 'If written in 1791, as is probable, this earliest extant specimen of Coleridge's epigrammatic style is better than a good many later ones.'

7–8 Charles James Fox (1749–1806) was leader of the liberal Whigs and a famous orator; his great rival, William Pitt (1759–1806), was the Tory Prime Minister.

Inside the Coach

First published in *1834*. The fair copy in MS O is entitled 'Ode to Sleep – Travelling in the Exeter Coach with three other Passengers over Bagshot heath after some vain endeavours to compose myself I composed this ode – August 17th 1791'.

15 *poppean* adjective formed from 'poppy', the flower from which opium is derived.
20 *pinions* wings, feathers. The dreaming traveller in these lines is figuratively astride Pegasus, the mythic winged horse of poetic inspiration.

Devonshire Roads

First published in *1834*. In MS O a note on the second line reads 'Plymtree Road, August 18, 1791'. Plimtree is some eight miles north of Ottery St Mary. Presumably this poem, 'Inside the Coach' and 'Music' were written on a visit home very near the end of STC's time at Christ's Hospital; see headnote to 'Sonnet on the Same').

17 *scritch owls* screech owls.
19 *wandering fires* will-o'-the-wisps.

Music

First published in *1834*; very likely written during the visit home in August 1791, along with 'In the Coach' and 'Devonshire Roads'. The title of the fair copy in MS O is 'Ode on the Ottery and Tiverton Church Music'.

8 *What time the Legion diabolic* Cf. *Paradise Lost* I. 36. Cf. also 'Lycidas' 28: 'What time the Gray-fly winds her sultry horn'.
20 *concords* an agreeable combination of musical tones heard simultaneously; a harmony.

Absence: A Farewell Ode on Quitting School for Jesus College, Cambridge

First published in the *Weekly Entertainer* (Sherborne, Dorset) for 21 October 1793 under the title 'Absence, an Ode', then in the *Cambridge Intelligencer* for 11 October 1794. Included in *1796*, *1803*, *1828*, *1829* and *1834* (Lamb protested at its being omitted from *1797*). There is a fair copy in MS E. STC formally left Christ's Hospital in September 1791 and took up residence in Cambridge the following month.

2 *Cam* the river which runs through Cambridge.

Sonnet on the Same

First published in *1834*, where, as here, it follows 'Absence: A Farewell Ode on Quitting School for Jesus College, Cambridge'. A fair copy in MS O is entitled 'Sonnet 9 on Quitting Christ's Hospital'.

14 *my widow'd Parent lorn* STC's mother was left a widow on 4 October 1781 with the sudden death of the Rev. John Coleridge. STC was nine at the time.

Happiness

First published in *1834*, where it is placed after 'Absence' and 'Sonnet on the Same'. But the poem was probably written before the other two, since it was sent in a letter to George Coleridge dated 22 June 1791 (*L* 1: 11–14). The speaker's imagined location in the poem is ambiguous: the reference to 'Devon's sod' (37) need not imply that the speaker is there, and 'this maternal seat' (77) is identified as 'Christ's Hospital' by a note in MS O, as 'Ottery St. Mary in Devonshire' by a note in MS O(c).

11 In MS O and MS O(c) this line is followed by the following: 'How pants my breast before my eyes / While Honour waves her radiant prize. / And Emulation', etc.

44 *own* acknowledge.

55 *magic* 'wonted' (MS O and MS O[c]).

80–1 In a revised version of lines 80–105 sent in a letter to Southey of 13 July 1794, STC wrote: ' 'Tis thine with faery forms to talk / And thine the philosophic walk'.

90–3 These four lines in the *1834* text replaced the following passage in the MS O fair copy:

> Ah! doubly blest, if Love supply
> Lustre to this now heavy eye,
> And with unwanted Spirit grace
> That fat vacuity of face.
> Or if e'en Love, the mighty Love
> Shall find this change his power above;
> Some lovely maid perchance thou'lt find
> To read thy visage in thy mind.

The last line of this passage echoes *Othello* I.iii.247: 'I saw Othello's visage in his mind'.

A Wish Written in Jesus Wood, Feb. 10th, 1792

First published in *1893*. This poem, a translation of a Latin poem by John Jortin called 'Votum', was included in the letter to Mary Evans of 13 February 1792 (*L* 1: 28–9) that also includes 'An Ode in the Manner of Anacreon' and 'A Lover's Complaint to His Mistress'. The present text follows that given in *L*.

2 *irriguous* irrigated, moistened, well-watered. Cf. 'irriguous Valley' in *Paradise Lost* IV. 255.
11 *forensic* belonging to public debate or discussion, especially of a legal kind; hence argumentative, rhetorical.

An Ode in the Manner of Anacreon

First published in *1893*; the poem was included in a second letter to Mary Evans of 13 February 1792 (*L* 1: 28), along with 'A Wish Written in Jesus Wood' and 'A Lover's Complaint to His Mistress'. The present text is from *L*.

3 *pinion* wing; 'Love' is represented as Cupid in the poem.
4 *minion* beloved, favourite.

To Disappointment

First published in *Letters of Samuel Taylor Coleridge*, ed. E. H. Coleridge (1895); included in a letter to Mrs Evans (Mary Evans's mother) of 13 February 1792 (*L* 1: 23).

10 *Prophetic* here an adverb: prophetically.
12 *Daemon* deity, supernatural power; also, characteristic indwelling power, genius.
17 *lists* listens to.
20 *Cambria's plains* 'Cambria' is an ancient name for Wales; the Evanses were planning a journey through Wales for the coming spring.
26 *lave* wash.

A Fragment Found in a Lecture-Room

First published in *Letters of Samuel Taylor Coleridge*, ed. E. H. Coleridge (1895); the present text is based on the earliest known version, in a letter to the Rev. George Coleridge of 2 April 1792 (*L* 1: 34–5; 'I wrote the following the other day under the title of a Fragment found in a Lecture Room'). A slightly different version appears in MS E.

1 *Cam* the river from which Cambridge takes its name.
3 *Boe[o]tia* an area and republic of ancient Greece.
4 *Mathesis* the ancient Greek and Latin word for 'mathematics', here imagined as an animate figure. Cf. prose introduction to 'A Mathematical Problem' above.
13 *lists* listens to.
15 *Cetera desunt* The rest is missing. This designation at the end of the text in the letter is odd, since the lines as they stand make a sonnet (with a turn at line 9).

Ode

First published in *The Watchman* for 24 March 1796 under the title 'A Morning Effusion' and signed 'G.A.U.N.T.'; a MS version appears in MS E. STC never collected this poem; E. H. Coleridge included it in *1912* and gives 1792 as the date of composition.

16 *small airs* 'light songs', but also 'light breezes', with 'the mourning Lyre' understood as an eolian harp. See headnote to 'The Eolian Harp' below.
19 *the fall of Harmony* As with 'small airs', the image is doubled through a pun: 'fall' means both the act of descending and, musically, a cadence.
34 *scythèd Car* a chariot whose wheels cut like scythes.

A Lover's Complaint to his Mistress

First published in *1893*, from the letter to Mary Evans of 13 February 1792 that also includes 'An Ode in the Manner of Anacreon' and 'A Wish Written in Jesus Wood'. In the letter STC introduces these lines more fully as 'A Lover's Complaint to His Mistress, who deserted him in quest of a more wealthy husband in the East Indies'.

1 *dubious* tenuous, uncertain.
5 *Julia* Cf. the early poem of this title from the Christ's Hospital Book.
6 *trust you* trust yourself.

With Fielding's Amelia

First published in *1834*. There is a fair copy in MS O entitled 'Sonnet 7 Sent to Mrs— with an Amelia'. According to E. H. Coleridge, 'the probable recipient . . . was the mother of Coleridge's first love, Mary Evans' (*1912* 1: 37 n.). *Amelia* is a novel by Henry Fielding published in 1751.

10 *on the page shall dwell* 'will linger over the pages of the novel'; but 'double pleasure' also encourages us to take the line as meaning 'will live within the pages of the novel'.

Written After a Walk Before Supper

First published in *1796*, from which the present text is taken. A MS version, described as 'A Simile', appears in a letter to STC's brother George of 9 August 1792 (*L* 1: 37-8). 'V—ker' in lines 2 and 6 is 'Vicar' in the MS: the reference is to the Rev. Fulwood Smerdon, who succeeded STC's father as vicar of Ottery St Mary after his death in 1781. When reconsidering the poems in *1796* for a second edition the following year, STC wrote to his friend Joseph Cottle: 'I am not solicitous to have anything omitted, except the sonnet to Lord Stanhope (see this poem below) and the ludicrous poem' (18 October 1796; *L* 1: 242). In his

Early Recollections; chiefly relating to the late S. T. Coleridge (1837), Cottle says
that STC was referring to 'Written After a Walk Before Supper' (1: 209). Lamb
urged STC not to include the poem in *1803*; it was in fact never published again
in STC's lifetime.

1 *flicker* move suddenly, bestir oneself.
14 *musk* an ingredient in perfumes.
16 'A good line' (STC's note in the letter to his brother).
18 *collops* folds or ridges of flesh.
20 *jack-boot* a high, heavy boot typically worn by the military.
21 *Pismire* ant.
25 *ween* think, believe.
31 *antic small with nimble crupper* little buffoon with nimble hind-quarters. The
MS version in the letter reads 'antic lean'; 'antic huge' appears in *1796*, but with
an errata note: 'For Antic huge read *antic small*'.

Imitated from Ossian

First published in *1796* as 'Effusion XXIX'; included in *1803*, *1828*, *1829* and
1834. A version appears in MS E. Beer follows Campbell and E. H. Coleridge in
giving 1793 as the date of composition. In *1796* and *1803* the following note
appears: ' – The flower hangs its head waving at times to the gale. "Why dost
thou awake me, O Gale?" it seems to say, "I am covered with the drops of Heaven.
The time of my fading is near, the blast that shall scatter my leaves. Tomorrow
shall the traveller come, he that saw me in my beauty shall come. His eyes will
search the field, they will not find me. So shall they search in vain for the voice
of Cona, after it has failed in the field." – Berrathon, see Ossian's *Poems*, vol ii.'
STC's poem complicates the relation of Lily-Maiden to Traveller-speaker ('The
Youth of simplest song') by making the 'faithful Maiden . . . seek / The Youth',
whereas in Ossian it is the 'traveller' whose 'eyes will search the field, they will
not find me'.

The Complaint of Ninathòma, from the Same

Another Ossian imitation first published in *1796*, with a parallel publication history
(see headnote to 'Imitated from Ossian'). This poem appears in a letter to Mary
Evans of 7 February 1793 (*L* 1: 52) and in MS E. A note in *1796* and *1803* again
quotes from Ossian's *Poems*: ' "How long will ye roll round me, blue-tumbling
waters of Ocean. My dwelling was not always in caves, nor beneath the whistling
tree. My feast was spread in Torthona's Hall. The youths beheld me in my
loveliness. They blessed the dark-haired Nina-thoma." – Berrathon.' STC's
mainly dactyllic metre here derives from the strong rhythmic patterns of Mac-
pherson's prose.

8–9 Between these lines the following passage appears in the letter to Mary Evans:
'By my friends, by my Lovers discarded, / Like the flower of the Rock now I
waste / That lifts her fair head unregarded, / And scatters its leaves on the blast.'
13 *disturbed* 'dispers'd' (letter to Mary Evans).

The Rose

First published in *1796*; included in *1797*, *1803*, *1828* and *1834*. In a letter to his brother George of 28 July 1793, STC says that he 'presented a moss rose to a lady – Dick Hart [George Coleridge's brother-in-law] asked if she was not afraid to put it in her bosom as perhaps there might be Love in it. I immediately wrote the following little ode or song or what you please to call it. It is of the namby pamby Genus' (*L* 1: 57–8). A note in *1852* says that this poem and 'Kisses' (see below) 'were addressed to a Miss F. Nesbitt, at Plymouth, whither the author accompanied his eldest brother, to whom he was paying a visit, when he was twenty-one years of age. Both poems are written in pencil on the blank pages of a copy of Langhorne's *Collins*. *Kisses* is entitled *Cupid turned Chymist*; is signed S. T. Coleridge, and dated Friday evening, 1793. *The Rose* has this heading: "On presenting a Moss Ross to Miss F. Nesbitt." In both poems the name of Nesbitt appears instead of Sara, afterwards substituted'. 'Sara' is Sara Fricker, to whom STC became engaged in the summer of 1794. Both this poem and 'Kisses' are Anacreontic adaptations; compare 'An Ode in the Manner of Anacreon' above. The pencil draft of 'The Rose' is now in the British Library; there are fair copies in MS E and in the Rugby MS.

12 *Sara's* 'Nesbitt's' (pencil draft); 'Angelina's' (letter to George Coleridge); 'Anna's' (MS E).
13 *unweeting* unconscious.
16 *faery* 'angry' (letter to George Coleridge).

Kisses

First published in *1796*, then in the supplement to *1797* and in *1803*, where it is first entitled 'Kisses' and from which the present text is taken. There is a pencil draft on the front flyleaves of an edition of William Collins's poetry now in the British Library (see W. Braekman, 'The Influence of William Collins on poems written by Coleridge in 1793', *Revue des Langues Vivantes* 31 [1965], 228–39), fair copies in MS E and the Rugby MS, and a version entitled 'A Specimen – Cupid turned Chymist –' in a letter to George Coleridge of 5 August 1793 (*L* 1: 60). On all three occasions when he published the poem, STC provided the following text of an eighteenth-century Latin lyric on which his poem is based:

> Effinxit quondam blandum meditata laborem
>   Basia lascivâ Cypria Diva manu.
> Ambrosiae succos occultâ temperat arte,
>   Fragransque infuso nectare tingit opus.
> Sufficit et partem mellis, quod subdolus olim
>   Non impune favis surripuisset Amor.
> Decussus violae foliis admiscet odores
>   Et spolia aestivis plurima rapta rosis.
> Addit et illecebras et mille et mille lepores,
>   Et quot Acidalius gaudia Cestus habet.

> Ex his composuit Dea basia; et omnis libens
>   Invenias nitidae sparsa per ora Cloës.
>
> > (*Carmina Quadragesimalia. Poetic Miscellanies*, Oxford, 1723–48,
> > vol. II. In his note on the poem in *1893*, Campbell says that it
> > is signed 'W. Thomas' in the Bristol Library copy)

6 *Idalian* pertaining to Idalium, an ancient town in Cyprus and a centre of the cult of Aphrodite.

11 *eyeless Chemist* Cupid, who is often blind in mythological tradition. In the letter to his brother STC calls the poem 'Cupid turn'd Chymist'.

17 *Cyprian Mother* Venus, Cupid's mother, because one of her homes was the island of Cyprus.

18 *Sara's lovelier lips* 'Nesbitt's' in all MS versions except MS E, where it is 'Mary's'.

Sonnet ('Thou gentle Look')

First published in *1796*; included as part of a sequence of sonnets in subsequent collections ('Sonnet III' in *1797* and *1803*; 'Sonnet VIII' in *1828, 1829, 1834*). The poem was sent in a letter to Southey of 11 December 1794, where STC makes clear that the last four lines were written by Charles Lamb (*L* 1: 136). He never himself used the title given in *1893* and *1912*, 'The Gentle Look'. Given the traditional Shakespearian rhyme-scheme and metrical arrangement, it is unclear why the poem is headed 'Irregular Sonnet' in MS E.

5 *What time* The force of the Miltonic phrase is unclear here; perhaps simply 'When' or 'At such time as when' is meant.

Sonnet to the River Otter

First published in *1797*. Lines 2–11 were published in *The Watchman* for 2 April 1796 as lines 17–26 of 'Recollection' (see below), and the entire poem was included in 'A Sheet of Sonnets' sent by STC to John Thelwall on 17 December 1796. These 'Sonnets' were never published as such; in MS form they were bound in a copy of *Sonnets and Other Poems* by the Rev. W. L. Bowles (see George Whalley, 'Coleridge's Sheet of Sonnets', *TLS*, 23 November 1956, 697). The poem subsequently appeared in *1803, 1817, 1828, 1829* and *1834*. The date of composition is conjecturally put at 1793 in *1893, 1912* and *Everyman*.

9 *marge with willows grey* 'margin's willowy maze' (*1797, Watchman*, 'Sheet of Sonnets', *1803*).

Lines on an Autumnal Evening

First published under the title 'Absence' in the *Weekly Entertainer* (Sherborne, Dorset) for 28 October 1793. An intermediate MS version, entitled 'An Effusion at Evening. Written in August *1792*', appears in MS E and is printed in *1912* 1: 49–50. The final version was published as 'Effusion XXXVI. Written in Early Youth, The Time, An Autumnal Evening' in *1796*; this version was included in *1797, 1803, 1828, 1829, 1834*. In *Social Life at the English Universities* (1874) Christopher Wordsworth recalls that STC read this poem at a college party on 7 November 1793. Fair copies of the intermediate and final versions appear in the Rugby MS. In his 'Advertisement' to the *Supplement* published in *1797* (244–45), STC discusses 'Lines on an Autumnal Evening' as among the poems from *1796* which he was originally 'determined to omit' but which 'Some intelligent friends' persuaded him to '*reprieve* from immediate oblivion'. He apologizes to Samuel Rogers 'and the Public' for having suggested in the *1796* note on line 57 below that the tale of Florio in the *Pleasures of Memory* might have been stolen from Michael Bruce: '. . . my sense of honesty would not have been satisfied by the bare omission of the note. No one can see more clearly the *littleness* and futility of imagining plagiarisms in the works of men of Genius; but *nemo omnibus horis sapit*; and my mind, at the time of writing that note, was sick and sore with anxiety, and weakened through much suffering. I have not the most distant knowledge of Mr Rogers, except as a correct and elegant Poet. If any of my readers should know him personally, they would oblige me by informing him that I have expiated a sentence of unfounded detraction, by an unsolicited and self-originating apology.'

18 *meed* reward.

21 *thrilled* Etymologically the word means 'pierced'; see 'shot' and 'electric dart'.

31 *paly* pale; the adverbial *-y* form is common in eighteenth-century verse.

34 *list* listen to.

39 *pinions* wings.

57 In *1796* the following note on this line appears: ' – I entreat the Public's pardon for having carelessly suffered to be printed such intolerable stuff as this and the thirteen following lines. They have not the merit even of originality: as every thought is to be found in the Greek Epigrams. The lines in this poem from the 27th to the 36th, I have been told are a palpable imitation of the passage from the 355th to the 370th lines of the Pleasures of Memory Part 3. I do not perceive so striking a similarity between the two passages; at all events I had written the Effusion several years before I had seen Mr Rogers' Poem – It may be proper to remark that the tale of Florio in the "Pleasures of Memory" is to be found in Lochleven, a poem of great merit by Michael Bruce. – In Mr Rogers' Poem the names are Florio and Julia; in the Lochleven Lemond and Levina – and this is all the difference.' STC ends the note by quoting ten lines from Bruce's poem as an 'exquisite passage, expressing the effects of a fine day on the human heart'.

58 *Proteus* in the *Odyssey*, a sea god who knows all things and has the power to change shape to avoid being questioned.

61 *Myrtle* in classical myth, a plant associated with Venus and love.

79 *my native brook* the River Otter.

92 *lambent* radiant, shining.

93–4 Cf. lines 16–20 of Shelley's 'To a Sky-Lark': 'Keen as are the arrows / Of that silver sphere / Whose intense lamp narrows / In the white dawn clear, / Until we hardly see – we feel that it is there'.

To Fortune: On Buying a Ticket in the Irish Lottery

First published in the *Morning Chronicle* for 7 November 1793, with the following letter 'To the Editor': '*Sir*, – The following poem you may perhaps deem admissible into your journal – if not, you will commit it εἰς ἱερὸν μένος Ἡφαίστοιο [to the temple of Hephaestus, i.e. the fire]. – I am, with more respect and gratitude than I ordinarily feel for Editors of Papers, your obliged, &c., Cantab. – S.T.C.' First collected in *1893*; Campbell thought it 'probable that this was Coleridge's first appearance in print' (567 n.). He also suggests that STC bought the ticket in the lottery, the drawings for which began five days after the poem was published, to escape financial embarrassment at Cambridge. A few weeks later, in early December, STC left the university to enlist, under an assumed name, in the Light Dragoons; see Table of Dates.

2 *that circling bandage* The goddess Fortune is traditionally blind.
15 *durance* endurance.
18 *scrip* small bag or wallet.
29 *relume* relight; cf. *Othello* V. ii. 13.
31 *haply* perhaps.

Perspiration: A Travelling Eclogue

First published in *Letters of Samuel Taylor Coleridge* (1895). STC sent the lines to Southey in a letter of 6 July 1794 (*L* 1: 84), on which the present text is based. Though the term 'eclogue' is associated with pastoral poetry, as in Virgil's *Eclogues*, it originally had a broader meaning: a short poem in the form of a dialogue or soliloquy; a choice poem (from the Greek verb for 'to choose'). In eighteenth-century poetry 'eclogue' recovered some of its earlier breadth of application – as in Lady Mary Wortley Montagu's *Town Eclogues*.

1 *Wheels* 'Wheel' (*1912*).
8 *Grots* grottos.

Lines written at the King's Arms, Ross, formerly the House of the 'Man of Ross'

First published in the *Cambridge Intelligencer* for 27 September 1794; included in *1796*, *1797*, *1803*, *1828*, *1829*, *1834*. The poem was also published in J. Hucks, *A Pedest'rian Tour through North Wales* (1795). Hucks was a Cambridge friend who joined STC on a walking tour in Wales during the summer of 1794. STC wrote to Southey on 13 July 1794: 'At Ross . . . we took up our quarters at the King's Arms, once the House of Kyrle, the M[an] of R[oss]. I gave the window-shutter the following effusion' (*L* 1: 87). The Man of Ross had been famously represented in Pope's 'Epistle to Bathurst'.

In *1796* lines 5 – 10 were included in 'A Monody on the Death of Chatterton' and excluded from this poem. In *1797* the lines were restored to this poem but in

1803 excluded again (though in that collection they were not transferred to the 'Monody'). The 20-line version of *1797* was printed with very slight differences in all subsequent editions.

9–10 'And o'er the dowried maiden's glowing cheek, / Bade bridal love suffuse its blushes meek' (letter to Southey).

19 *cheat* ease or eliminate by redirecting the attention.

Imitated from the Welsh

First published in *1796*; included in *1803*, *1828*, *1829*, *1834*. Probably written during the trip to Wales in the summer of 1794 (see headnote to previous poem).

Lines to a Beautiful Spring in a Village

First published in *1796*; included in the 1796 edition of the *Annual Register*, and in *1797*, *1803*, *1828*, *1829*, *1834*. Campbell dates the poem 1793 in *1893* and associates it with 'Sonnet' ('Thou gentle Look') and 'Sonnet to the River Otter'; in *1912* and in *Everyman* it is dated 1794. There is a version in MS E entitled 'Lines addressed to a Spring in the Village of Kirkhompton [sic] near Bath', and a revised fair copy in a notebook in the Pierpont Morgan Library, New York.

4 *Pierian* pertaining to Pieria in ancient Macedonia, where worship of the Muses supposedly originated.

18 *lorn* forlorn.

Imitations Ad Lyram

Published in *The Watchman* for 9 March 1796 but never included in any collection in STC's lifetime. The poem was accompanied by the following 'Advertisement': 'If we except Lucretius and Statius, I know not of any Latin poet, ancient or modern, who has equalled Casimir in boldness of conception, opulence of fancy, or beauty of versification. The Odes of this illustrious Jesuit were translated into English about 150 years ago, by a Thomas Hill, I think [according to *1912*, the *Odes* of Casimir were translated by "G. Hils." in 1646]. I never saw the translation. A few of the Odes have been translated in a very animated manner by [Isaac] Watts. I have subjoined the third ode of the second book, which, with the exception of the first line, is an effusion of exquisite elegance. In the imitation attempted, I am sensibile that I have destroyed the *effect of suddenness*, by translation into two stanzas what is one in the original.

> AD LYRAM.
> Sonori buxi Filia sutilis,
> Pendebis alta, Barbite, populo,
>   Dum ridet aer, et supinas
>   Solicitat levis aura frondes:
> Te sibilantis lenior halitus

> Perflabit Euri: me iuvet interim
>   Collum reclinasse, et virenti
>   Sic temere iacuisse ripa.
> Eheu! serenum quae nebulae tegunt
> Repente caelum! quis sonus imbrium!
>   Surgamus – heu semper fugaci
>   Gaudia praeterita passu!'

Though the lyre in STC's imitation is the traditional musical instrument and not an eolian harp, the imagery connecting its music to the changing force of the wind and to the speaker's shifting mood invites comparison with 'The Eolian Harp' (12 ff.) and with 'Dejection: An Ode' (6–8).

1 *air* vocal song, as distinguished from the lyre's sound ('thy kindred lay!').

The Sigh

First published, as 'Effusion XXXII', in *1796*; included in all subsequent collections in STC's lifetime except *1817*. STC sent the poem to Southey in a letter of 3–4 November 1794 (*L* 1: 124). In *1796* he dates the poem 'June 1794', but E. H. Coleridge is probably right to suggest that the reference to the Pantisocracy scheme in lines 19 ff. makes it unlikely that it was written in full before August. There are fair copies in the Pforzheimer Library (bound together with STC's autograph fair copy of Southey's lines 'On Bala Hill'), in MS E and in the Rugby MS. The 'Mary' addressed in the poem is Mary Evans; see headnotes to 'A Lover's Complaint to His Mistress' and 'With Fielding's Amelia'. STC seems still to have been in love with Mary Evans when he became engaged to Sara Fricker; see his letter to Henry Martin of 22 July 1794 (*L* 1: 90–5).

4 *Prospect* scene, surrounding landscape.
19 ff. During the summer of 1794 STC met Southey and planned with him to establish a utopian community on the banks of the Susquehanna River in Pennsylvania; see Table of Dates and the headnote to 'Pantisocracy'.

The Kiss

First published, as 'Effusion XXVIII', in *1796*; included in all subsequent editions in STC's lifetime except *1817*. There is a MS version in MS E, and a draft of a 17-line version of lines 9–19 on a scrap inserted into a notebook now in the Pierpont Morgan Library. The title 'The Kiss' first appeared in *1797*; Lamb objected to the possible confusion with the poem 'Kisses', and in *1803* the title is 'To Sara'. The *1797* title returned in *1828*, when 'Kisses' was omitted from the collection. Campbell says 'There is reason for supposing that these verses were originally addressed, and not merely transferred, "To Sara" [Fricker]' (*1893*, 569 n.). Composition is conjecturally put at 1794 in *1893*, *1912* and *Everyman*.

5 *viewless* invisible; cf. 'A Monody on the Death of Chatterton' (2nd) 138.
20–8 The ending of this poem strikingly anticipates 'The Eolian Harp' 14–17,

with its image of the 'coy maid' whose 'sweet upbraiding . . . must needs / Tempt
to repeat the wrong'. The status of what counts as 'passive', and what STC means
by 'gentle violence', is important in both poems.

To a Young Lady, with a Poem on the French Revolution

First published in the first number of *The Watchman* (1 March 1796); included
in all collections in STC's lifetime except *1817*. STC sent the poem in a letter
to Southey of 21 October 1794 (*L* 1: 117–18). There is also a version in MS E,
and a fair copy in the Pierpont Morgan Library notebook. The date 'September
1794' appears at the end of the text in *1797* and *1803*, but in *1828*, *1829* and *1834*
this is changed to 'September, 1792', possibly to suggest that STC's disillusion-
ment with the Revolution (see lines 28 ff.) began earlier than it did. The retreat
from 'the reeking plains of France' (which STC had not in fact 'strode', line 26)
to 'peaceful Virtue' (line 30) was a characteristic reaction on the part of those in
England who had previously supported the Revolution. Campbell thought that
the 'Poem on the French Revolution' referred to in the title was the 'Destruction
of the Bastile'. This may be the case even if the present poem was written in 1794
and not 1792, as Campbell believed.

10 'LEE BOO, the son of ABBA THULE, Prince of the Pelew Islands came over to
England with Captain Wilson, died of the small-pox, and is buried in Greenwich
Church-yard. See Keate's *Account* [*of the Pelew Islands*, 1788]' (STC's note, first
published in *The Watchman*).
14 ' "And suffering Nature weeps that *one* should die." – Southey's *Retrospect*'
(STC).
19 *Dog-star* Cf. line 13 of 'The Nose' (above).
24 *Tyrtæan* of or pertaining to the Spartan poet Tyrtæus, famous for his martial
and patriotic songs. The lyre is 'empassion'd' in the letter to Southey, 'Alcaean'
in the two other MS versions and in all printed texts except *1834*.
41 *Nor, Sara!* Sara Fricker, to whom STC became engaged in the summer of
1794. In the letter to Southey this line begins 'Nor, BRYNTON!' – see headnote
to 'Translation of Wrangham's Hendecasyllabi" ' below. STC reworked the last
four lines of the poem several times; the variants are given in *1912* 1: 66.

Translation of Wrangham's 'Hendecasyllabi ad Bruntonam e Granta Exituram'

First published in Francis Wrangham, *Poems* (1795), along with the following
poem, 'To Miss Brunton'. Wrangham's Latin poem was addressed to the actress
Ann Brunton; the 'Miss Brunton' in STC's poem was her younger sister Elizabeth,
also an actress.

12 *Monimia's tale of woe* Thomas Otway's blank-verse tragedy *The Orphan* (1680),
in which the heroine Monimia commits suicide.
21–8 The reference here is to a play entitled *The Grecian Daughter*, in which
Ann Brunton, under the stage-name of Mrs Merry, appeared as the character
Euphrasia.

31 *Granta's sons* Cambridge University students, who have been watching Ann Brunton perform.

32 *Pierian* pertaining to Pieria in ancient Macedonia, where the cult of the Muses is said to have originated.

To Miss Brunton with the Preceding Translation

See headnote to the preceding poem.

3 *Thalia* in Greek mythology the Muse of comedy and bucolic poetry.

Epitaph on an Infant

First published in the *Morning Chronicle* for 24 September 1794; included in *The Watchman* for 5 May 1796 and in all collections published in STC's lifetime except *1817*. E. H. Coleridge says that these lines were probably based on 'An Epitaph on an Infant' in the churchyard of Birchington, Kent: 'Ah! why so soon, just as the blossom appears, / Drops the fair blossom in the vale of tears? / Death view'd the treasure in the desart given / And claim'd the right of planting it in Heav'n' (*1912* 1: 68 n.). There is a Greek version and accompanying English translation in MS E (printed in the notes to *1912*), and a revised fair copy in the Pierpont Morgan Library notebook.

[Pantisocracy]

Never published in STC's lifetime. This sonnet, untitled, was sent to Southey in a letter of 18 September 1794 (*L* 1: 104). The first eight lines were included in the version of 'A Monody on the Death of Chatterton' printed in Lancelot Sharpe's edition of Chatterton's *Poems* (1794). Southey himself attributed the poem to STC's friend S. Favell in a letter of 19 October 1794, and the poem was attributed to Favell when it was first published in full in the *Life and Correspondence of the late Robert Southey*, ed. Cuthbert Southey, 6 vols (London, 1849–50). In *1852* it was printed with a note apologizing for the apparent plagiarism. But E. H. Coleridge argues that the sonnet is entirely STC's and notes that it was included in MS E.

On the Prospect of Establishing a Pantisocracy in America

First published anonymously in the *Co-operative Magazine and Monthly Herald* for 6 March 1826. This poem was conjecturally attributed to STC by E. H. Coleridge in 1907 and included in *1912*, although he acknowledges that there is no proof of authorship. It is included as doubtful in *Everyman*. No MS is known to exist; the 1794 date of composition in *1912* and *Everyman* is deduced from the fact that it was in the summer of this year that STC and Southey planned their ideal community. See headnote to '[Pantisocracy]' above.

14 *Transatlantic shore* STC and Southey hoped to establish their community on the banks of the Susquehanna River in Pennsylvania.

Elegy, Imitated from One of Akenside's Blank-Verse Inscriptions

First published anonymously in the *Morning Chronicle* for 23 September 1794; included in *The Watchman* for 17 March 1796, where it was signed simply 'T'. It was published as STC's in *1817*, *1828*, *1829* and *1834*. The editors of *1852* doubted that it was STC's and omitted it. But as Campbell notes, it originally appeared in the *Morning Chronicle* with 'Epitaph on an Infant', a poem known to be by STC. E. H. Coleridge accepts it as STC's in *1912*. Mark Akenside (1720–71) is best known for *The Pleasures of Imagination*; the 'Inscription' imitated here (No. III, 'Whoe'er thou art whose path in summer lies') was published in Robert Dodsley's *Collection of Poems*, vol. 6 (1758).

21–4 The last stanza follows Akenside's conclusion very closely: 'Go, Traveller; relate / The mournful story. Haply some fair maid / May hold it in remembrance, and be taught / That riches cannot pay for truth or love' (*The New Oxford Book of Eighteenth-Century Verse*, ed. Roger Lonsdale, no. 262).

The Faded Flower

Unpublished in STC's lifetime. This poem first appeared in the *New Monthly Magazine* for August 1836, together with a letter to Henry Martin dated 22 July 1794 in which it was included (*L* 1: 95). The letter describes STC's chance meeting with Mary Evans at Wrexham (see headnote to 'The Sigh' above). There is a transcript by 'Miss A Evans' dated 19 July 1794 (*Index* CoS 157), and another in an unidentified hand dated 10 July 1794 now in the Pierpont Morgan Library.

11 *Abra's* 'Emma's' (Pierpont Morgan transcript).

Sonnet ('Pale Roamer through the Night!')

First published, as 'Effusion XV', in *1796*; included in 'A Sheet of Sonnets' bound in a copy of Bowles's *Sonnets and Other Poems* (1796), in *1797* and in all subsequent collections except *1817*, as part of a variously numbered sequence of sonnets (it is 'Sonnet IX' in *1828*, *1829* and *1834*). In the Preface to *1796* (p. xi) STC says that 'The first half of Effusion XV was written by the Author of "Joan of Arc", an Epic Poem' – i.e. by Southey. It is conjecturally dated 1794 in *1893*, *1912* and *Everyman*.

2 May remorse possess that man on his death-bed.

7 'Thy kindred, when they see thee, turn aside' (*1803*).

9 'O! I could weep to think' is 'O I am sad to think' in all editions before *1834*.

13–14 'May has no feeling for the sore Disgrace; / Keen blows the Blast upon the moulting Dove' (*1803*).

Domestic Peace

First published in 1795 as a song in *The Fall of Robespierre* (Act I, 210–24), the drama on which STC collaborated with Robert Southey in 1794. It was included as 'Song' in all collected editions of the poems except *1817*. The present title first appears in *1797*.

Sonnet ('Thou bleedest, my poor Heart!')

First published in *1796* where, as in all subsequent collections except *1817*, it appears as part of a sequence of sonnets ('Sonnet XI' in *1828, 1829, 1834*). This poem is also included in the 'Sheet of Sonnets' sent by STC to John Thelwall on 17 December 1796 and bound in a copy of Bowles's *Sonnets and Other Poems* (1796). In both *1893* and *1912* it is given the title it has in *1797* and *1803*, 'On a Discovery Made too Late'. STC sent the poem to Southey in a letter of 21 October 1794 (*L* 1: 115–16), where it clearly refers to STC's discovery that, though engaged since August to Sara Fricker, he was still in love with Mary Evans and jealous of her actual or imagined lover (see letter to her of early November 1794 [*L* 1: 129–31], quoted in the notes below).

2–4 'Doth Reason ponder with an anguish'd smile / Probing thy sore wound sternly, tho' the while / Her Eye be swoln and dim with heaviness' (letter to Southey; Griggs also gives a cancelled version of these lines in *L* 1: 116 n.).

7–8 'After infinite struggles of Irresolution I will at last dare to request of you, Mary! that you will communicate to me whether or no you are engaged to Mr⸺' (letter to Mary Evans; Griggs' note identifies STC's rival as Fryer Todd, whom Mary Evans married on 13 October 1795).

9–14 'It was a faint and rayless Hope! Yet I nursed it in my Bosom with an Agony of Affection, even as a Mother her sickly Infant' (letter to Mary Evans).

Sonnet to the Author of the 'Robbers'

First published in *1796*; included in the 'Sheet of Sonnets' and in all subsequent collections except *1817* as part of a sequence of sonnets ('Sonnet XII' in *1828, 1829, 1834*). 'To the Author of the "Robbers" ' is part of the title in all published versions except *1803*. STC appended the following note to the poem in *1796* and *1797*: 'One night in Winter, on leaving a College-friend's room, with whom I had supped, I carelessly took away with me "The Robbers" a drama, the very name of which I had never before heard of:– A Winter midnight – the wind high – and "The Robbers" for the first time! – The readers of SCHILLER will conceive what I felt. SCHILLER introduces no supernatural beings; yet his human beings agitate and astonish more than all the *goblin* rout – even of Shakespeare.' Compare this note with STC's account of reading Schiller's play in his letter to Southey of 3 November 1794 (*L* 1: 122); see also stanza VII of 'Dejection: An Ode', with its images of the raving wind and 'the rushing of an host in rout' (111). Friedrich

Schiller's *Die Räuber*, a major text in the German *Sturm und Drang* period, was published in 1781.

1–6 Lines 1–4 are printed in reverse order (4, 3, 2, 1) in 'Sheet of Sonnets', and lines 5–6 are altered as follows: 'That in no after moment aught less vast / Might stamp me human!' STC wrote to Thomas Pool on 1 November 1796: 'It is strange that in the Sonnet to Schiller I wish to die – *die* that nothing may stamp me *mortal* – this *Bull* never struck me till Charles Lloyd mentioned it – the Sense is evident enough – but the word is ridiculously ambiguous' (*L* 1: 243). STC kept line 5 as altered in 'Sheet of Sonnets' but restored the word 'mortal' in *1797* and *1803*. In *1828* he returned to the *1796* version of lines 5–6 and stayed with it in *1829* and *1834*.
4 *a famished Father's cry* 'The Father of *Moor* in the Play of the Robbers' (STC's note in *1803*).

Melancholy: A Fragment

First published in the *Morning Post* for 12 December 1797. Included, with an additional three and a half lines, in *1817*; STC returned to the original shorter version when he published the poem in *1828*, *1829* and *1834*. It was sent in a letter to William Sotheby of 26 August 1802 (*L* 2: 855–6). A 1794 date of composition is given in *1893* and *1912*, based on the following note in *1817*: 'First published in the *Morning Chronicle*, in the year 1794.' Since the name of the paper in this note is incorrect, the year may be as well; Beer conjectures 1797 in *Everyman*.

2 *Where ruining ivies* 'Whose running ivies' (*Morning Post*).
3 *pall* cloak, cloth.
6 *adder's tongue* 'A Plant found on old walls and in wells and mois[t] [h]edges. – It is often called the Hart's Tongue' (STC's note in *Morning Post*). In *1817* this was corrected: 'A botanical mistake. The plant I meant is called the Hart's Tongue, but this would unluckily spoil the poetical effect. *Cedat ergo Botanice.*' A version of this latter note appears in *1828* and *1829* but not in *1834*.
13 In *1817* the ending is extended: 'Strange was the dream that fill'd her soul, / Nor did not whisp'ring spirits roll / A mystic tumult, and a fateful rhyme, / Mix'd with wild shapings of the unborn time.'

Songs of the Pixies

First published in *1796*; included (with revisions) in *1797*, *1803*, *1828*, *1829* and *1834*. There is a MS version in MS E Estlin, and a fair copy in a notebook in STC's hand containing materials used for *The Watchman*. STC's prose preface, which says that the poem was written in 1793, appears in all editions. The versions of the preface and of the poem itself given here are those of *1834*; STC made several changes in the text for this edition. He calls the poem an 'Irregular Ode', and the shifts in rhyme-scheme and metre between and within stanzas are striking.

14–15 Between these lines the following passage appears in the MSS and in *1796* and *1828*: 'Richer than the deepen'd bloom / That glows on Summer's lily-scented plume'.

17 *scouting* watching, looking out for.

21 *pinion* wing.

23 *fiery-tressed* Some editors have added a stress to the last syllable of 'tressed', but it is not clear that this is metrically necessary.

36 STC portrays himself here in the conventional guise of a young poet of 'sensibility'.

40 *grot* grotto.

47 *car* chariot; the 'dewy star' (48) is Venus, the Evening Star.

57 *turtle* turtle dove.

59 'The Electric Flash that from the melting eye' (both MSS and all texts printed prior to *1834*).

61 *mystic ringlets* magical circles.

68 *lonely Otter's* Refers to the River Otter.

79 *ebon* black; the colour of ebony.

85 *What time* 'At which time' – a Miltonic Latinism common in late eighteenth-century verse.

91 *proclaimed our Faery Queen* See the last paragraph of STC's preface. This is not primarily or exclusively a reference to Edmund Spenser's *The Faerie Queene*; the Pixies think of themselves as belonging more generally to the realm of 'Faery'.

95 *artless stole* long, loose, casual garment.

101 *snow-drop* the flower of this name.

106 *Zephyr* west wind, personified.

To a Young Ass, its Mother being Tethered Near it

First published in the *Morning Chronicle* for 30 December 1794; included in *1796* and in all subsequent collections except *1817*. There is a revised fair copy now at Harvard University entitled 'Monologue to a young Jackass in Jesus Piece – it's Mother near it chained to a Log' and dated 'Jesus College, 24 October 1794', a version in a letter to Southey of 17 December 1794 (*L* 1: 142–3), and another fair copy in the Rugby MS. STC also sent revisions to the poem in a letter to Joseph Cottle of 6 January 1797 (*L* 1: 300). In *Coleridge's Verse: A Selection*, William Empson and David Pirie print the earliest MS version because, they argue, only by returning to it can 'the original blend of sincere social protest with humorous hyperbole . . . be regained' (p. 218 n.); see also *1893* 477–8. Only STC's most important revisions are noted below. This is the poem that provoked Byron to satirize STC as 'the laureat of the long-ear'd kind' in *English Bards and Scotch Reviewers* (264).

4 *pat* 'scratch' (Harvard MS, *Morning Chronicle*).

8 *moveless* 'moping' (Harvard MS, letter to Southey, *Morning Chronicle*).

9 *Fears* 'soul' (Harvard MS).

12 Cf. *Hamlet* III.i.74.

21 'For much I fear, that he lives e'en as she' (*1796*).

23 *footsteps hither bend* 'steps toward me tend' (Harvard MS); 'footsteps t'ward me bend' (*1796*).

28 In the Harvard MS, this line and the six that follow make even more obvious the reference to STC's Pantisocracy scheme:

> Where high-soul'd Pantisocracy shall dwell!
> Where mirth shall tickle Plenty's ribless side,
> And smiles from Beauty's Lip on sunbeams glide,
> Where Toil shall wed young Health that charming Lass!
> And use his sleek cows for a looking-glass –
> And Mice with Pussy's Whiskers sport in Love.

E. H. Coleridge quotes a note in the Harvard MS – not by STC – to the second line of this passage: 'This is a truly poetical line of which the author has assured us that he did not *mean* it to have any meaning' (*1912* 1: 75).

35–6 'Than Handel's softest airs that soothe to rest / The tumult of a scoundrel Monarch's Breast' (Harvard MS). Empson and Pirie say that 'In the published version Coleridge suppressed . . . that last line [of the MS version] which was too dangerously "republican"' (p. 218). But in fact that line, in both the *Morning Chronicle* and in *1796*, reads 'The tumult of some *Scoundrel* Monarch's breast'.

Lines on a Friend Who Died of a Frenzy Fever Induced by Calumnious Reports

First published in *1796*; included in all subsequent collections except *1817*. The poem appears in a letter to Southey of 3–4 November 1794 (*L* 1: 121–4), in a letter to George Coleridge of 6 November 1794 (*L* 1: 127–8), in MS E and in the *Watchman* notebook now in the Pierpont Morgan Library. The friend was the Rev. Fulwood Smerdon, vicar of Ottery St Mary, who had died in August of 1794; see the headnote to 'Written After a Walk Before Supper' and STC's letter to Thomas Allsop of 29 June 1822 (*L* 5: 239).

1 *Edmund* In the letter to Southey the name is left blank; in the letter to George Coleridge it is 'Smerdon'.

4 *Ithuriel* The guardian angel who touched Satan with his spear in *Paradise Lost* 4. 810–11.

17–20 'Fierce-eyed' in line 17 is 'frantic' in both letters; 'squatting' in line 19 is 'couching' in the letter to George Coleridge. Charles Lamb wrote to STC on 10 June 1796: 'In *Edmund*, "Frenzy, fierce-eyed child" is not so well as "frantic", though that is an epithet adding nothing to the meaning. Slander *couching* was better than *squatting*'.

24 *zoneless* unbound, unconfined.

25 *firmer* 'generous' in both letters; 'manly' (MS E).

29 *rolled* 'prowl'd' in both letters and in MS E.

33 *grateful prayer* 'prayer of praise' (*1796*).

40 *Energic* in a state of action. Cf. 'Dejection: An Ode' 86: 'My shaping spirit of Imagination'.

To a Friend, Together with an Unfinished Poem

First published in *1796*; included in *1797* and *1803* (on which the present text is based). Lines 12–19 were published as a separate poem in *1834* under the title 'The Same', referring to the preceding poem in that edition, 'On Seeing a Youth Affectionately Welcomed by a Sister' (see headnote to that poem above). STC sent this poem in a letter to Southey of 29 December 1794, with the title 'To C. Lamb' (*L* 1: 147–8). The 'Unfinished Poem' of the printed title is 'Religious Musings', which STC began on Christmas Eve 1794.

1–3 'Thus far my sterile Brain hath fram'd the Song / Elaborate & swelling – but the Heart / Not owns it' (letter to Southey).

7 This line does not appear in the letter to Southey. Between lines 13 and 14 'On her soft Bosom I repos'd my Cares / And gain'd for every wound an healing Tear' (letter to Southey).

15 This image of STC as patient and his sister as nurse is striking, not only because it is Ann Coleridge's death that is being recalled here, but because Charles Lamb is represented as nursing his sister Mary.

17 'That shrink asham'd from even Friendship's eye' (letter to Southey, *1796*, *1797*).

19–21 Cf. 'This Lime-Tree Bower My Prison' 68–76: 'My gentle-hearted Charles! . . . to whom / No sound is dissonant which tells of life'.

21 *warm . . . high . . .* 'high . . . warm . . .' (letter to Southey).

24–5 An odd echo of Dryden's 'Mac Flecknoe': 'And lambent dullness played around his face' (111).

25 *sainted* 'holy' (letter to Southey).

28 In *1797* and *1803* STC added a note on the word 'implore': 'I utterly recant the sentiment contained in the lines [quotes 27–8], it being written in Scripture, "*Ask*, and it shall be given you", and my human reason being moreover convinced of the propriety of offering *petitions* as well as thanksgivings to the Deity.'

SONNETS ON EMINENT CHARACTERS

These twelve sonnets were contributed by STC to the *Morning Chronicle* between 1 December 1794 and 31 January 1795. The series was introduced by the following letter: '*Mr Editor* – If, Sir, the following poems will not disgrace your poetical department, I will transmit you a series of *Sonnets* (as it is the fashion to call them) addressed like these to eminent Contemporaries. STC. Jesus College, Cambridge.' STC later incorporated many of these poems, variously ordered, into a sequence of sonnets within his collected poetry: ten of the twelve appear in *1796*, for instance; seven in *1828*, *1829* and *1834*. The 'Sonnets on Eminent Characters' are printed here in the order in which they appeared in the *Morning Chronicle*, even though in some cases this represents a departure from the principle of compositional chronology observed elsewhere in this edition. The original sequence offers a coherent reflection in verse of STC's early political views. The omissions and rearrangements in later collections, described in the notes to individual sonnets in the series, likewise reflect his later political conservatism.

1. To the Honourable Mr Erskine

First published in the *Morning Chronicle* for 1 December 1794; included in *1796*, *1803* ('Sonnet X'), *1828*, *1829*, *1834* ('Sonnet IV'). The present text is that of *1834*. At the end of the *Morning Chronicle* version was this note: 'Our elegant correspondent will highly gratify every reader of taste by the continuance of his exquisitely beautiful productions. No. II. shall appear on an early day.' Thomas Erskine (1750–1823) was a distinguished jurist and Lord Chancellor in 1806–7; he defended Thomas Paine and other radicals during the French Revolution.

4 *For dreadless* 'Where fearless' (*Morning Chronicle*).
5 *censer* a vessel in which incense is burned.
6 *the insulted* 'her injur'd' (*Morning Chronicle*).
10 'With heav'n-breath'd blessings; and, when late the doom' (*Morning Chronicle*).
11 *die* 'rise' (*1803*).
13–14 'Though the great Sun not meets our wistful gaze / Still glows wide Heaven with his distended blaze' (*Morning Chronicle*).

2. Burke

First published in the *Morning Chronicle* for 9 December 1794; included in all collections except *1797* and *1817* ('Sonnet VII' in *1803*, 'Sonnet II' in *1828*, *1829*, *1834*). There is a MS version in a letter to Southey of 17 December 1794 (*L* 1: 142) and a revised fair copy, on a leaf with 'To the Rev. W. L. Bowles', at Harvard University. Edmund Burke (1729–97), the famous statesman and orator, had supported the American Revolution and other progressive causes as a member of the Whig Party, but his denunciation of the French Revolution in *Reflections on the Revolution in France* (1790) became an influential articulation of conservative, traditional English values.

2 *in a mourner's guise* English repression against citizens who in any way sympathized with the Revolution had reached its height in 1794–5. Habeas Corpus was suspended in May 1794; STC's friends John Thelwall and Horne Tooke were tried for treason (and acquitted) in November 1794; the 'Two Acts' against seditious meetings and other activities opposed to the government were passed in 1795.
8 *wizard spell* Burke's parliamentary oratory, even more than his writing, was famous for its spell-binding power.
9 STC added the following note to this line in *1796*: 'When I composed this line, I had not read the following paragraph in the *Cambridge Intelligencer* (of Saturday, November 21, 1795.) "When Mr Burke first crossed over the House of Commons from the Opposition to the Ministry, he received a pension of 1200 l. a year charged on the Kings Privy Purse! When he had completed his labors, it was then a question what recompense his service deserved. Mr Burke wanting a present supply of money, it was thought that a pension of 2000 l. *per annum* for *forty years certain*, would sell for eighteen year purchase, and bring him of course 36,000 l. a year *for three lives*, to be charged on the King's Revenue of the West India

4 1/2 per cents. This was tried at the market, but it was found that it would not produce the 36,000 l. which were wanted. In consequence of this a pension of 2500 l. per annum, *for three lives* on the 4 1/2 West India Fund, the lives to be nominated by Mr Burke, that he may accommodate the purchasers, is *finally* granted to this disinterested patriot! He has thus retir'd from the trade of politics, with pensions to the amount of 3700 l. a year.'

10 *stormy Pity* William Pitt, the Tory Prime Minister; see headnote to sonnet '6. Pitt' below.

3. Priestley

First published in the *Morning Chronicle* for 11 December 1794; included by STC in all collections except *1797* and *1817* ('Sonnet IX' in *1803*; 'Sonnet III' in *1828*, *1829*, *1834*). STC sent the sonnet to Southey in a letter of 17 December 1794 (*L* 1: 140). Joseph Priestley (1733–1804), an important scientist and leader of the Unitarians, was an influential political radical. In 1791 anti-Jacobin rioters set fire to his house in Birmingham, which had become a centre of political and intellectual dissent, and in 1794 he was forced to emigrate to the United States. Compare STC's lines on Priestley in *Religious Musings* 371–6.

1 *Vizir* Also 'vizier'; a high officer in an Islamic government, especially in the old Turkish Empire. Here the term is part of STC's effort to moderate or disguise the poem's original politics. In the version first printed in the *Morning Chronicle* the sonnet begins: 'Tho' king-bred rage with lawless uproar rude / Hath driv'n . . .'; the version sent in the letter to Southey begins: 'Tho' king-bred Rage with lawless Tumult rude / Have driv'n . . .'

4 *his mild radiance* Probably a reference to Priestley's membership in the Lunar Society, a group of Birmingham dissenters, politically liberal industrialists, writers and scientists (it included James Watt, Erasmus Darwin and Josiah Wedgwood) who met between 1766 and 1791 whenever the moon was full to discuss their papers and projects.

4. La Fayette

First published in the *Morning Chronicle* for 15 December 1794; included by STC in all collections except *1797* and *1817* ('Sonnet XIII' in *1803*; 'Sonnet VII' in *1828*, *1829*, *1834*). There is a revised fair copy in the Rugby MS, entitled 'Effusion 9'. The Marquis de La Fayette (1757–1834), French general and statesman, famously served the American cause during the War of Independence. He was at first a moderate supporter of the French Revolution but eventually came to defend the monarchy. He was imprisoned in Austria in 1792, escaped briefly in 1794, and was eventually released by Napoleon in 1797. The following note accompanied the poem in the *Morning Chronicle*: 'The above beautiful sonnet was written antecedently to the joyful account of the Patriot's escape from the Tyrant's Dungeon.'

3 *matin bird* the lark, which traditionally soars and sings in the early morning light.

5. Koskiusko

First published in the *Morning Chronicle* for 16 December 1794; included in *1796* and in *1828, 1829, 1834* ('Sonnet VI'). STC sent the poem to Southey in a letter of 17 December 1794 (*L* 1: 140). Tadeusz Kosciuszko (1746–1817), Polish general, fought with the colonists in the American Revolution and on his return to Poland championed Polish independence.

4 *swart* dark; 'list'ning' in the letter to Southey.

6. Pitt

First published in the *Morning Chronicle* for 23 December 1794, then in *The Watchman* for 2 April 1796. Included in *1796* and *1803* ('Sonnet VIII'). In *1852* the following note is attached: 'This sonnet, and the ninth, to Stanhope [see the last of these 'Sonnets on Eminent Characters' below], were among the pieces withdrawn from the second edition of 1797. They reappeared in the edition of 1803, and were again withdrawn in 1828, solely, it may be presumed, on account of their political vehemence. They will excite no angry feelings, and lead to no misapprehension now, and as they are fully equal to their companions in poetical merit, the Editors [Derwent and Sara Coleridge] have not scrupled to reproduce them. These Sonnets were originally entitled "Effusions" [in *1796*, but not in the *Morning Chronicle*].' William Pitt the Younger (1759–1806) was Prime Minister from 1783 to 1801 and from 1804 to 1806. He led England in its opposition to the French Revolution and was responsible for governmental policies and practices aimed at repressing dissent at home.

4 *Beseem thee, Mercy!* are appropriate to you, Mercy. This sonnet was entitled 'To Mercy' when published in *The Watchman*.
7 *Iscariot* Judas Iscariot, the disciple who betrayed Jesus.
8 *apostate* traitor or, literally, deserter. Pitt's father (also William), 1st Earl of Chatham (1708–78), had been a liberal Whig statesman. In the *Morning Chronicle* and *The Watchman* this line reads: 'Staining most foul a Godlike Father's name'.
12 *stern-brow'd Sister* Justice, whose blindness in this line implies dereliction rather than impartiality.
13 *terrible* terribly, in the sense of terrifyingly.

7. To the Rev. W. L. Bowles

First published in the *Morning Chronicle* for 26 December 1794. STC sent this version to Southey in a letter of 11 December 1794 (*L* 1: 136). He revised the sonnet substantially before including it in *1796*; a fair copy of the revised version, headed 'Effusion 1', is at Harvard University. The second version, with a few additional changes, was included in all subsequent collections (as 'Sonnet I') except *1817*. The present text is that of *1834*, where it is preceded, as it had been in *1796*, by four lines from Bowles:

> Content, as random Fancies might inspire,
> If his weak harp at times or lonely lyre
> He struck with desultory hand, and drew
> Some softened tones to Nature not untrue.

William Lisle Bowles (1762–1850) was a major influence on STC's early poetry. STC offered the following note on him when this sonnet appeared in the *Morning Chronicle*: 'Author of Sonnets and other Poems, published by Dilly. To Mr Bowles's poetry I have always thought the following remarks from Maximus Tyrius peculiarly applicable:– "... I am not now treating of that poetry which is estimated by the pleasure it affords to the ear – the ear having been corrupted, and the judgment-seat of the perceptions; but of that which proceeds from the intellectual Helicon, that which is *dignified*, and appertaining to *human* feelings, and entering into the soul." – The 13th Sonnet for exquisite delicacy of painting; the 19th for tender simplicity; and the 25th for manly pathos, are compositions of, perhaps, unrivalled merit. Yet while I am selecting these, I almost accuse myself of causeless partiality; for surely never was a writer so equal in excellence! –'

7 *thought-bewilder'd man* Cf. 'The Eolian Harp' 62–3: 'A sinful and most miserable man, / Wilder'd and dark ...'

11–14 Cf. 'The Eolian Harp' 44–8; the final lines of this sonnet also recall *Paradise Lost* 1. 21–2. STC would later develop theoretically (as in *BL* ch. XIII) the implied comparison between poetic inspiration and divine creation.

13 *plastic* Here and in 'The Eolian Harp' 47 the word means giving form or shape, creative (Greek *plassein*, to form, mould).

13–14 Note the change from 'formless' (without form) to 'unformed' (not yet formed) in the final lines of the revised version. In *1797* and *1803* the poem concluded with a different couplet: 'As made the soul enamour'd of her woe; / No common praise, dear Bard! to thee I owe.'

8. Mrs Siddons

First published in the *Morning Chronicle* for 29 December 1794 and signed 'S.T.C.'. In *1796* and *1797* ('Sonnet VIII') the sonnet was assigned to Charles Lamb; in *1803* ('Sonnet XII') it was again attributed to STC. E. H. Coleridge says that the poem 'may have been altered by Coleridge, but was no doubt written by Lamb and given by him to Coleridge to make up his tale of sonnets for the *Morning Chronicle*' (*1912* I: 85 n.). The fact that the poem was not included by STC in any collection after *1803*, which provides the present text, supports this view. Sarah Kemble Siddons (1755–1831) was the most distinguished actress of the age.

4 *listens* listens to.

5 *to wretch* to a wretched person.

   necromantic having to do with black magic or sorcery; specifically, with the art of conjuring up the spirits of the dead in order to predict the future.

6 *Or of those hags* 'Of Warlock Hags that' (*Morning Chronicle*).

10 *Beldame* an old woman, a hag.

9. To William Godwin, Author of 'Political Justice'

First published in the *Morning Chronicle* for 10 January 1795; never included in any collection by STC during his lifetime. The last six lines were sent to Southey in a letter of 17 December 1794 (*L* 1: 141). William Godwin (1756–1836), philosopher, novelist, political radical and subsequently an important friend and correspondent of STC, published the first edition of *An Enquiry Concerning Political Justice* in 1793. The book argued for the rational perfectibility of humanity and against all governmental and organized social constraints.

3 *Mimic Morn* STC's own note indicates a reference to the Aurora Borealis or Northern Lights; but 'false morn' is a traditional poetic locution for illusory optimism or promise.

10. To Robert Southey, of Balliol College, Oxford, Author of the 'Retrospect', and Other Poems

First published in the *Morning Chronicle* for 14 January 1795; not included by STC in any collection. STC sent the sonnet to Southey in a letter of 17 December 1794 (*L* 1: 143). They first met in the summer of 1794 (see Table of Dates).

8 *Myrtles* sacred to Venus and traditionally associated with erotic love.
   sear withered or scorched, an adjective here.
9 *Blossom* a verb.

11. To Richard Brinsley Sheridan, Esq.

First published in the *Morning Chronicle* for 29 January 1795; included by STC in all collections except *1797* and *1817*. There are MS versions in a letter to Southey of 17 December 1794 (*L* 1: 141–2) and in MS E, and a revised fair copy in the Rugby MS. Sheridan's best-known plays are *The Rivals* (1775) and *The School for Scandal* (1777); from 1780 he was a Whig MP and minister and became a famous parliamentary orator.

1–3 STC reworked the opening lines several times. The version in the letter to Southey begins: 'Some wingèd Genius, Sheridan! imbreath'd / His *various* influence on thy natal hour: / My fancy bodies forth the Guardian power'; the *Morning Chronicle* version begins as a question: 'Was it some spirit, *Sheridan*! that breath'd / His various influence . . .'.
4 'Hymetian Flowrets. Hymettus, a mountain near Athens, celebrated for its honey. This alludes to Mr Sheridan's classical attainments, and the following four lines to the exquisite sweetness and almost *Italian* delicacy of his poetry. In Shakespeare's *Lovers Complaint* there is a fine stanza almost prophetically characteristic of Mr Sheridan [quotes lines of Shakespeare's poem]' (STC's note in *1796*, *1803*). A shorter note appeared in the *Morning Chronicle*: 'Hymettus, a mountain famous for honey.'

5–6 Laura is the beloved addressed in Petrarch's lyric poetry, much of which was written in the Provençal town of Vaucluse.

12–13 The order of these lines is reversed in the letter to Southey and in MS E.
Apostate Cf. line 8 of the sonnet to Pitt above.

14 elder Fiend 'other Fiend' (Morning Chronicle); the reference, of course, is to Satan.

12. To Lord Stanhope, on Reading his Late Protest in the House of Lords / To Earl Stanhope

The first of these two sonnets – it can hardly be called a 'version' of the second – was published in the Morning Chronicle for 31 January 1795, signed 'One of the People'. It was first published as STC's in 1893; E. H. Coleridge accepts Campbell's attribution in 1912. The second sonnet was first published in 1796 and included in 1803. STC wrote to Mary Cruikshank in September 1807: '. . . in that first edition [1796] there was inserted (without my consent) a Sonnet to Lord Stanhope, in direct contradiction, equally to my then, as to my present principles – a Sonnet written by me in ridicule and mockery of the bloated style of French Jacobin declamation, and inserted by the fool of a Publisher in order, forsooth, that he might send the book, and a letter, to Earl Stanhope; who, to prove that he was not mad in all things, treated both book and letter with silent contempt' (L 3: 27). Campbell argues that STC's effort to pass the 1796 sonnet off as parody was in fact merely a manoeuvre to disguise his earlier radicalism (1893 576 n.).

'To Lord Stanhope' – Morning Chronicle
6 Corruption's bowl Cf. sonnet '2. Burke' 9.
13–14 Compare this image of the sun to '1. To the Honourable Mr Erskine' 12–14 and '4. La Fayette' 13–14.

'To Earl Stanhope' – 1796, 1803
7 Abdiel the zealous angel who opposes Satan's plans in Paradise Lost V. 803–907.
9 her liberty as represented in the French Revolution and as celebrated by its British sympathizers.

Lines to a Friend in Answer to a Melancholy Letter

First published in 1796; included in 1803, 1828, 1829, 1834. In an annotation in a copy of 1828, STC says that the poem is 'very like one of Horace's odes, starched' (1893 576 n.). There is a fair copy in the Rugby MS. A 1795 date of composition is proposed conjecturally in 1893, 1912 and Everyman. The ABBA quatrain, which had been used by Sir Philip Sidney, Ben Jonson and Lord Herbert of Cherbury, suggestively anticipates Tennyson's In Memoriam stanza. See Christopher Ricks, The Poems of Tennyson (Longman, 1969), p. 859.

14–16 A reference to new political possibilities opened up to peasants and workers by the French Revolution.
18 sanguinary bloody.
22 purple since Roman times the colour of nobility.

To an Infant

First published in *1796*; included by STC in all subsequent collections except *1817*. The version in MS E contains some differences from the printed text. Composition is put at 1795 in *1893*, *1912* and *Everyman*. The infant addressed in the poem could not have been STC's son Hartley, who was born several months after *1796* was published.

1–4 In MS E the poem begins as follows: 'How you sweet Child my Bosom's grief beguiles / With soul-subduing Eloquence of smiles! / Ah lovely Babe! in thee myself I scan – / Thou weepest! sure those Tears proclaim thee Man!' There are other, minor differences in the first ten lines between this version and the printed text.

14 'Whose kindly Heavings lull thy cares to Rest' (*1797*).

15 *Man's breathing Miniature!* Cf. Wordsworth's 'Ode: Intimations of Immortality from Recollections of Early Childhood' 85–6, 109–10.

19 *tetchy* irritable, touchy; in *1797* STC substituted 'fretful'.

22 *Seraph* Cf. 'Rime of the Ancyent Marinere' (1798) 517 ff.

To the Rev. W. J. Hort, while teaching a young lady some song-tunes on his flute

First published in *1796*, from which the present text is derived; not included by STC in any subsequent collection. The 1795 date of composition in *1893*, *1912* and *Everyman* is conjectural. W. J. Hort (only the initials 'W.J.H.' are given in the *1796* title) was a teacher in the school of Dr John Prior Estlin, a famous Unitarian and a friend and supporter of STC.

14 *correctly wild* with a wildness appropriate to lyric intensity and in keeping with the formal demands of the music.

15–24 Cf. the vision of the 'damsel with a dulcimer' near the end of 'Kubla Khan' 37–54. In both poems the focus of inspiration shifts from male poet to female musician. The 'rude romantic glen' in this poem (18) also anticipates 'that deep romantic chasm' in 'Kubla Khan'.

Sonnet ('Sweet Mercy! how my very heart has bled')

First published in *1796*; included by STC in 'Sheet of Sonnets' and in all subsequent collections except *1817*. In the *1796* table of contents the title is 'To an Old Man; it is 'Sonnet VI' in *1797*, 'Sonnet V' in *1803*, 'Sonnet X' in *1828*, *1829*, *1834*. The 1795 date of composition in *1893*, *1912* and *Everyman* is conjectural. In a letter to Thelwall of 13 November 1796 STC said: 'I was glad to hear . . . that you abhor the morality of my Sonnet to Mercy – it is indeed detestable & the poetry is not above mediocrity' (*L* 1: 254).

5 *My Father!* STC's actual father died in 1781.
9 *My Sara* STC's wife.
11 *purple* noble, aristocratic.
13 *Lazars* beggars afflicted with disease, lepers; see the parable of the rich man and the beggar Lazarus in Luke xvi.

To the Nightingale

First published in *1796*; included in *1803*, from which the present text is derived. The date of composition is conjecturally set at 1795 in *1893*, *1912* and *Everyman*. Many features of this poem are reworked and incorporated into 'The Nightingale', first published in *LB*.

1 *Philomel* mythological name for the nightingale, based on the name of the young woman Philomela who is transformed into a nightingale (most famously in Ovid's *Metamorphoses*).
4 *kennell'd* washed into a small channel or gutter.
17 *'Most musical, most melancholy'* The phrase is from Milton's 'Il Penseroso' 62; cf. STC's use of it in the later nightingale poem (13), along with his own note.
21 *What time* at which time (a Miltonic locution).

Lines composed while climbing the left ascent of Brockley Coomb, Somersetshire, May, 1795

First published in *1796*; included by STC in all subsequent collections except *1817*. In *1797* it is headed 'Sonnet V', in *1803* 'Sonnet XIV': structurally it is a Shakespearian sonnet with an unfortunate extra couplet at the end. Otherwise, the specificity of landscape description in this poem, finely adjusted to the sonnet movement, marks a fresh departure in STC's verse.

1 *reverted* turned back.
5 *scour* run quickly.
7 *deep* 'forc'd' in all versions prior to *1834*.
13 *cots* cottages.

Lines in the Manner of Spenser

First published in *1796*; included by STC in all collections except *1817*. A 1795 date of composition is conjectured in *1893*, *1912* and *Everyman*. The imitation here of Edmund Spenser's stanza form and artificially archaic diction ('withouten', 'yplucked') in *The Faerie Queene* (1590–96) is partly comic.

2 *olive tree* The speaker is looking to appease 'Sara's frowns' (5).
9 *recreant wight* unfaithful person.
11 Filled with thoughts of the beautiful being from whom I was separated.
12 *willow* traditionally associated with sadness, weeping.
17 'Like snowdrop opening to the solar ray' (*1796*).

23 *ken her altered mien* know her altered demeanour, her different attitude.
24 *ambushed* in the older sense of lying in wait to attack.
43 *living image of* actual person represented in.

To the Author of Poems published anonymously at Bristol in September 1795

First published in *1796* (Epistle IV); included in the Supplement to *1797* and in *1803*, on which the present text is based. The *1797* title and an *1803* footnote identify the 'Author' as Joseph Cottle, the Bristol bookseller and poet who published *1796*, *1797* and *LB*. In the 'Advertisement' to the Supplement of *1797*, STC explains why he included this poem among those which he finally decided not to exclude from the second edition: 'The first in order of the verses which I have thus endeavoured to reprieve from immediate oblivion was originally addressed "To the Author of Poems published anonymously at Bristol". A second edition of these poems has lately appeared with the Author's name prefixed: and I could not refuse myself the gratification of seeing the name of that man among my poems without whose kindness they would probably have remained unpublished; and to whom I know myself greatly and variously obliged, as a Poet, a man, and a Christian.' This poem is written in Spenserian stanzas; cf. 'Lines in the Manner of Spenser' above.

1 *Unboastful Bard!* 'My honor'd friend' (*1797*).
3 *'never-sere'* Cf. Milton's 'Lycidas' 2 ('with Ivy never sere').
29 *th' unfinish'd wreath* 'War, a Fragment' (STC's note) – the first of Cottle's poems to which STC here refers. The figure of the poem as garland or wreath is traditional.
30 *that holier chaplet* 'John the Baptist, a poem' (STC's note); a chaplet is a wreath for the dead.
32 *your Henderson* 'Monody on John Henderson' (STC's note).
42 *Pomona* Roman goddess of fruit, wife of Vertumnus.

The Production of a Young Lady, addressed to the author of the poems alluded to in the preceding epistle

First published in *1796*; not included by STC in any subsequent collection. The poem is signed 'Sara' in *1796*, but in the supplement to the 1847 edition of *BL*, STC's daughter (also Sara) says that her mother (Sara Fricker Coleridge) told her that she 'wrote but little' of this poem. There is a revised transcript of lines 1–60 in the hand of Sara Fricker, and of lines 61–4 in the hand of Joseph Cottle, signed and dated by Sara Fricker 17 August 1795, in the Rugby MS. In both *1893* and *1912* the title is 'The Silver Thimble'.

9 *viewless* invisible.
12 *Faery* specifically, the realm of British legend and myth represented in Spenser's *The Faerie Queene* (see 'Lines in the Manner of Spenser').
26 *cerulean* sky-blue.

29–46 The story of Arachne, the woman who challenged Pallas Athene to a weaving contest and was punished by the goddess, committed suicide, and eventually transformed into a spider, is told in Ovid's *Metamorphoses* and elsewhere.

48 *vestal* chaste, pure; in ancient Roman religion the vestal virgins were the king's daughters of the regal period, charged with preserving the fire in the Temple of Vesta.

53 *enthusiast* enthusiastic, lit. inspired or possessed by a god.

55–6 Reference to John the Baptist; see 'To the Author of Poems' 30–1 above.

Effusion XXXV. Composed August 20th, 1795, at Clevedon, Somersetshire

This is the earliest printed version of 'The Eolian Harp'. See headnote and notes to that poem below.

The Eolian Harp

First published in *1796* (see preceding text); included by STC in all subsequent collections. Because this is one of STC's most important and influential poems, and because its textual history is particularly complicated, both the earliest printed version and the version that appeared in *1817* and later editions are given in this edition (the later text is that of *1834*). The famous passage about 'the one Life' (26–33) in the later version was first printed among the Errata at the beginning of *1817*. The date given in the title of the *1796* version, 20 August 1795, indicates that STC originally wrote the poem before his marriage to Sara Fricker on 4 October of that year. An eolian harp, also called a wind-harp (it is named after Eolus or Aeolus, classical god of the winds), is a rectangular sounding box with eight or ten strings across its open side; when placed in a strong flow of air it produces musical sounds. Compare STC's use of the figure in the first stanza of 'Ode to the Departing Year' and in the first and seventh stanzas of 'Dejection: An Ode'. In the later version of this poem the figurative status of the harp shifts as it is variously associated with 'Sara' (12–19), with the speaker (40–3) and with 'all of animated nature' (44–8). The five verse paragraphs in the later version correspond to the number in Wordsworth's 'Tintern Abbey', which was clearly influenced by the *1796* version and which in turn influenced STC's later revisions. Line references for the following notes are to the *1834* text.

3 *cot* cottage.

5 *meet* fitting. This line was omitted in *1803*.

7 *star of eve* Venus.

8 This line also was omitted in *1803*.

11 *stilly* still, quiet. *1803* reads 'Hark!' the still murmur of the distant sea'.

12 *And that simplest lute* 'And th' Eolian lute' (*1803*).

13 Omitted in *1803*.

18 *sequacious* following one another in connected, pliant order. The specifically moral meaning of the word – slavishly compliant – may have some bearing on the imagery of lines 14–20.

21–33 Lines 21–9 were omitted in *1803*; line 20 is followed by the following version of 30–3: 'Methinks it should have been impossible / Not to love all things in a world like this, / Where even the breezes, and the common air, / Contain the power and spirit of Harmony.' Lines 26–33 in their present form, first printed in the Errata to *1817* (except that 'her instrument' is 'its instrument'), were first included within the text in *1828*.

26 *O the one life* Cf. Wordsworth, 'Tintern Abbey' 49: 'We see into the life of things'.

47 *Plastic* giving form or shape, creative; cf. 'To the Rev. W. L. Bowles' 11–14 and note.

Intellectual apprehended only by the intellect or understanding; non-material, spiritual.

55 *unregenerate* sinful, wicked, bad.

60 In *1796*, and again in *1797* and *1803*, STC included as a note on this line a quotation from *Appel à l'impartiale posterité* (*Appeal to Impartial Posterity*), Part III, p. 67, by 'Citoyenne Roland' (Madame Roland, 1754–93, a leader of the Girondists during the French Revolution, executed by the Jacobins): 'L'athée n'est point à mes yeux un faux esprit; je puis vivre avec lui aussi bien et mieux qu'avec le dévot, car il raisonne davantage, mais il lui manque un sens, et mon âme ne se fond point entièrement avec la sienne: il est froid au spectacle le plus ravissant, et il cherche un syllogisme lorsque je rends une action de grâce' ('In my eyes the atheist is not in the least a false person; I can live with him, as well as, and better than the devout, for he reasons further; but he lacks a certain sense and my mind does not blend entirely with his: he is cold to the most ravishing spectacle and he looks for a syllogism when I return a thanksgiving').

63 *Wildered* bewildered; lost, perplexed.

Lines written at Shurton Bars, near Bridgewater, September, 1795, in answer to a letter from Bristol

First published in *1796* under the general heading *Poetical Epistles*; included by STC in all subsequent collections except *1817*. There is a fair copy in the Rugby MS. The four-line motto or epigraph, although signed 'Anon.', is assumed by Campbell to be STC's own composition (*1893* 577 n.). It was omitted in *1797* and *1803*. Bristol was the home of STC's fiancée Sara Fricker (they were married in October 1795) and of her sister Edith, who was living there with her husband, Robert Southey; the second and third stanzas refer to STC's estrangement from Southey at this time and to consequently strained feelings between the two sisters. In *1797* and *1803* the poem is titled 'Ode to Sara, Written at Shurton Bars'.

5 'The expression "green radiance" is borrowed from Mr Wordsworth, a Poet whose versification is occasionally harsh and his diction too frequently obscure; but whom I deem unrivalled among the writers of the present day in manly sentiment, novel imagery, and vivid colouring' (STC, *1796* and *1797*). 'Green radiance' appears in Wordsworth's *An Evening Walk* (1793) 268. In a copy of *1797* STC later wrote, under the note quoted above, 'This note was written before I had ever seen Mr Wordsworth, *atque utinam opera ejus tantum noveram*' (quoted in *1893* 577 n.).

22 *untenanting* giving up residence in.

30 *viewless* invisible; cf. 'Monody on the Death of Chatterton' 138 and note above.

31–4 There are echoes here of 'The Eolian Harp', written the previous month.

33 *In bold ambitious sweep* 'With broad impetuous sweep' (*1797*, *1803*).

37 *the channelled Isle* 'The Holmes, in the Bristol Channel' (STC).

41 *tar* sailor.

53 *uncouth* in the older sense of strange, unknown.

80 *my kisses chaste and meek* Cf. 'The Eolian Harp' 5, '(Meet emblems they of Innocence and Love!)'.

85 *shapings* Cf. 'The Eolian Harp' 55, 'These shapings of the unregenerate mind'.

91–6 In *1796* and *1797* STC included a note on this passage: 'Light *from plants*. In Sweden a very curious phenomenon has been observed on certain flowers, by M. Haggern, lecturer in natural history. One evening he perceived a faint flash of light repeatedly dart from a marigold. Surprised at such an uncommon appearance, he resolved to examine it with attention; and, to be assured it was no deception of the eye, he placed a man near him, with orders to make a signal at the moment when he observed the light. They both saw it constantly at the same moment.

'The light was most brilliant on marigolds of an orange or flame colour; but scarcely visible on pale ones. The flash was frequently seen on the same flower two or three times in quick succession; but more commonly at intervals of several minutes; and when several flowers in the same place emitted their light together, it could be observed at a considerable distance.

'This phenomenon was remarked in the months of July and August at sun-set, and for half an hour when the atmosphere was clear; but after a rainy day, or when the air was loaded with vapours nothing of it was seen.

'The following flowers emitted flashes, more or less vivid, in their order:–

'1. The marigold, *galendula* [sic] *officinalis*.

2. Monk's hood, *tropaelum* [sic] *majus*.

3. The orange-lily, *lilium bulliferum*.

4. The Indian pink, *tagetes patula et erecta*.

'From the rapidity of the flash, and other circumstances, it may be conjectured that there is something of electricity in this phenomenon.'

The entire stanza, and of course the note, were omitted in *1803*; the stanza was replaced, without the note, in *1828*, *1829* and *1834*.

Reflections on Having Left a Place of Retirement

First published in the *Monthly Magazine* for October 1796; included by STC in *1797* and in all subsequent collections. The original title was 'Reflections on entering into active life. A Poem which affects not to be Poetry'. The motto, from Horace's *Satires* I.iv.42, means 'more akin to prose'; it was added in *1797* and signals STC's move towards a more informal and conversational style. The Coleridges left the cottage near Clevedon, celebrated in 'The Eolian Harp', in the spring of 1796. The two poems are in many respects companion pieces and share numerous descriptive details (the cottage surrounded by myrtle and jasmine, the sound of the sea in the distance).

1 *Cot* cottage.
12 *Bristowa's* Bristol's. The language in lines 12–14 referring to the merchant's 'thirst of idle gold' being supplanted momentarily by 'wiser feelings' is not in the *Monthly Magazine* version; Empson and Pirie criticize the later versions for making this 'wealthy son of commerce' too obvious a 'moral exemplum' (*Coleridge's Verse*, p. 219 n.).
19–20 *viewless* Cf. 'Monody on the Death of Chatterton' 138 and note.
25 *When the soul seeks to hear* Cf. 'Dejection: An Ode' 47–8: '. . . we receive but what we give, / And in our life alone does Nature live'.
31 *spot* here a verb.
36 *Channel* the Bristol Channel.
40 *Seemed imaged* 'Was imaged' (*Monthly Magazine*); Empson and Pirie comment that 'Later editions made the pantheism more tentative' (*Coleridge's Verse*, p. 219 n.).
49 *Howard's eye* John Howard (1726–90), prison reformer, died in Russia while tending the sick during one of his surveys of prisons.
55 'Seizes my Praise, when I reflect on those' (*1797, 1803, 1817*; the present version of this line was first introduced in Errata to *1817*.
70–1 These lines were omitted in *1803*.

On Donne's Poetry

First published in *LR* (1836) 1: 148. Beer dates the earliest version of this epigram '1795 or after' (*Everyman* 100). STC's marginalium in a copy of *1817* suggests a date at least as early as August 1798: 'This [comment of Lamb's on some lines in 'Human Life'] reminds me of some lines I wrote after leaving Stowey, in a poetic Epistle to my Friend, T. Poole: describing my our pursuits and conversation' [quotes a variant of the epigram; see *Marginalia* 2: 16 and n. in *CC*].

4 *Furnace* 'fire-blast' (*LR*); *Mangle-press* 'meaning's' (*LR*).

The Hour When We shall Meet Again

First published in *The Watchman* for 17 March 1796; included by STC in *1797* and *1803* (the present text derives from the latter edition). Conjecturally dated 1795 in *1893* and *1912*, 1796 in *Everyman*. In their note on this poem in *1852*, Derwent and Sara Coleridge say that it was written 'in half-mockery of [Erasmus] Darwin's style with its *dulcia vitia* [sweet corruption]' (p. 885; the reference is to the heroic couplets in Darwin's *The Loves of the Plants*, 1789).

2 *Turtles* turtle-doves.
3 *traces* ropes or straps, attached to a draught animal's collar, by which the vehicle is drawn.

The Destiny of Nations

First published in *1817*; included with successive minor alterations in *1828*, *1829*, *1834*. Some 361 lines of the earliest version of the poem were originally drafted in the autumn of 1794 (see George Whalley, 'Coleridge, Southey, and "Joan of Arc" ', *Notes & Queries* 199 [1954], pp. 67–9, and Morton D. Paley, 'Coleridge's "Preternatural Agency" ', *European Romantic Review* 1 [1991], pp. 135–43) and were included in Book II of Robert Southey's *Joan of Arc, An Epic Poem* (1796). A copy of Southey's poem annotated by STC is in the Berg Collection, New York Public Library. Much of the remaining poem in its *1817* version exists in drafts written in 1796 and intended to be part of a poem – variously titled *The Progress of Liberty*, *The Vision of the Maid of Orleans*, *Visions of the Maid of Orleans*, *Visions of the Maid of Arc*, *The Vision of the Patriot Maiden* – which was to appear in *1797*; see STC's letters to Thomas Poole of 13 December 1796 (*L* 1: 275) and to John Thelwall of 17 December 1796 (*L* 1: 285). For variant drafts from 1796 never included in published texts, see *1912* Appendix I.C.

It was Lamb's sharp criticism of the poem in a letter of 5 January 1797, together with STC's own 'anxieties and . . . slothfulness' (see his letters to Joseph Cottle of early February and late June 1797 [*L* 1: 309, 329]), that kept the rest of the poem from appearing in *1797*. STC did publish 148 lines of this version, beginning with what became line 127 of the *1817* text ('If there be beings of higher class than Man'), as a separate poem under the title 'The Visions of the Maid of Orleans. A Fragment, by S. T. Coleridge' in the *Morning Post* for 26 December 1797. For variants between this published 'Fragment' and the *1817* text of 'The Destiny of Nations' see David V. Erdman, 'Unrecorded Coleridge Variants', *Studies in Bibliography* 11 (1958), pp. 144–53. It is unclear just when STC returned to the drafts and to his contribution to Southey's *Joan of Arc* and combined them to produce the unfinished poem that appeared in *1817*. In a copy of Southey's *Joan of Arc* annotated by STC in 1814 he claims to have authored several passages in Books I, III and IV of the poem; see *Index* CoS 98. These annotations were first published in the *North British Review* 40 (January 1864), pp. 78–92 and are reproduced in *1893* 585–6 and in *1912* Appendix I.D.

A letter to J. J. Morgan of 16 June 1814 contains these broader judgments of his and Southey's writing in *Joan of Arc*: 'I looked over the 5 first Books . . . yesterday, at [Thomas] Hood's request, in order to mark the lines written by me. – I was really astonished, 1. at the school-boy wretched Allegoric Machinery – 2. at the transmogrification of the fanatic Virago into a modern novel-pawing Proselyte of the age of Reason, a Tom Paine in Petticoats, but *so* lovely! – & in love, moreover: . . . 3. at the utter want of all rhythm in the verse, the monotony & dead *plumb down* of the Pauses – & the absence of all Bone, Muscle, and Sinew in the single Lines' (*L* 3: 510). Yet in Ch. I of *BL* STC says: '. . . the compositions of my twenty-fourth and twenty-fifth year (*ex. gr.* the shorter blank verse poems, the lines which are now adopted in the introductory part of the VISION in the present collection in Mr. Southey's Joan of Arc, 2nd book, 1st edition, and the Tragedy of REMORSE) are not more below my present ideal in respect of the general tissue of the style, than those of the latest date' (1: 25–6). In an annotated copy of *1828*, which contains some specific comments included here in the notes,

STC says at the end: '*N.B.* – Within 12 months after the writing of this Poem, my bold Optimism, and Necessitarianism, together with the Infra, seu plusquam-Socinianism, down to which, step by step, I had *un*believed, gave way to the day-break of a more genial and less shallow system. But I contemplate with pleasure these Phases of my Transition. – S. T. Coleridge.'

1 In *Joan of Arc* Part II what eventually became the poem's opening lines begin differently: 'No more of Usurpation's doom'd defeat . . '

5–6 'Beneath whose shadowy banners wide unfurl'd / Justice leads forth her tyrant-quelling hosts' (*Joan of Arc*, *1817*). In *1828* and *1829* these lines are replaced by a single line, 'THE WILL, THE WORD, THE BREATH, THE LIVING GOD'; in *1834* STC expands this characterization of God into two lines as in the present text. On God as 'the infinite I AM', see *BL* XIII.

10 *Brutus and Leonidas* Lucius Junius Brutus (not Marcus Junius Brutus, one of the conspirators who overthrew Julius Caesar) led the liberation of Rome from the Tarquin kings and helped found the Roman republic in 510 BC. Leonidas was king of Sparta and commander of Greek forces in the Battle of Thermopylae.

12 *Man's* 'Earth's' (*1817*, *1828*, *1829*).

17 *Effulgent* shining, radiant.

19 *one mighty alphabet* The idea of the physical world as divinely authored text is recurrent in STC's verse and philosophical prose. e.g. 'Frost at Midnight' 60–2 and '[Lines from a Notebook – July 1807]' 27.

20–3 The allusion here is to the allegory of the cave in Book VII of Plato's *Republic*.

23 *The substance from its shadow* 'Things from their shadows' (*Joan of Arc*). STC made other changes in the last lines of this verse paragraph in the successive versions of the poem; see *1912* 1: 132 n.

24 *latence* latency, the condition of being obscured or concealed.

31 There is a long note on this line in *Joan of Arc* attacking Newton and Hartley. STC never reprinted it.

32 *impacts* Cf. *BL* VIII (1: 133): '. . . in any given perception there is something which has been communicated to [the mind] by an impact, or an impression ab extra'.

36 *properties* attributes, qualities (here, of the physical world).

37 This line, omitted in *Joan of Arc*, refers to the arguments of Berkeley and other radical idealist philosophers against the existence of a material world distinct from mind.

46 This line is not in *Joan of Arc*; cf. *BL* XIII and STC's idea of 'the infinite I AM'; also 'Religious Musings' 106, 415.

47 *Monads* individual elementary units of being, fundamentally psychical or spiritual in their identities but underlying material reality as well. The term is especially important in the philosophy of Leibniz (1646–1716), though it does not appear in the quotations from Leibniz used by STC at the beginning of *BL* XIII. STC's use of the concept in fact differs importantly from Leibniz's. He offers a philosophical alternative here to the doctrines of Newton and Hartley attacked in 31–5.

54 *volleying* rushing, rolling vehemently ahead.

61 *train up* lead up in a train.

62 *unconfirmed for day* unable to see in the full light (of truth).

68 *Boreal Morn* the Northern Lights or Aurora Borealis, also known as the False Morn.

70 *Niemi lake* lake in the Alban Hills in Italy.

71 'Balda-Zhiok, i.e. mons altitudinis, the highest mountain in Lapland'. This and STC's other notes quoted below, unless otherwise indicated, appeared in *Joan of Arc*, then in *1817* and subsequent editions.

72 ' "Solfar-kapper: capitium Solfar, hic locus omnium, quotquot veterum Lapponum superstitio sacrificiisque religiosoque cultui dedicavit, celebratissimus erat, in parte sinus australis situs, semimilliaris spatio a mari distans. Ipse locus, quem curiositatis gratia aliquando me invisisse memini, duabus praealtis lapidibus, sibi invicem oppositis, quorum alter musco circumdatus erat, constabat". – LEEMIUS, *De Lapponibus* ("Cape Solfar, this place was the most frequented of all that superstition dedicated to the Lapps' sacrifices and religious worship, situated on the southern side of the bay, about half a mile from the sea. The place itself, which I remember I once visited out of curiosity, consisted of two very high stones, facing each other, one of them covered with moss".)' In this and later notes STC quotes Knud Leem, or Leemius (1697–1774), *De Lapponibus Finmarchiae*.

74 'The Lapland women carry their infants at their back in a piece of excavated wood, which serves them for a cradle. Opposite to the infant's mouth there is a hole for it to breathe through . . .' STC extends this note with another Latin quotation from Leemius, *De Lapponibus*.

80 *Fancy* STC had not yet developed the theoretical distinction between Fancy and Imagination so prominent in *BL* XIII.

81 *unsensualizes* renders independent of the senses or of bodily desire.

91 *uncouth* crude or primitive, but also with the older sense of unknowing.

95 *unutterable shape* 'Jaibme Aibmo' (STC's note).

98 *Greenland Wizard* See STC's note on line 110.

99–100 Between these lines the following appear in *Joan of Arc*, *1817*, *1828*, *1829*: '(Where live the innocent as far from cares / As from the storms and overwhelming waves / Dark tumbling on the surface of the deep.)'

103 *Fury Form* See note to line 110. The *OED* cites a later example (1866) of the combination 'fury-form'. 'Fury' was used since Chaucer to designate the Eumenides, the avenging goddesses with snakes in their hair of classical mythology, and more generally any ferociously angry or malignant woman (*OED*).

105 This line does not appear in *Joan of Arc*.

110 'They call the Good Spirit, Torngarsuck. The other great but malignant spirit is a nameless Female; she dwells upon the sea in a great house, where she can detain in captivity all the animals of the ocean by her magic power. When a death befalls the Greenlanders, an Angekok or magician must undertake a journey thither: he passes through the kingdom of souls, over an horrible abyss into the palace of this phantom, and by his enchantments causes the captive creatures to ascend directly to the surface of the ocean. – See [David] *Crantz's History of Greenland*, vol. i.206' (STC's note).

124 *Bethabra* Betharabah or Bethabara, city in Palestine where John began baptizing (John i: 28). There is an allusion to the spreading of the word of God emphasized at the beginning of this gospel ('In the beginning was the Word . . . And the light shineth in darkness . . .').

127 STC's poem on Joan of Arc of 1796–7 began with this line.

138 *that warrior-maid of France* Joan of Arc (1412?–31), the spiritually inspired young woman who came to the aid of the future King Charles VII and led French forces in the defence of Orleans and other towns against the English during the Hundred Years War.

144 *doomed* destined, ordained.

150 *sweltry* sweating.

164 *front* forehead.

165 *flexile* flexible.

189 *predoomed* predetermined.

192 *unconcerning* indifferent; or perhaps unimportant, not concerning or pertaining.

194 *Neufchatel['s]* city in north-west Switzerland.

204 *thwart wain* wagon or cart resting across the road.

233 *husbandman* farmer.

242 *clipped* encircled closely, embraced; also, perhaps, cut.

255 *startful* apt to start, skittish.

278 The note in square brackets preceding this line is STC's and appears in the early printed text, as here. *1912* quotes STC's MS note on the following passage: 'These are very fine Lines, tho' I say it, that should not; but, hang me, if I know or ever did know the meaning of them, tho' my own composition.'

283–4 Cf. *Paradise Lost* I. 20–1: '[the Holy Spirit] with mighty wings outspread / Dove-like sat'st brooding on the vast abyss'.

285 *pestful* pestiferous, pest-bearing.

290 *Protoplast* the first-made thing or being of its kind; the first created human being.

295 *Gehenna's massy roots* In Jewish history, Gehenna is the Valley of Hinnon near Jerusalem where some of the Israelites sacrificed their children to Moloch, and which was therefore regarded as a place of abomination. In the New Testament it is identified with Hell.

296 *beldam* an aged woman.

301 *uncouth* in the older sense of unknown.

306 *evening hind* the farmworker at evening.

308 *plaining* complaining.

314 *tyrants* 'Monarchs' in *Joan of Arc, 1817, 1828, 1829*. See *1912* 1: 141 for an additional passage that follows this line in *Joan of Arc*.

316 *dam* mother, female parent (usually of animals).

319 *Ague, the biform hag* Ague is a malarial fever characterized by a succession of chills and fever (hence 'biform').

320 See *1912* 1: 142 n. for an additional passage that follows this line in *Joan of Arc*.

334 *white-robed* 'Rev. vi. 9, 11. – And when he had opened the fifth seal, I saw under the altar the souls of them that were slain for the word of God, and for the testimony which they held. And white robes were given unto every one of them, and it was said unto them, that they should rest for a little season, until their fellow servants also and their brethren, that should be killed as they were, should be fulfilled' (STC's note in *1817, 1828, 1829*).

335 *gratulant* expressing joy or satisfaction, congratulatory.

338 *confused* here either an adjective or a verb.

340 *relique* relic; that which is left behind; *1817* has 'relict'.

363 *precursive* preceding, as the harbinger or messenger of something.

369 'Like hideous features blended with the clouds' (*1817*). An Errata note on this line in *1817* says 'for "*blended*", &c., read "*looming on the mist*" '; 'booming on the mist' in *1834* is clearly a misprint. In *Joan of Arc* the passage corresponding to 369–71 reads: 'His hideous features blended with the mist, / The long black locks of SLAUGHTER. PEACE beheld . . .'

372 *reverted* turned back.

378–9 The present text of these lines is first given in an emendation in the Errata of *1817*. In *Joan of Arc* the lines read: 'The name of JUSTICE written on thy brow / Resplendent shone . . .' STC's 'name all light' here may be a source for Shelley, *The Triumph of Life* 352–3: ' "A shape all light, which with one hand did fling / Dew on the earth . . .' (notice that STC's figure 'flings the cool drops on a feverous cheek', 386).

384 'A grievous defect here is the rhyme recalling assonance of Peace, sweet, eve, cheek. Better thus:– Sweet are thy Songs, O Peace! lenient of care' (STC's MS note in a copy of *1828*).

388–93 'Southeyan. To be omitted' (STC's MS note in a copy of *1828*).

389 'A vile line' (STC's MS note in a copy of *1829*; he underlined the word 'foul' in this line).

410 *Bothnic* Bothnian, an area above the northern part of the Baltic Sea between Sweden and Finland.

412 *Leviathan* a mythical sea creature, frequently mentioned in the Bible and in Hebrew poetry.

417 *skin* form a skin or scab over.

421 Between this and the next line the following passage appears in *Joan of Arc*: 'A Vapor rose, pierc'd by the MAIDEN'S eye. / Guiding its course OPPRESSION sate within, / With terror pale and rage, yet laugh'd at times / Musing on Vengeance: trembled in his hand / A Sceptre fiercely-grasp'd. O'er Ocean westward . . .' STC wrote the following MS note after the second line of this passage: 'These images imageless, these *Small-Capitals* constituting themselves Personifications, I despised even at that time; but was forced to introduce them, to preserve the connection with the machinery of the Poem, previously adopted by Southey.'

426 *incumbent* lying or resting upon, pressing its weight upon.

435 *the healing God* 'The Apollo Belvedere' (STC's note). Apollo established his oracle at Delphi by killing the 'Huge Python' (437) that guarded the shrine of Mother Earth previously located there.

437–8 'Shriek'd AMBITION's ghastly throng / And with them those the locust Fiends that crawl'd . . .' (*Joan of Arc*). STC's MS note on this variant: ' – if Locusts how could they *shriek*? I must have caught the contagion of *unthinkingness*.'

445 *Eboe, or Koromantyn's plain* 'Eboe' ('Ibo') is the name of a group of tribes living along the lower Niger River in West Africa; 'Koromantyn' or 'Kormantyne' was a village in the central province of what used to be called the Gold Coast (now Ghana); many people from both areas were forced into slavery and taken to the West Indies and America. STC's own note on this passage is as follows: 'The Slaves in the West-Indies consider death as a passport to their native country. This sentiment is thus expressed in the introduction to a Greek Prize-Ode on the Slave Trade, of which the thoughts are better than the language in which they are conveyed.' STC here quotes the first four stanzas of his ode on the slave trade (1792; see Appendix 1), followed by this 'Literal Translation': 'Leaving the gates of darkness, O Death! hasten thou to a race yoked with misery! Thou wilt not be received with lacerations of cheeks, nor with funeral ululation – but with circling dances and the joy of songs. Thou art terrible indeed, yet thou swellest with Liberty, stern Genius! Borne on the dark pinions over the swelling of Ocean, they return to their native country. There, by the side of fountains beneath citron-groves, the lovers tell to their beloved what horrors, being men, they had endured from men.'

461 'Tho' these lines may bear a sane sense, yet they are easily, and more naturally interpreted with a very false and dangerous one. But I was at that time one of the *Mongrels*, the Josephidites [Josephides, the sons of Joseph], a proper name of distinction from those who believe *in*, as well as believe Christ the only begotten Son of the Living God before all Time' (STC's MS note).

463 *Love* 'Law' (*Joan of Arc*).

467 *predooming* prejudging.

470–4 These lines were originally lines 136–40 of Book II of *Joan of Arc*.

Religious Musings

First published in *1796*; included by STC in all subsequent collections except *1817*. Lines 260–357 were published in *The Watchman* for 9 March 1796 (*1796* was issued during the same month), under the title 'The Present State of Society'. Although the sub-title says that STC began the poem on Christmas Eve 1794, it is evident that he continued working on it into early 1796; in fact Joseph Cottle says that much of the poem was written while *1796* was being printed, some of it after everything in the volume except 'Religious Musings' was in type. STC altered the text of the poem and his own notes on it many times between *1796* and *1834*. There is a revised fair copy in the Rugby MS. In *1796*, *1797* and *1803* he prefixed the following lines, adapted from the First Book of Mark Akenside's *The Pleasures of Imagination* (1744, 1757; retitled *The Pleasures of the Imagination* in *Poems*, 1772):

> What tho' first,
> In years unseason'd, I attun'd the lay
> To idle Passion and unreal Woe?
> Yet serious Truth her empire o'er my song
> Hath now asserted; Falsehood's evil brood,
> Vice and deceitful Pleasure, she at once
> Excluded, and my Fancy's careless toil
> Drew to the better cause!

These three early editions also included, on a separate page, the following 'Argument': 'Introduction. Person of Christ. His prayer on the Cross. The process of his Doctrines on the mind of the Individual. Character of the Elect. Superstition. Digression to the present War. Origin and Uses of government and Property. The present State of Society. The French Revolution. Millenium. Universal

Redemption. Conclusion.' STC wrote to his friend John Thelwall, political radical and religious sceptic, in late April 1796: 'I build all my poetic pretensions on the Religious Musings, – which you will read with a POET'S Eye, with the same unprejudicedness, I wish, I could add, the same pleasure, with which the atheistic Poem of Lucretius. A Necessitarian, I cannot possibly disesteem a man for his religious or anti-religious Opinions – and as an *Optimist*, I feel diminished concern. – I have studied the subject deeply & widely – I cannot say, without prejudice: for when I commenced the Examination, I was an Infidel' (*L* 1: 205). The war between Britain and France, which began in 1794, and the continuing slave trade are the key historical influences on STC's poetic rethinking of conventional Christianity.

48–9 Adore Him as Nature's essence, etc. The grammar in this verse paragraph and throughout the poem is influenced by the compressed Latinate style of *Paradise Lost*.

55–6 For they dare to recognize that what may seem deformed is also the work of the Supreme Being alone.

58 *educing* bringing forth, eliciting.

64 *Who* those who. Many sections of this verse paragraph were substantially revised and expanded in *1803*. In place of lines **65–71** in the present text, for instance, *1803* reads:

> a VISION gathers in my soul,
> Voices and shadowy shapes! In human guise
> I seem to see the phantom, FEAR, pass by,
> Hotly-pursued, and pale! From rock to rock
> He bounds with bleeding feet, and thro' the swamp,
> The quicksand and the groaning wilderness,
> Struggles with feebler and yet feebler flight.
> But lo! an altar in the wilderness,
> And eagerly yet feebly lo! he grasps
> The altar of the living God! and there
> With wan reverted face the trembling wretch
> All wildly list'ning to his Hunter-friends
> Stands, till the last faint echo of their yell
> Dies in the distance. Soon refresh'd from Heaven . . .

79 *immitigable* not capable of being softened or appeased.

84 A note on this line in *1796* selectively quotes Revelation xvi. 1: 'And I heard a great voice out of the Temple saying to the seven Angels, pour out the vials of the wrath of God upon the earth.' The lines in *1796* corresponding to 78–84 in the present text are built around the figure of the 'seven Angels'.

89 'Our evil Passions, under the influence of Religion, become innocent, and may be made to animate our virtue – in the same manner as the thick mist melted by the Sun, increases the light which it had before excluded. In the preceding paragraph, agreeably to this truth, we had allegorically narrated the transfiguration of Fear into holy Awe' (STC's note in *1797, 1803*).

94–104 Compare this simile to Wordsworth's account of the moon flashing through an enveloping fog in the ascent of Snowdon (1805 *Prelude* XIII.39 ff.).

See also STC's own description of the optical phenomenon popularly called a 'Glory' in 'Constancy to an Ideal Object', lines 25-32 below.

106 *Omnific* all-creating; cf. *Paradise Lost* VII. 217.

107 *subliming* transmuting into something higher, more elevated.

113 STC here imagines the perceiving human mind re-enacting, at its own level, God's original act of creation. The idea is developed metaphysically in *BL* XIII and elsewhere in STC's prose.

119-21 The reference to Cain in this difficult passage was omitted in *1803*.

126 *unhelmed* unhelmeted, unprotected – or perhaps unguided, with no one at the helm.

127 *to know ourselves* See headnote to STC's late poem 'Self-Knowledge' below, first published in *1834*.

132-3 *him except / Aught to desire* to desire anything except him. In *1797* and *1803* the following note appeared to the line corresponding to 133 in the present text: 'If to make aught but the Supreme Reality the object of final pursuit, be Superstition; if the attributing of sublime properties to things or persons, which those things or persons neither do or can possess, be Superstition; then Avarice and Ambition are Superstitions: and he who wishes to estimate the evils of Superstition, should transport himself, not to the temple of the Mexican Deities, but to the plains of Flanders, or the coast of Africa. – Such is the sentiment convey'd in this and the subsequent lines.'

139-42 These lines referring to conventional religion's condoning of the slave trade are a condensed revision of the following passage in *1796*:

> But (whether ye th'unclimbing Bigot mock
> With secondary Gods, or if more pleas'd
> Ye petrify th'imbrothell'd Atheist's heart,
> The Atheist your worst slave) I o'er some plain
> Peopled with Death, and to the silent Sun
> Steaming with tyrant-murder'd multitudes;
> Or where mid groans and shrieks loud-laughing TRADE
> More hideous packs his bales of living anguish . . .

See the modern English translation of STC's prize Greek ode on the slave trade in Appendix 1.

147 *disherited* disinherited; cf. line 329.

148-9 Man knows no common centre, no common sire. STC's Latinate style again departs considerably from idiomatic phrasing.

155 *Fancy's wing* STC had not yet developed the distinction between Fancy and Imagination so important in his later philosophical writing (see *BL* XIII).

159 'January 21st, 1794, in the debate on the address to his Majesty, on the speech from the Throne, the Earl of Guildford moved an amendment to the following effect:– "That the House hoped his Majesty would seize the earliest opportunity to conclude a peace with France," &c. This motion was opposed by the Duke of Portland, who "considered the war to be merely grounded on one principle – the preservation of the Christian Religion." May 30th, 1794, the Duke of Bedford moved a number of resolutions, with a view to the establishment of a peace with France. He was opposed (among others) by Lord Abingdon in these remarkable words: "'The best road to Peace, my Lords, is War! and War carried on in the same manner in which we are taught to worship our Creator, namely, with all our souls, and with all our minds, and with all our hearts, and with all our strength"' (STC's note in *1797*, *1803*, *1828*, *1829*, *1834*).

164–5 The reference here is to the elaborate network of domestic spies which the Pitt government developed in the course of the 1790s to detect and punish political activity thought to be sympathetic to the French Revolution.

167 There is no punctuation at the end of this line in *1834*; the exclamation mark in the present text follows *1829* and all previous printings.

171 *that foul Woman of the North* Catherine the Great, Tsarina of Russia, was thought to have ordered the murder of her husband, Peter III, after deposing him.

173 *And he, connatural mind!* Frederick William II of Prussia, Catherine the Great's ally in the exploitative partitioning of Poland in 1793 ('connatural' means 'of the same nature'). STC included the following note at this point in *1796*: 'That Despot who received the wages of an hireling that he might act the part of a swindler, and who skulked from his impotent attacks on the liberties of France to perpetrate more successful iniquity in the plains of *Poland*.'

180 'The Father of the present Prince of Hesse Cassell supported himself and his strumpets at Paris by the vast sums which he received from the British Government during the American War for the flesh of his subjects' (STC's note, *1796*).

185 *Moloch* The rebel angel who counsels 'open war' in *Paradise Lost* II.49 ff.

192 *Lord of unsleeping Love* 'Art thou not from everlasting, O Lord, my God, mine Holy One? We shall not die. O Lord, Thou hast ordained them for judgment, &c. Habakkuk i.12' (STC's note, *1796*, *1828*, *1829*, *1834*). In *1797* and *1803* STC's note added the following to the Biblical quotation: 'In this paragraph the Author recalls himself from his indignation against the instruments of Evil, to contemplate the *uses* of the Evils in the great process of divine Benevolence. In the first age, Men were innocent from ignorance of Vice; they fell, that by the knowledge of consequences they might attain intellectual security, i.e. Virtue, which is a wise and strong-nerv'd Innocence.'

215 'I deem that the teaching of the gospel for hire is wrong; because it gives the teacher an improper bias in favour of particular opinions on a subject where it is of the last importance that the mind should be perfectly unbiased. Such is my private opinion; but I mean not to censure all hired teachers, many among whom I know, and venerate as the best and wisest of men – God forbid that I should think of these, when I use the word PRIEST, a name, after which any other term of abhorrence would appear an anti-climax. By a Priest I mean a man who holding the scourge of power in his right hand and a bible (translated by authority) in his left, doth necessarily cause the bible and the scourge to be associated ideas, and so produces that temper of mind which leads to Infidelity – Infidelity which judging of Revelation by the doctrines and practices of established Churches honours God by rejecting Christ. See "Address to the People". p. 57, sold by Parsons, Peternoster Row' (STC's note, *1796*; the reference at the end is to his own *Conciones ad Populum* of 1795).

223 *blind Ionian* Homer; this line was omitted in *1796* and *1803*.

225 *science* knowledge in a general sense.

234 *patriot Sage* 'Dr Franklin' (STC's note, *1796*).

246 *plastic* Cf. line 405.

249 *the summer noon* during a noontime in summer. Compare the image in 249–51 to Keats, 'To Autumn' 13–15.

257 *gazed* gazed at, looked at. In *1803* 254–55 read: 'The wafted perfumes, gazing on the woods / The many tinted streams and setting sun'.

264 *Their cots' transmuted plunder* the product of their cottage labour exploitatively transformed (into the luxuries of 'pageant Power').

266 *disbranchèd* cut off, severed (like the branches of a tree).

269 *Simoom* A powerful hot wind laden with dust, generated by the deserts and sandy plains of the middle east. STC's *1796* note quotes a long passage from James Bruce's *Travels to discover the source of the Nile* (1790), vol. IV, 557, which reads in part: 'I saw from the S.E. an haze come on, in colour like the purple part of the rainbow, but not so compressed or thick. It did not occupy twenty yards in breadth, and was about twelve feet high from the ground. – We all lay flat on the ground, as if dead, till . . . it was blown over. The meteor, or purple haze . . . was indeed passed; but the light air that still blew was of heat to threaten suffocation.' In the proof-sheets to *1797* STC indicates an addition to this note, never actually printed: 'The Simoon is here introduced as emblematical of the pomp and powers of Despotism.'

275 *Behemoth* 'Behemoth, in Hebrew, signifies wild beasts in general. Some believe it is the elephant, some the hippopotamus; some affirm it is the wild bull. Poetically, it designates any large quadruped' (STC's note in *1797* and subsequent editions through *1834*; a shorter and somewhat different note appears in *1796*).

292 *Lazar-house* a house for the poor and diseased – sometimes, specifically, for lepers.

294–5 'Forc'd or ensnar'd, who swept by Slaughter's scythe / Stern nurse of Vultures! stream in putrid heaps' (*1796*); 'O ye that streaming to the silent Noon, / People with Death red-eyed Ambition's plains!' (*The Watchman*).

302 *stream* 'steam' (*1796*, *The Watchman*, *1797*, *1803*).

304 'See the sixth chapter of the Revelation of St John the Divine. – And I looked and beheld a pale horse; and his name that sat on him was Death, and Hell followed with him. And power was given unto them over the FOURTH part of the Earth to kill with sword, and with hunger, and with pestilence, and with the beasts of the Earth. – And when he had opened the fifth seal, I saw under the altar the souls of them that were slain for the word of God, and for the testimony which they held; and white robes were given unto every one of them; and it was said unto them, that they should rest yet for a little season, until their fellow servants also, and their brethren that should be killed as they were should be fulfilled. And I beheld when he had opened the sixth seal, the stars of Heaven fell unto the Earth, even as a fig-tree casteth her untimely figs when she is shaken of a mighty wind: And the kings of the earth, and the great men, and the rich men, and the chief captains, &c.' (STC's note, *1796*).

315 *the storm begins* 'This passage alludes to the French Revolution: and the subsequent paragraph to the downfall of Religious Establishments. I am convinced that the Babylon of the Apocalypse does not apply to Rome exclusively; but to the union of Religion with Power and Wealth, wherever it is found' (STC's note, *1797* and *1803*; shorter versions of the note appear in *1796* and *1834*). Understanding the French Revolution in terms of biblical apocalypse and millennium was widespread among its English sympathizers during the 1790s.

323 *The abhorred Form* 'And there came one of the seven Angels which had the seven vials, and talked with me, saying unto me, come hither! I will show unto thee the judgment of the great Whore, that sitteth upon many waters: with whom the kings of the earth have committed fornication, &c. Revelation of St. John the Divine, chapter the seventeenth' (STCs note, *1796*). In the Protestant tradition the Whore of Babylon had long been a figure for the corruption of the Roman Catholic Church.

337 *Haunted* 'Hunted' in *1797, 1803, 1828, 1829*.

346-8 'The sapphire-blazing gates of Paradise / Are thrown wide open, and thence voyage forth / Detachments wild of seraph-warbled airs' (*1796, The Watchman*).

349 *amaranth* a mythical flower that never fades.

359 *Thousand Years* 'The Millenium:– in which I suppose, that Man will continue to enjoy the highest glory, of which his human nature is capable.– That all who in past ages have endeavoured to ameliorate the state of man will rise and enjoy the fruits and flowers, the imperceptible seeds of which they had sown in their former Life: and that the wicked will during the same period, be suffering the remedies adapted to their several bad habits. I suppose that this period will be followed by the passing away of this Earth and by our entering the state of pure intellect; when all Creation shall rest from its labours' (STC's note, *1797* and *1803*).

364 *Coadjutors* those who work with and assist others.

Milton's trump the trumpet of Milton's prophetic poetry in its called-for social and religious renovation; cf. Wordsworth's sonnet 'London, 1802' ('Milton! Thou shouldst be living at this hour: / England hath need of thee . . .').

369 *he first who marked the ideal tribes* 'David Hartley' (STC's note, in all editions). Hartley's associationist philosophy was still an important positive influence on STC, who named his first son (born on 19 September 1796) 'David Hartley'. For his later repudiation of Hartley's philosophy, see *BL* VII.

371 *Priestley* See STC's sonnet on Priestley ('Though roused by the dark Vizir Riot rude / Have driven our Priestley o'er the ocean swell') and headnote.

380 'Rev. chap. iv. v.2 and 3. – And immediately I was in the Spirit: and behold, a Throne was set in Heaven and one sat on the Throne. And he that sat was to look upon like a jasper and a sardine stone, &c.' (STC's note, *1797* and subsequent editions).

388 'The final destruction impersonated' (STC's note, *1797* and subsequent editions).

395 'This paragraph is intelligible to those, who, like the Author, believe and feel the sublime system of Berkeley; and the doctrine of the final Happiness of all men' (STC's note, *1797* and *1803*). The idealist philosopher George Berkeley (1685–1753) argued that there is no such thing as a material world separate from mind, that all existing reality is an idea in the mind of God.

400 This line was omitted from *1803*.

402 *Contemplant* contemplating.

408 *Monads* ultimate, absolutely simple units of being; see line 47 of 'The Destiny of Nations' above.

414 *empyreal* of or pertaining to the empyrean, the highest heaven.

From an Unpublished Poem

First published under the present title in *The Watchman* for 25 March 1796; reprinted in *LR* with the following extract from the essay in *The Watchman* 'On the Slave Trade' in which it had been included as part of some opening conjectures on the divine purpose in allowing the existence of evil: 'In my calmer moments I have the firmest Faith that all things work together for Good. But alas! it seems a long and dark Process!' The present text is from *The Watchman* (*CC* 2: 132).

On Observing a Blossom on the First of February, 1796

First published in *The Watchman* for 11 April 1796 as 'Lines on Observing a Blossom . . . , Written near Sheffield'; included in *1797* and all subsequent collections in STC's lifetime. Campbell suggests that the poem records an experience during STC's travels in search of subscribers to *The Watchman* (*1893* 581).

3 *frieze-coated* 'Frieze' is a coarse woollen cloth with a nap on one side, usually of Irish manufacture. 'Frieze-coat' was a common designation for an Irish peasant.
12 *Bristowa's bard* 'Chatterton' (STC's note).
13 *amaranth* in literary tradition, an imaginary flower that never fades.
16 *poor Poland's hope* In 1794 Kosciuszko led an unsuccessful rebellion against the Russians and the Prussians to halt the partition of Poland.
24 *attempered* attuned, harmonized.

Verses addressed to J. Horne Tooke

First published in *The Telegraph* for 9 July 1796, then in *Transactions* of the Philobiblon Society (*1796*). Not collected until *1893*. The present text is based on *1912* but follows more closely the punctuation of the MS version sent in a letter to the Rev. John Prior Estlin, prominent Unitarian and schoolmaster in Bristol, on 4 July 1796 (*L* 1: 224–5). STC introduced the poem to Estlin as follows: 'I shall finish with some Verses which I addressed to Horne Tooke & the Company who met on June 28th to celebrate his Poll. – I begin by alluding to the comparatively small number which he polled in his first contest for Westminster – You must read the lines, two abreast.' John Horne Tooke was a noted philologist and political radical. In 1794 he was tried for treason because of his activities as founder of the Society for Constitutional Information, but acquitted. At the general election of 1796 he stood as a candidate for Westminster and polled 2,819 votes, third behind Charles James Fox (5,160) and Admiral Sir Alan Gardner (4,814). Horne Tooke's most important philological work appears in ΕΠΕΑ ΠΤΕΡΟΕΝΤΑ *[Winged Words], or the Diversions of Purley* (Part I, 1786; Part II, 1798).

1–12 Horne Tooke first stood as a parliamentary candidate for Westminster in the election of 1790; on that occasion he lost to Fox by a very large majority.
13 *breeze-like Spirit* ' "Επεα πτερόεντα' (STC's note in the letter to Estlin); the

Greek phrase, a Homeric locution meaning 'winged words', is part of the title of
Horne Tooke's dialogic treatise on language.

20 *imposthum'd* abscessed.

24 *1912* has 'lightning's flash'; the present reading follows the letter to Estlin.

27–31 Horne Tooke is imagined as appealing to Parliament on behalf of those
who had suffered during the violence of the French Revolution. Belgium was
invaded by the French republican army in September 1792; in the Vendée, a
district in the west of France, a royalist and pro-Catholic insurrection was savagely
suppressed by the republican army. Though he supported many of the political
objectives of the Revolution, Horne Tooke consistently opposed the use of violence
to achieve them. Lines 31–2 are repeated in early editions of 'Ode on the Departing
Year' between lines 83 and 84 of *1834* text followed in this edition.

45–8 'Dundas left thief-takers in Horne Tooke's House for three days – with his
two Daughters *alone*; for Horne Tooke keeps no servant' (STC's note in the letter
to Estlin). Henry Dundas was Home Secretary during the early 1790s and
responsible for spying on and persecuting anti-government activists. Horne Tooke
had two illegitimate daughters, Mary and Charlotte, who lived with him in his
house in Wimbledon. A 'thief-taker' is someone hired to detect and catch thieves.

49 *Rome's 'first consul'* Lucius Junius Brutus, who led the uprising against Tarquin
and liberated Rome; Lucretia (Lucrece), who committed suicide after having been
raped by Tarquin, was of Brutus's family.

On a Late Connubial Rupture in High Life

First published in the *Monthly Magazine* for September 1796 under the present
title (STC first sent the poem to Lamb for publication in the *Morning Chronicle*
in July, but this never materialized). It was reprinted in *Felix Farley's Bristol
Journal* for 8 October 1796 and in the *Poetical Register* for 1806–7, but not
collected until *1877–80*. STC sent the poem in a letter of 4 July 1796 to John
Prior Estlin under the title 'To an unfortunate Princess' (*L* 1: 223–4; this letter
also contains 'Verses Addressed to John Horne Tooke'). The present text, with a
few clarifications in punctuation, follows that in Griggs's edition of the *Letters*.
There is a fair copy in Joseph Cottle's 'Bristol Album' (a collection of some 60
MS texts by various authors, including STC), under the title 'To the Princess
of Wales written during her separation from the Prince' and dated July 1796, and
two additional MS versions (see *Index* CoS 448 and 449). The Prince of Wales,
the future George IV, married Caroline of Brunswick in 1795. The couple
separated in 1796 and Caroline was deprived of her daughter, to whom she had
given birth earlier that year.

8 'Cytherea' is an alternate name for Venus.

11 *The* 'Those' (*Monthly Magazine*).

13 *Then o!* 'O then' (*Monthly Magazine*).

17 *could* 'might' (*Monthly Magazine*).

18 *thy* 'the' (*Farley's Bristol Journal*).

20 *bosom'd* 'meeting' (*Monthly Magazine*).

Sonnet written on receiving letters informing me of the birth of a Son,
I being at Birmingham

First published in the 'Biographical Supplement' to *BL* (1847); collected in *1877–80*. The poem was sent, along with the two following sonnets, in a letter to Thomas Poole dated 1 November 1796 (*L* 1: 245–6). STC added a note: 'These Sonnets put in no claim to poetry – (indeed as a composition I think so little of them that I neglect[ed] to repeat them to you) but it is a most faithful picture of my feelings on a very interesting event – When I was with you, they were indeed, excepting this first, in a rude & undrest state.' The present text is based on the version in the letter to Poole. STC's first son, David Hartley, was born on 19 September 1796, while STC was visiting Charles Lloyd and his family at Moseley, near Birmingham.

3 *but inly felt* 'but I felt' (cancelled phrase in MS).

Sonnet composed on a journey homeward; the author having received
intelligence of the birth of a son, Sept. 20th, 1796

First published in *1797*; included by STC in all subsequent collections. This is the second of the three sonnets sent to Poole in the letter of 1 November 1796 (see headnote to preceding poem). It also appears in a letter to John Thelwall of 19 November 1796 (*L* 1: 260–1), with this comment: 'My little David Hartley Coleridge is marvellously well, & grows fast. – I was at Birmingham when he was born – I returned immediately on receiving the unexpected news (for my Sara had strangely miscalculated) & in the Coach wrote the following Sonnet. It alludes in its first lines to a *Feeling* which if you never had yourself, I cannot explain to you.' STC offers the following additional comment in the letter to Poole: 'Almost all the followers of Fénelon [François Fénelon, 1651–1715, French theologian associated with the heretical movement known as Quietism] believe that *men* are degraded Intelligences, who had once all existed, at one time & together, in a paradisaical or perhaps heavenly state. – The first four lines express a feeling which I have often had. The present has appeared like a vivid dream or exact similitude of some *past* circumstances' (*L* 1: 246). STC dates the birth of his son, David Hartley, 20 rather than 19 September.

1–6 In the letter to Poole these lines are as follows:

> Oft of *some unknown Past* such Fancies roll
> Swift o'er my brain, as make the Present seem,
> For a brief moment, like a most strange dream
> When, not unconscious that she dreamt, the Soul
> Questions herself in sleep! and Some have said
> We liv'd ere yet this *fleshly* robe we wore.

5 As a note to this line in *1797* and subsequent editions, STC quotes, in Greek, from Plato's *Phaedo* 72e: '. . . our souls existed somewhere before they entered this human shape' (trans. Hugh Tredennick). Cf. *BL* XXII.
8 *art* 'Wert' (letter to Poole).

Sonnet to a friend who asked, how I felt when the nurse first presented my infant to me

First published in *1797*; included by STC in all subsequent collections. This is the third of the sonnets sent to Poole in the letter of 1 November 1796 (*L* 1: 246–7), headed 'Sonnet to a friend who wished to know how I felt when the Nurse first presented my Infant to me'. It also appears in the letter to John Thelwall of 19 November 1796 (*L* 1: 261). The friend may be either Charles Lloyd or Charles Lamb. STC seems to have sent the sonnet to Lamb in early November 1796; see Lamb's letter to STC of 8 November: '. . . I love you for those simple, tender, heart-flowing lines with which you conclude your last, and, in my eyes, best "Sonnet" (as you call 'em)–[quotes lines 13–14 of this poem] Cultivate simplicity, Coleridge; or, rather, I should say, banish elaborateness; for simplicity springs spontaneous from the heart, and carries into daylight its own modest buds and genuine, sweet, and clear flowers of expression. I allow no hotbed in the garden of Parnassus.' Campbell (*1893* 582) calls this sonnet 'a mere versification' of a passage in a letter to Poole of 24 September 1796 (*L* 1: 236).

Sonnet [to Charles Lloyd]

First published in *Poems on the Death of Priscilla Farmer. By her Grandson* [Charles Lloyd] (1796). Included in *1797*, again grouped with the poems by Lloyd included in that volume, and in Lloyd's *Nugae Canorae* (1819).

13 In a copy of Lloyd's *Nugae Canorae* now in the British Library, STC altered this line to read: 'Comforts on this late *eve*, whose youthful breast'.

To a Young Friend, on his Proposing to Domesticate with the Author. Composed in 1796

First published in *1797*; included by STC in all subsequent collections. The title in *1797* begins 'To C. Lloyd'. Campbell observes that 'The scenery of Coleridge's lines is that of the Quantocks, but they were written before Coleridge went to live at Stowey' (*1893* 583). STC made revisions in copies of *1797* and of *1817*; see *Index* CoS 708.

8 *those still* 'stilly' (*1797*); 'stillest' (*1803*).

11 *cliff* 'clift' (*1817, 1828, 1829*).

16 *How more than sweet* 'How heavenly sweet' (*1797, 1803*).

20–2 Compare the scene with the ash tree here and in the preceding verse paragraph to 'This Lime-Tree Bower My Prison' 9–20.

36 *basoned* basined, enclosed in a geological basin or declivity.

42 *youth* 'Lloyd' (*1797*); 'Charles' (*1803*).

43 *cheat* take advantage of.

46 *lone* 'low' (*1797, 1803*).

60 'And mad oppression's thunder-clasping rage' (*1797, 1803*).

69 'We'll laugh at wealth, and learn to laugh at fame' (*1797, 1803*).

72–6 These concluding lines were omitted from *1803*, presumably because of a breach in STC's friendship with Lloyd in 1797. They were restored in *1817*.

72 *hath drunk* 'has drank' (*1797*); 'hath drank' (*1817*, *1828*, *1829*).

75 'She whom I love, shall love thee. Honour'd youth' (*1797*, *1803*, *1828*, *1829*). The line was punctuated as in the present text in *1834*.

Addressed to a Young Man of Fortune Who Abandoned Himself to an Indolent and Causeless Melancholy

First published in the *Cambridge Intelligencer* for 17 December 1796; included in the quarto edition of 'Ode on the Departing Year' (1796) and in *1817*, *1828*, *1829*, *1834*. The poem, dated 11 December 1796, was sent in a letter to Benjamin Flower of the same date (*L* 1: 268). It was also sent in a letter to John Thelwall of 17 December 1796 (*L* 1: 286). The 'young man' addressed is Charles Lloyd.

6–7 These two lines are omitted in the version sent to Thelwall, with the query 'Were they rightly omitted?' and the comment 'I love Sonnets; but *upon my honour* I do not love *my* Sonnets' (*L* 1: 287; the omission gave this poem 14 rather than 16 lines). They are also omitted in the version published with 'Ode to the Departing Year' (1796).

8 *Pace round some widow's grave* 'Or seek some WIDOW's grave' (letter to Thelwall).

11 *eye* 'eyes' (letters to Flower and Thelwall, *Cambridge Intelligencer*).

15 *life's* 'Earth's' (letters to Flower and Thelwall, *Cambridge Intelligencer*, 'Ode to the Departing Year', 1796).

16 'A prey to the thron'd Murderess of Mankind' (letters to Flower and Thelwall, *Cambridge Intelligencer*, 'Ode to the Departing Year', 1796).

To a Friend Who Had Declared his Intention of Writing No More Poetry

First published in an unidentified Bristol newspaper in aid of a subscription for the family of Robert Burns, who died on 21 July 1796; a cutting containing the text of the poem is in the Forster Collection of the Victoria and Albert Museum. It was reprinted with minor alterations in the *Annual Anthology* (1800) and included by STC in *1817* and all subsequent collections. In *1834* it is dated '1796'. The 'Friend' is Charles Lamb, who renounced writing poetry on the occasion of his mother's tragic death in a letter to STC of 27 September 1796.

3 *Hight Castalie* called 'Castalie', an archaic Spenserian name for Castalia or the Castalian spring, sacred to Apollo and the Muses, on Mount Parnassus.

10 Thetis, divine mother of Achilles, plunged her infant son in the river Styx and thereby made him invulnerable, except for the heel by which she held him.

11 *recreant* false, unfaithful to one's duty or allegiance.

16 STC included as a note on 'arrows' in *1817* and subsequent collections a reference to 'Pind.[ar] Olym. ii. l. 156'.

17 Campbell (*1893* 583) quotes an unpublished letter from STC to John Thelwall: '[I send you] a poem of mine on Burns which was printed to be dispersed among

friends. It was addressed to Charles Lamb' (not in *L*). He also quotes Joseph Cottle, *Early Recollections; chiefly relating to the late S. T. Coleridge, during his long residence in Bristol* (1837, 1: 243) as saying that 'Coleridge used to read the bit about Burns with a "rasping force" which was "inimitable" '.

19 A slight misquotation of Milton's 'Lycidas' 14: 'Without the meed of some melodious tear'.

21–2 STC's note in *1817* and later editions says that the quoted passage here is 'Verbatim from Burns's dedication of his Poem to the Nobility and Gentry of the Caledonian Hunt'.

23 *Mæcenas* trusted counsellor of Augustus and enlightened literary patron of Virgil, Horace and other Roman poets.

25 *To gauge ale-firkins* to measure the amount of ale in a standard wooden cask. 'Gauge' was originally 'guard' in *1817*, then changed to 'guage' in the Errata.

26 *Aonian mount* Helicon, home of the ancient Muses; see *Paradise Lost* I. 15.

33, 34 *henbane . . . night-shade* deadly poisonous plants. The first printing and the *Annual Anthology* both have 'stinking hensbane'.

Ode to the Departing Year

First published in full in a quarto pamphlet with a Preface dated 26 December 1796. A shorter version of 102 lines was published in the *Cambridge Intelligencer* for 31 December 1796, the day on which STC took possession of his cottage at Nether Stowey. The 'Ode' was included in *1797*, with the Argument added for the first time, and then in all subsequent collections. STC sent revisions altering the quarto pamphlet version to that printed in *1797* in a letter to Joseph Cottle of 6 February–15 March 1797 (see Peter Mann, 'Two Autograph Letters of S. T. Coleridge', *Review of English Studies*, NS 25 [1974], 312–14). In *1803* the various sentences of the Argument were printed as notes to the relevant sections of the poem. A footnote added to the title in *1797* and subsequent editions says: 'This Ode was written on the 24th, 25th, and 26th days of December, 1796; and published separately on the last day of the year.' In the *Cambridge Intelligencer* the title was 'Ode for the last day of the year'; in all other published versions in STC's lifetime except *1834* it is 'Ode on the Departing Year'.

The quarto pamphlet contains a dedicatory letter to Thomas Poole commenting on the circumstances of composition: 'Soon after the commencement of this month, the editor of the *Cambridge Intelligencer* . . . requested me, by letter, to furnish him with some lines for the last day of the year. I promised him that I would make the attempt; but almost immediately after, a rheumatic complaint seized on my head, and continued to prevent the possibility of poetic composition till within the last three days. So in the course of the last three days the following Ode was produced. In general, when an author informs the public that his production was struck off in a great hurry, he offers an insult, not an excuse. But I trust that the present case is an exception, and that the peculiar circumstances which obliged me to write with such unusual rapidity give a propriety to my professions of it. . . . For me to discuss the *literary* merits of this hasty composition were idle and presumptuous. If it be found to possess that impetuosity of transition, and that precipitation of fancy and feeling, which are the *essential* excellencies of the sublimer Ode, its deficiency in less important respects will be easily pardoned by those from whom alone praise could give me pleasure: and whose minuter criticism will be disarmed by the reflection, that these lines were conceived "not in the soft obscurities of retirement, or under the shelter of Academic Groves, but amidst inconvenience and distraction, in sickness and in sorrow". I am more anxious lest the *moral* spirit of the Ode should be mistaken. You, I am sure, will not fail to recollect that among the ancients, the Bard and the Prophet were one and the same character; and you *know* that although I prophesy curses, I pray fervently for blessings . . .' (*L* 1: 288–9).

In a copy of *1817* STC wrote at the end of the poem: 'Let it not be forgotten during the perusal of this Ode that it was written many years before the abolition of the Slave Trade by the British Legislature, likewise before the invasion of Switzerland by the French Republic, which occasioned the Ode that follows ['France: An Ode'], a kind of Palinodia' (see Campbell, *1893* 588 and Mary Lynn Johnson, 'How Rare Is a "Unique Annotated Copy" of Coleridge's *Sibylline Leaves*', *Bulletin of the New York Public Library* 78 [1975], 451–81). In *1817* and subsequent collections Wordsworth's sonnet of 1802, 'When I have borne in memory what has tamed', is printed facing a page with the poem's title and epigraph:

> When I have borne in memory what has tamed
> Great nations, how ennobling thoughts depart
> When men change swords for ledgers, and desert
> The student's bower for gold, some fears unnamed
> I had, my country! Am I to be blamed!
> But, when I think of Thee, and what thou art,
> Verily, in the bottom of my heart,
> Of those unfilial fears I am ashamed.
> But dearly must we prize thee; we who find
> In thee a bulwark of the cause of men;
> And I by my affection was beguiled.
> What wonder if a poet, now and then,
> Among the many movements of his mind,
> Felt for thee as a Lover or a Child.

The epigraph consists of lines 1173–5 and 1199–1200 from the *Agamemnon* of Aeschylus. The speaker is Cassandra: 'Ha, ha! Oh, oh the agony! Once more the dreadful throes of true prophecy whirl and distract me with their ill-boding onset . . . . What is to come, will come. Soon thou, present here thyself, shalt of thy pity pronounce me all too true a prophetess' (Loeb Classical Library translation).

1 *Spirit* 'Being' (*1803*).
5 *free* 'freed' (1796 quarto).
6 *and a bowèd* 'and submitted' (*1803* and all subsequent editions until *1834*).
7 'When lo! far onwards waving on the wind' (*Cambridge Intelligencer*, 1796 quarto, *1797*, *1803*).
8 *train* 'skirts' (*Cambridge Intelligencer*, 1796 quarto, *1797*, *1803*).
11 'Ere yet he pierc'd the cloud and mock'd my sight' (*Cambridge Intelligencer*).
  foreclosed 'forebade' (1796 quarto, *1797*, *1803*).

22 'Ye Sorrows, and ye Joys advance' (*Cambridge Intelligencer*).

25 'Forbids its fateful strings to sleep' (*Cambridge Intelligencer*, 1796 quarto, *1797, 1803*).

31 'O'er the sore travail of the common Earth' (*Cambridge Intelligencer*, 1796 quarto).

33 'The Name of Liberty, which at the commencement of the French Revolution was both the occasion and the pretext of unnumbered crimes and horrors' (STC's note, *1803*).

36 *thy* 'the' (*1797, 1803*).

40 *wherefore* 'whither' (*Cambridge Intelligencer*, 1796 quarto). The Argument identifies the 'Northern Conqueress' as the Empress of Russia, Catherine the Great, who died in 1796. See 'Religious Musings' 171. The capture in 1790 of Ismail, a Turkish city on the Danube, and the sack of Warsaw in 1794, were recent instances of her aggressive ambition. STC included the following note on this line in the 1796 quarto: 'A subsidiary Treaty had been just concluded; and Russia was to have furnished more effectual aid than that of pious manifestoes to the Powers combined against France. I rejoice – not over the deceased Woman (I never dared figure the Russian Sovereign to my imagination under the dear and venerable character of WOMAN–WOMAN, that complex term for Mother, Sister, Wife!) I rejoice, as at the disenshrining of a Daemon! I rejoice, as at the extinction of the evil Principle impersonated! This very day, six years ago, the massacre of Ismail was perpetrated. THIRTY THOUSAND HUMAN BEINGS, MEN, WOMEN, AND CHILDREN, murdered in cold blood, for no other crime than that their garrison had defended the place with perseverance and bravery. Why should I recall the poisoning of her husband, her iniquities in Poland, or her late unmotivated attack on Persia, the desolating ambition of her public life, or the libidinous excesses of her private hours! I have no wish to qualify myself for the office of Historiographer to the King of Hell –! December 23, 1796.'

45 *The insatiate . . . drunken* 'That tyrant . . . frenzied' (*Cambridge Intelligencer*).

46 *Manes* in ancient Roman religion, spirits of the dead and gods of the underworld.

51–2 Between these lines in the *Cambridge Intelligencer*, the 1796 quarto, *1797* and *1803* the following lines appear: 'Whose shrieks, whose screams were vain to stir / Loud-laughing, red-eyed Massacre'.

61 *tyrant-murderer's* 'scepter'd Murderer's' (*Cambridge Intelligencer*, 1796 quarto, *1797, 1803*). After this line in the *Cambridge Intelligencer* the following lines appear:

> When shall scepter'd SLAUGHTER cease?
> A while he crouch'd, O Victor France!
> Beneath the lightning of thy lance;
> With treacherous dalliance courting PEACE –
> But soon upstarting from his coward trance
> The boastful bloody Son of Pride betray'd
> His ancient hatred of the dove-eyed Maid.
> A cloud, O Freedom! cross'd thy orb of Light,
> And sure he deem'd that orb was set in night:
> For still does MADNESS roam on GUILT's bleak dizzy height!

A slightly modified version of this passage appears in the 1796 quarto (see *1912* 1: 163 n.). In the *Cambridge Intelligencer* STC included a note on the fourth line: 'To juggle this easily-juggled people into better humour with the supplies (and themselves, perhaps, affrighted by the successes of the French) our Ministry sent an Ambassador to Paris to sue for Peace. The supplies are granted: and in the meantime the Archduke Charles turns the scale of victory on the Rhine, and Buonaparte is checked before Mantua. Straightways our courtly messenger is commanded to *uncurl* his lips, and propose to the lofty Republic to *restore* all *its* conquests, and to suffer England to *retain* all *hers* (at least all her *important* ones), as the only terms of Peace, and the ultimatum of the negotiation! [STC here quotes the Greek of Aeschylus, *Agamemnon* 222–4; the Loeb Classical Library translation is: 'For mankind is emboldened by wretched delusion, counsellor of ill, primal source of woe'.]

'The friends of Freedom in this country are idle. Some are timid; some are selfish; and many the torpedo torch of hopelessness has numbed into inactivity. We would fain hope that (if the above account be accurate – it is only the French account) this dreadful instance of infatuation in our Ministry will rouse them to one effort more; and that at one and the same time in our different great towns the people will be called on to think solemnly, and declare their thoughts fearlessly by every method which the *remnant* of the Constitution allows.'

62 *no earthly* 'an awful' (*Cambridge Intelligencer*).

63 *My soul beheld thy vision!* 'i.e. thy Image in a vision' (STC's note, 1796 quarto).

65 *thy robe inscrib'd with gore* 'there garmented with gore' (*Cambridge Intelligencer*, 1796 quarto, *1797*); 'thy vest profan'd with gore!' (*1803*).

67 *Thou storied'st thy sad hours!* 'Gav'st reck'ning of thy Hours' (*1803*).

68 *ethereal* 'choired' (*Cambridge Intelligencer*).

69 'Whose purple locks with snow-white glories shone' (*Cambridge Intelligencer*, 1796 quarto). In *1797* and *1803* 'purple locks' becomes 'wreathed locks'.

70 *wild* 'strange' (*Cambridge Intelligencer*).

74–9 These six lines replace a briefer sequence in the *Cambridge Intelligencer*, 1796 quarto, *1797*, *1803* (the last two lines are slightly changed in *1803*):

> On every Harp on every Tongue
> While the mute Enchantment hung:
> Like Midnight from a thunder-cloud
> Spake the sudden Spirit loud.

76 *Lampads* lamps or candlesticks – a biblical term referring to Revelation 4:5: 'And out of the throne proceeded lightnings and thunderings and voices; and there were seven lamps of fire burning before the throne, which are the seven Spirits of God.' Cf. 'Ne Plus Ultra' 18–21.

83 *Arm* 'God' (*Cambridge Intelligencer*). Between 83 and 84 the following lines appear in the *Cambridge Intelligencer*, 1796 quarto, *1797*, *1803*: 'By Belgium's corse-impeded flood, / By Vendée steaming [streaming, *Cambridge Intelligencer*] Brother's blood.' The cancelled lines refer to violent conflicts in the aftermath of the French Revolution.

87 *frost-winds* 'bleak winds' (*Cambridge Intelligencer*).
91 *Synod* 'Senate' (*1797*, *1803*). STC added a note on ' "full of gifts and lies" ' in the *Cambridge Intelligencer*: 'Gifts used in Scripture for Corruption.'
94–102 These lines replaced a shorter passage in the early editions. In the *Cambridge Intelligencer* the passage runs as follows:

> For ever shall the bloody island scowl?
> For ever shall her vast and iron bow
> Shoot Famine's evil arrows o'er the world,
> Hark! how wide Nature joins her groans below;
> Rise, God of Mercy, rise! why sleep the bolts unhurl'd?

There are slight variations in the 1796 quarto, *1797*, *1803*. STC included the following note on the third of these lines in the *Cambridge Intelligencer*: 'In Europe the smoking villages of Flanders and the putrified fields of La Vendée – from Africa the unnumbered victims of a detestable Slave-Trade. In Asia the desolating plains of Indostan, and the millions whom a rice-contracting Governor caused to perish. In America the recent enormities of the Scalp-merchants. The four quarters of the globe groan beneath the intolerable iniquity of the nation.'
103 *vision* 'Phantoms' (1796 quarto, *1797*, *1803*).
106 *phantom* 'vision' (1796 quarto, *1797*, *1803*).
113 *stranger* 'uglier' (1796 quarto).
121 'O doom'd to fall, enslav'd and vile' (1796 quarto, *1797*, *1803*).
133 *proud invader's* 'sworded Foeman's' (1796 quarto, *1797*); 'sworded Warrior's' (*1803*).
135 *Abandoned* 'Disclaim'd' (1796 quarto, *1797*). Other relatively minor changes were made in the 1796 quarto, *1797* and later editions of 135–9 (see *1912* for variants). In the 1796 quarto, *1797* and *1803* STC included the following note: '*Disclaim'd of Heaven!*' – The Poet from having considered the peculiar advantages, which this country has enjoyed, passes in rapid transition to the uses, which we have made of these advantages. We have been preserved by our insular situation, from suffering the actual horrors of War ourselves, and we have shewn our gratitude to Providence for this immunity by our eagerness to spread those horrors over nations less happily situated. In the midst of plenty and safety we have raised or joined the yell for famine and blood. Of the one hundred and seven last years, fifty have been years of War. Such wickedness cannot pass unpunished. We have been proud and confident in our alliances and our fleets – but God has prepared the canker-worm, and will smite the *gourds* of our pride. "Art thou better than populous No, that was situate among the rivers, that had the waters round about it, whose rampart was the Sea? Ethiopia and Egypt were her strength and it was infinite: Put and Lubim were her helpers. Yet she was carried away, she went into captivity: and they cast lots for her honourable men, and all her great men were bound in chains. Thou also shalt be drunken: all thy strongholds shall be like fig trees with the first ripe figs; if they be shaken, they shall even fall into the mouth of the eater. Thou hast multiplied thy merchants above the stars of heaven. Thy crowned are as the locusts; and thy captains as the great grasshoppers which camp in the hedges in the cool-day; but when the Sun ariseth they flee away, and their place is not known where they are. There is no healing of thy bruise; thy

wound is grievous: all, that hear the report of thee, shall clap hands over thee: for upon whom hath not thy wickedness passed continually? *Nahum*, chap. iii.'' '

144 'Stretch'd on the marge of some fire-flashing fount / In the black Chamber of a sulphur'd mount' (1796 quarto).

red volcanic stream 'roar of blazing stream' in *1797*.

152 *pennons* wings; pinions. Also a pennant, a triangular flag or streamer.

156 'Soliciting my scant and blameless soil' (1796 quarto).

159–60 'In the long sabbath of high self-content / Cleans'd from the fleshly passions that bedim' (1796 quarto). In *1797* this becomes 'In the deep sabbath of blest self-content / Cleans'd from the fears and anguish that dim'; in *1803*, 'In the blest sabbath of high self-content / Cleans'd from bedimming Fear, and Anguish weak and blind'.

The Raven

First published in the *Morning Post* for 10 March 1798, with the following introductory letter: 'Sir, – I am absolutely certain that the following Poem was written by EDMUND SPENSER, and found by an Angler buried in a fishing-box:–

> 'Under the foot of Mole, that mountain hoar,
> Mid the green alders, by the Mulla's shore.'

But a learned Antiquarian of my acquaintance has given it as his opinion that it resembles SPENSER's minor Poems as nearly as Vortigern and Rowena [the title of a Shakesperean forgery by W. H. Ireland, published in 1795] the Tragedies of WILLIAM SHAKESPEARE. – The Poem must be read in *recitative*, in the same manner as the Aegloga Secunda of the Shepherd's Calendar. CUDDY.'

Included in the *Annual Anthology* for 1800 and in *1817, 1828, 1829, 1834*. The subtitle was first added in *1817*. Campbell conjecturally dates the poem 1791 in *1893*; E. H. Coleridge dates it 1797 on the basis of a reference to the poem, under the title of 'Your *Dream*', in a letter to STC from Lamb of 5 February 1797. E. H. Coleridge provides textual variants from what he refers to as 'MS. S.T.C. . . . A single MS. poem in the handwriting of S. T. Coleridge'. No such MS is recorded by Rosenbaum and White in the *Index*; they do cite an undated 'Transcript in an unidentified hand' in the Berg Collection, New York Public Library.

1 'Under the arms of a goodly oak-tree' (*Morning Post, Annual Anthology*). For other minor differences in the opening eight lines between the present text and the early printings, see the textual notes in *1912*.

3 *mast* a general term for nuts, commonly beechnuts, fed to hogs.

17 'Seventeen or eighteen years ago an artist of some celebrity was so pleased with this doggerel that he amused himself with the thought of making a Child's Picture Book of it; but he could not hit on a picture for these four lines. I suggested a *Round-about* with four seats, and the four seasons, as Children, with Time for the shew-man' (STC's note on *Travelled* in *1817*).

23 *enow* archaic form of 'enough'.

25 *pent-house* a subsidiary structure, usually with a sloping roof, attached to the wall of a main house and serving as a porch, shed or outhouse.

37 *bulged* bilged; broken open through the bilge, the curved part of a ship between the bottom and the straight vertical topsides.

44 In *1817* two additional lines are added to the poem: 'We must not think so; but forget and forgive, / And what Heaven gives life to, we'll still let it live'. STC wrote the following note in a copy of *1817*: 'Added thro' cowardly fear of the Goody! What a Hollow, where the Heart of Faith ought to be, does it not betray? this alarm concerning Christian morality, that will not permit even a Raven to be a Raven, nor a Fox a Fox, but demands conventicular justice to be inflicted on their unchristian conduct, or at least an antidote to be annexed.'

To an Unfortunate Woman at the Theatre

First published in the *Morning Post* for 7 December 1797; included in the *Annual Anthology* (1800) and in *1817*, *1828*, *1829* and *1834*. The poem was sent to Joseph Cottle in a letter dated 10 March 1797 (*L* 1: 313–14), where it is headed 'To an unfortunate woman, whom I knew in the days of her Innocence. Composed at the Theatre'; it was meant to be included in *1797* but did not appear in that collection. As Campbell points out, this poem was intended to appear together with 'To an Unfortunate Woman', also sent in the letter to Cottle (*1893* 570).

1 *Maiden* 'Sufferer' (*Annual Anthology*).

5–12 These two stanzas are replaced by the following in the letter to Cottle and the *Annual Anthology*:

> Inly gnawing, thy distresses
>   Mock those starts of wanton glee;
> And thy inmost soul confesses
>   Chaste Affection's [affliction's, *Annual Anthology*] majesty.

14 *Maiden* 'Sufferer' (*Annual Anthology*).

15 *cot* cottage.

25 *sky-lark* 'Lavrac' (letter to Cottle, *Annual Anthology*, with a note by STC identifying this as 'The Lark').

31 *day-star* sun.

To an Unfortunate Woman

First published in *1797*; included by STC in all subsequent collections. It was sent to Cottle in the letter of 10 March 1797 that also contains 'To an Unfortunate Woman in the Theatre', where it is headed 'Allegorical Lines on the same subject'. Some revisions to this poem appear in STC's letter to Cottle of 15 March 1797 (*L* 1: 315–16). For the figure of the wind or 'gale' as ravishing male lover, see 'The Eolian Harp' 14–15.

To the Rev. George Coleridge

First published as the Dedication to *1797*, where it is dated 'Nether-Stowey, Somerset, May 26, 1797'; included in all subsequent collections. In a copy of *1797* STC wrote the following note on this poem: 'N.B. If this volume should ever be delivered according to its directions, *i.e.* to Posterity, let it be known that the Reverend George Coleridge was displeased and thought his character endangered by the Dedication.' STC's older brother George (1764–1828) had acted as a kind of second father to his younger siblings after the death of their father in 1781 (see lines 45, 51). The epigraph is from Horace's *Epode* II ('Notable to his brothers for his fatherly spirit'), a poem used by Pope as the model for his 'Ode on Solitude' ('Happy the man whose wish and care / A few paternal acres bound').

10 'Thine and thy Brothers' favourable lot' (*1803*).
20 Campbell quotes from a poem by STC's friend John Hucks: 'Deem not the friendships of your earlier days / False tho' "chance-started"; haply yet untried, / They are judg'd hardly' (*1893* 588).
21 *pelting* striking with a succession of blows or falling objects or particles, as a pelting rain.
26 *Manchineel* a poisonous tropical American tree having blistering milky juice and apple-shaped fruit. See *BL* I (1: 10), where STC recalls Bowyer's rigorous disciplining of his students' stylistic exuberance: 'Nay certain introductions, similies, and examples, were placed by name on a list of interdiction. Among the similies, there was, I remember, that of the Manchineel fruit, as suiting equally well with too many subjects.' In citing this passage Campbell refers to STC's 'life-long addiction to this rococo simile' (*1893* 588), but Engell and Bate observe that in fact this is the 'one occasion' in his poetry where STC 'yielded to the temptation to use the image' (*BL* 1: 10 n.).
30 'That I woke prison'd! But (the praise be His' (*1803*).
32 *one friend* Thomas Poole.
47–9 'Rebuk'd each fault, and wept o'er all my woes. / Who counts the beatings of the lonely heart' (*1797, 1803*).
52–3 Between these lines the following line appears in *1797*: 'My eager eye glist'ning with memry's tear'.
66–7 Between these lines in *1797* and *1803*: 'Or the high raptures of prophetic Faith'.
68 *strains* 'songs' (*1797, 1803*).

On the Christening of a Friend's Child

First published in *1797* (Supplement), but never reprinted in STC's lifetime. The present text follows *1797*. The poem was addressed to Anna Cruikshank, STC's neighbour at Nether Stowey.

2 *fontal* from the baptismal font.
39 *stud* stem, branch.

Inscription by the Rev. W. L. Bowles in Nether Stowey Church

First published in *LR* (1836). STC's lines are a translation of a Latin inscription on a tablet erected to the memory of Richard Camplin, who died on 20 January 1792. The text of Bowles's Latin is given in *1893* and *1912*:

> Laetus abi! mundi strepitu curisque remotus;
>> Laetus abi! caeli quâ vocat alma Quies.
> Ipsa fides loquitur lacrymamque incusat inanem,
>> Quae cadit in vestros, care Pater, Cineres.
> Heu! tantum liceat meritos hos solvere Ritus,
>> Naturae et tremulâ dicere Voce, Vale!

For Bowles's influence on STC's early verse, see *BL* I and 'To the Rev. W. L. Bowles' below.

This Lime-Tree Bower My Prison

First published in the *Annual Anthology* (1800) with the subtitle 'A Poem Addressed to Charles Lamb, of the India House, London'; reprinted in the *Poetical Classbook* (1810). STC included it in *1817* and in all subsequent collections. The poem was sent to Robert Southey in a letter dated c. 17 July 1797 (*L* 1: 334–6), with this account of its occasion: 'I had been on a visit to Wordsworth's at Racedown near Crewkherne – and I brought him & his Sister back with me & here I have *settled them* [at Alfoxden, four miles from Nether Stowey] . . . Charles Lamb has been with me for a week – . . . The second day after Wordsworth came to me, dear Sara accidentally emptied a skillet of boiling milk on my foot, which confined me during the whole of C. Lamb's stay & still prevents me from all *walks* longer than a furlong. – While Wordsworth, his Sister, & C. Lamb were out one evening; sitting in the arbour of T. Poole's garden, which communicates with mine, I wrote these lines, with which I am pleased.'

STC sent another copy of the poem in a 1797 letter to Charles Lloyd (see *L* 1: 334 n. and *1893* 591). STC made extensive manuscript revisions on the poem and added ten important lines in a copy of the *Annual Anthology* now in the Beinecke Library, Yale University; he made further alterations in a copy of *1817* now in the Houghton Library, Harvard University. Additional minor changes appear in *1829* and *1834*. Campbell records the following note written in a copy of *1834* 'when the poet was on his death-bed' over against the introductory note by STC: 'Ch. and Mary Lamb – dear to my heart, yea, as it were, my heart. – S.T.C. Æt. 63, 1834. 1797–1834 = 37 years!'

1–28 These opening lines are much less fully elaborated in the MS versions contained in the letters to Southey and Lloyd; in particular, much of the detail in the description of the 'roaring dell' (9 ff.) does not appear. Between 1 and 2 the following line appears in the letter to Southey: 'Lam'd by the scathe of fire, lonely and faint'; see *1912* 1: 178.

7 *springy* 'Elastic, I mean' (STC's note, letter to Southey).

17 *long lank weeds* 'The Asplenium Scolopendrium, called in some countries the Adder's Tongue, in others the Hart's Tongue; but Withering gives the Adder's Tongue as the trivial name of the Ophioglossum only' (STC's note in *1817* and later editions).

20 *blue* 'dim' (*Annual Anthology*). Cf. Dorothy Wordsworth's entry for 10 February 1798 in her *Alfoxden Journal*.

24 *whose sails light up* 'which lightly touches' (*Annual Anthology*).

30 *In the great City pent* Cf. STC's characterization of his experiences as a schoolboy in London in 'Frost at Midnight': 'For I was reared / In the great city, pent 'mid cloisters dim' (51–2). The main source for these instances is the simile applied to Satan in *Paradise Lost* IX.445: 'As one who long in populous City pent'.

31 *patient* 'bowed' (letter to Southey).

32 *strange calamity* In 1796 Charles Lamb's sister, Mary, had stabbed their mother to death in a fit of insanity.

34 *beams* 'heaven' (letter to Southey).

40 *On the wide landscape* 'On the wide view' (letter to Southey, with this note on the phrase: 'You remember I am a Berkeleyan'). *Wide* is 'wild' in *1817*, but this is corrected in the Errata.

41–2 'Less gross than bodily, a living thing / Which acts upon the mind and with such hues / As cloathe the Almighty Spirit' (*Annual Anthology*, *1817*). Empson comments: 'The later published versions tone down the views implied in the climax, omitting the description of Nature as "a living thing / That acts upon the mind", and suggesting that God was revealed as much in spite of the "hues" as because of them. In the final version they "veil" the Almighty Spirit, rather than "clothe" him and a "yet" is interposed before "he makes / Spirits perceive his presence [42–3]" ' (*Coleridge's Verse* 220).

48 The shift to past tense produces a striking effect here, after the present and present perfect tense of the previous lines. Notice the return to present tense at 55.

55 *branches* 'foliage' (letter to Southey).

60 Cf. Wordsworth, 'Tintern Abbey' 121–2: 'Knowing that Nature never did betray / The heart that loved her'. Lines 60–4 are omitted in the letter to Lloyd.

61–2 'No scene so narrow but may well employ' (letter to Southey, *Annual Anthology*).

68 *My gentle-hearted Charles!* 'My Sister and my Friends' (letter to Southey); 'My Sara and my Friends' (letter to Lloyd).

71 Omitted in the letter to Lloyd.

72 'Cross'd like a speck the blaze of setting day' (letter to Southey); 'Had cross'd the mighty orb's dilated blase' (letter to Lloyd).

73 *thou* 'ye' (letter to Southey); 'you' (letter to Lloyd).

74 *Flew creeking* 'Some months after I had written this line, it gave me pleasure to find that Bartram had observed the same circumstances of the Savanna Crane. "When these Birds move their wings in flight, their strokes are slow, moderate and regular; and even when at a considerable distance or high above us, we plainly hear the quill-feathers; their shafts and webs upon one another creek as the joints or working of a vessel in a tempestuous sea." ' (STC's note, *1817* and later editions.)

75 'For you my Sister and my Friends' (letter to Southey); 'For you my Sara and my Friends' (letter to Lloyd).

The Foster-Mother's Tale

First published in *LB* (1798); reprinted in the *LB* editions of 1800 (where it is subtitled 'A Narration in Dramatic Blank Verse'), 1802, 1805. It was originally part of Act IV of *Osorio*, written in 1797, a play which STC subsequently revised and retitled *Remorse*. The poem was printed in an Appendix to the second edition of *Remorse* (1813), included as the second poem in *1817*, then returned to the Appendix to *Remorse* in *1828*, *1829* and *1834*. In *Remorse* (1813) and in *1828*, *1829* and *1834* the speakers are Teresa (Maria) and Selma (Foster-Mother), and the fragment begins: '*Ter.* 'Tis said, he spake of you familiarly / As mine and Alvar's common foster-mother.' The following note is prefixed to the fragment in *1828* and *1829*; the first sentence only appears in *1834*: 'The following scene as unfit for the stage was taken from the Tragedy in 1797, and published in the *Lyrical Ballads*. But this work having been long out of print, and it having been determined, that this with my other poems in that collection (the *Nightingale*, *Love*, and the *Ancient Mariner*) should be omitted in any future edition, I have been advised to reprint it as a Note to the Second Scene of the Fourth . . .' The present text is taken from *1817*, the latest edition in which STC presented 'The Foster Mother's Tale' as a poem in its own right.

16 In *LB* (1800) the poem begins with 'But that entrance', in the Appendix to *Remorse* with 'But that entrance, Selma!' See line 67 below.
19 *Leoni* 'Sesina' (*Remorse* [1813], *1828*, *1829*, *1834*).
27 *Valez* ' 'Velez' ' (all editions of *LB*); 'Valdez' ' (*Remorse* 1813, *1828*, *1829*, *1834*).
41 *very learnèd* 'rare and learned' (*Remorse* [1813], *1828*, *1829*, *1834*).
57 *hole* 'cell' (*LB* 1800); 'den' (*Remorse* [1813]).
59 *in the cellar* 'near this dungeon' (*Remorse* 1813, *1828*, *1829*, *1834*).
62 *wild* 'wide' (*Remorse* [1813], *1828*, *1829*, *1834*).

The Dungeon

First published in *LB* (1798); reprinted in *LB* (1800) but not included as a separate poem again in any collection of STC's verse until *1893*. The lines were originally part of *Osorio* (V.i.107 ff.) and subsequently became part of *Remorse* (1813). The present text is from *LB* (1798).

1 *our* 'my' (*Remorse* [1813], *1828*, *1829*, *1834*).
   man 'men' (*Remorse* [1813], *1828*, *1829*, *1834*).
2 *process* progress, advance.
11 *mountebanks* boastful and unscrupulous tricksters; charlatans.
15 *steams and vapour* 'steaming vapours' (*Remorse* [1813], *1828*, *1829*, *1834*).

SONNETS ATTEMPTED IN THE MANNER OF CONTEMPORARY WRITERS

These three sonnets were first published in the *Monthly Magazine* for November 1797, signed 'Nehemiah Higginbottom'. They were reprinted in the *Poetical Register* for 1803 (1805), and by STC in a note to *BL* I (1: 26–8). The present texts are taken from *BL*. STC wrote to Joseph Cottle c. 20 November 1797: 'I sent three mock Sonnets in ridicule of my own, & Charles Lloyd's, & Lamb's, &c &c – in ridicule of that affectation of unaffectedness, of jumping & misplaced accent on common-place epithets, flat lines forced into poetry by Italics (signifying how well & *mouthis[h]ly* the Author would read them) puny pathos &c &c – the instances are almost all taken from mine & Lloyd's poems – I signed them Nehemiah Higginbottom. I think they may do good to our young Bards. –' (*L* 1: 357–8).

In *BL* STC introduces the Sonnets as follows: 'Every reform, however necessary, will by weak minds be carried to an excess, that itself will need reforming. The reader will excuse me for noticing, that I myself was the first to expose *risu honesto* [with honest laughter] the three sins of poetry, one or the other of which is the most likely to beset a young writer. So long ago as the publication of the second number of the monthly magazine, under the name of NEHEMIAH HIGGINBOTTOM I contributed three sonnets, the first of which had for its object to excite a good-natured laugh at the spirit of *doleful egotism*, and at the recurrence of favorite phrases, with the double defect of being at once trite, and licentious. The second, on low, creeping language and thoughts, under the pretence of *simplicity*. And the third, the phrases of which were borrowed entirely from my own poems, on the indiscriminate use of elaborate and swelling language and imagery. The reader . . . will I trust regard them as reprinted for biographical purposes, and not for their poetic merits.'

Engell and Bate note that 'Though the first sonnet is certainly a parody of Lloyd . . . and though the third could be viewed as a less convincing parody of himself, in the second C may have been thinking as much of R[obert] S[outhey] as of Lamb. Certainly Lamb assumed this [*L* 1: 404], and so did RS, to whom C wrote a passionate letter of denial [*L* 1: 358–9]. Later, still smarting, RS wrote four sonnets supposedly in C's most flaccid style and published them as by "Abel Shufflebottom".' (*BL* 1: 29 n).

Sonnet I

4 *saddens* 'darkens' (*Monthly Magazine*).
8 *the wretched ones that pass* 'Those wretched ones who pass' (*Monthly Magazine*).
9 *bleak* 'black' (*Monthly Magazine*).
14 *Oh* 'Ah!' (*Monthly Magazine*).

Sonnet II

This sonnet is titled 'To Simplicity' in the *Monthly Magazine*.

4 *haply* by chance, luck, accident.
5 *pad* cushioned saddle ('amble' in the next line suggests the grotesque image of the poet riding Lady Fortune).
6 *and yet* 'yet, though' (*Monthly Magazine*).
8 *Frown, pout and part, then* 'Gnaw cool and miff, O!' (*Monthly Magazine*).
10 *pall* cover with or as with a pall or cloak (but perhaps also with an ironic sense: make faint, insipid).

Sonnet III

This sonnet is titled 'On a Ruined House in a Romantic Country' in the *Monthly Magazine*.

1-2 'The house that Jack built' See STC's introduction of these sonnets in *BL* I. The phrase is also the title of a nursery tale of very ancient origins, and with an accumulative structure. The popular tale would be used to satirical political effect by William Hone and George Cruickshank in *The Political House that Jack Built* (1819).
8, 9 *aye* still,
     erst before, previously.
10 *brogues* trousers (the use of the word in this sense is now obsolete).
13 *Ah! thus* 'As when' (*Monthly Magazine*).

Parliamentary Oscillators

First published in the *Cambridge Intelligencer* for 6 January 1798 and signed 'Laberius'. (Decimus Laberius, c. 105-43 BC, was a writer of mimes. Because of his outspoken political criticism he was required by Julius Caesar to act in his own mimes.) STC included the poem in *1817* but not in subsequent collections. The poem is dated '1794' in *1817*, but there is nothing to support this early date. In the *Cambridge Intelligencer* the title is 'To Sir John Sinclair, S. Thornton, Alderman Lushington, and the whole Troop of Parliamentary Oscillators'. The *OED* suggests that *oscillator* had some idiomatic currency in the early nineteenth century as a term for politicians who swing back and forth.

11 *Mr PITT* William Pitt the Younger (1759-1806), Tory prime minister from 1783 to 1802, and again from 1804 until his death.
15-16 Cf. *Paradise Lost* IX. 526, where Satan, in serpent form, 'Fawning, . . . licked the ground whereon [Eve] trod', and IX. 549: 'So glozed the Tempter . . .'
42 *peasecod* pea pod.

THE RIME OF THE ANCIENT MARINER

First published anonymously in *LB* (1798), as the first poem in the volume; reprinted with many alterations in the 1800, 1802 and 1805 editions of *LB* (with the phrase 'A Poet's Reverie' added to the title). The revisions for *LB* (1800) were sent in a letter to the publishers, Biggs and Cottle, in mid-July 1800 (*L* 1: 598–602). The poem was included by STC in *1817* and in *1828*, *1829* and *1834*. The marginal glosses, composed in 1815–16 when a new collection of the poems was being prepared, were first printed in *1817*.

STC describes the origin of the poem in *BL* XIV, as part of an account of his collaboration with Wordsworth: 'The thought suggested itself (to which of us I do not recollect) that a series of poems might be composed of two sorts. In the one, incidents and agents were to be, in part at least, supernatural, and the excellence aimed at was to consist in the interesting of the affections by the dramatic truth of such emotions, as would naturally accompany such situations, supposing them real. And real in *this* sense they have been to every human being who, from whatever source of delusion, has at any time believed himself under supernatural agency. For the second class, subjects were to be chosen from ordinary life. . . . In this idea originated the plan of the "Lyrical Ballads"; in which it was agreed, that my endeavours should be directed to persons and characters supernatural, or at least romantic; yet so as to transfer from our inward nature a human interest and a semblance of truth sufficient to procure for these shadows of imagination that willing suspension of disbelief for the moment, which constitutes poetic faith. . . . With this view I wrote the "Ancient Mariner".' (*BL* 2: 5–7).

The 'Ancient Mariner' was criticized by most readers – including friends of STC such as Southey ('a Dutch attempt at German sublimity') – upon its first appearance in *LB* (1798). Wordsworth himself wrote to Joseph Cottle on 24 June 1799: 'From what I can gather it seems that the Ancyent Mariner has upon the whole been an injury to the volume, I mean that the old words and the strangeness of it have deterred readers from going on. If the volume should come to a second Edition I would put in its place some little things which would be more likely to suit the common taste.' STC wanted to withdraw the poem, but Wordsworth decided to include it, adding this note: 'I cannot refuse myself the gratification of informing such Readers as may have been pleased with this Poem, or with any part of it, that they owe their pleasure in some sort to me; as the Author was himself very desirous that it should be suppressed. This wish had arisen from a consciousness of the defects of the Poem, and from a knowledge that many persons have been much displeased with it. The Poem of my Friend has indeed great defects; first, that the principal person has no distinct character, either in his profession of Mariner, or as a human being who having been long under the controul of supernatural impressions might be supposed himself to partake of something supernatural; secondly, that he does not act, but is continually acted upon; thirdly, that the events having no necessary connection do not produce each other; and lastly, that the imagery is somewhat too laboriously accumulated. Yet the Poem contains many delicate touches of passion, and indeed the passion is every where true to nature; a great number of the stanzas present beautiful images, and are expressed with unusual felicity of language; and the versification, though the metre is itself unfit for long poems, is harmonious and artfully varied, exhibiting the utmost powers of that metre, and every variety of which it is capable. It therefore appeared to me that these several merits (the first of which, namely that of the passion, is of the highest kind), gave to the Poem a value which is not often possessed by better Poems. On this account I requested of my Friend to permit me to republish it.'

In 1835 Wordsworth told the Rev. Alexander Dyce: 'The *Ancient Mariner* was founded on a strange dream, which a friend of Coleridge [John Cruikshank] had, who fancied he saw a skeleton ship, with figures in it. We had both determined to write some poetry for a monthly magazine, the profits of which were to defray the expenses of a little excursion we were to make together. The *Ancient Mariner* was intended for this periodical, but was too long. I had very little share in the composition of it, for I soon found that the style of Coleridge and myself would not assimilate. Besides the lines (in the fourth part):

> And thou art long, and lank, and brown,
> As is the ribbed sea-sand –

I wrote the stanza (in the first part):

> He holds him with his glittering eye –
> The Wedding-Guest stood still,
> And listens like a three-years' child:
> The Mariner hath his will –

and four or five lines more in different parts of the poem, which I could not now point out. The idea of *"shooting an albatross" was mine; for I had been reading Shelvocke's Voyages, which probably Coleridge never saw*. I also suggested the reanimation of the dead bodies, to work the ship' (Rev. Alexander Dyce to H. N. Coleridge, recorded in a note to *1852*). Captain George Shelvocke's *A Voyage Round the World by the Way of the Great south Sea, Perf. in the Years 1719–20–1–2* was published in London in 1726.

In 1843 Wordsworth offered further commentary on the composition of 'The Ancient Mariner' as part of his remarks to Isabella Fenwick about his own poem, 'We Are Seven': 'In the spring of the year 1798, he [STC], my sister, and myself, started from Alfoxden, pretty late in the afternoon, with a view to visit Lenton and the valley of Stones near it; and as our united funds were very small, we agreed to defray the expense of the tour by writing a poem, to be sent to the new *Monthly Magazine*. . . . Accordingly we set off and proceeded along the Quantock Hills towards Watchet, and in the course of this walk was planned the poem of *The Ancient Mariner*, founded on a dream, as Mr Coleridge said, of his friend, Mr Cruikshank. Much the greatest part of the story was Mr Coleridge's invention; but certain parts I myself suggested:– for example, some crime was to be committed which should bring upon the old navigator, as Coleridge afterwards delighted to call him, the spectral persecution, as a consequence of that crime, and his own wanderings. I had been reading in Shelvock's *Voyages* a day or two before that while doubling Cape Horn they frequently saw albatrosses in that latitude, the largest sort of sea-fowl, some extending their wings twelve or fifteen feet. "Suppose," said I, "you represent him as having killed one of these birds on entering the South Sea, and that the tutelary Spirits of those regions take upon them to avenge the crime." The incident was thought fit for the purpose and adopted accordingly. I also suggested the navigation of the ship by the dead men, but do not recollect that I had anything more to do with the scheme of the poem. The Gloss with which it was subsequently accompanied was not thought of by either of us at the time; at least, not a hint of it was given to me, and I have no doubt it was a gratuitous afterthought. We began the composition together on that, to me, memorable evening. I furnished two or three lines at the beginning of the poem, in particular:–

> And listened like a three years' child;
> The Mariner had his will.

These trifling contributions, all but one (which Mr C. has with necessary scrupulosity recorded) slipt out of his mind as they well might. As we endeavored to proceed conjointly (I speak of the same evening) our respective manners proved so widely different that it would have been quite presumptuous in me to do anything but separate from an undertaking upon which I could only have been a clog. We returned after a few days from a delightful tour, of which I have many pleasant, and some of them droll-enough, recollections. We returned by Dulverton to Alfoxden. *The Ancient Mariner* grew and grew till it became too important for our first object, which was limited to our expectation of five pounds, and we began to talk of a volume, which was to consist, as Mr Coleridge has told the world [in *BL* XIV], of poems chiefly on supernatural subjects taken from common life, but looked at, as much as might be, through an imaginative medium . . .' (Note dictated to Isabella Fenwick in 1843; first published in *The Poetical Works of William Wordsworth*, 6 vols, 1857).

In *Table Talk* (30 May 1830 and 31 March 1832) STC offers additional remarks on the poem: 'Mrs Barbauld [Anna Letitia Barbauld, 1743–1825, prominent poet and essayist] told me that the only faults she found with the Ancient Mariner were – that it was improbable, and had no moral. As for the probability – to be sure that might admit some question – but I told her that in my judgment the chief fault of the poem was that it had too much moral, and that too openly obtruded on the reader. It ought to have had no more moral than the story of the merchant sitting down to eat dates by the side of a well and throwing the shells aside, and the Genii starting up and saying he must kill the merchant, because a date shell had put out the eye of the Genii's son' (*CC* 272–3).

No poem in English literature has had a richer or more complex interpretative history than 'The Ancient Mariner'. For contemporary reaction, see *Coleridge: The Critical Heritage*, ed. J. R. de J. Jackson (1970), esp. pp. 14–17, 51–3, 56–60; for a valuable survey of twentieth-century approaches, see Max F. Schulz in *The English Romantic Poets: A Review of Research and Criticism* (1985), pp. 386–93. Robert Penn Warren's essay in the *Kenyon Review* (1946), 'A Poem of Pure Imagination', has been especially influential in establishing the Christian thematic pattern of transgression, punishment and redemption, and in coordinating such a reading with an emphasis on the poem's dramatization of the imagination's potential for unifying perception. John Beer's readings of the poem in *Coleridge the Visionary* (1959) and *Coleridge's Poetic Intelligence* (1977) are especially helpful in connecting key philosophical and psychological issues to Coleridge's wide-ranging and often abstruse reading. Among the most provocative recent readings of the poem are those by Raimonda Modiano in *Modern Language Quarterly* (1977), Frances Ferguson in the *Georgia Review* (1977), Leslie Brisman in *Romantic Origins* (1978), David Simpson in *Irony and Authority in Romantic Poetry* (1979), Jerome J. McGann in *Critical Inquiry* (1981), and Arden Reed in *Romantic Weather* (1983). William Empson opened up crucial historical and political questions about 'The Ancient Mariner' in his 1964 essay in the *Critical Quarterly*, where he connects the power of neurotic guilt in the poem to disguised anxieties about European maritime exploitation and the slave trade. Empson and David Pirie extend this approach in the introduction and notes to *Coleridge's Verse: A Selection* (1972). For an important elaboration and clarification of Empson's insights, see J. R. Ebbatson, 'Coleridge's Mariner and the Rights of Man' (*Studies in Romanticism*, 1972).

Empson's conviction that 'The Ancient Mariner' is 'a splendid poem which was much mangled by its author for reasons of conscience' (*Coleridge's Verse* 27) is widely regarded as extreme and eccentric. Yet Empson's and Pirie's insistence on printing the text of the poem that appeared in *LB* (1798) has brought home what a different poem this is from the version familiar to us from later collections. See also Stillinger, *Coleridge and Textual Instability*, pp. 60–73. Accordingly, the text as it was first published in *LB* (1798) is here presented along with the text published in *1834*. Notes to the *LB* version are followed by notes to *1834*; significant revisions to *LB* that do not appear in *1834* are given in the first set of notes.

The Rime of the Ancyent Marinere (1798)

Argument 'How a Ship, having first sailed to the Equator, was driven by Storms to the cold Country towards the South Pole; how the Ancient Mariner cruelly and in contempt of the laws of hospitality killed a Sea-bird and how he was followed by many and strange Judgements: and in what manner he came back to his own Country' (*LB* 1800). The Argument was not included by STC in printings of the poems after *LB* (1800).

20 This line, which Wordsworth claimed among his contributions to the poem, is ambiguous: 'his' may refer either to the Wedding-Guest's or to the Mariner's own 'will'.

27 *Kirk* church.

29–32 The directions of the rising and setting sun indicate that the ship is sailing south.

34 The position of the sun here indicates that the ship has reached the equator or 'Line'.

45–8

> But now the Northwind came more fierce,
> There came a Tempest strong!
> And Southward still for days and weeks
> Like Chaff we drove along

> (*LB* 1800)

55 *ken* recognize.

60 *swound* swoon; see line 397. This line was changed in *LB* 1800 to 'A wild and ceaseless sound'.

62 *Thorough* older form of 'through'.

63 *And* an as if.

73 *shroud* rope supporting the mast of the ship.

74 *vespers nine* In ecclesiastical terms, 'vespers' is the sixth canonical hour of the breviary and is sung or said towards evening (Evensong). In poetry the word was traditionally applied to the evening song of birds.

81 The ship is now sailing north (see line 69, 'And a good south wind sprung up behind'), having rounded Cape Horn at the southern tip of South America.

83 *weft* in weaving, the threads carried by the shuttle across the warp. This line was changed in *LB* (1800): 'Still hid in mist; and on the left'.

93 *like God's own head* 'like an Angel's head' (*LB* 1800).

100 *The furrow follow'd free* In *1817* this line becomes 'The furrow stream'd off free', and STC adds a note to explain the change: '. . . I had not been long on board a ship, before I perceived that this was the image as seen by a spectator from the shore, or from another vessel. From the ship itself, the *Wake* appears like a brook flowing off from the stern.' STC restored the original version of the line in *1828*.

109 See line 34 and note.

124 *Death-fires* an atmospheric electrical phenomenon on a ship's mast or rigging, also commonly called St Elmo's fire or the 'corposant'. It was popularly believed to portend disaster.

139–40

> So past a weary time; each throat
> Was parch'd, and glaz'd each eye,
> When, looking westward, I beheld
> A something in the sky.
>
> (*LB* 1800)

144 *wist* knew.

147 *an* as if (as in *1834*).

149 *unslack'd* STC kept this form of 'unslak'd' through *1817* and first altered it in *1828*.

156 *Gramercy!* great thanks (from French *grand-merci*).

160 *weal* good.

175 *her* STC kept the possessive pronoun italicized here and in lines 177 and 186 through *1829*, removing the added emphasis only in *1834*.

176 *gossameres* filmy cobwebs that float in the air.

177–80

> Are those *her* Ribs, thro' which the Sun
> Did peer as thro' a grate?
> And are those two all, all her crew,
> That Woman, and her Mate?
>
> (*LB* 1800)

In a copy of *LB* 1798 there is a MS revision of this stanza identical to *LB* 1800 except for the first two lines, which read

> Are those *her* ribs which fleck's the Sun
> Like the bars of a dungeon grate?

180 *Pheere* 'Fere'; companion, mate.
181 STC wrote the following stanza in the margins of a copy of *LB* 1798, apparently to be inserted before 181–5. It was first published in *1912*:

> This Ship it was a plankless thing,
> – A bare Anatomy!
> A plankless spectre – and it mov'd
> Like a Being of the Sea!
> The Woman and a fleshless Man
> Therein sate merrily.

182 *ween* suppose, think.
186–90 All the present-tense verbs in the stanza are changed to past tense in *LB* (1800).
195 *sterte* started.
199–203 In *1893* Campbell first printed a MS revision of these lines, found 'Among papers . . . dated variously from 1806, 1807, and 1810' now in the British Library:

> With never a whisper on the main
>   Off shot the spectre ship;
> And stifled words and groans of pain
>   murmuring
>   Mix'd on each trembling   lip.
> And we look'd round, and we look'd up,
> And fear at our hearts, as at a cup,
>   The Life-blood seem'd to sip –
> The Sky was dull, and dark the night,
> The helmsman's face by his lamp gleam'd bright,
>   From the sails the dews did drip –
> Till clomb above the Eastern Bar,
> The hornèd Moon, with one bright star
>   Within its nether tip.

'It is a common superstition among sailors that something evil is about to happen whenever a star dogs the moon' (STC's MS note, first printed in *1877–80*).
207 *ee* eye.
216–19 'For the last two lines of this stanza, I am indebted to Mr WORDSWORTH. It was on a delightful walk from Nether Stowey to Dulverton, with him and his sister, in the Autumn of 1797, that this poem was planned, and in part composed' (STC's note in *1817*; cf. Wordsworth's own remarks on the composition of the poem quoted in the headnote).

234 *eldritch* weird, ghostly, frightful (an archaic word probably related to 'elf'); STC changed this to 'ghastly' in *LB* (1800).

237 *or* ere, before.

277 *unaware* His unconscious blessing of the water-snakes, which gains the Mariner partial and momentary absolution, parallels the unmotivated killing of the albatross at the end of Part I.

286 *yeven* archaic form of 'given', which STC introduced in *LB* (1800).

289 *silly* in the now obsolete sense of plain, simple, rustic, homely.

304 *sere* thin, worn, but perhaps also with something of the sense of withered, dried.

306 *fire-flags* meteor-like flashes of light, caused by lightning (see lines 317 and 321) or possibly by the Aurora Australis or Southern Lights.

 sheen shone (verb).

311 *sedge* grass-like plant that grows in wet or marshy places.

319–20 STC introduced in *LB* (1800) the revision of these lines that appears in the *1834* text.

337–8 Omitted in *LB* (1800) and thereafter.

338 Following this line STC added the stanza in which the Mariner responds to the Wedding-Guest's fear by explaining that the bodies of the dead crew-members were inhabited by 'spirits blest' in *LB* (1800) (see *1834* 345–9).

348 *Lavrock* colloquial name for the skylark. STC substituted the latter in *LB* (1800).

351 *jargoning* warbling, twittering (the original sense of the word in Old French and Middle English).

362–77 These lines were omitted in *LB* (1800) and thereafter.

363 Cf. line 20 and note.

368–9 Cf. lines 657–8.

375 *n'old* would not.

399 *have not* i.e. have not the knowledge.

404, 406 Compare the 'cross' / 'Albatross' rhyme that here frames the reference to the Mariner's cross-bow with the internal rhyme in line 59.

415–17 Campbell quotes Sir John Davies, *Orchestra; or, A Poem of Dancing*, st. 49 (*1893* 598).

419 As a source for the image here Campbell cites a line from *Osorio*, later *Remorse*: 'I have stood silent like a slave before thee' (V.i; see *1893* 598).

421 *great bright eye* Perhaps the reflected image of the moon, here imagined to be looking back at the moon itself.

445 *een* archaic plural of *ee* (eye), as in line 207; STC substituted the modern form in *LB* (1800).

461 *it fann'd my cheek* Cf. Wordsworth, *The Prelude* (1850) I. 1–2.

478 *strewn* See *OED* 6 under *strew*: 'To level, calm (stormy waves); to allay (a storm). Cf. L. *stenere aequor*'.

480 *shadow* The *OED* cites this passage under 'loose or extended use' of the word to mean 'A reflected image'. The effect is strange, however, given the preceding reference to 'moon light'. See 'shadows' in lines 483, 486 and 509, where the sense of *shade* as supernatural spectre is evident and again linked to effects of light ('Like as of torches came', 484). The marginal gloss to *1834* 480–7 is pertinent.

481–502 Omitted in *LB* (1800).

490 *rood* cross.

515 *corse* corpse.

517 *seraph-man* a seraph, highest in the ranks of angels, is usually represented as a shining red celestial being.

531–6 Omitted in *LB* (1800). In a copy of *LB* (1798), STC revised these lines as follows:

> Then vanish'd all the lovely lights,
>   The spirits of the air,
> No souls of mortal men were they,
>   But spirits bright and fair.

549 *rears* raises.

562 *look* STC retained the present tense through *1817*, changing it to past in *1828*.

565–6 This is the only instance in the poem when one stanza runs grammatically into the next.

566 *The skeletons* Changed to 'Brown Skeletons' in the Errata for *1817*.

  lag archaic form of 'lay'.

568 *Ivy-tod* ivy clump or bush.

607 *shrieve me* hear my confession and grant me absolution; in 608 the Hermit makes the sign of the cross on his brow.

615–18 These lines were revised in *LB* (1800) and given the form they have in *1834*, except that the second line of the stanza reads 'That agency returns'. In *LB* (1802) 'agency' was changed to 'agony'.

643 *Farewell, farewell!* 'The comma to be omitted' (Errata *LB* 1798).

656 *forlorn* forsaken.

The Rime of the Ancient Mariner (1834)

Motto, first printed in *1817*; adapted from the *Archaeologiae philosophicae* of Thomas Burnet (1635?–1715): 'I readily believe that there are more invisible than visible Natures in the universe. But who will explain for us the family of all these beings, and the ranks and relations and distinguishing features and functions of each? What do they do? What places do they inhabit? The human mind has always sought the knowledge of these things, but never attained it. Meanwhile I do not deny that it is helpful sometimes to contemplate in the mind, as on a tablet, the image of a greater and better world, lest the intellect, habituated to the petty things of daily life, narrow itself and sink wholly into trivial thoughts. But at the same time we must be watchful for the truth and keep a sense of proportion, so that we may distinguish the certain from the uncertain, day from night.'

12 *Eftsoons* at once.

41 *he* The masculine personification of the storm was added in *1817*.

55 *clifts* E. H. Coleridge says that this is 'probably a misprint. It is not corrected in the *Errata*' (*1912* 1: 189). But the *OED* shows 'clift' as a 'by-form of CLIFF, due to confusion between the word and *clift*, CLEFT, a fissure. Exceedingly common in 16–18th c., and used by some writers in the 19th c.' (an example is given from Shelley). See *Ancyent Mariner* (1798) 53.

429 The dialogue between the two voices ends here, although quotation punctuation is not used for the first six stanzas of Part VI in *1834* as it is in *1798*.
517 *marineres* In later editions STC kept the archaic spelling of 'mariners' here, apparently to preserve the rhyme with 'rears'.

Christabel

First published in a pamphlet titled *Christabel: Kubla Khan, A Vision; The Pains of Sleep* (1816), reissued twice in this year; included by STC in *1828*, *1829* and *1834*. The account of the various MSS of the poem given by E. H. Coleridge in *1912* should be supplemented and corrected by Rosenbaum and White, *Index CoS* 51–66 and by *Stillinger* 79–91. STC's own autograph MS, supposedly given to J. P. Collier, has never been located. 'The Conclusion to Part II' was sent by STC to Robert Southey in a letter dated 6 May 1801 (*L* 2: 728). The Preface was prefixed to the poem in all editions in STC's lifetime. The following passage appears in the 1816 version of the Preface, after the second sentence: 'Since the latter date, my poetic powers have been, till very lately, in a state of suspended animation. But as, in my very first conception of the tale, I had the whole present to my mind, with the wholeness, no less than the liveliness of a vision; I trust that I shall be able to embody in verse the three parts yet to come, in the course of the present year'. In *1828* and *1829* the clause following the last semi-colon was changed to 'I trust I shall yet be able to embody in verse the three parts yet to come'; in *1834* the entire passage was omitted. For the original of the 'two monkish Latin hexameters', first translated on 1 November 1801, see *1912* 2: 997 ('Fragment 4').

Arrangements were made with the printers to include *Christabel* in the second volume of *LB* (1800). On 4 October 1800 STC visited the Wordsworths at Grasmere and read the poem aloud to them, apparently much to their delight. But on 6 October Dorothy Wordsworth wrote in her *Journal*: 'Determined not to print *Christabel* with the L.B.' (*Journals of Dorothy Wordsworth*, ed. Mary Moorman [1958]). How much this decision had to do with the poem's being unfinished and how much with other kinds of judgment is unclear. STC wrote to Humphry Davy on 9 October 1800: 'The Christabel was running up to 1300 lines – and was so much admired by Wordsworth, that he thought it indelicate to print two Volumes with *his name* in which so much of another man's was included – & which was of more consequence – the poem was in direct opposition to the very purpose for which the Lyrical Ballads were published – viz – an experiment to see how far those passions, which alone give any value to extraordinary Incidents, were capable of interesting, in & for themselves, in the Incidents of common Life. – We mean to publish the Christabel therefore with a long Blank Verse Poem of Wordsworth's entitled the Pedlar – I assure you, I think very differently of CHRISTABEL. I would rather have written Ruth, and Nature's Lady than a million such poems / but why do I calumniate my own spirit by saying, *I* would rather – God knows – it is as delightful to me that they *are* written – I *know*, that at present (& I *hope*, that it *will* be so,) my mind has disciplined itself into a willing exertion of it's powers, without any reference to their *comparative* value' (*L* 1: 631–2). On 10 October 1800 William Wordsworth wrote to the printers cancelling the sheets of 'Christabel' already printed and the passage in the original version of the Preface which read: 'For the sake of variety and from a consciousness of my own weakness I have again requested the assistance of a Friend who contributed largely to the first volume, and who has now furnished me with the long and beautiful [long and beautiful *struck out in MS*] Poem of Christabel, without which I should not yet have ventured to present a second volume to the public'.

In a letter to Thomas Poole written only a day or so after Wordsworth's letter to the printers, STC says: 'The truth is, the endeavor to finish Christabel, (which has swelled into a Poem of 1400 lines) for the second Volume of the Lyrical Ballads threw my business terribly back – & now I am sweating for it –' (*L* 1: 634). Then on 1 November he wrote to Josiah Wedgwood about his effort to complete 'Christabel' for *LB* (1800): 'I tried to perform my promise; but the deep unutterable Disgust, which I had suffered in the translation of that accursed Wallenstein [Schiller's epic historical drama, the last two parts of which STC translated in 1799–1800] seemed to have stricken me with barrenness – for I tried & tried, & nothing would come of it. I desisted with a deeper dejection than I am willing to remember. . . . one day I dined out at the house of a neighbouring clergyman, & somehow or other drank so much wine, that I found some effort & dexterity requisite to balance myself on the hither Edge of Sobriety. The next day, my verse making faculties returned to me, and I proceeded successfully – till my poem grew so long & in Wordsworth's opinion so impressive, that he rejected it from his volume as disproportionate both in size & merit, & as discordant in it's character' (*L* 1: 643). STC makes clear in subsequent letters that the exclusion of 'Christabel' from *LB* (1800) increased his sense of faltering poetic power (see his letters to John Thelwall of 17 December 1800 [*L* 1: 655–6]; to Francis Wrangham of 19 December 1800 [*L* 1: 657–8], and to William Godwin of 25 March 1801 [*L* 2: 713–14]).

Plans to publish 'Christabel' separately emerge first in a letter to Poole of 6 January 1801 (*L* 2: 661), then in another letter to Poole of 16 March 1801: 'I shall therefore, as I said, immediately publish my CHRISTABEL, with two Essays annexed to it, on the Praeternatural – and on Metre' (*L* 2: 707). Wordsworth referred to this plea in a letter to Poole of 9 April 1801 – but nothing materialized. 'Christabel' circulated in MS: Scott says that he heard it recited in 1802, and he acknowledged its influence on *The Lay of the Last Minstrel* (1805, see the Preface to the 1830 edition of the *Lay*). Byron in turn heard Scott quote parts of 'Christabel' in June 1815 and expressed his admiration for it in letters to STC of 18 and 27 October 1815 (*Byron's Letters and Journals*, ed. Leslie Marchand, 4: 318–19, 321). In a note to stanza xix of *The Siege of Corinth* (1816) Byron acknowledges 'a close, though unintentional, resemblance in these twelve lines to a passage in an unpublished poem of Mr Coleridge, called "Christabel". It was not till after these lines were written that I heard that wild and singularly original and beautiful poem recited' (*Lord Byron: The Complete Poetical Works*, ed. Jerome J. McGann [1981] 3: 486). The famous account of Shelley's response to Byron's recitation from 'Christabel' at the Villa Diodati on the shores of Lake Geneva on 18 June 1816 is given in *The Diary of William Polidori*, ed. W. M. Rossetti. It was Byron who recommended to his publisher, John Murray, that he publish 'Christabel' in the volume containing 'Kubla Khan' and 'The Pains of Sleep'.

Contemporary critical response to 'Christabel' was disappointing, given the admiration expressed by Scott, Byron and others who knew the poem in MS. The *Critical Review* praised 'This very graceful and fanciful poem' (May 1816, 3: 509), but Hazlitt, writing in Leigh Hunt's *Examiner*, was sarcastically dismissive: ' "Christabel," which has been much read and admired in manuscript, is now for the first time confided to the public. . . . We wonder that Mr Murray, who has an eye for things, should suffer this 'mastiff bitch' to come into his shop. Is she a sort of Cerberus to fright away the critics? But – gentlemen, she is toothless.' He acknowledges that 'In parts . . . there is a great deal of beauty, both of thought, imagery, and versification; but the effect of the general story is dim, obscure, and visionary' (*Examiner*, 2 June 1816, 348–9).

In the last chapter of *BL*, STC addresses himself to the poem's contemporary reception. STC's latest comment on the poem is probably the one recorded in *Table Talk* for 1 July 1833: 'The reason of my not having finished Christabel is not that I don't know how to do it; for I have, as I always had, the whole plan entire from beginning to end in my mind; but I fear I could not carry on with equal success the execution of the Idea – the most difficult, I think, that can be attempted to Romantic Poetry – I mean witchery by daylight. I venture to think that Geraldine, as far as she goes, is successful – but I doubt any one being able to go much farther without recourse to some of the common shifts' (*CC* 1: 409–10). Dr James Gillman says in his *Life of S. T. Coleridge* (1838) that STC 'explained the story of *Christabel* to his friends', and that it is 'partly founded on the notion that the virtuous of the world save the wicked' (p. 283). Gillman goes on to report a plan for extending and completing the poem's narrative (pp. 301–3; Campbell quotes much of the plan in the notes to *1893* 604). STC's nephew Henry Nelson Coleridge reported the following comment made by Wordsworth in 1836: 'He said he had no idea how "Christabel" was to have been finished, and he did not think my uncle had ever conceived, in his own mind, any definite plan for it; that the poem had been composed while they were in habit of daily intercourse, and almost in his presence, and when there was the most unreserved intercourse between them as to all their literary projects and productions, and he had never heard from him any plan for finishing it. . . . I omitted to ask him, what seems obvious enough now, whether in conversing about it, he had never asked my uncle how it would end. The answer would have settled the question' (quoted in *1893* 604 n.).

Nineteenth-century commentators on 'Christabel' – including STC himself – divert attention from the central erotic aspect of the poem, with its inescapable suggestion of lesbian sexuality. This was true of most twentieth-century criticism until the 1970s: see Virginia L. Radley, '*Christabel*: Directions Old and New', *Studies in English Literature* (1964); Karen Swann, ' "Christabel": The Wandering Mother and the Enigma of Form', *Studies in Romanticism* 23 (1984); and Charles J. Rzepka, 'Christabel's "Wandering Mother" and the Discourse of the Self: A Lacanian Reading of Repressed Narration', *Romanticism Past and Present* 10 (1986).

6–7 In a copy of the second edition of 1816, the rhyme-words in these lines are changed by an unidentified hand to 'bold' and 'old', then to 'rich' and 'which'. As Rosenbaum and White note in *Index* CoS 64, these and other revisions made in this copy are not in STC's hand, as E. H. Coleridge claims in the notes to

1912. Yet the change of 'bitch' to 'which' in line 7 was included in *1828* and *1829*. *1834* returns to the original couplet.

16–20 Cf. Dorothy Wordsworth, *Alfoxden Journal* 31 January 1798: 'Set forward to Stowey at half-past five. A violent storm in the wood; sheltered under the hollies. When we left home the moor immensely large, the sky scattered over with clouds. These soon closed in, contracting the dimensions of the moon without concealing her.'

28–9 Between these lines the following passage appears in the first edition of 1816 only: 'Dreams, that made her moan and leap, / As on her bed she lay in sleep.'

30 *weal* well-being.

32 'The breezes they were still also' (*1816*).

34 *rarest mistletoe* According to ancient Celtic legend mistletoe was to be held in veneration when found in the rare circumstance of growing on an oak tree.

37 *sprang* 'leaps' (*1816*).

49–52 Cf. Dorothy Wordsworth, *Alfoxden Journal* 7 March 1798: 'William and I drank tea at Coleridge's. A cloudy sky. Observed nothing particularly interesting – the distant prospect obscured. One only leaf upon the top of a tree – the sole remaining leaf – danced round and round like a rag blown by the wind.'

61–5 These lines are an expansion of a briefer description in *1816*: 'Her neck, her feet, her arms were bare, / And the jewels disorder'd in her hair'. This revision appears as a marginal insertion in the copy of the second edition of *1816* cited in the notes to lines 6–7 above.

73 Though no quotation punctuation appears at this point in *1834* and in other earlier editions, it has been added in a way consistent with such punctuation elsewhere in *1834*.

87 *amain* at full speed.

88 *once* Three of the MSS have 'twice we cross'd the shade of night'.

92 *entranced* 'in fits' (*1816*).

I wis I believe (STC seems to have mistaken the meaning of the Middle English adverb 'ywis', 'certainly').

106–22

> Saying that she should command
> The service of Sir Leoline;
> And straight be convey'd, free from thrall,
> Back to her noble father's hall.
>
> So up she rose and forth they pass'd
> With hurrying steps yet nothing fast.
> Her lucky stars the lady blest,
> And Christabel she sweetly said –
> 'All our household are at rest,
> Each one sleeping in his bed;
> Sir Leoline is weak in health,
> And may not well awakened be.
> So to my room we'll creep in stealth,
> And you to-night must sleep with me.'
>
> (*1816*)

129–32 Geraldine's inability to enter the castle gate on her own power is the first of several suggestions that she is an evil spirit. According to legend, a witch cannot cross a threshold that has been blessed, without assistance.

148 The mastiff's 'angry moan' is a second sign of Geraldine's evil: animals are supposed to be able to sense the presence of an evil spirit.

152 *scritch* screech.

158–9 The 'fit of flame' is the third sign, again following folklore convention, of Geraldine's evil.

174 Rushes were commonly used in the medieval period as floor covering.

193 Two additional lines appear at the end of this verse paragraph in several of the MSS: ' "Nay, drink it up, I pray you do, / Believe me it will comfort you" '.

203 This is the first point in *1834* at which quotation punctuation appears.

205 *Peak* droop in health and spirit, waste away; the phrase 'peak and pine', originally from *Macbeth* 1.3.23, has become conventional.

252–3 Between these lines three of the existing MSS have an additional line: 'Are lean and old and foul of hue'. In his review in the *Examiner* for 2 June 1816, Hazlitt writes: 'The manuscript runs thus, or nearly thus:

> Behold her bosom and half her side –
> *Hideous, deformed, and pale of hue.*

This line is necessary to make common sense of the first and second part. "It is the keystone that makes up the arch". For that reason Mr Coleridge left it out' (349). Dr William Polidori's *Diary* indicates that this was also the version of these lines famously recited by Byron at the Villa Diodati on 18 June 1816.

254 'And she is to sleep by Christabel' (*1816*). In its present form this line first appears in *1828*.

255–61 These lines, which do not appear in the first edition of *1816*, were added in *1828*. Instead, *1816* reads: 'She took two paces and a stride, / And lay down by the maiden's side'.

258 *assay* effort, attempt.

286 Cf. Keats, 'The Eve of St Agnes' 220: 'Rose-bloom fell on her hands, together prest'.

288 *bale* evil, sorrow.

294 *I wis* I believe (see note to 92).

306 *Thou'st had thy will!* Cf. 'Ancient Mariner' (*1834*) 16: 'The Mariner hath his will'.

By tairn and rill There is a note on this phrase in the MS of the poem that STC presented to Sara Hutchinson in 1801: 'Tairn or Tarn (derived by Lye from the Icelandic *Tiorn*, stagnum, palus) is rendered in our dictionaries as synonymous with Mere or Lake; but it is properly a large Pool or Reservoir in the Mountains, commonly the Feeder of some Mere in the valley's. Tarn Watling and Blellum Tarn, though on lower ground that other Tarns, are yet not exceptions, for both are on elevations, and Blellum Tarn feeds the Wynander Mere.'

310 *fell* high moor, hill.

315–18 Cf. 'The Nightingale' 102–5.

332 Thomas Allsop reports a conversation during May 1821 in which STC praises a passage from 'Hymn to St Theresa' by Richard Crashaw (1621?–1649) beginning:

> Since 'tis not to be had at home
> She'll travel to a Martyrdome.
> No home for her, confesses she,
> But where she may a Martyr be.

'These verses were ever present to my mind whilst writing the second part of *Christabel*; if, indeed, by some subtle process of the mind they did not suggest the first thought of the whole poem' (*Letters, Conversation, and Recollections of S. T. Coleridge*, ed. Thomas Allsop, 1836).

339 *sacristan* sexton.

341 *tell* say prayers while counting the beads of a rosary.

344–59 'Bratha Head', 'Wyndermere', 'Langdale Pike' (Peak), 'Witch's Lair', 'Dungeon-ghyll' (a 'ghyll' is a ravine forming the bed of a stream) and 'Borodale' are all Lake District place-names.

365 *plight* plait.

408–26 Campbell notes in *1893* (607) that STC quoted this verse paragraph in a letter to Thomas Poole of 13 February 1813, in which STC acknowledges Poole's congratulations on the success of the play *Remorse* as putting an end to an estrangement that had begun in 1810: 'Dear Poole Love so deep & so domesticated with the whole Being, as mine was to you, can never cease *to be* –. To quote the best & sweetest Lines, I ever wrote – "Alas! they had been Friends in Youth! . . ."' (*L* 3: 435–6).

445 *kenned* recognized.

473 *ween* suppose, imagine.

495 *Knorren Moor, Halegarth Wood* Lake District place-names.

613 *And* 'But' (*1816*).

615 *the Baron's* 'her Father's' (*1816, 1828*).

656–77 In the letter to Southey of 6 May 1801 which contains the Conclusion to Part II, STC makes it evident that his son Hartley was the original provocation for these lines: 'Dear Hartley! we are at times alarmed by the state of his Health – but at present he is well – if I were to lose him, I am afraid, it would exceedingly deaden my affection for any other children I may have –

> A little child, a limber Elf . . .

A very metaphysical account of Fathers calling their children rogues, rascals, & little varlets – & c –' (*L* 2: 728–9). Empson comments that the lines 'have so little to do with *Christabel* that Coleridge had to reverse his account of Sir Leoline's emotions to avoid obvious self-contradiction. Sir Leoline's fatherly feelings which in the original [a MS now in the Wordsworth Library, Grasmere] had reinforced his anger "And did *not* work confusion there" had to be changed in the published version so that they "did *but* work confusion there"' (*Coleridge's Verse* 245).

674 *O sorrow and shame* Cf. line 296, where this phrase refers to Geraldine.

Lines to W. L. while he Sang a Song to Purcell's Music

First published in the *Annual Anthology* for 1800; included by STC in *1817* and all subsequent collections. There is a MS entitled 'To Mr William Linley', dated 12 September 1797, in the Buffalo and Erie County Public Library, Gluck collection. Linley was Richard Brinsley Sheridan's brother-in-law, whom STC had met on a visit to W. L. Bowles in September 1797; see *L* 1: 352.

3 *L*———! 'Linley' in MS.

The Three Graves

First published in *The Friend* No. 6 (21 September 1809), and subsequently included in *1817*, *1828*, *1829* and *1834*. A MS copy of the poem, written by Sarah Stoddart (later married to William Hazlitt) is in the Forster Collection, Victoria and Albert Museum, together with a MS of the Preface and emendations in STC's own hand: this, apparently, was the printer's copy for the initial publication (see *Index* CoS 686). The poem was printed continuously in *The Friend*, though it is divided into stanzas in the MS, as it is in *1817* and subsequent collections. Campbell and E. H. Coleridge both date the composition of the poem to 1798 (see *1912* 1: 267 n.), despite STC's referring in the 1809 Preface to his having 'composed the verses . . . somewhat more than twelve years ago' (i.e. 1796–7). Beer dates the poem 1797–8. On 9 October 1809 STC wrote to Poole: 'Strange! but the "Three Graves" is the *only* thing I have yet heard generally praised and enquired after!!' (*L* 3: 234). In a marginal annotation in a copy of *1817* STC commented: 'This very poem was selected [for *The Friend*], notwithstanding the preface, as a proof of my judgment and poetic diction, and a fair specimen of the style of my poems generally.' In the 1818 edition of *The Friend* (vol. II, Essay 1) STC wrote: 'In the homely ballad of the THREE GRAVES (published in my SIBYLLINE LEAVES) I have attempted to exemplify the effect, which one painful idea vividly impressed on the mind under unusual circumstances, might have in producing an alienation of the understanding; and in the parts hitherto published, I have endeavoured to trace the progress to madness, step by step. But though the main incidents are facts, the detail of the circumstances is of my own invention, that is, not what I know, but what I conceive likely to have been the case, or at least equivalent to it' (*CC* 1: 341). The present version of the Preface appeared in *1817*; in 1809 it began as follows: 'As I wish to commence the important Subject of – *The Principles* of political Justice with a separate number of THE FRIEND, and shall at the same time comply with the wishes communicated to me by one of my female Readers, who writes as the representative of many others, I shall conclude this Number with the following Fragment, or the third and fourth parts of a Tale consisting of six. The last two parts may be given hereafter, if the present should appear to have afforded pleasure, and to have answered the purpose of a relief and amusement to my Readers. The story . . . [continues essentially as in *1817* and later collections].' In *1893* Campbell printed as Parts I and II two fragmentary sequences of verse 'found among Coleridge's papers . . . from his autograph *MS*' (590); E. H. Coleridge followed Campbell in *1912* (1: 267 ff.). These fragments are now known to have been composed by William Wordsworth (see *The Friend*, *CC* 2: 89–96). Beer prints 'Part I' and 'Part II' in the Everyman Edition, suggesting only that Wordsworth may have contributed one substantial sequence and intermittently 'elsewhere' to them (155 n.).

PART III This heading does not appear in the texts printed in STC's lifetime; it was first added in *1893*.

6 *spikes* 'strikes' (*1817*), possibly a Somerset dialect word substituted in this edition; see *1912* 1: 276 n. Wagons loaded with corn (wheat) passing through the narrow lanes leave scattered stalks on the hedges.

18 *I've heard* The perfect tense here and in line 31 suggests that Mary may still be alive and talking to the sexton.

24 Compare the mother's spectral appearances in 'Christabel'. There are other verbal echoes and thematic links between the two poems.

70 *Commination prayer* in Anglican liturgy, a recital of divine threatenings against sinners; part of an office appointed to be read on Ash Wednesday and at other times (*OED*).

129 *dandled* moved (a child, etc) lightly up and down in the arms or on the knee.

257–60 The punctuation in this stanza has been modernized to avoid the confusion of the punctuation in previous printings.

273–6 Cf. 'Ancient Mariner' (*1834*) 601–6.

311–12 'He sat upright; and with quick voice / While his eyes seem'd to start' (MS).

Carmen reliquum in futurum tempus relegatum. 'The rest of the poem was postponed to a future time'; *To-morrow! and To-morrow! and To-morrow!* is from *Macbeth* (V.5.19). According to Beer, STC wrote this note in 1815.

The Wanderings of Cain

First published in its present form in *1828*; included in *1829* and *1834*, though in the latter printing, as here, without a paragraph of the Prefatory Note immediately following the passage of verse ('Encinctured with a twine of leaves'). The omitted passage runs as follows: 'I have here given the birth, parentage, and premature disease of the "Wanderings of Cain, a poem", – interesting, however, my Readers, not to think so meanly of my judgment as to suppose that I either regard or offer it as any excuse for the publication of the following fragment (and I may add, of one or two others in its neighbourhood) in its primitive crudity. But I should find still greater difficulty in forgiving myself were I to record pro *laedio* publico a set of petty mishaps and annoyances which I myself wish to forget. I must be content therefore with assuring the friendly Reader, that the less he attributes its appearance to the Author's will, choice, or judgment, the nearer to the truth he will be. S. T. Coleridge.' The prose headed 'Canto II' was first published in *The Bijou*, ed. W. Fraser (London, 1828), without the Prefatory Note and the verse. A draft of a prose continuation, or possibly of an alternative version, appears in a notebook, now in the British Library, containing material dated 1805–16 (*N* 2: 2780 and n.). E. H. Coleridge, who first published most of this notebook entry in the *Athenaeum* (1894) and quotes all of it in *1912* 1: 285–6 n., argues that 'The introduction of "alligators" and an "immense meadow" help to fix the date of

The Wanderings of Cain. The imagery is derived from William Bartram's *Travels in Florida and Carolina*, which Coleridge and Wordsworth studied in 1798'. But see Coburn on the difficulty of this dating (*N* 2: 2257 n.). Beer dates the poem 1797–8 in *Everyman*.

The verse was first published in the 'Conclusion' to *Aids to Reflection* with the following note: 'Will the Reader forgive me if I attempt at once to illustrate and relieve the subject [STC has been discussing 'enthusiastic Mystics'] by annexing the first stanza of the Poem, composed in the same year in which I wrote the Ancient Mariner and the first Book of Christabel' (*CC* 390–1). These verses also appear in a letter to Byron of 22 October 1815 (*L* 4: 602) and in a letter to an unidentified recipient of 12 May 1825 (*L* 5: 449).

Prefatory Note
A prose composition, one not in metre at least See Wordsworth's remarks about the language of prose and verse in the Preface to *Lyrical Ballads*, and STC's differing view of the matter in *BL*.

the draft of the plan and proposed incidents Among the Coleridge MSS in the British Library is a prose outline for a proposed continuation, headed 'Book 3rd'. Part of this MS was published by E. H. Coleridge in *The Athenaeum* article mentioned above; see *Index* CoS 793.

I have in vain tried to recover the lines Cf. Preface to 'Kubla Khan'.

[verse] . . . *a little child* . . . *Has he no friend, no loving mother near?* Cf. 'Dejection: An Ode' 121–5.

Fire, Famine, and Slaughter. A War Eclogue. With an Apologetic Preface

First published in the *Morning Post* for 8 January 1798, where it was signed 'Laberius' (see headnote to 'Parliamentary Oscillators'); included in the *Annual Anthology* (1800) and in *1817, 1828, 1829, 1834*. The Apologetic Preface, first published in *1817*, is printed in the Appendix to that edition. The Vendée, an area in the west of France on the Bay of Biscay, was the scene of a major counter-revolutionary insurrection in 1793, and of harsh reprisals by the Republican army. In 1796 a group of Vendéan royalist emigrés, backed by England, attempted an invasion but were defeated. In the version of the poem printed in the *Morning Post* the scene is set in 'a depopulated Tract in La Vendée'. STC dated the poem '1796' in *1817* and all subsequent editions, probably to suggest a date of composition closer to the historical events to which it refers.

2 'SLAUGHTER. I will name him in your ear' (*Morning Post*).
17–18 'FAMINE. Then sound it not, yet let me know; / Darkly hint it – soft and low!' (*Morning Post*).
19 *Letters four* P-i-t-t, English Prime Minister who had declared war on France.
20 *Both* 'FAMINE' (*Morning Post*).
22–3 'And I have spill'd the blood since then / Of thrice ten hundred thousand men' (*Morning Post*).
47 *Hedge* 'Huts' (*Morning Post*).

50 'As on I strode with monstrous strides' (*Morning Post*).
59 *I wist* 'I wish' (*Morning Post*).
65 'How shall I give him honour due?' (*Morning Post*).
76ff. In the *Morning Post* the poem ends as follows:

> [To *Slaughter*
> For *you* he turn'd the dust to mud
> With his fellow creatures' blood!
> [To *Famine*.
> And hunger scorch'd as many more,
> To make *your* cup of joy run o'er.
> [To *Both*.
> Full ninety moons, he by my troth!
> Hath richly cater'd for you both!
> And in an hour would you repay
> An eight years' debt? Away! away!
> I alone am faithful! I
> Cling to him everlastingly.

The Old Man of the Alps

First published in the *Morning Post* for 8 March 1798; never included in any collection in STC's lifetime and not published again until *1877–80*. The present text is from *1912*. The poem was signed 'Nicius Erythraeus', as was 'Lewti', published in the *Morning Post* five weeks later. Janus Nicius Erythraeus (Giovanni Vittorio d'Rossi, 1577–1647) was an Italian Latin scholar and poet.

13 *shiel* often 'shieling'; a hut or small cottage used by shepherds in summer.
37 *cot* cottage.
65 *NANSY'S murderous day* Nancy is the chief city of Lorraine in north-eastern France. During the French Revolution a mutiny in Nancy in August 1790 was put down with much bloodshed.
114 *Homestalls* homesteads; i.e. remains of farm houses.

The Apotheosis, or The Snow-Drop

Published in the *Express and Evening Chronicle* for 6–9 January 1798 (No. 516), where it was probably reprinted directly from the *Morning Post* for 3 January 1798 (there are no known surviving copies of this number of the *Morning Post*). This printed version is reprinted, in parallel with a new transcription of the surviving MS, in David V. Erdman, 'Lost Poem Found', *Bulletin of the New York Public Library* 65 (1961): 249–68. The best previous transcription of the MS is Griggs's in *L* 1: 639–42. The poem was never collected by STC himself. Campbell printed a six-stanza version derived from the MS in *1893* under the title 'The Snow-Drop'; E. H. Coleridge provides a poorly transcribed eight-stanza version in *1912*. The date of composition is mistakenly given as 1800 by both Campbell and E. H.

Coleridge because they were unaware of the poem's first printing and because the poem is addressed to Mary Robinson (1758–1800), to whom STC did address 'A Stranger Minstrel' in 1800. Beer in *Everyman* oddly follows the version in *1912*, but dates the poem December 1797. In the MS, which is in the Berg Collection at the New York Public Library, the poem is titled 'To the Snow Drop' and is addressed 'To the Editor of the Morning Post': 'Sir, I am one of your many readers who have been highly gratified by some extracts from Mrs Robinson's "Walsingham": you will oblige me by inserting the following lines [written] immediately on the perusal of her beautiful poem "The Snow Drop". – ZAGRI.' 'Zagri' appears as a name in STC's *Osorio*. When the poem was printed it was signed 'Francini', a name which Erdman, following Carl Woodring, connects with a famous Florentine family ('Lost Poem Found' 259). Mary Robinson was associated with the Della Cruscan movement in late eighteenth-century English poetry, which linked itself to the city of Florence. The style of STC's poem echoes the emotive, ornamented manner of much Della Cruscan verse.

5 *LAURA* Here Mary Robinson, but also the name of the Florentine woman addressed and celebrated in Petrarch's lyrics.
20 *Pierian* pertaining to Pieria, a region in ancient Macedonia sacred to the Muses.
28 *myrtle-tree* In mythological tradition sacred to Venus.
30 *Etesian* periodical or annual, particularly with reference to winds from the north in the Aegean Sea.
40 *Lethe* the river of forgetfulness in the classical underworld.
57–60 Cf. 'The Eolian Harp' 12–15: 'And that simplest Lute, / . . . How by the desultory breeze caress'd, / Like some coy maid half yielding to her lover'.

Frost at Midnight

First published in 1798 in a quarto pamphlet that also contained 'Fears in Solitude' and 'France. An Ode' (the publisher was Joseph Johnson, who had close ties to Blake, Wollstonecraft, Godwin, Paine, Priestley and Barbauld). The three poems were included in the *Poetical Register* for 1808–9, which was reissued in 1812; in 1812 they were again published in a pamphlet entitled *Poems*. STC included 'Frost at Midnight' in *1817, 1828, 1829* and *1834*. The poem is dated 'February 1798' in all editions except *1829* and *1834*, where it is undated. The major textual differences between earlier versions (the quarto pamphlet and the *Poetical Register*) and later ones concern lines 20–24 and the end of the poem.

7 *My cradled infant* Hartley Coleridge.
11 *This populous village* Nether Stowey.
15 *Only that film* 'In all parts of the kingdom these films are called *strangers* and supposed to portend the arrival of some absent friend' (STC's note, 1798 quarto).
18 *live* Subjunctive?
20–3 The present version of these lines first appeared in *1829*. The 1798 quarto reads:

> With which I can hold commune. Idle thought!
> But still the living spirit in our frame,

> That loves not to behold a lifeless thing,
> Transfuses into all its own delights,
> Its own volition, sometimes with deep faith
> And sometimes with fantastic playfulness.

In the *Poetical Register* this becomes:

> With which I can hold commune: haply hence,
> That still the living spirit in our frame,
> Which loves not to behold a lifeless thing,
> Transfuses into all things its own Will,
> And its own pleasures; sometimes with deep faith,
> And sometimes with a wilful playfulness
> That stealing pardon from our common sense
> Smiles, as self-scornful, to disarm the scorn
> For these wild reliques of our childish thought,
> That flit about, oft go, and oft return
> Not uninvited.

In *1817* and *1828* the passage is compressed as follows:

> To which the living spirit in our frame,
> That loves not to behold a lifeless thing,
> Transfuses its own pleasures, its own will.

23–4 In the 1798 quarto the opening lines of the second verse paragraph read:

> Ah me! amus'd by no such curious toys
> Of the self-watching subtilizing mind,
> How often in my earlier school-boy days
> With most believing superstitious wish . . .

In the *Poetical Register* the first three lines were changed to:

> Ah there was a time,
> When oft amused by no such subtle toys
> Of the self-watching mind, a child at school . . .

In *1817* the passage was compressed into the present version of line 24.

37 The 'stern preceptor' was the Rev. James Bowyer, headmaster of Christ's Hospital.

43 The reference is to STC's sister Ann; see the early poem 'On Receiving an Account that his Only Sister's Death was Inevitable'.

44 ff. Campbell observes in the notes to *1893* (610): 'When Coleridge wrote and [first] published these lines he had no prospect of living in the lake country. They must have been inspired by a purely prophetic vision.' See STC's letter to William Godwin, written from Greta Hall, Keswick on 22 September 1800: 'I look at my doted-on Hartley – he moves, he lives, he finds impulses from within & from without – he is the darling of the Sun and of the Breeze! Nature seems to bless him as a thing of her own! He looks at the clouds, the mountains, the living Beings of the Earth, & vaults & jubilates! Solemn Looks & solemn Words have been hitherto connected in his mind with great & magnificent objects only – with lightning, with thunder, with the waterfall blazing in the Sunset' (*L* 1: 625).

48 *thrills* 'fills' in 1798 quarto, *Poetical Register*, and *1817* – but changed to 'thrills' in the Errata for *1817*.

51–3 Cf. Wordsworth, *The Prelude* (1805) VI. 274–84.

72 ff. The 1798 quarto ends as follows:

> Or whether the secret ministery of cold
> Shall hang them up in silent icicles
> Quietly shining to the quiet moon,
> Like those, my babe! which ere tomorrow's warmth
> Have capp'd their sharp keen points with pendulous drops,
> Will catch thine eye, and with their novelty
> Suspend thy little soul; then make thee shout,
> And stretch and flutter from thy mother's arms
> As thou wouldst fly for very eagerness.

France. An Ode

First published in the *Morning Post* for 16 April 1798, under the title 'The Recantation: An Ode'. It was included, along with 'Fears in Solitude' and 'Frost at Midnight', in the quarto pamphlet published by Joseph Johnson in the same year. The poem was reprinted in the *Morning Post* for 14 October 1802, then included in the *Poetical Register* for 1808–9. In 1812 the quarto pamphlet of 1798 was reissued. 'France. An Ode' was included in *1817*, *1828*, *1829* and *1834*. Lines 85–98 are quoted, with a few minor changes, in *BL* Ch. X, where the poem is called 'FRANCE, a Palinode' (1: 199–200). Although it is dated 'February 1798' in the quarto pamphlet, the *Poetical Register* and *1817*, and (by mistake) 'February 1797' in *1828*, *1829* and *1834*, its immediate historical occasion was the French invasion of Switzerland in March 1798. In a MS note to 'Ode to the Departing Year' written in a copy of *1817*, STC refers to 'the invasion of Switzerland by the French Republic, which occasioned the Ode that follows, a kind of palinode'.

The following editorial note was prefixed to the poem when it first appeared in the *Morning Post*: 'The following excellent Ode will be in unison with the feelings of every friend to Liberty and foe to Oppression; of all who, admiring the French Revolution, detest and deplore the conduct of France towards Switzerland. It is very satisfactory to find so zealous and steady an advocate for Freedom as Mr COLERIDGE concur with us in condemning the conduct of France towards the Swiss Cantons. Indeed his concurrence is not singular; we know of no Friend to Liberty who is not of his opinion. What we most admire is the *avowal* of his sentiments, and public censure of the unprincipled and atrocious conduct of France. The poem itself is written with great energy. The second, third, and fourth stanzas contain some of the most vigorous lines we have ever read. The lines in the fourth stanza:–

> "To scatter rage and trait'rous guilt
> Where Peace her jealous home had built",

to the end of the stanza are particularly expressive and beautiful.'

When the poem was reprinted in the *Morning Post* in 1802 the following note and argument were prefixed: 'The following ODE was first published in this paper (in the beginning of the year 1798) in a less perfect state. The present state of France and Switzerland gives it so peculiar an interest at the present time that we wished to re-publish it and accordingly have procured from the Author a corrected copy. ARGUMENT. *First Stanza.* An invocation to those objects in Nature the contemplation of which had inspired the Poet with a devotional love of Liberty. *Second Stanza.* The exultation of the Poet at the commencement of the French Revolution, and his unqualified abhorrence of the Alliance against the Republic. *Third Stanza.* The blasphemies and horrors during the domination of the Terrorists regarded by the Poet as a transient storm, and as the natural consequence of the former despotism and of the foul superstition of Popery. Reason, indeed, began to suggest many apprehensions; yet still the Poet struggled to retain the hope that France would make conquests of no other means than by presenting to the observation of Europe a people more happy and better instructed than under other forms of Government. *Fourth Stanza.* Switzerland, and the Poet's recantation. *Fifth Stanza.* An address to Liberty, in which the Poet expresses his conviction that those feelings and that grand *ideal* of Freedom which the mind attains by its contemplation of its individual nature, and of the sublime surrounding objects (see Stanza the First) do not belong to men, as a society, nor can possibly be either gratified or realised, under any form of human government; but belong to the individual man, so far as he is pure, and inflamed with the love and adoration of God in Nature.'

2 'Veering your pathless march without controul' (1802 *Morning Post*).

6 *slope* 'steep' (1798 *Morning Post* and quarto, 1802 *Morning Post*, *Poetical Register*).

12 *way* 'path' (1802 *Morning Post*).

23 *smote* 'shook' (1802 *Morning Post*).

26 *lofty* 'eager' (1802 *Morning Post*).

30 *marched* 'moved' (1802 *Morning Post*). Prussia and Austria declared war against France in 1792, England and Holland in 1793.

35 *flung* 'spread' (1802 *Morning Post*).

43 *Blasphemy*['*s*] Atheist rationalism was an important aspect of the French Revolution, as was the appropriation and secularization of property previously held by the church.

53 *insupportably* 'irresistibly' (1802 *Morning Post*).

54 *ramp* Although this word appears in all versions of the poem up to *1817*, *1828* has 'tramp' – certainly a printer's error, but one which went uncorrected in *1829*, *1834* and subsequent collections until the edition of 1877–80. In *Tait's Magazine* (September 1834), De Quincey accused STC of plagiarizing the line from *Samson Agonistes* 1835–9. In a MS note to the copy of *1817* referred to in the headnote, STC says opposite this line: '*Samson Agonistes*, but never published the acknowledgment'. See Campbell, *1893* 608.

58 *reproached* 'rebuk'd' (1802 *Morning Post*).

62 *compel* 'persuade' (1802 *Morning Post*).

66 *Helvetia's* Switzerland's. The singular 'cavern' in *1834* is a departure – probably a printer's error – from 'caverns' in all previous texts.

69 *fleeing* 'flying' (1798 and 1802 *Morning Post*).

75 *stormy* 'native' (1802 *Morning Post*)

77 *taint* 'stain' (1802 *Morning Post*).

79 *patriot* 'patient' (1798 and 1802 *Morning Post*).

80 *Are these* 'Was this' (1802 *Morning Post*).

81 *Kings in the low lust* 'monarchs in the lust' (1802 *Morning Post*).

85-90 In the 1798 *Morning Post* version the following note appears after stanza IV: 'The fifth stanza, which alluded to the African Slave Trade as conducted by this country, and to the present Ministry and their supporters, has been omitted, and would have been omitted without remark if the commencing lines of the sixth stanza had not referred to it.

> VI
>
> Shall I with *these* my patriot zeal combine?
> No, Afric, no! They stand before my ken
> Loath'd as th'Hyaenas, that in murky den
> Whine o'er their prey, and mangle with their whine,
> Divinest Liberty! with vain endeavour,
> Have I pursued thee, many a weary hour, etc.'

The lines which now begin stanza V (referred to in the above note as stanza VI) first appeared in the 1798 quarto pamphlet, where there is no mention of an omitted stanza on the slave trade.

87 *burst* 'break' (1802 *Morning Post*).

91 *strain* 'pomp' (*BL* Ch. X).

95 *Priestcraft's* 'priesthood's' (1798 quarto, *Poetical Register*); 'superstitions' (*BL* Ch. X).

97 *subtle* 'cherub' (*BL* Ch. X).

98 'To live amid the winds and move upon the waves' (1798 *Morning Post* and quarto, *Poetical Register*); 'To live among the winds and brood upon the waves' (1802 *Morning Post*).

100 *scarce* 'just' (1802 *Morning Post*).

102 *temples* 'forehead' (1802 *Morning Post*).

104 *with intensest love* 'by intensest love' (1802 *Morning Post*).

Lewti, or the Circassian Love-Chaunt

First published in the *Morning Post* for 13 April 1798, signed 'Nicias Erythraeus' (see headnote to 'The Old Man of the Alps'). It was included in the *Annual Anthology* (1800) and in *1817*, *1828*, *1829* and *1834*. The three MSS of the poem now in the British Library (see *1912*, Appendix I.G) show its very close relationship to Wordsworth's 'Beauty and Moonlight': a transcription apparently in Dorothy Wordsworth's hand is almost identical to Wordsworth's 36-line poem, which was composed c. 1786. See *Index* CoS 296 and Jane Worthington Smyser, 'Coleridge's Use of Wordsworth's Juvenilia', *PMLA* 65 (1950), 419-26. The female figure addressed in these MS versions is at first 'Mary' and 'Sara' before eventually becoming 'Lewti'. 'Lewti' was to have been included in the first edition of *LB*, but at the last moment it was cancelled and 'The Nightingale' substituted for it. When first published in the *Morning Post* 'Lewti' was three times the length of the MS versions and contained two passages never again included in the poem (see notes below). It was also introduced by the following note: 'It is not amongst the least pleasing of our recollections, that we have been the means of gratifying the public taste with some exquisite pieces of Original Poetry. For many of them we have been indebted to the author of the Circassian's Love Chant. Amidst images of war and woe, amidst scenes of carnage and horror of devastation and dismay, it may afford the mind a temporary relief to wander to the magic haunts of the Muses, to bowers and fountains which the despoiling powers of war have never visited, and where the lover pours forth his complaint, or receives the recompense of his constancy. The whole of the subsequent Love Chant is in a warm and impassioned strain. The fifth and last stanzas are, we think, the best.' It is unclear why STC dated 'Lewti' 1795 in *1817* and subsequent editions, including *1834*. 'Circassian' refers to a group of tribes native to the Caucasus and noted for their physical beauty.

8–9 In a copy of the *Annual Anthology* annotated by STC he wrote between these lines: 'Two lines expressing the wetness of the rock'; see Campbell's note in *1893* 568.

10 *tressy* resembling long locks of hair.

14–15 Between these lines the following passage appears in the *Morning Post* version:

> I saw the white waves, o'er and o'er,
> Break against the distant shore.
> All at once upon the sight,
> All at once they broke in light;
> I heard no murmur of their roar,
> Nor ever I beheld them flowing,
> Neither coming, neither going;
> But only saw them o'er and o'er,
> Break against the curvèd shore:
> Now disappearing from the sight,
> Now twinkling regular and white,
> And LEWTI's smiling mouth can shew
> As white and regular a row.
> Nay, treach'rous image from my mind
> Depart; for LEWTI is not kind.

47 *lawny shroud* 'This image was borrowed by Miss Bailey in her Basil as the dates of the poems prove' (STC's MS note). Joanna Baillie (1762–1851), Scottish poet and dramatist, published *Basil*, one of a series of *Plays on the Passions*, in 1798. 'Lawny' is the adjective of 'lawn', a fine, sheer linen or cotton fabric.

52–3 Between these lines the following passage appears in the *Morning Post* version:

This hand should make his life-blood flow,
  That ever scorn'd my LEWTI so.

I cannot chuse but fix my sight
On that small vapour, thin and white!
So thin it scarcely, I protest,
  Bedims the star that shines behind it!
And pity dwells in LEWTI's breast
  Alas! if I knew how to find it,
And O! how sweet it were, I wist,
  To see my LEWTI's eyes to-morrow
Shine brightly thro' as thin a mist
  Of pity and repentant sorrow!
Nay treach'rous image! leave my mind –
Ah, LEWTI! why art thou unkind?

69–71 In the *Morning Post* and *Annual Anthology* these lines read as follows:

      Had I the enviable power
  To creep unseen with noiseless tread
  Then should I view . . .

Lamb sharply criticized 'enviable', and in a copy of the *Annual Anthology* STC altered the line to 'O beating heart had I the power'.

To a Young Lady on her Recovery from a Fever

First published in the *Morning Post* for 9 December 1799, with the title 'To a Young Lady, on Her First Appearance After a Dangerous Illness. Written in the Spring of 1799'. '1799' must be a slip for '1798': the poem is dated 'March 31, 1798' and signed 'Laberius' (see headnote to 'Parliamentary Oscillators'). There is a transcript in the British Library by J. Draper, entitled 'To Lavinia Poole' and beginning 'Why need I say, Lavinia dear', with a note saying that it was 'Copied from the original for Thomas Poole' and signed 'S. T. Coleridge March 31st 1798', in a letter from Draper to Thomas Poole of 22 October 1836 (*Index* CoS 709). Lavinia Poole was a cousin of STC's close friend Thomas Poole; she is addressed as 'Ophelia' in the *Morning Post* and in the *Annual Anthology* (1800). STC also included the poem in *1817*, *1828*, *1829* and *1834*.

6–7 'The breezy air, the sun, the sky, / The little birds that sing on high' (*Morning Post*, *Annual Anthology*).
12 *all* 'how' (*Morning Post*, *Annual Anthology*).
13 *grow* 'all' (*Morning Post*, *Annual Anthology*).

Fears in Solitude

First published in 1798 by Joseph Johnson, in the quarto pamphlet that included 'France. An Ode' and 'Frost at Midnight'; included in the *Poetical Register* for 1808–9 (1812), in an octavo pamphlet published by Law and Gilbert in 1812 again with 'France. An Ode' and 'Frost at Midnight', and in *1817* and all subsequent collections in STC's lifetime (the poem is dated 'Nether Stowey, April 28th, 1798' in the collections). Lines 129–97 were reprinted, together with 'France. An Ode', in the *Morning Post* for 14 October 1802, and in *The Friend* No. 2 (8 June 1809) under the title 'Fears of Solitude'. STC published the extract in *The Friend* as part of an effort to prove that his early writings did not have 'the least bias to Irreligion, Immorality, or Jacobinism' (footnote to *The Friend*, *CC* 4: 25). He introduces the extract in *The Friend* by asking: 'will any man, who loves his Children and Country, be slow to pardon me, if not in the spirit of vanity but of natural self-defence against yearly and monthly attacks on my character as an honest man and a loyal Subject, I prove the utter falsity of the charges by the only public means in my power, a citation from the last work published by me, in the close of the year 1798, and anterior to all the calumnies published to my dishonor. . . . The poem was written during the first alarm of Invasion, and left in the Press on my leaving my country for Germany. So few copies were printed, and of these so few sold, that to the great majority of my readers they will be any thing rather than a citation from a known publication – but my heart bears me witness, that I am aiming wholly at the moral confidence of my Readers in my principles, as a man, not at their praises of me, as a Poet; to which character, in its higher sense, I have already resigned all pretensions' (*CC* 4: 23). A revised fair copy signed 'S.T.C.', in the Pierpont Morgan Library, contains the following note: 'N.B. The above is perhaps not Poetry, – but rather a sort of middle thing between Poetry and Oratory – sermoni propriora. – Some parts are, I am conscious, too tame even for animated prose.' For STC's many annotations to the poem in a copy of the 1798 quarto, see B. Ifor Evans, 'Coleridge's Copy of "Fears in Solitude" ', *TLS* 18 April 1935, 255. Anxiety about an invasion of England by French forces was widespread in 1797–8.

33 'It is indeed a melancholy thing / And weighs upon the heart' (1798 quarto, *Poetical Register*, *1817*).

40 *groans* 'screams' (1798 quarto, *Poetical Register*).

48 Cf. 'The Destiny of Nations' 421–6.

53–60 'Meanwhile at home / We have been drinking with a riotous thirst. / Pollutions from the brimming cup of wealth / A selfish, lewd, effeminate race' (1798 quarto, *Poetical Register*). STC's alteration and expansion of this passage for *1817* and later editions is politically significant: 'Associations and societies', for instance, condemns pro-Revolutionary organizations such as the Society for Constitutional Information and the London Corresponding Society, along with 'the brimming cup of wealth', as sources of social corruption.

70 ff. In the late 1790s oaths of militant resistance were commonly sworn by members of newly emerging radical organizations. At the same time, conservative oaths of loyalty to church and crown in 'council and justice-court' took on heightened significance.

98 *on* 'or' in *1828* and subsequent collections. Campbell, E. H. Coleridge and Beer are here followed in the adoption of the earlier reading. But it may not be so obvious that the 'or' of later editions is a misprint.

112 *defeats* 'deceit' in *1817* (probably a misprint).

121 *translated* Printed in italics in the *1798* quarto and *Poetical Register*.

131 *drag* 'speed' in the extract printed in *The Friend*.

134 *breast* 'bosom' (*Morning Post* 1802 and *The Friend*).

138 *pure* 'strong' (*The Friend*).

139 *foe* 'race' (*The Friend*).

146 *we* 'ye' (*The Friend*).

148 *toss* 'float' (*The Friend*).

151 *fear* 'awe' (*The Friend*).

153 *foe* 'race' (*The Friend*).

157 *courage* 'freedom' (*Morning Post* 1802).

161-4 'Restless in enmity have thought all change / Involv'd in change of constituted power. / As if a Government were but a robe / On which our vice and wretchedness were sewn' (*The Friend*). In the *Morning Post* 1802 extract line 164 reads: 'To which our crimes and miseries were affix'd.'

165 *Like fancy-points and fringes* 'Like fringe, or epaulet' (*Morning Post* 1802).

166-71 Omitted in *The Friend*.

172-5 'and all / Who will not bow their heads, and close their eyes, / And worship blindly – these are enemies / Even of their country. Such have they deemed *me*' (*Morning Post* 1802). In *The Friend* the last clause is '*Such have I been deemed*', printed in italics.

177 *prove* 'be' (*Morning Post* 1802; *The Friend*); 'prove' in 183 is also changed to 'be' in these extracts.

179 *father* 'parent' (*The Friend*).

181 *limits* 'circle' (*Morning Post* 1802, *The Friend*).

214 *nook* 'scene' (1798 quarto, *Poetical Register*).

223 *the mansion of my friend* Thomas Poole's house in Stowey.

The Nightingale

First published in *LB* (1798), where it was inserted at the last minute to replace 'Lewti'; incuded in the 1800, 1802 and 1805 editions of *LB* and in *1817*, *1828*, *1829* and *1834*. Lines 43–9, dated to before April 1798, appear in the Gutch Memorandum Book, British Library (see *N* 1: 231). The 1798 subtitle was 'a Conversational Poem, written in April 1798'. 'Conversation Poem' was first used in *1817*, and the term has been extended to refer to the group of meditative-descriptive poems in blank verse written in the late 1790s.

13 '*Most musical, most melancholy*' 'This passage in Milton possesses an excellence far superior to that of mere description; it is spoken in the character of the melancholy Man, and has therefore a *dramatic* propriety. The author makes this remark, to rescue himself from the charge of having alluded with levity to a line in Milton; a charge than which none could be more painful to him, except perhaps that of having ridiculed his Bible' (STC's footnote, *LB* 1798 and in all subsequent editions except *LB* 1802 and 1805; in *1834* the note ends with the second mention

of 'Milton'). The reference is to 'Il Penseroso' 61–2: 'Sweet bird, that shunn'st the noise of folly, / Most musical, most melancholy'. Campbell quotes Wordsworth's letter to John Wilson: 'What false notions have prevailed, from generation to generation, of the true character of the Nightingale. As far as my Friend's Poem, in the *Lyrical Ballads*, is read, it will contribute greatly to rectify these' (*1893* 611). Campbell also quotes Wordsworth's 'Enterprise' (1820), with its reference to 'the sweet Bird, misnamed the melancholy'. The relevance of the brutal and tragic classical story of Philomela to later poetic treatments of the nightingale should always be considered (see line 39 below).

23 *conceit* pride, but also trope, figure of speech.

24 *Poet who hath been building up the rhyme* Cf. Milton, 'Lycidas' 10–11: 'he knew / Himself to sing, and build the lofty rhyme'.

39 Philomela, in classical myth, is the young woman raped by Tereus, husband of her sister Procne. Tereus cuts out Philomela's tongue to keep her from speaking, but she communicates the truth to Procne through a piece of needlework. Procne seeks revenge on Tereus by killing their son Itys and serving the flesh to him in a dish of food. Procne, Tereus and Philomela are transformed into birds of different species – Philomela, in Ovid's *Metamorphoses* VI and other Latin versions, into a nightingale.

40 *My Friend, and thou, our Sister!* 'My Friend, and my Friend's sister' (*LB* 1798, 1800); the reference is to William and Dorothy Wordsworth.

45 *his* The nightingale is again masculine in line 85, but cf. 'its' (12) and especially the feminine 'Philomela's' (39).

50–86 Campbell identifies this 'castle huge' as 'the ruined castle overhanging N[ether] Stowey' (*1893* 612); Elisabeth Schneider suggests a more exact identification: 'The castle of this passage is probably that of Enmore, seat of the Earl of Egmont. John Cruikshank . . . was the Earl's agent at Stowey. The "gentle maid" may have been an Ellen Cruikshank, who seems to have lived at Enmore; but there is some uncertainty about her identity' (*Selected Poetry and Prose* 641).

54 *king-cups* either the common buttercup or the marsh marigold.

60 *jug jug* According to the *OED*, the word 'jug' has been used since the early sixteenth century to represent the note of the nightingale.

64–9 The last sentence of this verse paragraph was omitted in *LB* 1800 and not restored until *1817*.

76 *What time* when, during a time when; this Latinate locution is recurrent in Milton.

81 'As if one quick and sudden gale had swept' (*LB* 1798, 1800, *1817*).

90 *That strain again!* Cf. Shakespeare, *Twelfth Night* I.i.4.

97–105 See *N* 1:219: 'Hartley fell down & hurt himself – I caught him up crying & screaming – & ran out of doors with him. – The Moon caught his eye – he ceased crying immediately – & his eyes & the tears in them, how they glittered in the Moonlight!'

106–9 Cf. 'Frost at Midnight' 48–64.

The Ballad of the Dark Ladie

First published in *1834*. A fair copy, dated 1827, appears in an album now in the British Library that belonged to Louisa Powles Plummer, and is entitled 'Introductory Stanzas of the Ballad of the "Dark Ladie", to which the Poem in the Sibylline Leaves entitled, *Love*, was originally composed as the Preface'. The fair copy is annotated: 'This is the first time that these stanzas have been committed to writing. S. T. Coleridge' (*Index* CoS 31). In an undated MS list of his poems STC gives the following information: '*Love*, 96 lines. *The Black Ladie*, 190 lines' (*1893* 614). If 'The Black Ladie' referred to here is 'The Ballad of the Dark Ladie', as Campbell and E. H. Coleridge both assume, then Louisa Plummer's fair copy represents about one-third of the poem as it was originally conceived. 'Love' was first published in the *Morning Post* for 21 December 1799, under the title 'Introduction to the Tale of the Dark Ladie'. But E. H. Coleridge notes that in *BL* XIV, STC says that he was simultaneously 'preparing the *Dark Ladie* and *Christabel*' for publication, which suggests that the poem existed in some form in 1798. In a prefatory letter to the editor of the *Morning Post* STC writes: 'The following Poem ['Love'] is the Introduction to a somewhat longer one, for which I shall solicit insertion on your next open day. The use of the Old Ballad word, *Ladie* (in some printings with a stress mark on the second syllable), for Lady, is the only piece of obsoleteness in it . . .' (quoted in Schneider, ed., *Selected Poetry and Prose* 645).

47–8 No break in the Ladie's speech to the Knight is indicated by the punctuation of *1834*, though these words appear to be spoken internally, to herself. Perhaps we are meant to take them as an aside, spoken so softly that the Knight cannot hear them. E. H. Coleridge and Beer both repunctuate the lines to exclude them from the Ladie's speech.

49 *1893, 1912* and *Everyman* all eliminate the commas from this line, so that 'my love' is read not as direct address, as in *1834*, but as the grammatical subject of 'Shall lead'. This makes better sense of the syntax of this stanza, but fits less well with the quotation marks indicating that the Ladie is speaking to, not of, the Knight. In line 57, however, *1834* treats 'my love' as grammatical subject.

Kubla Khan: Or, A Vision in a Dream

First published in 1816 by John Murray as an octavo pamphlet entitled *Christabel: Kubla Khan, A Vision; The Pains of Sleep*; included in *1828, 1829* and *1834*. A fair copy, slightly revised, is on permanent display at the British Library (Beer prints this as 'The Crewe Manuscript of *Kubla Khan*' in *Everyman* 204–6). A note at the end of the MS reads: 'This fragment with a good deal more, not recoverable, composed, in a sort of Reverie brought on by two grains of Opium, taken to check a dysentary, at a Farm House between Porlock & Linton, a quarter of a mile from Culbone Church, in the fall of the year, 1797. S. T. Coleridge.' Though in this note and in the prose introduction STC dates the original composition to the summer or fall of 1797, E. H. Coleridge and Campbell both argued for a date in 1798, primarily on the basis of a MS note of 3 November 1810 connecting STC's retirement to a house between Linton and Porlock to the distress of his quarrel with Charles Lloyd, which reached a crisis in May 1798. For further discussion see John Shelton, 'The Autograph Manuscript of "Kubla Khan" and an Interpretation', *REL* 7 (1966), 32–42, and Stillinger, *Coleridge and Textual Instability* 73–9, both of whom accept STC's own 1797 dating. Though differences in wording between the British Library fair copy and the versions printed in STC's lifetime are relatively minor, differences in stanzaic division are, as Stillinger argues, very interesting and important (see notes below). The present text follows the four-paragraph arrangement of the 1816 pamphlet and, possibly, of *1834*, though in the latter printing there is a page division between lines 36 and 37 which makes the existence of a paragraph break at this point uncertain. (The poem is divided into two paragraphs [1–36, 37–54] in the MS, and into three paragraphs [1–11, 12–30, 31–54] in *1828* and *1829*. Neither of these corresponds to the three-paragraph arrangement printed by E. H. Coleridge in *1912*.) And of course the addition of the prose introduction when the poem was first published in 1816 has had an enormous influence on the way it is read. In 1816 the prose introduction begins: 'The following fragment is here published at the request of a poet of great and deserved celebrity [Byron], and as far as the Author's own opinions are concerned, rather as a psychological curiosity, than on the ground of any supposed *poetic* merits'. This passage was retained in *1828* and *1829* but deleted in *1834*.

There is an extensive tradition of critical commentary on 'Kubla Khan', much of it concerned with the ways in which the imagery and narrative reflexively represent the poem's own compositional origins and fragmentary mode of existence. David Pirie opens up important political implications in his note in *Coleridge's Verse: A Selection*: 'Is Coleridge's Kubla supposed to be an ideal creator, or a self-indulgent tyrant who is culpably insensitive to the forces represented by the sacred river? . . . One possibility is that Coleridge vaguely had Napoleon in mind when writing the poem. Coleridge associated Napoleon's worst ambitions with the savagery traditionally ascribed by the 18th Century Englishman to the East' (249).

[Prose preface]
'Purchas's Pilgrimage' Samuel Purchas, *Purchas his Pilgrimage* (1613). The actual passage in this text reads: 'In Xamdu did Cublai Can build a stately Palace, encompassing sixteene Miles of plaine ground with a wall, wherein are fertile Meddowes, pleasant Springs, delightfull Streames, and all sorts of beasts of chase and game, and in the middest thereof a sumptuous house of pleasure, which may be removed from place to place.' The Mongol Kublai Khan was the founder of the Yuan dynasty in China in the thirteenth century.
Then all the charm . . . Lines 91–100 from 'The Picture; or, the Lover's Revolution' (see below).
Αὔριον ἄδιον ἄσω 'I shall sing a sweeter song tomorrow'; STC is recalling Theocritus, *Idyls* 1. 145: δ' ὕμμιν καὶ ἐς ὕστερον ἄδιον ᾀσῶ ('I shall sing a sweeter song on a later day'). In *1834* Αὔριον ('tomorrow') replaces Εαηερον ('today'), which appears in earlier printed versions of the preface.

3 *Alph* Probably from the Greek river Alpheus, which flows into the Ionian Sea; in myth, its waters are said to rise again as the fountain of Arethusa (see Milton, *Lycidas* 85, 132). Originary associations with *alpha*, the first letter of the Greek alphabet, are also important.
41 *Mount Abora* Probably an echo of *Paradise Lost* 4. 280–2: 'where Abassin Kings their issue guard, / Mount Amara, though this by some supposed / True Paradise under the Ethiop Line'.
54 Cf. Plato, *Ion* 534: 'So is it also with the good lyric poets; as the worshipping Corybantes are not in their senses when they dance, so the lyric poets are not in

their senses when they make their lovely lyric poems. No, when once they launch into harmony and rhythm, they are seized with the Bacchic transport, and are possessed – as the bacchants, when possessed, draw milk and honey from the rivers, but not when in their senses' (trans. Lane Cooper).

[Lines from a notebook – September 1798]

From *N* 1: 348; printed as 'Fragment 13' in *1912* 2: 999. Coburn says that the 'physiography of the notebook, and the last sentence of [*N* 1:] 335, suggest Sept 1798'.

1 Following this line in the notebook the following passage is crossed out: 'As silent as a sleeping Hermit's cell, / Mute as the cell of a sleeping anchoret, / As silent'.

[Hexameters:] William, My Teacher, My Friend!

First published in full in Christopher Wordsworth's *Memoirs of William Wordsworth* (1851) 1: 139–41, from a letter to Wordsworth of 10 December 1798 (*L* 1: 451–2; the present text is based on the one printed in Griggs's edition). Lines 28–34 were first published in *Friendship's Offering* (1834) under the title 'English Hexameters, written during a temporary blindness, in the year 1799', and in *1834* as 'English Hexameters'. A MS draft of lines 28–34, now in the Victoria College Library, Toronto, was probably sent for inclusion in *1834* in a letter of August 1833 from STC to H. N. Coleridge; see *L* 6: 948–9.

3 'False metre' (STC's note, letter to Wordsworth).
11 *yet flying still onwards* ' "*Still* flying onwards" were perhaps better' (STC's note, letter to Wordsworth).
25 'False metre' (STC's note, letter to Wordsworth).
33–4 In the letter to Wordsworth of 1798, only 'Is it the spirit?' is placed in inverted commas, but previous editors have clearly been right to follow the late MS draft of lines 28–34 and extend the quotation punctuation to include line 34.

[Translation of a passage in Ottfried's metrical paraphrase of the Gospel]

First published as a footnote in *BL* X (from which the present text is taken) and never again in STC's lifetime. The translation is introduced as follows: 'This paraphrase, written about the time of Charlemagne, is by no means deficient in occasional passages of considerable poetic merit. There is a flow, and a tender enthusiasm in the following lines (at the conclusion of Chapter V) which even in the translation will not, I flatter myself, fail to interest the reader. Ottfried is describing the circumstances immediately following the birth of our Lord' (1: 208). Following the translation in *BL* X, STC continues: 'Most interesting is it to consider the effect, when the feelings are wrought above the natural pitch by the belief of something mysterious, while all the images are purely natural. Then it is, that religion and poetry strike deepest.' STC says in *BL* X that he 'read through Ottfried's metrical paraphrase of the Gospel' when he visited Göttingen in 1799, so his translation has been dated to this year. In her 1847 edition of *BL*, Sara (Mrs H. N.) Coleridge corrects STC's reference to the original to 'Otfridi Evang. lib. i. cap. xi. 1. 73–108, contained in Schilter's *Thesaurus Antiquitatum Teutonicarum*, pp. 50, 51' and observes: 'The translation is a little condensed, but faithful in sense' (quoted in *1893* 620). Ottfried, or Otfrid (c. 800–875), was a monk in the abbey of Weissenburg, Alsace. He wrote the *Evangelienbuch* (c. 870), a 7416-line verse paraphrase of the Gospels; it is the most extensive surviving work in the Franconian dialect of Old High German.

[Fragmentary translation of the Song of Deborah]

First published in James C. McKusick, 'A New Poem by Samuel Taylor Coleridge', *Modern Philology* 84 (1987), 407–15, from an undated MS in the Berg Collection, New York Public Library. See *N* 3: 4116 n. The Old Testament Song of Deborah appears in Judges 5. McKusick comments that STC 'was comparing the English text with the Hebrew original, possibly with Assistance from the Septuagint and various biblical commentaries' (409), and that he was working with 'a concept of parallelism ... first used by Robert Lowth in his *Praelectiones de Sacra Poesi Hebraeorum* (1753) to explain what was "poetic" about a poetry that lacked any apparent rhyme or meter' (411). McKusick's conjectured date of composition, 1799, is entirely plausible.

1–6 Opposite these lines in the MS STC wrote: 'This is a mere annunciation, a *giving out* of the Hymn, which begins with "Ye Monarchs" &c.'

Catullian Hendecasyllables

First published in *1834*, with no acknowledgement that these lines are a loose translation of a section of Friedrich von Matthisson's *Milesisches Märchen*; for the original German text, see notes in *1852* and in *1893* (616). The lines are not in fact hendecasyllables (lines of 11 syllables), since STC has substituted a dactyl in place of a two-syllable foot at the beginning of each line. Campbell observes that Matthisson's German verse is hendecasyllabic and reasons therefore that the title of *1834* 'cannot have been given by Coleridge to his translation'. There is no evidence as to the date of composition; Campbell and E. H. Coleridge place this text among the poems of 1799, Beer gives a date of 1798, presumably because STC was in Germany from September 1798 until July 1799.

1 *Milesian* pertaining to Miletus, an ancient city of Asia Minor.
5 *plac'd* Emended to 'blest' in *1893* and *1912*, on the grounds that the latter more closely renders Matthisson's German word 'gesegnet' (blest, consecrated).
6 *bleat-resounding* 'bleak resounding' (*1834*); 'bleat-resounding' too is Campbell's emendation in *1893* and is very likely correct, given the German word 'Heerden-reichen' in Matthisson's text.

13 *son of Cytherea* Cupid, son of Venus.

16 *nightly* 'mighty' (*1834*); 'nightly' first appears in *1852* and is accepted in *1893* and *1912* – with good reason, given 'Oft by the moonlight' in line 7.

The Homeric Hexameter Described and Exemplified

First published, together with the following poem, in *Friendship's Offering* (1834); included in *1834*. In neither printing is it acknowledged that these lines are translated from Schiller's 'Der Epische Hexameter': 'Schwindelnd trägt er dich fort auf rastlos strömenden Wogen; / Hinter dir siehst du, du siehst von dir nur Himmel und Meer'. The source was first pointed out in a note to *1844*. In the Introduction to her edition of *BL* (1847) Sara Coleridge responded to charges of plagiarism against STC made in *Blackwood's Magazine* for March 1840: '. . . the verses from Schiller were added to the poetic works of Mr Coleridge [*1834*] by his late Editor [H. N. Coleridge]. Had the author himself superintended the edition into which they were first inserted, he would, perhaps, have made reference to Schiller . . . if he neglected to do so, it could not have been in any expectation of keeping to himself what he had borrowed from them' (1: xxxvi). But see Campbell's comment on this remark in *1893* (617). There are two MSS, each slightly different from the text printed in *1834*, and each also containing 'The Ovidian Elegiac Metre'; se *Index* CoS 225 and 226, and Kathleen Coburn, 'Original Versions of Two Coleridge Couplets', *N&Q* NS 5 (1958): 225–6. One of the MSS (University of South Wales) is undated, the other (Huntington Library) has a watermark of 1795. The lines are dated 1799 in *1893* and *1912*, 1798 in *Everyman*, again because of STC's stay in Germany during these years.

1 One MS has 'Proudly it drives us along thro leaping & limitless Billows'; the other has 'Strongly it tilts us along o'er leaping & limitless Billows'.

The Ovidian Elegiac Metre Described and Exemplified

First published in *1834*; see headnote to preceding poem for MSS sources, date of composition, and the failure to acknowledge Schiller's German original, which in this case is 'Das Distichon': 'Im Hexameter steight der Springquelle flüssige Säule; / Im Pentameter drauf fällt sie melodisch herab.' In the first of the two MSS mentioned in the headnote to 'The Homeric Hexameter', STC calls these lines 'Of the Hexameter & Pentameter from Schiller'; in the second, 'Specimen of English Elegiacs'.

2 'In the Pentameter still falling melodious down' (Huntington MS).

On a Cataract

First published in *1834*. There are two MSS: (1) a draft, untitled, in the Victoria College Library, Toronto, on a sheet also containing the unpublished hexameter lines beginning 'Hear, O ye Heavens!' and a list of poems, many composed c. 1797;

(2) a copy, entitled 'To a Cataract', in a letter to Mrs J. G. Lockhart of 26 July 1833 (*L* 6: 944–6). In the 1833 letter STC introduces the poem with the following comment on its metre: 'A fragmentary recollection of an Ode, in which the Writer attempted an accommodation of the regular Pindaric Scheme of metrical correspondence, by Strophe, Antistrophe, and Epode to a Language in which, as in the English, *Accent*, or the comparative *Stroke* of the voice on the Syllables, is substituted for the *Quantity*, or comparative *prolongation* of the Sounds . . .' He then provides a metrical analysis of the poem and concludes, following the 'Antistrophe': '*Meant* to have been finished, but *somebody* came *in*, or some*thing fell* out – & tomorrow – alas! tomorrow!' Nowhere does STC himself reveal that the lines are based on F. L. Stolberg's 'Unsterblicher Jüngling'; for the German text see *1844* 371–2 (where STC's source is first acknowledged) and *1893* 618. In the introduction to the 1847 edition of *BL* (referred to in the headnote to 'The Homeric Hexameter' above) Sara Coleridge remarks: 'Now the metre, language, and thoughts of Stolberg's poem are all in Coleridge's expansion of it, but those of the latter are not all contained in the former, any more than the budding rose contains all the riches of the rose full blown . . . That which is most exquisite in the *Lines on a Cataract* is Coleridge's own: though some may even prefer Stolberg's own striking original' (1: xxxvi). Once again, the reason for placing this text among the poems of 1799 in *1893*, *1912* and *Everyman* is STC's residence in Germany during that year.

2–3 'Thou streamest from forth / The cleft of thy ceaseless Nativity!' (MS draft); 'Thou leapest from forth / The Cell of thy ceaseless Nativity' (letter).
8–12

> The murmuring songs of the Son of the Rock,
> When he feeds evermore at the slumberless Fountain,
> There abideth a Cloud.
> At the Portal a Veil,
> At the shrine of thy self-renewing
> It embodies the Visions of Dawn.

> (MS draft; there are numerous differences in the letter)

20 *Above* 'Below' (MS draft).
22 *Madd'nest* 'Flockest' (MS draft).
23 'Wheelest, shatter'st, start'st' (MS draft); 'Plungest, shatter'st, whirl'st' (letter).

Tell's Birth-Place

First published in *1817* (where 'Imitated from Stolberg' is added to the title); included in *1828*, *1829* and *1834*. For the German text of F. L. Stolberg's 'Bei Wilhelm Tells Geburtsstätte im Kanton Uri', see *1893* 618–19. There is no basis for dating this poem to 1799, other than STC's trip to Germany of that year.

28 *Slavery* printed in italics in all editions before *1834*.

The Visit of the Gods

First published in *1817*; included in *1828*, *1829* and *1834*. There is a MS copy of the poem in a letter to John Whitaker of 30 April 1811 (*L* 3: 321–2). The Schiller poem on which STC's text is based is 'Dithyrambe'; the German text is given in *1893* 619. Placed among the poems of 1799 because STC was in Germany in that year.

5 *Iacchus* a deity celebrated along with Demeter and Persephone at the Eleusinian Mysteries.
13 *with your wings of upbuoyance* 'with delicious Upbuoyance' (letter to Whitaker).
14 *banquets* 'Banquet' (letter to Whitaker).
19 'Give, give [h]im the Nectar!' (letter to Whitaker).
21 *Hebe* daughter of Zeus and Hera, handmaiden to the gods.
22 *Quicken* 'Moisten' (letter to Whitaker).
23 *Styx* the main river in Hades, the underworld.

On an Infant which Died before Baptism

First published in *1834*. The lines were sent in a letter from STC, who was then in Göttingen, to his wife Sara on 8 April 1799; Berkeley, their second child, born on 15 May 1798, had died on 10 February 1799. 'Ah, my poor Berkeley!' STC wrote; 'A few weeks ago an Englishman desired me to write an epitaph on an infant who had died before its Christening. While I wrote it, my heart with a deep misgiving turned my thoughts homeward . . .' (*L* 1: 483). The original MS of the letter is lost; a transcript by Thomas Ward is in the Berg Collection, New York Public Library. A slightly different version entitled 'On an Infant who died before its Christening' is in one of the British Library notebooks (*N* 1: 625).

1 *called* Underlined in letter to Sara Fricker Coleridge.
3 *its* 'the' (letter to Sara Fricker Coleridge, notebook).
4 'The baby bow'd, and went without demur' (letter to Sara Fricker Coleridge, notebook).

Something Childish, but Very Natural

First published in the *Annual Anthology* (1800), signed 'Cordomi' (which STC annotates, in his own copy of the *Anthology*, '*i.e.* Heart-at-Home'); included in *1817*, *1828*, *1829*, *1834*. STC sent these lines to his wife in a letter from Göttingen of 23 April 1799 (*L* 1: 488–9); there is another version in a notebook (*N* 1: 625). In the *Biographical Memoir* written by Ferdinand Freiligrath for an edition of *1852* published in Leipzig in 1860, these lines are said to be 'an imitation of the German popular song "Wenn ich ein Vöglein wär" ' (see *1893* 621, where the text of this song from *Des Knaben Wunderhorn* is given).

3 *you* Underlined in the letter to Sara Fricker Coleridge.

Home-Sick. Written in Germany

First published in the *Annual Anthology* (1800), signed 'Cordomi' (see headnote
to previous poem); included in *1817, 1828, 1829, 1834*. A fair copy was sent to
Thomas Poole in a letter of 6 May 1799: 'O Poole! I am homesick. Yesterday, or
rather yesternight, I dittied the following hobbling Ditty; but my poor muse is
quite gone – perhaps she may return and meet me at Stowey' (*L* 1: 493).

13 *a wasting pang* 'no baby-pang' (1799 letter, *Annual Anthology*).
15 'There's only music in thy wings' (1799 letter).

The Virgin's Cradle-Hymn

First published in *The Courier* for 30 August 1811; incuded in *1817, 1828, 1829,
1834*. A MS version, together with the original Latin, appears in *N* 1: 409, headed
'At the bottom of a little Print in a Roman Catholic Village in the electorate of
Mentz – May 1799'.

Lines written in the album at Elbingerode, in the Hartz Forest

First published in the *Morning Post* for 17 September 1799; included in the *Annual
Anthology* (1800), *1817, 1828, 1829, 1834*. The lines were sent to Sara Fricker
Coleridge in a letter of 23 April 1799 (*L* 1: 504–5): 'At the inn they brought us
an Album, or Stamm-Buch, requesting that we would write our names and
something or other as a remembrance that we had been there. I wrote the following
lines which I send to you, not that they possess a grain of merit as poetry, but
because they contain a true account of my journey from the Brocken to Elbinrode
[Elbingerode].' STC made revisions to the poem in a copy of the *Annual Anthology*;
these revisions are published in *Marginalia* 1: 93 (*CC*) and, where significant, are
noted below.

In early January 1798 Daniel Stuart, owner of the *Morning Post* asked STC for
regular contributions in prose and verse. STC was already a contributor, but now
Stuart offered to pay him a guinea a week. This poem and the following sequence
of poems (up to 'Westphalian Song') first published in the *Morning Post* are
probably a response to Stuart's offer. The poems are printed here according to
the sequence of their appearance in the *Morning Post*, although there is no reason
to assume that this was the order in which they were written.

1 *Brocken's* 'The highest mountain in the Hartz, and indeed in North Germany'
(STC, *Annual Anthology*).
4 *Heavily* 'Wearily' (1799 letter).
6 *heaves* 'mov'd' (1799 letter).
9 *breeze* 'gale' (1799 letter).
11 *waterfall* 'waterbreak' (1799 letter).
12 *'mid* 'on' (1799 letter).
16 'With low and languid thought, for I had found' (1799 letter). In the *Annual*

Anthology and in subsequent collections the following passage from Southey's 'Hymn to the Penates' is quoted:

> – When I have gazed
> From some high eminence on goodly vales,
> And cots and villages embowered below,
> The thought would rise that all to me was strange
> Amid the scenes so fair, nor one small spot
> Where my tired mind might rest, and call it home.

16–18 Cf. 'Dejection: An Ode' 45–6: 'I may not hope from outward forms to win / The passion and the life, whose fountains are within'.
17 'That grandest scenes have but imperfect charms' (1799 letter, *Morning Post*, *Annual Anthology*).
18 'Where the eye vainly wanders nor beholds' (1799 letter); 'Where the sight . . .' (*Morning Post*, *Annual Anthology*).
19 'One spot with which the heart associates' (1799 letter, *Morning Post*, *Annual Anthology*).
19–20 'Fair cyphers of vague import, where the Eye / Traces no spot, in which the Heart may read' (*1817*, *1828*).
21 'Holy Remembrances of Child or Friend' (1799 letter); '. . . of Friend or Child' (*Morning Post*, *Annual Anthology*).
26 *eye* 'eyes' (1799 letter).
28–30 'Sweet native Isle / This heart was proud, yea mine eyes swam with tears / To think of thee: and all the goodly view' (1799 letter); 'O native land . . .' (*Morning Post*, *Annual Anthology*).
38 *family* 'brother-hood' (1799 letter).

The British Stripling's War-Song

First published in the *Morning Post* for 24 August 1799; printed in the *Annual Anthology* (1800), with 'Imitated from Stolberg' omitted, but not included in any of the collections published in STC's lifetime. The present text is based on that in the *Annual Anthology*. There is a revised and signed fair copy entitled 'The Stripling's War-song, imitated from the German of Stolberg' in the British Library; there are also revisions in a copy of the *Annual Anthology*, reprinted in *Marginalia* (*CC*) 1: 96. The original German poem on which this poem is based, F. L. Stolberg's 'Lied eines deutschen Knaben', is quoted in *1893* 617–18.

1 *Yes* 'My' (fair copy).
2 *our* 'your' (fair copy).
7 *march* 'move' (fair copy).
10 *sound* 'shrill [sounds]' (fair copy).
12 *Amid battle and tumult* 'Amid tumults and perils' (fair copy).
13 'My own eager shout in the heat of my trance' (fair copy; STC's correction in a copy of the *Annual Anthology* reads 'My own shout of onset, in the heat of my trance').
14 *visions* 'dreams full' (fair copy).

17 *with banners all streaming* 'with bannerets streaming ~~with a terrible beauty~~'
(fair copy).

20–1 Between these lines the following quatrain was erased from the fair copy:

> And the Host pacing after in gorgeous parade
> All moved to one measure in front and in rear;
> And the Pipe, Drum and Trumpet, such harmony made
> As the souls of the Slaughter'd would loiter to hear.

22 *For each nerve* 'For my soul' is erased from the fair copy.
28 *O lend me the sabre* 'Ah! give me the falchion' (fair copy).

Names

First published in the *Morning Post* for 17 August 1799, under the title 'Song
from Lessing'; reprinted in the *Poetical Register* for 1803 (1805) and in the *Keepsake*
for 1829, and included in *1834*. A MS version, untitled, appears in one of the
British Library notebooks (*N* 1: 625), and a copy made by Sara Hutchinson,
probably in 1802–3, is printed in Whalley, *Asra Poems* 16–17. See also J. D.
Campbell, 'Lessing and Coleridge', *N&Q*, 6th Ser. 8 (1883) 195. The German
text of Lessing's 'Die Namen' is given in *1893* 619–20.

9 *Choose thou* 'Take thou' (*Morning Post, Poetical Register*).
12 *Only, only call me Thine* 'But don't forget to call me *thine*' (*Poetical Register*).

The Devil's Thoughts

First published in the *Morning Post* for 6 September 1799, with the author
given as 'Richard Porson' (1759–1808, Greek scholar, writer, wine connoisseur);
included in *1828, 1829, 1834*. The poem was also published separately as an
illustrated pamphlet in 1830. Numerous other unauthorized editions, most of
them with illustrations, appeared in 1830–1. STC composed the poem in collabor-
ation with Southey; a MS version by Sara Hutchinson, with the stanzas composed
by Southey marked 'Σ', is printed in Whalley, *Asra Poems* 20–3 and following
32. For those stanzas of the present text composed by STC (4–8, 10–15, 17),
see the note from *1834* to line 28 below. In 1827 Southey himself expanded the
Morning Post version into a poem of 57 stanzas entitled 'The Devil's Walk'. In
the *Morning Post* the poem had fourteen stanzas (this version is printed in *1893*
621–2); in *1828* and *1829* it had ten. For additions, exclusions and repositionings
of various stanzas among the printings prior to *1834*, see *1912* 320 n. In his note
in *1893*, Campbell explains that 'The issue of the *M.P.* which contained the squib
had a great circulation, and in 1812 the verses were still remembered and quoted
as Porson's, for that great and good man took . . . little pains to disavow their
authorship' (622–3). Shelley wrote a parody of the poem in 1812 entitled 'The
Devil's Walk'; in 1813 Byron wrote 'The Devil's Drive'.

7 *switched* 'swish'd' (*Morning Post, 1828, 1829*).

8 *switches* 'swishes' (*Morning Post*, *1828*, *1829*).

9–12 This stanza did not appear in the *Morning Post*.

14 *dung hill* 'dung-heap' (*1828*, *1829*).

15–16 'Oh, oh; quoth he, for it put him in mind / Of the story of Cain and Abel' (*Morning Post*).

17 *Apothecary* 'A Potecary' (*1828*, *1829*).

18 *Ride* 'rode' (*Morning Post*, *1828*, *1829*).

vocations 'vocation' (*Morning Post*).

20 'And I looked, and beheld a pale horse, and his name that sat on him was Death, Rev. vi. 8' (note in *Morning Post*).

21 *saw* 'past' (*Morning Post*).

23 'And he grinn'd at the sight, for his favourite vice' (*Morning Post*).

25 *peep'd* 'went' (*Morning Post*, *1828*, *1829*).

28 *Hard by* 'Upon' (*Morning Post*); 'Fast by' (*1828*, *1829*). In the *Morning Post* the following note on this stanza appeared: 'This anecdote is related by that most interesting of the Devil's Biographers, Mr John Milton, in his *Paradise Lost*, and we have here the Devil's own testimony to the truth and accuracy of it.' In *1828*, *1829* and *1834* a longer note is given:

> 'And all amid them stood the tree of life
> High eminent, blooming ambrosial fruit
> Of vegetable gold (query paper money:) and next to Life
> Our Death, the tree of knowledge, grew fast by. –
> . . . .
> . . . .
> So clomb this first grand thief –
> Thence up he flew, and on the tree of life
> Sat like a cormorant.
>
> *Par. Lost. IV*

'The allegory here is so apt, that in a catalogue of various readings obtained from collating the MSS. one might expect to find it noted, that for "life" Cod. quid. habent, "Trade". Though indeed the trade, i.e. the bibliopolic, so called κατ' εξόχην, may be regarded as Life sensu eminentiori; a suggestion, which I owe to a young retailer in the hosiery line, who on hearing a description of the net profits, dinner parties, country houses, &c. of the trade, exclaimed, "Ay! that's which I call Life now!" – This "Life, our Death", is thus happily contrasted with the fruits of authorship. – Sic nos non nobis mellificamus apes.

'Of this poem, which with the Fire, Famine, and Slaughter, first appeared in the Morning Post, the 1st, 2nd, 3d, 9th, and 16th stanzas were dictated by Mr Southey, See Apologetic Preface, vol. i.

'If any one should ask who General ———— meant, the Author begs leave to inform him, that he did once see a red-faced person in a dream whom by the dress he took for a General; but he might have been mistaken, and most certainly he did not hear any names mentioned. In simple verity, the author never meant any one, or indeed any thing but to put a concluding stanza to this doggerel.'

In *1828* and *1829* the second prose paragraph of the note reads as follows, after the reference to the *Morning Post*: 'The three first stanzas, which are worth all the rest, and the ninth, were dictated by Mr Southey. See Apologetic Preface. Between the ninth and the concluding stanza, two or three are omitted, as grounded on subjects which have lost their interest – and for better reasons.'

29 *did glide* 'there plied' (*1828*, *1829*).

29–33 'He saw a pig right rapidly / Adown the river float, / That pig swam well, but every stroke / Was cutting his own throat' (*Morning Post*).

33–4 Between these lines in the *Morning Post*:

> Old Nicholas grinn'd and swish'd his tail
> For joy and admiration;
> And he thought of his daughter, Victory,
> And his darling babe, Taxation.

34–5 'As he went through —— —— fields he look'd / At a' (*Morning Post*).

39 *Unfetter* 'Hand-cuff' (*Morning Post*); 'Fetter' in *1912* must be E. H. Coleridge's unacknowledged emendation, since this stanza does not appear in the version printed in *1828* or *1829*.

42 *unfetter* 'unfettering' (*Morning Post*).

44 'And he laugh'd for he thought of the long debates' (*Morning Post*).

46 *saw* 'met' (*Morning Post*).

47 'Just by the Methodist meeting' (*Morning Post*).

48 *key* 'flag' (see note in *1912* 323: 'The allusion is to Archbishop Randolph consecrating the Duke of York's banners').

50–2
> She tip'd him the wink, then frown'd and cri'd
> 'Avaunt! my name's ——
> And turn'd to Mr W ——'

>   (*Morning Post*)

66 *General* ————— 'General ————— 's' (*Morning Post*). In a twelve-stanza version of the poem (and in some unauthorized printed versions) the blank is filled with 'Gascoigne' or 'Gascoyne'. See *1912* 1: 323 n., which goes on to say that 'in a MS copy taken at Highgate in June, 1820 by Derwent Coleridge the line runs "General Tarleton's"' (Sir Banastre Tarleton, 1754–1833, famous for his service in the American colonial war). In *1893* Campbell comments: 'In spite of Coleridge's disclaimer that he meant nobody in particular by "General —————," the stanza has been frequently and impudently misquoted with various names filled in – especially in "Thomas Clarkson: a Monograph" [1854, p. 212], where "Gascoyne" is inserted, meaning a pro-slavery M.P. for Liverpool in 1806' (623). See STC's note to line 28 quoted above.

Lines Composed in a Concert-Room

First published in the *Morning Post* for 24 September 1799; included in *1817*, *1828*, *1829*, *1834*. There is no existing MS of the poem and no clear evidence of the date of composition: see *1893* 623 and *1912* 1: 324, where the editors present the case for placing these lines among the poems of 1799. Compare the image of the 'Concert-Room' here to the reference to 'ball-rooms and hot theatres' in 'The Nightingale' 37.

14 *heartless* 'loathesome' (*Morning Post*).
19 *tedded* spread out for drying, usually with reference to hay.
24 *For round their roots* 'Around whose roots' (*Morning Post*, *1817*).
40 *thin* 'then' (*Morning Post*); the grammar of the final line is uncertain. In the *Morning Post* there followed three additional stanzas. The significance of the blanks in the last two lines is unclear:

> Dear Maid! whose form in solitude I seek,
>> Such songs in such a mood to hear thee sing,
>> It were a deep delight! – But thou shalt fling
> Thy white arm round my neck, and kiss my cheek,
>> And love the brightness of my gladder eye
>> The while I tell thee what a holier joy
>
> It were in proud and stately step to go,
>> With trump and timbrel clang, and popular shout,
>> To celebrate the shame and absolute rout
> Unhealable of Freedom's latest foe,
>> Whose tower'd might shall to its centre nod.
>
> When human feelings, sudden, deep and vast,
> As all good spirits of all ages past
>> Were armied in the hearts of living men,
> Shall purge the earth, and violently sweep
> These vile and painted locusts to the deep,
> Leaving un —————— undebas'd
> A ——— world made worthy of its God.

The Exchange

First published in *The Courier* for 16 April 1804; included in the *Poetical Register* for 1804 (1805) and in the *Literary Souvenir* for 1826. There is a notebook draft titled 'Timorous Love' (*N* 1: 625) among a series of drafts in verse dated 1799–1801; 1799 would therefore be the earliest conjectural date of composition.

1 'We plighted vows, my Love & I' (notebook).
2 'Me in her Arms, the Maiden clasping' (notebook).
3 *tell* 'guess' (*Courier*).
5 *love* 'leave' (notebook); *bade* 'bad' (notebook).
6 *and* 'but' (notebook; *Courier*).
7 *act the* 'be a' (notebook).

[Paraphrase of Psalm 46. Hexameters]

First published in *1912*. These lines appear in a letter to George Coleridge of 29 September 1799, introduced as follows: 'We were talking of Hexameters with you. I will, for want of something better, fill up the paper with a translation of one of my favourite Psalms into that metre which allowing trochees for spondees, as the nature of our Language demands, you will find pretty accurate a scansion' (*L* 1: 532–3). The present text is based on that in Griggs's edition; the metrical markings are STC's own.

Hymn to the Earth. Hexameters

First published in *Friendship's Offering* (1834); included in *1834*. In *Friendship's Offering* the poem appeared with several other pieces under the heading 'Fragments from the Wreck of Memory: or Portions of Poems Composed in Early Manhood: by S. T. Coleridge', and was prefaced by the following note. 'It may not be without use or interest to youthful, and especially to intelligent female readers of poetry, to observe that in the attempt to adapt the Greek metres to the English language, we must begin by substituting *quality* of sound for *quantity* – that is, accentuated or comparatively emphasized syllables, for what in the Greek and Latin Verse, are named long, and of which the prosodial mark is ‾; and *vice versa*, unaccented syllables for short marked ˘. Now the Hexameter verse consists of two sorts of *feet*, the spondee composed of two long syllables, and the dactyl, composed of one long syllable followed by two short. The following verse from the Psalms is a rare instance of a *perfect* hexameter (i.e. line of six feet) in the English language:–

> Gŏd cāme|ŭp wĭth ă|shōut: oūr|Lōrd wĭth thĕ|sōund ŏf ă|trūmpĕt.

'But so few are the truly *spondaic* words in our language, such as Ē̆gȳpt, ūprōar, tūrmōil, &c, that we are compelled to substitute, in most instances, the trochee; or ‾˘, i.e. in such words as mērrȳ, līghtlȳ, &c, for the proper spondee. It need only be added, that in the hexameter the fifth foot must be a dactyl, and the sixth a spondee, or trochee. I will end this note with two hexameter lines, likewise from the Psalms:–

> Thēre īs ă|rīvĕr thĕ|flōwĭng whĕre|ŏf shāll|glāddĕn thĕ|cītȳ,
> Hāllĕ|lūjăh thĕ|cītȳ ŏf|Gŏd Jē|hōvăh hăth|blēst hĕr.
>   S.T.C.'

E. H. Coleridge notes that 'On some proof-sheets, or loose pages of a copy of *The Hymn*, as published in *Friendship's Offering* for 1834 [now in the Pierpont Morgan Library, New York], which Coleridge annotated, no doubt with a view to his corrections being adopted in the forthcoming edition of his poems (1834), he adds in MS the following supplementary note:– "To make any considerable number of Hexameters feasible in our monosyllabic trocheo-iambic language, there must, I fear, be other licenses granted – in the *first* foot, at least – *ex.gr.* a superfluous ˘ prefixed in cases of particles such as 'of', 'and', and the like: likewise ‾ where the stronger accent is on the first syllable. – STC" ' (*1912* 1: 327 n.). In the Leipzig reprinting of *1852* it was first pointed out that this text is a loose translation of the opening lines of F. L. Stolberg's 'Hymne an die Erde'; the German text is given in *1893* 615.

8 *his* 'its' (*Friendship's Offering*).
9 *that rushing soft* 'that creep or rush' (*Friendship's Offering*).

Mahomet

First published in *1834*. In early September 1799, shortly after his return from Germany, STC and Southey planned to collaborate on a poem in hexameters about Mohammed. Southey seems to have written some 109 lines; these 14 lines (with no hint of sonnet structure) are apparently all that STC managed to produce. See STC's letter to Southey of 25 September 1799 (*L* 1: 531 and n.), *1893* 615–16 and *1912* 1: 329.

11 *ululation* loud howling, wailing, lamentation.
14 *dividuous* divided, distributed among a number.

Ode to Georgiana, Duchess of Devonshire

First published in the *Morning Post* for 24 December 1799; included in the *Annual Anthology* (1800) and in *1817, 1828, 1829, 1834*. STC made revisions to the poem in a copy of the *Annual Anthology*; these are printed in *Marginalia* (*CC*) 1: 96–7. The Duchess of Devonshire had published a poem entitled 'Passage over Mount Gothard' in the *Morning Chronicle* (20 December 1799) and again in the *Morning Post* (21 December). Compare the stanza of her poem quoted at the beginning here to STC's 'Tell's Birth-Place' above.

1 'Lady, Splendor's foster'd child' (*Morning Post*).
3–4 William Tell, according to Swiss legend, shot the oppressive Austrian bailiff Gessler with an arrow and led the revolt which succeeded in ousting him from the Canton of Uri in 1308.
7 *your days their circlets ran* 'your years their courses ran' (*Morning Post*).
11 *Obeisance, praises* 'Obeisant praises' (*Morning Post*).
14 *stately* 'gorgeous' (*Morning Post*).
15 This line is omitted from the version printed in *Annual Anthology*.
31–2 'But many of thy many fair compeers / Have frames as sensible of joys and fears' (*Morning Post* and *Annual Anthology*, except that the latter has 'your' instead of 'thy' in line 31).
34–5 '(Some few perchance to nobler being wrought), / Corrivals in the plastic powers of thought' (*Morning Post*).
40 *insidious* 'insulting' (*Morning Post*).
45 *penury* 'poverty' (*Morning Post, Annual Anthology*).
47 *You hailed the chapel* 'Hail'd the low Chapel' (*Morning Post, Annual Anthology*).

51 *Whence* 'Where' (*Annual Anthology*, *1817*, *1828*, *1829*; but STC returned to the *Morning Post* text in *1834*).

56 *caterpillar* 'Reptile' (*Morning Post*, *Annual Anthology*).

68–72 In a copy of the *Annual Anthology* STC made a mark with his pen through these lines. Campbell suggests that he did so in response to a remark by Lamb in a letter of 14 August 1800: 'By the bye, where did you pick up that scandalous piece of private history about the Angel and the Duchess of Devonshire? If it is a fiction of your own, why truly 'tis a very modest one *for you*' (*1893*, 624 n.).

72 *you* 'thee' (*Morning Post*).

73 *your* 'thy' (*Morning Post*).

76 'O Lady thence ye joy'd to see' (*Morning Post*).

A Christmas Carol

First published in the *Morning Post* for 25 December 1799; included in the *Annual Anthology* for 1800 and in *1817*, *1828*, *1829*, *1834*. The first five stanzas were sent to Southey in a letter of 28 December 1799 (*L* 1: 305–6). Campbell suggests that 'The Carol was probably inspired by the passage of Ottfried' (see 'Translation of a Passage in Ottfried's Metrical Paraphrase of the Gospel' above).

10 *While* 'And' (*Morning Post*).

15 Though obviously spoken by the 'Virgin-Mother', the last four words of this line are not printed in quotation marks in any edition.

35 'War is a ruffian Thief, with gore defil'd' (*Morning Post*).

37 *fiend* 'Thief' (*Morning Post*, *Annual Anthology*).

41 *rends* 'tears' (*Morning Post*).

43–8 Following this stanza another stanza appears in the *Morning Post* and *Annual Anthology*:

> Strange prophecy! Could half the screams
>   Of half the men that since have died
> To realise War's kingly dreams,
>   Have risen at once in one vast tide,
> The choral music of Heav'n's multitude
> Had been o'erpower'd, and lost amid the uproar rude!

On an Insignificant

First published in its present form from MS in *1893*; reprinted in *1912* 2: 954 as 'Epigram 11'. The last two lines were published separately, under this title, in *1834*. E. H. Coleridge says that the lines are adapted from Lessing's *Sinngedicht* No. 52 (*1912* 2: 954 n.).

Job's Luck

First published in the *Morning Post* for 26 September 1801, under the title 'The Devil Outwitted'; included in the *Annual Register* (1827), the *Keepsake* (1829) and *1834*. It appears in *1912* as 'Epigram 19', where E. H. Coleridge notes that the first stanza is adapted from Friedrich von Logan's *Sinngedicht, Hiobs Weib*, the second stanza from von Logan's *Sinngedicht, Auf den Hornutus* (*1912* 2: 957 n.); the German epigrams are themselves derived from a Latin epigram by John Owen. The poem is dated 1799 in both *1893* and *1912*, without evidence. There is a MS version in one of the British Library notebooks containing material dated 1799–1801; see *N* 1: 625 and *Index* CoS 270.

Love

First published as 'Introduction to the Tale of the Dark Ladie' in the *Morning Post* for 21 December 1799 (see headnote to 'Ballad of the Dark Ladie' above); included, under the title 'Love', in *LB* 1800, 1802 and 1805, and in *1817*, *1828*, *1829*, *1834*. The *Morning Post* version contains four preliminary and three concluding stanzas; this text and STC's introductory letter are printed as Appendix I.H in *1912*, where this text is collated with two MSS in the British Library: a thirty-two stanza draft of the first version, entitled 'The Dark Ladie' (MS 1), and a fair copy lacking stanzas 1–5 and 9–18 (MS 2). See J. D. Campbell, *Coleridge's Poems. A Facsimile Reproduction* (1899) and *Index* CoS 339 and 341. The *Morning Post* version was reprinted in *English Minstrelsy*, 1810 (2: 131–9) with the following prefatory note: 'These exquisite stanzas appeared some years ago in a London Newspaper, and have since that time been republished in Mr Wordsworth's Lyrical Ballads, but with some alterations; the Poet having apparently relinquished his intention of writing the Fate of the Dark Ladye.'

The printer's copy revised for publication in *LB* now at Yale University (see STC's letter of mid-July 1800 in *L* 1: 595–7) is reproduced in *A Description of the Wordsworth and Coleridge Manuscripts in the Possession of Mr T. Norton Longman*, ed. W. Hale White (1897), following p. 34; see *Index* CoS 342. For additional discussion of the circumstances and date of composition, see *1912* 1: 331 n. In *1817*, *1828* and *1829*, 'Love' is the first of a series of poems headed 'Love Poems', and it is preceded by an eleven-line quotation in Latin from Petrarch's *Epistola Barbata Sulmonensi*, part of which is also used as an epigraph to ch. X of *BL* (1: 222; Engell and Bate give an English translation in n. 2).

1 The poem begins with these four stanzas in the *Morning Post* version:

> O leave the Lilly on its stem;
>   O leave the Rose upon the spray;
> O leave the Elder-bloom, fair Maids!
>   And listen to my lay.
>
> A Cypress and a Myrtle bough,
>   This morn around my harp you twin'd,

Because it fashion'd mournfully
  Its murmurs in the wind.

And now a Tale of Love and Woe,
  A woeful Tale of Love I sing:
Hark, gentle Maidens, hark! it sighs
  And trembles on the string.

But most, my own dear Genevieve!
  It sighs and trembles most for thee!
O come and hear what cruel wrongs
  Befel the dark Ladie.

Lines 1–4 appear as the sixth stanza in the *Morning Post* and *English Minstrelsy*.
3 *All are* 'Are all' (*1817*, but this is changed back to 'All are' in Errata).
5–6 'Oft ever in my waking dreams / I dwell upon . . .' (*Morning Post*; these lines appear but have been erased in MS 1).
7 *lay* 'sate' (*Morning Post*).
15 *lay* 'harp' (*Morning Post*, MS 1, MS 2, *LB*).
21 *soft* 'sad' (*Morning Post*; the word is erased in MS 1).
23 *suited* 'fitted' (*Morning Post*, MS 1, MS 2, *LB*).
24 *That* 'The' (*Morning Post*, MS 1, MS 2, *LB*; the text in *English Minstrelsy* has 'The Ruins').
31 *that* 'how' (*Morning Post*; this stanza is omitted in MS 1).
34 *The deep, the low* 'The low, the deep' (*Morning Post*, MS 1, MS 2).
35 *With which I sang* 'In which I told' (*English Minstrelsy*).
43 *And that he crossed* 'And how he roam'd' (*Morning Post*).
44–45 Between these lines: 'And how he cross'd the Woodman's path / Thro' briars and swampy mosses beat; / How boughs rebounding scourg'd his limbs, / And low stubs gor'd his feet' (*Morning Post*).
45 *That* 'How' (*Morning Post*).
51 *that* 'how' (*Morning Post*).
53 *that* 'how' (*Morning Post*).
54 *murderous* 'lawless' (*Morning Post*).
59 *ever* 'meekly' (*Morning Post*).
61 *that* 'how' (*Morning Post*).
78 *virgin* 'maiden-' (*Morning Post*, MS 1, MS 2, *LB*).
79 *murmur* 'murmurs' (*Morning Post*).
81 *Her bosom heaved* 'I saw her bosom heave and swell, / Heave and swell with inward sighs – / I could not choose but love to see / Her gentle bosom rise' (*Morning Post*); 'I saw her gentle Bosom heave / Th' inaudible and frequent sigh; / And ah! the bashful modest Maiden mark'd / The wanderings of my eye' (MS 1). Compare the imagery and phrasing of this stanza to 'Christabel' 380, 553–4. This stanza represents a compression of two stanzas in the *Morning Post* version, where the second stanza begins 'Her wet cheek glow'd; she steps aside', etc.
95 *so* 'thus' (*Morning Post*).
96 Following this stanza in the *Morning Post* version are these three stanzas:

> And now once more a tale of woe,
>   A woeful tale of love, I sing:
> For thee, my Genevieve! it sighs,
>   And trembles on the string.
>
> When last I sang the cruel scorn
>   That craz'd this bold and lonely Knight,
> And how he roam'd the mountain woods,
>   Nor rested day or night;
>
> I promis'd thee a sister tale
>   Of Man's perfidious cruelty:
> Come, then, and hear what cruel wrong
>   Befel the Dark Ladie.

> *End of the Introduction.*

For MS variants in these three stanzas, see *1912* Appendix I.H.

The Madman and the Lethargist, an Example

First published, in a 39-line version entitled 'The Lethargist and Madman', in the *Morning Post* for 19 September 1799. A longer version appears in *N* 1: 625, from which the present text is taken (E. H. Coleridge published this version in *1912* 1: 414–16; no mention is made of the *Morning Post* publication).

3 *old king Olim's reign* In Latin, *olim* is an adverb meaning 'in times past', 'once upon a time'.
16 *Despots* 'monarch' is crossed out in the notebook.
22 *Citizen* Common term of address during the French Revolution.

On a Volunteer Singer

First published in the *Annual Anthology* for 1799–1800 as 'Epigram On a Bad Singer'; included among the epigrams in *1893* 445 and *1912* 2: 955–6. A draft appears in *N* 1: 625.

2 *Should* 'Did' (notebook).

Talleyrand to Lord Grenville

First published in the form presented here (including STC's introduction and notes) in the *Morning Post* for 10 January 1800 but never collected in STC's lifetime; it was reprinted in *Essays On His Own Time* (1850) and in *1877–80*. Lord Grenville was Foreign Secretary in Pitt's government from 1791 to 1801 and led the cause for repressive internal policies during the French Revolution.

To the Editor . . .

Duke of Portland Home Secretary under Pitt, 1794–1801.
oscitancy the act of gaping or yawning; drowsiness, sluggishness.
Sidonius Apollinaris Latin writer who flourished in Lyon, 455–75; also known as St Sidonius. The lines quoted here mean: 'Stones, and oaks, and fibrous horns / Are softened by the sweet and melodious sounds of art.'

11 *Cordelier* member of a French Revolutionary political club to which Danton and Marat belonged.

17 *Terrorists* A quite recent word in English; the *OED* cites Burke in 1795 as the earliest instance.

19 *the Moralist* 'This sarcasm on the writings of moralists is, in general, extremely just; but had Talleyrand continued long enough in England, he might have found an honourable exception in the second volume of Dr Paley's *Moral Philosophy*; in which both Secret Influence, and all the other *Established Forms*, are justified and placed in their true light' (STC). William Paley, English theologian, published *Principles of Moral and Political Philosophy* in 1785.

21 *Reps* 'A fashionable abbreviation in the higher circles for *Republicans*. Thus *Mob* was originally the Mobility' (STC).

29–30 These lines allude satirically to Burke's own reasoning about leaving the Whigs and joining the Tories.

34 *episcopal* (Literally) pertaining to bishops; see line 29 above.

36 '*Palma non sine pulvere.*' In plain English, an itching palm, not without the yellow dust' (STC).

44 *true line of beauty* The English satirical artist and theorist William Hogarth proclaimed the serpentine curve to be the 'line of beauty' in *The Analysis of Beauty* (1753).

51 'The word *Initiations* is borrowed from the new Constitution, and can only mean, in plain English, introductory matter. If the manuscript would bear us out, we should propose to read the line thus – "What a plentiful *Verbage*, what Initiations!" inasmuch as Vintage must necessarily refer to wine, really or figuratively; and we cannot guess what species Lord Grenville's eloquence may be supposed to resemble, unless, indeed, it be *Cowslip* wine. A slashing critic to whom we read the manuscript, proposed to read, "What a plenty of Flowers – what initiations!" and supposes it may allude indiscriminately to Poppy Flowers, or Flour of Brimstone. The most modest emendation, perhaps, would be this – for Vintage read Ventage' (STC).

60 'We cannot sufficiently admire the accuracy of this simile. For as Lord Grenville, though short, is certainly not the shortest man in the House, even so is it with the days in November' (STC).

68 'An evident plagiarism of the Ex-Bishop's from Dr Johnson:–

' "Existence saw him spurn her bounded reign,
And panting Time toil'd after him in vain:
His pow'rful strokes presiding Truth confess'd,
And unresisting Passion storm'd the breast." '

(STC)

Lines 5–8 from Johnson's 'Prologue Spoken at the Opening of the Theatre in Drury Lane, 1747' are misquoted here ('confess'd' should read 'impressed').

73 'This line and the following are involved in an almost Lycophrontic tenebricosity. On repeating them, however, to an *Illuminant*, whose confidence I possess, he informed me (and he ought to know, for he is a Tallow-chandler by trade) that certain candles go by the name of *sixteens*. This explains the whole, the Scotch Peers are destined to burn out – and so are candles! The English are perpetual, and are therefore styled Fixed Stars! The world *Geminies* is, we confess, still obscure to us; though we venture to suggest that it may perhaps be a metaphor (daringly sublime) for the two eyes which noble Lords do in general possess. It is certainly used by the poet Fletcher in this sense, in the 31st stanza of his *Purple Island*:–

> "What! shall I then need seek a patron out,
> Or beg a favour from a mistress' eyes,
> To fence my song against the vulgar rout,
> And shine upon me with her *geminies*?" '

(STC)

93 Emmanuel Joseph Sieyès (1748–1836), clergyman who supported the French Revolution in its early phases, including the execution of Louis XVI. He survived the Terror, participated in the Thermidor and Directory governments, and eventually helped Napoleon plan and execute his coup of 1799.

110 *basilicon plaister* 'Basilicon' is a type of ointment; etymologically, the word derives from the Greek for 'king'.

The Two Round Spaces on the Tomb-Stone

First published in the *Morning Post* for 4 December 1800 with the title 'The Two Round Spaces: A Skeltoniad'; reprinted in *Fraser's Magazine* in February and again in May 1833; first collected in *1834*, where the prefatory note first appears. The lines are included in a letter to Sir Humphry Davy of 9 October 1800 (*L* 1: 632–33) under the heading 'Skeltoniad (to be read in the Recitative Lilt)'. They are directed against the Scottish writer and political activist Sir James Mackintosh (1765–1832), who in 1791 wrote a powerful reply to Edmund Burke's *Reflections on the Revolution in France*, entitled *Vindicia Galliciae* (after 1796 he turned against the radicalism of the Revolution and eventually became a colonial official in India and a Member of Parliament). The apocalyptic millenarian association between the Revolution and the second coming of Christ which STC mocks here may be found in Blake's *The Marriage of Heaven and Hell* and in other radical texts of the 1790s. There are many minor differences not recorded here between the *1834* text and earlier printed and MS versions; see the notes in *1912* and *Index* CoS 775–80.
    A 'Skeltoniad' is a poem in the manner of John Skelton (? 1460–1529), whose satirical verses often create an irreverent headlong effect through colloquial diction and quick-recurring rhymes.

12 *fenced round* 'railed round' (letter to Davy); 'edg'd round' (*Fraser's* February 1833).
13–20 Omitted in the *Morning Post* printing. Daniel Stuart, editor of the *Morning*

Post, later wrote in the *Gentleman's Magazine* (May 1838) that he had refused to print STC's poem attacking Mackintosh, who was Stuart's brother-in-law. But in fact he had printed everything except these lines. With reference to line 15, Stuart says: 'Mackintosh had had one of his front teeth broken and the stump was black.'

19 *The Devil* 'Apollyon' (letter to Davy).

scotch Cf. *Macbeth* III.ii.13: 'We have scotched the snake, not killed it'. 'Scotch' means to cut, score, gash; here, as in Shakespeare's play, there is a punning overlap with 'Scots', 'Scottish'.

20 'a *humane* Wish' (STC's marginal note on this line in the letter to Davy).

21 *sixth of January* Twelfth Night, the Feast of the Epiphany.

24–5 Printed as a single line in *1912*, following earlier printings and the MS letter.

26 *stone* 'tall' (letter to Davy).

Between lines 26 and 27 'After sunset and before cockcrow' is printed in the *Morning Post* version, following the text in the letter to Davy.

27 *void* 'clear' (letter to Davy, *Morning Post*).

30–1 'In mansions not seen by the general eye / Of that right ancient family' (*Fraser's* February 1833). A stanza break is indicated after line 31 in the letter to Davy.

32 *void* 'clear' (letter to Davy, *Morning Post*).

34 Omitted in the letter to Davy and the *Morning Post*.

37 *Grannam* colloquial variant of 'grandam' (grandmother or old woman).

38 'With a snow-drift to fan 'em' (letter to Davy, *Morning Post*).

The Mad Monk

First published in the *Morning Post* for 13 October 1800; reprinted in a volume entitled *Wild Wreath* (1804), but never included in any collection in STC's lifetime. The full title of the *Morning Post* version was 'The Voice from the Side of Etna; or the Mad Monk: An Ode in Mrs Ratcliff's Manner'. 'Mrs Ratcliff' is Ann Radcliffe (1764–1823), author of Gothic novels (the most famous are *The Mysteries of Udolpho* and *The Italian*) which include a substantial amount of verse, and of a substantial body of poetry independent of the novels.

1 The semi-colon at the end of this line in previous printings (see *1912*) is confusing and has been replaced by a comma.

8 *to* 'an' (*Morning Post*).

14 *sorrows* 'motions' (*Morning Post*).

16 *If I must live to know* 'Then wherefore must I know' (*Morning Post*).

31 *murder'd maiden's* 'wounded woman's' (*Morning Post*).

38–9 'It is the stormy clouds above / That flash so red a gleam' (*Morning Post*).

47 Following this line: 'The twilight fays came forth in dewy shoon / Ere I within the Cabin had withdrawn / The goatherd's tent upon the open lawn – / That night there was no moon' (*Morning Post*).

A Stranger Minstrel

First published in *Memoirs of the late Mrs Robinson* (1801), where it is dated 'November 1800', and reprinted in *Poetical Works of the late Mrs Mary Robinson* (1806). Not collected until *1877–80*. Mary Robinson (1758–1800) had a famous career as an actress and published many volumes of poems. She was at work on her autobiography when she died on 26 December 1800. Campbell says that these lines 'were sent to Mrs Robinson a few weeks before her death' (*1893* 624 n.). In a letter to Poole of 1 February 1801, STC writes: 'Poor dear Mrs Robinson! you have heard of her Death. She wrote me a most affecting, heart-rending Letter a few weeks before she died, to express what she called her death-bed affection & esteem for me' (*L* 2: 669).

1 *Skiddaw's mount* In the letter to Poole cited above, STC quotes from Mary Robinson's recent letter to him: 'My little Cottage is retired and comfortable . . . But it is not surrounded with the romantic Scenery of your chosen retreat [Greta Hall, near Keswick]: it is not, my dear Sir! the nursery of sublime Thoughts – The abode of Peace – the solitude of Nature's Wonders. O! Skiddaw! – I think if I could but once contemplate thy Summit, I should never quit the Prospect it would present till my eyes were closed for ever!' (*L* 2: 669).

17 *sunny* 'sunshine' (*Memoirs* 1801).

34 This line ends with a comma in previously printed texts.

45 Campbell refers to this as an 'unhappy line' (*1893* 625 n.). Mary Robinson had earlier been the mistress of the Prince of Wales, later George IV.

55 *'haunted beach'* This was the title of a poem by Mary Robinson included in the *Annual Anthology* for 1800.

57 'Now to the maniac while he raves' (*Memoirs* 1801).

58 A line from Mary Robinson's 'Jasper', also published in the 1800 *Annual Anthology*.

Inscription for a Seat by the Road Side Half-Way Up a Steep Hill Facing South

First published in the *Morning Post* for 21 October 1800 (STC's birthday), but never included among the collected poems until *1912*. In the *Morning Post* the poem is signed 'Ventifrons'; E. H. Coleridge notes that 'Windy Brow' is a point in the Lake District 'immediately above the River Greta, on the lower slope of Latrigg. Here it was that on Wednesday, August 13, 1800, Wordsworth, his sister Dorothy, and Coleridge "made the Windy Brow Seat" ' (*1912* 1: 349 n.).

29 A dash has been substituted here for the comma at the end of this line in previous printings, to set off the exclamatory clause that begins after the dash in line 27.

Apologia Pro Vita Sua

First published in *Blackwood's Magazine* for January 1822, as part of *The Historie and Gests of Maxilian*; not included in any collected editions until *1877–80*. There is an untitled MS version in one of the British Library notebooks, dated 27–28 August 1800 (*N* 1: 791).

1–4

> The poet's eye in his tipsy hour
> Hath a magnifying power
> Or rather ~~he diverts his eyes~~ / his soul emancipates his eyes
> Of the accidents of size

> (Notebook)

In the *Blackwood's* printing 'eyes' in line 2 is singular, despite the plural in line 3.
7 *ken* 'eye' (notebook).

The Night-Scene: A Dramatic Fragment

First published in *1817*; included in *1828*, *1829*, *1834*. An early draft, part of an unfinished MS written in 1801 titled *The Triumph of Loyalty*, is printed as Appendix I.I in *1912* (2: 568–70).

28 'No leaflet stirr'd; – yet pleasure hung upon us' (*Triumph of Loyalty* 289).
49 *ear* 'Cheek' (*Triumph of Loyalty* 310).
52–6 In *The Triumph of Loyalty* these lines are spoken by Earl Henry, as a continuous part of his speech beginning at line 36.
58 *impatient* 'intolerant' (*Triumph of Loyalty* 319).

On Revisiting the Sea-Shore

First published in the *Morning Post* for 15 September 1801 under the title 'Ode After Bathing in the Sea, Contrary to Medical Advice'; included in *1817*, *1828*, *1829*, *1834*. The poem was included in a letter to Southey of 12 August 1801 (*L* 2: 409); there is also a second autograph MS dated 'Aug 1801'. For additional MS variants, see *Index* CoS 474–9.

3 *ceaseless* 'endless' (letter to Southey, *Morning Post*, MS).
4 *men* 'life' (letter to Southey, *Morning Post*, MS).
5 'Gravely said the sage Physician' (letter to Southey); 'Mildly said the mild Physician' (*Morning Post*).
6 'To bathe me on thy shores were death' (letter to Southey, *Morning Post*, MS).
10 'That love the city's gilded sty' (letter to Southey, *Morning Post*, MS).
13 *hopes* 'loves' (letter to Southey, MS).
16 *echoing* 'sounding' (letter to Southey, *Morning Post*, MS).
18 *Tearful raptures* 'Grief-like transports' (letter to Southey, *Morning Post*, MS).

Inscription for a Fountain on a Heath

First published in the *Morning Post* for 24 September 1801, under the title 'Inscription on a jutting Stone, over a Spring'; reprinted in the *Poetical Register* for 1802 (1803) and included in *1817, 1828, 1829, 1834*. A transcript by Sara Hutchinson, revised by STC, appears in Sara Hutchinson's commonplace book (*Asra Poems* 11).

3 *aged* 'darksome' (*Morning Post, Poetical Register*).
5 *Long may the Spring* 'Still may this spring' (*Morning Post, Poetical Register*).
7 *waters* 'water' (*Poetical Register*)
   to 'for' (*Morning Post, Poetical Register*).
9–12 E. H. Coleridge compares *Anima Poetae*: 'The Spring with the little tiny cone of loose sand ever rising and sinking to the bottom, but its surface without a wrinkle' (*1912* 1: 382 n.).
9 *soundless* 'noiseless' (*Morning Post, Poetical Register*).
13 'Here coolness dwell, and twilight' (*Morning Post, Poetical Register*).
16–19
> Here stranger, drink! Here rest! And if thy heart
> Be innocent, here too may'st thou renew
> Thy spirits, listening to these gentle sounds,
> The passing gale, or ever-murmuring bees.
>   (*Morning Post, Poetical Register*)

Drinking versus *Thinking*

First published, under the present title, in the *Morning Post* for 25 September 1801; included as 'Epigram 26' in *1893* and among the 'Jeux d'Esprit' in *1912* (2: 797).

14 *bishop* sweet drink made of wine, orange or lemon, and sugar; also applied to mulled port.

An Ode to the Rain

First published in the *Morning Post* for 7 October 1802; included in *1817*, from which the present text is taken. There is an untitled MS in the Wordsworth Library, Grasmere, and a transcript by Dorothy Wordsworth in William Wordsworth's commonplace book titled 'Lines Written by Coleridge in bed at Grasmere on Thursday night October 1st or rather on the morning of Friday, October 2nd 1801'. This dating of Dorothy Wordsworth's transcript calls into question E. H. Coleridge's speculation that the poem 'was written on the morning after the unexpected arrival of Charles and Mary Lamb at Greta Hall in August, 1802' (*1912* 1: 383 n.). The 'very worthy, but not very pleasant visitor' of the subtitle and lines 41–52 might instead have been Southey, who stayed with STC in Keswick from mid-August until Wednesday 7 October (see letter to Thomas Poole of 5 October 1801, *L* 2: 766); 'my sister dear' in line 42 would then have been Edith Fricker Southey, sister of STC's wife Sara. For STC's feelings of affections towards Edith and association of her with his sister Nancy, see *L* 1: 102. In a letter to Thomas Wedgwood of 20 October 1802, STC writes: 'I dedicate three days in the week to the Morning Post ... The Poetry, which I have sent, has been merely the emptying out of my Desk ... I never dreamt of acknowledging either [the epigrams] or the Ode to the Rain' (*L* 2: 876).

The Wills of the Wisp

First published in the *Morning Post* for 1 December 1801; included as 'Fragment 61' in *1893*, as 'Jeux d'Esprit 7' in *1912* (2: 979–80). STC sent the poem under the title 'To the Will o the Wisps' to Southey in a letter of 21 October 1801 (*L* 2: 769), with this comment: '... a couple of Sapphic Verses translated *in my way* from Stolberg – You may take your Oath for it, it was no admiration of the Thought, or the Poetry that made me translate them – ... It is more poetical than the original, of which this is a literal Translation – Still play, juggling Deceiver! still play thy wanton Dances, Fugitive child of Vapor, that fervently temptest onward the Wanderer's feet, then coyly fleest, at length beguilest into Ruin. These maiden Wiles – I know them – learnt them all out of thy blue eyes, fickle Nais.' The Latin epigraph means 'I scarcely call it mine'.

Ode to Tranquillity

First published in the *Morning Post* for 4 December 1801; included in *The Friend*, no. 1 (1 June 1809) and in *1817*, *1828*, *1829*, *1834*. There is a version in a letter to Sir George and Lady Beaumont of 22 September 1803 (*L* 2: 997–8) and a transcription by Sara Hutchinson, revised by STC and of uncertain date, in *Asra Poems* 8–9. The *Morning Post* version and the Sara Hutchinson transcription contain two additional stanzas at the beginning:

> What Statesman scheme and Soldiers work,
> Whether the Pontiff or the Turk,
> Will e'er renew th' expiring lease
> Of Empire; whether War or Peace
> Will best play off the CONSUL'S game;
> What fancy-figures, and what name
> Half-thinking, sensual France, a natural Slave,
> On those ne'er-broken Chains, her self-forg'd Chains, will grave;

> Disturb not me! Some tears I shed
> When bow'd the Swiss his noble head;
> Since then, with quiet heart have view'd
> Both distant Fights and Treaties crude,
> Whose heap'd up terms, which Fear compels,

(Live Discord's green Combustibles,
And future Fuel of the funeral Pyre)
Now hide, and soon, alas! will feed the low-burnt Fire.

8 *tempest* 'storm-wind' (*Morning Post*).

15 *To vex* 'And scare' (letter to Beaumonts).

17 *thy gentle hand* 'the power Divine' (*Morning Post*; letter to the Beaumonts, *The Friend*).

21 *Autumn* 'Summer' (*Morning Post*).

23 *Thou best the thought canst raise* 'The[e] best the thoughts will lift' (*Morning Post*); 'Thee best the thought will lift' (letter to Beaumonts).

26 *thee* 'HER' (letter to Beaumonts).

A Letter to ———, *April 4, 1802. – Sunday Evening*

This poem, STC's revised holograph fair copy of what would eventually become 'Dejection: An Ode', was originally written as a letter to Sara Hutchinson dated 4 April 1802. STC seems to have written the poem in part as a response to the first four stanzas of Wordsworth's 'Intimations Ode', which he heard in late March 1802. This MS is now in the Wordsworth Library, Grasmere, as is a possibly earlier transcript (also 339 lines – or 340 if one counts 'Yes, dearest Sara! yes!' at the beginning of line 231 as an additional line) in the hand of Mary Hutchinson, Sara's sister and William Wordsworth's wife. Both MSS are printed, along with photographic facsimiles, in *Coleridge's 'Dejection': The Earliest Manuscripts and the Earliest Printings*, ed. Stephen Maxfield Parrish (1988). The present text is derived from Parrish's edition; see also *L* 2: 790–8. Significant differences between this text and Mary Hutchinson's transcript are given in the notes below. For textual information concerning printed versions of 'Dejection' and later MS evidence, see the notes to that poem. For an especially useful discussion of 'A Letter to ———', see Gene W. Ruoff, *Wordsworth and Coleridge: The Making of the Major Lyrics, 1802–1804* (1989), ch. 3.

2 *grand* 'dear'.

10 *overspread* 'all suffus'd' (this phrase deleted in STC's holograph fair copy).

15 *O!* 'Ah'.

30–1 There is a stanza break between these lines in Mary Hutchinson's transcript.

37 *or* 'and'.

52 *These* 'Those'.

53 'O dearest Sara! what can they impart?'

54 *When even* 'Even when'.

61 *secret* 'gentle' (this word deleted in holograph fair copy).

63 *for cloister'd* 'far-cloister'd'.

66 *oft upon* 'often on'.

80 *O* 'Dear'.

83 *its* 'that'.

95 *Those* 'Thy'.

96 *Even now the* 'The very'.

99 *that* 'the'.

112 *The* 'My'.

134 *happy* 'quiet'.

135 'One Home the sure *Abiding* Home of All!'

143 *Loves & Quietness* 'Love and Happiness'.

146 *thine* 'thy'.

148 *shall be well* 'needs must be'.

158 *Mary, &* 'Mary,'.

174 *I may* 'shall I'.

185 *The* 'This'.

187 *rav'd* 'howl'd' (this word deleted in holograph fair copy).

190 'Or Crag, or Tairn, or lightning-blasted Tree'.

197 *Blossoms* 'blooms and'.

201 *the* 'a'.

203 *At once they groan with* 'That groan at once from'.

204 *'Tis hush'd!* 'But hush:'.

205 *all that* 'that dread'.

206 *Shudderings* 'Shuddering'.

216 *Thoughts* 'Hope' (this word deleted in holograph fair copy).

223–4 'Like elder Sisters, with love-twinkling Eyes! / Healthful, and light my Darling! mayst thou rise'.

231 'E'er I was wedded, tho' my path was rough' (corresponds to a line and a half in the holograph fair copy, which here are counted as a single line to retain parallel lineation between the two MSS).

237 *Ill Tidings* 'Misfortunes' (deleted in holograph fair copy).

247–8 There is no stanza break between these lines in Mary Hutchinson's transcript.

252 *if* 'when' (deleted in holograph fair copy).

258–9 The order of these lines is reversed in the Mary Hutchinson transcript.

262 *mourn'd* 'mourn'.

   might 'must'.

266 *And* 'Or' (deleted in holograph fair copy).

273 *still calls up a* 'ever calls up'.

275 *as well as* 'what well I'.

282 *Thoughts* 'Thought'.

283 *Philomel* 'Nightingale' (the holograph fair copy reading raises a question about gender in this allusion: 'Philomel' is female in the classical narrative). See the note on line 39 of 'The Nightingale' above.

291 *hop'd* 'hope'.

293 *I fear* 'to fear'.

308 *strong* 'strange'.

318 *strong* 'sweet'.

322 *of* 'from'.

322–3 There is no stanza break in the Mary Hutchinson transcript.

328 *those* 'these'.

333 *should'st* 'would'st'.

334–5 These lines were at first omitted, then written at the bottom of the page in the holograph fair copy, with marks indicating that they were to be inserted.

337 'Sara! thou Friend of my devoutest Choice!'

338 *O* 'As'.
339 *Thus* 'So'.

Dejection: An Ode

First published in the *Morning Post* for 4 October 1802 (the day on which William Wordsworth and Mary Hutchinson were married; also the seventh anniversary of STC's marriage to Sara Fricker); included, in much altered form, in *1817, 1828, 1829, 1834.* The *Morning Post* text is printed as Appendix I.K. in *1912* and in Parrish's *Coleridge's 'Dejection'*, facing the *1817* text. Subsequent to the two early MS versions of 'Letter to ————', two intermediate MS versions are important to the shape the poem took for the *Morning Post* publication: a 138-line fair copy included in a letter to William Sotheby of 19 July 1802, and a version of the sixth stanza of the printed text in a letter to Southey of 29 July 1802 (see *L* 2: 815–19, 831–2, and Parrish's *Coleridge's 'Dejection'* 35–43). Following the *Morning Post* publication STC included a version of lines 87–93 in a letter to Thomas Wedgwood of 20 October 1802 (*L* 2: 875) and a version of lines 1–86 in a letter to Sir George and Lady Beaumont of 13 August 1803 (*L* 2: 970–2). There is also a transcript in the hand of Sarah Stoddart of the entire poem in its later printed form, wanting lines 66 and 87–93, in a Malta notebook dated 1804–5. And finally, STC quoted two passages from 'Dejection' (47–75, 21–38) in the third of his essays 'On the Principles of Genial Criticism' in *Felix Farley's Bristol Journal* for 10 September 1814. Variants from these latter three MS sources are given in *Coleridge's 'Dejection'* 45–63. Perhaps the most interesting variation among these versions is the shift in the person addressed, from 'Wordsworth' and 'William' in the letter to Sotheby, to 'Edmund' in the *Morning Post*, to 'William' again in the letter to the Beaumonts, to 'Edmund' again in the Stoddart transcript, and finally to 'Lady' in *Felix Farley's Bristol Journal* and in *1817*. The original addressee, of course, was 'Sara'. The four-line epigraph from the 'Ballad of Sir Patrick Spence' ['Spens'] first appeared in the *Morning Post* printing.

2 *grand* 'dear' (letter to Sotheby).
5 *Than those which mould yon cloud* 'Than that which moulds yon clouds' (letters to Sotheby and Beaumonts); *cloud* is also plural in *Morning Post* and *1817*.
6 *the* 'this' (*Morning Post*).
   moans 'drones' (letter to Sotheby, *Morning Post*, letter to Beaumonts, Stoddart transcript).
7 *Upon* 'Amid' (letter to Beaumonts).
8 *were* 'was' (Stoddart transcript).
12 *by* 'with' (letters to Sotheby and Beaumonts).
17–20 Omitted in letter to Sotheby. *Rais'd* is 'rous'd' in the Stoddart transcript; *impulse* is 'Influence' in the letter to the Beaumonts.
21 *dark* 'dull' (Stoddart transcript).
21–38 These lines were published by STC in 1814 in *Felix Farley's Bristol Journal*, as an illustration of the following principle: 'We have sufficiently distinguished the beautiful from the agreeable, by the sure criterion, that when we find an object agreeable, the *sensation* of pleasure always precedes the judgement, and is its determining cause. We *find* it agreeable. But when we declare an object beautiful,

the contemplation or intuition of its beauty precedes the *feeling* of complacency, in order of nature at least: nay, in great depression of spirits may even exist without sensibly producing it.'

22 *stifled* 'stifling' (letter to Sotheby).

25–6 These lines are expanded and altered in the letter to Sotheby:

> This, William! well thou know'st,
> Is that sore Evil which I dread the most,
> And oft'nest suffer. In this heartless Mood,
> To other Thoughts by yonder Throstle woo'd
> That pipes within the Larch-tree, not unseen –
> (The Larch, that pushes out in Tassels green
> It's bundled Leafits) woo'd to mild Delights
> By all the tender Sounds & gentle Sights
> Of this sweet Primrose-month – & vainly woo'd!
> O dearest Poet, in this heartless Mood

STC carried this shift in addressing the poem to a male and not a female into the *Morning Post* version, where 'Edmund' and not 'Sara' or 'Lady' is the addressee in line 25.

29 *peculiar* 'celestial' (letter to Beaumonts, *Felix Farley's Bristol Journal*; also in two annotated copies of *1817*).

32 *motion* 'motions' (letter to Beaumonts).

35 *as fixed* 'that seems' (*Felix Farley's Bristol Journal*).

36 *cloudless, starless* 'starless, cloudless' (letter to Beaumonts). Following this line in the letter to Sotheby, 'A boat becalm'd! thy own sweet sky-canoe!'; in the *Morning Post*, 'A boat becalm'd! a lovely sky-canoe!'

37 There is a comma after *all* in the *Morning Post*.

38 In the letter to Sotheby, the *Morning Post* and the letter to Beaumonts, *see* and *feel* are in italics. In *Felix Farley's Bristol Journal*, the entire line is italicized.

39 *genial* here in its old sense as the adjectival form of 'genius', an individual's innate power or distinctive ability. The word also carried implications of 'generative', 'fecund'.

41 *smothering* Pronounced 'smoth'ring', and so printed in the letter to Sotheby, the *Morning Post*, the letter to the Beaumonts and *1817*.

47 *O Lady!* 'O Wordsworth' (letter to Sotheby); 'O Edmund' (*Morning Post*, Stoddart transcript); 'William' (letter to Beaumonts). *Receive* and *give* are underlined in the letter to the Beaumonts.

48 *our* Printed in italics in the *Morning Post*, where *nature* is capitalized.

51 In the *Morning Post*, *allowed* is printed in italics and preceded by a comma; it is underlined in the letters to Sotheby and to the Beaumonts.

54 *glory* In addition to the usual senses, here, as elsewhere in STC, also the striking natural visual phenomenon frequently experienced by mountain walkers, who see their own figure projected in the mist and enlarged by the sun, often with a circle of light around the head.

56 *there* 'that' (Stoddart transcript).

57 *potent* 'pow'rful' (letter to Sotheby).

58–9 There is no stanza break here in the letter to Sotheby, the *Morning Post* or the Stoddart transcript.

59 *me* Underlined in the letter to the Beaumonts.
60 There is a question mark at the end of this line in the *Morning Post*; in the letter to Sotheby, *What* is underlined.
61 *it doth* 'doth it' (letter to Beaumonts).
   exist 'subsist' (*Felix Farley's Bristol Journal*).
64 *virtuous Lady* 'blameless Poet' (letter to Sotheby); 'virtuous Edmund' (*Morning Post*, Stoddart transcript); 'dearest Bard' (letter to the Beaumonts); 'O beloved' (*Felix Farley's Bristol Journal*).
   Joy that 'but such as' (letter to Beaumonts).
66 Omitted in the letter to Sotheby, the *Morning Post*, letter to the Beaumonts, *Felix Farley's Bristol Journal*.
   effluence is printed as 'effulgence' in *1817* but corrected in the Errata and by STC in a copy of this edition.
67 *Lady* 'William' (letter to Sotheby); 'Edmund' (*Morning Post*, Stoddart transcript). In the letter to the Beaumonts, the line reads 'Joy, effluent, & mysterious, is the Power'; in *Felix Farley's Bristol Journal*, 'Life of our life, the parent and the birth'.
69 *Earth . . . Heaven* 'heaven . . . earth' (*Felix Farley's Bristol Journal*).
70 *Undreamt* 'Undream'd' (*Morning Post*, Stoddart transcript).
71 *the . . . the* 'that . . . that' (letter to Sotheby); 'This is the sweet Voice, This the luminous Cloud' (letter to Beaumonts, *Felix Farley's Bristol Journal*).
   In *Felix Farley's Bristol Journal*, *sweet* is 'strong', as it is in STC's holograph fair copy.
72 'We, we ourselves ~~rejoice~~' (letter to Sotheby, *Morning Post*, Stoddart transcript); 'Our hidden Selves rejoice!' (letter to Beaumonts); 'Our inmost selves rejoice' (*Felix Farley's Bristol Journal*).
73 *flows* 'comes' (letter to Sotheby); *sight* is mistakenly printed as 'light' in the *Morning Post*.
74 *the echoes* 'an echo' (letter to Sotheby).
75 After this line the following lines appear in the letter to Sotheby:

> Calm stedfast Spirit, guided from above,
> O Wordsworth friend of my devoutest Choice
> Great Son of Genius! full of Light & Love!
>   Thus, thus dost thou rejoice.
> To thee do all things live from pole to pole,
> Their Life the Eddying of thy living Soul!
> Brother & Friend of my devoutest Choice,
> Thus may'st thou ever, ever more rejoice.

All these lines except the fourth find their way into the final stanza of the *Morning Post* version.
76 Before this line in the letter to Sotheby, 'Yes, dearest Poet, yes!' 'Poet' becomes 'EDMUND' in the *Morning Post*, 'William' in the letter to the Beaumonts. In the letter to Southey, 'There was a time when' is simply 'Time when'.
77 *This joy within me* 'I had a heart that' (letter to Southey).
80 *For* 'When' near the end of ch. XXII of *BL*, where lines 80–1 are quoted as part of STC's desire to 'present myself to the Reader as I was in the first dawn of my literary life' (2: 159).

twining 'climbing' (letters to Sotheby, Southey, Beaumonts).

81 *fruits* 'fruit' (letter to Sotheby).

83 *care* 'car'd' (letter to Sotheby).

87–93 In the letter to Sotheby STC quotes these lines after saying: '(Here follows a dozen Lines that would give you no pleasure & then what follows –)' Parrish, *Coleridge's 'Dejection'* 38 n.). After line 86 in the *Morning Post* are the words 'The sixth and seventh stanzas omitted', and then three rows of asterisks (stanza VI in the present version was stanza V in the *Morning Post*). In the letter to Wedgwood STC again quotes lines 87–93, saying that 'These Lines in the original followed the line – My shaping Spirit of Imagination' (*L* 2: 875); the lines were incorporated into the printed version in *1817*. In the letter to the Beaumonts, STC ends the quoted extract with a row of asterisks and says, 'I am so weary of this doleful Poem that I must leave off'.

87 *think . . . feel* Both verbs are underlined in the letter to Southey.

91 *only* 'wisest' (letters to Sotheby and to Southey).

92 *Till* 'And' (letters to Sotheby, to Southey and to Wedgwood).

93 *habit* 'Temper' (letters to Sotheby, to Southey and to Wedgwood).

94–5 ' – Nay, wherefore did I let it haunt my mind / This dark distressful Dream?' (letter to Sotheby); 'O Wherefore . . .' (*Morning Post*).

96 *you* 'it' (letter to Sotheby, *Morning Post*).

wind 'sound' (Stoddart transcript).

99 'That Lute sent forth! O thou wild Storm without' (letter to Sotheby); *Thou Wind* is 'O wind' in the *Morning Post*; the change to 'Thou Wind' first appears in the Stoddart transcript.

100 *craig* 'crag' (*Morning Post*, Stoddart transcript, *1817*, *1828*, *1829*). 'Tairn is a small lake, generally if not always applied to the lakes up in the mountains, and which are the feeders of those in the vallies. This address to the Storm-wind will not appear extravagant to those who have heard it at night, in a mountainous country' (STC's note, which first appeared with minor variations in the *Morning Post*).

104 *who* 'that' (letter to Sotheby).

106 *Devils'* 'Devil's' (letter to Sotheby, the *Morning Post*); 'Devils' (Stoddart transcript).

yule 'yell' (Stoddart transcript).

111 *a host* 'an host' (*Morning Post*, Stoddart transcript, *1817*, *1828*, *1829*).

112 'With many groans from men . . .' (letter to Sotheby).

115 'Again! – but all that Noise . . .' (letter to Sotheby).

117 'And it has other sounds, less feaful & less loud.' (letter to Sotheby).

120 *As Otway's self had* 'As thou thyself had'st' (letter to Sotheby); 'As EDMUND's self had' (*Morning Post*, Stoddart transcript). Thomas Otway (1652–1685) was the author of many tragic dramas.

122 *lonesome wild* 'heathy Wild' (letter to Sotheby).

123 *hath* 'has' (letter to Sotheby).

124 *bitter* 'utter' (letter to Sotheby, *Morning Post*, Stoddart transcript).

125 *hear* Italicized and followed by an exclamation mark in the *Morning Post*.

126 *but* 'and' (*Morning Post*, Stoddart transcript).

128 *her* 'him' (*Morning Post*, Stoddart transcript).

129 The reading usually offered of this line is 'May this be a typical mountain storm, short though violent'.

130 *her* 'his' (*Morning Post*, Stoddart transcript). There is a comma at the end of this line in *1817*.
131 *watched* Printed in italics in the *Morning Post*.
132 *she* 'he' (*Morning Post*, Stoddart transcript).
134–9 The lines in the *Morning Post* version corresponding to these are as follows:

> And sing his lofty song, and teach me to rejoice!
> O EDMUND, friend of my devoutest choice,
> O rais'd from anxious dread and busy care,
> By the immenseness of the good and fair
> Which thou see'st ev'ry where
> Joy lifts thy spirit, joy attunes thy voice,
> To thee do all things live from pole to pole,
> Their life the eddying of thy living soul!
> O simple spirit, guided from above,
> O lofty Poet, full of light and love,
> Brother and friend of my devoutest choice,
> Thus may'st thou ever evermore rejoice!

134 *her . . . her* 'his' . . . 'his' (Stoddart transcript).
135 *her* 'him' (Stoddart transcript).
136 *her* 'his' (Stoddart transcript); 'Thy' (letter to Sotheby).
137 In the Stoddart transcript this line is the same as in the *Morning Post*.
138 'Brother & Friend of my devoutest choice' (letter to Sotheby); 'Dear Edmund! friend of my devoutest choice' (Stoddart transcript).
139 Following this line the poem is signed 'ΕΣΤΗΣΕ' in the *Morning Post*, a recurrently used Greek version of 'STC', which appears at the end of the Stoddart transcript.

[A Soliloquy of the full Moon, She being in a Mad Passion –]

Never published in STC's lifetime, these lines are written continuously as if they were prose, but with the use of the (/) to indicate line-endings, in a MS notebook or keepsake of Sara Hutchinson (*N* 1: 1193 n.). They are dated May–June 1802 by Coburn in *N*, April 1802 by Beer in *Everyman* 363. They are also published in *Asra Poems* 5–7.

24 *Voss* J. H. Voss, a German poet whose *Luise, ein ländliches Gedicht in drei Idyllen* (1795) STC admired and translated parts of.
45 *Naddle* Naddle Fell, in the Lake District between Ambleside and Keswick.

Answer to a Child's Question

First published in the *Morning Post* for 16 October 1802, titled 'The Language of Birds: lines spoken ex tempore, to a child, in early spring'; included in *1817*, *1828*, *1829*, *1834*. A MS version, included in a letter to Sir George and Lady Beaumont of 22 September 1803, is in the Pierpont Morgan Library and is titled

'Extempore – to a Child of six years old' (*L* 2: 998). There are also transcripts by an unidentified hand in the Wordsworth Library, Grasmere, and by Sara Hutchinson in her commonplace book (*Asra Poems* 7–8).

1 *The sparrow, the dove* 'The Linnet, the Dove' (letter to Beaumonts); 'The Chaffinch, the Dove' (Sara Hutchinson transcript).
6–7 Between these lines: ' "I love, and I love," almost all the birds say / From sunrise to star-rise, so gladsome are they' (*Morning Post*).
10 Adopted, E. H. Coleridge points out (*1912* 1: 306 n.), from the refrain of Matthew Prior's 'Song' ('One morning very early, one morning in the spring'): 'I love my love, because I know my love loves me'.
Following this line: ' 'Tis no wonder that he's full of joy to the brim, / When He loves his Love, and his Love loves him' (*Morning Post*).

A Day Dream

First published in *The Bijou* for 1828; included in *1828, 1829, 1834*. The address to 'Mary' (Mary Hutchinson) and references to 'Asra' (Sara Hutchinson) and to 'Our sister and our friend' (Dorothy and William Wordsworth) are characteristic of the poems of 1802 inspired by Sara Hutchinson. John Beer gives 27 March as the date of composition (*Everyman* 271); this could be consistent with the references to summer in the poem, given that these are part of an overtly fantasized and idealized moment.

4 *thee* Asra, Sara Hutchinson, though Mary is addressed directly in line 5.
8 *well* 'will' (*Bijou*).
20 *For dearly, Asra* 'For Asra, dearly' (*Bijou*).

The Day-Dream

First published in the *Morning Post* for 19 October 1802; not included in any collection in STC's lifetime (first collected in *1852*). There is a transcript in the hand of Mary Hutchinson, dated April–June 1802, in *Index* CoS 78, on leaves of her transcript of the 'Letter to ———'. The following note is attached to the poem in *1852*: 'This little poem first appeared in the *Morning Post* in 1802, but was doubtless composed in Germany. It seems to have been forgotten by its author, for this was the only occasion on which it saw the light through him. The Editors think that it will plead against parental neglect in the mind of most readers.' Though Campbell followed the *1852* editors' conjecture of a 1799 date of composition, E. H. Coleridge and John Beer both date the poem to 1801–2.

To Asra

First published in *1893*. The MS of this sonnet, now in the Victoria College Library, Toronto, is pasted on the inside front cover of the MS of 'Christabel' which STC gave to Sara Hutchinson in 1804. Campbell conjectures an 1803 date of composition, E. H. Coleridge 1801, both presumably based on STC's infatuation with Sara Hutchinson.

The Happy Husband

First published in *1817*; included in *1828, 1829, 1834*. There is no clear evidence as to the date of composition: E. H. Coleridge and John Beer both conjecture 1802.

19 *precipitated* produced rapidly, hurriedly; perhaps also with the sense of being thrown down.

A Thought Suggested by a View of Saddleback in Cumberland

First published in *The Amulet* (1833) and reprinted in *Friendship's Offering* (1834), but never included by STC himself in any collected edition. These lines appear in one of the 'Malta Notebooks' (now in the British Library) among entries dated 15 February–8 March 1806 (*N* 2: 2798). Another MS version appears in a letter to Thomas Pringle of 6 August 1833 (*L* 6: 951), and there is an undated fair copy at Harvard University. E. H. Coleridge argues that 'it is almost certain' that the lines were composed in the autumn of 1800 when STC first saw Saddleback (*1912* 1: 347 n.). But Beer's 'summer 1802' date of composition in *Everyman* seems more likely. A note accompanied the lines in *Friendship's Offering*: 'A Force is the provincial term in Cumberland for any narrow fall of water from the summit of a mountain precipice. The following stanza (it may not arrogate the name of poem) or versified reflection was composed while the author was gazing on three parallel *Forces* on a moonlight night, at the foot of Saddleback Fell' (*1893* 634 n.).

1 This line is apparently adapted from a poem by Isaac Ritson quoted in Hutchinson's *History of Cumberland* (*1912* 1: 347 n.).
3 'And streaming forth unquiet Light' (notebook).
6 *gentle* 'silent' (notebook).
7–8 Cf. Wordsworth, 'Tintern Abbey' 7–8: 'and connect / The landscape with the quiet of the sky'.
9 ~~'And Ah!~~ The Things ~~of~~ <that love the> Earth how full of Rage and Riot' (notebook).

[Untitled]

First published in *1893*, where it is titled 'A Sunset'. The lines appear in one of the Malta notebooks and are followed by the comment: 'These lines I wrote as nonsense verses merely to try a metre; but they are by no means contemptible – at least, on reading them over I am surprised at finding them so good / 16 Aug. 1805 – Malta Now will it be a more English Music if the first & fourth are double rhymes; & the 5th & 6th single? – or all single; or the second & 3rd double? Try' (*N* 2: 2224 f. 25). Beer gives '?1802–4' as the date of composition in *Everyman*.

STC included the lines in a letter to William Worship dated 22 April 1819 (see *L* 4: 937–8, where this letter is printed from a transcript without the verses). The MS letter is printed in 'Unpublished Letter and Poems of Samuel Taylor Coleridge', *The Archivist* 1 (1888), 11–12; see *Index* CoS 656. The present text is from *N*.

The Keepsake

First published in the *Morning Post* for 17 September 1802; included in *1817*, *1828*, *1829*, *1834*. In *1893* Campbell comments: 'It had been composed two years before, and, possibly, with Dorothy Wordsworth in the poet's mind, for "Emmeline" was Wordsworth's poetical name for his sister' (624 n.). Acknowledging that Campbell 'may have seen a dated MS', E. H. Coleridge says 'Internal evidence would point to the autumn of 1802' as the date of composition (*1912* 1: 345 n.).

1 This line was omitted in the *Morning Post*.
Tedded spread out for drying.
12–13 These lines appear in reverse order in the *Morning Post*.
13 'One of the names (and meriting to be the only one) of the *Myosotis Scorpioides Palustris*, a flower from six to twelve inches high, with blue blossom and bright yellow eye. It has the same name over the whole Empire of Germany (*Vergissmein nicht*) and, I believe, in Denmark and Sweden' (STC's note).
16 Printed with commas after 'worked' and 'loved' in the *Morning Post* and subsequently by STC.
17 *they* 'all' (*Morning Post*).
19 *joyous* 'joyless' (*1817*, *1828*).
20–1 'Leaving the soft bed to her sister, / Softly she rose, and lightly stole along, / Her fair face flushing in the purple dawn, / Adown the meadow to the woodbine bower' (*Morning Post*).
25 *scarcely moving* 'scarcely-flowing' (*Morning Post*).
34–5 Printed in the *Morning Post* and subsequently by STC with commas after 'voice' and 'weep'.
39 *thenceforth* 'henceforth' (*Morning Post*).

The Picture, or the Lover's Resolution

First published in the *Morning Post* for 6 September 1802, without lines 17–25; reprinted in the *Poetical Register* for 1802 and, in its present longer form, in *1817*, *1828*, *1829*, *1834*. There is a transcript of a 161-line version in Sara Hutchinson's hand, which probably dates to August–September 1803, in the Wordsworth Library, Grasmere.

3 *wild* 'blind' (*Morning Post*, *Poetical Register*).
16 *distant sea* Cf. 'The Eolian Harp' 11: 'The stilly murmur of the distant Sea'.
17–25 These lines, first added to the version printed in *1817*, appeared in altered form in a letter to Joseph Cottle of 27 May 1814 (*L* 3: 499).

26 Cf. 'Dejection: An Ode' 94–5: 'Hence, viper thoughts, that coil around my mind, / Reality's dark dream!' This line does not appear in the *Morning Post* or *Poetical Register*.

27 The myrtle was sacred to Venus (and Cupid).

these 'here' (*Morning Post*).

28–9 Expanded from a single line in the *Morning Post* and *Poetical Register* versions: 'For Love to dwell in; the low stumps would gore'.

31–3 '. . . till, like wounded bird / Easily caught, the dusky Dryades / With prickles sharper than his darts would mock' (*Morning Post*, *Poetical Register*).

32–42, 44 Omitted in the *Morning Post* and *Poetical Register*.

51 This line is hypermetrical; 'I' is omitted in the *Morning Post* and *Poetical Register*.

55 *brook* 'stream' (*Morning Post*, *Poetical Register*); in *1817* 'stream' again appears but is changed to 'brook' in the Errata.

56–7 *yet tinkling sound; / Or to the bees* 'yet bell-like sound/Tinkling, or bees' (*Morning Post*, *Poetical Register*, *1817*, *1828*).

58 *The* 'This' (*Morning Post*, *Poetical Register*, *1817*).

70 *That swells its* 'Who swells his' (*Morning Post*, *Poetical Register*, *1817*).

75 *the downcast* 'her downcast' (*Morning Post*, *Poetical Register*); in *1817* the line reads, 'Her face, her form divine, her downcast look'.

76–7 'Contemplative, her cheek upon her palm / Supported; the white arms and elbow rest' (*Morning Post*, *Poetical Register*); 'Contemplative! Ah see! her open palm' (*1817*).

79–80 *Who erewhile / Had* 'He, meanwhile, / Who' (*Morning Post*, *Poetical Register*, *1817*).

79–86 In a copy of *1817*, STC made a mark in the margin beside these lines, altered line 79 to its form in *1829* and *1834*, and commented: 'These lines I hope to fuse into a more continuous flow, at least to articulate more organically' (see *1893* 628 n.).

86 Not in the *Morning Post*, *Poetical Register*, *1817*.

87 *The* 'She' (*Morning Post*, *Poetical Register*, *1817*).

89 *Lychnis* campion.

91–100 See the prefatory note to 'Kubla Khan', where these lines are quoted.

94 *mis-shape* 'mis-shapes' (*Morning Post*).

108 *love-yearning by* 'love-gazing on' (*Morning Post*, *Poetical Register*).

114 *Spire* 'Tow'r' (*Morning Post*, *Poetical Register*, *1817*).

118 *emancipate* emancipated.

121 *and* ', to' (*Morning Post*, *Poetical Register*).

124 *waves* 'waters' (*Poetical Register*, *1817*).

126–32 'They meet, they join / In deep embrace, and open to the sun / Lie calm and smooth. Such the delicious hour' (*Morning Post*, *Poetical Register*, *1817*). The present version of 126–33 appears in the Errata of *1817*.

133 *feuds* 'quarrels' (*Morning Post*, *Poetical Register*).

134 *And* 'But' (*1817* Errata).

135 *I pass forth* 'I come out' (*Morning Post*, *Poetical Register*); 'come' is 'came' in *1817* but corrected to 'come' in Errata.

144 *At* 'Beneath' (*Morning Post*, *Poetical Register*, *1817*, but corrected to 'At' in Errata of latter).

152 *this* Italicized in the *Morning Post* and *Poetical Register*; all capitals in *1817, 1828, 1829*. Compare the image in this line to 'This Lime-Tree Bower My Prison' 13–16.

158 *Unfilletted* not wound into a circle or coronet.

Hymn Before Sun-Rise, in the Vale of Chamouni

First published in the *Morning Post* for 11 September 1802, under the title 'Chamouny; The Hour Before Sunrise. A Hymn' (for this version see *1912* Appendix I.J). Reprinted in the *Poetical Register* for 1802 (1803) and in *The Friend* no. XI for 26 October 1809 (*CC* 2: 156–8); included in *1817, 1828, 1829, 1834*. A MS version now in the Pierpont Morgan Library appears in a letter to Sir George and Lady Beaumont of 22 September 1803, where it is titled 'Mont Blanc, the summit of the Vale of Chamouny, an Hour before Sunrise – An Hymn' (*L* 2: 995–7). There are fair copies at Harvard and in the British Library, and a printer's copy for *The Friend* no. XI in the Victoria and Albert Museum.

This poem is an English expansion of Sophie Christiane Friederike Brun's 20-line 'Chamouny beym Sonnenaufgange'; see A. P. Rossiter, *TLS* (28 September 1951) 613. In the *Morning Post* and the *Poetical Register* the following note precedes the poem: 'Chamouni is one of the highest mountain valleys of the Barony of Faucigny in the Savoy Alps; and exhibits a kind of fairy world, in which the wildest appearances (I had almost said horrors) of Nature alternate with the softest and most beautiful. The chain of Mont Blanc is its boundary; and besides the Arve it is filled with sounds from the Arveiron, which rushes from the melted glaciers, like a giant, mad with joy, from a dungeon, and forms other torrents of snow-water, having their rise in the glaciers which slope down into the valley. The beautiful *Gentiana major*, or greater gentian, with blossoms of the brightest blue, grows in large companies a few steps from the never-melted ice of the glaciers. I thought it an affecting emblem of the boldness of human hope, venturing near, and, as it were, leaning over the brink of the grave. Indeed, the whole vale, its every light, its every sound, must needs impress every mind not utterly callous with the thought – Who *would* be, who *could* be an Atheist in this valley of wonders! If any of the readers of the MORNING POST [If any of those who have *Poetical Register*] have visited this vale in their journeys among the Alps, I am confident that they will not find the sentiments and feelings expressed, or attempted to be expressed, in the following poem, extravagant' (*1912* 1: 377 n.). The shortened version of this note preceding the present text appears in *1817, 1828, 1829, 1834*. In all these editions the poem is the first in a series titled 'III. Meditative Poems, in Blank Verse'.

3 *O sovran Blanc!* 'O Chamouny' (*Morning Post, Poetical Register*, letter to Beaumonts); the present phrase first appears in *The Friend*.

5 *Rave ceaselessly* Cf. Shelley, 'Mont Blanc' 10–11: 'and a vast river / Over its rocks ceaselessly bursts and raves'. This is the first of several important echoes of STC's 'Hymn' in Shelley's poem. It has been noted that 'Rave' is an anagram of 'Arve'.

> *most awful Form!* 'dread mountain form' (*Morning Post, Poetical Register*, letter to Beaumonts).

8 'Deep is the sky, and black: transpicuous, deep' (*Morning Post, Poetical Register*); 'Deep is the sky, transpicuous, deep, and black' (letter to Beaumonts).

11 *is thine* 'seems thy' (*Morning Post, Poetical Register*).

13 *Mount* 'form' (*Morning Post, Poetical Register*, letter to Beaumonts).

14 *the bodily sense* 'my bodily eye' (*Morning Post, Poetical Register*); 'my bodily sense' (letter to Beaumonts).

16 *Invisible* In capitals in the *Morning Post, Poetical Register*, letter to Beaumonts, *The Friend*.

17–19 'Yet thou, meantime, wast working on my soul, / E'en like some deep enchanting melody' (*Morning Post, Poetical Register*, letter to Beaumonts).

20–8

> But I awoke, and with a busier mind,
> And active will self-conscious, offer now
> Not, as before, involuntary pray'r
> And passive adoration! –
>   Hand and voice,
> Awake, awake! and thou, my heart, awake!
> Awake ye rocks! Ye forest pines, awake!
> Green fields, and icy cliffs! All join my hymn!
>
>   (*Morning Post, Poetical Register* and – with
>   minor variants – letter to Beaumonts)

29–30 'And thou, O silent mountain, sole and bare, / O blacker, than the darkness, all the night' (*Morning Post, Poetical Register*); 'And thou, thou silent Mountain, lone and bare! / O struggling with the Darkness all the Night' (letter to Beaumonts); STC adds a note to line 30 in the letter: 'I had written a much finer Line when Sca' Fell was in my Thoughts – viz –

> O blacker than the Darkness all the Night,
> And visited & c –'

In *The Friend*, no. XIII, 16 November 1809, another version of line 29 is given: 'Thou first and chief, stern Monarch of the Vale!'

38 *parent* 'Father' (*Morning Post, Poetical Register*, letter to Beaumonts).

41 'From darkness let you loose and icy dens' (*Morning Post, Poetical Register*, letter to Beamonts).

46 'Eternal Thunder and unceasing foam' (letter to Beaumonts).

48 *Here let the billows stiffen* 'Here shall the billows stiffen' (*Morning Post, Poetical Register*); 'Here shall your billows stiffen' (letter to Beaumonts).

49 *the mountain's brow* 'yon dizzy heights' (*Morning Post, Poetical Register*).

50 'Adown enormous ravines steeply slope' (*Morning Post, Poetical Register*, letter to Beaumonts). In the letter STC adds this note: '*a bad line*; & I hope to be able to alter it'.

56–7 'Who with lovely Flowers / Of living blue' (*Morning Post, Poetical Register*, letter to Beaumonts). STC adds this note on 'lovely Flowers' in the letter: 'The *Gentiana major* grows in large companies a stride's distance from the foot of several of the Glaciers – Its *blue* Flowers, the Colour of Hope – is it not a pretty Emblem of Hope creeping onward even to the edge of the grave – to the very Verge of utter Desolation?' See STC's introductory note to 'Hymn' above.

58–63

> GOD! GOD! The torrents like a shout of nations,
> Utter! The ice-plain bursts, and answers GOD!
> GOD, sing the meadow-streams, with gladsome voice,
> And pine groves with their soft, and soul-like sound,
> The silent snow-mass, loos'ning, thunders GOD!

> > (*Morning Post*, *Poetical Register*, and with minor changes
> > in letter to Beaumonts, where the fifth of these lines reads,
> > 'Ye perilous Snow-towers, fall and thunder, GOD!')

64 'Ye dreadless flow'rs! That fringe th' eternal frost!' (*Morning Post*, *Poetical Register*); 'Ye azure Flowers, that skirt the eternal Frost!' (letter to Beaumonts).
65 *sporting round* 'bounding by' (*Morning Post*, *Poetical Register*, letter to Beaumonts).
66 *mountain-storm* 'mountain blast' (*Morning Post*, *Poetical Register*).
70–80

> And thou, O silent Form, alone and bare
> Whom, as I lift again my head bow'd low
> In adoration, I again behold,
> And to thy summit upward from the base
> Sweep slowly with dim eyes suffus'd by tears,
> Awake, thou mountain form! rise, like a cloud!

> > (*Morning Post*, *Poetical Register*)

> And thou, thou silent Mountain, lone and bare!
> Whom as I lift again my Head, bow'd low
> In Adoration, I again behold!
> And from thy Summit upward to the Base
> Sweep slowly with dim Eyes suffus'd with Tears!
> Rise, mighty Form! even as thou *seem'st* to rise!

> > (Letter to Beaumonts)

70 *Thou too, hoar Mount!* 'Once more, hoar Mount' (British Library fair copy).
72 *through the pure serene* 'in the pure serene' (*The Friend*); 'in the blue serene' (British Library fair copy).
75 'Who, as once more I lift my Head bow'd low' (*The Friend*; altered in the changes given in *The Friend* no. XIII to 'That, as once more I raise my head bow'd low').
83–4 'Great Hierarch! tell thou the silent Stars, / Tell the blue Sky, and tell the rising sun' (letter to Beaumonts).
84 *yon* 'the' in the *Morning Post* and *Poetical Register*.
85 'Earth with her thousand voices calls on God!' (*Morning Post*, *Poetical Register*, letter to Beaumonts).

The Good, Great Man

First published in the *Morning Post* for 23 September 1802, as 'Epigram' and signed 'ΕΣΤΗΣΕ'; reprinted in the *Poetical Register* for 1802 (1803) and in *The Friend* no. XIX for 28 December 1809, but never included by STC in any collection in his lifetime. There is a transcript in Sara Hutchinson's hand in the printer's copy for *The Friend* no. XIX.

The Knight's Tomb

First published in *1834*. In his *Life of Coleridge*, Gillman says that these lines were composed 'as an experiment for a metre' and that they were recited by STC to 'a mutual friend' who in turn quoted them the following day to Sir Walter Scott, who quoted them in chapter VIII of *Ivanhoe* and in chapter IX of *Castle Dangerous*. See E. H. Coleridge's note in *1912* 1: 432. There is a MS at Cornell University including a note to an unidentified correspondent dated 20 October 1824; another MS in the Berg Collection, New York Public Library, where the poem is titled 'The knightly Sword, a Ballad'; and an undated and signed MS at Yale University. The date of composition is uncertain: Beer tentatively follows Mrs H. N. Coleridge in *1852* in dating the poem to 1802 in *Everyman* 378, and this date has been provisionally adopted here.

1 *Sir Arthur O'Kellyn* 'Sir Arthur O'Relhan' (Cornell MS, Berg MS); 'Sir Arthur O'Rellian' (Yale MS).

To Matilda Betham from a Stranger

First published in a privately printed *Autobiographical Sketch* of Matilda Betham (1802), in which it was introduced as follows: 'One of our most celebrated poets, who had, I was told, picked out and praised the little piece "On a Cloud", another had quoted (saying it would have been faultless if I had not used the word *Phoebus* in it, which he thought inadmissible in modern poetry), sent me some verses inscribed "To Matilda Betham, from a Stranger"; and dated "Keswick, Sept. 9, 1802, S.T.C." I should have guessed whence they came, but dared not flatter myself so highly as satisfactorily to believe it, before I obtained the avowal of the lady who had transmitted them' (quoted from a copy of the *Autobiographical Sketch* in the Forster Collection, Victoria and Albert Museum, in *1912* 1: 374). Lines 34–41 are quoted in a letter to William Sotheby of 10 September 1802 (*L* 2: 864).

3 Catherine Rose Rouse-Boughton visited STC at Greta Hall with her husband Sir Charles Rouse-Boughton in September 1802.
12 *quit-rent* a fixed rent paid by a tenant, originally as a substitute for services owed to a feudal lord.
15 *gadding* running about profusely, wildly.
16 *coronal* coronet, garland.
27 *th' impassioned Lesbian* Sappho.

Westphalian Song

First published in the *Morning Post* for 27 September 1802; never included in any collection in STC's lifetime. Placed among the poems of 1799 in *1893* and *1912* because of STC's stay in Germany that year. Beer places it later in *Everyman*, and that dating has been followed here. 'Mr Dibdin' referred to in the prefatory note is Charles Dibdin (1745–1814), actor, dramatist and popular song-writer.

The Pains of Sleep

First published in *Christabel: Kubla Khan, A Vision; The Pains of Sleep* (1816); included in *1828*, *1829* (but not in the table of contents), *1834*. A MS draft appears in a letter to Southey of 10 September 1803 (*L* 2: 982–4); a 17-line version of lines 18–32 appears in a letter to Poole of 3 October 1803 (*L* 2: 1009–10). In the letter to Southey STC writes: 'I have abandoned all opiates except Ether be one; & that only in *fits* – & that is a blessed medicine! – & when you see me drink a glass of Spirit & Water, except by prescription of a physician, you shall despise me – but still I can not get quiet rest' (*L* 2: 982). At the end of the letter he continues: 'I do not know how I came to scribble down these verses to you – my heart was aching, my head all confused – but they are, doggrels [sic] as they may be, a true portrait of my nights. – What to do, I am at a loss: – for it is hard thus to be withered, having the faculty & attainments, which I have. –' (*L* 2: 984).

1 This line also begins 'A Child's Evening Prayer'.
   Ere 'When' (letter to Southey).
9 *sense.* Underlined in letter to Southey, italicized in *Christabel*, *1828*, *1829*. In the letter *sense* is also underlined in line 10.
12 'Since round me, in me, everywhere' (letter to Southey).
13 *wisdom* 'Goodness' (letter to Southey).
16 *Up-starting* 'Awaking' (letter to Southey).
18–26
> Desire with Loathing strangely mixt,
> On wild or hateful Objects fixt:
> Pangs of Revenge, the powerless Will,
> Still baffled, & consuming still,
> Sense of intolerable Wrong,
> And men whom I despis'd made strong
> Vain-glorious Threats, unmanly Vaunting,
> Bad men my boasts & fury taunting
> Rage, sensual passion, mad'ning Brawl,
>
> (letter to Southey)

18 *trampling* 'ghastly' (letter to Poole).
19 *intolerable* 'insufferable' (letter to Poole).
20 *those* 'they' (letter to Poole).
22–23 Between these lines: 'Tempestuous pride, vain-glorious Vaunting, / Base Men my vices justly taunting ———' (letter to Poole).
27 *which* 'that' (letters to Southey, Poole).
28 *could* 'might' (letters to Southey, Poole).
30 'For all was Horror, Guilt & Woe' (letter to Southey); 'For all was Guilt, & Shame, & Woe –' (letter to Poole).
33 *So* 'Thus' (letter to Southey).
34 *coming* 'boding' (letter to Southey).

35–6 'I fear'd to sleep: sleep seem'd to be / Disease's worst malignity' (letter to Southey).

38 *waked* 'freed' (letter to Southey – 'wak'd' is cancelled).

39 'O'ercome by Sufferings dark & wild' (letter to Southey).

42 *anguish* 'Trouble' (letter to Southey).

43 *said* 'thought' (letter to Southey).

45–6 'Still to be stirring up anew / The self-created Hell within' (letter to Southey).

47 *deeds* 'Crimes' (letter to Southey).

49–50 'With such let Fiends make mockery – / But I – O wherefore this on *me*?' (letter to Southey).

50–1 Between these lines: 'Frail is my Soul, yea, strengthless wholly, / Unequal, restless, malancholy; / But free from Hate, & sensual Folly!' (letter to Southey).

51 *be* 'live' (letter to Southey).

52 At the end of this line in the letter to Southey, STC writes '& &c &c &c &c &c –'.

[Lines from a notebook – September 1803]

First published as 'Fragment 7' in *1912* 2: 998. From *N* 1: 1506, where it is printed without verse lineation, but with (/) after 'given', 'Heaven' and 'Unconquered'. Printed in its present form by Beer in *Everyman* 380.

[Lines from a notebook – February–March 1804]

These three adaptations from *Paradise Lost* appear as sequential notebook entries: *N* 2: 1945 (*PL* IX. 227–8), *N* 2: 1946 (*PL* IX. 288–9), *N* 2: 1947 (*PL* IX. 309–12). The first and third passages were published in *1912* 2: 1004, 999; the second was published in *1893* 461. The third passage follows Milton exactly except for the punctuation.

[What is Life?]

First published in the *Literary Souvenir* for 1829; included in *LR* 1: 60 and collected in *1844*. These lines appear in *N* 2: 2224 f. 25, where they are dated October 1804. In the notebook draft the first two lines are separated from the rest, though they have been printed as a single text since 1829. In a letter to William Worship of 22 April 1819 STC included a copy of these lines following the first four lines of 'A Monody on the Death of Chatterton' and titled them 'On the same Subject, but composed two years later, namely between 15 and 16 (What is Life?)'; see *L* 4: 937 n.

1 *deem'd* 'held' (notebook).

2 *ample* 'simple' (notebook).

6 'Is Life pure act *per se* (in its own nature) itself by consciousness unbounded,' (notebook).

[Lines from a notebook – April 1805]

First published in *1893* 461 as 'Fragment 68', then in *1912* 2: 1000 as 'Fragment 15'. From *N* 2: 2532.

[Lines from a notebook – May–June 1805]

First published in *1893* 461 as 'Fragment 66', then in *1912* 2: 999 as 'Fragment 14'. From *N* 2: 2597.

Phantom

First published in *1834* immediately following 'Phantom or Fact', which was first published in *1828* and probably written around that time. The lines appear in one of STC's Malta notebooks, dated 8 February 1805, with the following introduction: 'Of Love in Sleep, the seldomness of the Feeling, scarcely ever in short absences, or except after very long Absence / a certain indistinctness, a sort of *universal-in-particularness* of Form, seem necessary – vide the note preceding, and my Lines' (*N* 2: 2441). See also *N* 2: 2055 n. The variants below are all from the notebook text.

1 *and* 'or'.
2 *and* 'or'.
3 *was* 'seem'd'.
4 'Of Aught upon her brighten'd Face'.
6 *But* 'Save'.
8 *thro'* 'in'.

[An Angel Visitant]

Unpublished in STCs lifetime, these lines were first published in *LR* 1: 280, then in *1877–80*. The MS, from which the present text is taken, is in a British Library notebook (actually several notebooks combined) containing material dating from 1800–07 (*N* 2: 2224 f. 81). Coburn says: 'The lines were probably composed earlier than Malta; they read like 1800–1' (*N* 2: 2224, note on no. 42). E. H. Coleridge conjecturally dates the lines 1801, Beer 1804. Coburn goes on to describe them as an adaptation and translation of some lines of German verse by Friedrich von Hagedorn quoted by STC in the same notebook (*N* 2: 2224 f. 15).

2 'holly peep' cancelled following *Beneath this* in notebook.
3 'it is' cancelled following *How warm,* in notebook.

Reason for Love's Blindness

First published in *1828*; included in *1829* and *1834*. No MS source is listed in *Index*. Beer dates the poem February 1805 in *Everyman*.

[Untitled]

First published in *1893* under the title 'An Exile'; these lines appear without title in one of the Malta notebooks, dated October 1805 (*N* 2: 2691).

Constancy to an Ideal Object

First published in *1828*; included in *1829* and *1834*. There is no surviving MS and no clear evidence as to the date of composition. Beer places the poem in early 1806 in *Everyman* 385 but notes: 'The date is unusually uncertain, the main clue being in a letter by Coleridge of June 1825 referring to part at least of it as ". . . those lines which a long time ago I sent to Mrs Green" ' (*L* 5: 467).

7 *Fond* foolish.
12 *She* Identified by some commentators as Sara Hutchinson.
17 *meed* reward.
30 *An image* 'This phenomenon, which the author has himself experienced, and of which the reader may find a description in one of the earlier volumes of the Manchester Philosophical Transactions, is applied figuratively in the following passage of the Aids to Reflection. "Pindar's fine remark respecting the different effects of music, on different characters, holds equally true of Genius; as many as are not delighted by it are disturbed, perplexed, irritated. The beholder either recognises it as a projected form of his own being, that moves before him with a glory round its head, or recoils from it as a spectre." – Aids to Reflection, p. 220' (STC's note). *Glory* was a term for a mountain phenomenon in which one's own enlarged image is seen projected by the sun in the mist, with a circle of light around the head; see 'Dejection: An Ode' 54.

[Lines from a notebook – March 1806]

First published as 'Fragment 8' in *1912* 2: 998; from *N* 2: 2799.

[Lines from a notebook – June 1806]

First published in *Letters of Samuel Taylor Coleridge* (1895), then in *1912* as 'Fragment 19' (2: 1001). From *N* 2: 2866. E. H. Coleridge identifies the source as the ballad 'Waly, Waly, Love be bonny' in Thomas Percy's *Reliques of Ancient English Poetry*.

Farewell to Love

First published in *The Courier* for 27 September 1806; reprinted in the *Morning Post* for 11 October 1806 and in the *Gentleman's Magazine* for November 1815. Included in *LR* 1: 280 and in Thomas Allsop's *Letters, Conversations* (1836), 1: 143. As E. H. Coleridge points out in *1912* 2: 402 n., this sonnet, modelled on Sonnet 74 of Fulke Greville's *Coelica*, was inscribed on the margin of Charles Lamb's copy of Greville's *Works* (1633).

Time, Real and Imaginary

First published at the end of the preface to *1817*; included in *1828, 1829, 1834*. STC introduces the poem in *1817* as follows: 'At the request of the friends of my youth, who still remain my friends, and who were pleased with the wildness of the compositions, I have added two school-boy poems [the second is 'The Raven'] . . . Surely, malice itself will scarcely attribute their insertion to any other motive, than the wish to keep alive the recollections from early life. – I scarcely knew what title I should prefix to the first. By imaginary Time, I meant the state of a school boy's mind when on his return to school he projects his being in his day dreams, and lives in his next holidays, six months hence: and this I contrasted with real Time' (iii). In fact, an earlier version of lines 2–11 of this poem, written not when STC was a schoolboy but sometime between 1802 and 1807, forms the end of a 25-line MS poem in the hand of Sara Hutchinson printed by Whalley in *Asra Poems* 17–18 and by Beer in *Everyman* under the title 'Hope and Time' (388). The MS poem begins as follows:

> In the great City rear'd, my fancy rude
> By natural Forms unnurs'd & unsubdued
> An Alien from the Rivers & the Fields
> And all the Charms, that Hill or Woodland yields,
> It was the pride & passion of my Youth
> T' impersonate & color moral Truth[:]
> Rare Allegories in those Days I spun,
> That oft had mystic senses oft'ner none.
> Of all Resemblances however faint,
> So dear a Lover was I, that with quaint
> Figures fantastically grouped I made
> Of commonest Thoughts a moving Masquerade.
> 'Twas then I fram'd this obscure uncouth Rhyme,
> A sort of Emblem 'tis of HOPE & TIME.
>
> In ancient Days, but when I have not read,
> Nor know I, where – but 'twas some elfish Place . . .

E. H. Coleridge links 'Time, Real and Imaginary' with a notebook entry dated January–March 1811 (see *N* 3: 4048 and Coburn's note).

3 *pinions* 'pennons' ('Hope and Time' 17).
4 *lovely* 'winged' ('Hope and Time' 18).
6 'But HOPE outruns the other –' ('Hope and Time' 20).
7 *runs* 'flies' ('Hope and Time' 21).
9 'Time is his Name – & he, alas! is blind' ('Hope and Time' 23).
10 'With regular Step o'er rough & smooth he past' ('Hope and Time' 24).
11 *be* 'is' ('Hope and Time' 25).

[Lines from a notebook – 1806]

First published in *1893* 469 as 'Fragment 115'; included in *1912* 2: 998 as 'Fragment 9'. From *N* 2: 2921. Coburn points out in her note on this entry that these lines, like the following two verse fragments from the notebooks, are derived from Fulke Greville's *Alaham* (c. 1600–01).

[Lines from a notebook – October–November 1806]

First published with many alterations in *LR* 1: 277; included the *Poetical and Dramatic Works* of 1887 and in *1912* 2: 1005–6 as 'Fragment 39'. From *N* 2: 2926; see *N* 2: 2921 n. for source in Greville's *Alaham*.

[Lines from a notebook – 1806]

First published in Mrs Henry Sandford's *Thomas Poole and His Friends* (1888); included in *1912* 2: 1001 as 'Fragment 21'. From *N* 2: 2932; see *N* 2: 2921 n. for source in Greville's *Alaham*.

[Lines from a notebook – November–December 1806]

First published in *1912* 2: 1013 as 'Fragment 63'; from *N* 2: 2951.

[Lines from a notebook – February 1807]

First published in *1912* 2: 1001 as 'Fragment 20'; from *N* 2: 3004, which includes other cancelled versions.

9 *Faquir* usually spelled 'fakir'; a member of a Moslem sect who has taken a vow of poverty; a dervish.

[Lines from a notebook – February 1807]

The opening three lines first published in *1912* 2: 1002 as 'Fragment 25', the following eight lines first published on the same page of *1912* as 'Fragment 26'. These lines appear as three sequential entries in *N* 2: 2995, 2996, 2997; Beer prints them together in *Everyman* 402. Lines 4–11 are printed together in *Asra Poems* 173.

[Lines from a manuscript – 1807–8]

First published in *1893* 469 as 'Fragment 114': lines 1–6 in verse, as here, and the rest as prose. The same format is followed in *1912* 2: 997–8, as 'Fragment 6'. See Beer, *Everyman* 400.

[Lines from a notebook – July 1807; includes lines previously published separately as 'Coeli enarrant']

These lines appear together in *N* 2: 3107. Lines 22–32 were first published separately in *1912* 1: 486 under the title 'Coeli Enarrant', 'The heavens are telling', with an allusion to Psalm 19. Beer comments: 'They are based by Coleridge on a childhood memory of an occasion when he was punished so hard by his father in the schoolroom that instead of the required lesson he could only cry "O" ' (*Everyman* 401). At the end of the notebook entry STC writes: 'I wrote these Lines, as an imitation of Du Bartas, as translated by our Sylvester.' The French poet Guillaume de Salluste, Signeur Du Bartas (1544–90), wrote an influential creation epic titled *La Semaine* in 1578; it was translated by Joshua Sylvester in 1605 and given the title *Divine Weekes and Workes*.

29–31 Compare the language here to 'Dejection: An Ode' 114–25.

[Lines from a notebook – January 1808]

First published in *1893* 461 as 'Fragment 71'; included in *1912* 2: 1003 as 'Fragment 30'. From *n* 3: 3234.

To William Wordsworth

First published in *1817*; included in *1828, 1829, 1834*. STC sent a version of the poem (127 lines) to Sir George Beaumont in a letter dated January 1807 (printed in *1893* Appendix H, 525–6; the letter is apparently now lost and does not appear in *L*). Another version (119 lines), described by E. H. Coleridge as 'earlier' but 'of about the same date', was given to Wordsworth and is printed in *1912* Appendix I.L and, more accurately, in *The Prelude 1799, 1805, 1850*, ed. Jonathan Wordsworth, M. H. Abrams and Stephen Gill (1979), 542–45 and in *Everyman* 392–99 (the MS is now in the Wordsworth Library, Grasmere). Both these early versions differ strikingly from the text printed in *1817* and later. Lines 12–47 appear in a letter to Wordsworth of 30 May 1815 (*L* 4: 573–4); lines 69–75 in a letter to William Mudford of 18 February 1818 (*L* 4: 838). Lines 65–75 are printed near the end of *BL* X, as an extension of the following self-judgment: 'On my own account I may perhaps have had sufficient reason to lament my deficiency in self-controul, and the neglect of concentrating my powers to the realization of some permanent work. But to verse rather than to prose, if to either, belongs the "voice of mourning" for "Keen panges of love awakening as a babe . . ." ' (1: 221).

Title 'To a Gentleman' (letter to Beaumont, *1817, 1828, 1829*). In the Wordsworth Library MS the title is 'To William Wordsworth. Lines Composed, for the Greater Part on the Night, On Which He finished the Recitation of His Poem (in Thirteen Books) Concerning the Growth and History of His Own Mind'.
1 'O Friend! O Teacher! God's great Gift to me!' (MS, letter to Beaumont).
6–12

> Of thy own Spirit, thou hast lov'd to tell
> What may be told, to th' understanding mind
> Revealable; and what within the mind
> May rise enkindled. Theme as hard as high!
> Of Smiles spontaneous and mysterious Fear
>
> (MS)

> Of thy own spirit thou hast loved to tell
> What *may* be told, by words revealable;
> With heavenly breathings, like the secret soul
> Of vernal growth, oft quickening in the heart,
> Thoughts that obey no mastery of words,
> Pure self-beholdings! theme as hard as high,
> Of *smiles* spontaneous and mysterious *fear*
>
> (letter to Beaumont)

9 'By vital breathings like the secret soul' (*1817, 1828*).
11 *Thoughts all too deep for words!* Cf. Wordsworth, 'Intimations Ode' 203: 'Thoughts that do often lie too deep for tears'.
   Theme hard as high! Cf. Milton, *Paradise Lost* 1. 26, 9. 13–14 and 42–3.
16 *Or by some inner power* 'Or by interior Power' (MS); 'Or by some central breath' (letter to Wordsworth).
17 *inner* 'hidden' (MS, letter to Beaumont).
19 Cf. 'Intimations Ode' 56 and esp. 69–76 ('But He beholds the light, and whence it flows . . .'); also Wordsworth's 'Elegiac Stanzas Suggested By A Picture of Peele Castle' 13–16.
18–40

> Mid festive crowds, *thy* Brows too garlanded,
> A Brother of the Feast: of Fancies fair,
> *Hyblaean murmurs of poetic Thought*,
> *Industrious in its Joy*, by lilied Streams
> *Native or outland, Lakes and famous Hills!*
> *Of more than Fancy*, of the Hope of Man
> *Amid the tremor of a Realm aglow* –
> *Where France in all her Towns lay vibrating*
> Ev'n as a Bark becalm'd on sultry seas
> Beneath the voice from Heav'n, the bursting crash

> *Of Heaven's immediate thunder! when no cloud*
> *Is visible, or Shadow on the Main*
> Ah! soon night roll'd on night, and every Cloud
> Open'd its eye of Fire: and Hope aloft
> Now flutter'd, and now toss'd upon the storm
> Floating! Of *Hope afflicted and struck down*
> *Thence summoned homeward* – homeward to thy Heart,
> Oft from the *Watch-tower of Man's absolute self*,
>
>   (MS)

28 'Distending, and of man' (letter to Beaumont).

29–37 Cf. Wordsworth, *The Prelude* (1805) 6. 352 ff.

30 'Even as a bark becalm'd on sultry seas / Quivers beneath the voice from Heaven, the burst' (letter to Beaumont). In the 1815 letter to Wordsworth and in *1817* and *1828*, the image is compressed to a single line: 'Ev'n as a bark becalm'd beneath the burst'.

38 *struck down* 'amazed' (letter to Wordsworth).

39 *summoned homeward* 'homeward summoned' (letter to Wordsworth).

40 *From the dread watch-tower* 'As from the watch-tower' (letter to Beaumont).

44 *controlling* In the Wordsworth Library MS, '?impelling, ?directing' appear as alternatives.

45–6 'Virtue and Love! An Orphic Tale indeed, / A Tale divine' (MS). *Song* is also 'tale' in these lines in the letter to Beaumont.

46 *thoughts* 'Truths' (letter to Wordsworth).

47 Cf. Wordsworth, *The Prelude* (1805) 1.64–5.
    O great Bard! 'Ah! great Bard' (MS).

48 *strain* 'Swell' (MS).

49 *eye* 'ken' (MS), 'eyes' (letter to Beaumont).
    viewed 'saw' (letter to Beaumont).

52 *They, both in power and act* 'For they, both power and act' (letter to Beaumont).

53–4 'and Time is not with *them*, / Save as it worketh *for* them, they *in* it' (*1817, 1828, 1829*).

58, 59 *lay* 'Song' (MS, letter to Beaumont).

61–4 These lines replace the following more extended passage in the Wordsworth Library MS and the letter to Beaumont (variants between the MS and letter are given in square brackets):

> Dear shall it be to every human heart,
> To me how more than dearest! me, on whom
> Comfort from thee, and utterance of thy love,
> Came with such heights and depths of harmony
> Such sense of wings uplifting, that the storm
> Scatter'd and whirl'd me, till my thoughts became
> [Such sense of wings uplifting, that its might
> Scatter'd and quell'd me – till my thoughts became
>
>   (letter to Beaumont)]

> A bodily tumult; and thy faithful hopes,
> Thy hopes of me, dear Friend! by me unfelt!
> Were troublous to me, almost as a voice,
> Familiar once, and more than musical;
> To one cast forth, whose hope had seem'd to die
> A wanderer with a worn-out heart
> [As a dear woman's voice to one cast forth
> A wanderer with a worn-out heart forlorn.
>
> (letter to Beaumont)]
>
> Mid strangers pining with untended wounds.
> O Friend, too well thou know'st of what sad years
> The long suppression had benumb'd my soul,
> That even as life returns upon the drown'd,
> The unusual joy awoke a throng of pains –

73 *thee* In italics in *1817*, *1828*, *1829*.

74 *Strewed* 'Strewn' (letter to Beaumont, *1828*, *1829*).

82 *thy* In italics in *1817*, *1828*, *1829*.

  Nor do thou 'Thou too, Friend!' (MS, letter to Beaumont).

83 'O injure not the memory of that Hour' (MS); 'Impair thou not the memory of that Hour' (letter to Beaumont).

90 *halcyon* legendary bird with the power to calm the sea, where it nested.

93 'Becomes most sweet! hours for their own sake hail'd' (MS).

96 *thy* 'the' (letter to Beaumont).

98 *my* 'her' (letter to Beaumont).

99 ' "A beautiful white cloud of Foam at momentary intervals coursed by the side of the Vessel with a Roar, and little stars of flame danced and sparkled and went out in it: and every now and then light detachments of this white cloud-like foam dashed off from the vessel's side, each with its own small constellation, over the Sea, and scoured out of sight like a Tartar Troop over a wilderness." *The Friend* [no. XIV, 23 November 1809], p. 220' (STC's note).

102 *and* 'my' (MS, letter to Beaumont).

104 *Song* 'Lay' (MS).

106 *my* 'mine' (MS, letter to Beaumont).

107–8 Between these lines: 'All, whom I deepliest love, in one room all!)' (MS, letter to Beaumont). In the former text, there is a parenthesis from 'yet thou thyself' in line 105 to this line; in the latter text, only this line is contained in parentheses.

Metrical Feet. Lesson for a Boy

First published in *1834*. The lines were written as a verse letter to Derwent Coleridge dated 3 March 1807, where they are introduced thus: '[The chi]ef and most common metrical Feet expressed in corresponding [metre]' (*L* 3: 5–6). In the MS the individual metrical feet are, inconsistently, marked off with strokes (/), and the names of the feet are written in capital letters.

1 *shōrt* Metrically unmarked in MS.
2 'Frōm lōng / tŏ lōng / ĭn sōl/ĕmn sōrt' (MS).
4 *trĭsȳllăblĕ* 'trī / syllable' (MS).
6 *the swift Anapæsts throng* Metrically unmarked in MS.
7 *with one short at each side* 'with two short at each side' (MS).
10–11 There is space separating these lines in the MS.
15 *May . . . must* Underlined in MS.

Recollections of Love

First published in *1817*; included in *1828, 1829, 1834*. A five-stanza version, including two drafts of the first stanza, appears in a notebook containing material of various and uncertain date (*N* 2: 2224); E. H. Coleridge conjecturally dates this draft to 1807, while Beer indicates a range of 1807–17. There is a partly cancelled draft of lines 11–12 in another notebook dated February 1807 (*N* 2: 3003).

1–5 In the variant draft of this stanza in the notebook, *Recess* and *caress* are 'recesses' and 'caresses'; *you* in line 5 is 'thee'. STC then writes, introducing the version printed in *1817* and later: 'A variety of the same [metre], & more melodious in our Language by substituting single for the two double rhymes'.
7 *sea ward* 'Southern' (notebook).
9 *here and there, like things astray* 'upward on the fav'ring wind' is cancelled in the notebook, as is 'I reclin'd' at the end of line 6, which would have made a different rhyme.
10 In the notebook STC drafted, cancelled, then redrafted a stanza to follow this line, which does not appear in any printed text:

> On such a bed of heath as this
> I lay, a stranger to ~~thine~~ your eye.
> Yet whence that ~~sense of~~ aching Hope? that sign
> Those yearnings ~~after~~ for an unknown bliss?
> Beloved! flew thy Spirit by?

12 *your* 'thy' (notebook).
13 *That asking look?* 'That seeking [Doze / Dream / Gaze]?' (notebook).
14 'That promise without whence or where' (notebook).
15 *your* 'thy' (notebook).
17 *rose-mark* 'sure mark' (notebook).
18 '~~I have seen first seen~~ I lov'd thee, maiden mild' (notebook).
19 'my Heart' cancelled after 'As whom' (notebook).
20 'was the my Soul' cancelled after 'So deeply' (notebook).
21–30 These stanzas do not appear in the notebook draft.
25 *Greta* the River Greta, near which STC's house Greta Hall stood.

The Blossoming of the Solitary Date-Tree. A Lament

First published in *1828*, then in *1829* and *1834*. The last three stanzas were published separately in *New Times* (31 January 1818). A transcript of these stanzas in the hand of John Taylor Coleridge appears in a copybook of poems by members of the Coleridge family, where it is headed: 'An Imitation of one of the Minnesingers of the Thirteenth Century, introduced by Mr Coleridge into his Lecture on the Literature of the Middle Ages' (see *Index* CoS 38). STC's prefatory account of this poem's fragmentary survival, the eastern imagery and the speaker's imaginative and emotional self-subordination to a 'Dear Maid' all suggest links with 'Kubla Khan'. The date of composition is given as 1805 in *1893* and *1912*. In *Everyman* 404 Beer comments: 'The date of this poem is uncertain, but a letter of 1822 [5: 216] recalling that lines 76–8 were addressed to Sara Hutchinson suggests that the verse part of the poem belongs to the time of his love for her. The prologue, which in diction resembles that of the introduction to *Kubla Khan* and some of the glosses for *The Ancient Mariner*, may well have been added later on similar lines to such framing devices.'

5 *stood* 'were yet standing' (*1828*).

8 *mediator* 'moderator' (*1828*).

9 *'not so'* Omitted in *1828*.

11–16 The rest of the paragraph from here reads as follows in *1828*: ' ". . . remain here all the days of his now mortal life, and enjoy the respite thou mayest grant him, in this thy Paradise which thou gavest to him, and hast planted with every tree pleasant to the sight of man and delicious fruitage." And the word of the Most High answered Satan: "The *tender mercies of the wicked are cruel*. Treacherous Fiend! guilt deep as thine could not be, yet the love of kind not extinguished. But if having done what thou hast done, thou had'st yet the heart of man within thee, and the yearning of the soul for its answering image and completing counterpart, O spirit, desperately wicked! the sentence thou counsellest had been thine own." '

18 *Linnaeus* Swedish botanist (1707–78).

47 'Hope, Imagination, honourable aims,' (*1828*).

52 *voices* 'voices mute' (*1828*).

54 *O no! no!* 'No! No!' (*1828*).

60 thy '*thy*' in italics (*1828*).

76 thee '*thee*' in italics (*1828*).

To Two Sisters

First published in *The Courier* for 10 December 1807, signed 'SIESTI' ('STC' phonetically jumbled); never collected in this form in STC's lifetime (first included in *1877–80*). There is a signed fair copy of a 12-line version (1–5, 45–52), titled 'To M[ary] M[organ] and C[harlotte] B[rent]', dated November 1807; see *Index* CoS 759 and W. Braekman, 'A Reconsideration of the Genesis of S. T. Coleridge's Poem "On Taking Leave Of —" ', *Notes and Queries* 209 (1964), 21–4; see also *Index* CoS 760, 761, 762. A much shorter and altered version was included in *1834*; see following poem.

On Taking Leave Of ———, 1817

First published in *1834*. This is a much shortened and altered version of the preceding poem, 'To Two Sisters', and is accordingly included at this point in the chronological sequence. The 1817 date in the title suggests that STC may have originally revised the text for inclusion in *1817*.

A Child's Evening Prayer

First published in *1834* (not in *1852*, as E. H. Coleridge and *Index* say). There is a transcript, probably in the hand of Sara Coleridge and headed 'Sara Coleridge's prayer by her Father', in the Victoria College Library, Toronto. The date of composition is given as 1806 in *1893*, *1912* and *Everyman* – but with no supporting evidence.

1 This is also the opening line of 'The Pains of Sleep'.

Ad Vilmum Axiologum

First published in *1893*. A draft of these lines appears in a notebook entry among material dated 1807–10 (*N* 2: 3231). Rosenbaum and White date these lines 1807–8, Beer dates them ?1810 – both seem more likely than E. H. Coleridge's guess of 1805. The lines follow a cancelled version of a Latin poem also titled 'Ad Vilmum Axiologum' (see *Everyman* 309, which includes an English prose translation); an uncancelled draft of the Latin lines appears at the end of this notebook entry. Another draft of the first six English lines appears earlier in the same notebook (*N* 2: 3220), where they follow an effort to render three German distichs of Goethe and Schiller (see Coburn's note on *N* 2: 3220 and 'Fragment 17' in *1912* 2: 1000). 'Axiologus' is Wordsworth's own Latinization of his name; in 1787 he thus signed his first published poem, 'A Sonnet on seeing Miss Helen Maria Williams weeping at a tale of distress'.

1 *creates* 'awakens to' (first notebook draft).
2 'in' is cancelled after 'awake' in the second notebook draft. In the first notebook draft the following alternative is given: 'Welcoming Hearts: is it their voice, or is it thy own voice?' At the bottom of the draft the line is written again and becomes: 'Welcoming Souls! is it their Voice, sweet Poet! or is it thy own Voice?'
6 'Meet and' is cancelled at the beginning of this line in the second notebook draft; 'Song' is cancelled following 'thy'. In the first notebook draft one version of this line is cancelled and changed to 'Meet the Song, they *receive*, and retain, and resound, & prolong it!'
7 'things' is cancelled following 'and' in the second notebook draft.

Psyche

First published in *BL* (1817) 1: 78, with the following note: 'The fact, that in Greek Psyche is the common name for the soul, and the butterfly, is thus alluded to in the following stanza from an unpublished poem by the author.' It was included in *The Amulet* (1833), in *LR* and in *1844*; in the last two publications it is dated 1808. There is a revised fair copy in the Houghton Library, Harvard University, entitled 'Psyche: a reflection', and a transcript by Sara Hutchinson in the Wordsworth Library, Grasmere (*Asra Poems* 17). For evidence supporting an 1808 date of composition, see *N* 3: 3264 n. and 3: 3362. Two later MSS in the Berg Collection, New York Public Library, are recorded in *Index* CoS 546, 547.

[Sonnet – translated from Marino]

First published in *1893*, from a notebook draft among material dated 1–22 September 1808 (*N* 3: 3377). Campbell gives the Italian text of Giambattista Marino (or Marini) (1569–1625) in his note in *1893* 632, as does E. H. Coleridge in *1912* 2: 1131–2. Coburn notes in her comment on this translation: 'In the manuscript the lines are indicated only by capitalization, the page of the notebook being too narrow to take the full lines.' She also notes the relation of imagery and source to *N* 3: 3379, which contains the fragment 'Two wedded Hearts, if e'er were such'.

[Fragment: 'Two wedded Hearts']

First published in *1893*; included as 'Fragment 31' in *1912*. In a notebook entry for September 1808 (*N* 3: 3379) these two variant fragments follow STC's meditation on himself and Sara Hutchinson and are introduced as follows: 'N.B. This put in simple & elegant verse, as an imitation of Marini – and of too large a part of the Madrigals of Guarini himself' (Giovanni Battista Guarini, 1537–1612). Coburn notes that in these lines STC is 'identifying his own story with the story of Pyramus and Thisbe of Ovid's *Metamorphoses* IV' (*N* 3: 3379 n.). See headnote to preceding poem.

Version 1
5 *there* 'where' (*1893, 1912*).
Version 2
4 'Still' is cancelled at the beginning of this line in the notebook.

A Tombless Epitaph

First published in *The Friend*, no. XIV, for 23 November 1809, without title and with the following footnote: 'Imitated, though in the movements rather than the thoughts, from the viith, of Gli Epitafi of *Chiabrera* . . .' (Gabriello Chiabrera, 1552–1638, Italian poet whose epitaphs also impressed Wordsworth). Included in *1817, 1828, 1829, 1834*. In Spenser's *The Faerie Queene* I.6, Sir Satyrane ('A Satyres son yborne in forrest wylde') rescues Una from the satyrs. STC explains at the beginning of *The Friend* no. XIV that he has received 'numerous Letters . . . from the Friend, with a slight sketch of whose character I have introduced the present Number under the name, which he went by among his friends and familiars, of SATYRANE, the Idoloclast, or breaker of Idols'.

13 '(Too much of all!)' (*The Friend*).
16 *inlets* 'outlets' (*The Friend*).
24 *Hippocrene* the spring at the foot of Mount Helicon, sacred to the Muses and source of poetic inspiration.
33 *odorous* 'od'rous' (*The Friend*).
36 *Philosopher!* 'Philosopher,' (*The Friend*).

On a Clock in a Market-Place

First published in *LR*. These lines appear in a notebook entry dated July–September 1809 (*N* 3: 3546), where they are headed 'On a clock in A Market-place (proposed)', and in a letter to Thomas Poole of 9 October 1809 (*L* 3: 236). The present text is based on that in the notebook. In the letter STC explains that he 'was asked for a motto for a *market*-clock' and that he 'uttered the following literally without a moment's premeditation'.

1 'What now, O Man! thou does or mean'st to do' (letter to Poole, *LR*).
2 *rue* Spelled 'rew' in the notebook.
3–4 'When hov'ring o'er the line this Hand will tell / Thy last dread moment. Twill be Heaven or Hell!' is partially cancelled in the notebook.
4 'None of the previous publications of the lines indicates Coleridge's noticeable enlargement here of the two final nouns. The last two lines are written in an unusually large hand for Coleridge, and with a special deliberateness about the words *Heaven* and *Hell*' (Coburn, *N* 3: 3546 n.).

Separation

First published in *1834*. There is a notebook draft, quite different from the printed version, dated 1809–10 (*N* 3: 3653). The occasion of the poem was probably Sara Hutchinson's leaving Grasmere for a visit to Wales. A note to the 1848 one-volume edition of STC's *Poems* says that 'The Fourth and last stanzas are adapted from the twelfth and last of Cotton's *Chlorinda* . . . The fifth stanza is the eleventh of Cotton's poem'; in *1852* the note reads: 'The fourth and last stanzas are from Cotton's *Chlorinda*, with very slight alteration.' Charles Cotton's *Poems on Several Occasions* (1681) are praised in chapter XIX of *BL* (2: 91–2) and in Wordsworth's Preface to *Poems* (1815).

1 The notebook draft begins with three lines not in the printed version: 'Made worthy by excess of Love / A wretch thro' power of Happiness, / A poor from wealth, I dare not use'.
5–8 STC may have worried that Sara Hutchinson would marry her cousin John

Monkhouse, whose new farm on the banks of the Wye at Hindwell she visited (see Coburn's note to *N* 3: 3653).

13 *Asra* Written with the Greek letters ΑΣΡΑ throughout the notebook draft.

16 'That Treasure would supply desert!' (notebook).

17–20 This stanza constitutes lines 4–7 of the notebook draft.

21–2 'Death, erst contemn'd, O ΑΣΡΑ! why / ~~With~~ Now terror-stricken do I see?' (notebook).

The Visionary Hope

First published in *1817*; included in *1828*, *1829*, *1834*.

22 *can* In italics in *1817*, *1828*, *1829*.

[Lines from a notebook – March 1810]

First published in *1893* 462 as 'Fragment 75'; included in *1912* 2: 1004 as 'Fragment 34'. From *N* 3: 3747.

[Lines from a notebook – April–June 1810]

First published in *1912* 2: 1001 as 'Fragment 22'; from *N* 3: 3764.

[Lines from a notebook – May 1810]

First published in *1893* 462 as 'Fragment 76'; included in *1912* 2: 1004–5 as 'Fragment 35'. From *N* 3: 3796. On the inner and outer margin of the notebook page are STC's anagrams, in Greek capitals, for Sara Hutchinson.

7 *disrent* This word is not in the *OED*; presumably it means torn away or torn apart.

Epitaph on an Infant

First published in *The Courier* for 20 March 1811, signed 'Aphilos' (without love, friendless, but also unloving, unfriendly). Included in *1817*, *1828*, *1829*, *1834*. There is a fair copy written in a copy of *1797* in the Beinecke Library, Yale University. Beer gives the date of composition as 1809 in *Everyman*, without explanation. Berkeley Coleridge died in infancy in February 1799.

1 *balmy* 'milky' (*Courier*, fair copy).

5 *infant's* 'darling's' (*Courier*).

6 *O tell, rude stone!* 'Tell simple stone' (*Courier*).

7 *the* 'a' (*Courier*).

[Lines from a notebook – 1811]

First published in *1893* 462 as 'Fragment 77'; included in *1912* 2: 1005 as 'Fragment 36'. From *N* 3: 4052.

[Fragment of an ode on Napoleon]

First published in *1912* 2: 1003 as 'Fragment 29'; from *N* 3: 4073, where it is conjecturally dated 1811.

2 *Hippocrene* the spring on Mount Helicon, thus in myth a source of poetic inspiration.
5 Phlegethon and Cocytus are two of the four rivers running through Hades, the underworld of ancient Greek myth.
9 *Euterpe* one of the nine Muses, associated with music, specifically with flute-playing.

[Lines inscribed on the fly-leaf of Benedetto Menzini's 'Poesie' (1782)]

First published in *1893* 467 as 'Fragment 100'; included in *1912* 2: 1010 as 'Fragment 52'.

[Lines from a notebook – May–June 1811]

First published in *1912* 2: 1005 as 'Fragment 37'; from *N* 3: 4045. Coburn notes that the top of this notebook page has been cut off and that these lines may therefore have been the last lines of a longer poem (*N* 3: 4045 n.).

1 *O me miserable man!* Cf. Satan's words in *Paradise Lost* 4. 73–5: 'Me miserable! which way shall I fly / Infinite wrath, and infinite despair? / What way I fly is Hell; myself am Hell'.

[Lines from a notebook – May–July 1811]

First published in *1893* 462 as 'Fragment 78'; included in *1912* 2: 1005 as 'Fragment 38'. From *N* 3: 4092–3. The first two lines, used in *Remorse* IV.ii.96–7, are a versification of a sentence of Jean Paul (Johann Paul Richter, 1763–1825): 'Durch die ganze Nacht ging ein halb verlorner Donner, gleichsam als zürnte er im Schlafe.' The last four lines, written as a separate fragment in the notebook, are also a versified adaptation from Jean Paul – in this case, from a passage in *Geist* (1801) quoted at length in *N* 3: 4088 n. See Coburn's note on 3: 4093 for the religious and psychological significance of these lines.

[Lines from a notebook – May 1814?]

First published in *1912* 2: 997 as 'Fragment 2'; from *N* 3: 4194, where they are found among material dated 1814–15.

[Lines from a notebook – 1815–16]

First published in *1893* 469 as 'Fragment 109'; included in *1912* 2: 1007 as 'Fragment 42'. From *N* 3: 4283. Campbell compares lines 19–22 of 'The Destiny of Nations'. Compare also the sentence near the end of Shelley's *A Defence of Poetry*: 'Poets are . . . the mirrors of the gigantic shadows which futurity casts upon the present.'

[Lines from a notebook – 1815–16]

First published in *1893* 469 as 'Fragment 110'; included in *1912* 2: 1008 as 'Fragment 46'. From *N* 3: 4298; Coburn says in her note on this entry that the lines are 'an attempted versification, condensation, and paraphrase of Jean Paul's *Geist* (1801) 2: 78. STC's "klumps" is directly from the German "Klumpen" '.

On Donne's First Poem

The opening twelve lines were first published among the 'Jeux d'Esprit' in *1912* (2: 980–81). The draft of the complete text appears in a notebook entry dated April–May 1811, where it is followed without break by drafts of 'Limbo' and 'Ne Plus Ultra' (*N* 3: 4073). Beer's 32-line text in *Everyman* (425) follows the first eighteen lines from f. 145v and f. 146, then introduces seven lines from f. 149, then concludes with the remaining seven lines from f. 146; see Coburn's note on *N* 3: 4073 for a justification for this procedure. The present text follows *Everyman*. STC's poem is inspired by Donne's 'The Flea'.

Limbo

First published in its present form in *1834*. The MS draft is part of the notebook entry of April–May 1811 (*N* 3: 4073) that includes 'On Donne's First Poem' and 'Ne Plus Ultra'. Five lines clearly related to this poem (they appear as lines 6–10 in the 38-line version of 'Limbo' printed in *1893* and *1912*) were published in a note to Essay IX, Section the Second, in vol. 3 of *The Friend* (1818; *CC* 4: 494) and reprinted as a separate poem entitled 'Moles' in *1834* (see below). Beer's 32-line version of 'Limbo' in *Everyman* follows the sequence of lines in the notebook draft but does not include the lines that STC published separately as 'Moles'. There is also a 32-line fair copy in an album of Sara Coleridge, signed by STC and dated 'Highgate, 15 October 1827' (*Index* CoS 306). Lines 1–20 of the present text appear in a letter to Alaric A. Watts dated December 1828 (*L* 6: 779–80).

1 ff. These lines are preceded in the notebook draft by a six-line cancelled passage and by a version of the lines printed separately in *1834* as 'Moles'.

2 *so* 'such' (1827 fair copy).

5 *branny* covered with bran or husks of grain (which has presumably been cut and ground despite Time's being 'scytheless').

6 *the* 'his' (1827 fair copy).

7 *Not mark'd by flit of Shades* 'Mark'd but by Flit of Shades' (notebook, 1827 fair copy).

20 *at* 'on' (1827 fair copy).

20 In the 1827 fair copy line 20 is followed by these lines:

> In one sole Outlet yawns the Phantom Wall,
> And through this grim road to [a] worser thrall
> Oft homeward scouring from a sick Child's dream
> Old Mother Brownrigg shoots upon a scream;
> And turning back her Face with hideous Leer,
> Leaves Sentry there *Intolerable Fear*!
> > A Horrid thought is growthless dull Negation:
> > Yet that is but a Purgatory Curse,
> > > SHE knows a fear far worse
> > Flee, least thou hear its Name! Flee rash
> > > Imagination!

21 *immure* wall in, surround, enclose.

26–28 In the notebook draft the present version of these three lines follows a passage not printed in *1834*:

> For skimming in the wake, it mock'd the care
> Of the Old Boat-God for his Farthing Fare,
> Tho' Irus' Ghost itself he neer <frown'd> blacker on.
> The skin and skin-pent Druggist crost the Acheron,
> Styx and with Puriphlegethon Cocytus:
> The very names, methinks, might thither fright us –
> Unchang'd it cross'd & shall &c

There then follows a comment in prose: 'A Specimen of the Sublime dashed to pieces by cutting too close with her fiery Four in Hand round the corner of Nonsense –'. In the sequence of verse comprising the *1834* printed text the following variant of lines 26–28 appears:

> But the Hag, Madness, scalds the Fiends of Hell
> With frenzy-dreams, all incompassible
> Of aye-unepithetable ~~Priv~~ Negation

Moles

First published in *The Friend* (1818), where the lines are applied to 'the partizans of a crass and sensual materialism'; included under the present title in *1834*. See headnote to 'Limbo' for a discussion of how these lines relate to the rest of the notebook draft (*N* 3: 4073).

1 'Even now it shrinks them! they shrink in, as Moles' (notebook); 'They, like moles' (*The Friend*).
2 This line is not in parentheses in *The Friend*.
3 'Shrink from the light, then listen for a sound' (*The Friend*).

Ne plus ultra

First published in *1834*. Though these lines appear in a separate notebook entry (*N* 3: 4074) from the drafts of 'On Donne's First Poem', 'Limbo' and 'Moles', Coburn says that 'Limbo' and 'Ne plus ultra' 'are two parts of one poem, two sides of one coin (as EHC indeed points out), negative light or timelessness and positive darkness or hell. It is difficult to separate them even graphically in the manuscript. . . . Nor did Coleridge indicate two poems by supplying separate titles' (*N* 3: 4074 n.). She goes on to say that ' "Ne plus ultra" ['no further'] appears to be HNC's [Henry Nelson Coleridge's] title, given when he included the lines in *PW* (1834). Coleridge may, however, have seen it'.

1 Cf. 'Limbo' 28: '. . . 'tis positive Negation!'
2 *Antipathist* 'One possessed by an antipathy or constitutional aversion; a natural enemy' (*OED*; this line of 'Ne plus ultra' is cited as the earliest example, though the source and date are incorrectly given as *1817*).
9 There is a comma after 'shadow' in the notebook draft.
18, 20 *Lampads Seven* Cf. 'ode to the Departing Year' 76-7: '. . . The Lampads seven (the mystic Words of Heaven)'. In Revelation iv.5 these are the seven 'lamps of fire' burning before the throne of God.

The Suicide's Argument

First published in *1828*; included in *1829* and *1834*. There is a notebook draft dated 1811 (*N* 3: 4106) that includes two additional opening lines ('Complain'd of, complaining, There shov'd & here shoving, / Every One blaming me, never a one loving!') and an additional line at the end ('Be thy own heart our common arbiter'). There is also a signed fair copy in the Victoria College Library, Toronto (*Index* CoS 654).

[An Invocation: from 'Remorse']

First published as a separate poem in *1844*; published in 1813 as III, i, lines 69–82 of *Remorse*, STC's tragedy of the Spanish Inquisition produced at Drury Lane in 1811 (originally composed in 1797 and titled *Osorio*). Though never treated as a separate poem by STC, the lines are included here because they have become a traditional part of his poetic oeuvre.

God's Omnipresence, a Hymn

Unpublished in STC's lifetime; first collected in *1852*. A MS version with the present title, now at Princeton University, is dated 19 June 1814 (see *Index* CoS 232).

To a Lady. With Falconer's 'Shipwreck'

First published in *1817*; included in *1828*, *1829*, *1834*. A version with numerous changes was published in *Felix Farley's Bristol Journal* for 21 February 1818, under the title 'Written in a Blank Leaf of Faulkner's Shipwreck, presented by a friend to Miss K'. The poem is dated June 1814 by Beer in *Everyman* (431–2), though his grounds for doing so are not indicated. William Falconer (1732–69) went to sea at the age of eighteen on the *Britannia* and was one of three survivors when the ship went down; *The Shipwreck* was published in 1762. All variants given below are from the version in *Felix Farley's Bristol Journal* unless otherwise indicated.

2 *archèd* 'cloyst'ring'.
4 *lady's* 'woman's'.
5 *sublimer* 'diviner'.
6 'On torrent falls, on woody mountain dell'.
8 'Attuning wild tales to the ocean's swell'.
10 *thee* In italics in *Felix Farley's Bristol Journal*.
11 *Now mounts, now totters* 'It mounts it totters'.
12 *Now groans, and shivers* 'It groans, it shivers'.
14 *of* 'and'.
15 *Forlorn the* 'the toil worn'.
17–20
    Say then what power evoked such genial strains
        And beckon'd godlike to the trembling Muse?
    The thought not pleasureless of suffer'd pains
        But *chiefly* friendship's voice, her holy dues.

21 'Demanding dear remembrances of friend'.
23 *Which Love makes substance! Hence* 'Which love make real! Thence'.
24 *life* 'love'.
26 'Sweet Maid for friendship framed this song to thee'.
28 *Falconer* 'Falkner' (*1817*), 'Faulkner' (*Felix Farley's Bristol Journal*).
  me 'ME' (*1817*, *1828*, *1829*).

Human Life, On the Denial of Immortality

First published in *1817*; included in *1828, 1829, 1834*. E. H. Coleridge conjectures an 1815 date of composition; Beer gives 1811–15.

5 In *1817, 1828* and *1829* 'are' and 'whole' are in italics.

[Song from 'Zapolya']

First published as part of STC's drama *Zapolya* (II, i, 65–80) in 1817; first published as a separate poem in *1844*. Beer gives the date of composition as ?April 1815–Feb. 1816; he also notes that the lines are adapted from 'Herbstlied' by Johann Ludwig Tieck (1773–1853). E. H. Coleridge prints what he calls a manuscript 'prose version' of the German in *1912* Appendix IV.B.

[Hunting Song from 'Zapolya']

First published as part of *Zapolya* (IV, 2, 56–71) in *1817*; first published as a separate poem in *1844*. As with the preceding song from this play, the date of composition is probably April 1815–Feb. 1816.

[Faith, Hope, and Charity. From the Italian of Guarini]

First published in *1912*. There is a complete draft, together with a slightly different version of the first twenty lines, in the hand of Hartley Coleridge in the British Library (see *Index* CoS 160; E. H. Coleridge's note implies that only the 20-line version is in Hartley Coleridge's hand, *1912* 1: 427 n.). Beer gives the date of composition as '?1812 ?1815' in *Everyman*. For the Italian original of 'Dialogo: Fede, Speranza, Carità' from *Madrigali* by Giovanni Battista Guarini, see *1912* Appendix VI.P. See also the note to '[Fragment: "Two Wedded Hearts"]'.

Fancy in Nubibus

First published in *The Courier* for 30 January 1818, then in *Blackwood's Magazine* for November 1819; included in *1828, 1829, 1834*. The poem was enclosed in an undated letter to Dr James Gillman, where it is headed 'Fancy in Nubibus, A Sonnet composed at Little Hampton, 29 Oct 1817' (*L* 4: 780 – from a printed source). A fair copy titled 'Fancy in the Clouds' was sent to Charles Lamb in October 1818 (*The Letters of Charles Lamb*, ed. E. V. Lucas [1935], 2: 223–4); Lamb also made a transcript of the poem, with the title 'Fancy in the Clouds: a Marine Sonnet', in a copy of *1817* (see *Index* CoS 163). E. H. Coleridge, following Freiligrath's preface to the 1852 German edition of STC's *Poems*, notes that the last five lines are indebted to Friedrich Leopold Stolberg's 'An das Meer' (*1912* 2: 435 n.) and provides the German text in Appendix VI.Q.

4 *let* 'bid' (*Blackwood's*).
5 *Own* 'Owe' (*Courier*).
  quaint 'strange' (*Blackwood's*).
6 *head* 'heart' (letter to Gilman).
  bent 'bow'd' (*Blackwood's*).
9 *through* 'o'er' (*Blackwood's*).

Israel's Lament

First published as an octavo pamphlet, also containing the Hebrew text facing, in 1817 (reprinted by the Society of Jewish Bibliophiles, 30 May 1962, with an introduction by Henry Hofheimer); not included in any of the editions published in STC's lifetime. The present text is that of the 1817 pamphlet. Princess Charlotte, granddaughter of George III and daughter of the Prince and Princess of Wales, died on 6 November 1817; her death produced a massive display of public mourning.

50 *Jeshurun's Sons* Jeshurun is a poetical Old Testament name for Israel.

A Character

First published in *1834*. E. H. Coleridge conjectured that the lines were written in response to Hazlitt's character-sketch of STC in *The Spirit of the Age* (1825) and accordingly gives 1825 as the date of composition. Beer, who agrees with the Hazlitt connection, nevertheless dates the lines '?November 1819'. A MS draft of the poem in the British Library is undated.

1 *for* ' 'mongst' (MS).
11 *had a* 'had but' (MS).
22 *denounced* 'disowned' (MS).
31 *sharp* 'smoke' (MS).
36 *Joseph* 'Judas' (MS).
46 *sic vos non vobis* Abbreviation of a line attributed to Virgil: 'Sic vos non vobis mellificatis apes' ('So you bees make honey, not for yourselves'). Beer notes that the line is adopted in STC's note on line 28 of 'The Devil's Thoughts' (*Everyman* 438).
66 There is a comma after *rivals* in the *1834* text.
69–74
  Yet still pursu'd thro' scoff and gibe
  From A. to Z. his old A.B.C.
  Content that he could still subscribe
  In symbol just his name ΕΣΤΗΣΕ;
  (In punic Greek that's He hath stood:)
  Whate'er the men, the cause was good.
               (MS; 'ΕΣΤΗΣΕ', a Greek punning transliteration of
               'STC', was frequently used as a signature
               for newspaper and magazine publication)

84 'Poor witless Bard, unfed, untended' (MS).

Lines to a Comic Author, on an Abusive Review

First published in *Friendship's Offering*, ed. H. Inglis (London, 1834), with the title 'Lightheartedness in Rhyme'; included in *1834*. There is a quite different undated and untitled draft (printed in *1912* 2: 476 n.), as well as a revised fair copy titled 'To a Comic Author on an abusive review of his Aristophanes', in the British Library; a fair copy of a 19-line version at Harvard University signed 'Highgate, 15 September 1819'; and a corrected copy (possibly a proof) of the first publication in the Pierpont Morgan Library. E. H. Coleridge's conjectured date of composition is 1825; the *Everyman* date of November 1819 is certainly more accurate.

1–3 The British Library draft begins as follows:

> They fled; –
> Friend yet unknown! What tho' a brainless rout
> *Usurp the sacred title of the Bard –*
> What tho' the chilly wide-mouth'd chorus
> From Styx or Lethe's oozy Channel croak:
> So was it, Peter, in the times before us . . .

4 *Momus* ancient Greek god of ridicule and satire; often a figure for the fault-finding and captious critic.

6–10

> The plighted coterie of Phoebus he bespoke
> And laughing with reverted faces ran
> And somewhat the broad freedom to excuse
> They had allow'd the audacious Greek to use

> (British Library draft)

12–17 These lines in the printed version have no equivalent in the British Library draft, which instead ends:

> If the good dulness be the home of worth
> Duller than Frogs co-ax'd, or Jeffrey writ
> We, too, will Aristoff and welcome it –

13 *maugre* in spite of.

To Nature

First published in *Letters, Conversation and Recollections* (1836), 1: 144. Beer follows E. H. Coleridge in conjecturing 1820 as the date of composition (*Everyman* 440), though he does not identify the MS source of the text he prints. No surviving MS is recorded in *Index*.

The Tears of a Grateful People

First published, with the Hebrew text, in a pamphlet dated 1820; never included in any edition in STC's lifetime. George III died on 29 January 1820.

17 'The author, in the spirit of Hebrew Poetry, here represents the Crown, the Peerage, and the Commonality, by the figurative expression of the Sun, Moon, and Stars' (STC's note).
37 *Jeshurun* a poetical name for Israel in the Bible.

First Advent of Love

First published in *1834*. A version of lines 3-4 appears in a notebook entry dated January–September 1821 (*N* 4: 4810; a date of 17 February 1821 is given for this entry in *Index*): 'A pretty unintended Couplet in the Prose of Sidney's Arcadia

> And sweeter than a gentle South-west wind
> O'er flowry fields and shadow'd Waters creeping
> In summer's extreme heat. –'

In her note on this entry, Coburn quotes a passage from the early pages of Book 1 of Sir Philip Sidney's *Arcadia*.

[Reason]

First published as the conclusion of *On the Constitution of the Church and State* (1830; *CC* 10: 184-5), where the lines are introduced as follows: 'Finally, what is Reason? You have often asked me; and this is my answer.' Beer gives 1821-2 and 1829 as dates of composition: the former refers to a draft of these lines in a notebook dated 1821-2 (*N* 4: 4844). The lines from Dante are *Paradiso* 1. 88-90; the 1814 translation by Henry Francis Cary, which STC refers to in 1818, is as follows: 'With false imagination thou thyself / Makest dull; so that thou seest not the thing / Which thou hadst seen, had that been shaken off'. Accent marks to the Italian have been added in the present text.

1 *mist* 'Self' (notebook).
2 *Defecates* frees itself from impurities; refines or purifies itself.
4 *reign* Spelled 'rein' in 1830 *On the Constitution*; the notebook draft has 'reign'. In the first edition of *On the Constitution*, 'There' in this line is 'Then'. *Her* is underlined in the notebook draft.

[Lines from a notebook – 1822]

First published in *1893* 469 as 'Fragment 108'; included in *1912* 2: 1011 as 'Fragment 57'. There is a notebook draft followed by a fair copy among material from 1822; the present text is based on the fair copy, which is printed by Coburn in *Inquiring Spirit* 127. Beer gives the lines the title 'The Philosophical Trinity' in *Everyman* 441.

From the German

First published in *1834*. A fair copy – signed but untitled, undated and written out as 12 lines instead of 6 – is in the Speck Collection at Yale University (see *Index* CoS 187, and W. L. Phelps, 'A Literary Discovery', *Scribner's Magazine*, 93 [1933], 60). The German original is Mignon's famous song from Goethe's *Wilhelm Meister* ('Kennst du das Land'). Beer gives a conjectural date of composition of 1823–4 in *Everyman*.

The Reproof and Reply

First published in *Friendship's Offering* for 1834 (see headnote to 'Lines to a Comic Author' above), introduced by the following motto: 'I expect no sense, worth listening to, from the man who never does talk nonsense. – *Anon.*' Included in *1834*, from which the present text is taken. E. H. Coleridge says that the text in *1912* follows a 'MS version . . . in the possession of Miss Edith Coleridge', but no such MS is identified in *Index*. Both E. H. Coleridge and Beer preface the poem with the following subtitle given in *Friendship's Offering*: 'Or, the Flower-Thief's Apology, for a robbery committed in Mr and Mrs ———'s garden, on Sunday morning, 25th of May, 1823, between the hours of eleven and twelve'.

14 *fair* ——— 'fair Chisholm' (*1912*, from MS). In the *Friendship's Offering* text the name here and in lines 35, 43, 56 and 60 is given as 'C———' or 'C———m'. E. H. Coleridge supplies the name 'Chisholm' throughout, apparently from the MS.

31 *Mary* ——— 'Mary H———' (*1912*, from MS). She is not identified in any previous edition of the poem. *Polly Hymnia* puns on the Greek for 'hymned, celebrated by many'.

34 *thee* In italics in *1912* text (from MS).

35 *Mol Pomene* Comic English variant on 'Melpomene', the Greek muse of tragedy.

38 *Lured the wild fancies forth* 'Did lure the fancies forth' (*1912*, from MS).

46 *day-dreams* In italics in *1912* (from MS).

47 'And if I pluck'ed "each flower that *sweetest* blows," –' (*1912*, from MS); the phrase in inverted commas here may be a variation on line 202 of Wordsworth's 'Intimations Ode': 'To me the meanest flower that blows can give . . .'

48 *nose* In italics in *1912* (from MS). This line marks the end of a verse paragraph in *1912*.

49 'The English Parnassus is remarkable for its two summits of unequal height, the lower denominated Hampstead, the higher Highgate' (STC's note in MS, quoted in *1912* 1: 442).

63 *The Eighth Commandment* 'Thou shalt not steal' (Exodus xx: 15).

Youth and Age

First published in its present form in *1834*. Lines 1–38 were published in the *Literary Souvenir*, ed. Alaric A. Watts (1828) and in *The Bijou* (1828) and were included in *1828* and *1829*. Lines 39–49 were published as 'The Old Man's Sigh' in *Blackwood's Magazine* for June 1832. A draft of a 20-line version appears in a notebook entry with the title 'Aria Spontanea' and the date '10 Septr 1823. Wednesday Morning, 10 o'clock' (*N* 4: 4993). Another draft, extensively revised (50 lines) and untitled, appears later in the same notebook (*N* 4: 4996). Both drafts are printed in *1912* Appendix I.M. There is a fair copy of lines 1–43, plus one additional line, untitled and undated but written on paper watermarked 1822, in the Victoria College Library, Toronto. Several other partial fair copies and transcripts are listed in *Index* CoS 821–31; see also F. L. Beaty, 'Two Manuscript Poems of Coleridge', *Review of English Studies* n.s. 7 (1956), 185–7, and Warren E. Gibbs, 'Samuel Taylor Coleridge's "The Knight's Tomb" and "Youth and Age" ', *Modern Language Review*, 28 (1933), 83–5. E. H. Coleridge concluded that 'lines 1–43 were composed in 1823, and . . . the last six lines of the text which form part of *An Old Man's Sigh* were composed, as an afterthought, in 1832' (*1912* 1: 439 n.).

1 *Verse, a* 'Verse is a' (1822 fair copy, as alternative).

2 *clung* 'clings' (1822 fair copy, *Bijou*).

6 *When I* Printed in italics in *1828*, *1829*.

8 *This breathing house* 'This house of clay' (1822 fair copy, *Bijou*).

10 'O'er hill and dale and sounding sands' (1822 fair copy, *Bijou*).

11 *then* In italics in *1828*, *1829*.

12 *skiffs* 'boats' (1822 fair copy, *Bijou*).

20 *came* 'come' (*Bijou*).

21 'Of Beauty, Truth, and Liberty!' (1822 fair copy, *Bijou*).

23 *woful* 'mournful' (*Literary Souvenir*).

25 *many* 'merry' (*Bijou*).

27 *fond* 'false' (1822 fair copy, *Bijou*).

32 *make believe* Printed in italics in *1828*, *1829*.

34 *drooping* 'dragging' (1822 fair copy, *Bijou*).

42 *us* 'me' (1822 fair copy).

43–4 'Now I am old! / Now I am old, – ah woful Now' (1822 fair copy).

44–5 Between these lines: 'In our old age / Whose bruised wings quarrel with the bars of the still narrowing cage' inserted in 1832 draft of 'An Old Man's Sigh'.

49 'O might Life cease! and Selfless Mind, / Whose total Being is Act, alone remain Behind' added in 1832 draft of 'An Old Man's Sigh'.

Desire

First published in *1834*. There is a notebook draft, dated 24 April 1824: 'Desire of pure Love born itself the same; / A pulse that animates the outer frame, / And takes the impress of the nobler part, / It but repeats the Life, that of the Heart'

(*N* 4: 5146). These four lines follow a six-line version of lines 29–32 of 'Love's Apparition and Evanishment' (see below) without a break.

The Delinquent Travellers

First published in *1912*, 'From an hitherto unpublished MS, formerly in the possession of Coleridge's friend and amanuensis Joseph Henry Green' (1: 443 n.). No evidence is given for the 1824 date of composition – and no manuscript of this poem is listed in *Index*. Beer follows the *1912* text and accepts the date of composition (*Everyman* 450–3).

3 '*The Private Journal of Captain G. F. Lyon of the Mt Hecla, during the recent voyage of discovery under Captain Perry*, was published by John Murray in 1824' (*1912* 1: 444 n.).
43 *Planet* From Greek πλανητεσ, 'wanderer'.
50 *old King Log* proverbially, a king who rules quietly, never displaying his power. In mythology the frogs asked Jupiter for a king. He threw down a log of wood, and the frogs complained about having such a passive king. Jupiter then sent a stork, who ate all the frogs.
73 *demireps* an eighteenth-century term for women whose reputations are only half reputable; women of doubtful character.
81 *Dumpton Bay* 'A coast village near Ramsgate. In several years, including 1824, Coleridge passed some weeks at Ramsgate during the late autumn' (*Everyman* 452 n.).

Song, ex improviso

First published in *The Keepsake*, ed. F. M. Reynolds (London, 1830); never collected in STC's lifetime. The present text is from *1912*. There is an untitled transcript in a commonplace book inscribed 'To Susan Ayling ... from Dora Wordsworth, Rydal Mount, July 7th 1824' (*Index* CoS 627).

Work Without Hope

First published in *The Bijou* (1828) under the title 'Lines composed on a day in February'; included in *1828*, *1829*, *1834*, with the subtitle 'Lines composed 21st February, 1827'. There is a 35-line notebook draft – extensively revised, untitled and signed 'Jacob Hodiernus' – in an entry also containing a draft of a letter to an unidentified recipient dated 21 February 1825 (*N* 4: 5192; the draft of the poem is also printed in *1912* 2: 1110–11).

1 *Slugs* 'Snails' (erased in notebook draft); 'Stags' (*1828*, *1829*).
5 *the sole unbusy thing* Cf. 'Frost at Midnight' 16: 'The sole unquiet Thing'.
7 *amaranths* in myth and literary tradition, an imaginary flower supposed never to fade.
11 The notebook draft contains two variants of this line: 'With unmoist lip and wreathless brow I stroll'; 'With lips unmoistened wreathless brow I stroll'.

The Two Founts

First published in the *Annual Register* for 1827 as 'Stanzas addressed to a Lady on her Recovery from a Severe attack of Pain'; included in *The Bijou* for 1828 and in *1828, 1829, 1834*. A MS version headed 'To Eliza in Pain' was sent to Elizabeth Aders on 3 June 1826 (*L* 6: 664–5). The text printed in *L* is derived from a fair copy in an album of Elizabeth Aders, possibly dating from January 1828 (*Index* CoS 772).

8 *wished* 'meant' (MS).
11 *That . . . this* Underlined in MS, printed in italics in *1828, 1829*.
14 'Will ope *that* Fount alone by no Distress' (MS); *that* printed in italics in *1828, 1829*.
17–20 A draft of these lines appears in a notebook entry dated 1826; they are preceded by the following additional stanza:

> Was ne'er on earth Seen beauty like to this,
> The concentrated satisfying Sight
> In its deep quiet ask no further bliss,
> At once the form and Substance of Delight!

Lines 19–20 in the notebook draft read: 'Looks forth upon the troubled air below / Unmoved, entire, inviolately bright' (*N* 4: 5368).
31 *tort'ring* 'fost'ring' (*Annual Register, Bijou*).
34 *fount of pain* In capitals in MS.
44 *. . . less . . . less . . . less* Underlined in MS, printed in italics in *1828, 1829*.
45 *barbed* 'venom'd' (MS).
47 *any* Printed in italics in *1828, 1829*.

The Pang More Sharp Than All

First published in *1834*. There is a draft related to lines 36–43 in the British Library, on paper watermarked 1819. The date of composition is particularly uncertain: in *Everyman* 457 Beer says '1807 onwards? 1823–5 onwards?' The draft is printed in *1912* 1: 457 n. and in *Asra Poems* 176.

7 *guerdons* honours, rewards.
36–43 The draft corresponding to these lines runs as follows:

> – into my Heart
> As 'twere some magic Glass the magic child
> Transfused his Image and full counterpart;
> And then he left it like a Sylph beguiled
> To live and yearn and languish incomplete!
> Day following day, more rugged grows my path,
> There dwells a cloud before my heavy eyes;
> A Blank my Heart, and Hope is dead and buried,

Yet the deep yearning will not die; but Love
Clings on and cloathes the marrowless remains,
Like the fresh moss that grows on dead men's bones,
Quaint mockery! and fills its scarlet cups
With the chill dewdamps of the Charnel House.
O ask not for my Heart! my Heart is but
The darksome vault where Hope lies dead and buried,
And Love with Asbest Lamp bewails the Corse.

39 '*Faerie Queene*, B. III. c. 2. s 19' (STC's note in *1834*). The reference is to Spenser's description of the magic looking-glass devised by Merlin, which had the power to represent everything in the world exactly as it was in truth. It is in this looking glass that Britomart first sees Artegall.

Sancti Dominici Pallium

First published in the *Evening Standard* for 21 May 1827, titled 'A Dialogue written on a Blank Page of Butler's Book of the Roman Catholic Church'. Included in *1834*. Beer's note in *Everyman* 457 provides a concise account of the title and context: ' "The Robe of St Dominic". The poem reflects the heat of religious debate in the mid 1820s, when the question of Roman Catholic emancipation was being discussed, along with that of the Church of England and its authority. Southey's *Book of the Church* (1825) had been answered by Charles Butler's *Book of the Roman Catholic Church* and an anonymous pamphlet written by John Milner titled *Merlin's Strictures*; Southey had then returned to the fray with *Vindiciae Ecclesiae Anglicanae* (1826). The title of the poem refers obliquely to the part played by St Dominic and his black-robed order in such things as the Inquisition and the persecution of the Albigenses.' See also the headnote in *1912* 1: 448 n. An undated MS headed 'Facit Indignatio Versus', signed by STC, was sold at auction in 1931; its present location is unknown. A revised fair copy of lines 1–42, also undated, is in the Victoria College Library, Toronto. E. H. Coleridge supplies the names of the disputants in lines 7, 17, 34 and 39 in accordance with the MS because, he says, 'The poem as published in 1834 and every subsequent edition (except 1907) is meaningless.' Beer also follows this practice in *Everyman*. The present text, in keeping with the principle of following *1834* as closely as possible, reserves the names for the notes.

7 ——— 'Milner' (MS, *Evening Standard*).
10 *John Huss* Bohemian reformer, buried alive in 1415.
17 *Yet* ——— 'Yet Miln –' (*Evening Standard*), 'Yet Milner' (MS).
 Enough of ——— 'Enough of Milner' (MS, *Evening Standard*).
21 ——— 'Butler' (MS, *Evening Standard*).
22 *milky queen* Queen Mary I ('Bloody Mary'), who during her reign attempted to restore Catholicism to England.
25 'Who with a zeal that passed her sex's bounds' (*Evening Standard*).
30 *spear* 'helm' (*Evening Standard*).
32 *beck'ning* 'proffered' (*Evening Standard*).

Caduceus the winged staff entwined with two serpents, a symbol of the medical profession.

34 'What Milner boasts tho' Butler may deplore' (MS); 'What Milner lauds tho' Butler may deplore' (*Evening Standard*).

35 *repeat* 'reply' (*Evening Standard*).

36 *shown* Underlined in MS and fair copy, printed in italics in the *Evening Standard*.

37 ——— 'Butler' (MS, *Evening Standard*). The following note on this line appears in the MS, the fair copy and the *Evening Standard*: ' "Smooth Butler". See the Rev. Blanco White's Letter to C. Butler, Esq.'

38 *haut-gout* literally 'high taste', i.e. fancy dish.

39 ———'s 'Milner's' (MS, *Evening Standard*).

42 *Irish* 'the O'Gorman' (MS, *Evening Standard*).

46 *blood and soot* 'soot and blood' (*Evening Standard*). William Cobbett (1763–1835) was a prominent radical journalist and political leader; in 1824 he published a *History of the Protestant 'Reformation' of England and Ireland*.

47 Francis Jeffrey (1773–1850) was founder and editor of the *Edinburgh Review* and a prominent Whig.

glairy covered with glair, the white of an egg used as a varnish to preserve paintings and in glazes.

55 *lights* 'sights' (*Evening Standard*).

The Improvisatore

First published, with a prose introduction headed 'New Thoughts on Old Subjects', in *The Amulet*, ed. S. C. Hall (1828); included in *1829* and *1834* (the running title in *1834* is 'New Thoughts on Old Subjects'). There is a fair copy of two fragments of the dramatic prologue and of lines 5–48 of the verse 'Answer'. E. H. Coleridge in *1912*, and after him Beer in *Everyman*, follow the *Amulet* text of 1828. But it is not true, as E. H. Coleridge says, that 'The text of 1834 is identical with that of the *Amulet*': for example, in the dramatic prologue Eliza says 'what an elevating idea' in the *Amulet* text, 'what an elevating thought' in *1834*; Katherine then says 'If it be only an *idea*' in the *Amulet* text, 'If it be not only a mere fancy' in *1834*. The present text is that of *1834*.

Improvisatore means 'improviser'; *John Anderson, My Jo, John* is the title of a well-known poem by Robert Burns, based on an old Scottish ballad. *Moore's Irish Melodies* refers to an extremely popular collection of lyric poems by Thomas Moore (1779–1852), first published in 1807. *Beaumont and Fletcher* are Francis Beaumont (1584–1616) and John Fletcher (1579–1625), Jacobean dramatists whose collaborative works were greatly admired in the early nineteenth century. *The Elder Brother* was completed by Fletcher (and probably by Philip Massinger) about 1635; the speech quoted in STC's dramatic prologue here is from III, ii, and was originally printed as prose.

9 There is no verse paragraph break here in *The Amulet* (see *1912*, *Everyman*).

22 *belief* Printed in italics in *The Amulet*.

23 *had* Printed in italics in *The Amulet*.

25 *was* Printed in italics in *The Amulet*.

32 the 'a' (*The Amulet*).
62 is Printed in italics in *The Amulet*.

Love's Burial-Place: A Madrigal

First published in *1828*, with the title 'The Alienated Mistress: A Madrigal (From an Unfinished Melodrama)'; printed in *The Amulet* for 1833, but not included in *1829* or *1834*. The present text is from *The Amulet*. There is a fair copy of the poem, with the title 'Love's Burial-place: a Madrigal', sent by STC to S. C. Hall, editor of *The Amulet*, for this printing (see *L* 6: 698 n.). There is also a transcript by Sara Coleridge, dated 1827, in the Bodleian Library (see *Index* CoS 356). Beer conjectures an 1826 date of composition (*Everyman* 465).

1–2 '*Lady*. If Love be dead (and you aver it!) / Tell me Bard! where Love lies buried' (*1828*). The opening of Sara Coleridge's transcript is identical.
5 *Oh, gentle dame!* 'Ah faithless nymph' (*1828*).
7 *call* 'name' (*1828*).
9 *seem'd* 'was' (*1828*).
10 *caught* 'took' (*1828*).

Lines Suggested by the Last Words of Berengarius

First published in the *Literary Souvenir*, ed. Alaric A. Watts (1827), with 'Epitaphium Testamentarium' printed as a footnote to the title. Included in *1828*, *1829*, *1834*. There is a MS version of both poems on a single leaf in the Huntington Library (see *Index* CoS 319 and 150); Beer follows this MS in *Everyman* 466–7 and gives 1826 as the conjectured date of composition.

1–2 Beer prints these lines with a comma following 'Pope' and a stroke (/) and no comma following 'appear'.
13 *learned* Printed in italics in *Literary Souvenir* and underlined in MS. *Fear* is in capitals in the MS.
19 *recreant* Underlined in MS; printed in italics in *Literary Souvenir*, *1828*, *1829*.
23 *his* Underlined in MS; printed in italics in *Literary Souvenir*.
32 *shall* 'will' (*Literary Souvenir*, *1828*, *1829*).
33 *dawn* In capitals in MS.
34 *th' approaching* 'the coming' (*Literary Souvenir*).
   noon In capitals in the MS.
35 *morn* In capitals in the MS.

Epitaphium testamentarium

First published in the *Literary Souvenir* (1827); see headnote to preceding poem. Not included in any edition in STC's lifetime. The Greek and Latin epigraph means: 'The epitaph of STC, written by himself on the point of death'. Beer offers the following translation of the poem itself: 'The things I shall leave are either nothing, or of no value, or scarce my own. The dregs I give to Death: I restore the rest, O Christ! to thee.'

Duty Surviving Self-Love

First published in *1828*; included in *1829*, *1834*. There is a draft MS in the British Library, initialled and dated 2 September 1826, which is prefaced with the following note:

'QUESTION, ANSWER, AND SOLILOQUY
And are you (said Alia to Constantius, on whose head sickness and sorrow had antedated Winter, ere yet the time of Vintage had passed), Are you the happier for your Philosophy? And the smile of Constantius was as the light from a purple cluster of the vine, gleaming through snowflakes, as he replied, The Boons of Philosophy are of higher worth, than what you, O Alia, mean by Happiness. But I will not seem to evade the question – Am *I* the happier for my Philosophy? The calmer at least and the less unhappy, answered Constantius, for it has enabled me to find that selfless Reason is the best Comforter, and only sure friend of declining Life. At this moment the sounds of a carriage followed by the usual bravura executed on the brazen knocker announced a morning visit: and Alia hastened to receive the party. Meantime the grey-haired philosopher, left to his own musings, continued playing with the thoughts that Alia and Alia's question had excited, till he murmured them to himself in half audible words, which at first casually, and then for the amusement of his ear, he *punctuated* with rhymes, without however conceiting that he had by these means changed them into poetry.'

4 'When thy own body first the example set' (MS).

[Homeless]

First published in *The Literary Magnet* for January 1827; never collected in STC's lifetime. Campbell included the poem in *1893* and gave it the title 'Homeless'. E. H. Coleridge describes 'A transcript, possibly in Mrs Gillman's handwriting . . . inscribed on the fly-leaf of a copy of Bartram's *Travels in South Carolina* which Coleridge purchased in April 1818' (*1912* 1: 460 n.), but this is not listed in *Index*. An 1826 date of composition is given both in *1912* and, conjecturally, in *Everyman*.

Ἔρως ἀεὶ λάληθρος ἑταῖρος

First published in *1828*, where, as in *1829*, it serves as a motto for the concluding section of poems headed 'Prose in Rhyme; and Epigrams, Moralities, and Things without a Name'; included in *1834*, where it serves as a motto for 'Miscellaneous Poems'. The Greek title means 'Love, always a talkative companion'. There is a notebook draft in an entry dated 1826, and a signed undated MS version in the Wordsworth Library, Grasmere (see *Index* CoS 833 and 834). Beer gives 'before May 1827' as the date of composition.

1 *does the full heart* 'I own, do we' (notebook).
2 *it* 'we' (notebook).
3 'But in how many more do we let know' (notebook).
4 *which yet it fain* 'we found' (notebook).

Song

First published in *1828*; not included in *1829* or *1834*. There is a notebook draft, untitled, in an entry dated 1826 (see *Index* CoS 626).

1 'Tho' hid in spiral myrtle wreath' (notebook).
2 *that* 'which' (notebook).
3 *clefts* 'slits' (notebook).
  has 'hath' (notebook).
4 *flashes* 'glitter' (notebook).
5 *clefts* 'slits' (notebook).
6–8 'We spy no less, too, that the Blade, / Is cut away or snapt atwain / And nought but Hilt or Stump remain' (notebook).

Profuse Kindness

First published in *1834*. There is a transcript by Sara Coleridge (dated 1827) in Louisa Powles Plummer's album, which also contains a fair copy by STC of 'The Ballad of the Dark Ladie' and a transcript by Sara Coleridge of 'Love's Burial-Place' (see *Index* CoS 540, 31, 356). The epigraph is from Hesiod's *Works and Days*, line 40: 'They know not how much more the half is than the whole.'

Written in an Album

First published in *1834*. There is an untitled MS version in a letter to J. H. Green of 30 May 1827 (*L* 6: 686); the metrical markings are STC's:

> Parry seeks the Pólar Ridge:
> But rhymes seeks S. T. Cólĕridge
> Fit for Mrs Smudger's *Ol*bum
> Or to wipe her Baby's small bum.

There is a fair copy of the published version in an album of William Upcott dated 'Highgate, 28 September 1827'. Sir William Edward Parry (1790–1855) was making an unsuccessful but important attempt to reach the north pole in 1827. STC had come to know his brothers Charles and Frederick in Göttingen.

To Mary Pridham

First published in *1893*. Two MS sources are known: one dated 'Grove, Highgate, 15th October, 1827' and followed by Campbell in *1893*, another inscribed on the first page of an album presented to Mary Pridham at the time of her marriage to Derwent Coleridge and followed by E. H. Coleridge in *1912* and by Beer in *Everyman*. E. H. Coleridge dates this latter MS 16 October 1827. The present text follows *1912*.

1 *I have left behind* 'hard has been my lot' (15 October MS).
2 'And rough my path thro' life, I murmur not' (15 October MS).
3 *Now I revive* 'Rather rejoice' (15 October MS).
5 'That all this shaping heart has yearned to see' (15 October MS).
7–10 Identical to lines 5–8 of the verse section of 'The Improvisatore' above, except that lines 7 and 8 are transposed.
8 *his . . . his* 'the . . . the' (15 October MS).

Verses Trivocular

First published in *1912* 2: 985, from a draft on the inside back cover of a notebook, untitled and initialled (*Index* CoS 786). Beer dates these lines January 1828 in *Everyman* 470.

Water Ballad

First published in *The Athenaeum* for 29 October 1831; never collected in STC's lifetime. According to *Index* (CoS 794), there is a transcript in an unidentified hand in a commonplace book in the Bristol Reference Library. E. H. Coleridge, who conjecturally dates these lines 1799, says that they are based on the 'Bacarolle de Marie' by François Antoine Eugène de Planaid. Beer dates the lines June–July 1829 in *Everyman* 470–1.

Cologne

First published in *Friendship's Offering*, ed. H. Inglis (1834), under the title 'Expectoration the Second'; included in *1834*. The poem was written on the front endpaper, together with 'Epitaph' below, of a copy of the Galignani *Poetical Works of Coleridge, Shelley, and Keats* (Paris, 1829). Beer gives the date of composition as July 1828 in *Everyman* 471.

On my Joyful Departure from the Same City

First published, with the preceding poem ('Cologne'), in *Friendship's Offering* (1834) under the title 'An Expectoration, or Splenetic Extempore, on my joyful departure from the City of Cologne'. Included in *1834*. In two copies of the first publication, possibly proofs, STC inserted 'a' before 'rhymer' in line 1 (*Index* CoS 468; *1912* 1: 477 n.). Beer gives the date of composition as 'July 1828' (*Everyman* 471).

3 *Rudesheimer* 'The *apotheosis* of Rhenish wine' (STC).

[The Netherlands]

First published as 'Fragment 49' in *1912* 2: 1009, from an untitled notebook draft. See Kathleen Coburn, *The Self-Conscious Imagination* (1974) 52, and Beer, *Everyman* 472, where the date of composition is August 1828.

The Garden of Boccaccio

First published in *The Keepsake*, ed. F. M. Reynolds (1829); included in *1829* and *1834*. There is a fair copy, revised and initialled, in the Huntington Library (*Index* CoS 195). Beer gives the date of composition as '?June–August 1828'. The division of verse paragraphs is quite different in *1834* from the earlier printing; the present text departs from *1834* and follows Beer's *Everyman* text in beginning new verse paragraphs at lines 19 and 57.

11 E. H. Coleridge identifies the 'Friend' in this line as Mrs Gillman.
35 *Scalds* ancient Scandinavian bards.
38 *Hertha* or Nerthus: the name given by Tacitus to a Scandinavian or northern Germanic goddess of fertility.
50 *pardie* indeed, verily (archaic).
49–56 The following variant appears in a notebook draft (see *Index* CoS 196):

> And there was young Philosophy
> Unconscious of herself, pardie;
> And now she hight poesy,
> And like a child in playful glee
> Prattles and plays with flower and stone,
> As youth's fairy playfellows
> Revealed to Innocence alone.

98 'Boccaccio claimed for himself the glory of having first introduced the works of Homer to his countrymen' (STC).
    Mæonides an ancient literary name for Homer.
100 'I know few more striking or more interesting proofs of the overwhelming influence which the study of the Greek and Roman classics exercised on the judgments, feelings, and imaginations of the literati of Europe at the commencements of the restoration of literature, than the passage in the Filocopo of Boccaccio: where the sage instructor, Racheo, as soon as the young prince and the beautiful girl Biancofiore had learned their letters, sets them to study the Holy Book, Ovid's Art of Love. "Incominciò Racheo a mettere il suo officio in esecuzione con intera sollecitudine. E loro, in breve tempo, insegnato a conoscer le lettere, fece leggere

il santo libro d'Ovvidio, nel quale il sommo poeta mostra, come i santi fuochi di Venere di debbano ne' freddi cuori accendere" ' (STC's note). In *Everyman* 475 n., Beer provides an additional note written by STC on the fly-leaf of his copy of vol. 1 of Boccaccio's *Opera* (1723): 'Deeply interesting – but observe, p. 63, 11. 33–5 (*loc. cit.*), The *holy Book* – Ovid's *Art of Love*!! This is not the result of mere Immorality: "Multum, Multum / Hic jacet sepultum".'

Alice du Clos: Or The Forked Tongue. A Ballad

First published in *1834*. There is a revised draft, described by E. H. Coleridge as 'an early if not a first draft' and by Rosenbaum and White as a 'fair copy', in the Berg Collection, New York Public Library, which has been dated c. 1828–9 (see *Index* CoS 9). E. H. Coleridge also records some variants from 'a second draft (MS b) of lines 97–112', but this MS is not recorded in *Index*. See *1912* 1: 470 n. for variants of these lines erased in the fair copy.

25 A new verse paragraph is begun here in *1912* and in *Everyman*, but on what textual basis is unclear.
48 'Go tell him I am well at home' (erased in MS).
49 *speed* 'fly' (erased in MS).
50 *stronger* 'sweeter' (erased in MS).
51 *gentler* 'lovelier' (erased in MS).
53 *reel'd* 'pass'd' (erased in MS).
54–7 STC's revisions of this simile, though eventually erased, are as follows:

> Like a ~~tall Wave that~~ $\frac{\text{stormy}}{\text{huge and dark.}}$
> Reels sideway from a toiling Bark
> Toil'd in the deep sea-trough
> Is traversed by
> ~~Catches askance~~   the Lightning flash
>
> *or* Like a huge Billow, rude and dark
>   as it falls off from a Bark
> That ~~tumbling mainward from~~
>   Toil'd in the deep Sea-trough

He also erased 'wheeling' as an alternative to *shouldering* in line 56.
61 *A moment* 'A moment's pause' (erased in MS).
65 'Yon May-thorn tree dimly –' and 'O fairly flower yon may-thorn tree' (variants erased from MS).
69 *lightsome* 'glittery' (MS).
71 *With* 'The' (MS).
76 'Lord Julian in the Greenwood stays' (erased in MS).
87 'With buskins and with quiver' (erased in MS).
89 *een* archaic plural, 'eyes'.
91 *Ellen* E. H. Coleridge describes this as 'a slip of the pen for "Alice" ' (*1912* 1: 469 n.).

110 *sore* 'sair' (erased in MS).
122 'With all his gay hunt round' (MS).
126 *When* 'And' (MS).
128 'And dark of Brow, with a word' (MS).
135 *stifled* 'muttering' (erased in MS).
136 *And look'd askance* 'And Look askance' (MS; 'Yet not unheard' erased).
153–9 See *1912* 1: 474 n. for variants of these lines erased in MS.
159 'She bade me tell you' (erased in MS).
167 'For as she clos'd her scoffing phrase' (erased in MS).
173–4 'And who from twixt those opening Trees / Pricks on with laughing cheer' (erased in MS).

Love, Hope, and Patience in Education

First published in *The Keepsake* for 1830; included in *1834* (3: 331). There are two MSS: one in an album belonging to Emily Trevenen, titled 'Reply to a Lady's Question respecting the accomplishment most desirable in an Instructress' and dated 1 July 1829; another (now lost – see *Index* CoS 345) titled 'Lines in a Lady's Album in answer to her Question respecting the Accomplishments most desirable in the Mistress or Governess of a Preparatory School' and enclosed in a letter to William Sotheby of 13 July 1829 (*L* 6: 798–9).

2 *And* 'Yet' (letter to Sotheby).
9–11 'Methinks I see them now, the triune group, / With straiten'd arms uprais'd, the Palms aslope / Robe touching Robe beneath, and blending as they flow' (letter to Sotheby).
12 *like snow emboss'd in snow* Cf. 'Alice du Clos' 24: 'A snow-drop on a tuft of snow!' In both cases STC may be thinking of Shakespeare's *Venus and Adonis* 362: 'A lily prison'd in a gaol of snow'.
15 *doth* 'will' (*Keepsake*).
24–6 STC added the following note in the letter to Sotheby: 'In the first copy the Lines stood thus:

> "Then like a Statue, with a Statue's Strength,
> And with a Smile, the Sister-Fay of those
> >   Who at meek Evening's Close
> >   To teach our Grief repose
> Their freshly-gathered Store of Moonbeams wreathe
> On Marble Lips, a CHANTREY has made breathe,
> Stands the mute" &c –

but they were struck out by the Author, not because he thought them bad lines in themselves (quamvis Della Cruscam fortasse paullulo nimis redolere videantur) but because they diverted and retarded the stream of the Thought and injured the Organic Unity of the Composition. PIÙ NEL UNO is Francesco de Salez' brief and happy definition of the Beautiful: and the shorter the poem, the more indispensable is it, that the Più should not overlay the Uno, that the unity should be *evident*. But to sacrifice the *gratification*, the sting of *pleasure*, from a fine *passage* to the *satisfaction*, the sense of *Complacency* arising from the contemplation of a symmetrical *Whole*, is among the last Conquests atchieved by men of genial powers. S.T.C.'

[Lines written in commonplace book of Miss Barbour]

First published in the *New York Mirror* for 19 December 1829 and dated 'Grove, Highgate, August 1829'; never collected in STC's lifetime, and no MS is known to exist. The present text is from *1912*. The poem is not included in *Everyman*.

To Miss A.T.

First published in *Essays on His Own Time* (1850). There is a fair copy, signed, titled 'To Miss Jones' and dated 1 September 1830 (*Index* CoS 733). The poem is not included in *Everyman*. The present text is from *1912*.

Love and Friendship Opposite

First published in *Friendship's Offering* for 1834, where the title is 'In Answer to a Friend's Question'; included in *1834*. No MS is known to exist; the date of composition is conjectured to be 1830 in *1912* and *Everyman*.

Not at Home

First published in *1834*. No MS is known to exist; *1912* and *Everyman* both give 1830 as a conjectural date of composition.

5 *ee* eye (archaic).
6 *swart* dark.

W.H. Eheu!

STC never published this epitaph on Hazlitt, a version of the poem he had published in the *Morning Post* for 22 September 1801 as 'Epitaph on a Bad Man' (see Epigram 34 in *1912* 2: 961–2 and *Everyman* 485). There is a fair copy in a notebook, headed 'Obit Saturday Septr 18 [10?], 1830 W.H. Eheu!' (*Index* CoS 140) and followed by this note: 'With a sadness at heart, and an earnest hope grounded on his misanthropic sadness, when I first knew him in his twentieth or twenty-first year, that a something existed in his bodily organism that in the sight of the All-Merciful lessened his responsibility, and the moral imputation of his acts and feelings.' 'Eheu!' is the Latin equivalent of 'Alas!' For Hazlitt's view of Coleridge, see especially 'On My First Acquaintance with Poets', first published in *The Liberal* for April 1823.

Phantom or Fact?

First published in *1834*. No MS is known to exist; *1912* and *Everyman* both give 1830 as a conjectural date of composition.

4 *unnethe* 'uneath'; not easily, scarcely (archaic).

Charity in Thought

First published in *1834*. No MS is known to exist; *1912* and *Everyman* both give 1830 as a conjectural date of composition.

Humility the Mother of Charity

First published in *1834*. There is a signed but untitled and undated fair copy in the Bodleian Library (see *Index* CoS 231). 1830 is the conjectured date of composition in *1912* and *Everyman*.

['Gently I took that which ungently came']

First published in *1834*, without a title but with the epigraph from 1 Corinthians (the title 'Forbearance' was assigned to the poem in *1893*). No MS is known to exist; E. H. Coleridge gives '?1832' as the date of composition in *1912*; Beer gives '?1819 ?1832' in *Everyman*. E. H. Coleridge notes the relation of the first line to a passage in Spenser's *Shepherd's Calendar* ('Februarie'): 'Ne ever was to Fortune foeman, / But gently took, that ungently came' (cf. also 'foe' in lines 11–12 of STC's poem).

Cholera Cured Before Hand

First published in *1834*. The lines were enclosed in a letter to J. H. Green dated 26 July 1832, with the following variant of the introduction printed in *1834*: 'Address premonitory to the Sovereign People; or the Cholera cured beforehand, promulgated *gratis* for the use of the Useful Classses, specially of those resident in St Giles's, Bethnal Green, Saffron Hill, &c – by their Majesties', i.e. the People's, loyal Subject, DEMOPHILUS MUDLARKIADES' (*L* 6: 917–18). A second version was enclosed in a letter to H. N. Coleridge of 28 August 1832: here the prefatory note varies only slightly from that in the letter to Green through the list of working-class areas of London; it then continues as follows – 'and likewise, inasmuch as the good man is merciful even to the Beasts, for the benefits of the Bulls and Bears of the Stock Exchange' (*L* 6: 924–5). A third version was enclosed in a letter to 'G. Williams, surgeon', dated 5 September 1832 and signed 'Philodemos Coprophibus' – 'Lover-of-the-people Living-off-excrement' (this letter is not in Griggs's edition; see *Index* CoS 50). Variants from the letters to

Green and to H. N. Coleridge are given below. According to Campbell's note in *1893* 653 n., there was a cholera epidemic in 1832. This poem is not included in *Everyman*.

1–6 These lines do not appear in the letter to Green.

4 'For Damns, Grins and Wry Faces' (letter to HNC).

7 'To escape Belly-ache' (letter to Green).

11 *Dispipsy* 'Dys Pipsy' (letter to Green); 'Dis Pipsy' (letter to HNC, in which STC includes this note: 'Sometimes erroneously written Dyspepsia: but there can be little doubt, that Dis is the Diminutive of Dyonesia, or some such Christian Name. The Sir-name, Pipsy, is probably but a fondling name for an infant Daughter of the Pip Family').

12 'And there*fore* don't get tipsy!' (letters to Green, HNC).

15 *to Dispipsy* 'for Dys Pipsy' (letter to Green), 'to Dys Pipsy' (letter to HNC).

16 *with this gipsy* 'of Dys Pipsy' (letter to Green).

19 *Cholery Morpus* 'Cholera morbus' is a non-infectious, rarely fatal form of cholera, usually caused by contaminated food.

20–1 These lines are not in the letter to Green.

22 'And on! och! my dear Honeys!' (letter to Green)

23 'There is no Cure for *You*' (letter to Green).

24 'And you'll find it . . .' (letter to Green).

28 *offal-fed* 'horn and hoof'd' (letter to Green).

32 *'Till* 'Then' (letter to Green).

33 *last* 'length' (letter to Green).

36 *Dear mudlarks* See STC's comic Latin pseudonym in the prefatory notes included in the letters to Green and to HNC.

38 *and* 'with' (letter to HNC).

42 *pig* 'live' (letter to Green).

43 *Cobbett's, O'Connell's* See notes on lines 42 and 47 of 'Sancti Dominici Pallium' above. Daniel O'Connell (1775–1847) was an important Irish political leader and agitator.

Love's Apparition and Evanishment

First published in *Friendship's Offering* for 1834, signed and dated 'S. T. Coleridge, August 1833'; included in *1834*. Three fair copies of this 28-line version of the poem exist, all of them dated August 1833 (see *Index* CoS 350, 351, 352 and *L* 6: 954). There is also a draft of lines 4 and 7–17 in a fragment of a letter to J. G. Lockhart dated 6 November 1833 (*Index* CoS 353; *L* 6: 971–3). A 21-line draft in the British Library begins with a version of four lines never published as part of this poem by STC himself but added as 'L'Envoy' by Derwent and Sara Coleridge in *1852* and printed as part of the poem in *1893*, *1912* and *Everyman*. The MS is printed in *1912* 2: 1087–8 and begins as follows:

> In vain I supplicate the Powers above;
> There is no Resurrection for the Love
> That, nursed with tenderest care, yet fades away
> In the chilled heart by inward self-decay.

'The Envoy' printed in *1852* and other editions substitutes 'we' for 'I' in the first of these lines and 'gradual' for 'inward' in the fourth. Two 6-line MS versions of these lines exist, one dated 24 April 1824 and another 27 April 1824 (*Index* CoS 348 and 349, and *L* 6: 954; Campbell printed the first of these MSS in *1893*, E. H. Coleridge the second in *1912* 1: 489 n.).

3 *Who* 'That' (British Library draft).
4 'Where basking Dipsad's hiss and swell' (*Friendship's Offering*, with the following note: 'The Asps of the sand-desert, anciently named Dipsads').
5 'And hangs his wistful head aslant' (British Library draft).
6 'Some sound he fain would catch' (British Library draft).
7 *And now* 'Anon' (*Friendship's Offering*).
10–21 The corresponding passage in the British Library draft runs as follows:

> Suspended there, as it befell,
>   O'er my own vacancy,
>   And while I seemed to watch
> The sickly calm, as were of heart
>   A place where Hope lay dead,

12 'A "Seat of Camomile" had long before been associated with Sara Hutchinson' (Beer, *Everyman* 488 n.; cf. 'Letter to Sara Hutchinson' above, line 86).
14 *idle brain* Cf. 'The Eolian Harp' 40–1; in *Friendship's Offering* this line is 'Flitting across the idle sense the while'.
22 'The spirit of departed Love' (British Library draft).
23 'Stood close beside my bed' (British Library draft).
24 'She bent methought to kiss my lips' (British Library draft).
26 *but* 'with' (British Library draft).
27 *Woke just enough* 'That woke enough' (*Friendship's Offering*); 'That awoke just enough' (British Library draft).
28 *Hope* 'it' (British Library draft).

To the Young Artist, Kayser of Kaserwerth

First published in *1834*, with the date '1833' attached. There is a fair copy, signed and dated '1833' (*Index* CoS 758). J. Kayser made a pencil-sketch of STC in this year; STC commented on it in a letter to the well-known artist E. F. Finden of 6 November 1833: '. . . a Likeness, certainly; but with such unhappy Density of the Nose & ideotic Drooping of the Lip, with a certain pervading *Wooden[n]ess* of the whole Countenance, that it has not been thought guilty of any great Flattery by Mr Coleridge's Friends' (*L* 6: 974, with facing illustration). Beer gives the date of composition as 'August–October 1833' in *Everyman* 489.

4 *The parting friend's 'alas!'* 'The parting friend's, alas!' (*1834*). The clarification in punctuation was introduced in *1893* and followed in *1912*.

Know Thyself

First published in *1834*, with the epigraph from Juvenal (*Satires* xi.27 – 'And from heaven descends *know thyself*') but without a title ('Self-Knowledge' was assigned in *1893* and has been followed in subsequent editions). The present title was used by STC himself in a MS draft signed and dated 10 January 1834 (*Index* CoS 594).

My Baptismal Birth-Day

First published in *Friendship's Offering* for 1834, under the title 'Lines composed on a sick-bed, under severe bodily suffering, on my spiritual birthday, October 28th'; included in *1834*. There is a MS version in a letter from STC to Thomas Pringle dated 6 August 1833 (*L* 6: 950–1), and another in Mrs William Ellis's album, signed and dated 1833 (*Index* CoS 384). E. H. Coleridge says that 'Emerson heard Coleridge repeat an earlier version of these lines on Aug. 5, 1833' (*1912* 1: 490 n.). There is a transcript of the poem by Eliza Louisa Emmerson at Yale University (*Index* CoS 382).

1 'Born unto God in CHRIST – in Christ, my ALL!' (*Friendship's Offering*, letter to Pringle).
3 *I* 'we' (letter to Pringle, *Friendship's Offering*).
4 *my* 'our' (letter to Pringle, *Friendship's Offering*).
7 *fear* 'dread' (letter to Pringle, *Friendship's Offering*).
9–10 'Let Sea, and Earth, and Sky / Wage war against me!' (letter to Pringle, *Friendship's Offering*).
11 *they* Printed in italics in *Friendship's Offering*.
12 *that* 'who' (letter to Pringle, *Friendship's Offering*).
14 *his . . . there* Printed in italics in *Friendship's Offering*. This line echoes the last line of Donne's *Holy Sonnets* X: 'And death shall be no more; Death, thou shalt die.'

Epitaph

First published in *1834* with the date, as shown. Seven MSS versions in STC's hand (one of them now lost) and a transcript by Elizabeth Aders from a letter sent to her by STC, probably in November 1833, are listed in *Index* CoS 131–6. Variants from the following MSS are given in the notes below: (1) two versions in a single MS in the British Library, entitled (a) 'Epitaph in Hornsey Churchyard Hic Jacet S.T.C.' and (b) 'ETESI's [sic] EPITAPH', both printed in *1912* 2: 1088–9; (2) a version in a letter to J. H. Green dated 28 October 1833 (*L* 6: 963); (3) a version in a letter to J. G. Lockhart dated 5 November 1833 (*L* 6: 973); (4) the Elizabeth Aders transcript (*L* 6: 969–70). See E. H. Coleridge's headnote, *1912* 1: 491 n., for other MS titles and for information about STC's practical intentions concerning his epitaph: 'From the letter to Mrs Aders it appears that Coleridge did not contemplate the epitaph being inscribed on his tombstone, but that he intended it to be printed "in letters of distinctly visible and legible size" on the outline of a tombstone to be engraved as a vignette to be published in a magazine, as to illustrate the last page of his "Miscellaneous Poems" in the second volume of his *Poetical Works*.'

1 *Passer-by* 'Visitor' (British Library MS a).
2 *breast* 'heart' (British Library MS b, letters to Aders, Green, Lockhart).
3 'There lies a Poet: or what once was He' (British Library MS a).
  A Poet lies 'Here lies a Poet' (British Library MS b).
  seem'd he 'was he' (letter to Green).
5 *toil of* 'toilsome' (letter to Aders).
7 *to be forgiven* Underlined in letters to Aders and Green.
8 After this line the following appears in British Library MS b: 'Inscription on the Tombstone of one not unknown; yet more commonly known by the Initials of his Name than by the Name itself.'

Appendix 1: On the Wretched Lot of the Slaves in the Isles of Western India

This modern English translation of STC's greek Sapphic ode on the slave trade was originally published in *An Infinite Complexity: Essays in Romanticism*, ed. J. R. Watson (Edinburgh: Edinburgh University Press for the University of Durham Press, 1983). The Greek text of the ode was first published by Campbell in *1893* (Appendix B, 476–7), from the official manuscript copy at Cambridge University. In June 1792, STC was awarded the Brown Gold Medal for this poem; the epigraph indicates that STC formally read it before 'the highest Assembly' on 3 July. The West Indian slave trade had been hotly debated in 1792, both in parliament and in the Cambridge University Senate. The poem is written in Sapphic stanzas: three longer logaoedic hendecasyllabic lines followed by a shorter adonic line. It has its technical limitations: Richard Porson, the Professor of Greek at Cambridge, claimed to have found 134 instances of bad Greek in it (see Richard Holmes, *Coleridge: Early Visions*, p. 43). STC quoted four stanzas of the ode, followed by a 'Literal Translation' of them into English (see *1893* 585), as part of his note to line 438 of 'The Destiny of Nations' (originally line 327 of STC's contribution to 'Joan of Arc').

Appendix 2: [Notebook draft of an essay on punctuation]

This essay, dated April–July 1809 by Kathleen Coburn in her edition of the *Notebooks* (3: 3504), appears in a notebook now in the Victoria College Library, University of Toronto. There is a transcript in the hand of Henry Nelson Coleridge in the Humanities Research Center, University of Texas, Austin.

INDEX OF TITLES

INDEX OF FIRST LINES